DISCARDED BY
SUFFOLK UNIVERSITY
SAWYER LIBRARY

COLLEGE LIBRARY
SUFFOLK UNIVERSITY
BOSTON. MASS.

Effects of Petroleum on Arctic and Subarctic Marine Environments and Organisms

VOLUME II

BIOLOGICAL EFFECTS

The National Marine Fisheries Service (NMFS) does not approve, recommend, or endorse any proprietary product or proprietary material mentioned in this publication. No reference shall be made to NMFS, or to this publication furnished by NMFS, in any advertising or sales promotion which would indicate or imply that NMFS approves, recommends, or endorses any proprietary material mentioned herein, or which has as its purpose an intent to cause directly or indirectly the advertised product to be used or purchased because of this NMFS publication.

Effects of Petroleum on Arctic and Subarctic Marine Environments and Organisms

VOLUME II

BIOLOGICAL EFFECTS

EDITED BY

Donald C. Malins

Environmental Conservation Division
Northwest and Alaska Fisheries Center
National Marine Fisheries Service
National Oceanic and Atmospheric Administration
U.S. Department of Commerce
Seattle, Washington

ACADEMIC PRESS, INC. **New York San Francisco London** 1977
A Subsidiary of Harcourt Brace Jovanovich, Publishers

QH
545
.O5
E34
Vol. II

103524

COPYRIGHT © 1977, BY ACADEMIC PRESS, INC.
ALL RIGHTS RESERVED.
NO PART OF THIS PUBLICATION MAY BE REPRODUCED OR
TRANSMITTED IN ANY FORM OR BY ANY MEANS, ELECTRONIC
OR MECHANICAL, INCLUDING PHOTOCOPY, RECORDING, OR ANY
INFORMATION STORAGE AND RETRIEVAL SYSTEM, WITHOUT
PERMISSION IN WRITING FROM THE PUBLISHER.

ACADEMIC PRESS, INC.
111 Fifth Avenue, New York, New York 10003

United Kingdom Edition published by
ACADEMIC PRESS, INC. (LONDON) LTD.
24/28 Oval Road, London NW1

Library of Congress Cataloging in Publication Data

Main entry under title:

Effects of petroleum on arctic and subarctic marine
     environments and organisms.

    Bibliography: p.
    CONTENTS: v.
v. 2   Biologicals effects.
     1.   Oil spills—Environmental aspects—Arctic regions.
  2.   Petroleum—Physiological effect.   3.   Aquatic animals,
Effect of water pollution on.   I.   Malins, D. C.
QH545.05E34   628.1′683   77-8559
ISBN 0–12–466902–6

PRINTED IN THE UNITED STATES OF AMERICA

Contents

CHAPTER 1

ACUTE TOXIC EFFECTS OF PETROLEUM ON ARCTIC AND SUBARCTIC MARINE ORGANISMS

Donovan R. Craddock   1

CHAPTER 2

MARINE FISH AND INVERTEBRATE DISEASES, HOST DISEASE RESISTANCE, AND PATHOLOGICAL EFFECTS OF PETROLEUM

Harold O. Hodgins, Bruce B. McCain, and Joyce W. Hawkes   95

CHAPTER 3

METABOLISM OF PETROLEUM HYDROCARBONS: ACCUMULATION AND BIOTRANSFORMATION IN MARINE ORGANISMS

Usha Varanasi and Donald C. Malins   **175**

CHAPTER 4

SUBLETHAL BIOLOGICAL EFFECTS OF PETROLEUM HYDROCARBON EXPOSURES: BACTERIA, ALGAE, AND INVERTEBRATES

Frederick G. Johnson   **271**

CHAPTER 5

SUBLETHAL BIOLOGICAL EFFECTS OF PETROLEUM HYDROCARBON EXPOSURES: FISH

Benjamin G. Patten   **319**

CHAPTER 6

EFFECTS OF PETROLEUM ON ECOSYSTEMS

Herbert R. Sanborn   337

CHAPTER 7

BIOLOGICAL EFFECTS OF PETROLEUM ON MARINE BIRDS

W.N. Holmes and J. Cronshaw   359

CHAPTER 8

CONSEQUENCES OF OIL FOULING ON MARINE MAMMALS

Joseph R. Geraci and Thomas G. Smith   **399**

CHAPTER 9

EFFECTS OF OIL SPILLS IN ARCTIC AND SUBARCTIC ENVIRONMENTS

Robert C. Clark, Jr., and John S. Finley   **411**

Contributors

ROBERT C. CLARK, JR.
DONOVAN R. CRADDOCK
JOHN S. FINLEY
JOYCE W. HAWKES
HAROLD O. HODGINS
FREDERICK G. JOHNSON
BRUCE B. McCAIN
DONALD C. MALINS
BENJAMIN G. PATTEN
HERBERT R. SANBORN
USHA VARANASI

Environmental Conservation Division
Northwest and Alaska Fisheries Center
National Marine Fisheries Service
National Oceanic and Atmospheric Administration
U.S. Department of Commerce
2725 Montlake Boulevard East
Seattle, Washington 98112

J. CRONSHAW
W.N. HOLMES

Department of Biological Sciences
University of California
Santa Barbara, California 93106

JOSEPH R. GERACI

Wildlife Disease Section
Department of Pathology
Ontario Veterinary College, University of Guelph
Guelph, Ontario, Canada

THOMAS G. SMITH

Arctic Biological Station
Fisheries and Marine Service
Department of Fisheries and the Environment
P.O. Box 400
Ste. Anne de Bellevue, Quebec, Canada

Preface

As oil transport and drilling operations intensify in the Arctic and Subarctic in response to pressing demands for energy it becomes increasingly important to understand the biological effects of petroleum on marine organisms (see Preface to Volume I). The impact of these intrusions on the biota of the often pristine areas is poorly understood, despite certain relevant data from laboratory experiments with indigenous organisms and a lesser amount of field information; the latter is particularly lacking from arctic regions.

In this volume an attempt is made to compile these data, evaluate the implications to possible alterations in organisms and ecosystems, and offer suggestions for future work where significant gaps in knowledge exist. I will not attempt to reiterate nor elaborate on the views of individual specialists contributing to this volume. Yet in the general sense it seems especially worthwhile to point out that more information is needed on long-term (chronic) biological effects through both laboratory and field studies. Ideally, both approaches should be conducted in a *concerted* and *complementary* way to develop a better understanding of the impact of petroleum operations on the arctic and subarctic marine resources. Realistically translating the laboratory findings to the field is, by nature, a difficult and formidable task in view of the many interacting factors existing in the marine environment. Equally difficult problems arise in conducting field studies where great importance must be attached to the attainment of a comprehensive view of possible effects on organisms and ecosystems through the identification of a *variety* of relevant parameters. The study of only a few select parameters may provide a myopic perspective and lead to invalid conclusions. Hopefully, these challenges will receive a dedicated and enthusiastic response from all concerned both with requirements for energy and with efforts to preserve a viable and healthy marine environment for ourselves and future generations.

Acknowledgments

Preparation of this book was encouraged and partially supported by the Outer Continental Shelf Environmental Assessment Program, Environmental Research Laboratories, National Oceanic and Atmospheric Administration, with funding furnished by the Bureau of Land Management, U.S. Department of the Interior.

We are grateful to our colleagues at the Northwest and Alaska Fisheries Center, Department of Oceanography at the University of Washington, and other institutions for help and advice during preparation of this book and for review of drafts of the manuscripts. A special note of appreciation is due to several individuals: Mr. Maurice E. Stansby for guidance in production and in obtaining literature through retrieval services and personal contacts; Mr. Frank Piskur for his dedicated and conscientious efforts editing manuscripts and in organizing materials; Mr. James Peacock, Ms. Carol Oswald, and Mr. Steve Jensen for preparation of figures and illustrations and design of cover; Ms. Gail Siani for her tireless efforts in typing drafts and for her fine contribution to the organization of materials; Mrs. Isabell Diamant for her typing skill and review of literature references; Mrs. Enid Renaud for assistance in preparing and for typing of the index; Mrs. Margurite Morey for typing and proofreading; Ms. Susan Stranahan, Mr. Michael Uhler, and Mrs. Patricia Kummer for proofreading and editorial support; Mrs. Nellie Nickels for general and administrative assistance.

Especial indebtedness is due to the following specialists who kindly reviewed drafts of the manuscripts:

JACK W. ANDERSON, Battelle Pacific Northwest Laboratories, Sequim, Washington

LAURA M. BECKNER, Northwest and Alaska Fisheries Center, Seattle, Washington

R.A.A. BLACKMAN, Fisheries Laboratory, Ministry of Agriculture, Fisheries, and Food, Essex, England

JACQUES M. CHILLER, National Jewish Hospital, Denver, Colorado

WALTER J. CRETNEY, Environment Canada, Victoria, British Columbia, Canada

EDWARD E. DeNIKE, Washington State Department of Ecology, Olympia, Washington

CLARE DION, Northwest and Alaska Fisheries Center, Seattle, Washington

MELVIN W. EKLUND, Northwest and Alaska Fisheries Center, Seattle, Washington

JOHN W. FARRINGTON, Woods Hole Oceanographic Institution, Woods Hole, Massachusetts

CHARLES I. GIBSON, Battelle Pacific Northwest Laboratories, Seattle, Washington

COLIN K. HARRIS, University of Washington, Seattle, Washington

HUGH L. HUFFMAN, JR., EXXON Research and Engineering Co., Linden, New Jersey

ALAN J. KOHN, University of Washington, Seattle, Washington

C. BRUCE KOONS, EXXON Production Research Co., Houston, Texas

MARSHA L. LANDOLT, University of Washington, Seattle, Washington

JERRY LARRANCE, Pacific Marine Environmental Laboratory, Seattle, Washington

RICHARD F. LEE, Skidaway Institute of Oceanography, Savannah, Georgia

EDWARD R. LONG, Environmental Research Laboratories, Marine Ecosystems Analysis, Puget Sound Project, Seattle, Washington

CLAYTON D. McAULIFFE, Chevron Oil Field Research Co., La Habra, California

SEELYE MARTIN, University of Washington, Seattle, Washington

ALLAN D. MICHAEL, University of Massachusetts, Gloucester, Massachusetts

ROY E. NAKATANI, University of Washington, Seattle, Washington

DONALD J. REISH, California State University, Long Beach, California

STANLEY D. RICE, Northwest and Alaska Fisheries Center, Auke Bay, Alaska

WILLIAM T. ROUBAL, Northwest and Alaska Fisheries Center, Seattle, Washington

TERESA I. SCHERMAN, Northwest and Alaska Fisheries Center, Seattle, Washington

MARIBETH SPENCER, University of Washington, Seattle, Washington

JAMES T. STALEY, University of Washington, Seattle, Washington

JOHN H. VANDERMEULEN, Bedford Institute of Oceanography, Dartmouth, Nova Scotia, Canada

J. ROBERT WAALAND, University of Washington, Seattle, Washington

DOUGLAS D. WEBER, Northwest and Alaska Fisheries Center, Seattle, Washington

FRED T. WEISS, Shell Development Co., Houston, Texas

MARLEEN M. WEKELL, University of Washington, Seattle, Washington

SEFTON R. WELLINGS, University of California, Davis, California

JEANNETTE A. WHIPPLE, Southwest Fisheries Center, Tiburon, California

WILLIAM T. YASUTAKE, U.S. Fish and Wildlife Service, Seattle, Washington

CLAUDE E. ZoBELL, Scripps Institution of Oceanography, La Jolla, California

The authors of Chapters 7 and 8 give special acknowledgments as follows:

Chapter 7. The cost of preparing this manuscript was defrayed by funds from the University of California and the National Science Foundation, Washington, D.C. Some of the data reported were obtained in the course of research studies conducted in these laboratories; this work was supported by funds awarded to W.N. Holmes from the American Petroleum Institute (Contract No. OS12C), the National Science Foundation (Grants No. GB 20806 and BNS 74-17367), and the University of California, Committee on Research. The bibliographic search was completed through a grant to Professor M. Marcus, Institute for the Interdisciplinary Applications of Algebra and Combinatorics, from the Office of Science Information Services of the National Science Foundation (Grant No. DSI 76-09080). We also wish to express our appreciation to Mrs. Ilene Hames, who assisted in the preparation of the manuscript.

Chapter 8. We thank Dr. R. Thomson, Messrs. D.St. Aubin, T. Austin, and A. Gilman, of the Pathology Department, University of Guelph, and Dr. F.R. Engelhardt, Southeastern Massachusetts University. Hakgagiak of Holman, Northwest Territories, assisted in the field studies. We wish to thank the Polar Continental Shelf Project for logistic support, Mr. J. Holer, Niagara Marineland and Game Farm, for providing maintenance facilities for some of the seals, and Dr. J. Schroder and Mr. J. Parsons for seal maintenance at Guelph. This chapter is modified from the publication; Geraci, J.R. and T.G. Smith, J. Fish. Res. Board Can. 33:1976-84 (1976).

Contents of Volume I

NATURE AND FATE OF PETROLEUM

Chapter 1

ACUTE TOXIC EFFECTS OF PETROLEUM ON ARCTIC AND SUBARCTIC MARINE ORGANISMS

DONOVAN R. CRADDOCK
Environmental Conservation Division

Northwest and Alaska Fisheries Center
National Marine Fisheries Service
National Oceanic and Atmospheric Administration
U.S. Department of Commerce
Seattle, Washington 98112

INTRODUCTION

Petroleum exploration, production, and transportation in Arctic and Subarctic areas and the attendant pollution have caused concern for the welfare of the marine biota. Acute

toxicity tests or bioassays have played an important part in
the study of the short-term effects of petroleum pollution on
the biota.

The terms toxicity test and bioassay are frequently used
interchangeably. Bioassays were normally associated with the
measurement of drugs where the prime interest was in determining from the degree of response of the test organism the
strength of the stimulus [1]. A true bioassay technically
requires that a standard preparation be used both for a comparison of activity with the test material and as a means of
defining the unit in which the activity is to be expressed.
Sprague [2] defined a bioassay as "a test in which the quantity or strength of material is determined by the reaction of
the living organism to it." He felt that this definition adequately covered the usual pharmacological tests of drugs as
well as the toxicity tests conducted in pollution studies.
Toxicity tests are studies in which the effects of subjecting
living organisms to various concentrations of a particular
substance or to a range of physical conditions are compared
with the effects produced in control groups. Controls consist
of the same living organisms subjected to the same treatment
except for exposure to the test pollutant or condition. In
acute toxicity tests, the effect of the treatment is measured
by the time to death of the test animal. Standard Methods,
American Public Health Association [3] simply state that "In a
bioassay, experimental organisms are subjected to a series of
concentrations of a known or suspected toxicant under adequately controlled conditions."

The objectives of this chapter are to review the literature on acute toxicity bioassay techniques using aquatic
(mainly marine) organisms and to review the results of bioassays of petroleum relative to the toxicity of the various
products tested and the sensitivity of the various marine
organisms used (mainly arctic and subarctic species).

BACKGROUND

Acute toxicity studies have long played an important role
in man's effort to monitor and modify the effects of his activities on the biota. Tarzwell [4] provided a brief history
of these activities in the United States and stated that in
the early part of this century studies were initiated to determine the effect of various substances, including gashouse
wastes, on fishes. He further stated that during the 1920's
and 1930's techniques and methods were refined, but noted the
great diversity in methods and reporting that continued, the
lack of description of methods used, and the wide range of
toxicities reported for the same materials when tested with
the same species. During the 1940's the need for ·standardiza-

tion was recognized and considerable effort was expended in trying to achieve some degree of uniformity in methods and reporting. A report [5] of the Subcommittee on Research of the Water Pollution Federation was published in 1951 as "Bioassay methods for the evaluation of the acute toxicity of industrial wastes to fish." These recommendations have been widely used and accepted as standard methods for short-term acute bioassays with fish. They were improved and included in Standard Methods, American Public Health Association [3]. Katz [6] also prepared an excellent review of the historical background and methods of toxicity bioassay. Although many have worked for standardization and much has been accomplished, even more remains to be done.

IMPORTANCE AND SCOPE

Acute toxicity tests or bioassays have almost unlimited uses, but the primary uses of these short-term tests are to answer one or more of the following general questions about some material [2]: (1) Is it toxic? (2) How toxic? (3) Does it vary in toxicity? (4) Which fractions of the material are most toxic? and (5) Do treatment methods and dilution effectively protect the aquatic biota? Other important uses of acute toxicity tests would be to (1) determine the relative sensitivity of various species and life stages to a pollutant, (2) develop criteria for establishing water-quality standards, and (3) determine the variable toxicity of a substance synergistic with other substances or conditions. Acute toxicity studies are especially useful in determining the sensitive species of an ecosystem that can then be used as indicator species for a particular type of pollution. Acute toxicity studies are a useful preliminary step to determining concentrations to be tested in long-term or sublethal exposures.

Many industrial wastes, including petroleum materials, are very complex mixtures of chemicals; often incomplete information is available on the toxicity of the various chemical components. Frequently analytical methods for measuring the individual chemicals are not sensitive enough or are otherwise inadequate, and consequently estimating the toxicity of a waste from information on individual components is very difficult. Bioassays can help solve this problem since they can be used to directly evaluate the toxicity of chemically complex wastes in probably the quickest most economical way [7]. Acute toxicity studies are normally of short duration (frequently seven days or less) and have the advantages of being comparatively easy to conduct and are economical [8].

For these reasons, acute toxicity tests have been far more frequently employed than chronic exposure tests, but they are ordinarily only the first step toward acquiring meaningful information that can be gained only through long-term studies.

LIMITATIONS

Although acute toxicity tests have a wide range of uses, they also have some rather severe limitations. One of the greatest of these is that only the time to death of the test organism is considered, whereas a wide range of behavioral and physiological responses are completely ignored. Another serious limitation is the great difficulty in translating the lethal concentrations determined in acute toxicity tests into concentrations that might be safe over a long period of exposure. After an initial mortality of weaker individuals there may be an extended period of no loss. It is equally difficult to relate the time of death in 96 hr acute toxicity studies to the effects of exposures of shorter duration. Brungs [9] noted that some toxic substances continue to exhibit direct lethal effects for as long as several months and suggested that the standard lethal test should be extended from 96 hr to two weeks. Furthermore, the various life history stages of a particular species may show different sensitivities to toxic materials; also, organisms may show interspecies and intraspecies differences in tolerance. Variations in water quality may also have a profound influence on the results of the acute toxicity test. Consequently, the information obtained may only be directly applicable to the particular species and life stage tested at the temperature and water quality used [10]. General inferences of importance may surely be made, but there is considerable debate concerning the extension of results from species-to-species and life stage-to-life stage. A continuing problem is the difficulty in standardizing methods of testing and assessment of data, because so many tests are conducted for specific purposes under a specific set of circumstances.

ACUTE BIOASSAY TECHNIQUES

Several reports have been published that outline and describe in some detail the techniques to be followed to help insure useful and standardized results from acute toxicity tests with aquatic organisms. An early paper was by Hart et al. [11]; however, one of the better known papers by Doudoroff et al. [5] was an early effort at standardization and formed the basis for the section on toxicity to fish in Standard Methods, American Public Health Association [3]. Other papers by Henderson and Tarzwell [7], Lennon and Walker [12], Sprague [2,13-15], Daugherty [16], and Burdick [17] provide supplementary data and describe refined techniques or special situ-

ations. Tarzwell [18] and LaRoche et al. [19] specifically
directed their studies toward the bioassay of petroleum. The
following summary of bioassay methods was drawn from the foregoing works in general and especially from the papers by
Doudoroff et al. [5], Sprague [2], and Tarzwell [18]; the
methods will apply to laboratory conditions generally.

Recently a shift in the emphasis of acute toxicity tests
has been made. Previously, the acute toxicity of a particular
material, or waste product, to a specific indicator species
was determined; currently, the tests are carried out on a variety of marine organisms and their various life stages under
a variety of conditions. This has come about because of the
widespread pollution of the marine environment by petroleum
and other products and the realization that the effect on all
members of the ecosystem and their various life stages must be
known to adequately assess the impact of pollution.

The procedure and techniques employed in acute toxicity
testing will vary depending on the objectives of the investi-
gator. Doudoroff et al. [5] and Sprague [2] described the
methods and procedures of conducting simple lethal tests;
Turnbull et al. [20] discussed the testing and toxicity of refinery materials; and Tarzwell [18] and LaRoche et al. [19]
described a procedure to indicate the relative toxicity of
dispersants and oil-dispersant mixtures. Brungs [9] described
the procedure for continuous flow tests. Regardless of the
specific objectives, all acute toxicity or bioassay studies
have several common features, which are considered in the
remainder of this section.

TEST ANIMALS

Most of the guides for conducting bioassays with aquatic
organisms deal with finfish, but concern for the entire ecosystem demands that bioassay procedures for all marine organisms be developed. The determination of the toxicity of a
particular substance requires a test species that is common
and is important economically, recreationally, or ecologically
to the body of water concerned. The indicator species should
be sensitive to adverse conditions, but capable of existing
well in captivity. If a specific species is of interest and
does not meet the foregoing requirements, the research will
have to allow for its peculiarities. Different species may
show important variations in sensitivity to a particular toxicant and generalizations from the results may be very risky.
Too frequently in the past extremely hardy species were selected as bioassay animals because they were easy to maintain
in the laboratory. This practice could, of course, provide
misleading results. The same is true in the assessment of
data on acute toxicity tests of various life stages of an

individual species; the ova, larva, or juvenile stage may be more or less sensitive to the toxicant than the adult stage. Moreover, the spawning stage of the adults may be a critically sensitive stage often overlooked. All of the test animals should be collected from the same area at the same time and should be of the same species and life stage, and approximately the same size. There are different criteria for size of fish, but one that is usually accepted is that the length of the largest fish should not be more than 1.5 times the length of the smallest. Other investigators believe that this range is too great and that it should be reduced. Although size variation in invertebrates may be just as significant, it is often ignored. Small specimens are preferred because of the convenience of smaller test chambers. There should be no objection to large specimens as long as proper adjustments are made in the volume and/or flow of water provided per animal.

Doudoroff et al. [5] prepared a list of suggested indicator species for freshwater fishes and Becker et al. [21] prepared lists of bioassay animals for each of eight regions of the United States. An excellent list that includes fish, crustacea, mollusca, and algae was presented by Vaughan [22] for the Pacific Northwest. The standard fish for petroleum studies suggested by Tarzwell [18] were the fathead minnow (*Pimephales promelas*) for fresh water and the mummichog (*Fundulus heteroclitus*) for east coast salt water. If the problem at hand is to determine the relative toxicity of a pollutant, the use of one of the standard species would naturally be advisable. If, however, interest is in the effect of the pollutant on the environment generally, all species that can be maintained in a healthy condition in the laboratory may serve as indicator species.

HOLDING TEST FISH

Holding facilities may be almost any arrangement that provides adequate volume and flow for the numbers of animals to be held. Circular fiberglass tanks are very convenient because they may be obtained in various sizes and can be set up with an inlet, central drain, and standpipe arrangement. This system will provide a gentle circular current in the tank for exercise for the animals as well as adequate drainage for removing debris and minimizing cleaning problems. Flowing water is preferred; Sprague [2] advised that, ideally, there should be a flow of one liter of water per minute for every kilogram of fish being held and a volume of at least one liter of water for every 10 grams of fish. Additionally, the total volume of flow over 2-3 hr should be equal to the total volume of the tank. Aeration may also be provided and is advisable if dissolved oxygen levels are much below saturation. General recommendations for holding invertebrates were not given, but the foregoing should suffice in most cases. Special arrangements are necessary for holding larval stages.

Acclimation of the test animals to the dilution water and to the approximate test temperatures of the experiment may take from 10 to 30 days. A period of at least two weeks would normally suffice. Acclimating an organism to a temperature lower than that of its environment requires more time than acclimating one to a temperature higher than that of its environment [23,24], and each species has an upper and lower ultimate incipient lethal level. Changes from the water quality of the organisms' natural environment should be kept to a minimum. Test animals should be fed during the acclimaation period to maintain them in a healthy condition. Many fish species adapt readily to frozen moist pelleted food that is specially formulated and available in a range of sizes; however, providing adequate food for some invertebrate species can be a much more difficult problem.

Diseased organisms should not be used in a bioassay, and any sign of disease or other abnormality in physical condition or behavior would render them unsuitable. A mortality of more than 5% during the four days prior to testing is considered excessive. A mortality curve staying at an asymptotic level for at least a week at the end of the acclimation period is an indication of healthy organisms. Perkins [25] discussed the pitfalls to avoid in collecting and holding marine animals for toxicity testing.

DILUTION WATER

The source of the dilution water for toxicity studies depends in part on the objective of the study. If the objective is to determine the toxicity of some material alone then any source of clean nontoxic water is suitable as long as it is not contaminated with chlorine, copper, zinc, or other toxic elements. Well water may be suitable, or natural unpolluted waters from streams or bays may be used. Instructions for the preparation of standard seawater and fresh water are given by Tarzwell [18]. In the case of seawater, care should be taken to provide the salinity requirements of the test animal. If the objective is to determine the effect of the pollutant on organisms from a particular body of water, then, of course, the dilution water should be obtained from that source. More specifics on water quality may be found in the sources previously mentioned.

TEST TANKS

Test containers should normally be of glass, certainly of an inert nontoxic substance, and the volume, shape, and color should be commensurate with the behavior of the organisms. Cylindrical tanks offer the advantages of better circulation, reduced cannibalism, and a better environment for schooling species. The tank size depends on the size and number of organisms to be tested and on the provision for adequate volume for each animal. An adequate volume of water is necessary to prevent depletion of the toxicant, lowering of the dissolved oxygen level, and fouling of the water with wastes. In static tests the guideline of one gram of tissue per liter of test solution is often followed. A guideline by Sprague [2] suggested the need of 2-3 liters of new test water per gram of fish per day either supplied by inflow in a constant flow system or by replacment in a static system. In static bioassays, this level of test solution could be met by changing the test water daily. Such practice would have the added advantage of maintaining the test concentrations of the toxicants. In continuous flow conditions, the same volumes of new test water should be maintained (2-3 l/g per day). In addition, the volume of flow should equal the volume of the test tank during 8 hr. If the test material is very unstable or volatile, such as a water-soluble fraction (WSF) of petroleum, replacement rate of the media should be faster so that the flow equals the volume of the tank during 3-5 hr. Depth of water should be more than 6 inches, but the surface area should be small, especially when testing volatile substances.

TEST TEMPERATURES

Although standard temperatures have been suggested and some support is evident for 15°C for cold water species and 25°C for warm water species when testing the relative toxicity of a substance, little deviation from the ambient temperature at time of collection or normal habitat temperature of the organism should be allowed. All comparative toxicity tests should be carried out at the same temperature, inasmuch as temperature may have an impact on toxicity and volatility of the test material.

DISSOLVED OXYGEN

The oxygen content of the test solution must be maintained at a suitable level for the well-being of the particular test animal; usually not less than 5-10 parts per million (ppm), depending on the species and temperature, or more than saturation. Artificial aeration is not generally acceptable because volatile toxicants or volatile components of the toxicant may be driven off. If reducing the number of fish and increasing the volume of solution does not solve the problem of depressed oxygen levels, special methods may be employed [5]. The best solution is to use a continuous flow system.

NUMBER OF TEST ANIMALS

Ten animals per test chamber is an accepted standard; however, more or fewer may be used if conditions of volume or flow dictate. If fewer than 10 animals must be tested per vessel, additional units of the same concentration should be set up so that the total tested at each concentration is at least ten, otherwise confidence in the results is reduced. Simultaneous replicate tests should be provided to obtain a value as close as possible to the true mean.

TESTING PROCEDURE

All conditions should be as identical as possible in each tank (including the control tanks). Tanks should be of identical construction and volume and contain the same number and size of organisms. Physical and chemical conditions, such as water flow, temperature, lighting, and dissolved oxygen content, as well as parameters indicating metabolite build up, should be monitored frequently during the course of the experiment. Location of test lots should be randomized to eliminate position effects in the laboratory and the organisms should be distributed serially to the various test tanks to provide random selection of the organisms within a test lot. The test material should be stored in completely full, tightly stoppered bottles at 0°-4°C until ready for use. The dilutions for all concentrations of the test samples should be prepared from the same source material and should be prepared at the same time. If continuous flow conditions are to be used, the source container should be properly stoppered and vented through a water tube arrangement to reduce loss of volatile material. Guides for the selection of the range of concentrations to be tested are given by the American Public Health Association [3] and by Doudoroff et al. [5]. Exploratory tests, using a small number of organisms, are also advised to provide a general idea of the levels to use in the actual tests. The concentrations of toxicant used should ideally provide from 0% mortality to 100% mortality. The concentrations are frequently a logarithmic or geometric series.

The nature of the toxicant and the method of its release into the environment may determine or dictate the method of testing. If the material is relatively stable in a water solution and is discharged into the environment over short intervals, it would lend itself to short-term static testing. On the other hand, if the toxicant is volatile, easily degradable, rapidly detoxified, or high in oxygen demand, and is released into the environment continuously, it would lend itself to continuous flow bioassay methods. A continuous flow system has the added advantages of providing constant test conditions; continuous renewal of unstable contaminants; replacement of dissolved oxygen and nutrients; removal of metabolic waste; and testing over a long period, in some cases a life cycle of the organism. There are two general techniques of continuous toxicant flow delivery: dilution and adjustment of two flow rates. Brungs [9] discussed several types of these two systems and provided references to them. The dilution system has the advantage of being fail-safe, that is if the flow of dilution water stops so does the flow of toxicant.

Numerous methods have been used to expose marine organisms to petroleum in bioassays in an effort to simulate conditions during an actual spill. Conditions encountered on a beach have been simulated by raising organisms through a layer of whole oil [26], and by letting oil floating on the water surface settle on the organisms by repeatedly lowering and raising the water level [27]. In some cases benthic organisms were exposed to oil settled to the bottom by sand mixtures [28] and intertidal organisms were exposed by pouring oil on the sand surface [27]. Oil has even been introduced in the food of the test animals. In most instances oil was added to seawater volumetrically to obtain the desired initial concentration, mixing the oil and seawater in some manner and then introducing the test animals.

Preparation of the test media for the bioassay of petroleum with marine organisms has ranged from simply using the whole oil to mixing oil in seawater in various ways, to the fairly complicated extraction of the WSF. An oil-in-water dispersion (OWD) may be prepared by merely layering oil on the surface [29], by mixing initially by mechanical or water agitation [30-33], or stirring constantly during the bioassay. Different methods of continuous flow bioassay with oil include metering oil and seawater through a static mixer [22] or using a series of tanks or baffles to allow the mixed oil particles to settle up before exposing the organisms [30]. Most of the mixing methods mentioned provide an OWD, whereas the last method provides a WSF. The material resulting from an OWD is chemically the same as the parent oil, whereas the WSF is considerably different.

Recently investigators have been standardizing the preparation of test materials by following the methods of Anderson et al. [32] with only some slight modification in the preparation of OWD and WSF. The OWD was prepared by adding a specific volume of oil to seawater and shaking vigorously for 5 min

at approximately 200 c/m. The oil and water layers were allowed to separate for 30-60 min before the test organisms were
introduced through the surface oil film into the aqueous layer
by means of glass tubing. The WSF was prepared by adding 1
part of oil to 9 parts of seawater in a capped 19 liter bottle
and stirring slowly for 20 hr at room temperature with a mag-
netic stirrer. The oil and water phases were allowed to separate for 1-6 hr before the water phase was siphoned off from
beneath the slick for immediate use in testing. Gordon et al.
[34] showed that the concentrations of oil accomodated in seawater under laboratory conditions were directly related to the
amount of oil added and the degree of mixing, but inversely
related to temperature.

Mount and Brungs [35] and Benoit and Puglisi [36] described apparatus for maintaining a series of constant concentrations in flowing water; Lichatowich et al. [37] also made
specific reference to the problems of testing the toxicity of
crude and refined oils. Vaughan et al. [22] pointed out the
importance of standardizing the methods and conditions under
which oil and water are mixed and the resulting dispersion in
the test tanks during the bioassay period. A serious problem
with continuous flow studies of crude petroleum oils has been
the difficulty of obtaining a consistent WSF of the material
on a continuous basis. The petroleum may form an emulsion so
that the test solution contains both dispersed oil and the
WSF, or the character of the WSF may change during the testing
period.

Static tests usually run for 96 hr, whereas continuous
flow tests may run for 96 hr to 2 weeks or even longer. Feeding of the organisms is not recommended in static bioassays,
but is used in continuous flow tests because of the length of
the test period and to eliminate feeding stress. All components of a diluter apparatus (used to dispense various concentrations of the test material to the test tanks) should be
made of glass to avoid sorption and leaching of toxic materials, particularly if testing petroleum.

Observations of the behavior of the test animal and for
mortality should start almost immediately after placing the
animals in the test solution; often much relevant data are
lost otherwise. Sprague [2] suggested a series of observations in a logarithmic series that can be accomplished mainly
within regular working hours; 15 min, 30 min, 60 min, 2 hr, 4
hr, 8 hr, 14 ± 2 hr, 24 hr, 33 ± 3 hr, 2 day, 3 day, 4 day,
etc. Death of the fish should be assumed if no respiratory or
other movement is detectable, even following gentle stimulation of the animal with a glass rod or other suitable probe.
Similar criteria for death have been established for other
organisms. Daily observations should be made and any deaths
recorded and the dead animals removed. It is also a good

practice to hold the test animals in fresh flowing water for some time after the test to check for delayed death which may be significant, especially in invertebrates [38].

ANALYSIS OF TEST MEDIA

Analytical monitoring of concentrations of individual compounds or groups of compounds in the test media during the course of the experiment is essential for meaningful and comparable results when testing petroleum hydrocarbons due to their complex and unstable nature (e.g., tendency toward photooxidation). Monitoring and in depth analysis of crude and refined oils used in bioassay studies was first reported by Anderson et al. [32]. Currently, many investigators are incorporating analysis of the test media in their studies. These include Vaughn [22], Bean et al. [30], Rossi et al. [39], Rossi and Anderson [40], Vanderhorst et al. [41], Rice et al. [42] and Rice et al. [38].

Several analytical techniques have been used to monitor the petroleum hydrocarbon content of test media. A detailed discussion of analytical methods used with petroleum hydrocarbons may be found in Chapter 1 of Volume I. Infrared spectrophotometry (IR) has probably been used most frequently and it gives a measure of the total hydrocarbon content of the media. However, considerable difficulty may be encountered with IR analysis because of problems arising from difficulties in the preparation of the standards and the samples. IR analysis determines the overall or total hydrocarbon content of the sample by measuring certain carbon-hydrogen bonds.

Ultraviolet (UV) spectrophotometry can be used to monitor the unsaturated petroleum hydrocarbon content of the medium, but here again problems arise in preparing the proper standard. The UV absorption varies depending on the compound and therefore it is not practical to make up an adequate standard for complex petroleum hydrocarbon samples. Consequently UV is usually measured in equivalents of some specific compound such as naphthalene [43]. Both IR and UV are non-specific for determining the presence of individual compounds.

Fluorescence spectrophotometry has been used to monitor certain types of compounds; however, a very small proportion of petroleum hydrocarbon compounds fluoresce and for this reason it is not as widely used as IR and UV for routine analysis.

Chromatography is an analytical technique that can be used to separate specific compounds in a complex mixture for subsequent analyses. Gas chromatography (GC) has the widest application since it can both separate and quantify hydrocarbons ranging from methane to complex six-ring aromatic compounds. Liquid (LC) and thin-layer (TLC) chromatography may be used in specific applications and are especially useful with compounds that are not suitable (e.g., not readily volatilized) for GC analysis.

Mass spectrophotometry (MS) is a method used for the identification of specific compounds and is often interfaced with a gas chromatograph.

When dealing with complex mixtures such as petroleum hydrocarbons the test media may be monitored using one of the simple and rapid methods such as IR, UV, or GC, depending on the petroleum material being used.

REPORTING TEST RESULTS

There are numerous ways of reporting the results of bioassays, but almost all relate to the concentration of the contaminant tolerated or survived by 50% of the test animals over the experimental period. Some of the designations include lethal dose (LD), lethal concentration (LC), effective concentration (EC), effective dose (ED), and tolerance limit (TL). Median tolerance limit (TLm or TL_{50}) is the recommended designation and is used most commonly. However, LC_{50} (lethal concentration for 50% of the individuals) is frequently used. The two terms have the same numerical value. The unit designation should also indicate the exposure period: for example, 24 hr TL_{50}, 48 hr TL_{50}, or 96 hr TL_{50}. The TL may be calculated for mortality levels other than 50% and is reported as TL_{25}, TL_{75}, etc. In 1949 Litchfield and Wilcoxon [44] described a method of evaluating bioassay results using a rapid graphic method of estimating EDm (median effective dose), calculation of the slope of dose-percent effect curves and calculation of confidence limits. Confidence limits should be reported to facilitate comparison with other studies. The nomogram developed by these authors is simple and quick to use as is their chi-square goodness of fit test.

Acute toxicity data may be plotted on semilogarithmic coordinate graph paper [3]; concentrations of toxicant used are indicated on the logarithmic scale and percentage survival of test animals are indicated on the arithmetic scale. The data is plotted and a straight line is drawn through the points representing the true concentrations where survival was just below and just above 50%. The concentration where this line crosses the 50% survival line is the TL_{50} value. Sprague [2] explained how to calculate LC_{50} during the progress of the experiment by constructing graphs using special paper having a logarithmic scale and probability (probit) scale to guide the researcher. He also explained the method of constructing a toxicity curve, the final estimation of LC_{50} or the incipient LC_{50}, and how to use computer and alternate methods of analysis.

Reported results of acute toxicity studies should include the final TL_{50}, confidence limits of the data, and the slope of the probit line. In addition, a complete description of the fish, the material, the methods, and test conditions should be given. The following seven point rating system for evaluating reliability and usefulness of bioassay data was taken from Cairns and reported by Sprague [2]: (1) test organisms clearly identified as to species, size, and weight; (2) dilution water quality stated; (3) bioassay organisms preconditioned or acclimated to test environment; (4) methods and procedures clearly stated; (5) appropriate controls included; (6) adequate control of environmental conditions; and (7) statistical evaluation of data.

Items falling under (4) that should be clearly reported are the method and frequency of sampling of the test solution and the method of analysis for the test toxicants. This information is especially important in tests of unstable materials. Other papers on bioassay apparatus, analysis, and presentation of data were reported by Bean et al. [30], Vaughan [22], Vanderhorst et al. [31], Tarzwell [4,45], Skidmore [46], Brown [1], Graham and Dorris [47], Weiss and Botts [48], Mount and Brungs [35], Hart et al. [49], and Benville and Korn [50].

ACUTE TOXICITY OF PETROLEUM

Although many toxicants have been bioassayed with many marine species, it is only within the last few years that much attention has been focused on the toxicity of crude oil, refined petroleum products, and their components. Only a few of these studies have been related to the arctic or subarctic marine species which might be affected by oil pollution resulting from the development and transportation of Alaskan North Slope oil. In the tables that follow, information is presented on the results of laboratory studies on petroleum-related acute toxicity tests on generally arctic or subarctic marine species. Many field studies have been reported in the literature, but are not included because the original reports contained no information on the levels of toxicants or on other important parameters. In this tabulation, I have attempted to include as much information from the laboratory studies as practicable regarding the life stage of the species tested, the nature and preparation of the test material, and other important parameters of the experiment including type of test (static or continuous flow), size of test chambers, volume of water, temperature, salinity, aeration conditions, replacing the test material, duration of tests, and nature of the reported data (TLm or percentage survival). Concentrations are usually reported in ppm, and the method of analysis of the toxicant, if any, is given, as well as remarks or other important observations by the author of the paper being reviewed or by the author of this review.

Although the tabulation is directed toward the acute toxicity of oil on arctic and subarctic species, comparatively little work has been done on arctic species, whereas considerable information is available on work done in other areas. A few of these studies have been included if they deal with a widely distributed species or if they provide an example of a particularly well conducted study. In an attempt to bring some order from the mass of published data, the tables have been organized on a phylogenetic basis, and consequently a single paper may be repeated in more than one table if the author studied animals from more than one phyla. Studies on plants, bacteria, and protozoa have not been included.

In each case reported the common name of the organism is followed by the scientific name and life history stage (first column of tables). If no life history stage is mentioned, it should be assumed that the adult stage was involved. The second column contains a description of the material tested and may include information on material preparation. The third column describes the test parameters as well as possible in the necessarily small space. It includes information on the type of test (static or continuous flow), type of water (seawater or fresh water), temperature, salinity, dissolved oxygen content, duration of exposure, and nature of reported data (TLm, LC_{50}, EC_{50}, percentage survival or mortality). The fourth column gives the concentration of the material eliciting the response described in the previous column. These concentrations are usually expressed in volume-to-volume basis in ppm if no detailed analysis of individual components of the media was made. When original data were presented in units other than ppm, a conversion was made to ppm if practical. The fifth column presents pertinent observations regarding the study and especially makes note if an analysis was made of the actual test material, either before, during, or after the test. The first six tables are in phylogenetic order: Table 1 - Coelenterata, Table 2 - Echinodermata, Table 3 - Mollusca, Table 4 - Annelida, Table 5 - Arthropoda, Table 6 - Chordata; Table 7 deals with general studies.

INTERPRETATION OF RESULTS

Great difficulty persists in interpreting and comparing the results of the various workers in the study of acute toxicity of petroleum to marine animals, mainly because of the lack of standardization of experimental methods and the frequent lack of monitoring of the hydrocarbon concentrations of the experimental media during the bioassay period. These same difficulties were noted by Moore and Dwyer [99], Anderson

et al. [32], and Rice et al. [38] in their assessments of published data on the effects of oil on marine organisms. The
levels of the fractions in the test media should be measured
frequently, because petroleum materials show great variability
in composition, weather rapidly, and are only slightly soluble
in water; and the fractions are often volatile. Test concentrations reported are frequently only those used initially to
prepare the material and not those actually encountered by the
test animals as determined by periodic analysis of the test
media. The mode of presenting petroleum material to the test
animals also influences the results and comparability of the
data, and differences in handling the test media can radically
alter the actual content of volatile components. Initial concentrations may be reported in a manner making comparison difficult and in some cases the material tested is not properly
identified or described. Often because of the complex nature
and expense of the analytical procedures, sufficient data for
proper interpretation of results are not always obtained on
levels of specific hydrocarbons in the test media and in the
animals.

The preceding tables illustrate the difficulty in making
comparisons of the relative tolerance of various phyla to toxic petroleum materials and the relative tolerance of classes
and orders within a phyla. Moore et al. [100] estimated the
range of concentrations of various petroleum materials showing
acute toxicity to various, arbitrarily-classified, groups of
marine organisms (Table 7). Data from the table indicate that
larvae of all species of marine organisms would be the least
resistant to water-soluble hydrocarbons of petroleum, No. 2
fuel oil, and fresh crude oil; gastropods would be the most
resistant; and pelagic crustaceans, benthic crustaceans, bivalves, and finfish would be intermediately resistant.

Although early bioassays with petroleum, where no chemical analyses of the test media were made, contributed little
to an understanding of the relative sensitivity of various
phyla and classes, they did provide the necessary developmental stages in the refinement of petroleum toxicity testing
techniques. They also provided a general knowledge of the
relative toxicity of petroleum to the marine biota in that
they demonstrated the generally greater toxicity of more refined oils over that of crude oils. This relationship was
verified by Anderson et al. [32] who found the WSF and OWD of
refined oils considerably more toxic than those of crude oils.
On the other hand, Rice et al. [38] found no significant differences between the WSF toxicities of Cook Inlet crude oil
and No. 2 fuel oil to the bulk of 27 Alaskan marine species
tested. The three species that did show a difference (scallops, scooter shrimps, and pink salmon fry) were all more sensitive to the refined No. 2 fuel oil. It is generally agreed

by those doing in-depth analyses that the soluble aromatic hydrocarbon components, especially the naphthalenes may be the most acutely toxic constituents of the petroleum WSF. These authors [38] concluded that of the 27 Alaskan species tested, fish were among the most sensitive and that invertebrates included both sensitive and relatively resistant species. The resistant species were mostly intertidal and had some adaptation allowing temporary insulation from stress. They also compared six recent studies [22,30,32,38,39,41] using comparable analytical methods and generally similar mixing and exposure procedures to compare the sensitivity to oil of Alaskan species relative to species from warmer areas. They concluded that although Alaskan species seemed more sensitive, differences in TLm values between cold and warm water forms was probably due to differences in toxicity resulting from greater persistence of hydrocarbon in cold water rather than to differences in the sensitivity of the species. Others have observed that dispersions prepared at low temperatures were more toxic [51].

CONCLUSIONS

    In an arctic environment, the intertidal areas are continually scoured by ice, effectively minimizing the populations that may inhabit that area and consequently limiting the opportunity for potential damage to invertebrate fauna from petroleum deposited on the beaches. However, petroleum trapped under the ice does not weather and lose its toxic effects as it would on open water, and with the advent of the spring breakup the toxic components of the oil would be reintroduced into the water column at the time of greatest biological activity [51]. Thus, the sensitive larval stages of many species would be exposed to lethal and detrimental sublethal concentrations of oil.

    Adult neritic species would not be expected to suffer as adversely from petroleum spills or blowouts except in the immediate vicinity because the concentrations of petroleum components in the water area would not be high or persist for long. Most species are not acutely affected by whole crude oil at levels less than 100 ppm and most would be expected to avoid the higher concentrations.

    Benthic organisms may be subjected to petroleum contamination by direct contact and through the process of grazing on bottoms containing sedimented oil. The effect of such contamination is not known, but Percy and Mullin [51] found that benthic organisms were killed only when exposed to the high levels of petroleum that would be encountered in the immediate vicinity of an oil spill; such high levels would not likely be encountered elsewhere in nature.

Although it appears that the larval stages of marine organisms are most likely to be affected, the evidence is incomplete and conflicting. Rossi and Anderson [40] stated that there are indications of significant differences in sensitivity to petroleum hydrocarbons among life stages of marine invertebrates and pointed out the great resistance of larval stages of *Neanthes* as compared to the young adult.

Considerable information is available on the toxic effects of petroleum on marine organisms, but most of the data are incomplete, conflicting, and in many cases, not comparable; furthermore, few data relate to marine organisms or the environment of the arctic and subarctic regions. The works of Rice et al. [42] and Rice et al. [38] are the most extensive to date relative to the sensitivity of various arctic marine species to the WSF of crude and refined oil. In addition, their preparation and exposure procedure allow comparison. Analyses were made of the exposure concentrations by IR spectrophotometry. An average of the 96 hr TLm values reported by these authors for various species of the same phyla give a general indication of the relative sensitivity of the various phyla (Table 8). However, there may be wide species variation within a phyla and one should not assume a particular species is resistant because the phyla as a whole is resistant. As an example, a whelk had a 96 hr TLm of > 21.0 ppm, whereas a scallop had a 96 hr TLm of only 2.1 ppm. An examination of Table 8 indicates that Chordata (fishes) are generally the most sensitive to the WSF of crude oil as stated by the above authors. Molluscs and possibly echinoderms appear to be quite resistant, whereas anthropods may be either sensitive (crab and shrimp) or resistant (amphipod, isopod, mysid, and barnacle) to the WSF of crude oil. The range of sensitivity of the various phyla to the obviously more toxic WSF of No. 2 fuel oil was relatively small (96 hr TLm of 1.8-4.1 ppm). The greater toxicity probably is caused by higher concentrations of aromatic hydrocarbons.

The greatest losses in the arctic may occur in the plankton populated by the sensitive eggs and larvae of many species that are found in open water away from beaches. The intertidal areas of the arctic are rather narrow and are comparatively barren of marine life; however, subarctic intertidal areas may be quite extensive and are abundantly populated. Such areas would be expected to be increasingly affected by oil spills and blowouts.

Predictive capability relative to effects of petroleum pollution to marine organisms of the arctic, subarctic, or any other area will be achieved only after the collection of a comprehensive, comparable bank of pertinent data. Such data can be provided only after the adoption of standardized procedures involving (1) holding and exposure of the test organisms,

(2) preparation of test media, (3) type and frequency of analysis of test media, and (4) uniform assessment of pertinent results.

PROSPECTUS

Although there are considerable data available on the short-term toxicity of various petroleum oils to marine organisms, the early work was of little value in predicting the acute effects of short-term exposure during spills or blowouts in the natural environment. This was due to a lack of standardization of bioassay procedures making comparison of results and predictions almost futile. Methods and duration of exposure were not standardized, running the entire range from whole oil through dispersions and suspensions to the WSF; exposures ranged from hours to days to weeks. To improve the situation, standards should be set for preparation of test media and methods and duration of exposure for different classes of animals and different petroleums. Since the work of Anderson et al. [32], most recent investigators have attempted some standardization of preparation and exposure.

One of the major difficulties in making comparisons and subsequent predictions from existing data is the lack of knowledge of actual hydrocarbon concentrations to which the organisms are exposed. Frequently only the beginning volume-to-volume concentrations of oil to seawater are given which may have very little meaning depending on the bioassay procedure followed. The complex nature of petroleum products, their variable solubility and volatility make frequent monitoring of the test media a necessity [32,34]. However, in the past and even now many researchers do not have the expensive and complex analytical equipment needed for good results nor the expertise to operate it. The alternative is a multidisciplinary approach which is expensive and not always possible. Reliable, simplified methods for analysis of hydrocarbon concentration of bioassay test media are sorely needed.

Oftentimes laboratory bioassay conditions (physical parameters) are so dissimilar to natural conditions that the resulting information has little application to the real world. More effort must be expended to simulate natural conditions for bioassays.

A very important aspect of the petroleum pollution problem that apparently has received little attention is an assessment of the concentrations of the various components and phases of a petroleum that marine organisms might realistically encounter in nature. Few field studies following spills actually measure oil in water. Intertidal organisms may encounter whole oil, whereas neritic and benthic species would seldom be expected to contact this form of petroleum. What are the concentrations of dispersions, suspensions, and water-soluble fractions of various petroleums that marine species might be expected to encounter in Arctic and Subarctic seas and how long do they persist? These kinds of data would be invaluable in planning realistic and useful bioassays.

The major difficulty in predicting the short-term impact of oil pollution on arctic species is the lack of studies on the sensitivity of these species under arctic conditions. Some researchers [38,42] are making good progress in this area but until more well-planned studies of arctic species are completed, prediction of effects of short-term oil pollution will be little more than speculation.

Some general hypotheses relative to petroleum pollution of the marine environment that may assist in prediction of oil impact are: (1) Crude oils are generally less toxic than refined oils. Refined oils such as No. 2 diesel oil are more lethal because of a higher content of higher boiling aromatic hydrocarbons, such as naphthalenes, which are soluble but have low volatility [32]; (2) The lower boiling point and more soluble aromatic components are the most acutely toxic [32]; (3) Aromatic content of crude oils usually volatilizes appreciably with 12-24 hr of exposure, whereas refined oil may resist weathering; (4) A toxic WSF may persist longer in cold water than in temperate waters, consequently affecting all life stages to a greater degree in Arctic areas [51]; (5) The maximum WSF of crude oils in seawater is very low, probably in the range of 5-15 ppm; (6) Oil does not weather appreciably under ice and retains most of the toxic properties until the ice breaks up [51]; (7) A substantial OWD may persist for some time where extensive agitation occurs, but concentrations above 5 ppm may not persist much longer than 24 hr under normal conditions; much remains to be learned in this area.

Some short-term biological effects of exposure to petroleum have been hypothesized that may assist in making very general predictions of the impact on arctic and subarctic marine species: (1) Larvae of many species are probably the most sensitive to oil, possibly 10-100 times more sensitive than adults; (2) Eggs are generally less sensitive than larvae and apparently derive considerable protection from the chorion; (3) Confusion persists on the sensitivity of invertebrates in general. Some researchers report they are very sensitive, whereas studies in the arctic indicated some species are relatively tolerant; (4) Some adult marine species are relatively tolerant to crude oil WSF and it is believed that many adult species, especially finfish, will avoid lethal concentrations of oil; (5) Many benthic species are relatively tolerant and are killed only by high exposures not realistically expected in natural spill situations. Gastropods appear to be the most resistant to the WSF, bivalves are moderately resistant, and benthic crustaceans may be least resistant.

Considering the relatively high hydrocarbon concentrations required to cause significant short-term mortality in most adult neritic and adult benthic species, disastrous or massive kills would not be expected except in the immediate vicinity of the oil spill or blowout. This seems an even more reasonable conclusion when the facts of rapid weathering and avoidance by some species is considered. The very sensitive larval stages of many species could suffer extreme mortality, but probably only in very localized areas and over comparatively short periods.

Intertidal organisms may be damaged by both the toxic and coating properties of crude oil. Arctic intertidal areas are relatively barren and damage may not be great; however, in subarctic areas where intertidal life is abundant the reverse may be true. Oil trapped under the ice could cause serious losses to organisms inhabiting the ice-water interface as well as having serious consequences to larval and other stages exposed during the spring breakup.

The preceding short-term predictions, admittedly based on meager and sometimes conflicting information, do not appear too bleak, but many more studies using comparable preparation and exposure procedures and sophisticated media analyses are needed for confirmation.

REFERENCES

1. Brown, V.M. (1973). Concepts and outlook in testing the toxicity of substances to fish. In: Bioassay Techniques and Environmental Chemistry (G.E. Glass, ed.), p. 73-96. Ann Arbor Science Publishers, Inc., Ann Arbor, Michigan.
2. Sprague, J.B. (1973). The ABC's of pollutant bioassay using fish. In: Biological Methods for the Assessment of Water Quality. Am. Soc. Test. Mater., Spec. Tech. Publ. 528, p. 6-30.
3. American Public Health Association (1971). Standard Methods for the Examination of Water and Waste Water, 13th Ed., Washington, D.C., 874 p.
4. Tarzwell, C.M. (1971). I. Measurement of pollution effects on living organisms. Bioassays to determine allowable waste concentrations in the aquatic environment. Proc. R. Soc. Lond. B. Biol. Sci. 177:279-85.
5. Doudoroff, P., B.G. Anderson, G.E. Burdick, P.S. Galtsoff, W.B. Hart, R. Patrick, E.R. Strong, E.W. Surber, and W.M. VanHorn (1951). Bioassay methods for the evaluation of acute toxicity of industrial wastes to fish. Sewage Ind. Wastes 23:1380-97.

6. Katz, M. (1971). Toxicity bioassay techniques using
    aquatic organisms. In: Water and Water Pollution Hand-
    book (L.L. Ciaccio, ed.), Vol. 2, p. 763-800. Marcel
    Dekker, Inc., New York.

7. Henderson, C. and C.M. Tarzwell (1957). Bioassays for
    control of industrial effluents. Sewage Ind. Wastes
    29:1002-17.

8. Stephan, C.E. and D.I. Mount (1973). Use of toxicity
    tests with fish in water pollution control. In: Biolog-
    ical Methods for the Assessment of Water Quality. Am.
    Soc. Test. Mater., Spec. Tech. Publ. 528, p. 164-77.

9. Brungs, W.A. (1973). Continuous flow bioassays with
    aquatic organisms: Procedures and applications. In:
    Biological Methods for the Assessment of Water Quality.
    Am. Soc. Test. Mater., Spec. Tech. Publ. 528, p. 117-26.

10. LaRoche, G. (1972). Biological effects of short-term
    exposures to hazardous materials. In: Proceedings of
    Conference on Control of Hazardous Material Spills, March
    21-23, 1972, p. 199-206. Environmental Protection
    Agency, University of Houston, Houston, Tex.

11. Hart, W.B., P. Doudoroff, and J. Greenbank (1945). The
    evaluation of the toxicity of industrial wastes, chemi-
    cals and other substances to freshwater fishes. The
    Atlantic Refining Co., Philadelphia, Pa., 317 p.

12. Lennon, R.E. and C.R. Walker (1964). Investigations in
    fish control. I. Laboratories and methods for screening
    fish control chemicals. Bur. Sport Fish. Wildl. Circ.
    185, 15 p.

13. Sprague, J.B. (1969). Measurement of pollutant toxicity
    to fish. I. Bioassay methods for acute toxicity. Water
    Res. 3:793-821.

14. Sprague, J.B. (1970). Measurement of pollutant toxicity
    to fish. II. Utilizing and applying bioassay results.
    Water Res. 4:3-32.

15. Sprague, J.B. (1971). Measurement of pollutant toxicity
    to fish. III. Sublethal effects and "safe" concentra-
    tions. Water Res. 5:245-66.

16. Daugherty, F.M., Jr. (1951). A proposed toxicity test
    for industrial wastes to be discharged into marine
    waters. Sewage Ind. Wastes 23:1029-31.

17. Burdick, G.E. (1967). Use of bioassays in determining
    levels of toxic wastes harmful to aquatic organisms. In:
    A Symposium on Water Quality Criteria to Protect Aquatic
    Life. Am. Fish. Soc. Spec. Publ. 4, p. 7-12.

18. Tarzwell, C.M. (1969). Standard methods for determination of relative toxicity of oil dispersants and mixtures of dispersants and various oils to aquatic organisms. In: Proceedings of 1969 Joint Conference on Prevention and Control of Oil Spills, p. 179-86. American Petroleum Institute and Federal Water Pollution Control Agency, Washington, D.C.

19. LaRoche, G., R. Eisler, and C.M. Tarzwell (1970). Bioassay procedures for oil and oil dispersant toxicity evaluation. J. Water Pollut. Control Fed. 42:1982-9.

20. Turnbull, H., J.G. DeMann, and R.F. Weston (1954). Toxicity of various refinery materials to fresh water fish. Ind. Eng. Chem. 46:324-33.

21. Becker, C.D., J.A. Lichatowich, M.J. Schneider, and J.A. Strand (1973). Regional survey of marine biota for bioassay standardization of oil and oil dispersant chemicals. Am. Pet. Inst. Publ. 4167, 102 p.

22. Vaughan, B.E. (1973). Effects of oil and chemically dispersed oil on selected marine biota. Laboratory study. Am. Pet. Inst. Publ. 4191, 32 p.

23. Brett, J.R. (1956). Some principles in the thermal requirements of fishes. Q. Rev. Biol. 31:75-87.

24. Mihursky, J.A. and V.S. Kennedy (1967). Water temperature criteria to protect aquatic life. Am. Fish. Soc., Spec. Publ. 4, p. 20-32.

25. Perkins, E.J. (1972). Some problems of marine toxicity studies. Mar. Pollut. Bull. 3:13-4.

26. Dicks, B. (1973). Some effects of Kuwait crude oil on the limpet, *Patella vulgata*. Environ. Pollut. 5:219-29.

27. Taylor, T.L., J.F. Karinen, and H.M. Feder (1976). Responses of the clam *Macoma balthica* (Linnaeus), exposed to Prudhoe Bay crude oil as unmixed oil, water-soluble fraction and sediment-absorbed fraction in the laboratory. Northwest and Alaska Fisheries center, NMFS, NOAA, U.S. Dep. of Commerce, Auke Bay Fisheries Laboratory, P.O. Box 155, Auke Bay, Alaska. Processed Report, 27 p.

28. Chipman, W.A. and P.S. Galtsoff (1949). Effects of oil mixed with carbonized sand on aquatic animals. U.S. Bur. Sport Fish. Wildl., Spec. Sci. Rep. 1, p. 1-52.

29. Morrow, J.E. (1973). Oil-induced mortalities in juvenile coho and sockeye salmon. J. Mar. Res. 31:135-43.

30. Bean, R.M., J.R. Vanderhorst, and P. Wilkinson (1974). Interdisciplinary study of the toxicity of petroleum to marine organisms. Battelle Pacific Northwest Laboratories, Richland, WA, 99352, 31 p.

31. Vanderhorst, J.R., C.I. Gibson, and L.J. Moore (1976). The role of dispersion in fuel oil bioassay. Bull. Environ. Contam. Toxicol. 15:93-100.

32. Anderson, J.W., J.M. Neff, B.A. Cox, H.E. Tatem, and G.M. Hightower (1974). Characteristics of dispersions and water-soluble extracts of crude and refined oils and their toxicity to estuarine crustaceans and fish. Mar. Biol. (Berl.) 27:75-88.

33. Rice, S.D., D.A. Moles, and J.W. Short (1975). The effect of Prudhoe Bay crude oil on survival and growth of eggs, alevins, and fry of pink salmon, *Oncorhynchus gorbuscha*. In: Proceedings of 1975 Conference on Prevention and Control of Oil Pollution, p. 502-7. American Petroleum Institute, Washington, D.C.

34. Gordon, D.C., Jr., P.D. Keizer, and N.J. Prouse (1973). Laboratory studies of the accomodation of some crude and residual fuel oils in sea water. J. Fish. Res. Board Can. 30:1611-8.

35. Mount, D.I. and W.A. Brungs (1967). A simplified dosing apparatus for fish toxicology studies. Water Res. 1: 21-9.

36. Benoit, D.A. and F.A. Puglisi (1973). A simplified flow-splitting chamber and siphon for proportional diluters. Water Res. 7:1915-6.

37. Lichatowich, J.A., P.W. O'Keefe, J.A. Strand, and W.L. Templeton (1973). Development of methodology and apparatus for the bioassay of oil. In: Proceedings of 1973 Joint Conference on Prevention and Control of Oil Spills, p. 659-66. American Petroleum Institute, Washington, D.C.

38. Rice, S.D., J.W. Short, and J.F. Karinen (1976). Toxicity of Cook Inlet crude oil and No. 2 fuel oil to several Alaskan marine fishes and invertebrates. In: Symposium on Sources, Effects, and Sinks of Hydrocarbons in the Aquatic Environment, AIBS, 9-11 August 1976. American University, Washington, D.C., 12 p.

39. Rossi, S.S., J.W. Anderson, and G.S. Ward (1976). Toxicity of water-soluble fractions of four test oils for the polychaetous annelids, *Neanthes arenaceodentata* and *Capitella capitata*. Environ. Pollut. 10:9-18.

40. Rossi, S.S. and J.W. Anderson (1976). Toxicity of water-soluble fractions of No. 2 fuel oil and Louisiana crude oil to selected stages in the life history of the polychaete, *Neanthes arenaceodentata*. Bull. Environ. Contam. Toxicol. 16:18-24.

41. Vanderhorst, J.R., C.I. Gibson, and L.J. Moore (1976). Toxicity of No. 2 fuel oil to coon stripe shrimp. Mar. Pollut. Bull. 7:106-8.

42. Rice, S.D., J.W. Short, C.C. Broderson, T.A. Mecklenburg, D.A. Moles, C.J. Misch, D.L. Cheatham, and J.F. Karinen (1975). Acute toxicity and uptake-depuration studies with Cook Inlet crude oil, Prudhoe Bay crude oil, No. 2 fuel oil and several subarctic marine organisms. Dec. 1, 1975. Northwest and Alaska Fisheries Center, NMFS, NOAA, U.S. Dep. of Commerce, Auke Bay Fisheries Laboratory, P.O. Box 155, Auke Bay, Alaska. Processed Report, 144 p.

43. Neff, J.M. and J.W. Anderson (1975). An ultraviolet spectrophotometric method for the determination of naphthalene and alkylnaphthalenes in the tissues of oil-contaminated marine animals. Bull. Environ. Contam. Toxicol. 14:122-8.

44. Litchfield, J.T., Jr. and F. Wilcoxon (1949). A simplified method of evaluating dose-effect experiments. J. Pharmacol. Exp. Ther. 96:99-113.

45. Tarzwell, C.M. (1971). Toxicity of oil and oil dispersant mixtures to aquatic life. In: Water Pollution by Oil (P. Hepple, ed.), p. 263-72. Institute of Petroleum, London.

46. Skidmore, J.F. (1974). Factors affecting the toxicity of pollutants to fish. Vet. Rec. 94:456-8.

47. Graham, R.J. and T.C. Dorris (1968). Long-term toxicity bioassay of oil refinery effluents. Water Res. 2:643-63.

48. Weiss, C.M. and J.L. Botts (1957). Factors affecting the response of fish to toxic materials. Sewage Ind. Wastes 29:810-8.

49. Hart, W.B., R.F. Weston, and J.G. Demann (1945). An apparatus oxygenating test solutions in which fish are used as test animals for evaluating toxicity. Trans. Am. Fish. Soc. 75:228-36.

50. Benville, P.E., Jr. and S. Korn (1974). A simple apparatus for metering volatile liquids into water. J. Fish. Res. Board Can. 31:367-8.

51. Percy, J.A. and T.C. Mullin (1975). Effects of crude oils on arctic marine invertebrates. Beaufort Sea Tech. Rep. No. 11, Environment Canada, Victoria, B.C., 167 p.

52. Chia, F.-S. (1973). Killing of marine larvae by diesel oil. Mar. Pollut. Bull. 4:29-30.

53. Allen, H. (1971). Effects of petroleum fractions on the early development of a sea urchin. Mar. Pollut. Bull. 2:138-40.

54. Renzoni, A. (1975). Toxicity of three oils to bivalve gametes and larvae. Mar. Pollut. Bull. 6:125-8.

55. LeGore, R.S. (1974). The effect of Alaskan crude oil and selected hydrocarbon compounds on embryonic development of the Pacific oyster, *Crassostrea gigas*. Ph.D. Thesis, University of Washington, Seattle, 186 p.

56. Renzoni, A. (1975). Influence of crude oil, derivatives and dispersants on larvae. Mar. Pollut. Bull. 4:9-13.

57. Clark, R.C., Jr., J.S. Finley, and G.G. Gibson (1974). Acute effects of outboard motor effluent on two marine shellfish. Environ. Sci. Technol. 8:1009-14.

58. Griffith, D. de G. (1970). Toxicity of crude oil and detergents to two species of edible molluscs under arti-ficial tidal conditions. In: FAO Technical Conference on Marine Pollution and Its Effect on Living Resources and Fishing. FAO Fish. Rep. 99, FIRM/R99. Food and Agriculture Organization of the United Nations, Rome, 188 p.

59. Cardwell, R.D. (1973). Acute toxicity of No. 2 diesel oil to selected species of marine invertebrates, marine sculpins, and juvenile salmon. Ph.D. Thesis, University of Washington, Seattle, 124 p.

60. Swedmark, M., A. Granmo, and S. Kollberg (1973). Effects of oil dispersants and oil emulsions on marine animals. Water Res. 7:1649-72.

61. U.S. Environmental Protection Agency (1975). Semi-annual Report, January to July 1975. Environmental Research Laboratory, Narragansett, Rhode Island, 137 p.

62. Kanter, R. (1974). Susceptibility to crude oil with re-spect to size, season and geographic location in *Mytilus californianus* (Bivalvia). University of Southern Cali-fornia, Sea Grant Program (USC-SG-4-74), Los Angeles, Calif., 43 p.

63. Ehrsam, L.C., Jr., T.S. English, J. Matches, D. Weitkamp, R. Cardwell, R.S. LeGore, R.W. Steele, and R. Orhiem (1972). Biological assessment of diesel oil spill, Phase II, Anacortes, Washington, September 1971. Final Report prepared for EPA, Contr. No. 68-01-0017, Texas Instru-ments, Inc., Tex., 82 p.

64. Crapp, G.B. (1971). The ecological effects of stranded oil. In: Proceedings of the Ecological Effects of Oil Pollution on Littoral Communities (E.B. Cowell, ed.), p. 181-6. Institute of Petroleum, London.

65. Ottway, S. (1971). The comparative toxicities of crude oils. In: Proceedings of the Ecological Effects of Oil Pollution on Littoral Communities (E.B. Cowell, ed.), p. 172-80. Institute of Petroleum, London.

66. Portmann, J.E. (1969). Report of the ices working group on pollution of the North Sea. Int. Counc. Explor. Sea. Coop. Res. Rep. Ser. A13, 61 p.

67. Nelson-Smith, A. (1971). Effects of oil on marine plants and animals. In: Water Pollution by Oil (P. Hepple, ed.), p. 273-91. In: Proceedings of a Seminar held at Aviemore Inverness-Shire, Scotland, 4-8 May 1970. Institute of Petroleum, London.

68. Kasymov, A.G. and A.D. Aliev (1973). Experimental study of the effect of oil on some representatives of benthos in the Caspian Sea. Water Air Soil Pollut. 2:235-45.

69. Bender, M.E., J.L. Hyland, and T.K. Duncan (1974). Effect of an oil spill on benthic animals in the lower York River, Virginia. In: Marine Pollution Monitoring (Petroleum). Natl. Bur. Stand. Spec. Publ. 409, p. 257-9.

70. Neff, J.M., J.W. Anderson, B.A. Cox, R.B. Laughlin, Jr., S.S. Rossi, and H.E. Tatem (1976). Effects of petroleum on survival, respiration and growth of marine animals. In: Symposium on Sources, Effects, and Sinks of Hydrocarbons in the Aquatic Environment. AIBS, 9-11 August 1976. American University, Washington, D.C., 12 p.

71. Wells, P.G. (1972). Influence of Venezuelan crude oil on lobster larvae. Mar. Pollut. Bull. 3:105-6.

72. Wells, P.G. and J.B. Sprague (1976). Effects of crude oil on American lobster (*Homarus americanus*) larvae in the laboratory. J. Fish. Res. Board Can. 33:1604-14.

73. Karinen, J.F. and S.D. Rice (1974). Effects of Prudhoe Bay crude oil on molting tanner crabs, *Chionoecetes bairdi*. Mar. Fish. Rev. 36:31-7.

74. Davenport, J. (1973). A comparison of the effects of oil, B.P. 1100 and oleophilic fluff upon the porcelain crab, *Porcellana platycheles*. Chemosphere 1:3-6.

75. Mironov, O.G. (1969). The viability of larvae of some crustaceans in marine water polluted with oil products. Zool. Zh. 48:1734-7.

76. Nelson-Smith, A. (1970). The problem of oil pollution of the sea. Adv. Mar. Biol. 8:215-306.

77. Tatem, H.E. and J.W. Anderson (1973). The toxicity of four oils to *Palaemonetes pugio* (Holthuis) in relation to uptake and retention of specific petroleum hydrocarbons. Am. Zool. 13:1307-8.

78. Lichatowich, J.A., J.A. Strand, and W.L. Templeton (1972). Development of toxicity test procedures for marine zooplankton. Am. Inst. Chem. Eng. Symp. Ser. 68:372-8.

79. Sandberg, D.M., A.D. Michael, B. Brown, and R. Beebe-Center (1972). Toxic effects of fuel oil on haustoriid amphipods and pagurid crabs. Biol. Bull. 143:475-6.

80. Wolf, E.G. and J.A. Strand (1973). Determination of acute and chronic effects of treated ballast water on selected aquatic biota from Port Valdez, Alaska, 37 p. Final report to Alyeska Pipeline Service Co., Bellevue, Washington. Prepared by Battelle Pacific Northwest Laboratories, Richland, WA 99352.

81. Mironov, O.G. (1969). The effect of oil pollution on some representatives of the Black Sea zooplankton. Zool. Zh. 48:980-4.

82. Kontogiannis, J.E. and C.J. Barnett (1973). The effect
     of oil pollution on survival of the tidal pool copepod,
     Tigriopus californicus. Environ. Pollut. 4:69-79.

83. Katz, L.M. (1973). The effects of water soluble fraction
     of crude oil on larvae of the decapod crustacean, *Neo-
     panope texana* (Sayi). Environ. Pollut. 5:199-204.

84. Corner, D.S., A.J. Southward, and E.C. Southward (1968).
     Toxicity of oil spill removers ('detergents') to marine
     life. An assessment using the intertidal barnacle,
     Elminius modestus. J. Mar. Biol. Assoc. U.K. 38:29-47.

85. Milovidova, N.Y. (1974). The effect of oil pollution on
     some coastal crustaceans of the Black Sea. Hydrobiol. J.
     (Eng. Transl. Gidrobiol. Zh.) 4:76-9.

86. Rice, S.D. (1973). Toxicity and avoidance tests with
     Prudhoe Bay oil and pink salmon fry. In: Proceedings of
     1973 Joint Conference on Prevention and Control of Oil
     Spills, p. 667-70. American Petroleum Institute,
     Washington, D.C.

87. Brown, V.M., D.G. Shurben, and J.K. Fawell (1967). The
     acute toxicity of phenol to rainbow trout in saline
     waters. Water Res. 1:683-5.

88. Struhsaker, J.W., M.B. Eldridge, and T. Echeverria (1974).
     Effects of benzene (a water-soluble component of crude
     oil) on eggs and larvae of Pacific herring and northern
     anchovy. In: Pollution and Physiology of Marine Organ-
     isms (J.F. Vernberg and W.B. Vernberg, eds.), p. 253-84.
     Academic Press, New York.

89. Kuhnhold, W.W. (1969). Effect of water soluble sub-
     stances of crude oil on eggs and larvae of cod and her-
     ring. Fisheries Improvement Committee Int. Counc.
     Explor. Sea (CM 1969/E 17), Copenhagen, 15 p.

90. Kuhnhold, W.W. (1970). The influence of crude oils on
     fish fry. In: FAO Technical Conference on Marine Pol-
     lution and its Effects on Living Resources and Fishing.
     MP/70/E-64. Food and Agriculture Organization of the
     United Nations, Rome, 10 p.

91. James, M.C. (1926). Preliminary investigation of the
     effect of oil pollution on marine pelagic eggs, April
     1925. In: Preliminary Conference on Oil Pollution of
     Navigable Waters, June 8-16, 1926, Appendix 6, p. 85-92.
     U.S. Bureau of Fisheries Interdepartmental Committee,
     Washington, D.C.

92. Gilet, R. (1960). Water pollution in Marseilles and its
     relation with flora and fauna. In: Proceeding of the
     First International Conference for Waste Disposal in the
     Marine Environment, Berkeley, California, 1959, p. 39-56.
     Pergamon Press, New York.

93. Tagatz, M.E. (1961). Reduced oxygen tolerance and toxicity of petroleum products to juvenile American shad. Chesapeake Sci. 2:65-71.

94. Gardner, G.R., P.P. Yevich, and P.F. Rogerson (1975). Morphological anomalies in adult oyster, scallop, and Atlantic silversides exposed to waste motor oil. In: Proceedings of 1975 Conference on Prevention and Control of Oil Pollution, p. 473-7. American Petroleum Institute, Washington, D.C.

95. Mironov, O.G. (1967). Effect of low concentrations of oil and oil products upon the developing eggs of the Black Sea flatfish - Kalkan (*Rhombus maeoticus* (Pallas)). Vopr. Ikhtiol. 7:577-80.

96. Meyerhoff, R.D. (1975). Acute toxicity of benzene, a component of crude oil, to juvenile striped bass (*Morone saxatilis*). J. Fish. Res. Board Can. 32:1864-6.

97. Hakkila, K. and A. Niemi (1973). Effects of oil and emulsifiers on eggs and larvae of Northern pike (*Esox lucius*) in brackish water. Aqua Fenn., p. 44-59.

98. Sprague, J.B. and W.G. Carson (1970). Toxicity tests with oil dispersants in connection with oil spill at Chedabucto Bay, Nova Scotia. Fish. Res. Board Can. Tech. Rep. 201, 30 p.

99. Moore, S.R. and R.L. Dwyer (1974). Effects of oil on marine organisms: A critical assessment of published data. Water Res. 8:819-27.

100. Moore, S.F., R.L. Dwyer, and A.M. Katz (1973). A preliminary assessment of the environmental vulnerability of Machias Bay, Maine to oil supertankers. Mass. Inst. Technol. Sea Grant Rep. 73-6, 162 p.

TABLE 1

Acute toxicity of petroleum to Coelenterata

Organism	Material Tested	Test Parameters	Concentration		Remarks	Reference
Hydrozoan *Tubularia crocea*	Crude oil and carbonized sand mixture	Static bioassay; SW[a]; 200 ml vol.; 20.6°–21.3°C. Survival after 24 hr (%)	Oil:SW	$\widetilde{=}$ppm	Concentration is oil added to SW; sufficient carbonized sand mixed to completely absorb oil	28
		66	1:1000	1×10^3		
		24	1:400	25×10^2		
		14	1:200	5×10^3	Actual concentrations of hydrocarbons test animals subjected to are unknown	
		6	1:80	125×10^2		
		2	1:40	25×10^3		
		0	1:20	5×10^4		
	Water extract of crude oil: 200 ml oil mixed with 4 l SW for 6½ hr; WSF[b] separated for 48 hr	Static bioassay; SW; 200 ml vol.; 20.6°–21.3°C. Survival after 24 hr (%)	Oil:SW	$\widetilde{=}$ppm	SW soluble product	
		93	1:1000	1×10^3		
		88	1:400	25×10^2		
		46	1:200	5×10^3		
		0	1:40	25×10^3		
		13	1:20	5×10^4		
		33	1:8	125×10^3		
		27	1:4	25×10^4		
		0	1:2	5×10^5		
	Crude oil and carbonized sand mixture	Constant flow system; SW; 250 ml vessel; 65-70 l/hr-flow-over oil mixed with sand; 20.4°–20.7°C. Survival after 48 hr (%)	Crude oil in test jar (ml)			
		83	5			
		30	10			
		44	20			
		13	30			

a SW: Seawater

b WSF: Water-soluble fraction

Organism	Material Tested	Test Parameters	Concentration	Remarks	Reference
Tubularia crocea	Oil	Static bioassay; SW; 200 ml vol.; 21.2°–21.9°C. Survival after 24 hr(%)	Oil:SW ≅ppm		
	Crude	0	1:40 25 x 10^3		
	Fuel	19	1:40 25 x 10^3		
	Lubricating	58	1:40 25 x 10^3		
	Diesel	0	1:40 25 x 10^3		
Medusa *Halitholus cirratus*		Static bioassay; oil and SW dispersion; 450 ml vol.; 8°C; 17 °/oo sal.; aeration; test media replaced every 24 hr. 5–20 animals per beaker.		No appreciable mortality in light or medium concentrations. Light: 10–20 ppm Medium: 20–200 ppm Arctic sp.	51
	Crude oil	Mortality after 96 hr(%)			
	Atkinson Point	30 ⎫			
	Venezuela	100 ⎬	Heavy: 300–1,000 ppm		
	Norman Wells	100 ⎪			
	Pembina	100 ⎭			

TABLE 2

Acute toxicity of petroleum to Echinodermata

Organism	Material Tested	Test Parameters	Concentration	Remarks	Reference
	No. 2 diesel oil	Static bioassay; SW[a]; 50 ml beaker with 0.5% oil added; larvae placed in beaker; stirred frequently, oil covers surface.	%	Survival may be related to egg and larval size.	52
		Average survival		*Parent Egg diam. (μm)*	
Starfish					
Pisaster ochraceous (larva)		Gastrula stage, 12 hr	0.5	120	
Luidia foliata (larva)		Bipinnaria stage, 15 hr	0.5	150	
Crossaster papposus (larva)		Brachiolaria stage, 200 hr	0.5	700	
Sand dollar					
Dendraster excentricus (larva)		Pluteus stage, 21 hr	0.5	110	
Sea urchin, purple *Strongylocentrotus purpuratus* (egg)	WSF[b] of the following oils prepared by shaking 25 ml oil in 500 ml SW; WSF drawn off bottom.	Static bioassay; 5 ml of WSF SW mixture. Eggs fertilized in 0.5 ml SW, then added to 5 ml of each dilution.		Exposure to even the highest concentrations of the WSF (50 or 100%) of the various oils had little effect, in most cases, on fertilization.	53
	Jet fuel JP-8, Distillate heating oil No. 2	Development of test embryos not significantly different from development of control embryos; 4 hr exposure.	12.5%	The lighter, more highly refined oils were the least toxic.	

Organism	Material Tested	Test Parameters	Concentration	Remarks	Reference
Strongylocentrotus purpuratus (egg)	Diesel fuel No. 2 Diesel fuel No. 2 Argentina crude oil Wilmington, Calif., crude oil Jet fuel A-50 Cook Inlet, AK, crude oil Central Libyan crude oil Waxy crude oil Residual heating oil No. 5 Bunker C fuel oil (residual) 4-Corner crude oil Bunker fuel oil Bunker oil No. 6	Development of test embryos significantly different from development of control embryos - 4 or less cells after 4 hr exposure.	12.5%		
	WSF of following oils, prepared by stirring 1 l. oil/100 l. SW for 20 hr and allowed to settle for 3 hr.	Static bioassay; SW; 18 l vol.; 4-12°C, aerated; 8-12 animals per dose.		IR Analysis	38
Sea cucumber *Eupentacta quinquesemita*	Cook Inlet crude oil No. 2 fuel oil	96 hr TLm 96 hr TLm	ppm >6.9 >2.28		
Cucumaria vega cf.	Cook Inlet crude oil	96 hr TLm 96 hr TLm	>14.7 >2.11		

a SW: Seawater

b WSF: Water-soluble fraction

TABLE 3

Acute toxicity of petroleum to Mollusca

Organism	Material Tested	Test Parameters	Concentration	Remarks	Reference
Oyster, American *Crassostrea virginica* (gamete, embryo, larva)	WSF[b] of following oils:	Static bioassay; SW[a]; gametes sperm and eggs exposed to test media for 1 hr.	1 ppm	Nigerian crude oil more toxic than Alaskan or Kuwait.	54

	Prudhoe Bay crude oil	Fertilization -71.4%
		Development -68.5%
		  of embryos
		Survival of -55.0%
		  larvae			

	Nigeria (Bonny) crude oil	Fertilization -63.3%
		Development -50.4%
		  or embryos
		Survival of -43.3%
		  larvae			

	Kuwait crude oil	Fertilization -73.2%
		Development -69.3%
		  of embryos
		Survival of -53.8%
		  larvae			

a   SW: Seawater

b   WSF: Water–soluble fraction

c   DO: Dissolved oxygen

Organism	Material Tested	Test Parameters	Concentration	Remarks	Reference
Oyster, Pacific *Crassostrea gigas* (larva)	Prudhoe Bay crude oil:	Static bioassay; filtered SW; 1 l beakers; 20°–21.5°C; 25.3–30.8°/oo sal.; exposure 48 ± 2 hr; 30,000 larvae per beaker.		ED50 (50% effective dose) EMD50 (50% ecological mortality	55
				Less than 1.0 ml Alaskan crude oil per liter SW was required to consistently produce a 50% effect.	
	Whole oil	48 hr ED50	ppm 523	Concentrations less than threshold effect levels apparently stimulate larval development.	
	Water soluble fractions:		ppm		
	Whole extract A		323,600		
	n-Pentane		46,000		
	n-Hexane		41,000		
	n-Heptane		11,000		
	Total: $nC_5 + nC_6 + nC_7$		98,000		
	Cyclohexane	48 hr ED50	69,000		
			ppb		
	Benzene		9,355		
	Toluene		5,899		
	o-Xylene		359		
	m-Xylene		1,223		
	p-Xylene		359		

Organism	Material Tested	Test Parameters	Concentration	Remarks	Reference
Crassostrea gigas	Pure Hydrocarbons		ppm		
	Naphthalene		194		
	Cyclooctane		233		
	Isopropyl Benzene		236		
	o-Xylene		338		
	m-Xylene		626		
	p-Xylene	48 hr ED$_{50}$	695		
	Benzene		1,052		
	Ethyl benzene		1,182		
	Toluene		1,209		
	o-, m-, p-Xylenes		1,239		
	Cyclohexane		1,701		
	Cyclopentane		3,753		
		Static bioassay; SW; 22°–25°C; 30 ± 0.5°/oo sal; 6 hr exposure; aeration.		Stock solution 1:4 (oil:SW)	56
Oyster		Mortality(%)	ppm		
Crassostrea angulata (larva)	Venezuelan crude oil	30.7	1,000		
	No. 1 fuel oil	26.0	1,000		
Oyster, Pacific					
Crassostrea gigas (larva)	Venezuelan crude oil	31.4	1,000		
	No. 1 fuel oil	27.0	1,000		
Mussel					
Mytilus galloprovincialis (larva)	Venezuelan crude oil	28.4	1,000		
	No. 1 fuel oil	24.4	1,000		
Quahog *Venus mercenaria*	Crude oil Diesel oil Lubricating oil Fuel oil	SW siphoned over 20 ml oil or oil + carbonized sand, then into test bowl at 250 ml/min. No mortalities in 12½ days.	Unknown		28

Organism	Material Tested	Test Parameters	Concentration		Remarks	Reference
Oyster, American *Crassostrea virginica*		Static bioassay; SW; 10 gal; 13°/oo sal.; aerated, 12 oysters per tank.	oil:SW	≅ppm		
			%			
	Diesel oil	Survival-13 days - 33	1:189	5,291		
	Diesel oil and carbonized sand	Survival-13 days - 75	1:189	5,291		
	Crude oil	Survival-12 days - 75	1:500	2,000		
	Crude oil and carbonized sand	Survival-12 days - 75	1:500	2,000		
Mussel, Bay *Mytilus edulis* (47 mm avg)	Outboard motor effluent	Constant flow bioassay; 1 l/min (0.1 l/min effluent + 0.9 l/min SW), 10°-20°C.			Information on stress, gill degeneration, and uptake of hydrocarbons.	57
		24 hr exposure and 9 days holding - 66% mortality	10% effluent			
Oyster *Ostrea lurida* (37 mm avg)		10 day exposure - 14% mortality	10% effluent			
Periwinkle *Littorina littorea*	Aramco crude oil	Simulated tidal cycle in 5 l clean SW; circular tank 35 cm diam; 435 ml of evaporated oil poured on surface and mixed; tank drained, settling oil on animals; 7 hr later tank refilled and tidal cycles repeated.			Additional information on recovery and reattachment of treated animals. Temperature dependent effect important.	58

Tidal regime

Temp (°C)	TD$_{50}$	Evap. Oil(%)
4.6	10 hr	11
	12 hr	12.5
11.0	2 hr	11
	4 hr	12.5

Organism	Material Tested	Test Parameters	Concentration	Remarks	Reference
Mussel, bay *Mytilus edulis*		Tidal regime	Evap. Oil(%)		
		Temp (°C) TD$_{50}$			
		4.6 No effect	11		
		No effect	12.5		
		11.0 No effect	11		
		No effect	12.5		
	No. 2 diesel oil	Static bioassay; SW; 40 ml vol.		Survival may be related to egg and larval size.	52
Limpet *Acmaea (Notoacmaea) scutum* (larva)		Average survival	%	Parent Egg diam. (µm)	
		Veliger stage – 48 hr	0.5	182	
Bubble, white *Haminoea virescens* (larva)		Veliger stage – 31 hr	0.5	80	
Nudibranch *Melibe leonina* (larva)		Veliger stage – 15 hr	0.5	85	
Chiton *Katharina tunicata* (larva)		Trochophore stage – 72 hr	0.5	275	
Oyster, Pacific *Crassostrea gigas* (larva)		Veliger stage – 24 hr	0.5	60	
Mussel, bay *Mytilus edulis*	WSF of No. 2 diesel oil	Static bioassay; SW; 15 l vol.; 11.4°-12.2°C; 30°/oo sal.; oil layered on surface and stirred constantly at 1000-1500 r/min.	ml oil/l SW ppm(calc)	Emulsion rather than WSF.	59
		24 hr EC$_{50}$	0.0170 17.0	EC$_{50}$ = loss of substrate attachment and formation of byssus thread.	
		48 hr EC$_{50}$	0.0156 15.6		

Organism	Material Tested	Test Parameters	Concentration		Remarks	Reference
			ml oil/l SW	ppm(calc)		
Limpet					Concentrations are the	
Acmaea (Notoacmaea)		24 hr EC50	0.0417	41.7	initial volume of oil	
scutum		48 hr EC50	0.0229	22.1	layered on water divid-	
Snail, wrinkled purple					ed by volume of water.	
Thais lamellosa		36 hr EC50	0.113	11.3	Does not represent	
		48 hr EC50	0.059	59.0	hydrocarbon content.	
	Oman crude oil	Constant flow bioassay; SW; 500 ml/min.; 10°C; 32–34°/oo sal.; concentrations maintained by mixing standard solution and SW at predetermined ratios.			Tested 350, 650 and 1,000 ppm. Study deals mainly with dispersant and oil emulsions.	60
			ppm			
Scallop					<1,000 ppm, lowest	
Pecten opercularis		Shell diam – 45–70 mm 96 hr LC50	<1,000		medium concentration affecting shell closure.	
Cockle						
Cardium edule		Shell diam – 8–15 mm 96 hr LC50	<1,000			
Mussel, bay					<350 ppm, lowest medium concentration affecting byssal activity and shell closure. Crude less toxic than oil emulsions.	
Mytulis edulis		Shell diam – 60–70 mm 96 hr LC50	<1,000			

	WSF of No. 2 fuel oil	Continuous flow bioassay; ambient water conditions.			IR analysis.	61

			Expected ppm	Actual ppm		
Scallop, bay		Exposure	Mortality(%)			
Argopecten irradians		Control–91 days	17.3	0	0.006	
irradians (adult)		91 days	24.6	0.1	0.067	
		91 days	87.9	1.0	0.54	
		7 days	100.0	10.0	10.6	

Organism	Material Tested	Test Parameters		Concentration		Remarks	Reference
		Exposure	Mortality(%)	Expected ppm	Actual ppm		
Quahog							
Mercenaria mercenaria (juvenile)		Control-4 mo	0	0	0.006		
		4 mo	0	0.1	0.067		
		4 mo	1.6	1.0	0.54		
		20 days	100.0	10.0	10.6		
	Santa Barbara crude oil	Static bioassay; SW; 4,000 ml vol.; 15 ± 1°C; vigorous aeration; media changed every 48 hr; 20 animals per container.				Emulsified and soluble phases. Data taken from graphs. Suscepti- bility depended on size, season, and lo- cation.	62
Mussel				ppm			
Mytilus californianus		Pismo Beach 48-56 days exposure - 10-90% mortality		10,000		Larger, Pismo Beach and Catalina mussels most suseptible.	
		Coal Point 48-56 days exposure - 0-60% mortality		10,000			
		Palos Verdes 48-56 days exposure - 0-20% mortality		10,000			
		Santa Catalina Island 48-56 days exposure - 0-100% mortality		10,000			
	No. 2 diesel oil	Static bioassay; SW; 15 l or 45 l vol.; 11°-13°C; 25-31°/oo sal.; usually 30-31°/oo; 10 or more animals per aquaria. Oil layered on surface and stirred constantly for subsurface circulation. 10 or more animals per aquaria. Test mixtures renewed at 24 hr.				Test concentrations reported do not repre- sent hydrocarbon con- tent of water. Average shell length - 18.6 mm ± 5.2 mm.	63

Organism	Material Tested	Test Parameters	Concentration	Remarks	Reference
		EC50 (loss of attachment)	ppm		
Limpet					
Acmaea (Colisella) pelta		24 hr	41.0	Although many became moribund, few died during bioassay or recovery period.	
Acmaea (Notoacmaea) scutum		48 hr	23.5		
Acmaea sp. (3)					
Snail, wrinkled purple					
Thais lamellosa		48 hr	58.5	Average length - 44.2 mm ± 4.02 mm.	
		EC50 (Failure to reattach to substrate)			
Mussel, bay				Average length - 9.80 mm ± 2.33 mm.	
Mytilus edulis		24 hr	16.6	Virtually complete recovery in 24 hr of running SW.	
		48 hr	15.0		

Organism	Material Tested	Test Parameters			Concentration	Remarks	Reference
	Kuwait crude oil	Static bioassay; SW; 10°-18°C; animals exposed to whole oil for 6 hr, then washed and returned to clean SW.				Kuwait residue is crude oil with fractions that boil below 370°C removed.	64
	Kuwait residue						
		Temp. (°C)	Kuwait crude (% mortality)	Kuwait residue (% mortality)			
Gastropod							
Monodonta lineata		14	0	0			
Gibbula umbilicalis		17	6	0			
		17	4	0			
Periwinkle							
Littorina littorea		14	34	0	Whole oil		
Littorina obtusata		10	44	0			
Littorina saxatilis rudis		18	80	0			
Limpet							
Patella vulgata		12	100	-			
Mussel, bay							
Mytilus edulis		17	0	0			

Periwinkle Littorina littorea / Littorina obtusata / Littorina littoralis — oil toxicity data

Organism	Material Tested	Test Parameters	Concentration	Remarks	Reference
Periwinkle *Littorina littorea*	Gasoline (leaded); Kerosine; Dieselect; No. 2 fuel oil; 3500 fuel oil; Crude oil	50 animals per lot immersed in oil for various time periods and returned to SW; 16°C. (see mortality table below)	Whole oil		
Periwinkle *Littorina littorea* / *Littorina obtusata*	Kuwait crude oil	50 animals per lot exposed for 6 hr to oil (2.5 l crude oil poured onto 10.0 l SW) vigorously aerated for various periods before exposing organisms. (see mortality table below)	Unknown	Mortalities may have been caused by water soluble portion.	
Periwinkle *Littorina littoralis*	Crude oils (coded)	Static bioassay; SW; 16°C; aerated; 50 animals treated for 5 days.	Whole oil	Darkest, thickest crudes have highest percent asphaltenes and are less toxic than lighter crudes.	65

Mortality(%) per time immersed:

Material	6 min	30 min	1 hr	1 hr	6 hr
Gasoline (leaded)	78	80	76	78	70
Kerosine	10	14	20	50	68
Dieselect	0	0	0	0	0
No. 2 fuel oil	0	0	0	2	2
3500 fuel oil	0	0	0	0	0
Crude oil	12	10	28	48	62

Mortality(%) per time in evaporation vessel (aeration):

	0 hr	0.5 hr	1 hr	6 hr	24 hr
Littorina littorea	58	66	48	50	44
Littorina obtusata	94	88	78	82	70

Organism	Material Tested	Test Parameters		Concentration	Remarks	Reference
		Oil / Mortality (%)	Asphaltenes (%, by wt.)			
Littorina littoralis	Oil				Oils not identified.	
		CT10 1	5.8			
		CT18 55	0.4			
		CT 4 63	2.8			
		CT14 57	5.0			
		CT12 85	1.4			
		CT 6 72	1.4			
		CT 5 56	0.5			
		CT 7 48	0.7			
		CT11 52	0.5			
		CT 9 21	0.7			
		CT19 17	0.1			
		CT 8 32	0.17			
		CT17 70	0.4			
		CT16 29	0.0			
		CT20 44	0.1			
		CT 2 74	0.05			
		CT 1 89	0.05			
		CT15 52	0.0			
		CT 3 83	0.0			
		CT13 64	0.0			
Limpet *Patella vulgata*	Kuwait crude oil	Static bioassay; SW; 12°C; 20-30 specimens to tank. Animals attached to rocks raised through oil on surface. Detachment after various times in oil. After 6 hr 40-60% After 12 hr 30-55%		Whole oil	Detachment not sign of mortality, 100% recovery after 3 hr wash in clean SW. However, detached animals move, and are susceptible to predation and mechanical damage. Rate of detachment depends on activity related to time of day.	26
Cockle *Cardium edule*	Phenol	48 hr LC50		500 ppm		66,67

Organism	Material Tested	Test Parameters	Concentration	Remarks	Reference
Clam *Macoma balthica*	Prudhoe Bay crude oil	Continuous flow; SW and tide simulation; 7°-12°C; oil poured on surface of falling tide for 5 successive days.		Simulated oil spill. Clams coming to surface would presumably die.	27
	Whole Oil	No significant mortality 2 mo after exposure	1.2, 2.4, and 5 μl/cm^2 per day	Arctic species.	
	WSF: Prepared by mixing 1 l oil in 100 l SW; siphoned off below slick. 100% WSF = 0.379 naphthalene equivalents.	Static bioassay; SW; 8°-18°C.			
		50% burrow to surface (ECm) in 3 days	0.436 ppm		
		20% mortality 11 days	0.036 ppm		
		Continuous flow bioassay; SW;			
		50% burrow to surface (ECm) in 3 days	0.367 ppm		
		No mortality	0.019-0.302 ppm		
	Oil-contaminated sediment	Continuous flow bioassay; SW; 9°-12°C; oil depth over clam beds 0.25 and 0.5 cm (1 part oil:2 parts dry sediment).	Depth of oil contaminated sediment		
		Significant mortality	0.5 cm		
		50% burrow to surface in 1 day	0.669 cm		

Organism	Material Tested	Test Parameters	Concentration	Remarks	Reference
	WSF of Artem oil	Static bioassay; SW; 19.3°-24.4°C; 0.3-5.0 l vol.; DOC 4.5-7.0 mg/l.		Actual concentrations not analyzed.	68
		Avg. survival (days)	ppm		
Gastropod *Pyrgohydrodia dubia*		12 6	4.0 14.0		
Cerastoderma lamarcki		3 5	4.0 14.0		
	WSF of Bunker C oil	Closed continuous flow bioassay; SW; 12-18°/oo sal.; test animals in flasks.		IR analysis test 5.53 ppm	69
Gastropod *Nassarius obsoletus*		No effect	5.53 ppm		
Bivalve *Modiolus demissus*		No effect	5.53 ppm		
	WSF of following oils prepared by stirring 1 l oil/100 l SW for 20 hr and allowing to settle for 3 hr.	Static bioassay; SW; 18 l vol.; 4°-12°C; aerated; 8-12 animals per dose.		IR analysis	38
		TLm	ppm		
Clam, littleneck *Protothaca staminea*	Cook Inlet crude oil No. 2 fuel oil	96 hr 96 hr	>14.7 >2.11		
Mussel, bay *Mytilus edulis*	Cook Inlet crude oil No. 2 fuel oil	24 hr 96 hr 24 hr 96 hr	>5.15 >5.15 >3.11 >3.11		
Limpet *Notoacmaea scutum*	Cook Inlet crude oil No. 2 fuel oil	96 hr 24 hr 96 hr	3.65 >4.19 5.04		

Organism	Material Tested	Test Parameters	Concentration		Remarks	Reference
Notoacmaea sp.	Cook Inlet crude oil	24 hr	>5.15			
		96 hr	4.19			
	No. 2 fuel oil	24 hr	>1.77			
		96 hr	4.27			
Chiton						
Cryptochiton stelleri	No. 2 fuel oil	24 hr	>1.13			
		96 hr	1.24			
Katharina tunicata	No. 2 fuel oil	24 hr	1.03			
		96 hr	0.44			
Periwinkle						
Littorina sitkana	Cook Inlet crude oil	24 hr	>20.97			
		96 hr	>20.97			
Snail						
Margarites pupillus	No. 2 fuel oil	24 hr	>1.13			
		96 hr	>1.13			
Whelk						
Nucella lima	Cook Inlet crude oil	24 hr	>20.97			
		96 hr	>20.97			
	WSF prepared by mixing 1 l oil/100 l SW for 20 hr and allowing to stand for 3 hr. OWD prepared by high speed stirring of oil and 18 l SW for 1 min and allowing to stand for 1 hr.	Static bioassay; SW; 18 l vol.; 3.7°-10.2°C; aerated; 8-12 animals per dose.			IR and UV analysis. Arctic and subarctic species.	42

			ppm(UV)	ppm(IR)		
Scallop, pink		TLm				
Chlamys rubida	WSF of following oils:					
	Prudhoe Bay crude oil	96 hr	168	2.07		
	Cook Inlet crude oil (treated)	96 hr	162	3.15		
	Cook Inlet crude oil (untreated)	96 hr	146	1.57		
	No. 2 fuel oil	96 hr	199	0.80		

Organism	Material Tested	Test Parameters	Concentration		Remarks	Reference
		TLm	ppm(UV)	ppm(IR)		
Chlamys rubida	OWD of following oils:					
	Prudhoe Bay crude oil	96 hr	155	9.34		
	Cook Inlet crude oil	96 hr	148	8.04		
	(treated)					

TABLE 4

Acute toxicity of petroleum to Annelida

Organism	Material Tested	Test Parameters	Concentration	Remarks	Reference
	No. 2 fuel oil (diesel oil)	Static bioassay; SW[a]; 50 ml beaker with 0.5% oil added; larvae placed in beaker and stirred frequently. Oil covered surface.		Survival may be related to egg and larval size.	52
		Average survival	%	Parent egg diam. (µm)	
Polychaete *Nereis vexillosa* (larva)		Metatroch stage, 48 hr	0.5	220	
Serpula vermicularis (larva)		Trochophore stage, 3 hr	0.5	90	
Nereis brandti (larva)		Trochophore stage, 48 hr	0.5	175	
	WSF[b] of Artem oil	Static bioassay; SW; 0.3–5.0 l vol.; 19.3°–24.4°C; O₂: 4.5–7.0 mg/liter		Actual concentrations not analyzed.	68
		Average survival	ppm		
Oligochaete *Nais elinguis*		5–6 day	4.0–14.0		
Polychaete *Nereis diversicolor*	WSF of following oils:	2–6 day	≅5.0–15.0	Data taken from graph.	39
		Static bioassay; synthetic SW; 50 ml vol.; 20±1°C; 32°/oo sal.; 1 animal/125 ml flask; no aeration. WSF prepared by stirring slowly for 20 hr, 9 parts SW to 1 part test oil.		Concentration values represent ppm of total hydrocarbons. UV analysis.	

Organism	Material Tested	Test Parameters	Concentration	Remarks	Reference
Polychaete			ppm		
Neanthes arenaceodentata	No. 2 fuel oil	TLM 48 hr	3.2		
		96 hr	2.7		
	Bunker C fuel oil	48 hr	4.6		
		96 hr	3.6		
	S. Louisiana crude oil	48 hr	13.9		
		96 hr	12.5		
	Kuwait crude oil	48 hr	>10.4		
		96 hr	>10.4		
Capitella capitata	No. 2 fuel oil	48 hr	3.5	*C. capitata* widely distributed and re- sistant to pollution.	
		96 hr	2.3		
	Bunker C fuel oil	48 hr	1.1		
		96 hr	0.9		
	S. Louisiana crude oil	48 hr	16.2		
		96 hr	12.0		
	Kuwait crude oil	48 hr	>10.4		
		96 hr	>9.8		
	WSF of Bunker C fuel oil.	Closed continuous flow bioassay; SW; 12-18°/oo sal.; test animals in flasks.		IR analysis tested 5.53 ppm.	69
Polychaete					
Nereis succinea			No effect		
Spiochaetopterus costarum oculatus		48 hr TL$_{50}$	5.53 ppm 4.92 ppm		
	WSF of Southern Louisiana crude oil. Prepared by mixing 1 part oil to 9 parts SW for 20 hr.	Static Bioassay; SW.		IR analysis.	70
Sargassum worm			ppm		
Platynereis dumerilii		48 hr LC50	12.3		
		96 hr LC50	9.5		

Organism	Material Tested	Test Parameters	Concentration	Remarks	Reference
			ppm		
Errant benthic worm *Neanthes arenaceodentata*		48 hr LC50 96 hr LC50	13.9 12.5		
Sedentary benthic worm *Capitella capitata*		48 hr LC50 96 hr LC50	16.2 12.0		
	WSF of following oils. Prepared by adding 1 part oil to 9 parts SW in 19 l bottle and stirred for 20 hr, allowed to settle 1-6 hr.	Static bioassay, synthetic SW; 50 ml vol.; 22°C; 32°/oo sal.; 10 juveniles or 1 adult per container.		UV analysis.	40
Polychaete *Neanthes arenaceo-dentata* Juvenile stages		_TLM_	ppm		
(4 segment, 9 days)	No. 2 fuel oil	24 hr 48 hr 96 hr	>8.7 >8.7 8.4		
(18 segment, 21 days)		24 hr 48 hr 96 hr	>8.7 >8.7 5.7		
(32 segment, 30 days)		24 hr 48 hr 96 hr	>8.7 7.8 5.2		
(40 segment, 40 days)		24 hr 48 hr 96 hr	>8.7 6.2 4.0		
(4 segment, 9 days)	South Louisiana crude oil	24 hr 48 hr 96 hr	>19.8 >19.8 >19.8		

Organism	Material Tested	Test Parameters TLM	Concentration ppm	Remarks	Reference
Neanthes arena-ceodentata					
(18 segment, 21 days)		24 hr	>19.8		
		48 hr	>19.8		
		96 hr	>19.8		
(32 segment, 30 days)		24 hr	>19.8		
		48 hr	>19.8		
		96 hr	17.8		
(40 segment, 40 days)		24 hr	>19.8		
		48 hr	17.0		
		96 hr	15.2		
Adult stages	No. 2 fuel oil				
(Immature Adults, 48 segments, 46 days)		24 hr	>8.7		
		48 hr	3.2		
		96 hr	2.7		
(Mature Males, 60 segments, 54 days)		24 hr	>8.7		
		48 hr	3.0		
		96 hr	2.6		
(Gravid Females, 60 segments, 54 days)		24 hr	>8.7		
		48 hr	5.6		
		96 hr	4.2		
(Immature Adults, 48 segments, 46 days)	South Louisiana crude oil	24 hr	18.0		
		48 hr	13.9		
		96 hr	12.5		
(Mature Males, 60 segments, 54 days)		24 hr	18.1		
		48 hr	13.6		
		96 hr	12.0		
(Gravid Females, 60 segments, 54 days)		24 hr	>19.8		
		48 hr	18.0		
		96 hr	17.6		

a SW: Seawater

b WSF: Water-soluble fraction

TABLE 5

Acute toxicity of petroleum to Arthropoda

Organism	Material Tested	Test Parameters	Concentration	Concentration	Remarks	Reference
Lobster, American *Homarus americanus* (larva)	Venezuelan crude oil (emulsions)	Static bioassay; SW[a]; 20°- 21°C; 4 l vol.; 4-10 day tests; larval stages 1-4, 4-5 larvae per concentration; emulsion removed from under surface and diluted.			Long-term, low level exposure adversely affected molting and development.	71
			ml/l	ppm		
		24 hr - 100% mortality	0.1	100		
		96 hr - variable mortality	0.01	10		
		96 hr - low mortality	0.001	1		
		96 hr - low mortality	0.0001	0.1		
		96 hr LC$_{50}$	0.03-0.002	2-30		
Lobster, American *Homarus americanus* (larva)	Venezuelan crude oil, stirred, ultrasonic dispersion.	Static bioassay, SW; 800 ml vol.; 20°C; DO[d] 4.8 mg/l; fed artimea daily.			UV analysis of average initial concentration given.	72
			ppm			
1st Stage		96 hr LC$_{50}$	0.86			
3rd & 4th Stage		96 hr LC$_{50}$	4.90			
1st Stage		30 day LC$_{50}$	0.14			

a   SW: Seawater

b   WSF: Water-soluble fraction

c   OWD: Oil water dispersion

d   DO: Dissolved oxygen

52

Organism	Material Tested	Test Parameters	Concentration		Remarks	Reference
Crab, tanner						
Chionoecetes bairdi (juvenile)	Prudhoe Bay crude oil	Static bioassay; SW; 4°-5°C; 15 l in 20 l vessel; aerated; 1 crab (70-110 mm carapace) per vessel; oil poured into jar and mixed 1 min at 2,240 r/min.			Concentrations tested 0.18, 0.32, 0.56, and 1.00 ml/l. Author states the material may be more toxic than test indicates. Behavior-increased activity followed by contraction of legs and death. Lower concentrations caused reduction in molting success and autotomizing of limbs.	73
			ml/l	ppm		
Pre-molt		24 hr TLm	0.56	560		
		48 hr TLm	0.56	560		
Past molt		24 hr TLm	0.83	830		
		48 hr TLm	0.56	560		
Crab, Dungeness						
Cancer magister	No. 2 fuel oil	Flow-through bioassay; SW; 8°-12°C; 29.3-32.4 °/oo sal.; pH 7.4-8.4; DO 7.9-9.4 ppm; oil + water metered into common funnel and then to static mixer.			Concentration based on metered inflow. IR analysis. Good section on test animal selection, techniques, and equipment.	22
		96 hr TLm	4,778 ± 1,071 ppm			
		Static bioassay; SW; 800 ml vol.; aerated 75 bubbles/min.				
			ppm			
		TLm				
Crab, kelp						
Pugettia producta (larva)	No. 2 fuel oil	96 hr	10			
	Kuwait crude oil	96 hr	500			
	S. Louisiana crude oil	96 hr	450			
Crab, rock						
Cancer productus (larva)	No. 2 fuel oil	96 hr	4			
	Kuwait crude oil	96 hr	200			
	S. Louisiana crude oil	96 hr	250			

Organism	Material Tested	Test Parameters	Concentration	Remarks	Reference
Crab, porcelain *Porcellana platycheles*	Kuwait crude oil	Static bioassay; SW; 1 l bottles; 750 g mixture of oil and SW suspension; aerated; 10 crabs/bottle. Survival after 20 days 100% 100%	 10,000 ppm 1,000 ppm	Additional information on effects of oleophilic fluff and a dispersant.	74
Crab, marble *Pachygrapsus marmoratus* (larva)	Oil Bunker C fuel oil Solar oil	Static bioassay; SW; Koch's dishes; 10-15 specimens. Percent survival 5 days after exposure for: 5 min. 30 min. 60 min. 25 10 0 15 20 0 10 0 0	 ppm 100	"Oil" not specified. Mironov concludes that oil products in SW at concentrations of 1-100 ppm exert a definite toxic effect on larval shrimp and crabs. Concentrations estimated from graphs.	75
Crab *Pilumnus hirtellus*	Oil	96 hr TL50	10		
Shrimp *Leander adspersus*	Oil	96 hr TL50	50		
Crab, hairy hermit *Pagurus hirsutiusculus*	No. 2 diesel oil	Static bioassay; SW; 12°-13°C; exposed in 215 x 100 x 65 mm Pyrex container. Temp.(°C) LT50(min) 10.1±0.1 159 20.3±1.7 49 24.9±0.5 34	Whole Oil		59

Organism	Material Tested	Test Parameters Temp.(°C)	LT50(min)	Concentration	Remarks	Reference
Pagurus hirsutiusculus	Mineral oil	12.0±0.7 16.6±0.7	1,118 435	Whole oil		
Crab, hermit *Pagurus granosimanus*	No. 2 diesel oil	12.9±0.7	350			
Crab, shore *Hemigrapsus oregonensis*	No. 2 diesel oil	12.0±0.4 14.5±1.1 17.4±0.7 20.3±0.5 20.3±0.5 25.0±0.5 30.2±0.5	1,795 1,305 835 295 675 235 57			
	Mineral oil	13.3±0.9 17.9±2.1	1,510 782			
Crab, shore *Hemigrapsus nudus*	No. 2 diesel oil	14.0±1.0 20.5±0.4 25.0±0.1 30.5±0.8	812 364 149 42			
	Mineral oil	12.8±0.7 20.2±0.3	1,770 835			
Crab, rock *Cancer productus*	No. 2 diesel oil	13.1±0.7	730	Exposed in 50 x 100 mm crystallizing dishes. Whole oil	Indication of difference in toxicity depending size and sex.	
Amphipod *Orchestia traskiana*	No. 2 diesel oil	Temp.(°C) 12.2±0.3 13.4±0.4 19.7±0.7 24.8±0.5	LT50(min) 152 134 104 106			

Organism	Material Tested	Test Parameters		Concentration	Remarks	Reference
		Temp.(°C)	LT50 (min)			
Orchestia traskiana	Mineral oil	13.7±0.6	2,900	Whole oil		
		20.4±0.7	1,650			
Amphipod						
Calliopius laeviusculus	No. 2 diesel oil	15.5±0.4	103			
	Mineral oil	13.3±0.4	531			
Isopod						
Gnorimosphaeroma oregonesis oregonesis	No. 2 diesel oil	10.9±0.7	1,360			
		13.8±0.7	1,040			
		20.2±0.5	403			
		25.0±0.4	392			
		30.0±0.6	119			
	Mineral oil	12.9±0.7	3,400			
		18.5±1.7	2,120			
Shrimp, pandalid *Pandalus danae*		Static bioassay; SW; 6 l vol.; 9°C; narrow-mouth carboys.			No. of test animals assumed to be 10 per test vessel.	30
		Percent mortality after 24 hr exposure		(IR) ppm (GC)	Much additional information on analysis of oil:water solution and techniques of bioassays.	
	Filtered SW extract of Prudhoe Bay crude oil	0		0.6 1.23		
		20		1.2 3.19		
		100		2.3 5.63		
		100		3.3 11.55		
	Unfiltered SW extract of Prudhoe Bay crude oil	0		0.6 1.23		
		80		1.2 3.19		
		100		2.3 5.63		
		100		3.3 11.55		
	Filtered SW extract of S. Louisiana crude oil	0		0.6 1.23		
		0		1.2 3.19		
		60		2.3 5.63		
		100		3.3 11.55		

Organism	Material Tested	Test Parameters	Concentration	Remarks	Reference
Pandalus danae	Unfiltered SW extract of S. Louisiana crude oil	Percent mortality after 24 hr exposure	(IR)ppm(GC)		
		0	0.6 1.23		
		100	1.2 3.19		
		100	2.3 5.63		
		100	3.3 11.55		
		Continuous flow bioassay; SW; serially diluted; 8.5-9.0°C; DO 5.0-5.3 ppm.			
	WSF[b] of Prudhoe Bay crude oil	Percent mortality after 24 hr exposure	(IR)ppm(GC)		
		100	1.86 1.64		
		10	1.02 0.8		
		10	0.56 0.29		
Shrimp, pink *Pandalus montagui*	Phenol	48 hr LC$_{50}$	17.5 ppm		66,76
Shrimp, brown *Crangon crangon*	Phenol	48 hr LC$_{50}$	23.4 ppm		
Crab, shore *Carcinus maenas*	Phenol	48 hr LC$_{50}$	56.0 ppm		
Shrimp *Leander adspersus* var. *Fabricii* Rathke	Oman crude oil	Flow-through bioassay; SW; 500 ml/m; 10°C; 32-34°/oo sal.; concentration maintained by mixing standard solution and SW at predetermined ratios. 96 hr LC$_{50}$	<1,000 ppm	Study dealt mainly with dispersants and emulsions. Crude less toxic than oil emulsions. Tested 350, 650, and 1000 ppm. 350 ppm was lowest median concentration affecting locomotary behavior.	60

Organism	Material Tested	Test Parameters	Concentration		Remarks	Reference
Shrimp, grass *Palaemonetes pugio*	WSF of following:	Static bioassay; SW. Temp:(°C)		ppm	WSF prepared by mixing a 10% solution of oil and water for 20 hr and water phase tested. IR analysis. Information on uptake and retention.	77
		S. Louisiana crude oil 21		<16.80		
		Kuwait crude oil 21		<10.20		
		No. 2 fuel oil 21		5.50		
		Bunker C fuel oil 21		3.43		
		S. Louisiana crude oil 24		15.70		
		S. Louisiana crude oil 32 } 48 hr TLm		10.70		
		Benzene 21		33.00		
		Phenol 21		20.00		
		Naphthalene (N) 21		2.35		
		Methylnaphthalene (MN) 21		1.00		
		Dimethyl-napthalene (DMN) 21		0.70		
Shrimp, grass *Palaemonetes pugio*	WSF of No. 2 fuel oil	Continuous flow bioassay; ambient water conditions; Environ. Res. Lab., Narragansett, R.I.	Expected (ppm)	Actual (IR) (ppm)	IR analysis of test water.	61
		Exposure Mortality(%)				
		Control-4 mo 0.8	0.0	0.006		
		4 mo 6.2	0.1	0.067		
		100 days 73.8	1.0	0.54		
		6 days 100.0	10.0	10.6		
	WSF prepared by adding 1 part oil to 9 parts SW in 19 l bottle and stirring for 20 hr; allowed to settle 1-6 hr. OWD^C prepared by adding oil to SW and shaking vigorously for 5 min; allowed to settle 30-60 min.	Static bioassay; synthetic SW; 500 or 750 ml vol.; 15°-20°C; 20°/oo sal.; aerated 180 bubbles per min.			OWD concentrations expressed as ppm oil added to water; WSF concentrations as ppm total hydrocarbon in	32

Organism	Material Tested		Test Parameters	Concentration		Remarks	Reference
			TLm	ppm			
Mysid							
Mysidopsis almyra	S. Louisiana crude oil					First good coverage of total	
		OWD	48 hr	37.5		hydrocarbons and specific	
		WSF	48 hr	8.7		hydrocarbon content of WSF	
						and OWD of oils tested.	
	Kuwait crude oil					Not arctic or subarctic, but	
		OWD	48 hr	63.0		good example of a careful	
		WSF	48 hr	6.6		study.	
	No. 2 fuel oil						
		OWD	48 hr	1.3			
		WSF	48 hr	0.9			
	Bunker C oil - WSF		48 hr	0.9			
Shrimp, grass							
Palaemonetes pugio	S. Louisiana crude oil						
		OWD	48 hr	1,650			
		OWD	96 hr	200			
		WSF	48 hr	>16.8			
		WSF	96 hr	>16.8			
	Kuwait crude oil						
		OWD	48 hr	9,000			
		OWD	96 hr	6,000			
		WSF	48 hr	>10.2			
		WSF	96 hr	>10.2			
	No. 2 fuel oil						
		OWD	48 hr	3.4			
		OWD	96 hr	3.0			
		WSF	48 hr	4.1			
		WSF	96 hr	3.5			
	Bunker C oil						
		WSF	48 hr	2.8			
		WSF	96 hr	2.6			
Shrimp, brown							
Penaeus aztecus	S. Louisiana crude oil						
		OWD	48 hr	>1,000			
		OWD	96 hr	>1,000			

Organism	Material Tested	Test Parameters	Concentration	Remarks	Reference
Penaeus aztecus	No. 2 fuel oil	TLm	ppm		
	OWD	48 hr	9.4		
	OWD	96 hr	9.4		
	Bunker C fuel oil				
	WSF	48 hr	3.5		
	WSF	96 hr	1.9		
	WSF prepared by mixing 1 l oil/100 l SW for 20 hr and allowing to stand for 3 hr. OWD prepared by high speed stirring of oil in 18 l SW for 1 min and allowing to stand for 1 hr.	Static bioassay; SW:18 l vol.; 3.7°-10.2°C; aerated; 8-12 animals per dose.		IR and UV analysis. Arctic and subarctic species.	42
Crab, King	WSF of:		ppb(UV)	ppm(IR)	
Paralithodes camtschatica	Prudhoe Bay crude oil	TLm	202	2.35	
	Cook Inlet crude oil (treated)	96 hr	202	4.21	
	No. 2 fuel oil	96 hr	408	5.10	
		96 hr			
	OWD of:				
	Prudhoe Bay crude oil	96 hr	129	5.30	
	Cook Inlet crude oil (treated)	96 hr	82	7.89	
Shrimp, pandalid	WSF of:				
Pandalus goniurus	Prudhoe Bay crude oil	96 hr	92	1.26	
	Cook Inlet crude oil (treated)	96 hr	111	1.98	
	Cook Inlet crude oil (untreated)	96 hr	176	1.85	
	No. 2 fuel oil	96 hr	156	1.69	

Organism	Material Tested	Test Parameters TLm	Concentration ppb(UV)	Concentration ppm(IR)	Remarks	Reference
Pandalus goniurus	OWD of:					
	Prudhoe Bay crude oil	96 hr	31	2.31		
	Cook Inlet crude oil (treated)	96 hr	61	4.13		
Shrimp, *Eualus fabricii*	WSF of:					
	Prudhoe Bay crude oil	96 hr	158	1.94		
	Cook Inlet crude oil (treated)	96 hr	160	3.17		
	Cook Inlet crude oil (untreated)	96 hr	171	4.34		
	No. 2 fuel oil	96 hr	138	0.53		
	OWD of:					
	Prudhoe Bay crude oil	96 hr	151	13.91		
	Cook Inlet crude oil (treated)	96 hr	120	10.06		
Shrimp, pandalid *Pandalus hypsinotus*	WSF of:					
	Prudhoe Bay crude oil	96 hr	133	1.96		
	Cook Inlet crude oil (treated)	96 hr	122	2.72		
Pandalus borealis	WSF of:					
	Prudhoe Bay crude oil	96 hr	113	2.11		
	Cook Inlet crude oil (treated)	96 hr	88	2.43	IR and UV analysis. Arctic and subarctic species.	

WSF prepared by mixing 1 l oil/100 l SW for 20 hr and allowing to stand for 3 hr.

Static bioassay; SW; 60 ml vol.; 5°-5.5°C; not aerated.

Organism	Material Tested	Test Parameters	Concentration ppb(UV)	ppm(IR)	Remarks	Reference
	WSF of:					
Crab, King						
Paralithodes	Cook Inlet crude oil	96 hr TLm	74.5	3.0		
camtschatica	(treated)	96 hr ECm	74.5	3.0		
(larva)	Prudhoe Bay crude oil	96 hr TLm	>290	>6.4		
		96 hr ECm	57.8	1.4		
Crab, tanner						
Chionoecetes	Cook Inlet crude oil	96 hr TLm	>301	>10.8		
bairdi	(treated)	96 hr ECm	43.4	1.7		
(larva)		13°C temperature				
Crab, Dungeness						
Cancer magister	Cook Inlet crude oil	48 hr TLm	>212	>7.1		
(larva)	(treated)	48 hr ECm	41.1	1.6		
	Prudhoe Bay crude oil	48 hr TLm	>246	>5.5		
		48 hr ECm	87.8	2.14		
		3.5°C temperature				
Shrimp, pandalid						
Pandalus	Cook Inlet crude oil	96 hr TLm	–	7.94		
hypsinotus	(treated)	96 hr ECm	–	1.83		
(larva)	Prudhoe Bay crude oil	96 hr TLm	–	8.53		
		96 hr ECm	–	0.75		
Pandalus	Cook Inlet crude oil	96 hr TLm	–	1.72		
goniurus	(treated)	96 hr ECm	–	1.69		
(larva)						
Shrimp						
Eualus fabricii	Cook Inlet crude oil	96 hr TLm	–	5.89		
(larva)	(treated)	96 hr ECm	–	0.95		
	Prudhoe Bay crude oil	96 hr TLm	–	6.36		
		96 hr ECm	–	1.29		
	WSF of following oils, prepared by stirring 1 l oil/100 l SW for 20 hr and allowing to settle for 3 hr.	Static bioassay; SW; 18 l vol.; 4°–12°C; aerated; 8–12 animals per dose.			IR analysis	38

Organism	Material Tested	Test Parameters	Concentration	Remarks	Reference
		TLm	ppm		
Shrimp, pandalid					
Pandalus danae	Cook Inlet crude oil	24 hr	0.95		
		96 hr	0.81		
	No. 2 fuel oil	24 hr	1.68		
		96 hr	1.11		
Pandalus goniurus	Cook Inlet crude oil	24 hr	2.31		
		96 hr	1.98		
	No. 2 fuel oil	96 hr	1.69		
Shrimp					
Eualus fabricii	Cook Inlet crude oil	24 hr	2.52		
		96 hr	1.46		
	No. 2 fuel oil	24 hr	0.91		
		96 hr	0.53		
Shrimp, pandalid					
Pandalus hypsinotus	Cook Inlet crude oil	24 hr	2.87		
		96 hr	2.72		
Pandalus borealis	Cook Inlet crude oil	24 hr	2.89		
		96 hr	2.43		
	No. 2 fuel oil	24 hr	0.38		
		96 hr	0.21		
Crab, King					
Paralithodes camtschatica	Cook Inlet crude oil	24 hr	5.16		
		96 hr	4.21		
	No. 2 fuel oil	96 hr	5.10		
Crab, hermit					
Pagurus hirsutinsculus	Cook Inlet crude oil	96 hr	3.1		
	No. 2 fuel oil	96 hr	>5.59		
Amphipod					
Orchomene pinguis	Cook Inlet crude oil	24 hr	>7.40		
		96 hr	>7.40		
	No. 2 fuel oil	96 hr	>1.34		

Organism	Material Tested	Test Parameters	Concentration	Remarks	Reference
		TLm	ppm		
Isopod					
Idothea wosnesenskii	Cook Inlet crude oil	96 hr	>8.99		
	No. 2 fuel oil	96 hr	>5.59		
Mysid					
Acanthomysis pseudomacropsis	Cook Inlet crude oil	96 hr	>8.99		
	No. 2 fuel oil	96 hr	>0.95		
Barnacle					
Balanus glandula	Cook Inlet crude oil	24 hr	>8.51		
		96 hr	>8.51		
	OWD prepared by adding oil to SW and stirring constantly.	Static bioassay; SW; 900 ml vol.; ambient temperature; aeration; 10 animals per vessel; continuous mixing.		Includes test procedures for zooplankton.	78
		TLm	ppm	Data taken from graph.	
Crab, kelp					
Pugettia producta (megalops)	No. 2 fuel oil	96 hr	>10		
	Louisiana crude oil	96 hr	<100		
	Kuwait crude oil	96 hr	<1000		
	WSF of Southern Louisiana crude oil, prepared by mixing 1 part oil to 9 parts SW for 20 hr.	Static bioassay; SW.		IR analysis.	70
			ppm		
Shrimp, opposum					
Mysidopsis almyra		48 hr LC50	8.7		
		96 hr LC50	–		
Shrimp					
Leander terruicornis		48 hr LC50	10.2		
		96 hr LC50	6.0		

Organism	Material Tested	Test Parameters	Concentration	Remarks	Reference
Shrimp, grass *Palaemonetes pugio*		48 hr LC_{50} 96 hr LC_{50}	ppm >16.8 >16.8		
Shrimp, brown *Penaeus aztecus* (post larva)		48 hr LC_{50} 96 hr LC_{50}	>19.8 >19.8		41
	OWD of No. 2 fuel oil, prepared by vigorously mixing 2.4 ml/min oil and 15,000 mL/min SW followed by floatation and discard of insoluble oil. Waterborn oil mixed with raw SW.	Continuous flow bioassay; SW; 75 l vol.; flow 2 l/min; 30°/oo sal.; 10.5°C; DO 8.6 mg/l.		IR analysis.	
Shrimp, pandalid *Pandalus danae*		72 hr LC_{50} 96 hr LC_{50}	1.3 (ppm) 0.8 (ppm)		
Shrimp, oppossum *Neomysis awatschensis*	WSF of No. 2 diesel oil. Oil layered on surface and stirred constantly at 1,000–1,500 r/min.	static bioassay; SW; 5 gal glass aquaria with 15 l SW; 11°C; 25°/oo sal. 24 hr LC_{50} 48 hr LC_{50}	ml oil/l SW ppm 0.327 327 0.112 112	Emulsion rather than WSF. No analysis of test material.	59
Mysid *Neomysis* sp. (Size 2.74 mm ± 0.31 mm carapace length)	WSF of No. 2 diesel oil. Oil layered on surface and stirred constantly for subsurface circulation.	Static bioassay; SW; 15 l vol.; 11–13°C; 25–30°/oo sal.; test media renewed at 24 hr; 10 or more animals per aquaria. 24 hr LC_{50} 48 hr LC_{50}	ppm 350.0 95.0	Test concentrations do not represent hydrocarbon content of water. Mostly berried females. Less sensitive at 25°/oo than at 30°/oo sal.	63

Organism	Material Tested	Test Parameters	Concentration	Remarks	Reference
			ppm		
Amphipod *Anisogammarus* sp. (Size 14.67 mm ± 1.80 mm total length)		48 hr LC$_{50}$	100.0	Only one oil concentration tested – 100 ppm.	
Crab, shore *Hemigrapsus oregonensis*		48 hr LC$_{50}$	3,000.0		
	No. 2 fuel oil	Static bioassay; synthetic SW; 500 ml vol.		Test media stirred twice daily for 30 min.	79
			mg oil/l SW		
Amphipod *Neohaustorius biarticulatus*		Turbulent stirring, 25-33% vortex. 36 hr LD50	50 25	Toxicity decreases with increasing age of oil SW mixture.	
		Slow stirring, no vortex. 72 hr LD50	50 25		
		20 ml clean sand and oil-SW mixture 24 hr LD50	50		
Crab, hermit *Pagurus longicarpus*		20 ml clean sand and oil-SW mixture 12 hr LD50	50	Prelethal behavior: vacated shells and lost coordination several hr before death.	
		Static bioassay; SW; 1 l vol.; 12°-18°C; 8.5-11°/oo sal.			80
Amphipod *Anisogrammarus locustoides*	Treated Puget Sound ballast water	96 hr – no increase in mortality at any concentration	To 33 ppm		
	Treated Valdez ballast water		7.4 and 5.6 ppm		
Isopod *Idothea fewkesi*	Treated Valdez ballast water	1, 3, 10, 30, and 100% treated ballast water No effect			

66

Organism	Material Tested	Test Parameters	Concentration	Remarks	Reference
Crab, shore *Hemigrapsus oregonensis*	Treated Valdez ballast water	1, 3, 10, 30 and 100% treated ballast water No effect			
	Oil-SW dispersion of following oils:	Static bioassay; SW; 450 ml; 8°C; 17°/oo sal.; aeration; 5 to 20 animals; media replaced each 24 hr.		Light dispersion (10-20 ppm) of all crude oils - no mortality.	51
	Light - 25 µl oil/ 500 ml SW Med. - 250 µl oil/ 500 ml SW Heavy - 1000 µl oil/ 500 ml SW				
		Percent mortality after 96 hr exposure	Initial conc.		
Amphipod *Onisimus affinis*	Norman Wells Venezuelan Atkinson Point Pembina	95 100 88 25	300-1,000 ppm (Heavy)		
	Norman Wells Venezuelan	33 18	20-200 ppm (Medium)		
Copepod *Calanus hyperboreas*	Atkinson Point Venezuelan Norman Wells Pembina	0 0 10 37.5	300-1,000 ppm (Heavy)		
Isopod *Mesidotea entomon*	Norman Wells	0	300-1,000 ppm (Heavy)		
Mesidotea sibirica	Norman Wells	0			
Mesidotea sabini	Norman Wells	0			
Amphipod *Atylus carinatus*	Norman Wells	15	300-1,000 ppm (Heavy)		

Organism	Material Tested	Test Parameters	Concentration	Remarks	Reference
		Percent mortality after 96 hr exposure	Initial conc.		
Amphipod *Corophium clarencense*	Norman Wells	67.5	300–1,000 ppm (Heavy)	Great variation in test results of different groups of same species.	81
Copepod *Acartia clausi*	Crude oil } Black oil } Solar oil }	Static bioassay; SW; Koch's dishes; 10–15 specimens. Little difference in survival after 24 hr	0.01–0.05 ml/l (≅10–50 ppm)	No difference in reaction to different oils.	
		Great change in survival (toxic)	0.05–0.1 ml/l (50–100 ppm)		
Copepod *Paracalanus parvus* *Centropages ponticus* *Penillia avirostris* *Oithona nana*	} Black oil }	Little difference in survival after 24 hr Great change in survival (toxic)	0.01–0.05 ml/l (10–50 ppm) 0.05–0.1 ml/l (50–100 ppm)		
	Crude oil (not specified)	Static bioassay; SW; 20 x 150 mm test tubes; -17.5°C; 50 copepods per test tube. No aeration - 100% mortality in 3 days Aeration - 100% mortality in 5 days }	1.5 mm thick slick	0.5 ml crude added to 20 ml SW; made 1.5 mm thick slick. Crude oil probably acts as barrier to oxygen transfer and contains toxic substances.	82
Copepod, tidepool *Trigriopus californicus*	WSF of Venezuelan crude oil, made by adding 50 ml crude to 5 l of SW. Synthetic SW stirred 24 hr; in separation funnel 1 hr.	Static bioassay; SW; medium changed daily.		50% mortality value taken from graph. 4 ppm analyzed on Beckman (total organic carbon)	83

Organism	Material Tested	Test Parameters	Concentration	Remarks	Reference
Decapod *Neopanope texana* (larva)		96 hr LC$_{50}$	10 ml/l	Exposure retarded molting.	
Barnacle *Balanus cariosus* (larva)	No. 2 diesel oil	Static bioassay; SW; 40 ml vol. Average survival of Nauplius stage – 12 hr	0.5%	Survival may be re-lated to egg and larval size. Parent egg diam. (μm) = 170	52
Barnacle *Balanus balanoides*	Crude oil and carbonized sand	Static bioassay; SW; 250 ml vol.; 21.0°–21.8°C. Enough sand to keep oil on bottom. Time to 100% mortality 70 hr 54 hr 45 hr	Oil:SW $\tilde{=}$ppm 1:50 20,000 1:25 40,000 1:125 80,000	Additional informa-tion on behavior.	28
Barnacle *Eliminius modestus* (stage II nauplius)	*"Torrey Canyon Oil"* (weathered Kuwait crude oil) Suspension of oil and SW.	Static bioassay; SW; 200 ml finger bowls; 16°–20°C; 200 nauplii/bowl. Loss of swimming activity No observable effects in 24 hr	1,000 ppm 100 ppm	The study mainly con-cerned with toxicity of detergents.	84
(spat)	Kuwait crude oil Film on surface	4 hr – >50% normal cirral beat 48 hr – 28% normal cirral beat	100 ppm 100 ppm		
	Suspension of oil and water.	4 hr – 50% normal cirral beat 48 hr – 10% normal cirral beat	100 ppm 100 ppm		

Organism	Material Tested	Test Parameters	Concentration	Remarks	Reference
Barnacle *Eliminius modestus* (larva)	Fresh crude oil	1 hr LC_{50}	100 ppm		66,67
Barnacle *Balanus crenatus*	Norman Wells crude oil	Static bioassay; SW; 450 1 vol.; 8°C; 17°/oo sal.; aeration; 5-20 animals; media replaced at 24 hr intervals. 96 hr - 73% mortality	30-1,000 ppm	Oil and SW dispersion. Initial concentration. Arctic species.	51
	Anastasiyerka crude oil	Static bioassay; SW; 3°-18°C; 1-5 specimens per petri dish; water changed daily for adults and every 2 days for juveniles.		Emulsion of oil and SW. Concentrations reflect only the amount of oil added to water. Data taken from graph.	85

	Percent survival after 10 days	ml oil/1 SW	ppm
Isopod *Idothea baltica basteri* (adult)	75	1.0	1,000
	90	0.1	100
	100	0.01	10
	100	0.001	1
(juvenile)	0	1.0	1,000
	25	0.1	100
	60	0.01	10
	75	0.001	1
Amphipod *Gammarus marino-* *gammarus olivii* (adult)	0	1.0	1,000
	100	0.1	100
	80	0.01	10
	100	0.001	1
(juvenile)	0	1.0	1,000
	0	0.1	100
	20	0.01	10
	50	0.001	1

Organism	Material Tested	Test Parameters	Concentration	Remarks	Reference
	WSF of Bunker C fuel oil	Closed, continuous flow bioassay; SW; 12-18°/oo sal.; test animals in flasks.	$\frac{ppm}{}$		69
Isopod *Idothea tribola*		No effect	5.53		
Amphipod *Gammarus macronatus*		48 hr TL$_{50}$	0.42		
Crab, hermit *Pagurus longicarpus*		48 hr TL$_{50}$	0.62		

TABLE 6

Acute toxicity of petroleum to Chordata

Organism	Material Tested	Test Parameters	Concentration	Remarks	Reference
	Simulated Valdez ballast water. Prepared from Prudhoe Bay crude oil	Flow-through and static bio-assay; 30 l vol.; 12°–18°C; 8.5–11°/oo sal.		TLms not given. IR analysis.	80
Salmon, chum *Oncorhynchus keta*		Fish acclimated	ppm(avg.)	Number of fish tested	
0.35 g avg.	100% treated ballast water	<16 hr – 100% mortality	6.4	15	
	100% treated ballast water	<48 hr – 100% mortality	4.6	15	
1.83 g avg.	100% untreated ballast water	16 hr – 100% mortality	7.9	–	
	10% untreated ballast water	70 hr – 100% mortality	1.0	–	
		Fish not acclimated (stressed)			
0.38 g avg.	50% untreated ballast water	78 hr – 98% mortality	<1.0 to 3.5	300	
	Simulated Valdez ballast water	Fish acclimated			
5.36 g avg.	Puget Sound water 100% treated ballast water	7.5 hr – 100% mortality	13.3	8	
	Valdez water 100% treated ballast water	7.5 hr – 100% mortality	12.8	8	
1.90 g avg.	Valdez water 20%, 30%, and 50% treated ballast water	96 hr – 0% mortality	<1.0 to 1.2	–	

a SW: Seawater
b WSF: Water-soluble fraction
c OWD: Oil water dispersion

72

Organism	Material Tested	Test Parameters	Concentration	Remarks	Reference
			ppm(avg.)	Number of fish tested	
Oncorhynchus keta		Fish not acclimated (stressed)			
0.9 g avg.	Valdez water 50% treated ballast water	7 day – 75% mortality	3.4	24	
	Valdez water 30% treated ballast water	14 day – 63% mortality	2.0	–	
Salmon, pink *Oncorhynchus gorbuscha*	Simulated Valdez ballast water				
0.22 g avg.	100% treated ballast water	48 hr – 95% mortality	4.5	38	
0.47 g avg.	30% treated ballast water	96 hr – 13% mortality	<1.0	17	
Salmon, Chinook *Oncorhynchus tschawytscha* (fingerling)	WSF[b] of Prudhoe Bay crude oil	Continuous flow bioassay; SW[a]; 8.5°–9.0°C; DO: 5.0–5.3 ppm.		Serially diluted. Much additional information on analysis of components in solution and on techniques of flow-through bioassay.	30

Percent mortality after 24 hr	ppm (filtered medium)	
	(IR)	(GC)
100	1.86	1.64
70	1.02	0.8
0	0.56	0.29

Organism	Material Tested	Test Parameters	Concentration	Remarks	Reference
Salmon, Chinook *Oncorhynchus tschawytscha*	WSF of No. 2 diesel oil. Oil layered on surface and stirred (1,000 – 1,500 r/min).	Static bioassay; fresh water and SW; 5 gal glass aquaria, 15 l water; 6.9° ± 0.5°C.		Emulsion rather than WSF.	59

	ml oil/ l water	≅ppm
Fresh water		
48 hr LC50	1.19	1,190
96 hr LC50	0.349	349

Organism	Material Tested	Test Parameters	Concentration	Remarks	Reference
Salmon, Chum *Oncorhynchus keta*		25°/oo salinity 48 hr LC_{50} 96 hr LC_{50} 30°/oo salinity 48 hr LC_{50} 96 hr LC_{50}	ml oil/l water / ≅ppm 0.538 538 0.312 312 0.550 550 0.184 184		
Salmon, Pink *Oncorhynchus gorbuscha*	Prudhoe Bay crude oil	Static bioassay; SW; 4 day exposure.		Doses of oil quantitated volumetrically and corrected to ppm.	86
Salmon, Pink *Oncorhynchus gorbuscha* (fry)		June 5, 7.5°C 96 hr TLm Aug. 27, 11.5°C 96 hr TLm	213 ppm 110 ppm	Older fry held at higher temperature more susceptible to oil toxicity.	
Salmon, Pink *Oncorhynchus gorbuscha*	Prudhoe Bay crude oil	Static bioassay; fresh water and SW; 20 l glass jars; 4.0°–5.0°C; aerated 100 bubbles per min.		Mechanical and water agitation of oil-water dispersions. IR analysis made of concentrations resulting from different amounts of oil and different mixing methods.	33
Egg Early alevin Mid-alevin Late alevin Emergent fry	Mechanically mixed fresh water	96 hr – no deaths 96 hr TLm 96 hr TLm 96 hr TLm 96 hr TLm	ml/l 3.20 0.62 0.55 0.70 0.40(12 ppm,IR)		
Migrant fry	Mechanically mixed SW	96 hr TLm	0.042(6 ppm,IR)		
Egg Early alevin Mid-alevin Late alevin Emergent fry	Water agitation - fresh water	96 hr – no deaths 96 hr – mortality<50% 96 hr TLm 96 hr TLm 96 hr TLm	3.20 3.20 3.20 1.85 1.25		
Migrant fry	Water agitation - SW	96 hr TLm	0.075(0.7 ppm,IR)		

Organism	Material Tested	Test Parameters		Concentration	Remarks	Reference
	Prudhoe Bay crude oil, oil poured on surface.	Static bioassay; synthetic SW; 75 l vol.; 30°/oo sal.; DO 7-10.5 ppm; pH 8.1; aerated constantly; 96 hr exposure.			No analysis of test water. Material lost potency with storage. Mortality varied directly with concentration and inversely with temperature. Oil exposed to air for 30 days did not produce greater mortality than controls.	29
		Temp(°C)	Mortality(%)	ppm		
Salmon, Coho *Oncorhynchus* *kisutch* (advanced parr/ 11 mo old)		8	10	(Control)		
		8	56	3,500		
		13	0	(Control)		
		13	62.5	3,500		
		8	9.1	(Control)		
		8	80.5	3,500		
Salmon, Sockeye *Oncorhynchus* *nerka* (advanced parr/ 10 mo old)		8	10	(Control)		
		8	39.3	500		
		8	44.8	1,000		
		8	6.7	1,750		
		8	40.0	3,500		
		3-5	0	(Control)		
		3-4	55	500		
		3	100	1,750		
		4-5	90	3,500		
		13	0	(Control)		
		13	0	500		
		13	6.9	1,000		
		13	5	1,750		
		13	20	3,500		
	Phenol	Static bioassay; SW and fresh water; 40 l aquaria; 15.0°-15.8°C; pH 8.1-8.4; aeration; fish 200 mm avg.			Concentrations of phenol measured before and after change of fish; constant for 6 hr. Values taken from graph.	87
		48 hr LC at various % SW		mg/l (ppm)		
Trout, Rainbow *Salmo gairdneri* (yearling)		60		5.25		
		40		7.25		

Organism	Material Tested	Test Parameters	Concentration	Remarks	Reference
Salmo gairdneri (yearling)	Oil and water metered into common funnel and then through static mixer.	48 hr LC$_{50}$ at various %SW: 30 / 15 / 100(fresh water)	mg/l (ppm): 7.90 / 8.00 / 9.3	Increased salinity results in increased toxicity.	22
		Continuous flow bioassay; SW; 8°–12°C; 29.3–32.4 °/oo sal.; DO 7.9–9.4 ppm; pH 7.4–8.4.		Concentration based on metered inflow. EEC – estimated exposure concentration, calculated by IR. Good sections on test animals selection and bioassay methods.	
		Stage	hr TLm	ppm	
Perch, shiner *Cymatogaster aggregata*	No. 2 fuel oil S. Louisiana crude oil	Adult Adult	96 72	550±80 1,200(EEC 62)	
	Kuwait crude oil S. Louisiana crude oil	Adult Juvenile	96 72	1,300±260(EEC 65) 840±80(EEC 15)	
Sand lance, Pacific *Ammodytes hexapterus*	No. 2 fuel oil		96	43±6	
Salmon, chum *Oncorhynchus keta*	No. 2 fuel oil		96	1,040±260	
Sculpin, staghorn *Leptocottus armatus*	Kuwait crude oil		96	5,600±1,400	
Herring, Pacific *Clupea pallasii*	No. 2 fuel oil		96	20	
Pipefish, bay *Syngnathus griseolineatus*	Kuwait crude oil		96	<675(EEC 22)	
Capelin *Mallotus villosus*	S. Louisiana crude oil		72	150±360	

Organism	Material Tested	Test Parameters	Concentration	Remarks	Reference
		hr TLm	ppm		
Flounder, starry *Platichthys* *stellatus*	S. Louisiana crude oil	72	1,400±110		
Sole, sand *Psettichthys* *melanostictus* (egg and larva)	S. Louisiana crude oil	Static bioassay; SW; 8.0°C. <u>Mortality (%)</u> After 6 days – 100 100 100 100 100	ppm 10 30 50 100 500		
	No. 2 fuel oil	After 4 days – 0 0 0 0 20	1 5 10 25 50		
	Kuwait crude oil	After 5 days – 50 20 10 60 90	10 30 50 100 500		
	Benzene	Static bioassay; SW; 8 l vol.; 10.0°–19.2°C; 10–30 °/oo sal.; DO 7.4–8.1 ppm; 50 per container.		Concentrations measured with GC.	88
			ppm(initial)		
Herring, Pacific *Clupea pallasi* (egg) (larva)		96 hr TL50 48 hr TL50	40-45 20-25		
Anchovy, northern *Engraulis mordax* (egg) (larva)		48 hr TL50 48 hr TL50	20-25 20-25		

Organism	Material Tested	Test Parameters		Concentration		Remarks	Reference
		Age at start (days)	Mortality at 140 days deg. (%)	ml/l	ppm		
Cod	Oil poured on 30 l water, stirred and allowed to set 1 day.	Static bioassay; SW; 6°C.				Precentages of dead cod eggs as difference to mortality in controls. Data estimated from graphs.	89
Gadus morhua L. (egg)	WSF of Venezuelan crude oil	0-1	30				
		3.5	40 }	10	10,000		
		10.0	20				
		0-1	40				
		3.5	25 }	1	1,000		
		10.0	2.5				
		0-1 }	No difference from controls				
		3.5		0.1	100		
		10.0					
	WSF of Libya crude oil		Little difference from controls }	10 1 0.1			
	WSF of Iran crude oil	0-1	60				
		3.5-1.0	Little difference from controls }	0.1			
		0-1	45				
		3.5	35 }	1			
		10.0	12				
		0-1	70				
		3.5	60 }	10			
		10.0	5				
Herring							
Clupea harengus L. (egg)	Venezuelan crude	3.5	100				
	Iran crude	3.5 4.5	100 90 }	0.1-10	100-10,000		
	Libya crude	5.5	100				

Organism	Material Tested	Test Parameters	Concentration	Remarks	Reference
	Clear oil extract prepared by adding various amounts of oil to SW and circulating for 2 days.	Static bioassay; SW.		Analysis showed 10^4 ppm gave dissolved hydrocarbon in range of 10 ppm. Young eggs 5–30 hr after fertilization most sensitive.	90
Cod	WSF of following oils.	Percent Mortalities (>controls after 100 hr)	ppm		
Gadus morhua (egg)	Venezuelan crude oil	40	10^4		
	Iran crude oil	30	10^4	Taken from graph.	
		10–17	100		
	Libya crude oil	Practically nontoxic	2.1–10^6		
		Hatching rate (as % of controls) for eggs of age:			
		0.5 day 4 days 10 days			
	Venezuelan crude oil	20 25 50	10^4		
	Iran crude oil	20 40 –			
	Libya crude oil	40 95 –			
(larva)		Mean critical time (days) in WSF for larvae transferred at age of:		Larva with partly or entirely resorbed yolk sac were most sensitive.	
		1 day 3 days 5 days 10 days			
	Iran crude oil	14 10 8.2 5.5	10^2		
	Agha crude oil	8.4 7.5 5.9 4.5	10^3		
	Jari crude oil	4.2 3.5 2.5 0.5	10^4		
Cod	Bunker C fuel oil	Flow-through hatching box; SW; 2°–5°C; 96 hr exposure.			91
Gadus sp. (egg)		Mortality (%)	Oil(%)		
	(Control)	1.2	0		
	Light oil	2.9	0.1		
	Heavy oil	2.0	0.1		

Organism	Material Tested	Test Parameters	Concentration	Remarks	Reference
Gadus sp. (egg)		Static bioassay; SW; 8 liter pans; 2.5" deep; aeration-jet on surface; 100 hr exposures	Oil(%)		
		Mortality(%)			
	(Control)	5.6	0	Inadequate aeration.	
	Light oil	32.7	0.1		
	Heavy oil	37.0	0.1		
		Static bioassay; SW; 6 liter pans; 350 cc flow; 50 hr exposure.			
		Mortality(%)			
	(Control)	35.2	0		
	Light oil	77.0	0.1		
	Heavy oil	17.5	0.1		
		Static bioassay; SW; 1 liter dish; 3" deep; aeration at intervals; 30 hr exposure.			
		Mortality(%)			
	(Control)	6.8	0	Inadequate aeration	
	Light oil	35.8	0.1		
	Heavy oil	17.5	0.1		
		Same as above but more aeration, 42 hr exposure.			
		Mortality(%)			
	(Control)	3.0	0	No inhibitive effects observed on cod eggs under conditions similar to those in nature.	
	Light oil	24.0	0.1		
	Heavy oil + Gasoline	3.2	0.1		

Organism	Material Tested	Test Parameters	Concentration	Remarks	Reference
Flounder, winter *Pseudopleuronectes* sp. (larva) 8 hr		Static bioassay; SW; 1 liter dish; aeration; 42 hr exposure.	Oil(%) Mortality(%)		
	(Control)		0 0	Slight effect on flounder larvae.	
	Light oil		0.1 6.8		
	Oman crude oil	Flow-through bioassay; SW; 500 ml/min.; 10° ± 2°C; 32-34°/oo sal.; concentrations maintained by mixing standard solution and SW at predetermined ratios; fish 20-30 cm long.		Tested 350, 600 and 1,000 ppm. Study dealt mainly with oil dispersants and oil emulsions. <350 ppm affected locomotory behavior of cod.	60
Cod *Gadus morhua*		96 hr LC50	>1,000 ppm	Whole crude oil less toxic than its emulsions.	
Shad, American *Alosa sapidissima* (young)	Gasoline	48 hr LC50	91 ppm	Essentially, the water soluble component was being tested.	76,92
	Heavy fuel oil	48 hr LC50	2417 ppm		
	Diesel oil	48 hr LC50	167 ppm		
	WSF of following:	Static bioassay; fresh water; 113 l aquaria; DO 6 ppm; water circulated to permeate surface slick and extract WSF.		Mortality partly due to physical and partly due to toxicological causes. Gasoline and diesel oil lost much of toxicity with time.	93
		hr to TLm	ppm		
Shad, American *Alosa sapidissima* (juvenile)	Gasoline	24	91		
		48	91		
	Diesel fuel oil	24	204		
		48	167		
	Bunker oil No. 6	48	2,417		
		96	1,952		

Organism	Material Tested	Test Parameters	Concentration	Remarks	Reference
	No. 2 diesel oil	Static bioassay; SW; 45 l vol.; 11°-13°C; 30-31°/oo sal.; 10 animals per aquaria; oil layered on surface and stirred constantly for subsurface circulation.		Test concentrations reported do not represent hydrocarbon content of water. Test mixture not renewed.	63
Sculpin, tadpole *Psychrolutes paradoxus*		48 hr LC50	400 ppm	Tadpole 37.0 mm ± 3.14 mm.	
Sculpin, tidepool *Oligocottus maculosus*		48 hr LC50	400 ppm	Tidepool 45.5 mm ± 2.87 mm. No mortalities occurred during 48 hr at 251 and 398 ppm.	
Silverside, Atlantic *Menidia menidia*	Waste automotive crankcase oil	Static bioassay; SW; 2 l vol.; 20°±1°C; 30°/oo sal.; 5 fish per aquaria; continually aerated.		Additional information on oysters and scallops.	94
		48 hr LC50 96 hr LC50	2,200 ppm 1,700 ppm		
		Static bioassay; 500 liter recirculated SW.			
		7 days, 100% mortality 36 days, 0% mortality 60 days, 0% mortality	250 ppm 100 ppm 20 ppm		
Flatfish, Black Sea *Rhombus maeoticus* (egg)		Static bioassay; SW; 180 ml vol.; 16.5°-18.0°C; 20-30 developing eggs per dish.		Method of mixing oil and SW not stated.	95

Organism	Material Tested	Test Parameters				Concentration	Remarks	Reference
		Viable eggs (%) after:				ppm		
		1 day	2 days	3 days				
Rhombus maeoticus (egg)	Bunker C fuel oil	82	0	-		100		
		84	0	-		10		
		76	71	0		1		
		87	81	81		0.1		
		89	89	89		0.01		
		83	83	83		0.0 (control)		
	Solar oil	81	0	-		100		
		82	10	0		10		
		89	78	78		1		
		87	87	67		0.1		
		94	81	81		0.01		
		83	83	83		0.0 (control)		
	Malgobeck oil	80	0	-		100		
		87	74	0		10		
		81	81	81		1		
		72	67	55		0.1		
		67	67	67		0.01		
		83	83	83		0.0 (control)		

Same as above, after 5 days:

Organism	Material Tested	Hatch(%)	Abnormal(%)	Concentration ppm	Remarks
(larva)	Bunker C fuel oil	100	100	0.1	Mironov concludes that concentrations of oil of 0.01-1.0 ppm may be toxic to eggs of flatfish.
		100	37	0.01	
	Solar oil	100	All died	1.0	
		100	All died	0.1	
		100	23	0.01	
	Malgobeck oil	0	-	1.0	
		100	100	0.1	
		100	40	0.01	
		100	7	0.0 (control)	
	WSF of Bunker C fuel oil	2 days, 100% mortality		1.0	

Organism	Material Tested	Test Parameters	Concentration	Remarks	Reference
Bass, striped *Morone saxatilis* (juvenile)	Benzene – introduced from gas wash bottles.	Flow-through bioassay; SW; 40-70 l vol.; 17.4°C; 29°/oo sal.; fish, 1.5± 0.5 g. 72 hr LC50 96 hr LC50	10.9 µl/l (ppm) 10.9 µl/l (ppm)		96
Pike, Northern *Esox lucius* (egg and larva)	WSF of Russian crude oil	Static bioassay; SW; 500 ml vol.; 10°C; 5.8°/oo sal.; glass jar; no aeration; 10 eggs or larvae each; oil stirred in water for 30 min, clear extract used.		Compounds extracted from 1,000, 3,000, 10,000 ppm Russian crude. Dissolved fractions of crude oil seemed to have no effect.	97
			ppm		
		Stage I (eyed egg) 24 hr TLm 48 hr TLm	>10⁴		
		Stage II (yolk sac) 24 hr TLm 48 hr TLm	>10⁴		
		Stage III (free swimming) 24 hr TLm 48 hr TLm	>10⁴		
		Stage IV (ca. 1 mo old) 24 hr TLm 48 hr TLm	>10⁴		
Toadfish *Opsanus tau* (larva)	Diesel oil and carbonized sand	Static bioassay; SW; 22.1-23.1°C.		8-10 larvae per test.	28

	Survival after 52 hr(%)	Oil:SW	≅ppm
	100	1:40	25,000
	40	1:20	50,000
	0	1:10	100,000

Organism	Material Tested	Test Parameters	Concentration		Remarks	Reference

Organism	Material Tested	Test Parameters	Concentration			Remarks	Reference
Opsanus tau (larva)	Lubricating oil (SAE 20) and carbonized sand	Survival after 50 hr(%)	Oil:SW	≅ppm			
		80	1:40	25,000			
		100	1:20	50,000			
		80	1:10	100,000			
	Crude oil and carbonized sand	Survival after 48 hr(%)					
		100	1:200	5,000			
		100	1:80	12,500			
		40	1:40	25,000			
		0	1:20	50,000			
		0	1:10	100,000			
Tunicate *Boltenia velosa*	No. 2 diesel oil	Static bioassay; SW; 40 ml vol. Developmental stage – tadpole Survival time – 5 hr		0.5%		Egg diameter 154 μm. Survival may be related to egg and larval size.	52
Killifish *Cyprinodon variegatus*	Prepared from the following oils. WSF prepared by adding 1 part oil to 9 parts SW in 19 1 bottle and stirring for 20 hr; allowed to settle 1–6 hr. OWD prepared by adding oil to SW and shaking vigorously for 5 min.; allowed to settle 30–60 min.	Static bioassay; synthetic SW; 500 or 750 ml vol.; 15°–20°C; 20°/∘∘ sal.; aerated 180 bubbles per min.				OWD concentrations expressed as ppm oil added to water. WSF concentrations as ppm total hydrocarbon in aqueous phase determined by IR analysis. First good coverage of total hydrocarbon and specific hydrocarbon content of WSF and OWD of oils tested.	32

85

Organism	Material Tested	Test Parameters hr TLm	Concentration ppm	Remarks	Reference
Cyprinodon variegatatus	S. Louisiana crude – OWD oil	48	33,000	Not arctic or subarctic but a good example of a careful study.	
		96	29,000		
	– WSF	48	19.8		
		96	19.8		
	Kuwait crude oil – OWD	48	80,000		
		96	80,000		
	No. 2 fuel oil – OWD	48	200		
		96	93		
	– WSF	48	>6.9		
		96	6.3		
	Bunker C fuel oil – WSF	48	4.4		
		96	3.1		
Silverside *Menidia beryllina*	S. Louisiana crude – OWD oil	48	5,000		
		96	3,700		
	– WSF	48	8.7		
		96	5.5		
	Kuwait crude oil – OWD	48	15,000		
		96	9,400		
	– WSF	48	6.6		
		96	6.6		
	No. 2 fuel oil – OWD	48	125		
	– WSF	48	5.2		
		96	3.9		
	Bunker C fuel oil – WSF	48	2.7		
		96	1.9		
Killifish, longnose *Fundulus similus*	S. Louisiana crude – OWD oil	48 & 96	6,000		
	– WSF	48 & 96	16.8		

Organism	Material Tested	Test Parameters	Concentration	Remarks	Reference
Fundulus similus		hr TLm	ppm		
	Kuwait crude oil - OWD	48 & 96	14,800		
	- WSF	48 & 96	10.4		
	No. 2 fuel oil - OWD	48	36		
		96	33		
	- WSF	48	4.7		
		96	3.9		
	Bunker C fuel oil - WSF	48	2.27		
		96	1.69		
	Bunker C fuel oil	Static bioassay; fresh water and SW; 60 l vol.; 5°-15°C; no replacement. Oil-water dispersion stirred continually.		Bunker C fuel oil by itself was "practically" nontoxic; Information on toxicity of dispersants.	98
Salmon, Atlantic *Salmo salar* L. (parr)		96 hr LC50	mg/l		
		15°C	>10,000		
		5°C	>10,000		
Flounder, winter *Pseudopleuronectes americanus*		15°C	>10,000		
		5°C	>10,000		
	OWD of following oils. Prepared by adding oil to SW and stirring constantly.	Static bioassay; SW; 900 ml vol.; ambient temperature; aeration; 10 animals per vessel; continuous mixing.		Includes test procedures for zooplankton. Data taken from graphs.	78
Cabazon *Scorpaenichthys marmoratus* (larva)	No. 2 fuel oil	~96 hr TLm	<10 ppm		
	Louisiana crude oil	~96 hr TLm	>100 ppm		

Organism	Material Tested	Test Parameters	Concentration			Remarks	Reference
	WSF of Southern Louisiana crude oil. Prepared by mixing 1 part oil to 9 parts SW for 20 hr.	Static bioassay; SW.				IR analysis. Not arctic or sub-arctic species.	70
			hr LC$_{50}$		ppm		
Silverside *Menidia beryllina* (minnow)			48		8.7		
			96		5.5		
Killifish, Gulf *Fundulus similus*			48		16.8		
			96		16.8		
Sheepshead *Cyprinodon variegatus* (minnow)			48		>19.8		
			96		>19.8		
	Prepared materials from the following oils. WSF prepared by mixing 1 l oil with 100 l SW for 2 hr and allowing to stand for 3 hr. OWD prepared by high-speed stirring of oil in 18 l SW for 1 min and allowing to stand for 1 hr.	Static bioassay; SW;18 l vol.; 3.7°-10.2°C; aerated; 8-12 animals per dose.				IR and UV analysis. Arctic and subarctic species.	42
				ppb(UV)	ppm(IR)		
Salmon, pink *Oncorhynchus gorbuscha*	WSF of:						
	Prudhoe Bay crude oil			92	1.41		
	Cook Inlet crude oil (treated)		96 hr TLm	102	2.92		
	Cook Inlet crude oil (untreated)			100	1.47		
	No. 2 fuel oil			223	0.81		

Organism	Material Tested	Test Parameters	Concentration ppb(UV)	Concentration ppm(IR)	Remarks	Reference
Oncorhynchus gorbuscha	OWD of:					
	Prudhoe Bay crude oil	} 96 hr TLm	80	4.50		
	Cook Inlet crude oil (treated)		52	3.41		
Dolly Varden *Salvelinus malma*	WSF of:					
	Prudhoe Bay crude oil		67	1.10		
	Cook Inlet crude oil (treated)	} 96 hr TLm	109	2.94		
	Cook Inlet crude oil (untreated)		80	1.54		
	No. 2 fuel oil		357	2.29		
	OWD of:					
	Prudhoe Bay crude oil	} 96 hr TLm	124	16.41		
	Cook Inlet crude oil (treated)		202	7.30		
		Static bioassay; SW; 60 ml vol.; 4.5°-8°C; no aeration.	ppb(UV)	ppm(IR)	IR and UV analysis. Arctic and subarctic species.	
Herring *Clupea harengus pallasi* (larva)	WSF of Cook Inlet crude oil (treated)	96 hr TLm	74.5	3.0	IR analysis.	38
	WSF of following oils prepared by stirring 1 l oil per 100 l SW for 20 hr and allowing to settle for 3 hr.	Static bioassay; SW; 18 l vol.; 4°-12°C; aerated; 8-12 animals per dose.				
Salmon, pink *Oncorhynchus gorbuscha*		hr TLm	ppm			
	Cook Inlet crude oil	24	4.13			
		96	2.92			
	No. 2 fuel oil	24	0.89			
		96	0.81			

Organism	Material Tested	Test Parameters	Concentration	Remarks	Reference
		hr TLm	ppm		
Dolly Varden					
Salvelinus malma	Cook Inlet crude oil	24	3.25		
(smolt)		96	2.94		
	No. 2 fuel oil	96	2.29		
Cod, saffron					
Eleginus gracilis	Cook Inlet crude oil	24	2.48		
		96	2.28		
	No. 2 fuel oil	24	>4.56		
		96	2.93		
Tube-snout					
Aulorhynchus	Cook Inlet crude oil	96	1.34		
flavidus					

TABLE 7

Acute toxicity of petroleum to marine animals.

Organism	Material Tested	Lethal Concentration ppm	Reference
Finfish	Soluble hydrocarbons	5-50	61
Larvae and eggs		0.1-1.0	
Pelagic crustacea		1-10	
Benthic crustacea		1-10	
Gastropods		10-100	
Bivalves		5-500	
Other benthic invertebrates		1-10	
Finfish	No. 2 fuel oil/kerosine	550	
Larvae and eggs		0.1-4.0	
Pelagic crustacea		5-50	
Benthic crustacea		5-50	
Gastropods		50-500	
Bivalves		30,000-40,000	
Other benthic invertebrates		5-50	
Finfish	Fresh crude oil	88-18,000	
Larvae and eggs		0.1-100	
Pelagic crustacea		100-40,000	
Benthic crustacea		56	
Gastropods		?	
Bivalves		1,000-100,000	

Organism	Material Tested	Lethal Concentration ppm	Reference
Other benthic invertebrates	Fresh crude oil	100-6,100	
Finfish	Gasoline	91	
	Diesel fuel	240-420	
Finfish	Waste oil	1,700	
Larvae and eggs		1->25	
Pelagic crustacea		15->50	
Finfish	Residual oils	2,000-10,000	

TABLE 8

Acute toxicity of water-soluble fractions of a crude and refined oil to arctic marine species from four Phyla

Organism	Avg. 96 hr TLm (ppm) of WSF[a] of:	
	Crude oil	No. 2 fuel oil
Echinodermata Sea Cucumber (2 spp.)	10.8	2.3
Mollusca 10 species	9.8	2.3
Arthropoda Crabs (4 spp.) Shrimp (5 spp.)	2.3	2.3
Amphipod, Isopod, Mysid, and Barnacle (1 sp. ea.)	8.5	4.1
Chordata Fish (5 spp.)	1.8	1.8

Data taken from Rice et al. [42] and Rich, Short and Karinen [38].

a WSF: Water-soluble fraction.

Chapter 2

MARINE FISH AND INVERTEBRATE DISEASES, HOST DISEASE RESISTANCE, AND PATHOLOGICAL EFFECTS OF PETROLEUM

HAROLD O. HODGINS, BRUCE B. McCAIN, AND JOYCE W. HAWKES
Environmental Conservation Division

Northwest and Alaska Fisheries Center
National Marine Fisheries Service
National Oceanic and Atmospheric Administration
U.S. Department of Commerce
Seattle, Washington 98112

INTRODUCTION

Very little is known about pathological conditions of most anadromous and marine arctic and subarctic animals. Almost nothing is known about the effects of petroleum and related substances, and environmental modifications resulting from petroleum exploration, on the health of these species. In the absence of extensive existing knowledge, our approach to a review will be as follows.

First, we will direct our coverage in this section toward marine fish and invertebrates; however, certain aspects of disease and disease resistance mechanisms in mammals and birds will be included. We will eliminate from the present section a discussion of alterations from normal function that, in our judgment, more appropriately belong in the sections on physiological effects (See Chapters 4 and 5, Volume II), even though such alterations may fall within the scope of a broad definition of pathology. The discussions will begin with a review of the principal known diseases of arctic and subarctic fish and invertebrate species. The approach will be paradigmatic; little purpose would be served by a tedious listing of every reported abnormality. Next will be a review of knowledge concerning disease resistance mechanisms of vertebrates and invertebrates and environmental factors affecting disease and disease resistance; this is relevant because pathological changes reflect interactions--frequently complex--between host, pathogen, and the environment (Fig. 1). Existing information about pathological changes in marine and certain other representative species exposed to petroleum will then be presented. Finally, an attempt will be made to put all of this in the perspective of knowledge now available and still needed for attaining interpretative and predictive capabilities for effects of oil and oil exploration on diseases of potentially impacted marine animals.

Considerable emphasis will be placed on tumors or neoplasms. A number of marine fish species worldwide have tumors. There is no proof that the prevalence of tumors in fish is correlated with the activities of man, although there have been claims that greater numbers of tumors exist in fish from

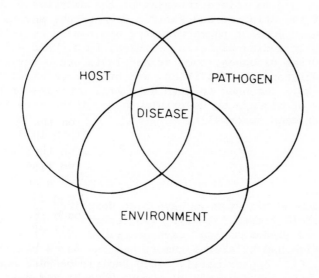

FIG. 1.   Diagrammatic description of the relationships between host defense, pathogens, environmental conditions, and disease.   From Snieszko, S.F. [307] with permission.

polluted waters than in fish from pristine areas [1].   Studies in which we have participated or collaborated [2,3] have revealed substantial numbers of tumors in fish from Puget Sound, Washington, and from the Bering Sea, the latter an area far removed from population centers and industrial pollution. Petroleum and petroleum products contain carcinogens [4-14] and the question is open as to whether increased environmental levels of these hydrocarbons will increase prevalence of tumors in marine animals, or even affect man as a result of consumption of contaminated species.

Consideration will be given to potential immunosuppressive effects of petroleum hydrocarbons and associated metals. According to some current concepts, impairment of cellular immunity would lead to a higher incidence of tumors of viral etiology, but probably would not markedly affect the incidence of tumors induced by chemical carcinogens [15].   A number of carcinogens and cytotoxic materials, including certain hydrocarbons and metals in petroleum, affect mechanisms of resistance to infectious disease in the host or are in other ways immunosuppressive [16-33].   Depression of immune responses, even if the incidence of tumors is not affected, could tip the balance in favor of a pathogen and lead to increased morbidity and mortality of marine species from infectious diseases.

PRINCIPAL DISEASES OF ARCTIC AND SUBARCTIC MARINE SPECIES

Fishes and macroinvertebrates of the arctic and subarctic regions of the Atlantic and Pacific Oceans have several types of diseases. Some of these diseases are caused by infectious organisms, including bacteria, viruses, fungi, and animal parasites. Other diseases, such as neoplasia and a variety of poorly understood abnormalities, are of unknown etiology. This review is intended to give a general overview of both categories of disease by describing some of the more important examples of each abnormality.

NEOPLASIA

Fish

Oral Tumors

Pseudobranchial tumors have been described in four species of Gadoid fishes [34-41]. Two reports on these tumors in Atlantic cod (*Gadus morhua*) each described two fish; in each case one fish had bilateral tumors and one had a unilateral tumor [34,36]. Approximately 8,000 Pacific cod (*G. macrocephalus*) with pseudobranchial tumors have been reported in the northeastern Pacific Ocean [37,38-41]. All of the tumors in these species have so far been reported to be bilateral. Tumor-bearing pollock (*Theragra chalcogrammus*) were found by Takahashi [35] (1 fish with bilateral tumors) and McCain et al. [40] (156 tumor-bearing fish, 7 with unilateral tumors). The cod, *Pollochrius brandti*, also has these tumors [35]; two cases were mentioned, one bilateral and one unilateral.

In general, these tumors are oval, ranging in size from slightly larger than the pseudobranchial gland to 4.5 x 3.5 x 2.0 cm. They are lobulated, smooth, and pale yellow to cream-colored, and portions of the tumors are sometimes necrotic (Fig. 2). The tumors are enclosed in a thick connective tissue capsule. The tumor tissue is soft and easily disrupted, while the reddish-brown pseudobranchial tissue is usually firm and can be located anywhere within the tumor.

Differences of opinion as to the internal structure of pseudobranchial tumors have been reported. Alpers et al. [38] and McCain et al. [3] described the tumors as containing normal-appearing pseudobranchial tissue separated from the tumor tissue by a thickened connective tissue capsule (Fig. 3). They suspected that the tumors were derived from the epidermal cells on the surface of this capsule. Lange [34], on the other hand, reported no definite boundary between the glandular and tumor tissue, and hypothesized that the pseudobranchial tissue was "actively engaged in tumor formation." In addition, the above-mentioned authors and Wellings [37] reported large cells with a pale-staining, granular cytoplasm, and an

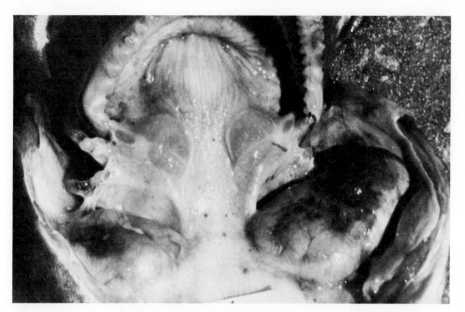

FIG. 2. Bilateral pseudobranchial tumors in the pharynx of a
Pacific cod (Gadus macrocephalus).

unusually large nucleolus. Alpers et al. [38] were unable to
find these cells in the tumor-associated pseudobranchial tissue, but Lange [34] found them in both types of tissue. Electron microscopic examination of these cells by Alpers et al.
[38] demonstrated that they were morphologically identical to
tumor-specific cells in epidermal papillomas of flatfishes,
known as X-cells (see section on epidermal tumors).

Two squamous cell carcinomas of the mandible and maxilla
of an Atlantic salmon (*Salmo salar* L.) were reported by
Roberts [42]. The lesions were invasive, and contained foci
of epithelial cells with frequent mitotic figures.

Oral tumors, probably fibroameloblastomas, on the jaws of
two chinook salmon (*Oncorhynchus tshawytscha*) were described
[43]. The tumors were large enough to prevent mouth closures,
and were composed of connective tissue containing foci of epithelial cells.

Epidermal Tumors

Epidermal papillomas occur in at least 19 species of
flatfish (Order Pleuronectiformes). Tumor-bearing flatfish
have been reported in the western [44], eastern [45-48], and
northern [3] Pacific Ocean, and in the northeastern Atlantic
Ocean [49].

One of the areas of the Pacific Ocean most intensively
studied for these tumors has been Puget Sound, Washington.

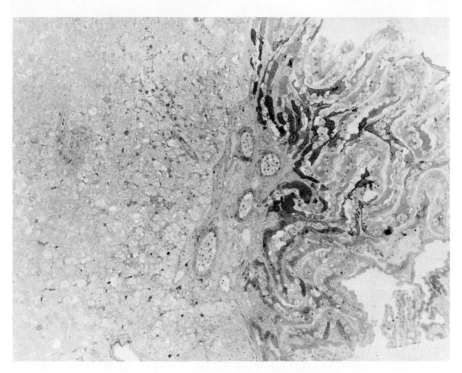

FIG. 3. A section of a pseudobranchial tumor from a Pacific cod. Normal-appearing pseudobranchial tissue is on the right, a portion of the connective tissue capsule is in the middle, and the epidermal tumor is on the left. (Stained with H & E)

Tumor frequencies of 5 to 20% have been reported for certain populations of English sole (*Parophrys vetulus*) [48,50], starry flounder (*Platichthys stellatus*) [47], and flathead sole (*Hippoglossoides elassodon*) [51]. In these species the young-of-the-year fish have the highest tumor frequencies, with the percentage of tumor-bearing fish decreasing rapidly after the first year. Tumor-bearing fish over four years old are rare. Although the disease has a definite seasonal pattern in which each year class first develops tumors during the late summer and fall of their first year, the distribution of diseased fish of a particular species can be quite variable. For example, one area may have a species with a high tumor frequency, while a nearby area may be tumor-free.

The epidermal papillomas have three morphologically and cytologically related forms: the angioepithelial nodule, the angioepithelial polyp, and the epidermal papilloma. The angioepithelial nodule lesion is most commonly found on young flatfish. In our laboratory, the angioepithelial nodule on certain flatfish progressed into epidermal papilloma. The angioepithelial nodules are 1 to 5 mm in diameter, hemispherical, pink to red, smooth-surfaced, and sessile. Microscopically, the angioepithelial nodules consist of a central mass of vascular connective tissue capped with a thin layer of hyperplastic epidermis. Epidermal papillomas account for most of the tumors that occur on flatfish one year of age or over. They are 0.5 to 10 cm in greatest dimension, and vary in thickness from about 0.5 to 2.5 cm. The color of epidermal papillomas varies from pink to brown to black, with the surface being "cauliflower-like" in appearance (Fig. 4). Epidermal papillomas are composed of a fibrovascular stroma supporting a thick papillomatous layer of epidermal cells (Fig. 5). Angioepithelial polyps resemble epidermal papillomas except that the epithelial layer has about the same thickness as normal skin.

Angioepithelial nodules, epidermal papillomas and angioepithelial polyps contain a tumor-specific cell known as an X-cell [52]. When viewed by light microscopy, these cells show a granular cytoplasm, a slightly basophilic nucleus, and a large nucleolus. X-cells stained by the Feulgen technique (a histochemical stain specific for DNA) appear to be devoid of DNA [53]. By electron microscopy, the nuclei show very diffuse chromatin-like material and large nucleoli, and the cyto-

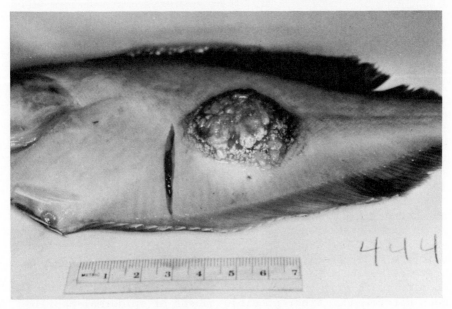

FIG. 4. Epidermal papilloma on the "blind" side of a rock sole (Lepidopsetta bilineata).

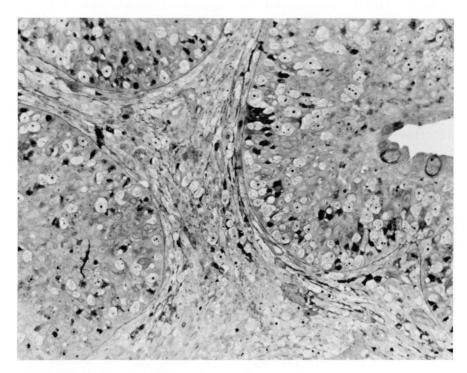

FIG. 5. *Section of an epidermal papilloma from a rock sole.*
Fibrovascular stroma extends up through hyperplastic epithe-
lium; both areas contain X-cells characterized by their large
size, pale nucleus and large, intensely stained nucleolus.
(Stained with H & E)

plasm contains large vesicular bodies and a variety of elec-
tron-dense cytoplasmic granules (Fig. 6). Some of these
granules appear to be virus-like particles of three general
types. However, efforts to detect tumor viruses, or to transmit the disease *in vitro* or *in vivo* have been unsuccessful
[2].

The etiologic agent of flatfish epidermal papillomas is
not known. A tumorigenic virus may be present in tumors, but
is in undetectable amounts or is not transmitted by techniques
used so far. The X-cells may be single-celled parasites which
elicit a hyperplastic response, or they may be transformed
host cells. Because these cells appear to be unable to undergo mitosis *in vivo* and *in vitro*, their identity has not yet
been determined. Other possible causes of epidermal papillomas include natural or manmade carcinogens, and genetic
factors.

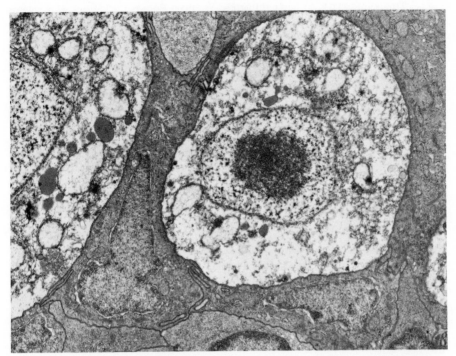

FIG. 6. Electron micrograph of an X-cell from an epidermal
papilloma on a rock sole (X 12,000).

Hyperplastic growths on the Japanese goby (*Acanthogobius
flavimanus*) which resemble flatfish epidermal papillomas have
been reported at several locations in Japan [54,55].   In addition to having gross similarity to the flatfish tumors, the
goby tumors also contained cells identical to X-cells.   These
goby tumor cells contained cytoplasmic virus-like particles
which were doughnut-shaped and about 150 nm across and 240 nm
long.

Two species of eel (*Anguilla anguilla* and *A. vulgaris*) in
the eastern Baltic Sea have epidermal papillomas.   Disease
frequencies in the eels in various regions ranged as high as
28% [56,57].   A seasonal fluctuation in prevalence was reported in eels in the Elbe River where there were peaks of tumor frequency in the early spring and mid-summer [58], and in
Dutch waters where the high-frequency period was in autumn and
the low-frequency period in the springtime [56].

Eel papillomas may occur on any part of the body, but are
usually associated with the head.   The tumors are red to gray,
are attached to the skin by a stalk, do not penetrate the epi-

dermis, and frequently have a diameter of less than 10 mm [56, 58]. The tumor cells appear to be of epidermal origin.

The cause(s) of eel tumors is not known, although a virus has been implicated. Virus-like particles have been observed in tumor cells, and in cells of fish cell lines infected with blood from tumor-bearing eels [57]. Attempts to transmit the disease *in vivo* and *in vitro* with tumor cell extracts have given variable results [56,57]. Peters [58] suggested that pollutants, including chemical carcinogens, were responsible for the eel tumors.

Epidermal Erythrophoroma

Smith [59] described a winter flounder (*Pseudopleuro-nectes americanus*) with an erythrophoroma of the skin. The red-pigmented tumor was composed of spindle-shaped cells which extended into the cutaneous layers and contained vermilion to orange granules. Secondary tumors, also red-colored, were found in the liver, kidney, and spleen.

Melanomas

Two pollock (*T. chalcogramma*) were reported by Takahasi [35] to have melanomas. One tumor was large and was mottled gray and black; and the other was smaller and was uniformly black. The mottled tumor contained a variety of cell types distributed in vascular connective tissue. The black tumor had invaded the musculature and may have metastasized to the peritoneum.

Several nodular melanomas on the surface of a halibut (*Hippoglossus hippoglossus*) were described by Johnstone [60]. Most of the tumor cells were spindle-shaped and had invaded the adjacent muscle tissue.

An Atlantic cod [61] had several invasive melanosarcomas in muscle tissue adjacent to the epidermis.

Fibromas

Several coho salmon (*O. kisutch*) captured off the coast of Oregon had fibromas located below the skin. One such tumor consisted of well-differentiated collagenous tissue covered by normal-appearing skin and scales [37].

Wellings [37] also reported two Pacific halibut (*H. stenolepis*) from Alaskan waters with single fibromas. One tumor was located on the mandible and the other on the body. They appeared to originate in the dermis and consisted of densely packed connective tissue.

Fibromas in the body musculature have also been found in pollock [35] and haddock (*Melanogrammus arglefinus*) [61]. In both cases, the tumors were composed of fibroblast-like cells and were not invasive.

Lipofibromas

Two cases of lipofibromas have been mentioned in the literature. One rockfish (*Sebastodes diploproa*) had an encapsulated subepithelial tumor with yellow tissue consisting of mature fat cells dispersed throughout collagenous tissue [62]. A round, 2 cm diameter, tumor on the surface of a Pacific halibut contained mature fatty tissue and a stroma of collagenous tissue [37].

Lipoma

A lipoma under the epithelium of a plaice (*Pleuronectes platessa*) was reported by Bergman [63]. The tumor was non-invasive and was composed largely of fat cells. Another lipoma, apparently originating in the striated muscles of the trunk of a halibut (*H. hippoglossus*) was described by Williams [64]. The tumor was very large (27.6 x 12.5 cm) and pale yellow and contained mature fat cells. A lipoma in the liver of a pollock (*Pollachius carbonarius*) has also been described. The tumor was green and encapsulated, and was composed of fat cells interspersed with hematopoietic tissue [65].

Osteomas and Osteosarcomas

Wellings [37] characterized two cases of bone tumors of Pacific halibut. Both tumors were located on the "blind side" operculum, and appeared as white masses covered by unbroken skin. One tumor contained cancellous bone surrounded by fibroadipose material, identified as a lipoosteoma; and the other had bony spicules interspersed in a fibrous matrix, classified as a fibro-osteoma.

Eight pollock (*T. chalcogramma*) were reported by Takahashi [35] to have bone growths on spines of the dorsal fins (6 fish) and in opercula (2 fish). Of the spine growths, the author had difficulty deciding if they were exostoses or osteomas. The operculum tumors were osteomas.

Two cod (*G. morhua*) were reported with bone tumors. One had a large (5 x 2 cm) osteoma on the premaxilla which was composed of normal bone tissue [64], and the other had an osteosarcoma which extended from the body surface to the peritoneal cavity with infiltrations into the adjacent muscles. The latter tumor contained a variety of tissue types, including osteoid tissue [66].

Rhabdomyomas

Two types of rhabdomyomas in herring (*Clupea harengus harengus*) have been described. One tumor had recognizable striated muscle fibers only on its periphery [67], and the other was composed largely of striated muscle fibers [61].

Thomas [68] characterized a muscle tumor that was present on the trunk of an Atlantic halibut (*H. hippoglossus*). The tumor was white and mildly invasive, and consisted of an area of undifferentiated cells and an area of normal-appearing striated muscle structure.

Lymphosarcomas

Two salmonid species with lymphosarcomas have been reported. Two aquarium-raised chum salmon (*O. keta*) were described with lymphosarcoma-like growths, one was a tumor composed of small lymphoid cells which appeared to be invasive of the adjoining muscle and connective tissue, and the other consisted of a swelling in the kidney that was made up largely of lymphocytes [69]. The other species was Atlantic salmon, for which one fish was described as having kidney lymphosarcomas which diffusely infiltrated the entire kidney and occluded the hemal arch [70].

An Atlantic cod captured in the western Atlantic had an ocular lymphosarcoma [71]. The tumor showed considerable necrosis and consisted of packed masses of lymphoid-like cells. The normal structure of the eye was destroyed.

Neural Tumors

A neurofibroma on the tip of the barbule of a Pacific cod was described by Wellings [37]. Another cod (*G. morhua*) was reported to have a large ganglioneuroma extending from the body surface which contained loci of ganglion cells [61].

Lucké [72] reported that 76 snapper (*Lutianus griseus, L. jocu, L. apodus*) had tumors involving the nerve sheaths. The tumors often occurred in the subcutaneous nerves of the head and dorsal areas. Tissue types and structures in these tumors often resembled neurilemomas in humans.

A single case of a neurofibroma on the snout of a snake prickleback (*Lumpenus sagitta*) has been reported [73]. The tumor was subcutaneous and cream-colored, and contained whorls of spindle cells interspersed with nerve fibers.

Miscellaneous Tumors of Internal Organs

Gastrointestinal Tract. Takahashi [35] described an adenocarcinoma in the rectal gland of a pollock (*T. chalcogramma*). The tumor was approximately 10 cm in diameter and grayish white, and had metastasized to the liver, stomach, spleen, and several other areas of the body. A stomach tumor of a coho salmon has also been reported [74]. This tumor, considered to be a reticulosarcoma, was encapsulated, and was made up of a mixture of reticulum and collagen fibers.

Kidney. Kidney neoplasia has been reported for only a few marine fishes. Takahashi [75] described a renal tumor in a Pacific mackerel (*Scomber japonicus*) and Harshbarger [76] listed a renal cyst-adenoma in a great sculpin (*Myoxocephalus polyacanthocephalus*). A nephroblastoma was reported in a striped bass (*Morone saxatilis*) [77]. The tumor had replaced a large portion of the kidney, and infiltration of neighboring tissues was suspected, but not confirmed. The bulk of tumor tissue consisted of cartilage.

Invertebrates

Mesenchymal Tumors

Tumors of mesenchymal origin have been described in two species of oysters. Two cases have been reported in the Pacific oyster (*Crassostrea gigas*) [78,79]. In one case, the tumor was located in the rectal area attached by a stalk. Histologically, the benign tumor was encapsulated, and had a stroma containing normal-appearing Leydig cells, vascularization with leukocytic infiltration, and unusually large amounts of collagen-like material. The second tumor was located on the dorsal surface of the oyster, but began in the ventral area of the body and penetrated the mantle. This tumor was also considered benign, although it contained unusual "pseudo-tubules" which consisted of ring-shaped arrangements of colla-gen-like fibers and cells appearing to be leukocytes. Newman [80] described the histological properties of a growth found in *C. virginica*. The growth was vascular with atypical cells distributed throughout. These hypertrophic cells had enlarged nuclei with one or more large nucleoli, and appeared to have a high frequency of mitotic figures.

Leukemia-like Neoplasms

Three species of oyster and one species of mussel are known to have neoplastic disorders involving hemocytes. Farley [81] described five cases in *C. virginica* and one in *C. gigas*. All six cases had in common the infiltration of tis-sues, especially connective tissue, with hyaline hemocytes. The invasive hemocytes were more than twice the size of normal hemocytes, often had large amounts of RNA in the cytoplasm, and had a high frequency of mitotic figures. The tissues of affected oysters were usually "watery" and the digestive gland was pale. A similar infiltrated lesion in *C. virginica* [82] contained atypical cells of apparent blastoid origin. These enlarged cells were also observed by Farley and Sparks [83] in *Ostrea lurida* and *C. virginica*. Generally such cells were pleomorphic, often spindle-shaped, and mitotically very ac-tive. In the more advanced stages of this particular disease, tissue degeneration occurred and led to emaciation and atrophy of various organs.

In 10 out of 100 blue mussels (*Mytilus edulis*) from the coast of Oregon examined histologically by Farley [84], neo-plastic lesions comprised of large undifferentiated cells sim-ilar to those described above were found. The lesions were in the form of foci or diffuse areas and were located in a variety of tissues, including connective tissue and hemolymph spaces. Animals with large or numerous lesions generally were in poor health or moribund.

Neoplasia in Miscellaneous Tissues

A tumor-like growth consisting of hard mass of fibrous connective tissue enclosed by a fibrous capsule was reported in a Pacific oyster [85]. The tumor contained sinusoids with leucocytes and gonadal-like cells. The presence of spindle-shaped cells with staining properties similar to muscle cells supported a muscle-origin hypothesis.

Tumor-like growths have been found on the siphon of one of 500 soft-shell clams (*Mya arenaria*) captured on the East coast of the United States [86] and a horse clam (*Tresus nuttallii*) [87]. The soft-shell clam tumor was a wrinkled enlargement of the siphon and consisted of hyperplastic smooth muscle tissue covered by an epithelial layer which was confluent with the rest of the siphon. The other tumor was also composed of smooth muscle, but was papillomatous in appearance.

Two butter clams (*Saxidomus giganteus*) from the Washington coast had wart-like tumors on the surface of the foot [88, 89]. Both growths were composed of essentially normal-appearing cells usually associated with foot tissues and contained no mitotic figures.

Approximately 10% of the clams (*Macoma balthica*) examined by Christensen et al. [90] in Maryland had a neoplastic disease primarily of the gills, characterized by atypical cells in the gill epithelia which infiltrated neighboring tissues and, in some cases, to more distant tissues, such as the foot and kidney. Clams with extensive infiltration were usually emaciated. The atypical cells were quite similar in appearance to those described in the previous section on leukemia-like neoplasms [80]. The disease appeared to be seasonal, with frequencies highest in the fall and lowest in the spring.

A hyperplastic, possibly precancerous, condition in the soft-shell clam (*M. arenaria*) was described by Barry et al. [91]. The affected organs were the gill filaments and kidney; the gill lesions were grossly visible as raised grayish-white growths, and the kidney lesions were detectable only by microscopic examination. Affected gill filaments were structurally altered, and the gill epithelium contained unusual basophilic cells with enlarged vesicular nuclei having large, intensely-staining nucleoli. A high frequency of mitotic figures was observed in affected epithelia. Similar basophilic cells were found in hyperplastic kidneys. In addition, the kidneys were often necrotic and had sufficient hyperplasia to make these organs appear nonfunctional. In the main area of study, Rhode Island, 211 of 588 clams had a form of this condition, with some samplings having a frequency as high as around 70%. No definite association with pollution was demonstrated. This same condition was found by these authors in *M. arenaria* over a wide geographical area, including the East and West coasts of the United States.

A more recent investigation of *M. arenaria* involved animals exposed to an oil spill in Maine [92]. About 25% of the surviving clams had gonadal tumors, which contained large multinucleated and pleomorphic mononuclear cells. The nuclei were often very basophilic and contained prominent nucleoli. Occasionally, the normal gonadal tissue was replaced by these neoplastic cells, and other tissues were infiltrated. Samplings from stations nearest the oil spill area had the highest frequencies of tumors.

Gonadal tumors were also found in the ovaries of the quahaug (*Mercenaria mercenaria*) [93]. A total of 15 cases were observed in 1,839 quahaugs examined histologically. The affected ovaries had a hyperplastic germinal epithelium and large atypical cells with vesicular nuclei often replacing the normal ovarian follicles. One of the tumors apparently metastasized to the red gland and the heart.

Blue crabs (*C. sapidus*) on the Atlantic coast of North America were reported by Newman [94] to have neoplastic blood disease. Unusual cells, larger and more basophilic than normal cells, accumulated in the circulatory vessels and sinuses.

Sparks and Lightner [95] described a papilloma-like growth on the carapace of a brown shrimp (*Penaeus aztecus*). No unusual cells or mitotic figures were found.

BACTERIAL DISEASES

Fish
Vibriosis

Eels (*A. vulgaris* and *A. anguilla*) have been known since the early 1700's [96] to develop a particular bacterial disease. Typical signs of the disease include red spots on the body surface which in severe cases spread over the entire exterior (Fig. 7). The bacterium most often isolated from these lesions is *Vibrio anguillarum* [97].

Vibrio organisms are gram-negative, non-spore-forming, rod-shaped bacteria which are cytochrome oxidase positive and are usually sensitive to vibriostat 0/129 (a compound which specifically inhibits the growth of *Vibrio* sp.). High frequencies of infections with *V. anguillarum* are often associated with increased water temperatures [98].

Several species of flatfish have been reported with hemorrhagic surface lesions from which *V. anguillarum* was isolated. Winter flounder with a vibriosis-like disease near Rhode Island yielded bacterial isolates; these bacteria, when

FIG. 7. Coho salmon (Oncorhynchus kisutch) with a ring-shaped
lesion caused by the bacterium Vibrio anguillarum.

injected into normal winter flounder, caused typical lesions
of vibriosis from which similar bacteria were re-isolated
[99].   In addition, vibriosis was described by Anderson and
Conroy [98] in lemon sole (P. macrocephalus), plaice, and tur-
bot (Rhombus maximum) caught off the British Isles.   Diseased
fish of all three species were anemic, as demonstrated by
their hemoglobin levels and erythrocyte concentrations.
        V. anguillarum has been described as a disease agent in a
variety of other marine fish species.   Atlantic cod with vibriosis have been found several times in the eastern and western Atlantic Ocean [98,100,101].   Numerous coalfish (Gadus
virens) with vibriosis have been found in Norwegian waters
[101].
        Most reports of vibriosis in salmonids have been con-
cerned with maricultured fish.   On the northwest coast of
North America, six species were affected, chum, sockeye (O.
nerka), pink (O. gorbuscha), coho, chinook salmon, and rainbow
trout (S. gairdneri) [102-105].   Atlantic salmon and rainbow
trout in northern European areas also develop vibriosis [101,
106].

Pseudomonas Infections
        Some confusion exists in the literature concerning the
taxonomic status of *Pseudomonas* organisms isolated from diseased marine fish.   ZoBell and Wells [107] described a bacterial dermatitis in gobies (Gillichthys mirabilis) and blen-
nies (Hypsoblennis gilberti) off California.   The bacteria
were confined to surface lesions which ranged in severity from
a whitish spot to ulcers.   The causative bacterium was identified as *Pseudomonas ichthyodermis* and was described as gram-
negative, asporogenous, motile, and halophilic.   In 1954, P.

ichthyodermis was isolated from a surface lesion on a plaice captured near Scotland [108]. However, in 1963, Shewan [109] recommended that this bacterial species be placed in the genus *Vibrio*.

Pseudomonads have often been isolated from diseased marine fishes [110], but they have been seldom reported as the primary causative agent [111]. A species often isolated is *P. fluorescens* [112].

Aeromonas Infections

The best known *Aeromonas* species causing fish disease in marine waters is *A. salmonicida* which causes the disease furunculosis. This bacterium has been a major problem in the mariculture of salmonid fishes [113,114]. Scott [115] demonstrated that the disease could be transmitted between salmonids through the water column. The organism has been isolated from diseased wild chinook salmon [116] and sablefish (*Anoplopoma fimbria*) [102] in the northeastern Pacific Ocean.

The bacterium is gram-negative, oxidase positive, fermentative, nonmotile, non-spore-forming and rod-shaped, and produces a brown, water-soluble pigment. Several forms of furunculosis have been described. Most commonly, infected fish develop "boil-like" lesions or hemorrhagic areas on the body surfaces. Internally, the kidney, spleen, and liver may be necrotic or hemorrhagic [112,115].

Mycobacteriosis

Most reports of marine fish mycobacteriosis have used the observation of acid-fast, gram-positive, rods in characteristic lesions as presumptive proof for diagnosis. Mycobacteriosis was identified in Atlantic cod [117], halibut (*H. hippoglossus*) [118], and several Pacific salmon and trout (*O. tschawytscha, O. kisutch, O. nerka* and *S. gairdneri*) [119]. Ross [120] was able with some difficulty to culture a mycobacterium isolated from a salmonid which he called *M. salmoniphilum*. However, he did not demonstrate that his isolate was the etiological agent.

Acute and chronic types of mycobacteriosis have been described. The acute form has few external signs; the chronic form is characterized by grayish lesions on the body surface and in the liver, spleen, kidney, and other internal organs [121]. Histopathologically, the lesions contain tubercles composed of epithelioid cells and histiocytes encompassed by a layer of fibroblasts [112].

Pasteurellosis

Four species of marine fish found off the Atlantic coast of the United States have experienced epizootics as a result of infection with *Pasteurella piscicida*. The first described case involved mostly white perch (*M. americana*) and some striped bass [122]. The signs of this condition were not given. In another incident, Atlantic menhaden (*Brevoortia tyrannus*) and striped mullet (*Mugil cephalus*) were affected [123]. Diseased fish had mucus-like material on the surface of the gills and purulent material in the peritoneal cavity. Bacteria isolated from these fish were able to kill other fish when added to their seawater aquaria. Although the gross signs of the experimentally infected fish were not the same as the naturally infected fish, the same bacterium was isolated.

The bacteria isolated from these two epizootics were classified as *Pasteurella* on the basis of their staining properties, bipolar gram-negativity, and physiological properties.

Corynebacteriosis

Kidney disease, a systemic disease caused by members of the genus *Corynebacterium* has been found almost exclusively in hatchery-reared salmonids [111]. The disease has been diagnosed in adult chinook salmon which had spent about two months in fresh water at an Oregon hatchery after returning from the Pacific Ocean [124], and in Atlantic salmon captured in Scotland [125]. Bell [126] described the disease in salt-water-reared pink salmon in western Canada.

The kidney disease-associated bacterium is gram-positive, aerobic, non-acid-fast and non-spore-forming, and grows slowly on even the most enriched medium [112]. Presumptive evidence of the disease is often based on the presence of small, gram-positive diplobacilli in the affected tissue. As the name indicates, the kidney is often the tissue most frequently affected by the disease. The kidney lesions are usually gray to white and necrotic. Other tissues are also involved including the body muscles, liver, and spleen [112,126].

Myxobacteriosis

The fish disease most often associated with myxobacteria is columnaris disease, caused by *Flexibacter columnaris*. This condition is essentially a disease of fish in fresh water [127]. Another myxobacterial disease is called bacterial gill disease and has been reported in maricultured sockeye salmon [114]. Bacterial gill disease results in hyperplasia and hypertrophy of the epithelial cells lining the gill lamellae [112].

Myxobacteria are gram-negative, are motile by means of cell flexing rather than flagella, and, under some conditions, can form fruiting bodies or microcysts.

Invertebrates
Diseases Caused by Gram-Negative Bacteria

Several crustacean diseases have been reported to be associated with chitin-destroying bacteria. King crabs (*Paralithodes* sp.) in Alaska have a condition known as "rust disease," which causes a darkening and softening of the exoskeleton [128]. The cause is thought to be either bacterial [129], or fungal [130], or a synergistic effect of both [131]. "Rust disease" is communicable, but does not appear to cause death. Of the larger king crabs captured in Kachemak Bay, Cook Inlet, in 1957, 11% had a "rust disease" [129].

Rosen [132] described a necrotic condition of the exoskeleton of the American blue crab (*Callinectes sapidus*). The condition began as small brown foci with a reddish depressed center, which, in the more advanced stages, coalesced to form extensive necrotic areas. In enrichment medium, isolates from the lesions yielded almost pure cultures of small gram-negative rods; the bacteria were not taxonomically identified. An effort was made by Cook and Lofton [133] to characterize the chitin-digesting, gram-negative bacteria isolated from normal-appearing and diseased Penaeid shrimp and blue crab. Representatives of the genus *Beneckea* were isolated from all of the shrimp that they examined. Attempts to transmit the condition with *Beneckea* isolates were inconclusive.

Another case, where similar bacterial isolates were obtained from a high frequency of diseased blue crab, was reported by Krantz et al. [134]. They isolated *Vibrio parahaemolyticus* from blue crab in Chesapeake Bay that were lethargic and had high bacterial concentrations in their hemolymph. No attempts to transmit the disease were described.

Lightner and Lewis [135] isolated *V. anguillarum, V. alginolyticus,* and an *Aeromonas* species from three species of Penaeid shrimp. Shrimp injected with these isolates changed to a white-opaque color and eventually died.

Bacteria classified as either *Aeromonas* or *Vibrio* species were implicated as etiological agents of a disease known as bacillary necrosis of hard clam (*M. mercenaria*) larvae [136]. This condition, which could be experimentally produced with pure bacterial cultures, caused massive mortalities of clam larvae. The moribund and dead larvae had extensive granular necrosis. The authors suggested that the bacterial isolates were part of the normal flora and that the disease was environmentally induced. Similar observations with hard clam larvae were reported by Guillard [137].

Diseases Caused by Gram-Positive Bacteria

A disease of American (*Homarus americanus*) and European (*H. vulgaris*) lobsters, characterized by a decrease in circulating hemocytes, prolonged clotting time, hemorrhaging, and a general weakened condition, has been extensively described in the literature. The etiological agent is *Aerococcus viridans homari*, a gram-positive coccus [138]. This disease is thought to be transmitted through surface wounds, and the lobsters appear to have no defense mechanisms against the bacterium [138]. Bell and Hoskins [139] were able to transmit the disease to Dungeness crabs (*Cancer magister*) and spot shrimp (*Pandalus platyceros*) by injecting the bacteria intramuscularly.

VIRAL DISEASES

Fish
Lymphocystis Disease
Lymphocystis disease is caused by a virus and has been often reported to be present in marine species in the northeastern and northwestern Atlantic Ocean. Reports of three investigations in the Irish Sea and nearby waters contained information on this condition in plaice, sanddab (*Limanda limanda*) and flounder (*Platichthys flesus*) [140-142]. Frequencies of fish with lymphocystis growths captured during the three studies were as high as 25% at some sampling stations and averaged between 2 and 15%.

Baltic herring (*C. harengus membras*) [143] and perch (*Acerina cernua*) [144] with lymphocystis disease have been found in the Baltic Sea. The relative frequency of lymphocystis was about 0.5% for the Baltic herring.

Off the eastern coast of North America, two species of flounder, the American plaice (*Hippoglossoides platessoides*), and the southern flounder (*Paralitchthys dentatus*), also have been found with this disease. The American plaice captured in 1964 on the Grand Bank had an overall average lymphocytis frequency of about 1%; affected fish had been seen since 1960 [145]. Murchelano and Bridges [146] reported lymphocystis disease in 44 out of 64 (68.7%) American plaice caught in Casco Bay, Maine, in 1975.

Off the northwestern coast of North America, yellowfin sole (*Limanda aspera*) and lingcod (*Phiodon elongatus*) showed lymphocystis disease. Of the 13,239 yellowfin sole examined by McCain et al. [3] in 1975 in the Bering Sea, 272 had the typical growths, an overall frequency of 2.1%. Two cases of lingcod with lymphocystis were described by Hoskins et al. [114] in British Columbia, Canada.

Lymphocystis disease is not known to be fatal. The virus causes extensive cellular hypertrophy of fibroblastic cells, increasing their size up to 1 to 1.5 mm in diameter. These cells occur singly [143] or in growths containing hundreds of cells [3] (Fig. 8). Depending upon the amount of blood supply associated with these growths, they can be gray to red to

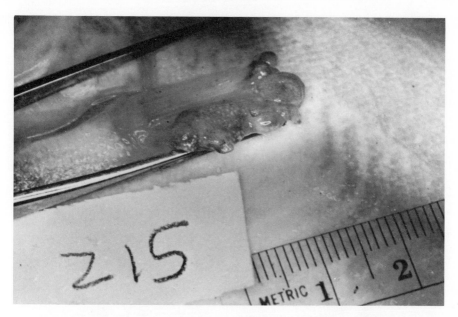

FIG. 8. *Lymphocystis growth on the "blind" side pectoral fin of a yellowfin sole* (Limanda aspera).

clear. Lymphocystis growths can occur on all body surfaces, fins, and less commonly in internal organs. Fins containing growths may become extensively eroded (Fig. 9) [3].

The most common sites for surface growths on fish vary with geographical location and between affected species. *P. flesus* and *P. platessa* in the Irish Sea had growths most often on the caudal, dorsal, and anal fins; while the "blind" and "eyed" surfaces were affected equally [141]. Templeman [145] found that in American plaice the fins and edge of the body between the anus and anal fin were the most common locations. McCain et al. [3] observed lymphocystis growths most often on the "blind" side of yellowfin sole, with the pectoral fin most often affected. This variation in lesion location between species and geographical locations probably reflects differences in the mode of virus transmission.

Lymphocystis cells have a capsule of hyaline mucopolysaccharide, an enlarged nucleus with one or more intensely staining nucleoli, and a granular cytoplasm containing inclusions [142,147] (Fig. 10). These inclusions contain hexagonal virus particles ranging in diameter from 200 to 300 nm (Fig. 11). Lymphocystis virus is a DNA virus and a member of the icosahedral cytoplasmic DNA virus group [3].

The mode of transmission of the virus is poorly understood. A commonly expressed theory is that injury sites serve as points of entry [3,141]. A freshwater form of lymphocystis

FIG. 9. *Lymphocystis growth accompanied by fin erosion on the "blind" side pectoral fin of a yellowfin sole.*

virus has been transmitted *in vivo* by injecting fish subdermally with filtered tissue extracts [148]. Various sources of infecting virus have been proposed: (a) lymphocystis virus is naturally present in the marine environment, and (b) fish are exposed to virus as the results of contact with fishing nets and suspended sediments from estuarine waters [141,145].

Piscine Erythrocytic Necrosis
     A recently described viral infection of marine fishes is characterized by the presence of cytoplasmic inclusion bodies in erythrocytes. Species affected include Atlantic cod, sea snail (*Liparis atlanticus*), shorthorn sculpin (*Myxocephalus scorpius*), and Atlantic herring (*C. harengus*) off the eastern coast of North America [149,150]; the blenny (*Blennius pholis*) from the northeastern Atlantic [151]; and Pacific herring, chum salmon, and pink salmon in the coastal waters of British Columbia [152,153].
     Affected fish are lethargic presumably due to anemia [153]. Erythrocytes with inclusion bodies contain nuclei in various stages of degeneration. The inclusions, when examined electron microscopically, contain virus-like particles with a size and morphology very similar to lymphocystis virus [151,

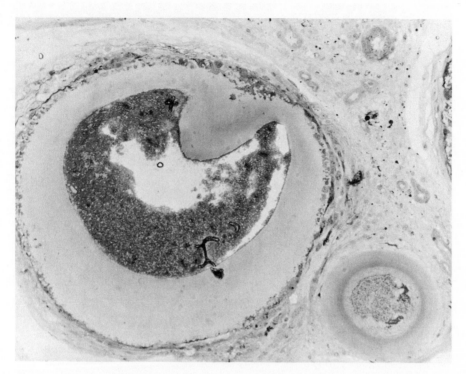

FIG. 10.   Two lymphocystis cells, approximately 0.3 and 0.1 mm
in diameter, from a yellowfin sole, respectively.   The larger
cell has a centrally located inclusion body from which the
electron micrograph in Figure 12 was taken.

154].   Successful *in vivo* transmission of the disease has
been accomplished using filtered tissue homogenates [153].

Infectious Hematopoietic Necrosis

        Infectious hematopoietic necrosis virus has caused epi-
zootics in trout and Pacific salmon cultured in fresh and seawater [111,152,155].   The effect of this virus upon wild populations of salmonids is not known.   Bell and Margolis [152]
reported the isolation of the virus from wild sockeye salmon.
        Infectious hematopoietic necrosis virus is a member of
the bullet-shaped group of viruses known as rhabdoviruses.
The gross signs of infected fish includes pale gills, darkened
coloration, exophthalmos, fecal casts, patches of hemorrhagic
tissue in the muscles at the bases of fins, and extensive necrosis of the hematopoietic tissue (kidney and spleen) [147].

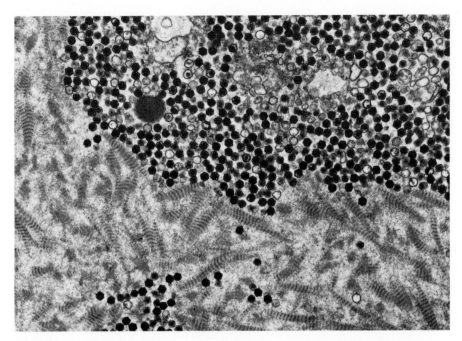

FIG. 11.   *Electron micrograph of an inclusion body of a lymphocystis cell containing hexagonally-shaped, 200 nm virus particles (X 16,000).*

Invertebrates
    Reports of viruses in shrimp, crabs, and octopus in the
Gulf of Mexico and the Mediterranean have appeared in the literature, but, since this review is concerned with arctic and
subarctic species, these examples will not be mentioned further.

Herpes-Type Viral Infections
    Oysters (*C. virginica*) from the northeastern coast of the
United States showed high mortalities when experimentally exposed to water temperatures between 28° and 30°C.   Generally
this temperature range has no adverse effects.   Cells in dead
oysters contained intranuclear inclusions.   Electron microscopic examination of these inclusions demonstrated the presence of herpes-type virus-like particles [156].   The relationship between the virus-like particles and the temperature-
related oyster mortalities has not yet been established.

Diseases Causes by Unclassified Viruses
    Bang [157] reported the isolation of a virus from the
shore crab (*Carcinus maenas*) from the coast of France.   The

diseased animals had lost their blood-clotting ability and had abnormal amoebocytes. He was able to transmit the disease to European and American shore crabs.

MYCOSES

Fish
Infections by Ichthyophonus species

   Ichthyophonus hoferi (sometimes referred to as *Ichthyosporidium hoferi*) is recognized as an extremely important marine fish pathogen in the Atlantic Ocean. Off the northeastern coast of North America, several documented epizootics have occurred since the early 1900's involving Atlantic herring [158]. During these epizootics, about 25% of the herring were infected, usually with an acute form of the disease involving extensive hyphal invasion of the musculature, heart, and gastrointestinal tract. Externally, the affected fish have numerous raised papules which may become necrotic and ulcerated. Sindermann [158] estimated that between epizootics the enzootic disease frequency was less than 1%.

   Ichthyophonus spp. have been isolated from several marine species in the coastal regions of Europe, including mackerel (*Scomber scomber*) [159] and over 30 other teleost fish [160].

Infections by Saprolegnia species

   Saprolegnia spp. are generally regarded as secondary invaders and are usually confined to estuarine or fresh water [161]. Spawning salmonids are especially susceptible to these fungi [160]. Stuart and Fuller [162] isolated *Saprolegnia* sp. from lesions of the disease ulcerative dermal necrosis on Atlantic salmon captured in a British estuary. Fish infected with these fungi develop white, cotton-like patches on their surface; the hyphae from these patches can eventually penetrate the epidermis and invade the musculature.

Infections by Dermocystidium species

   Another group of fungi which infect salmonid fishes in fresh and brackish water is *Dermocystidium* sp. Allen et al. [163] described adult dead and moribund chinook salmon in Washington State with massive hyphal cysts in their gills and spleens from which *Dermocystidium* sp. was isolated. This fungus has also been associated with mortalities of wild, spawning sockeye salmon in British Columbia [152].

Invertebrates
Infections by Lagenidium species

   Lagenidium spp. have been isolated from the eggs and larvae of several species of marine crustacea. Wild populations of blue crab on the eastern coast of North America have been reported to have *L. callinectes* associated with their egg masses [164]. Scott [165] reported on a survey in which 40% of the blue crabs were found to have eggs infected with this fungus. Usually only the outer layers of eggs in the mass are affected. Infection ultimately involves invasion of entire ova by fungal hyphae [166].

The larvae of maricultured shrimp (*Penaeus setiferus*) [167], lobsters (*Homarus americanus*) and crab (*Cancer magister*) are also infected by *Lagenidium* spp. [168]. Infected larvae usually died after being immobilized as the result of extensive internal hyphal growth.

Infections by Dermocystidium species

Adult oysters (*C. virginica*) along the Atlantic coast of the United States have been reported to develop a systemic fungal infection as the result of invasion by *Dermocystidium marinum* [169]. The infection may retard growth, inhibit normal gonad development, or cause death [97].

Infections by Saprolegnia species

A fungus, identified as *Leptolegnia marina*, was isolated from several different cases of fungus-infected pea crabs (*Pinnotheres pisium*) in the waters of the British Isles [170]. The gills and eggs were most often affected, and infected animals usually died.

Miscellaneous Fungal Infections

Maricultured clams (*Venus mercenaria*) and oyster (*C. virginica*) in the western Atlantic have been reported to have fungus-infected larvae [171]. The fungi, which were classified as *Sirolpidium zoophthorum*, invaded the interior of the larvae and caused epidemic-proportion mortalities.

Tanner crabs (*Chioncecetes* sp.) captured in the Gulf of Alaska had an exoskeletal disease involving a "...mat of black, encrusting nodules or pustules forming a dense, hard, almost tar-like covering..." [172]. Although a fungus has been isolated and cultivated from the diseased crabs, the cause of the disease has not been definitely established. Large numbers of tanner crab (approximately 2 to 3% of the catch) captured in the Bering Sea in 1975 and 1976 had this condition [40] (Fig. 12). Crab with this disease did not appear to be adversely affected.

HELMINTHIASIS AND OTHER PARASITIC INFESTATIONS

Because the relationship between host, parasite, and pathogenicity is poorly understood for most of the parasites associated with arctic and subarctic fishes and invertebrates,

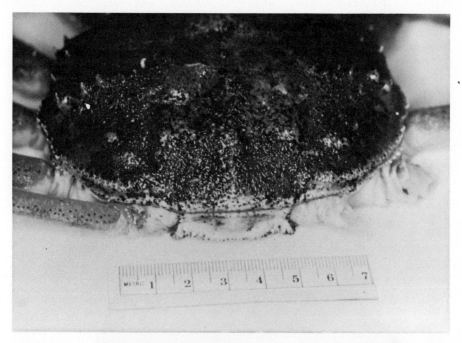

FIG. 12.   Tanner crab (Chioncecetes *sp.) with "black mat"
disease.*

only a brief description of some of the better known examples
will be discussed.

Fish

The helminths, including trematodes, cestodes, and nematodes, produce disease signs in marine fish in greatly varying
degrees.   Trematode species have metacercariae which form
cysts under the skin, but are thought not to cause serious
disease [173].   Cestodes have been reported in several fishes
in Canadian Pacific waters [174].   The larval cestodes may be
found in the musculature, but few gross pathological problems
have been observed.   Larval nematodes are present in the muscles of a large number of marine species [175,176].   In some
cases, pathological damage results from the movement of these
larvae to other parts of the fish; for example, the liver may
become heavily infested and dysfunctional.

Protozoan parasites infest a great many bottom-dwelling
fish along the Pacific coast of North America [177].   The
presence of these organisms does not always result in pathological damage to the host.   Myxosporidia, however, are known
to cause a condition in fish muscles referred to as "milki-

ness." Several marine fish species are affected including
halibut (*H. stenolepis*), starry flounder, and hake (*Merluccius
productus*) [178,179]. In most cases the disease is not obvious in freshly captured fish, but the condition can be readily
detected after the affected fish have been refrigerated for 4-
24 hr. During this period, proteolytic enzymes present in the
spores, when released into muscle tissue, are thought to cause
foci of softened and liquefied muscle in which cysts containing spores can be macroscopically observed.

Another group of protozoans, the microsporidia, form
easily detected cysts or "tumors" in the somatic muscles of
many groundfishes. Members of the families Gasterosteidae,
Zoarcidae, and Gadidae have been reported with this disease
[180-182].

Many copepod species attach to the gills and body surfaces of a wide variety of marine fishes in the northeastern
Pacific Ocean [183] (Fig. 13). Some of these parasites are
able to invade internal organs, such as the heart [184], and
some cause skin ulcerations.

*FIG. 13. Caudal fin of a Pacific cod with two copepod
parasites.*

Invertebrates

Parasitic protozoans, including gregarines, microspori-
dans, and ciliates, invade gills, blood, muscles, and the intestinal caeca of several crustacean species [128]. Several
early life stages of helminths are commonly isolated from
crabs and shrimps [113]. Larval trematodes and cestodes are

the most common and cause negligible to severe damage.
Leeches have also been reported on the abdomens of Dungeness
crab (*C. magister*) in British Columbia [185].

Crustacean parasites, such as isopods, copepods, and
rhizocephalans, have been reported in a large variety of crabs
and shrimp. Alaskan king crab are occasionally parasitized by
rhizocephalans [128]. Many shrimp of the family Hippolytidae
in the Chukchi Sea, Alaska, were parasitized by an isopod
(probably *Phryxus abdominalis*) [186].

Molluscs harbor a variety of parasites; the most pathogenic are the haplosporidans and crustacea. Haplosporidans
(*Minchinia* sp.) have been associated with extensive oyster (*C.
virginica*) mortalities on the East Coast of North America
[187]. Sparks [188] reported pathological effects in the epithelium and other tissues of Pacific oysters (*C. gigas*) as the
result of invasion by the copepod *Mytilicola orientalis*.
Another species of copepod (*M. intestinalis*) reportedly caused
emaciation, discoloration, and death in European mussels (*M.
edulis*) [189].

MISCELLANEOUS ABNORMALITIES OF UNKNOWN ETIOLOGY

In this section, emphasis will be placed on those pathological conditions of unknown etiology affecting large numbers
of individuals.

Fish
Mass Mortalities
Two cases of large-scale deaths among Pacific herring
were reported in British Columbia, Canada. In one, occurring
in 1942, heavy mortalities were observed for about one month,
followed by a one to two month period of lethargy and abnormal
behavior by populations of herring [190]. Moribund fish were
lethargic, but generally normal appearing. A high percentage
of the livers showed grossly abnormal texture and color.
Also, the red blood cells were abnormal. No bacteria could be
cultured. The authors suggested that an infectious agent was
responsible, and Sindermann [97] hypothesized that the agent
was an *Ichthyophonus* sp. Another possibility could be a viral
cause, since the disease signs were similar to those observed
by Evelyn [153] in Pacific herring infected with piscine
erythrocytic necrosis virus. An outstanding feature of
piscine erythrocytic necrosis virus-infected fish are inclusions in erythrocytes; and Tester [190] found that moribund
herring had "abnormal" erythrocytes. A similar epizootic
among Pacific herring was reported by Stevenson [191] in 1949
in the same general area.

Menhaden (*B. tyrannus*) in the coastal waters of the
northeastern United States have been reported to have periodic

epizootics [192]. Moribund fish swim erratically and have
exophthalmos. Suggested causes of this disease include:
changes in salinity, reduced oxygen content, pollution, and
viruses [97].

Pacific sardines (*Sardinops sagax*), also in British
Columbian waters, were described with high mortalities in 1941
[193]. Individuals from affected populations were lethargic
and had respiratory difficulties; hemorrhagic areas were present on the body surface. Little natural food was found in the
areas where mortalities were occurring, and dead fish had empty stomachs. The health of the sardines seemed to improve
when food became available, and the authors suggested that
lack of food caused the condition. Sindermann [97] found
similar disease signs among fungus-infected Atlantic herring
and suggested that the Pacific sardine epizootic could have
been caused by a fungus.

Fin Erosion

Two estuarine areas of the subarctic, the New York Bight
and the Duwamish River, Seattle, Washington, are known to have
pleuronectid fishes with fin erosion. Starry flounder and
English sole in the Duwamish River show fin erosion [194].
Affected fish have signs ranging from hemorrhagic granulation
tissue on or at the base of the fins to complete loss of fins
(Figs. 14,15). Eroded fins examined histologically were char-

FIG. 14. A starry flounder (Platichthys stellatus) with an
early form of fin erosion associated with anal fin on the
blind side (arrow).

FIG. 15. A starry flounder with severe erosion of the dorsal
fin. Flaps of skin extend over the body in the anterior
region of the dorsal fin.

acterized by extensive bone resorption, fibrosis, epidermal
hyperplasia, hyperplasia of mucous cells, and, in some cases,
necrosis of the epithelium (Fig. 16). No bacteria, parasites,
or fungi were found in eroded fin tissue. The average frequency of fin erosion among starry flounder and English sole
collected in the Duwamish River in 1975 was 8 and 0.5%,
respectively.

     The gross and histopathological characteristics of fin
erosion in winter flounder in the New York Bight have several
features in common with the characteristics of the disease in
fish from the Duwamish River [195]. In 1974, Ziskowski and
Murchelano [196] reported the overall frequency of fin erosion
in winter flounder to be 14.1%. In addition, they found four
other species of flatfish with fin erosion; *L. ferruginia, P.
dentatus, P. oblongus,* and *Scophthalmus aquosus.*

     The cause of fin erosion in marine flatfish is not known.
Mahoney et al. [110] found numerous gram-negative bacteria
associated with affected fins, and classified most of them in
the bacterial genera *Aeromonas, Pseudomonas,* and *Vibrio.* The
fin rot condition was induced in normal fish by abrading fins
and inoculating the areas with selected isolates of either of
the three genera. The disease could not be produced by inoculating unabraded fins with bacteria. These authors concluded
that fin rot was caused by a combination of environmental

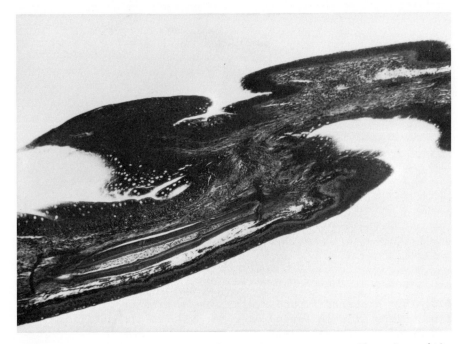

FIG. 16. A section of fin tissue from a starry flounder with fin erosion. Normal-appearing bone spicules (lower left) are being resorbed and replaced by fibrosis and granulosis. Fin tissue which has lost fin ray (upper right) has collapsed and folded back onto itself.

stress resulting from sewage pollution and secondary invasion by heavy populations of gram-negative bacteria. In a review of fin rot among marine and freshwater fish, Bullock et al. [197] concluded that there are three possible causes of fin rot:

> 1. bacteria, usually of the Aeromonas-Pseudomonas group, are the direct cause;
> 2. these bacteria and also aquatic myxo-bacteria are secondary invaders which attack fins damaged by injury...; 3. the condition accompanies other bacterial disease...

In the Duwamish River, starry flounder [198] and English sole [194] have elevated levels of polychlorinated biphenyls. Couch [199] was able to induce fin erosion and liver lesions in spot (Leiostomus xanthurus) by exposure to polychlorinated biphenyl (Aroclor 1254). Fin-eroded starry flounder also have

liver abnormalities [200] very similar to those described by
Couch [199]. Attempts to isolate disease-specific microorganisms from Duwamish River fish with fin erosion were unsuccessful.

Ulcerative Dermal Necrosis

A condition of Atlantic salmon known as ulcerative dermal
necrosis has been found in fish from several rivers in the
British Isles [201]. Although most cases of this disease occur in fresh water, a brief description will be presented here
because the condition may originate in marine waters [162].
Ulcerative dermal necrosis affects adult salmon almost exclusively. Ulcers are usually found on the head where they begin
as grayish areas and develop into extensive areas with hemorrhagic borders. The ulcers are often secondarily infected
with the fungus *Saprolegnia parastica*. Ulcerated fish usually die. No disease-specific bacteria or viruses have been
isolated. The cause of this disease is not known; however,
the cause is probably multifactorial, with the migration of
Atlantic salmon from salt to fresh water being one of the factors [201].

Ulcerative Skin Condition of Cod

During a sampling expedition in the Bering Sea in 1976,
McCain et al. [40] observed skin ulcers on 3.7% of the Pacific
cod they examined. Two main types of ulcers were found; a
round hemorrhagic, open type (Fig. 17) and a raised, round,
ring-like, yellowish mucoid lesion with the center sometimes
appearing to be normal skin and other times being hemorrhagic
(Fig. 18). Both types of ulcers often occurred on the same
fish. Gram-negative bacteria with identical morphological and
biochemical properties identified as pseudomonad-like, were
routinely isolated from cauterized ulcers. Whether these bacteria were the primary cause or secondary invaders has not
been established.

Fused Viscera of Salmon

Sockeye salmon captured in the Northeast Pacific during
the years 1957 through 1964 had a high prevalence (0.02 to
25%) of fish with tightly compacted viscera attached to the
body wall "with mesenteric and peritoneal adhesions" [202].
The individual organs appeared to be normal and the effects of
the adhesions were not known. One suggested cause of this
condition was nematodes of the *Philonema* sp. These parasites
were reported to cause visceral adhesions in other salmonid
species, and *P. oncorhynchi* were isolated in varying numbers
from affected sockeye salmon.

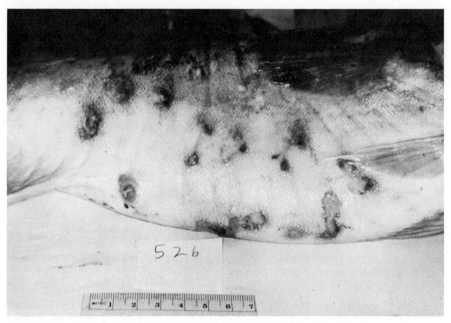

FIG. 17. *Skin ulcers on the lower ventral surface of a Pacific cod.*

Invertebrates
Oyster Mortalities

Among the Pacific oyster along the northwest coast of the United States, mass mortalities prior to 1959 had occurred almost annually at various sites [203]. Environmental conditions seemed to have little relationship to the deaths, and no disease-specific microorganisms were detected. Usually, oysters in their second growing season were affected. A pathological syndrome known as "focal necrosis" was suggested as being involved [97].

On the eastern coast of the United States, extensive epizootics in oyster (*C. virginica*) populations were thought to have been caused by a fungus (*D. marinum*) or a haplosporidan (*Minchiria nelsoni*) [97]. The pathogenicity of these two agents appears to be dependent upon salinities above 15% and warm water temperatures.

The European oyster (*Ostrea edulis*) has also experienced severe mass mortalities characterized by emaciation [97]. No microorganism was routinely isolated from diseased oysters.

The sea scallop (*Placopecten magellanicus*) in the waters off eastern Canada were reported to have "natural" annual mortalities of over 10% [204]. The deaths were attributed to

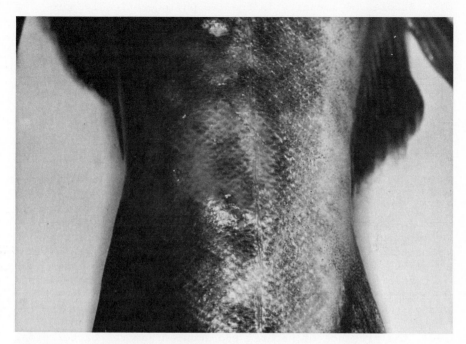

FIG. 18. A ring-like lesion near the caudal region of a Pacific cod.

the cumulated effects of environmental conditions, fishing practices, and predation. Involvement of microorganisms was discounted.

DISEASE RESISTANCE MECHANISMS OF VERTEBRATES AND INVERTEBRATES

Considerable progress has been made in recent years in understanding immunological mechanisms. For example, in about the last fifteen years lymphocytes have emerged from the obscurity of morphologically identifiable cells of unknown or debated function to their present status as a functionally diverse group of cells known to be primary mediators of immunological phenomena. The structure of immunoglobin molecules has been elucidated and new information has been obtained about the genetics of immune responses. There is, however, much about immune mechanisms and disease resistance that is still not defined. It is generally not yet possible to graft tissue completely successfully to any but genetically very closely related immunocompetent hosts; the role of immune responses in cancer is not clear; and the exact roles of humoral and cellular mechanisms of resistance to infectious disease in various species is not well-defined.

Studies on immunity in species phylogenetically more
primitive than mammals date back to around the turn of the
century. In 1882, the Russian zoologist, Elie Metchnikoff,
described phagocytosis after viewing cells in transparent
starfish embryos [205], and in the early 1900's production
of antibacterial agglutinins in fish was demonstrated [206].

In the 1960's a surge of interest in the phylogeny of immunity occurred, largely initiated and furthered by the group
associated with Robert A. Good at the University of Minnesota.
Their findings with various primitive vertebrates and their
claim that adaptive immunity was not evident in the most primitive living vertebrate, the hagfish (*Eptatretus stouti*)
[207], stimulated a number of studies. Hildemann and coworkers [208] later found, however, that if appropriately exposed
to immunogen, the hagfish was immunologically competent. With
the demonstration that adaptive immunity exists in all vertebrate groups, increased emphasis was placed on immune responses in invertebrates and the relation of these responses
to vertebrate mechanisms. Although no inducible molecule that
is completely analogous to vertebrate antibody has been demonstrated in invertebrates, a variety of phenomena have been observed that are analogous or homologous to responses in vertebrates. These include the action of phagocytic cells [209,
210], the presence of natural and induced humoral bactericidal
activity [211-215], the existence of humoral factors possessing phagocytosis-promoting (opsonic) activity [216], the recognition of self from non-self [217], and the specific rejection of foreign tissue grafts [218].

All animal species possess certain innate mechanisms of
disease resistance in order to survive; all vertebrate groups
and some invertebrates have, in addition, demonstrable adaptive or inducible immunological responses. Much of the information available on certain aspects of immunity, however, was
obtained from studies of laboratory mammals and from birds and
man and may not apply in all instances to other species.

INNATE IMMUNITY

Innate immunity is defined as immunity that is constitu-
tive for the species; that is, it is naturally present and
characteristic for a species. This type of immunity includes
anatomical barriers and substances in body fluids, as well as
the activity of phagocytic cells. Even in mammals, the animals most studied, factors which determine innate immunity are
not well-defined [219], and less is known about such factors
in lower species.

Mechanisms in Higher Vertebrates
External
     In mammals, external defense mechanisms relate both to
surface integuments that act as physical barriers to protect
against invasion of pathogenic microorganisms and to factors
associated with integuments that contribute to disease resistance. Among these factors are the "normal flora," microorganisms that may inhibit or compete with pathogens. In cases
of alterations of the immune state of the host, microorganisms
of normal flora can actually invade and cause disease. Mucous
secretions on integumentary surfaces are important in antimicrobial defense because of their ability to trap microorganisms, which are then carried away, and because they contain
antimicrobial substances such as the enzyme lysozyme. Phagocytic cells also exist at mucosal surfaces and engulf pathogens. Antibodies--particularly of the IgA class--are present
in mucus of mammals and are thought to be an important first
line of defense. The acidity of the skin and the long-chain
fatty acids produced in sebaceous glands also exert antimicrobial effects.
     The digestive tract of mammals contains special innate
systems of defense against microbes. The mouth has stratified
epithelium which is an effective mechanical barrier and which
heals rapidly after injury. The flushing action of saliva
also clears foreign material. In addition, there are antimicrobial substances in saliva, and the normal microbial flora
are thought to maintain homeostasis. Most microorganisms that
reach the stomach in mammals are rapidly destroyed as a result
of the gastric acid. The intestinal tract, other than the upper duodenum, is alkaline; factors other than pH, such as the
actions of normal flora and phagocytes, are principal defense
mechanisms in this area [219].

Internal
     A number of nonspecific, internal defense mechanisms
await a potential pathogen which penetrates beyond surface
anatomical barriers. These include both cellular and humoral
mechanisms. The phagocytic cell system of the host constitutes the major internal innate means of defense. The polymorphonuclear leukocytes are the first line of resistance and
are chemotactically attracted to sites of injury by substances
released from damaged tissues. Many microbial invaders induce
an inflammatory response in the host that results in a local
and early extravascular accumulation of polymorphonuclear leukocytes, macrophages, lymphocytes and fluid, and the eventual
formation of fibrin. This response serves to mobilize cellular and humoral antimicrobial components in the host that
phagocytize the invaders, dilute their toxicity, and wall them
off, and establish micro-environments unfavorable for micro-

bial growth. In many instances, bacteria are transported to
lymph nodes which act as filters because of their structure
and the concentration of phagocytic cells present.

The system of mononuclear phagocytic cells termed the reticuloendothelial system also functions to clear and destroy
invading microbes. This system includes fixed tissue phagocytes, such as the Kupffer cells of the liver, peritoneal and
alveolar macrophages, monocytes of the blood, and progenitor
cells in bone marrow. Many of these cells located at a local
lesion arise from monocytes and progenitors in bone marrow,
although they can also occur as the result of local cell mitosis and differentiation.

A number of nonantibody, antimicrobial substances present
in body fluids act nonspecifically on invading microorganisms.
In mammals, these substances include organic acids, basic
polypeptides, lysozyme, interferon, and others. There are
also antibody molecules present, which may react with an invading pathogen, which occur in the absence of known antigenic
stimuli. In many instances this simply means that these molecules were induced in the host during the course of a previous, perhaps subclinical, infection with the homologous or an
antigenically related microbe or by contact with cross-reac-
tive antigens in the diet. It is possible, however, that some
of these so-called "natural antibodies" occur constitutively
and are part of the innate system of defense against disease
[219,220].

Mechanisms in Lower Vertebrates and Invertebrates
External
The concept that integuments are vital disease resistance
barriers in lower species rests more on observation and anal-
ogy than on experimental evidence, although some studies on
this subject have been reported [221,222]. Clearly, extensive
surface damage to aquatic animals residing in hypo- or hypertonic environments disrupts osmoregulatory homeostatic mechanisms. In addition, damage to the skin of fish, particularly
if water temperature is elevated, may well result in fungus
infections.

There are several published reports on the detection of
agglutinins or immunoglobulin antigens in the mucus of fish
[223-227] and one report of *in vitro* antibacterial activity
detected in the body mucus of trout [227]. Whether or not
these factors play a substantial role in disease resistance
is not yet clear.

Internal
More experimentation has been done on innate mechanisms
of immunity in invertebrates than in lower vertebrates. Probably this is due to the fact that antimicrobial mechanisms

have been identified in invertebrates, but they have not been shown to be induced or enhanced by exposure to disease organisms. Invertebrates possess both humoral and cellular innate internal mechanisms which react against microbes; bactericidins and agglutinins have been demonstrated. Phagocytic cells have been studied in a number of invertebrates and probably represent the principal defense mechanism after surface barriers have been penetrated by pathogens. For recent reviews of invertebrate immunology see references 228-233.

Lower vertebrates possess phagocytic cells and lymphoid elements that appear to function similarly in many respects to those in higher animals. Very little direct evidence is available, however, on the nature of innate immunity in lower vertebrates. Certainly an added important variable to be considered for the poikilotherms is the effect of temperature. For recent reviews on immunology of lower vertebrates see references 228,233-239.

ACQUIRED IMMUNITY

Mechanisms in Higher Vertebrates
Humoral

Specific, humoral, adaptive or acquired immunity against microorganisms is an important function of antibody and antibody-related mechanisms in higher vertebrates. Among the ways antibodies are known or are presumed to act against pathogenic bacteria are by neutralizing toxins, by facilitiating phagocytosis (opsinization), and by interaction with a series of serum proteins collectively termed complement to kill gram-negative bacteria. Antibodies may also inhibit pathogenic bacteria by clumping or agglutinating them, thereby preventing their dissemination. Specific anti-viral antibodies effectively inhibit the hematogenous spread of viral infections and are thought to inhibit viral replication by preventing attachment of virus to receptor sites on cells (e.g., poliovirus), by sterically hindering the discharge of nucleic acid from adsorbed virus into cells, or by preventing virus from escaping from phagocytic vacuoles of phagocytic cells to allow viral replication in the cytoplasm [240].

Evidence gained from study of patients with hereditary immunodeficiencies or with secondary immunodeficiencies arising from a variety of causes has delineated some of the major components of human bodily defenses against disease [241]. Similar information has been obtained as the result of experiments with laboratory animals, particularly with mice, rats, rabbits, and chickens [242]. Clinical evidence from immunodeficient human patients implicates humoral responses as the primary defense mechanisms against a number of pathogenic bacteria and one virus, the hepatitis virus [243].

Cellular

In addition to humoral immunity, there are acquired cellular disease-resistance mechanisms [244]. Acquired cellular immunity can be demonstrated under appropriate experimental conditions as immunity that can be transferred from an immune animal to a nonimmune animal with living cells but not with serum. Acquired antimicrobial cellular immunity is effected principally by the activity of cells of the reticuloendothelial system, that is, the mononuclear phagocytes and not the polymorphonuclear leukocytes. Although mechanisms of acquired cellular immunity are not yet well defined, clear evidence exists that such immunity arises partially as a result of the activity of one of the two major types of lymphoid cells, the thymus-derived or T-lymphocytes [245,246]. The thymus-derived cells arise and/or differentiate in the thymus gland during development and are seeded to peripheral lymphoid organs or tissues where they undergo changes and perform specific functions. These include specific activation of the thymus-derived cells by immunogens. This results in cell division followed by production of factors (lymphokines) which induce macrophages to undergo changes (activation) making them more efficient in neutralizing and destroying foreign material. The activation by immunogen (afferent limb) of such cellular immunity is specific, but the effector action (efferent limb) is nonspecific [247]. Thymus-derived cells may also act either directly or indirectly to destroy foreign cells, such as those present in a kidney or skin graft received from a genetically nonidentical donor, and to recognize and implement destruction of cells that have undergone malignant changes. This latter function has been proposed as the major reason for the existence and conservation of acquired cellular immunity during phylogeny. That is, it has been proposed that membrane changes in cells reflecting cancerous potential are recognized as foreign by the immune system of the host and the aberrant cells are destroyed before they can divide and form tumors [245]. In this context, tumors form only when aberrant cells escape or overcome this immunosurveillance either because of some property of the transformed cell or because of weakening or failure of thymus-dependent immune mechanisms [248].

There is considerable evidence that increased numbers of tumors occur in human patients and laboratory animals that have immunodeficiencies or that have been treated with immunosuppressive agents such as chemicals or irradiation [15,249-256]. The picture is not a simple one, however, and the role of immune responses in tumor formation is not yet fully defined [15,254,257]. There is evidence, however, that little relationship exists between immune status and activity of polycyclic hydrocarbon carcinogens [258].

In addition to their function in cellular immunity, T-cells also interact with the other major type of lymphoid cells termed B-cells (originally, because they are derived from the Bursa of Fabricius in the chicken, but now usually interpreted as indicating bone-marrow derived). Cells of the B-cell line differentiate and produce antibody, but in many tests this occurred only after interaction with T-cells. It has been shown, therefore, that there are T-dependent antigens that require T-cell participation for antibody production by B-cells and a few T-independent antigens that can stimulate B-cells directly to form antibody [259].

Depression of cellular immunity in man has been correlated with increased susceptibility to a number of viral diseases, yeast infections, and tuberculosis, as well as with possible increased incidence of tumors [243].

Mechanisms in Lower Vertebrates and Invertebrates
Humoral

Experiments dating back more than 50 years have demonstrated that teleost fish are capable of producing specific antibody [206]. It is now generally accepted that all vertebrates possess this capability. However, fishes mostly have only one major class of immunoglobulin, whereas five classes have been defined in man, and other vertebrates have intermediate numbers of classes [233]. Antibodies of lower vertebrates are capable of high levels of specificity for antigen [260-264]. Their antibodies are also capable of most of the *in vitro* immunological reactions that mammalian antibodies develop, such as precipitation, agglutination, and interaction with complement to lyse erythrocytes [234,260,265]. Multicomponent complement activity has also been clearly demonstrated in serum of lower vertebrates [228]. There is, however, little information on the role of acquired humoral immunity of lower vertebrates, particularly poikilotherms, in disease resistance. Passively transferred specific antibody will protect trout and salmon from bacterial diseases [266,267] and antibody and complement from trout will inhibit *in vitro* growth of pathogenic bacteria [267]. A marked increase in specific bacteria-agglutinating antibody in the sera of fish after natural exposure to pathogens has not been generally found, although there are reports of apparent moderate increases [268-270]. Fish have specific, natural agglutinins; their presence may be a source of confusion in assessing antibody titers in wild fish. Also, titers of agglutinins and precipitins may not quantitatively reflect humoral immunity; this fact has been little appreciated, particularly in earlier studies. Recent observations [271] on bacterial disease resistance acquired by salmon subsequent to feeding bacterial antigens have suggested that the degree of immunity developed did not correlate with titers of antibacterial agglutinins. In these experiments, oral immunization of salmon with antigens from the saltwater pathogen, *Vibrio anguillarum*, resulted in demonstrable protection in the absence of increased levels of agglutinins. There was evidence that bactericidal antibody levels in the serum did increase.

The mucus of fish contains immunoglobulin and agglutinins, as well as apparent complement-like activity. It is not known, however, if these factors play a role in acquired humoral immunity. Bacterial flora reflective of that in the immediate environment can be isolated from the body surface of wild fish [272,273]. This would argue against the presence of a wide-spectrum, strongly bactericidal activity in normal mucus, even though low levels of bactericidal or bacteriostatic activity have been demonstrated in fish mucus *in vitro* [227]. It is possible, however, that agglutinins in mucus bind bacteria and prevent their penetration through skin, or that specific antibody in mucus of immune fish may, with complement, selectively destroy certain pathogens.

Cellular

Lower vertebrates are capable of recognizing and rejecting foreign tissue grafts (allografts and xenografts) whereas control autografts are accepted [228]. This is evidence for a system of cellular immunological functions analogous or homologous to that of mammals. Experiments have shown that even lower invertebrates are capable of recognition phenomena, that is, they can differentiate self from non-self [228]; but there is little evidence that most invertebrates can manifest specific, acquired cellular immune responses. There are exceptions such as earthworms, which are capable of specifically recognizing and rejecting foreign tissue grafts [274,275].

Whether or not acquired cellular immune reactions are of importance in infectious disease resistance in lower species is still not known. It appears, however, that lower vertebrates possess mechanisms of cellular immunity against foreign cells similar to those that have been implicated in mammalian immunity against tumors.

GENETIC AND ENVIRONMENTAL INFLUENCES

In man the occurrence of repeated infections signals a deficiency in his resistance mechanisms against disease. Specific defects in cellular or humoral immunity result in increased susceptibility to certain infections. Immune deficiencies are classified as either primary or secondary. Primary immune deficiencies results from genetic abnormalities; secondary deficiencies result from nongenetic factors that prevent the expression of a mature immune system [276,277].

Such secondary immune deficiencies may result from naturally occurring disease or from exposure to various immunosuppressive agents [278].

In domestic animals evidence has also been obtained that genetic resistance to disease exists [279,280]. Different strains of animals are able to develop high or low titers of antibodies in response to antigenic stimulation. With the use of inbred strains of mice and other animals, much new information has been gained on the genetic control of immune responses [281-287].

Nutrition is an important factor in disease. It has been generally observed in humans during recorded history that famine and an increased incidence of infectious disease go hand-in-hand. Within the last few decades, the relationship between nutrition and disease has been explored experimentally and is becoming much better understood [288-294].

A number of chemical and physical agents inhibit immune responses and, in some instances, have been linked with increased incidence of, or susceptibility to, disease. Examples of known immunosuppressives are ionizing radiation and cytotoxic drugs, including alkylating agents such as nitrogen mustard and cyclophosphamide (Cytoxan); and antimetabolites such as methotrexate, 6-mercaptopurine, and azathioprine [295]. Some of these agents are used extensively in man to control rejection of grafted organs. Certain chemical environmental contaminants have been implicated in decreased immune responses and/or increased incidence of diseases. These include polychlorinated biphenyls [296-298], organochlorine insecticides [299-301], and the metals lead and cadmium [25-29,31-33]; it has been recently reported, however, that lead or cadmium, depending on the dose or route of administration, could either increase or decrease formation of antibody in mice [302]. It has also been well-documented that many chemical carcinogens are immunosuppressive agents [16-33].

It has been clearly demonstrated that temperature is an important variable in development of circulating antibody in poikilothermic animals [303-306]. It is also clear that water temperature is a dominant factor in the experimental induction of bacterial and viral diseases of fishes [307]. There is, however, little information on the relative effects of temperature on the pathogen, in relation to the effects of temperature on specific acquired resistance of the poikilothermic host and on the innate resistance and physiologic well-being of the host.

EFFECTS OF PETROLEUM ON DISEASE AND DISEASE RESISTANCE

PETROLEUM, PETROLEUM PRODUCTS AND PETROLEUM-ASSOCIATED METALS IMPLICATED IN NEOPLASIA

It has recently been claimed that from 50% to as high as 90% of all cancers in man are causatively related to environmental factors [22,308,309]. Considerable evidence exists that certain hydrocarbons in petroleum and petroleum derivatives are carcinogens for various species and that petroleum and petroleum products are implicated in hyperplasia and neoplasia. For example, Hieger and Woodhouse [12] reported on the carcinogenic activity for rabbits and mice of three crude oils and five fractions of each oil obtained under conditions to prevent cracking. In general, the greatest carcinogenic activity occurred in the designated heavy fractions of the oils although skin tumors appeared in animals treated with two of the three unfractionated crude oils and with each of the fractions. Cahnmann [11] reported that American shale oil, which was known to possess carcinogenic properties, contained between 0.003 and 0.004% of the potent polynuclear aromatic hydrocarbon carcinogen, benzo[a]pyrene. In later studies, however, Hueper and Cahnmann [10] found that the carcinogenic effect of American shale oil was not restricted to the benzo-[a]pyrene-containing fractions, but that, in addition, fractions having a boiling point below that of benzo[a]pyrene possessed appreciable carcinogenic properties when injected intramuscularly into mice.

Cook et al. [9] reviewed evidence that lubricating and cutting oils caused skin cancer in humans and that the components of three crude oils carcinogenic for mice or rabbits were in the fraction boiling between 300°-400°C, with most the activity in the fraction boiling between 350°-400°C [9]. Solvents known to extract aromatic constituents also extracted almost all of the carcinogenic activity. Mastromatteo [310] reported on six cases of squamous cell carcinoma in employees of a single machine-operating plant that seemed to be related to exposure to cutting oil. Hueper and Payne [8] presented evidence that four road asphalts applied to the skin of or injected into mice elicited cancer in some of the animals at the sites of injection, whereas fumes from petroleum roofing asphalt did not produce cancers of the lungs in rats and guinea pigs for periods of up to two years. Falk et al. [7] briefly described cancers attributed to mineral oil in a general review of the carcinogenicity for man of polycyclic aromatic hydrocarbons. Carruthers and Douglas [311] and Carruthers et al. [6] reported on the isolation of 1,2-benzanthracene derivatives from a Kuwait crude oil and that biological tests (personal communication from D.L. Woodhouse cited in Carruthers et al. [6]) of extracts from high-boiling fractions of Kuwait crude oil were carcinogenic. Bingham et al. [5] found that repetitive application of certain refined mineral oils to the skin of mice produced papillomas or squamous cell carcinomas. These benign or malignant tumors occurred in frequencies ranging from zero or very low after exposure to a number of oils to a high, for one oil, of 29 out of 30 mice developing skin tumors after an average of about 13 weeks exposure.

Wallcave et al. [312] reported epidermal carcinomas occurred in over 90% of 58 mice treated with coal-tar pitch, but only one carcinoma and five papillomas occurred in 218 mice treated with eight asphalts. It was not clear whether or not there was a relation between aromatic hydrocarbon content of asphalts and tumorigenicity.

ZoBell [313] reviewed the sources and biodegradation of environmental carcinogenic hydrocarbons and pointed out these compounds are widely distributed in air, soil, marine mud, water, vegetable oils, mineral oils, and other materials. He presented evidence for the biosynthesis of carcinogenic hydrocarbons by bacteria, algae, and higher plants and discussed biodegradation of the chemicals by animals and bacteria. Nelson-Smith [314] also discussed the widespread distribution of polycyclic aromatic hydrocarbons, including those having potential carcinogenic activity, in the marine environment.

Hueper [4] reviewed the relation between exposure of marine species to mineral oils and the incidence of tumors and presented indirect evidence that development of tumors in such species was related to exposure to petroleum. Blumer [315] has also reviewed evidence that oil contamination of the sea can increase the risk of cancer in humans, and raises the question as to whether oil pollution can contaminate beaches and fisheries resources to the extent it constitutes a severe public health hazard. Moore et al. [316] reviewed the distribution of carcinogenic polycyclic aromatic hydrocarbons in the environment and emphasized that these compounds can slowly accumulate in tissues of a number of fish and shellfish. Sullivan [317] also reviewed reports on the polycyclic aromatic hydrocarbon content of petroleum, estimates of discharges of these compounds into the ocean, and concentrations of benzo[a]pyrene in seafood and other foods. He reported that concentrations of benzo[a]pyrene in marine animals can vary from nondetectable levels to over 2,000 µg/kg and concluded that the amount of benzo[a]pyrene in seafood is appreciably higher than the amount in non-marine food. He stated that the higher values in marine foods "are undoubtedly due to petroleum contamination from neighboring sources." He also stated that the relatively high levels of benzo[a]pyrene found in marine animals off Greenland and in the Arctic Ocean "indicate possibly high levels of benzopyrene in the entire world ocean."

Blumer and Youngblood [318] applied techniques, having greater analytical resolution than those previously used, in studies of environmental polycyclic aromatic hydrocarbons. They suggested that most of these compounds in recent sediments are from a single source because of the consistency of the hydrocarbon patterns among their samples. They found, however, that the relative abundance of unsubstituted aromatic hydrocarbons and certain other hydrocarbon compounds is not the same as that of crude oil. They suggested that most of the hydrocarbons in recent sediments were formed in forest and prairie fires and were subsequently distributed widely in the environment. They considered it unlikely that these compounds have a biosynthetic origin and cite literature documenting that it is still unresolved and controversial as to whether polycyclic aromatic hydrocarbons are even synthesized by organisms.

Certain compounds containing metals that may be associated with crude oil or with petroleum exploration have also been implicated in carcinogenesis. These metals include cadmium, chromium, iron, lead, nickel, zinc, and possibly others [319].

There are a number of published reports on aquatic animals in polluted waters exhibiting tumors or hyperplastic diseases that are not found in the same frequencies in less polluted areas, although the etiology of the diseases is usually not known. Brown and coauthors in a series of papers and abstracts [1,320-323] reported a higher frequency of tumors in freshwater fish from a polluted watershed than that in fish from nonpolluted waters. They found a tumor frequency of 1.03% in 4,639 fish of all species examined from a Canadian nonpolluted control watershed as compared to a 4.38% tumor frequency in 2,121 fish of all species from polluted Fox River (Illinois) waters. Among the pollutants found in the Fox River were mercury, lead, arsenic, toluene, crude oil, gasoline, benzanthracene, chlorinated hydrocarbons, phosphates, sulfates, and coliform bacteria. Dissolved oxygen content, temperature, and nutrients were similar in the two watersheds. In addition to tumors, two types of leukemia were found in northern pike (*Esox lucius*) in the Fox River. A lymphosarcoma of the jaw of pike was also found; the disease was transmissible by cell-free homogenates of the tumor, suggesting a viral etiology.

Gardner et al. [324] reported finding an incidence of 22% cancerous animals in one soft-shelled clam population recovered from the vicinity of a jet fuel spill. There was no mention of tumor frequency in control clams from a non-spill area. They also reported the occurrence of "precancerous lesions" in olfactory organs of a marine fish exposed under laboratory conditions to a salt-water-soluble fraction of crude oil.

Butler and Berkes [325] described cancer-like growths in marine animals taken from polluted waters.

Powell et al. [326] found that hyperplasia of the ovicells in an estuarine bryozoan, *Schizoporella unicornis* (an aquatic invertebrate), was induced experimentally by placing colonies, having normal numbers of ovicells, close to coal-tar derivatives in an estuary. But, Straughan and Lawrence [327] found no instances of hyperplasia of ovicells in bryozoans from surface, subsurface, and benthic kelp fronds in an area chronically exposed to natural oil seepage.

Other experimental studies have been reported. Aromatic compounds isolated from marine muds caused "cancerous growths" in certain seaweeds [328]. A number of aromatic hydrocarbons, including some not reported as carcinogens, stimulated growth of algae [329]. Sea urchin eggs treated with 3,4-benzopyrene cleaved and developed abnormally [330]. Tumors were induced in some of 1,220 guppies (*Poeciliea reticulata*) and 40 zebra fish (*Danio rerio*) following multiple exposures to nine carcinogens [331]; 7-12-dimethylbenz[a]anthracene, 3-methylcholanthrene, and benzidine did not produce tumors, but N-2-fluorenylacetamide, o-aminoazotoluene, 4-dimethylaminoazobenzene, diethylnitrosamine, dimethylnitrosamine, and nitrosomorpholine did.

EVIDENCE FOR TISSUE AND CELLULAR DAMAGE RESULTING FROM EXPOSURE TO PETROLEUM AND ASSOCIATED METALS

The study of organ, tissue, and cell structure is one approach to understanding alterations of life processes in arctic and subarctic marine species after exposure to petroleum. There is a paucity of work in this field, but there are trends in the available data that point to similarities in cellular dysfunction after exposure of fish to several different contaminants, even though the experimental conditions vary considerably.

In fish, the gills have been identified as excellent biological indicators of the effects of toxic materials in the environment. Several changes in the gills have been noted at the cellular level after exposure to contaminants. In six species of marine fish sampled from an area near an oil slick off the Louisiana and Texas coast, a loss of epithelial cells occurred. Mucous cells were also depleted and an acidophilic cell type was reduced [332].

In laboratory studies, both phenols and crude oil from several sources have been used for experiments which range from sublethal exposures to 48 hr LC_{50} studies. Phenol is a common compound in crude oil and occurs in low amounts, less

than 0.10% [333]; however, the biological importance of phenol
may be compounded because some components of crude oil, i.e.,
benzene, are oxidized to phenol in liver [334]. A concentration of 1 part phenol per 100,000 parts fresh water caused no
detectable changes in the gill of the goldfish, *Carassius
auratus*, but the same concentration produced destructive effects on liver, spleen, and kidney [335]. However, the gills
were inflammed and mucous glands completely discharged in 14
species of fish from the Rhine and Elbe Rivers that were polluted with phenol at the time of sampling [336]. Rainbow
trout in fresh water at levels of phenol between 6.5 and 9.6
mg/l developed inflammed gills and epithelial cell sloughing
[337]. At the highest concentrations, fish were killed in a
few hours. At lower concentrations and in longer term experiments with bream, *Abramis brama*, the gill epithelium disinte-
grated and lesions developed in blood vessel walls with ex-
travasation of blood into the gill lamellae [338].

The gill response common to each treatment was the loss
of integrity of the epithelial cell layer and discharge of the
mucous glands. This could increase other toxic effects since
penetration into blood would be more direct and protective
flushing of mucous secretions would be exhausted.

Skin of a number of species of fish was affected by phenol exposure in a similar manner: the epidermis became inflammed and swollen to twice its normal thickness [336] and
mucous cells were dilated and numerous [338].

A probable major route of entry of contaminants such as
phenol to other organs is through the gills to the blood.
Visualization of phenol concentrations using bromine to form
tribromophenol crystals demonstrated the greatest concentrations of phenol in blood plasma when compared with other body
fluids of the bream [338]. Both red and white blood cells of
bream incurred damage from phenol exposure; a decrease of one-
half million red blood cells per cubic millimeter of blood was
observed [339].

After exposure to both No. 2 fuel oil [340] and phenol
[338], there was evidence of damage to the liver of coho salmon and bream. The color of the liver changed from the normal
dark brownish-red to a light brown with a blotchy rather than
uniform pigmentation. These color changes probably reflect
circulatory system damage, which is known to occur in a variety of fish species after exposure to several petroleum hydrocarbon products as well as other types of contaminants such as
chlorobiphenyls [337,341,346]. Erythrocytes were damaged by
high concentrations of phenols [342], so that there was a decrease in the number of red blood cells and those surviving
were swollen [343]. Histological sections of livers showed
local hematomas, occluded vessels, and regions of extravasated
blood after exposure to crude oil and coal tar [335], chloro-

biphenyls [341], and phenol [338]. When levels of phenol were high enough to cause the death of the fish within a few hours after exposure, there was extensive internal hemorrhage [337].

In addition to circulatory changes that affect the liver, there is evidence for a depletion of energy reserves in the parenchymal cells of the livers of *Fundulus* from petroleum-contaminated waters. Electron microscopy demonstrated decreases in glycogen and lipid, as well as increases in rough endoplasmic reticulum and free ribosomes, possibly reflecting increased enzyme synthesis [344]. Glycogen depletion in liver was the common effect on ten fresh water and three marine fish in laboratory studies with 30 pesticides and chlorobiphenyls. The most frequently tested species were lake trout, *Salvelinus namaycush*, and bluegills, *Lepomis macrochirus*. In general, lipid reserves were depleted after exposure to some pesticides but there was fatty infiltration following exposure to chlorobiphenyls as well as lipid vacuole formation [199]. These fatty livers had an abnormal proliferation of endoplasmic reticulum.

Alterations in the pigment inclusions in liver cells were observed in goldfish exposed to crude oil and coal tar; there was an accumulation in bilirubin crystals, and of a "yellow haemoglobinogenetic" pigment which gave reactions for both iron and lipid [335]. In bream, phenol treatment resulted in an accumulation of lipofuscin granules in the hepatic arterial and venous vessels and the endothelial cells lining the lumen of the vessels [338].

Contaminants that damage blood may also affect the spleen. This organ was found to change from a black-red hue to light tan in coho salmon after exposure to No. 2 fuel oil [340], or lighten perceptibility when bream were immersed in phenol [338]. With a 2.6 mg/l phenol treatment, the splenic tissue in bream was less tightly structured and cellular changes included increased lipofuscin and hemosiderin but no change in bilirubin. Under the same conditions, the blood vessels of the kidney of bream were dilated and filled with masses of blood; discoloration of skin, gills, cerebrospinal fluid, cardiac muscle, liver, spleen, and kidney, was also noted [338].

The pink shrimp (*Penaeus duorarum*) has been used as a test species for toxicant effects; the hepatopancreas, with its variety of cell types, was the organ primarily affected. Changes in hepatopancreatic cells in many ways paralleled alterations observed in fish liver. When shrimp were exposed to chlorobiphenyls, glycogen was depleted and there was excess lipid accumulation in the hepatopancreas. In addition, electron microscopical examination revealed severe cell damage: loss of the microvillar surface at the lumenal side of the cells and generalized pathological changes, such as swollen mitochondria, hypertrophic nuclei, and presence of myelin bodies [345].

In summary, very little is known specifically about the effects of petroleum hydrocarbons on the structure of tissues and cells of arctic and subarctic marine species. The few studies on fresh water and temperate marine species indicate which tissues are vulnerable to such contaminants and the specific types of damage which may result from exposure.

Trace metals such as cadmium, lead, and others which may be associated with petroleum hydrocarbons are among the more toxic metals known to affect marine and other organisms [347]. More is known about the effects of cadmium on the morphology of fish and mammals than about lead, nickel, or chromium. The effects of all four metals, but predominantly cadmium, on testis and ovaries, the central nervous system, gills, intestine, liver, and kidney, will be discussed.

The toxicity of cadmium to humans [348] and mammals [349] has been recognized for some time; a major site of damage is the testis. Testicular atrophy occurred in rats and mice injected subcutaneously with 0.02 mM cadmium chloride per kilogram of body weight. Both the seminiferous epithelium and interstitial tissue were severely damaged; no regeneration of spermogenic epithelium was evident as long as 133 days after the last cadmium injection [348]. Some areas of the testes did recover; within 20 days after cadmium exposure, new blood vessels were formed and later, new Leydig cells were observed and there was a gradual restoration of endocrine function.

The reproductive tissues of fish can also be affected by exposure to trace metals. Seven days after a 24-hr exposure to 25 ppm cadmium in the water, brook trout, *Salvelinus fontinalis*, developed haemorrhagic necrosis of the testis. Androgen production was disturbed but the primordial germ cells were not changed [350]. Testicular damage also occurred in goldfish after five intraperitoneal injections of 10 mg cadmium chloride per kilogram of body weight. The number of primary germ cells decreased as the seminiferous tubules became depleted and were replaced by collagen fibrils [351]. In the same study, but with female goldfish, histological integrity of the ovaries was maintained, but both the number of mature oocytes and relative weights of the ovaries decreased. In addition, lead may affect gonadal tissue. Sexual maturation was retarded in newborn guppies, *Lebistes reticulatus*, exposed to 2 ppm lead nitrate or 1.25 ppm lead [352].

Toxic effects of cadmium have been observed on the central nervous system of 190 g Sprague-Dawley rats injected subcutaneously with 5.5 mg/ml cadmium chloride. Some ganglionic cells were lysed and others had pyknotic nuclei; massive hemorrhages also occurred in the ganglionic tissues [353]. In subsequent experiments, young rats and rabbits had damaged

central nervous systems after receiving cadmium chloride in
the first few days after birth; both nerve fibers and cells
were destroyed [354].

Effects of cadmium on other tissues did not involve hemorrhagic lesions. The cells of target organs appeared to be
directly damaged by cadmium. The gills of *Fundulus heteroclitus* were damaged after the fish were exposed for 64 hr to
28 mg cadmium per liter in fresh water. The mucous epithelium
sloughed and necrotic tissues were evident on both the lamellae and filaments [355]. In 20 ^{o}/oo salinity and at cadmium
levels "considered to be acutely toxic" [356], *F. heteroclitus*
responded with an excessive production of mucus from the gill.
The gill epithelium was destroyed in four species of fish, including rainbow trout, exposed to both nickel and cadmium and
the fish suffocated [357]. Lead contamination of other species of fish produced a similar response [358,359].

Apparently, the salinity of the water is a factor in the
toxic action of cadmium on fish: *F. heteroclitus* treated with
cadmium in seawater were more resistant to poisoning [360]
than when exposed in fresh water [355]. In addition, the intestine, rather than the gills, showed damaged mucous cells
and a swollen epithelium after a one-hour exposure to 50 ppm
cadmium chloride, and, after 48 hr, the submucosa was edema-
tous. Some hypertrophied and necrotic areas were observed in
the gills of these fish but not all the filaments were affected and not to the extent reported in fresh water exposures
[361]. According to Voyer et al. [355] the differences in osmoregulatory mechanisms in fresh and marine fishes may explain
the differences in gill and intestinal damage. In freshwater
fishes there is a flow of water into the fish through the
gills and oral tissues with minimal ingestion; however, marine
fish swallow water and excrete salts to compensate for the de-
hydrating effects of the surroundings.

After entry to internal tissues, cadmium can be accumulated in both kidney and liver. Overall histological integrity was maintained in the livers of goldfish injected intraperitoneally with ten doses of 20 mg/l cadmium, but occasional
focal granulomas developed. The kidneys of the same fish had
an abundant invasion of macrophages which aggregated at some
sites and formed granulomas [351].

Newman [362] found that the kidney structure changed in
five of six cunners, *Tautogolabrus adspersus*, which were exposed to 48 ppm cadmium chloride ($CdCl_2 \cdot 2-1/2 \ H_2O$) in seawater. There was diffuse and focal necrosis in the kidney tubules, and, in one cunner, the necrosis had progressed to form
overt lesions. The proximal segment of the tubule was most
affected; however, the glomeruli were not damaged. After a
year's exposure to 5 mg/l of cadmium in seawater (20 ^{o}/oo

salinity), no lesions were found in the liver and kidney tissue of *Fundulus* [356].

The blood spaces of the kidney of the cunner treated with 48 ppm cadmium chloride in seawater had large numbers of immature thrombocytes. In addition, changes in circulating blood cells occurred: the numbers of thrombocytes and lymphocytes decreased and the percentage of neutrophils increased [362]. Similar changes in the percentage of neutrophils and lymphocytes occurred in rabbits fed food containing 160 ppm cadmium for 200 days. Each rabbit consumed 14.9 mg cadmium per kilogram of body weight per day [363]. Thrombocyte, neutrophil and basophil levels changed in white perch, *Morone americana*, and hogchokers, *Trinectes maculatus*, exposed to Baltimore Harbor water for 7-30 days [364]. The water contained at least six heavy metals, among them cadmium and chromium.

EFFECTS OF PETROLEUM HYDROCARBONS AND ASSOCIATED METALS ON IMMUNE RESPONSES AND DISEASE RESISTANCE

There is experimental evidence that certain polycyclic aromatic hydrocarbons inhibit immune responses. For example, Stjernswärd in a series of studies [18-21] established that injection of single, low, tumor-inducing doses of 3-methylcholanthrene and dibenz[a]anthracene into mice prior to administration of antigen resulted in depressed levels of antibody-forming cells. Also, 3-methylcholanthrene caused suppression of cell-mediated immunity [17,365]. Other potent polycyclic hydrocarbon carcinogens such as 9,10-dimethyl-1,2-benzanthracene, 1,2,5,6-dibenzanthracene, and 3,4-benzpyrene produced a markedly diminished capacity for rejection of tumors or foreign tissue grafts in mice, whereas a number of non-carcinogenic hydrocarbons produced little or no such effect on this aspect of cellular immunity [365]. Other hydrocarbons showing immunosuppressive activity are *p*-dimethylaminoazobenzene [366, 367] and "mineral oil" [24].

Compounds containing certain metals such as cadmium and lead, which may be associated with petroleum, have been found to be immunosuppressive. Koller et al. [26] reported a remarkable decrease in antibody forming cells in mice exposed to 3 ppm cadmium in drinking water for 70 days and Koller and Kovacic [29] found a decrease in antibody formation in mice exposed to lead (14-1,375 ppm as lead acetate in deionized water for 56 days).

Cook et al. [27] reported that intravenous administration of cadmium acetate (0.60 mg/100 g) and lead acetate (2.00 mg/ 100 g) enhanced the susceptibility of rats to intravenous challenge with *Escherichia coli* by approximately a thousand-fold. It appeared that the effect was mediated by increased susceptibility to endotoxin, since equivalent vulnerability of metal-treated rats to exposure to killed *E. coli* occurred.

Hemphill et al. [28] reported that mice treated with subclinical doses of lead nitrate (100 µg/l or 250 µg/l per day) for 30 days were more susceptible to challenge with *Salmonella typhimurium*.

Trejo et al. [31] found that a single injection of lead acetate (5.0 mg) had no effect on antibody production of rats but that it did impair phagocytic activity and significantly reduced the ability of liver and spleen to detoxify endotoxin.

Jones et al. [368] found that the effects of metals on immune respones depend on dose and time of administration in relation to antigen. For example, cadmium chloride (0.6 mg/kg Cd^{2+}) injected daily 5 days/week into rats beginning 14 days before antigen enhanced both primary and secondary antibody responses. If the metal treatment was initiated one week before antigen, the primary immune responses was delayed and the secondary response depressed. It was postulated that cadmium may be involved in a number of physiological processes in cells or may affect cell permeability.

Koller et al. [369] reported that a single dose of lead (4 mg) administered orally or intraperitoneally to mice stimulated formation of IgM antibody. Conversely, lead by either route of administration significantly reduced IgG antibody formation. Cadmium (0.15 mg), in comparison, caused an increase in IgM antibody formation when injected intraperitoneally, a slight decrease of IgM when given orally, a reduced IgG antibody response when given orally, and an increased IgG antibody response when given intraperitoneally. Subclinical doses of lead in drinking water (2,500 ppm lead acetate over 10 weeks), cadmium (300 ppm cadmium chloride over 10 weeks), or mercury (10 ppm mercuric chloride over 10 weeks) suppressed immunocompetence of rabbits [25], but various subclinical dietary doses of lead had no effect on immunocompetence of chickens [370].

Nickel affected interferon synthesis of cells in tissue cultures whereas iron, chromium, and cadmium had no effect [30,371].

Robohm and Nitkowski [32] have reported that exposure of a fish, the cunner, to 3 to 24 ppm Cd^{2+} in artificial seawater had no demonstrable effect on the ability of the fish to produce antibody. Exposure to 12 ppm cadmium increased the rates of bacterial uptake in phagocytes of the liver and spleen but significantly decreased the rates of bacterial killing within cells, probably increasing susceptibility of the fish to disease.

Therefore, it appears that effects of at least certain trace metals on immune responses vary markedly depending on dose and time of administration in relation to antigen, and on route of metal administration. These factors must be considered as well as the species in evaluating trace metal effects on disease resistance of arctic and subarctic marine animals.

PROSPECTUS

Two effects of exposure to petroleum and constituent hydrocarbons and trace metals appear to be particularly relevant to the pathology of marine species and to the prospect of increased oil exploration activity in northern seas. The first is the development of hyperplasia and neoplasia in man and laboratory animals after exposure to hydrocarbons and metals. Tumors have been found, sometimes in high frequency, in marine animals in the North Pacific, in the Bering Sea, and in many other areas of the world. There is no definitive evidence that petroleum is an etiological factor in these lesions; in fact, their cause is unknown at present. Any significant increase in levels of environmental carcinogens from petroleum or other sources could, however, be reflected in increased incidence of tumors in susceptible marine species.

The other effect of exposure to petroleum that may have considerable impact on diseases of marine animals is its potential for suppressing immune responses and disease resistance. Many carcinogens are immunosuppressive for laboratory animals, and predictably at some exposure levels would have similar effects on disease resistance mechanisms of marine vertebrates and, possibly, invertebrates. Bacterial and other infectious diseases are enzootic in northern marine waters; thus, a reduction of humoral and cellular immunity could substantially increase mortalities of marine species directly because of disease or indirectly because of reduced vitality.

A key tissue is whether or not petroleum at levels it is introduced in northern marine waters can induce tumors or suppress immunity in species of the area. Well-designed laboratory examinations of indigenous species conducted at physiological temperatures would go a long way toward determining the existence, nature, and severity of such potential problems.

REFERENCES

1. Brown, E.R., J.J. Hazdra, L. Keith, I. Greenspan, J.B.G. Kwapinski, and B. Parker (1973). Frequency of fish tumors found in polluted watershed as compared to non-polluted Canadian waters. Cancer Res. 33:189-98.
2. Wellings, S.R., B.B. McCain, and B.S. Miller (1976). Papillomas in pleuronectid fishes: the current state of knowledge, with particular reference to etiology. Prog. Exp. Tumor Res. 20:55-74.

3. McCain, B.B., S.R. Wellings, C.E. Alpers, M.S. Myers, and W.D. Gronlund (1976). The frequency, distribution, and pathology of three diseases of demersal fishes in the Bering Sea. J. Fish. Biol., In press.

4. Hueper, W.C. (1963). Environmental carcinogenesis in man and animals. Ann. N.Y. Acad. Sci. 108:963-1038.

5. Bingham, E., W.A. Horton, and R. Tye (1965). The carcinogenic potency of certain oils. Arch. Environ. Health 10:449-51.

6. Carruthers, W., H.N.M. Stewart, and D.A.M. Watkins (1967). 1,2-Benzanthracene derivatives in a Kuwait mineral oil. Nature 213:691-2.

7. Falk, H.L., P. Kotin, and A. Mehler (1964). Polycyclic hydrocarbons as carcinogens for man. Arch. Environ. Health 8:721-30.

8. Hueper, W.C. and W.W. Payne (1960). Carcinogenic studies on petroleum asphalt, cooling oil, and coal tar. Arch. Pathol. 70:372-84.

9. Cook, J.W., W. Carruthers, and D.L. Woodhouse (1958). Carcinogenicity of mineral oil fractions. Br. Med. Bull. 14:132-5.

10. Hueper, W.C. and H.J. Cahnmann (1958). Carcinogenic bioassay of benzo[a]pyrene-free fractions of American shale oils. Arch. Pathol. 65:608-14.

11. Cahnmann, H.J. (1955). Detection and quantitative determination of benzo[a]pyrene in American shale oil. Anal. Chem. 27:1235-40.

12. Hieger, I. and D.L. Woodhouse (1952). The value of the rabbit for carcinogenicity tests on petroleum fractions. Br. J. Cancer 6:293-9.

13. Gräf, W. and C. Winter (1968). 3,4-Benzpyren im erdöl. Arch. Hyg. (Athens) 152:289-93.

14. Twort, C.C. and J.M. Twort (1931). The carcinogenic potency of mineral oils. J. Ind. Hyg. 13:204-26.

15. Haughton, G. and A.C. Whitmore (1976). Genetics, the immune response and oncogenesis. Transplant. Rev. 28:75-97.

16. Baldwin, R.W. (1973). Immunological aspects of chemical carcinogenesis. Adv. Cancer Res. 18:1-75.

17. Prehn, R.T. (1963). Function of depressed immunologic reactivity during carcinogenesis. J. Natl. Cancer Inst. 31:791-805.

18. Stjernswärd, J. (1965). Immunodepressive effect of 3-methylcholanthrene. Antibody formation at the cellular levels and reaction against weak antigenic homografts. J. Natl. Cancer Inst. 35:885-92.

19. Stjernswärd, J. (1966). Effect of noncarcinogenic and carcinogenic hydrocarbons on antibody-forming cells measured at the cellular level *in vitro*. J. Natl. Cancer Inst. 36:1189-95.

20. Stjernswärd, J. (1967). Further immunological studies of chemical carcinogensis. J. Natl. Cancer Inst. 38:515-26.

21. Stjernswärd, J. (1969). Immunosuppression by carcinogens. Antibiot. Chemother. (Basel) 15:213-33.

22. Maugh, T.H. (1974). Chemical carcinogenesis: A long-neglected field blossoms. Science 183:940-4.

23. Matsuoka, Y., H. Senoh, T. Kawamoto, T. Kohmo, T. Hamaoka, and M. Kitagawa (1972). Failure of immunological memory in DMBA-treated mice. Nat. New Biol. 238: 273-4.

24. Kripke, M.L. and D.W. Weiss (1970). Studies on the immune responses of BALB/c mice during tumor induction by mineral oil. Int. J. Cancer 6:422-30.

25. Koller, L.D. (1973). Immunosuppression produced by lead, cadmium, and mercury. Am. J. Vet. Res. 34:1457-8.

26. Koller, L.D., J.H. Exon, and J.G. Roan (1975). Antibody suppression by cadmium. Arch. Environ. Health 30:598-601.

27. Cook, J.A., E.O. Hoffman, and N.R. Di Luzio (1975). Influence of lead and cadmium on the susceptibility of rats to bacterial challenge. Proc. Soc. Exp. Biol. Med. 150:748-54.

28. Hemphill, F.E., M.L. Kaeberle, and W.B. Buck (1971). Lead suppression of mouse resistance to *Salmonella typhimurium*. Science 172:1031-2.

29. Koller, L.D. and S. Kovacic (1974). Decreased antibody formation in mice exposed to lead. Nature 250:148-9.

30. Treagan, L. and A. Furst (1970). Inhibition of interferon synthesis in mammalian cell cultures after nickel treatment. Res. Commun. Chem. Pathol. Pharmacol. 1: 395-402.

31. Trejo, R.A., N.R. Di Luzio, L.D. Loose, and E. Hoffman (1972). Reticuloendothelial and hepatic functional alterations following lead acetate administration. Exp. Mol. Pathol. 17:145-58.

32. Robohm, R.A. and M.F. Nitkowski (1974). Physiological response of the cunner, *Tautogolabrus adspersus*, to cadmium. IV. Effects of the immune system. U.S. Natl. Mar. Fish. Serv. Spec. Sci. Rep. Fish. 681:15-20.

33. Treagan, L. (1975). Metals and the immune response. A review. Res. Commun. Chem. Pathol. Pharmacol. 12:189-220.

34. Lange, E. (1973). Carcinoid-like tumours in the pseudobranch of *Gadus morhua* L. Comp. Biochem. Physiol. 45: 477-81.

35. Takahashi, K. (1929). Studie über die fischgeschwülste. Z. Krebsforsch. 29:1-73.

36. Peyron, A. and L. Thomas (1929). Contribution à l'étude des tumeurs du revêtement branchial chez les poissons. Bull. Assoc. Fr. Etude Cancer 18:825-37.

37. Wellings, S.R. (1969). Neoplasia and primitive vertebrate phylogeny: Echinoderms, prevertebrates and fishes - A review. Natl. Cancer Inst. Monogr. 31, p. 59-128.

38. Alpers, C.E., B.B. McCain, M.S. Myers, and S.R. Wellings (1977). Pathology of pharyngeal tumors in Pacific cod, *Gadus macrocephalus*, of the Bering Sea. J. Natl. Cancer Inst., In press.

39. Stich, H. and C.R. Forrester (1977). Prevalence of gill tumors in Pacific cod (*Gadus macrocephalus*) off British Columbia. Cancer Res. Ctr., Univ. Brit. Col., Vancouver, B.C., Canada. In preparation.

40. McCain, B.B., M.S. Myers, W.D. Gronlund, and S.R. Wellings (1977). Baseline data on diseases of fishes from the Bering Sea for 1976. U.S. Natl. Mar. Fish. Serv., NWAFC, Seattle, Wash. Submitted for publication.

41. Levings, C.D. (1968). Report on groundfish cruise of C.G.S. *G.B. Reed* to Hecate Strait in February 1968. Fish. Res. Board Can. Rep. 62, 41 p.

42. Roberts, R.J. (1972). Oral carcinomata in a salmon (*Salmo salar* L.). Vet. Res. 91:199.

43. Schlumberger, H.G. and M. Katz (1956). Odontogenic tumors of salmon. Cancer Res. 16:369-70.

44. Kimura, I., T. Miyake, and Y. Ito (1967). Papillomatous growth in sole from Wakosa Bay area. Proc. Soc. Exp. Biol. Med. 125:175-7.

45. Mearns, A.J. and M. Sherwood (1974). Environmental aspects of fin erosion and tumors in southern California dover sole. Trans. Am. Fish. Soc. 103:799-810.

46. Cooper, R.C. and C.A. Keller (1969). Epizootiology of papillomas in English sole, *Parophrys vetulus*. Natl. Cancer Inst. Monogr. 31, p. 173-86.

47. Wellings, S.R., R.G. Chuinard, and M. Bens (1965). A comparative study of skin neoplasma in four species of pleuronectid fishes. Ann. N.Y. Acad. Sci. 146:479-501.

48. McArn, G.E., R.G. Chuinard, R.E. Brooks, and B.S. Miller (1968). Pathology of skin tumors found on English sole and starry flounder from Puget Sound, Washington. J. Natl. Cancer Inst. 41:229-42.

49. Johnstone, J. (1925). Malignant tumours in fishes. Proc. Liverp. Biol. Soc. 39:169-200.

50. Angell, C.L., B.S. Miller, and S.R. Wellings (1975). Epizootiology of tumors in a population of juvenile English sole (*Parophrys vetulus*) from Puget Sound, Washington. J. Fish. Res. Board Can. 32:1723-32.

51. Miller, B.S. and S.R. Wellings (1971). Epizootiology of tumors on flathead sole (*Hippoglossoides elassodon*) in East Sound, Orcas Island, Washington. Trans. Am. Fish. Soc. 100:247-66.

52. Brooks, R.E., G.E. McArn, and S.R. Wellings (1969). Ultrastructural observations on an unidentified cell type found in epidermal tumors of flounders. J. Natl. Cancer Inst. 43:97-100.

53. McCain, B.B. (1974). A tumor-specific cell in flatfish (Heterosomata) papillomas with an abnormally low DNA content. Proc. Am. Assoc. Cancer Res. 15:116.

54. Oota, K. (1952). An epidemic occurrence of tumor-like hyperplasia of epidermis in a species of fish, *Acanthogobius flavimanus*. Gann 43:264-5.

55. Imai, T. and N. Fujiwara (1959). An electron microscopic study of a papilloma-like hyperplastic growth in a gobi. Kyushu J. Med. Sci. 10:135-47.

56. Deys, B.F. (1969). Papillomas in the Atlantic eel, *Anguilla vulgaris*. Natl. Cancer Inst. Monogr. 31:187-94.

57. Koops, H., H. Mann, I. Pfitzner, O. Schmid, and G. Schubert (1970). The cauliflower disease of eels. Am. Fish. Soc. Spec. Publ. No. 5, p. 291-5.

58. Peters, G. (1975). Seasonal fluctuations in the incidence of epidermal papillomas of the European eel *Anguilla anguilla* L. J. Fish. Biol. 7:415-22.

59. Smith, G.M. (1934). A cutaneous red pigmented tumor (erythrophoroma) with mitostases, in a flatfish (*Pseudopleuronectes americanus*). Am. J. Cancer 21:596-9.

60. Johnstone, J. (1915). Diseased and abnormal conditions of marine fishes. Proc. Liverp. Biol. Soc. 29:80-113.

61. Mawdesley-Thomas, L.E. (1972). Some tumors of fish. In: Diseases of Fish (L.E. Mawdesley-Thomas, ed.), p. 191-284. Academic Press, London.

62. Harshbarger, J.C. and C.W. Bane (1969). Case report of fibrolipoma in a rockfish, *Sebastodes diploproa*. Natl. Cancer Inst. Monogr. 31:219-22.

63. Bergman, A.M. (1921). Einige geschwülste bei fischen: Rhabdomyom, Lipome und Melanom. Z. Krebsforsch. 18:292-302.

64. Williams, G. (1929). Tumourous growths in fish. Proc. Trans. Liverp. Biol. Soc. 43:120-48.

65. Thomas, L. (1933). Sur un lipome abdominal chez un colin. Bull. Assoc. Fr. Etude Cancer 22:419-35.

66. Thomas, L. (1932). Deux cas de tumeurs osseuses chez des téléosteens. Bull. Assoc. Fr. Etude Cancer 21:280-94.

67. Williams, G. (1931). On various fish tumors. Proc. Trans. Liverp. Biol. Soc. 45:98-104.

68. Thomas, L. (1932). Rhabdomyome chez un flet. Bull. Assoc. Fr. Etude Cancer 21:225-33.

69. Honma, Y. and Y. Hirosaki (1966). Histopathology on the tumors and endocrine glands of the immature chum salmon, *Onchorynchus keta*, reared in the Enoshima aquarium. Jpn. J. Iththyol. 14:74-83.

70. Haddow, A. and I. Blake (1933). Neoplasms in fish: A report of six cases with a summary of the literature. J. Pathol. Bacteriol. 36:41-7.

71. Wolke, R.E. and D.S. Wyand (1969). Ocular lymphosarcoma of an Atlantic cod. Bull. Wildl. Dis. Assoc. 5:401-3.

72. Lucké, B. (1942). Tumors of the nerve sheaths in fish of the snapper family (*Lutranidae*). Arch. Pathol. 34:133-50.

73. McArn, G. and S.R. Wellings (1967). Neuofibroma in a teleost fish, *Lumpenus sagitta*. J. Fish. Res. Board Can. 24:2007-9.

74. Ashley, L.M., J.E. Halver, and S.R. Wellings (1969). Case reports of three teleost neoplasms. Natl. Cancer Inst. Monogr. 31, p. 157-66.

75. Takahashi, K. (1934). Studies on tumours of fishes from Japanese waters. Proc. Pac. Sci. Congr. 5:4151-5.

76. Harshbarger, J.C. (1972). Work of the registry of tumours in lower animals with emphasis on fish neoplasms. In: Diseases of Fish (L.E. Mawdesley-Thomas, ed.), p. 285-303. Academic Press, London.

77. Helmboldt, C.F. and D.S. Wjand (1971). Nephroblastoma in a striped bass. J. Wildl. Dis. 7:162-5.

78. Sparks, A.K., G.B. Pauley, R.R. Bates, and C.S. Sayce (1964). A mesenchymal tumor in a Pacific oyster, *Crassostrea gigas* (Thurberg). J. Invertebr. Pathol. 6:448-52.

79. Sparks, A.K., G.B. Pauley, and K.K. Chew (1969). A second mesenchymal tumor from a Pacific oyster (*Crassostrea gigas*). Proc. Natl. Shellfish. Assoc. 59:35-9.

80. Newman, M.W. (1972). An oyster neoplasm of apparent mesenchymal origin. J. Natl. Cancer Inst. 48:237-43.

81. Farley, C.A. (1969). Probable neoplastic disease of the hematopoietic system in oyster, *Crassostrea virginica* and *Crassostrea gigas*. Natl. Cancer Inst. Monogr. 31, p. 541-55.

82. Couch, J.A. (1969). An unusual lesion in the mantle of the American oyster, *Crassostrea virginica*. Natl. Cancer Inst. Monogr. 31, p. 557.

83. Farley, C.A. and A.K. Sparks (1970). Proliferative diseases of hemocytes, endothelial cells, and connective tissue cells of mollusks. Comp. Leukemia Res. 36:610-7.

84. Farley, C.A. (1969). Sarcomatid proliferative disease in a wild population of blue mussels (*Mytilus edulis*). J. Natl. Cancer Inst. 43:509-16.

85. Pauley, G.B. and C.S. Sayce (1968). An internal fibrous tumor in a Pacific oyster, *Crassostrea gigas*. J. Invertebr. Pathol. 10:1-8.

86. Pauley, G.B. and T.C. Cheng (1968). A tumor on the si-
phons of a soft-shell clam (*Mya arenaria*). J. Invertebr.
Pathol. 11:504-6.

87. Des Voigne, D.M., M.C. Mix, and G.B. Pauley (1970). A
papilloma-like growth on the siphon of the horse clam,
Tresus nuttali. J. Invertebr. Pathol. 15:262-70.

88. Pauley, G.B. (1967). A butter clam (*Saxidomus giganteus*)
with a polypoid-tumor on the foot. J. Invertebr. Pathol.
9:577-9.

89. Sparks, A.K. (1972). Invertebrate Pathology: Noncommu-
nicable diseases. Academic Press, New York, 387 p.

90. Christensen, D.J., C.A. Farley, and F.G. Kern (1974).
Epizootic neoplasms in the clam *Macoma balthica* (L.) from
Chesapeake Bay. J. Natl. Cancer Inst. 52:1739.

91. Barry, M.M., P.P. Yevich, and N.H. Thayer (1971). Atypical hyperplasia in the soft-shell clam *Mya arenaria*. J.
Invertebr. Pathol. 17:17-27.

92. Barry, M. and P.P. Yevich (1975). The ecological, chemical, and histopathological evaluation of an oil spill
site: Part III. Histopathological studies. Mar.
Pollut. Bull. 6(11):171-3.

93. Barry, M.M. and P.P. Yevich (1972). Incidence of gonadal
cancer in quahaug *Mercenaria mercenaria*. Oncology 26:
87-96.

94. Newman, M.W. (1970). A possible neoplastic blood disease
of blue crabs. Comp. Leukemia Res. 36:648.

95. Sparks, A.K. and D.V. Lightner (1973). A tumor-like pap-
illiform growth in the brown shrimp (*Penaeus aztecus*).
J. Invertebr. Pathol. 22:203-12.

96. Oppenheimer, C.H. (1962). On marine fish diseases. In:
Fish as Food (G. Borgstrom, ed.), Vol. 2, p. 541.
Academic Press, New York.

97. Sindermann, C.J. (1970). Principal Diseases of Marine
Fish and Shellfish. Academic Press, New York, 369 p.

98. Anderson, J.I.W. and D.A. Conroy (1970). *Vibrio* disease
in marine fishes. Am. Fish. Soc. Spec. Publ. 5,
p. 266-72.

99. Levin, M.A., R.E. Wolke, and V.J. Cabelli (1972). *Vibrio
anguillarum* as a cause of disease in winter flounder
(*Pseudopleuronectes americanus*). Can. J. Microbiol. 18:
1585-92.

100. Traxler, G.S. and M.F. Li (1972). *Vibrio anguillarum*
isolated from a nasal abscess of the cod fish (*Gadus
morhua*). J. Wildl. Dis. 8:207-14.

101. Haastein, T. and G. Holt (1972). The occurrence of
Vibrio disease in wild Norwegian fish. J. Fish. Biol.
4:33-7.

102. Evelyn, T.P.T. (1971). An aberrant strain of the bacterial fish pathogen *Aeromonas salmonicida* isolated from a marine host, the sablefish (*Anoplopoma fibria*), and from two species of cultured Pacific salmon. J. Fish. Res. Board Can. 28:1629-34.

103. Rucker, R.R. (1959). *Vibrio* infections among marine and freshwater fish. Prog. Fish-Cult. 21:22-4.

104. Cisar, J.O. and F.L. Fryer (1969). An epizootic vibriosis in chinook salmon. Bull. Wildl. Dis. Assoc. 5:73-6.

105. Harrell, L.W., A.J. Novotny, M.H. Schiewe, and H.O. Hodgins (1976). Isolation and description of two *vibrios* pathogenic to Pacific salmon in Puget Sound, Washington. Fish. Bull. 74:447-9.

106. McCarthy, D.H., J.P. Stevenson, and M.S. Roberts (1974). Vibriosis in rainbow trout. J. Wildl. Dis. 10:2-7.

107. ZoBell, C.E. and N.A. Wells (1934). An infectious dermatitis of certain marine fishes. J. Infect. Dis. 55: 299-305.

108. Hodgkiss, W. and J.M. Shewan (1950). *Pseudomonas* infection in a plaice. J. Pathol. Bacteriol. 62:655-7.

109. Shewan, J.M. (1963). The differentiation of certain genera if gram negative bacteria frequently encountered in marine environments. In: Symposium on Marine Microbiology (C.H. Oppenheimer, ed.), p. 499. Thomas, Chicago.

110. Mahoney, J.B., F.H. Midlige, and D.G. Deuel (1973). A fin rot disease of marine and eurhyanline fishes in the New York Bight. Trans. Am. Fish. Soc. 102:596-605.

111. Rucker, R.R., B.J. Earp, and E.J. Ordal (1954). Infectious diseases of Pacific salmon. Trans. Am. Fish. Soc. 83:297-312.

112. Wolke, R.E. (1975). Pathology of bacterial and fungal diseases affecting fish. In: The Pathology of Fishes (W.E. Ribelin and G. Migaki, eds.), p. 33-116. University of Wisconsin Press, Madison.

113. Sindermann, C.J. (1974). Diagnosis and control of mariculture diseases in the United States. U.S. Natl. Mar. Fish. Serv. Rep. 2, 306 p.

114. Hoskins, G.E., G.R. Bell, and T.P.T. Evelyn (1976). The occurrence, distribution and significance of infectious diseases and of neoplasms observed in fish in the Pacific region up to the end of 1974. Fisheries Marine Service of Canada Tech. Rept. 609, 37 p.

115. Scott, M. (1968). The pathogenicity of *Aeromonas salmonicida* (Griffin) in sea and brackish waters. J. Gen. Microbiol. 50:321-7.

116. Wood, J.W. (1959). Ichthyophthiriasis and furunculosis in adult Pacific salmon. Prog. Fish-Cult. 21:171.

117. Johnstone, J. (1913). Diseased conditions in fishes. Proc. Liverp. Biol. Soc. 27:196-218.

118. Sutherland, P.L. (1922).   A tuberculosis-like disease in a saltwater fish (halibut) associated with the presence of an acid-fast tubercle-like bacillus.   J. Pathol. Bacteriol. 25:31-5.

119. Wood, J.W. and E.J. Ordal (1958).   Tuberculosis in Pacific salmon and steelhead trout.   Fish. Commission Oregon Contrib. 25, 38 p.

120. Ross, A.J. (1970).   Mycobacteriosis among Pacific salmonid fishes.   Am. Fish. Soc. Spec. Publ. 5, p. 279-83.

121. Conroy, D.A. (1970).   Piscine tuberculosis in the sea water environment.   Am. Fish. Soc. Spec. Publ. 5, p. 273-8.

122. Snieszko, S.F., G.L. Bullock, E. Hollis, and J.G. Boone (1964).   *Pasteurella* sp. from an epizootic of white perch (*Roccus americanus*) in Chesapeake Bay tidewater areas.   J. Bacteriol. 88:1814-5.

123. Lewis, D.H., L.C. Grumbles, S. McConnell, and A.I. Flowers (1970).   *Pasteurella*-like bacteria from an epizootic in menhaden and mullet in Galveston Bay.   J. Wildl. Dis. 6:160-2.

124. Wood, J.W. and F. Wallis (1955).   Kidney disease in adult chinook salmon and its transmission by feeding to young chinook salmon.   Oregon Fish. Comm. Res. Briefs 6:32-40.

125. Smith, I.W. (1964).   The occurrence and pathology of the Dee disease.   Scotl. Dep. Agric. Fish. Mar. Res. 34:3.

126. Bell, G.R. (1961).   Two epidemics of apparent kidney disease in cultured pink salmon (*Oncorhynchus gorbuscha*).   J. Fish. Res. Board Can. 18:559-62.

127. Pacha, R.E. and E.J. Ordal (1970).   Myxobacterial diseases of salmonids.   Am. Fish. Soc. Spec. Publ. 5, p. 243-57.

128. Sindermann, C.J. and A. Rosenfield (1967).   Principal diseases of commercially important marine bivalve mollusca and crustacea.   Fish. Bull. 66:335-85.

129. Bright, D.B., F.E. Durham, and J.W. Knudsen (1960).   King crab investigations of Cook Inlet, Alaska.   Unpublished report.   Allen Hancock Foundation, University of Southern California, Los Angeles.

130. Schaperclaus, W. (1954).   Fischkrankheiten I-XII. Akademie-Verlag, Berlin, 708 p.

131. Rosen, B. (1970).   Shell disease of aquatic crustaceans. Am. Fish. Soc. Spec. Publ. 5, p. 409-15.

132. Rosen, B. (1967).   Shell disease of the blue crab *Callinectes sapidus*.   J. Invertebr. Pathol. 8:348-53.

133. Cook, D.W. and S.R. Lofton (1973).   Chitinoclastic bacteria associated with shell disease in *Penaeus* shrimp and the blue crab (*Callinectes sapidus*).   J. Wildl. Dis. 9: 154-9.

134. Krantz, G.E., R.R. Colwell, and E. Lovelace (1969).
Vibrio parahaemolyticus from the blue crab *Callinectes sapidus* in Chesapeake Bay. Science 164:1286-7.

135. Lightner, D.V. and D.H. Lewis (1975). A septicemic bacterial disease syndrome of penaeid shrimp. U.S. Natl. Mar. Fish. Serv. Mar. Fish. Rev. 37:25-8.

136. Tubiash, H.S., P.E. Chanley, and E. Leifson (1965). Bacillary necrosis, a disease of larval and juvenile bivalve mollusks. I. Etiology and epizootiology. J. Bacteriol. 90:1036-44.

137. Guillard, R.R.L. (1959). Further evidence of the destruction of bivalve larvae by bacteria. Biol. Bull. (Woods Hole) 117:258-66.

138. Stewart, J.E. (1975). Gaffkemia, the fatal infection of lobsters (genus *Homarus*) caused by *Aerococcus virdinans* (var) *homari*: A review. U.S. Natl. Mar. Fish. Serv. Mar. Fish. Rev. 37:20-4.

139. Bell, G.R. and G.E. Hoskins (1966). Experimental transmission of the lobster pathogen, *Gaffkya homari*), to Pacific crabs and prawns. In: 16th Annual Meeting, Canadian Society of Microbiology, Saskatoon, 1 p. (abstract).

140. Perkins, E.J., J.R.S. Gilchrist, and O.J. Abbott (1972). Incidence of epidermal lesions in fish of the northeast Irish Sea area, 1971. Nature 238:101-3.

141. Shelton, R.G.J. and K.W. Wilson (1973). On the occurrence of lymphocystis, with notes on other pathological conditions, in the flatfish stocks of the northeast Irish Sea. Aquaculture 2:395-409.

142. Russell, P.H. (1974). Lymphocystis in wild plaice *Pleuronectes platessa* (L.), and flounder, *Platichthys flesus* (L.), in British coastal waters: A histopathological and serological study. J. Fish. Biol. 6:771-8.

143. Aneer, G. and O. Ljungberg (1976). Lymphocystis disease in Baltic herring (*Clupea harengus* var. *membras* L.). J. Fish. Biol. 8:345-50.

144. Weissenberg, R. (1965). Fifty years of research on the lymphocystis virus disease of fishes (1914-1964). Ann. N.Y. Acad. Sci. 126:362-81.

145. Templeman, W. (1965). Lymphocystis disease in American plaice of the eastern Grand Bank. J. Fish. Res. Board Can. 22:1345-56.

146. Murchelano, R.A. and D.W. Bridges (1976). Lymphocystis disease in the winter flounder, *Pseudopleuronectes americanus*. J. Wildl. Dis. 12:101-3.

147. Yasutake, W.T. (1975). Fish viral diseases: Clinical, histopathological and comparative aspects. In: The Pathology of Fishes (W.E. Ribelin and G. Migaki, eds.), p. 247. University of Wisconsin Press, Madison.

148. Wolf, K. (1962). Experimental propagation of lympho-cystis disease in fishes. Virology 18:249-56.
149. Laird, M. and W.L. Bullock (1969). Marine fish hemato-zoa from New Brunswick and New England. J. Fish. Res. Board Can. 26:1075-102.
150. Sherburne, S.W. (1973). Erythrocyte degeneration in the Atlantic herring, *Clupea harengus harengus* L. Fish. Bull. 71:125-34.
151. Johnston, M.R.L. and A.J. Davies (1973). A pirhemocyton-like parasite of the blenny, *Blennius pholis* L. (Tele-ostei:Blenniidae) and its relationship to *Immunoplasma neuman*, 1909. Int. J. Parasitol. 3:235-41.
152. Bell, G.R. and L. Margolis (1976). The fish health pro-gram and the occurrence of fish diseases in the Pacific region of Canada. Fish Pathol. 10:115-22.
153. Evelyn, T.P.T. (1975). Personal communication. Fisheries Research Board of Canada Biological Station, Nanaimo, B.C., Canada.
154. Walker, R. (1971). PEN, a viral lesion of fish erythro-cytes. Am. Zool. 11:707 (abstract).
155. Amend, D.F. and F.W. Wood (1972). Survey for infectious hematopoietic necrosis (IHN) virus in Washington salmon. Prog. Fish-Cult. 34:143-7.
156. Farley, C.A., W.G. Banfield, G. Kasnic, Jr., and W.S. Foster (1972). Oyster herpes-types virus. Science 178: 759-76.
157. Bang, F.B. (1971). Transmissible disease, probably viral in origin, affecting the amebocytes of the European shore crab, *Carcinus maenas*. Infect. Immun. 3:617-33.
158. Sindermann, C.J. (1963). Disease in marine populations. Trans. N. Am. Wildl. Nat. Resour. Conf. 28:336-56.
159. Sproston, N.G. (1947). *Ichthyosporidium hoferi* (Plehn and Mulsow), on internal fungoid parasite of the mackerel. J. Mar. Biol. Assoc. U.K. 26:72-98.
160. Reichenbach-Klinke, H. (1955). Pilze in tumoren bei fischen. Verhandl-Deut. Zool. Ges. Tubingen, p. 351-7.
161. Reichenbach-Klinke, H. and E. Elkan (1965). The Princi-pal Diseases of Lower Vertebrates. Academic Press, London, 600 p.
162. Stuart, M.R. and H.T. Fuller (1968). Mycological aspects of diseased Atlantic salmon. Nature 217:90-2.
163. Allen, R.L., T.K. Meekin, G.B. Pauley, and M.P. Fujihara (1968). Mortality among chinook salmon associated with the fungus *Dermocystidium*. J. Fish. Res. Board Can. 25: 2467-75.
164. Umphlett, C.J. and E.M. McCray, Jr. (1975). A brief re-view of the involvements of *Lagenidium*, an aquatic fungus parasite, with arthropods. U.S. Natl. Mar. Fish. Serv. Mar. Fish. Rev. 37:61-4.

165. Scott, W.W. (1962). The aquatic phycomycetous flora of marine and brackish waters in the vicinity of Gloucester Point, Virginica. Va. Inst. Mar. Sci. Spec. Sci. Rep. 36, 16 p.

166. Johnson, T.W., Jr. (1970). Fungi in marine crustaceans. Am. Fish. Soc. Spec. Publ. 5, p. 405-8.

167. Lightner, D.V. and C.T. Fontaine (1973). A new fungus disease of the white shrimp *Penaeus setiferus*. J. Invertebr. Pathol. 22:94-9.

168. Nilson, E.H., W.S. Fisher, and R.A. Shleser (1976). A new mycosis of larval lobster (*Homarus americanus*). J. Invertebr. Pathol. 27:177-83.

169. Mackin, J.G., H.M. Owen, and A. Collier (1950). Preliminary note on the occurrence of a new protistan parasite, *Dermocystidium marinum* n.sp. in *Crassostrea virginica* (Gmelin). Science 111:328-9.

170. Atkins, D. (1954). A marine fungus *Plectospira dubia* n.sp. (Saprolegniaceae), infecting crustacean eggs and small crustacea. J. Mar. Biol. Assoc. U.K. 33:721-32.

171. Davis, H.C., V.L. Loosanoff, W.H. Weston, and C. Martin (1974). A fungus disease in clam and oyster larvae. Science 120:36-8.

172. Van Hyning, J.M. and A.M. Scarborough (1973). Identification of fungal encrustation on the shell of the snow crab (*Chionoecetes bairdi*). J. Fish. Res. Board Can. 30:1738-9.

173. Wolfgang, R.W. (1954). Studies of the trematode *Stephanostomum baccatum* (Nicoll). II. Biology, with special reference to the stages affecting the winter flounder. J. Fish. Res. Board Can. 11:963-87.

174. Arai, H.P. (1967). Ecological specificity of parasites of some embiotocid fishes. J. Fish. Res. Board Can. 24:2161-8.

175. Scott, D.M. and W.R. Martin (1957). Variation in the incidence of larval nematodes in Atlantic cod fillets along the southern Canadian mainland. J. Fish. Res. Board Can. 14:975-96.

176. Templeman, W., H.J. Squires, and A.M. Fleming (1957). Nematodes in the fillets of cod and other fishes in Newfoundland and neighboring areas. J. Fish. Res. Board Can. 14:831-97.

177. Margolis, L. (1970). A bibliography of parasites and diseases of fishes of Canada: 1879-1969. Fish. Res. Board Can. Tech. Rep. 185, 38 p.

178. Margolis, L. (1953). Milkiness in lemon sole fillets. Fish. Res. Board Can. Ann. Rep. Pac. Biol. Stn. 11953, p. 158.

179. Patashnik, M. and H.S. Groninger (1964). Observations on the milky condition of some Pacific coast fishes. J. Fish. Res. Board Can. 21:335-46.

180. Weissenberg, R. (1921). Zur wirtsgewegesabteilung des plasmakorpers der *Glugea anomalacysten*. Arch. Protistenkd. 43:400-21.

181. Nigrelli, R.F. (1946). Studies on the marine resources of southern New England. V. Parasites and diseases of the ocean pout *Macrozoarces americanus*. Bull. Bingham Oceanogr. Collect. Yale Univ. 9:187-221.

182. Polzanski, Y.I. (1955). Contributions to the parasitology of fishes of the northern seas of the USSR. Tr. Zool. Inst. Akad. Nauk. SSSR 19:5-170.

183. Arai, H.P. (1969). A new trematode of the genus *Lepidophyllum* (Digenea:Steganodermatidae) from a cottid fish, *Hemilepidotus hemilepidotus*. J. Fish. Res. Board Can. 26:799-803.

184. Mann, H. (1954). Die wirtschaftliche bedeutung von krankheiten bei seefischen. Fischwirtschaft 6:38-9.

185. MacKay, D.C. (1942). The Pacific edible crab, *Cancer magister*. Fish. Res. Board Can. Bull. 62:1-32.

186. Sparks, A.K. and W.T. Pereyra (1966). Benthic invertebrates of the southeastern Chukchi Sea. In: Environment of the Cape Thompson Region, Alaska (N.J. Wilimovsky, ed.), p. 811-38. U.S. Atomic Energy Commission, Washington, D.C.

187. Rosenfield, A. (1964). Studies of oyster microparasites. U.S. Fish Wildl. Serv. Circ. 200, p. 30-7.

188. Sparks, A.K. (1962). Metaplasia of the gut of the oyster, *Crassostrea gigas* (Thunberg) caused by infection with the copepod *Mytilicola orientalis* Mori. J. Insect Pathol. 4:57-62.

189. Korringa, P. (1968). On the ecology and distribution of the parasitic copepod *Mytilicola intestinalis* Steuer. Bijdr. Dierkd. 38:47-57.

190. Tester, A.L. (1942). Herring mortality along the southeast coast of Vancouver Island. Fish. Res. Board Can. Prog. Rep. 52, p. 11-5.

191. Stevenson, J.C. (1949). The mortality of herring at Mud Bay, March, 1949. Fish. Res. Board Can. Circ. 18, p. 1-3.

192. Westman, J.R. and R.F. Nigrelli (1955). Preliminary studies of menhaden and their mass mortalities in Long Island and New Jersey waters. N.Y. Fish Game J. 2:142-3.

193. Foerster, R. (1942). The mortality of young pilchards, 1941. Fish. Res. Board Can. Prog. Rep. 48, p. 3-8.

194. Wellings, S.R., C.E. Alpers, B.B. McCain, and B.S. Miller (1976). Fin erosion disease of starry flounder (*Platichthys stellatus*) and English sole (*Parophrys vetulus*) in the estuary of the Duwamish River, Seattle, Washington. J. Fish. Res. Board Can. 33:2577-86.

195. Murchelano, R.A. (1975). The histopathology of fin rot disease in winter flounder from the New York Bight. J. Wildl. Dis. 11:263-8.

196. Ziskowski, J. and R. Murchelano (1975). Fin erosion in winter flounder (*Pseudopleuronectes americanus*) from the New York Bight. Mar. Pollut. Bull. 6:26-8.

197. Bullock, G., D.A. Conroy, and S.F. Snieszko (1971). Bacterial diseases of fishes. In: Diseases of Fishes (S.F. Snieszko and H.R. Axelrod, eds.), p. 7-151. T.F.H. Publications, Jersey City, N.J.

198. Sherwood, M. and B. McCain (1976). A comparison of fin erosion disease: Los Angeles and Seattle. In: Coastal Water Research Project. Annual Report of the Southern California Coastal Water Research Project, El Segundo, Calif., p. 143-7.

199. Couch, J.A. (1975). Histopathological effects of pesticides and related chemicals on the livers of fishes. In: The Pathology of Fishes (W.E. Ribelin and G. Migaki, eds.), p. 1003. University of Wisconsin Press, Madison.

200. Pierce, K., B. McCain, and S.R. Wellings (1976). Histopathology of abnormal livers and other organs in the starry flounder from the Duwamish River, Seattle, Washington. Dep. Med.-Path., Univ. Calif., Davis. Manuscript in preparation.

201. Roberts, R.J. (1972). Ulcerative dermal necrosis (UDN) of salmon (*Salmo salar* L.). In: Diseases of Fish (L.E. Mawdesley-Thomas, ed.), p. 380. Academic Press, London.

202. French, R.F. (1965). Visceral adhesions in high-seas salmon. Trans. Am. Fish. Soc. 94:177-81.

203. Woelke, C.E. (1961). Pacific oyster *Crassostrea gigas* mortalities with notes on common oyster predators in Washington waters. Proc. Natl. Shellfish. Assoc. 50: 53-66.

204. Medcof, J.C. and N. Bourne (1964). Causes of mortality of the sea scallop, *Placopecten magellanicus*. Proc. Natl. Shellfish. Assoc. 53:33-50.

205. Davis, B.D., R. Dulbecco, H.N. Eisen, H.S. Ginsberg, B.W. Wood, and M. McCarty (1973). Microbiology, p. 629-30. Harper & Row, New York.

206. Ridgway, G.J., H.O. Hodgins, and G.W. Klontz (1966). The immune response in teleosts. In: Phylogeny of Immunity (R.T. Smith, P.A. Miescher, and R.A. Good, eds.), p. 199-207. University of Florida Press, Gainesville.

207. Papermaster, B.W., R.M. Condie, J. Finstad, and R.A. Good (1964). Evolution of the immune response. I. The phylogenetic development of adaptive immunologic responsiveness in vertebrates. J. Exp. Med. 119:105-30.

208. Hildemann, W.H. (1970). Transplantation immunity in fishes: Agnatha, Chondrichthyes, and Osteichthyes. Transplant. Proc. 2:253-9.

209. Bang, F.B. (1975). Phagocytosis in invertebrates. In: Invertebrate Immunity (K. Maramorosch and R.E. Shope, eds.), p. 137-51. Academic Press, New York.

210. Anderson, R.S. (1975). Phagocytosis by invertebrate cells in vitro: Biochemical events and other characteristics compared with vertebrate phagocytic systems. In: Invertebrate Immunity (K. Maramorosch and R.E. Shope, eds.), p. 153-80. Academic Press, New York.

211. Tripp, M.R. (1975). Humoral factors and molluscan immunity. In: Invertebrate Immunity (K. Maramorsch and R.E. Shope, eds.), p. 201-23. Academic Press, New York.

212. Chadwick, J.S. (1975). Hemolymph changes with infection or induced immunity in insects and ticks. In: Invertebrate Immunity (K. Maramorsch and R.E. Shope, eds.), p. 241-71. Academic Press, New York.

213. Evans, E.E., P.F. Weinheimer, R.T. Acton, and J.E. Cushing (1969). Induced bactericidal response in a sipunculid worm. Nature 223:695.

214. Acton, R.T., P.F. Weinheimer, and E.E. Evans (1969). A bactericidal system in the lobster Homarus americanus. J. Invertebr. Pathol. 12:463-4.

215. Weinheimer, P.F., R.T. Acton, S. Sawyer, and E.E. Evans (1969). Specificity of the induced bactericidin of the West Indian spiny lobsters, Panulirus argus. J. Bacteriol. 98:947-8.

216. Prowse, R.N. and N.N. Tait (1969). In vitro phagocytosis by amoebocytes from the haemolymph of Helix aspera (Muller). I. Evidence for opsonic factor(s) in serum. Immunology 17:437-43.

217. Burnet, F.M. (1974). Invertebrate precursors to immune responses. In: Contemporary Topics in Immunobiology (E.L. Cooper, ed.), Vol. 4, p. 13-24. Plenum Press, New York.

218. Cooper, E.L. (1969). Specific tissue graft rejection in earthworms. Science 166:1414-5.

219. Weiser, R.S., Q.N. Myrvik, and N.N. Pearsall (1969). Fundamentals of Immunology, p. 305-22. Lea & Febiger, Philadelphia.

220. Boyden, S.V. (1966). Natural antibodies and the immune response. Adv. Immunol. 5:1-28.

221. Harvey, W.R. and J.T. Blankenmeyer (1975). Epithelial structure and function. In: Invertebrate Immunity (E. Maramorsch and R.E. Shope, eds.), p. 3-23. Academic Press, New York.

222. Orihel, T.C. (1975). The peritrophic membrane: Its role as a barrier to infection of the arthropod host. In: Invertebrate Immunity (K. Maramorsch and R.E. Shope, eds.), p. 65-73. Academic Press, New York.

223. Fletcher, T.C. and P.T. Grant (1969). Immunoglobulins in the serum and mucus of the plaice (*Pleuronectes platessa*). Biochem. J. 115:65.

224. Fletcher, T.C. and A. White (1973). Antibody production in the plaice (*Pleuronectes platessa* L.) after oral and parenteral immunization with *Vibrio anguillarum* antigens. Aquaculture 1:417-28.

225. Bradshaw, C.M., A.S. Richard, and M.M. Sigel (1970). IgM antibodies in fish mucus. Proc. Soc. Exp. Biol. Med. 136:1122-4.

226. Di Conza, J.J. (1970). Some characteristics of natural haemaglutinins found in serum and mucus of the catfish, *Tachysurus australis*. Aust. J. Exp. Biol. Med. Sci. 48: 515-23.

227. Harrell, L.W., H.M. Etlinger, and H.O. Hodgins (1976). Humoral factors important in resistance of salmonid fish to bacterial disease. 2. Anti-*Vibrio anguillarum* activity in mucus and observations on complement. Aquaculture 7:363-70.

228. Cooper, E.L. (1976). Comparative Immunology. Prentice-Hall, Englewood Cliffs, N. J., 338 p.

229. Cooper, E.L. (1974). Contemporary Topics in Immunobiology, Vol. 4. Plenum Press, New York, 299 p.

230. Maramorsch, K. and R.E. Shope (1975). Invertebrate Immunity. Academic Press, New York, 365 p.

231. Anon. (1972). Invertebrate Immune Defense Mechanisms. MSS Inf. Corp., New York, 204 p.

232. Hildemann, W.H. (1974). Phylogeny of immune responsiveness in invertebrates. Life Sci. 14:605-14.

233. Marchalonis, J.J. and R.E. Cone (1973). The phylogenetic emergence of vertebrate immunity. Aust. J. Exp. Biol. Med. Sci. 51:461-88.

234. Corbel, M.J. (1975). The immune response in fish: A review. J. Fish. Biol. 7:539-63.

235. Ellis, A.E. and A.L.S. Munroe (1976). Defense mechanisms in fish. 1. A study of the phagocytic system and the fate of intraperitoneally injected particulate material in the plaice (*Pleuronectes platessa* L.). J. Fish. Biol. 8:67-78.

236. Cooper, E.L. (1973). The thymus and lymphomyeloid system in poikilothermic vertebrates. In: Contemporary Topics in Immunobiology (A.J.S. Davies and R.L. Carter, eds.), Vol. 3, p. 13-38. Plenum Press, New York.
237. Anon. (1972). Phylogenetic Development of Vertebrate Immunity: I. MSS Inf. Corp., New York, 208 p.
238. Anon. (1972). Phylogenetic Development of Vertebrate Immunity: II. MSS Inf. Corp., New York, 174 p.
239. Hildemann, W.H. and A.A. Benedict (1975). Immunologic Phylogeny. Advances in Experimental Medicine and Biology. Vol. 64. Plenum Press, New York, 485 p.
240. Weiser, R.S., Q.N. Myrvik, and N.N. Pearsall (1969). Fundamentals of Immunology, p. 322-5. Lea & Febiger, Philadelphia.
241. Park, B.H. and R.A. Good (1974). Principles of Modern Immunobiology, p. 274-85. Lea & Febiger, Philadelphia.
242. Park, B.H. and R.A. Good (1974). Principles of Modern Immunobiology, p. 268-74. Lea & Febiger, Philadelphia.
243. Park, B.H. and R.A. Good (1974). Principles of Modern Immunobiology, p. 284. Lea & Febiger, Philadelphia.
244. Weiser, R.S., Q.N. Myrvik, and N.N. Pearsall (1969). Fundamentals of Immunology, p. 325-7. Lea & Febiger, Philadelphia.
245. Davis, B.D., R. Dulbecco, H.N. Eisen, H.S. Ginsberg, B.W. Wood, and M. McCarty (1973). Microbiology, p. 558-81. Harper & Row, New York.
246. Zinkernagel, R.M. (1976). Cell-mediated response to *Salmonella typhimurium* infection in mice: Development of nonspecific bactericidal activity against *Listeria monocytogenes*. Infect. Immun. 13:1069-73.
247. Mackaness, G.B. and R.V. Blanden (1970). Cellular immunity. In: Infectious Agents and Host Reactions (S. Mudd, ed.), p. 22-60. Saunders, Philadelphia.
248. Burnet, F.M. (1970). The concept of immunological surveillance. Prog. Exp. Tumor Res. 13:1-27.
249. Ritts, R.E. and H.B. Neel (1974). An overview of cancer immunology. Mayo Clin. Proc. 49:118-31.
250. Zisblatt, M. and F. Lilly (1972). The effect of immunosuppression on oncogenesis by murine sarcoma virus. Proc. Soc. Exp. Biol. Med. 141:1036-40.
251. Cerilli, J. and D. Hattan (1974). Immunosuppression and oncogenesis. Am. J. Clin. Pathol. 62:218-23.
252. Kersey, J.H., B.D. Spector, and R.A. Good (1973). Immunodeficiency and cancer. In: Advances in Cancer Research (G. Klein, S. Weinhouse, and A. Haddow, eds.), Vol. 18, p. 211-30. Academic Press, New York.
253. Penn, I. and T.E. Starzl (1973). Immunosuppression and cancer. Transplant. Proc. 5:943-7.

254. Kripke, M.L. and T. Borsos (1974). Immunosuppression and carcinogenesis: A review. In: Immunological Parameters of Host-Tumor Relationships (D.A. Weiss, ed.), Vol. 3, p. 74-89. Academic Press, New York.

255. Kersey, J.H., B.D. Spector, and R.A. Good (1973). Primary immunodeficiency diseases and cancer: The immunodeficiency-cancer registry. Int. J. Cancer 12:333-47.

256. Schein, P.S., and S.H. Winokur (1975). Immunosuppressive and cytotoxic chemotherapy: Long-term complications. Ann. Intern. Med. 82:84-95.

257. Wagner, J.L. and G. Haughton (1971). Immunosuppression by anti-lymphocyte serum and its effect on tumors induced by 3-methylcholanthrene in mice. J. Natl. Cancer Inst. 46:1-10.

258. Stutman, O. (1974). Tumor development after 3-methylcholanthrene in immunologically deficient athymic-nude mice. Science 183:534-6.

259. Davis, B.D., R. Dulbecco, H.N. Eisen, H.S. Ginsberg, B.W. Wood, and M. McCarty (1973). Microbiology, p. 456-63. Harper & Row, New York.

260. Hodgins, H.O., R.S. Weiser, and G.J. Ridgway (1967). The nature of antibodies and the immune response in rainbow trout (*Salmo gairdneri*). J. Immunol. 99:534-44.

261. Hodgins, H.O. (1972). Serological and biochemical studies in racial identification of fishes. In: The Stock Concept in Pacific Salmon (R.C. Simon and P.A. Larkin, eds.), p. 199-208. University of British Columbia, Vancouver.

262. Evelyn, T.P.T. (1971). The agglutinin response in sockeye salmon vaccinated intraperitoneally with a heat-killed preparation of the bacterium responsible for salmonid kidney disease. J. Wildl. Dis. 7:328-35.

263. Haimovich, J. and L. DuPasquier (1973). Specificity of antibodies in amphibian larvae possessing a small number of lymphocytes. Proc. Natl. Acad. Sci. 70:1898-1902.

264. Oosterlee, C.C. (1972). Chicken iso-immune red cell agglutinins produced by plasma injections. Anim. Blood Groups Biochem. Genet. 3:181-4.

265. Chiller, J.M., H.O. Hodgins, and R.S. Weiser (1969). Antibody response in rainbow trout (*Salmo gairdneri*). II. Studies on the kinetics of development of antibody-producing cells and on complement and natural hemolysin. J. Immunol. 102:1202-7.

266. Spence, K.D., J.L. Fryer, and K.S. Pilcher (1965). Active and passive immunization of certain salmonid fishes against *Aeromonas salmonicida*. Can. J. Microbiol. 11:397-405.

267. Harrell, L.W., H.M. Etlinger, and H.O. Hodgins (1975). Humoral factors important in resistance of salmonid fish to bacterial disease. I. Serum antibody protection of rainbow trout (*Salmo gairdneri*) against vibriosis. Aquaculture 6:211-9.

268. Hodgins, H.O., F.L. Wendling, B.A. Braaten, and R.S. Weiser (1973). Two molecular species of agglutinins in rainbow trout (*Salmo gairdneri*) serum and their relation to antigenic exposure. Comp. Biochem. Physiol. 45B:975-7.

269. Fujihara, M.P. and R.L. Tramel (1968). *Columnaris* exposure and antibody production in seaward and upstream migrant sockeye salmon. Annual Report for 1967 to the U.S. Atomic Energy Commission, Division of Biological Medicine. Vol. I. Biological Sciences, p. 916-21. Battelle Memorial Institute, Pacific Northwest Laboratories, Seattle, Washington.

270. Janssen, W.A. and C.D. Meyers (1968). Fish: Serologic evidence of infection with human pathogens. Science 159: 547-8.

271. Rohovec, J.S. (1975). Oral and parenteral immunization for the control of *Vibrio anguillarum*, the etiological agent of vibriosis in salmonid fish. Ph.D. Thesis, Oregon State University, Corvallis, 82 p.

272. Colwell, R.R. (1961). Commensal bacteria of marine animals, a study of their distribution, physiology and taxonomy. Ph.D. Thesis, University of Washington, Seattle, 198 p.

273. Potter, L.E. and G.E. Baker (1961). The role of fish as conveyors of microorganisms in aquatic environments. Can. J. Microbiol. 7:595.

274. Cooper, E.L. (1970). Transplantation immunity in helminths and annelids. Transplant. Proc. 2:216-21.

275. Chateaureynaud-Duprat, P. (1970). Specificity of allograft reaction in *Eisenia foetida*. Transplant. Proc. 2: 222-5.

276. Sell, S. (1975). Immunology, Immunopathology, and Immunity, 2nd Ed., p. 300. Harper & Row, New York.

277. Park, B.H. and R.A. Good (1974). Principles of Modern Immunobiology, p. 289-316. Lea & Febiger, Philadelphia.

278. Sell, S. (1975). Immunology, Immunopathology, and Immunity, 2nd Ed., p. 313-22. Harper & Row, New York.

279. Hutt, F.B. (1970). Genetic resistance to infection. In: Resistance to Infectious Disease (R.H. Dunlap and H.W. Moon, eds.), p. 1-11. Saskatoon Modern Press, Saskatoon, Saskatchewan.

280. Hildemann, W.H. (1973). Genetics of immune responsiveness. In: Annual Review of Genetics (H.L. Roman, L.M. Sandler, and A. Campbell, eds.), Vol. 7, p. 19-36. Annual Reviews, Palo Alto, California.

281. Davis, B.D., R. Dulbecco, H.N. Eisen, H.S. Ginsberg, B.W. Wood, and M. McCarty (1973). Microbiology, p. 477-80. Harper & Row, New York.
282. Grumet, F.C. (1975). Genetic control of the immune response. Am. J. Clin. Pathol. 63:646-55.
283. Balcarova, J., K. Hala, and T. Hraba (1973). Differences in the intensity of antibody formation to different antigens in inbred lines of chickens. Folia Biol. (Prague) 19:329-36.
284. Thiele, E.H. (1974). Induction of host resistance in different mouse strains. Proc. Soc. Exp. Biol. Med. 146: 1067-70.
285. Plant, J. and A.A. Glynn (1974). Natural resistance to *Salmonella* infection, delayed hypersensitivity and Ir genes in different strains of mice. Nature 248:345-7.
286. Jacobson, R.H. and N.D. Reed (1974). The immune response of congenitally athymic (nude) mice to the intestinal nematode *Nippostrongylus brasiliensis*. Proc. Soc. Exp. Biol. Med. 147:667-70.
287. Darnell, M.B., H. Koprowski, and K. Lagerspetz (1974). Genetically determined resistance to infection with Group B arboviruses. I. Distribution of the resistance gene among various mouse populations and characteristics of gene expression *in vivo*. J. Infect. Dis. 129:240-7.
288. Gontzea, I. (1974). Nutrition and Anti-Infectious Defense. S. Karger, Basel, 287 p.
289. Faulk, W.P. (1974). Nutrition and immunity. Nature 250: 283-4.
290. Faulk, W.P., E.M. Demaeyer, and A.J.S. Davies (1974). Some effects of malnutrition on the immune response in man. Am. J. Clin. Nutr. 27:638-46.
291. Worthington, B.S. (1974). Effect of nutritional status on immune phenomena. J. Am. Diet. Assoc. 65:123-9.
292. Walford, R.L., R.K. Liu, M. Gerbase-Delima, M. Mathies, and G.S. Smith (1973/1974). Longterm dietary restriction and immune function in mice: Response to sheep red blood cells and to mitogenic agents. Mech. Ageing Dev. 2: 447-54.
293. Axelrod, A.E. (1971). Immune processes in vitamin deficiency states. Am. J. Clin. Nutr. 24:265-71.
294. Krishnan, S., Y.N. Bhuyan, G.P. Talwar, and V. Ramalingaswami (1974). Effect of vitamin A and protein-calorie undernutrition on immune responses. Immunology 27: 383-92.
295. Park, B.H. and R.A. Good (1974). Principles of Modern Immunobiology, p. 251-7. Lea & Febiger, Philadelphia.

296. Vos, J.G. and T. DeRoij (1972). Immunosuppressive activity of a polychlorinated biphenyl preparation on the humoral immune response in guinea pigs. Toxicol. Appl. Pharmacol. 21:549-55.

297. Friend, M. and D.O. Trainer (1970). Polychlorinated biphenyl: Interaction with duck hepatitis virus. Science 170:1314-6.

298. Hansen, D.J., P.R. Parrish, J.I. Lowe, A.J. Wilson, Jr., and P.D. Wilson (1971). Chronic toxicity, uptake, and retention of Aroclor 1254 in two estuarine fishes. Bull. Environ. Contam. Toxicol. 6:113-9.

299. Gabliks, J., T. Al-zubaidy, and E. Askari (1975). DDT and immunological responses. Arch. Environ. Health 30: 81-4.

300. Wassermann, M., D. Wassermann, Z. Gershon, and L. Zellermayer (1969). Effects of organochlorine insecticides on body defense systems. Ann. N.Y. Acad. Sci. 160:393-401.

301. Wassermann, M., D. Wassermann, E. Kedar, and M. Djavaherian (1971). Immunological and detoxication interaction in p,p-DDT fed rabbits. Bull. Environ. Contam. Toxicol. 6:426-35.

302. Koller, L.D., J.H. Exon, and J.G. Roan (1976). Humoral antibody response in mice after single dose exposure to lead or cadmium. Proc. Soc. Exp. Biol. Med. 151:339-42.

303. Avtalion, R.R., A. Wojdani, Z. Malik, R. Shahrabani, and M. Duczyminer (1973). Influence of environmental temperature on the immune response in fish. Curr. Top. Microbiol. Immunol. 61:1-35.

304. Cone, R.E. and J.J. Marchalonis (1972). Cellular and humoral aspects of the influence of environmental temperature on the immune response of poikilothermic vertebrates. J. Immunol. 108:952-7.

305. Lin, H.H. and D.T. Rowlands, Jr. (1973). Thermal regulation of the immune response in South America toads (*Bufo marinus*). Immunology 24:129-33.

306. Cooper, E.L. (1976). Comparative Immunology, p. 241-9. Prentice-Hall, Englewood Cliffs, New Jersey.

307. Sniezko, S.F. (1974). The effect of environmental stress on outbreaks of infectious diseases of fish. J. Fish. Biol. 6:197-208.

308. Levin, W., A.W. Wood, H. Yagi, P.M. Dansette, D.M. Jerina, and A.H. Conney (1976). Carcinogenicity of benzo[a]-pyrene 4,5-, 7,8-, and 9,10-oxides on mouse skin. Proc. Natl. Acad. Sci. 73:243-7.

309. Wynder, E.L. (1976). Nutrition and cancer. Fed. Proc. 35:1309-15.

310. Mastromatteo, E. (1955). Cutting oils and squamous-cell carcinoma. Part I: Incidence in a plant with a report of six cases. Brit. J. Ind. Med. 12:240-3.

311. Carruthers, W. and A.G. Douglas (1961). 1,2-Benzanthracene derivatives in a Kuwait mineral oil. Nature 192: 256-7.

312. Wallcave, L., H. Garcia, R. Feldman, W. Lijinsky, and P. Shubik (1971). Skin tumorigenesis in mice by petroleum asphalts and coal-tar pitches of known polynuclear aromatic hydrocarbon content. Toxicol. Appl. Pharmacol. 18: 41-52.

313. ZoBell, C.E. (1971). Sources and biodegradation of carcinogenic hydrocarbons. In: Proceedings of 1971 Joint Conference on Prevention and Control of Oil Spills, p. 441-51. American Petroleum Institute, Washington, D.C.

314. Nelson-Smith, A. (1972). Pollution and Marine Ecology. Elek Science, London, 260 p.

315. Blumer, M. (1972). Oil contamination and the living resources of the sea. In: Marine Pollution and Sea Life (M. Ruivo, ed.), p. 476-81. Fishing News (Books), London.

316. Moore, S.F., R.L. Dwyer, and A.M. Katz (1973). A preliminary assessment of the environmental vulnerability of Machias Bay, Maine to oil supertankers. Mass. Inst. Technol. Rep. MITSG 73-6, 162 p.

317. Sullivan, J.B. (1974). Marine pollution by carcinogenic hydrocarbons. In: Marine Pollution Monitoring (Petroleum). Natl. Bur. Stand. Spec. Publ. 409, p. 261-3.

318. Blumer, M. and W.W. Youngblood (1975). Polycyclic aromatic hydrocarbons in soils and recent sediments. Science 188:53-5.

319. Sunderman, F.W. (1971). Metal carcinogenesis in experimental animals. Food Cosmet. Toxicol. 9:105-20.

320. Brown, E.R., L. Keith, J.B.G. Kwapinski, and J. Hazdra (1972). The incidence of fish tumors found in a polluted watershed as compared to nonpolluted Canadian waters. Proc. Am. Assoc. Cancer Res. 13:45.

321. Brown, E.R., L. Keith, J.B.G. Kwapinski, J. Hazdra, and P. Beamer (1973). Frequency of tumors in fish populating a polluted water system. Proc. Am. Assoc. Cancer Res. 14:1.

322. Brown, E.R., L. Keith, J. Hazdra, and T.F. Sinclair (1974). Oncogenic agents found in fish inhabiting a polluted water system: Implications for leukemia and lymphosarcoma. Proc. Am. Assoc. Cancer Res. 15:22.

323. Brown, E.R., L. Keith, J.J. Hazdra, and T. Arndt (1975). Tumors in fish caught in polluted waters: Possible explanations. In: Comparative Leukemia Research 1973, Leukemogenesis (Y. Ito and R.M. Dutcher, eds.), University of Tokyo Press, Tokyo, Bibl. Haemat. 40, p. 47-57.

324. Gardner, G., P. Yevich, M. James, and J.C. Prager (1974). The microscopic perils of marine pollution. Underwater Nat. 8:15-9.

325. Butler, M.J.A. and F. Berkes (1972). Biological aspects of oil pollution in the marine environment: A review. McGill University, Montreal, Mar. Sci. Cent. Manuscr. Rep. No. 22, p. 62-4.

326. Powell, N.A., C.S. Sayce, and D.F. Tufts (1970). Hyperplasia in an estuarine bryozoan attributable to coal tar derivatives. J. Fish. Res. Board Can. 27:2095-6.

327. Straughan, D. and D.M. Lawrence (1975). Investigation of ovicell hyperplasia in bryozoans chronically exposed to natural oil seepage. Water Air Soil Pollut. 5:39-45.

328. Ishio, S., T. Yano, and H. Nakagawa (1972). Cancerous disease of *Porphyra tenera* and its causes. In: Proceedings Seventh International Seaweed Symposium, p. 373-6. Cited in: Boney, A.D. (1974). Aromatic hydrocarbons and the growth of marine algae. Mar. Pollut. Bull. 5:185-6.

329. Boney, A.D. (1974). Aromatic hydrocarbons and the growth of marine algae. Mar. Pollut. Bull. 5:185-6.

330. Ceas, M.P. (1974). Effects of 3,4-benzopyrene on sea urchin egg development. Acta Embryol. Exp. 3:267-72.

331. Pliss, G.B. and V.V. Khudoley (1975). Tumor induction by carcinogenic agents in aquarium fish. J. Natl. Cancer Inst. 55:129-36.

332. Blanton, W.G. and M.C. Robinson (1973). Some acute effects of low-boiling petroleum fractions in the cellular structures of fish gills under field conditions. In: The Microbial Degradation of Oil Pollutants (D.G. Ahearn and L.P. Meyers, eds.), p. 265-73. Publ. No. LSU-SG-73-01. Center for Wetland Resources, Louisiana State University, Baton Rouge, La.

333. Keith, L.N. (1976). Identification and Analysis of Organic Pollutants in Water, p. 593. Ann Arbor Science Publishers, Inc., Ann Arbor, Mich.

334. Brocksen, R.W. and H.T. Bailey (1973). Respiratory response of juvenile chinook salmon and striped bass exposed to benzene, a water-soluble component of crude oil. In: Proceedings of 1973 Joint Conference on Prevention and Control of Oil Spills, p. 783-92. American Petroleum Institute, Washington, D.C.

335. Vishnevetskii, F.E. (1961). Pathomorphology of fishes poisoned with phenol and water-soluble components of crude oil, coal tar and mazut (an experimental study). Tr. Astrakh. Gos. Zapov. 5:350-2.

336. Reichenbach-Klinke, H.-H. (1965). Der Phenolgehalt des Wassers in seiner Auswirkung auf den Fischorganisnus. Arch. Fischereiwiss. 16:1-16.

337. Mitrovic, U.V., U.M. Brown, D.G. Shurben, and M.H. Berryman (1968). Some pathological effects of sub-acute and acute poisoning of rainbow trout by phenol in hard water. Water Res. 2:249-54.

338. Waluga, D. (1966). Phenol effects on the anatomico-histopathological changes in bream (Abramis brama L.). Acta Hydrobiol. 8:55-78.

339. Waluga, D. (1966). Phenol induced changes in the peripheral blood of the bream, Abramis brama (L.). Acta Hydrobiol. 8:87-95.

340. Cardwell, R.C. (1973). Acute toxicity of No. 2 diesel oil to selected species of marine invertebrates, marine sculpins and juvenile salmon. Ph.D. Thesis, University of Washington, Seattle, 124 p.

341. Couch, J., G. Gardner, J.C. Harshbarger, M.K. Tripp, and P.P. Yevich (1974). Evaluation of responses in marine organisms. Histological and physiological evaluations in some marine fauna. In: American Petroleum Institute Marine Bioassays, Workshop Proceedings, 1974, p. 156-73. American Petroleum Institute, Washington, D.C.

342. Linhardt, H. (1951). Spektroskopische Blutuntersuchungen an Fischen nach Vergiftung mit Blut und Abwassergiften. Diss. Tierärztl-Fak, University of Muchen. Cited in reference 337.

343. Halsband, E. and I. Halsband (1963). Veranderungen des Blutbildes von Fischen infolge toxischer Schaden. Arch. Fischereiwiss. 14:68-85.

344. Sabo, D.J., J.J. Stegeman, and L.S. Gottlieb (1975). Petroleum hydrocarbon pollution and hepatic lipogenesis in the marine fish, Fundulus heteroclitus. Fed. Proc. 34(3):810.

345. Couch, J. and D. Nimmo (1974). Ultrastructural studies of shrimp exposed to the pollutant chemical, polychlorinated biphenyl (Aroclor 1254). Bull. Pharmacol. Environ. Pathol. 11:17-20.

346. Gardner, G.R., P.P. Yevich, and P.F. Rogerson (1975). Morphological anomalies in adult oyster, scallop, and Atlantic silversides exposed to waste motor oil. In: Proceedings of 1975 Conference on Prevention and Control of Oil Pollution, p. 473-7. American Petroleum Institute, Washington, D.C.

347. Bryan, G.W. (1971). The effects of heavy metals (other than mercury) on marine and estuarine organisms. Proc. R. Soc. Lond. B. Biol. Sci. 177:389-410.

348. Parizek, J. (1957). The destructive effect of cadmium ion on testicular tissue and its prevention by zinc. J. Endocrinol. 15:56-63.

349. Singhal, R.L., Z. Merali, and P.D. Hrdina (1976). Aspects of the biochemical toxicology of cadmium. Fed. Proc. 35(1):75-80.
350. Sangalang, G.B. and M.J. O'Halloran (1972). Cadmium-induced testicular injury and alterations of androgen synthesis in brook trout. Nature 240:470-1.
351. Tafanelli, R. and R.C. Summerfelt (1975). Cadmium-induced histopathological changes in goldfish. In: The Pathology of Fishes (W.E. Ribelin and G. Migaki, eds.), p. 613-45. University of Wisconsin Press, Madison.
352. Crandall, C.A. and C.J. Goodnight (1962). Effects of sublethal concentrations of several toxicants on growth of the common guppy, *Lebistes reticulatus*. Limnol. Oceanogr. 7:233-8.
353. Gabbiani, G. (1966). Action of cadmium chloride on sensory ganglia. Experientia 22:261-2.
354. Gabbiani, G., D. Baic, and C. Deziel (1967). Toxicity of cadmium for the central nervous system. Exp. Neurol. 18:154-60.
355. Voyer, R.A., P.P. Yevich, and C.A. Barszcz (1975). Histological and toxicological responses of the mummichog, *Fundulus heteroclitus* (L.) to combinations of levels of cadmium and dissolved oxygen in freshwater. Water Res. 9:1069-74.
356. Gardner, G.R. (1975). Chemically induced lesions in estuarine or marine teleosts. In: The Pathology of Fishes (W.E. Ribelin and G. Migaki, eds.), p. 657-93. University of Wisconsin Press, Madison.
357. Schwiger, G. (1957). The toxic action of heavy metals salts on fish and organisms on which fish feed. Arch. Fischereiwiss. 8:54-78.
358. Carpenter, K.E. (1927). The lethal action of soluble metallic salts on fishes. J. Exp. Biol. 4:378-90.
359. Haider, G. (1964). Heavy metal toxicity to fish. I. Lead poisoning of rainbow trout (*Salmo gairdnerii*) and its symptoms. Z. Angew. Zool. 51:347-68.
360. Voyer, R.A. (1975). Effect of dissolved oxygen concentration on the acute toxicity of cadmium to the mummichog, *Fundulus heteroclitus* (L.) at various salinities. Trans. Am. fish. Soc. 104:129-34.
361. Gardner, G.R. and P.P. Yevich (1970). Histological and hematological responses of an estuarine teleost to cadmium. J. Fish. Res. Board Can. 27:2185-96.
362. Newman, M.W. and S.A. MacLean (1974). Physiological responses of the cunner, *Tautogolabrus adspersus*, to cadmium. VI. Histopathology. U.S. Natl. Mar. Fish. Serv. Spec. Sci. Rep. Fish. 681:27-33.

363. Stowe, H.D., M. Wilson, and R.A. Goyer (1972). Clinical and morphologic effects of oral cadmium toxicity in rabbits. Arch. Pathol. 94:389-405.

364. Morgon, R.P. II, R.F. Fleming, V.J. Rasin, Jr., and D. Heinle (1973). Sublethal effects of Baltimore Harbor water on the white perch, *Morone americana*, and the hogchoker, *Trinectes maculatus*. Chesapeake Sci. 14:17-27.

365. Rubin, B.A. (1964). Carcinogen-induced tolerance to homotransplantation. Prog. Exp. Tumor Res. 5:217-92.

366. Malmgren, R.A., B.E. Bennison, and T.W. McKinley (1952). Reduced antibody titers in mice treated with carcinogenic and cancer chemotherapeutic agents. Proc. Soc. Exp. Biol. Med. 79:484-8.

367. Baldwin, R.W. and D. Glaves (1973). Unpublished observation cited in Baldwin, R.W., Immunological aspects of chemical carcinogenesis. In: Advances in Cancer Research (G. Klein, S. Weinhouse, and A. Haddow, eds.), p. 1-75. Academic Press, New York.

368. Jones, R.H., R.L. Williams, and A.M. Jones (1971). Effects of heavy metal on the immune response. Preliminary findings for cadmium in rats. Proc. Soc. Exp. Biol. Med. 137:1231-6.

369. Koller, L.D., J.H. Exon, and J.G. Roan (1976). Humoral antibody response in mice after single dose exposure to lead or cadmium. Proc. Soc. Exp. Biol. Med. 151:339-42.

370. Vengris, V.E. and C.J. Mare (1974). Lead poisoning in chickens and the effects of lead on interferon and antibody production. Can. J. Comp. Med. 38:328-35.

371. Pribyl, D. (1975). The effect of metal on the interferon system *in vitro*. In Preparation. Cited in: Treagan, L. (1975). Metals and the immune response, a review. Res. Commun. Chem. Pathol. Pharmacol. 12:189-220.

Chapter 3

METABOLISM OF PETROLEUM HYDROCARBONS: ACCUMULATION AND BIOTRANSFORMATION IN MARINE ORGANISMS

USHA VARANASI AND DONALD C. MALINS
Environmental Conservation Division

Northwest and Alaska Fisheries Center
National Marine Fisheries Service
National Oceanic and Atmospheric Administration
U.S. Department of Commerce
Seattle, Washington 98112

INTRODUCTION

Until 1962 it was generally believed that marine organisms lacked the enzyme systems to metabolize the aromatic petroleum hydrocarbons. Little attention was given at that time to the metabolic fate of other petroleum hydrocarbons in

marine organisms, such as the alkane components. In fact, our
knowledge of the biochemical consequences of exposing marine
life to petroleum hydrocarbons was acquired to a large measure
in the last 15 years. In considering the narrower area of
arctic and subarctic organisms and ecosystems, it should be
emphasized that even less information exists which directly
relates to biochemical effects of petroleum hydrocarbons under
conditions pertaining in these geographic areas. Consequently, in attempting to review the subject, we chose to cover
studies conducted primarily on indigenous species and include,
wherever possible, the relatively small amount of data which
relate to the influence of environmental conditions (e.g., low
temperatures). Much of the review will include discussion on
the uptake, metabolism, and discharge of petroleum hydrocarbons in marine organisms exposed to sublethal levels of petroleum. We will discuss resultant biochemical alterations in
challenged organisms to ascertain overall effects of long-term
exposures to sublethal concentrations of petroleum hydrocarbons. Major emphasis will be on laboratory bioassay studies
or simulated field experiments. In addition, certain relevant
information about concentrations of petroleum hydrocarbons in
animals obtained from known areas of petroleum contamination
will be included. (A more comprehensive discussion of field
studies is given by Clark and Finley in Chapter 9 of Volume
II). The present treatment of the subject should afford an
understanding of the mode of accumulation, biotransformation,
and discharge of petroleum and associated products in tissues
of marine organisms. Furthermore, we will attempt to evaluate
the status of knowledge on these subjects and pinpoint areas
where information is lacking. We will also delineate areas
where more work is required to form a cohesive understanding
of the biochemical consequences of exposing arctic and subarctic marine species and ecosystems to petroleum.

UPTAKE, DISTRIBUTION, AND DISCHARGE
OF PETROLEUM AND CONSTITUENTS

A survey of the literature shows that most reported studies can be divided into two groups of major importance. The
first group consists of challenge studies with crude oil, and
the second group consists of studies with individual petroleum
hydrocarbons. These two types of experiments provide complementary information; thus, they are vitally important in understanding the overall consequences of petroleum pollution in
the aquatic system.

FRACTIONS OF PETROLEUM

Numerous studies have been documented on the uptake and

biological effects of various oils in marine organisms. However, comparison of the data obtained from these studies is
rather difficult because the chemical composition of petroleum used in the experiments varied considerably and because
several different exposure techniques were employed. A later
discussion will show that the mode of entry of petroleum hydrocarbons into organisms is an important factor in determining
the accumulation and distribution, as well as the degree and
extent of discharge of petroleum hydrocarbons. Accordingly,
for convenience, we have compared the results of various challenge experiments on the basis of exposure conditions. The
experiments are divided into the following categories:
(a) Field studies involving organisms taken from "polluted"
areas, (b) laboratory studies using oil-in-water dispersion(s)
(OWD) and a water-soluble fraction (WSF) of oil, and (c) feeding studies incorporating petroleum in the diet.

Plankton and Invertebrates
     Plankton are of interest with respect to their important
position in the initial stages of the food chain and also
because of their vital role in photosynthesis. Limited information is available on the uptake and assimilation of petroleum in plankton. Because of their general lack of mobility,
plankton communities have been considered as potentially the
foremost victims of oil spills, but evidence seems to suggest
that these organisms are able to cope with oil pollution
better than higher animals.

Field Studies
     Most of the information on the levels of petroleum hydro-
carbons in plankton was obtained from analyses of samples
taken from areas of known contamination. A study by Conover
[1] showed that Bunker C fuel oil spilled during the wreck of
the tanker *Arrow* was taken up by zooplankton and accumulated
to a significant degree. As much as 10% of the oil in the
water column was apparently associated with zooplankton, such
as copepods. In this study, the plankton were not rinsed to
remove external oil particles; however, fecal material contained large amounts of oil, thereby indicating that oil was
ingested to some degree and was not just adsorbed on the surface of the organisms. About 70% of the ingested oil was discharged unaltered in fecal material. Conover [1] estimated
that 2% of the total Bunker C fuel oil in the water column may
have been deposited in sediment by this process. The oil in
the sediment may be more prone to bacterial degradation. Such
degraded oil would then be available to benthic organisms.
     Morris [2] reported that barnacles living on weathered
tar balls contained small amounts of petroleum-associated
hydrocarbons. These hydrocarbons comprised 5% of the total

lipid, which in turn constituted 7-8% of the total wet weight of the barnacles. The data indicated that aromatic hydrocarbons were assimilated in the barnacles to a slightly greater extent than straight-chain hydrocarbons.

Clark et al. [3] examined algae *(Fucus gardneri)*, goose barnacles *(Mitella polymerus)*, and purple shore crabs *(Hemigrapsus nudus)* from the wreckage area of the *General M. C. Meigs* which carried Navy special fuel oil. Gas-liquid chromatography (GLC) of contaminated and uncontaminated specimens, together with the oil, indicated the presence of paraffinic hydrocarbons in specimens from the contaminated area. The false eel grass *(Phyllospadix scouleri)* collected 1 mo after the spill retained as much as 41% of its dry weight as oil; *F. gardneri* accumulated as much as 160 ppm of paraffinic hydrocarbons at the end of 1 yr following the oil spill. One and one-half years later, however, the algae did not contain significant levels of petroleum hydrocarbons indicating that probably new growth had replaced contaminated *Fucus*. The authors [3] did not detect any measurable concentrations of petroleum hydrocarbons in coraline algae *(Calliarthron schmitti)*; however, they reported significant levels (2-4 ppm, dry weight) in purple sea urchin. In purple shore crabs, the concentration of petroleum hydrocarbons was twice the biogenic baseline concentrations.

Blumer and coworkers [4] examined oysters and scallops from a coastal area of Massachusetts two months after a spill of No. 2 fuel oil. The oysters and scallops contained 69 and 14 ppm (µg/g, wet weight) of petroleum hydrocarbons, respectively. Significant levels of hydrocarbons were detected in the adductor muscle of scallops. The authors stated that the oil was being continuously released from the sediments and this was the cause for high concentrations of petroleum hydrocarbons found in the animals.

Oil-in-Water Dispersion(s) (OWD) Studies

Oil-in-water dispersion studies are most frequently used in assessment of rates of uptake and accumulation of petroleum hydrocarbons in marine biota. This system simulates natural conditions of the aquatic environment after an oil spill. To prepare the OWD, a known amount of oil is vigorously stirred with water for a short period (e.g., 5-10 min). The oil and water layers are allowed to separate for 30-60 min. The surface slick is not removed; thus, small amounts of soluble hydrocarbons are continuously leached into the water. In addition, the oil slick tends to retard evaporation of volatile fractions from the aqueous phase, although continuous losses of volatile (short-chain paraffins and aromatics) hydrocarbons from the oil slick undoubtedly take place. These experiments are usually carried out under static bioassay conditions.

The animals must be introduced into challenge aquaria with great care in order not to contaminate them with the oil slick.   In this type of experiment, the composition of petroleum hydrocarbons in the aqueous phase depends on the type and amount of oil (Table 1).   Anderson et al [5] noted that crude oils exhibited a nearly linear relation between the amount of added oil and the concentration of petroleum hydrocarbons in water after 1 hr.   The authors [5] demonstrated that even when the amount of added oil (No. 2 fuel oil) was as high as 1,000 ppm, the concentration of petroleum hydrocarbons in water was rather small (50 ppm) (Fig. 1).

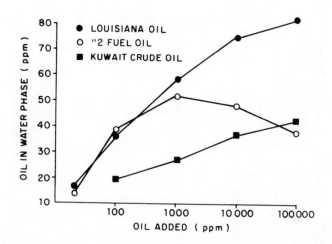

Fig. 1.   *Relationship between amount of oil added (ppm, v/v) and total concentration of dissolved and dispersed oil hydrocarbons in aqueous phase of oil-in-water dispersions prepared with three oils in 20 °/oo salinity Instant Ocean Seawater. From Anderson et al. [5] with permission.*

The OWD studies pose several experimental difficulties because of continuously fluctuating exposure conditions (Fig. 2).   For example, OWD are not very stable systems.   Various hydrocarbons (aromatic, alicyclic, and aliphatic) are selectively partitioned between aqueous and oil phases, with low molecular weight structures (e.g., benzenes, naphthalenes) being more soluble in the aqueous phase than the higher molecular weight structures.   Therefore, the organisms are initially exposed to relatively high concentrations of aromatic hydrocarbons in water but because of their volatile nature these compounds soon begin to evaporate from the aqueous phase. Accordingly, the animals are exposed to varying concentrations of petroleum hydrocarbons during a single experiment.

TABLE 1

Hydrocarbon composition of the aqueous phase of oil-in-water dispersions before and after aeration

Hydrocarbons	Kuwait crude oil[a]		South Louisiana crude oil[a]		No. 2 fuel oil[a]	
	Initial (ppb)	Final (ppb)	Initial (ppb)	Final (ppb)	Initial (ppb)	Final (ppb)
C_{12}–C_{24} n-paraffins	1,320	71	1,988	64	4,234	820
Tri- and tetra-methylbenzenes	260	70	135	99	547	79
Naphthalene	19	15	64	53	671	292
1-Methylnaphthalene	12	1	40	24	416	132
2-Methylnaphthalene	16	17	46	25	646	159
Dimethylnaphthalenes	33	4	108	32	1,430	179
Trimethylnaphthalenes	19	3	56	6	872	105
Phenanthrene	2	2	34	2	214	65
Methylphenanthrenes	2	2	20	2	152	46
Total n-paraffins	1,320	71	1,988	64	4,234	820
Percent decrease	95%		97%		81%	
Total aromatics	359	110	506	241	4,950	1,057
Percent decrease	69%		52%		79%	
Total hydrocarbons measured	1,679	181	2,494	305	9,184	1,877
Percent decrease	89%		88%		80%	

Adapted from Anderson et al. [5].

a Oil-in-water dispersions containing 1,000 mg (ppm) oil per liter. Aeration period was 24 hr.

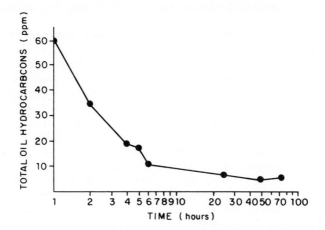

Fig. 2. Relationship between aeration time and total oil-hydrocarbon concentration in water phase of 1,000 ppm (oil added) oil-in-water dispersions of South Louisiana crude oil. From Anderson et al. [5] *with permission.*

Uptake of oil by barnacle larvae (Nauplius phase of *Balanus balanoides)* and copepods *(Calanus finmarchicus)* was studied by Parker and coworkers [6]. To assess whether the animals are capable of distinguishing between food particles and oil droplets, live copepods and barnacle larvae were placed in seawater containing a culture of diatom *(Phaeodactylum tricornutum)* and a fine suspension (2-10 ppm) of oil at 10°C. After 18 hr of exposure, the test animals and their fecal pellets were analyzed. The authors [6] noted that there was a considerable amount of oil in the gut of the exposed animals and a substantial amount in the fecal pellets. It was inferred from these findings that the organisms were not capable of distinguishing between food particles and oil droplets. Another study [7] with corals demonstrated, with the use of gas chromatography, that petroleum hydrocarbons could be incorporated into these organisms. A marked uptake of aliphatic hydrocarbons having chain lengths C_{11}-C_{15} and chain lengths greater than C_{23} was observed in corals exposed to 10 ppm of Iranian crude oil for 96 hr under static bioassay conditions. The amount of petroleum hydrocarbons was less than 1% of their natural (biogenic) hydrocarbon content. It was noted that when colonies of corals were exposed to only 3 ppm of petroleum, paraffinic hydrocarbons of chain lengths C_{11}-C_{15} were not detected, whereas chain lengths greater than C_{23} were accumulated to detectable levels. The author [7] attributed this result to a more rapid evaporation of short-chain hydro-

carbons from the more dilute (3 ppm) solutions. The concentration of aromatic hydrocarbons in the challenged organism
was not determined.

Most of the studies on OWD have been carried out on bivalves (with special emphasis on oysters) and crustaceans.
Lee and coworkers [8] investigated the uptake and discharge of
mineral oil by the mussel, *Mytilus californianus,* a common intertidal filter feeder. Mineral oil contains essentially
straight- and branched-chain paraffins together with cyclo-
paraffins. Solutions of 1 g of oil in seawater (sonicated)
containing celite were used. Levels and profiles of paraffins
in the aqueous phase were not determined. It was observed
that young mussels (0.30 g, dry weight excluding shell) rapidly accumulated 5.9 mg of hydrocarbons per gram total weight in
24 hr. The levels of hydrocarbons were assessed from the
analyses of extracted lipids. A maximum concentration of
hydrocarbons (6.1 mg) was reached after a 4-day exposure and
then levels began to decline slightly (4.8 mg) over a period
of the next 6 days (Table 2) [8]. It was suggested that the

TABLE 2

Uptake of mineral oil by the mussel, Mytilus californianus

Time of exposure[a] (days)	Hydrocarbon Content of mussel (mg/g)	Hydrocarbon content of the lipid in mussel (%)
0	0.5	3
2	5.9	30
4	6.1	36
10	4.8	--

Adapted from Lee et al. [8] *with permission of California
Marine Research Committee.*

a The mussels were placed in a 7 liter aquarium and a mineral
   oil "slick" was formed by adding approximately 1 gram of
   oil. Mussels were taken out at various time intervals, for
   analyses.

hydrocarbons arising from the mineral oil were stored in lipid
deposits (1% of total body weight) and constituted as much as
36% of total lipid on a 4-day exposure. Lee and coworkers [8]
noted from the GLC profiles of the hydrocarbons extracted from
the test animals that the mineral oil had accumulated in the
mussels without any apparent change in composition. When the
exposed mussels were placed in uncontaminated seawater, the
discharge of mineral oil was rapid and in 4 days 99% of the
oil was lost from the test mussels; however, small amounts of

oil persisted in the animals even after 120 hr of depuration, as determined by GLC.

Stainken [9] reported on the mode of accumulation of OWD of No. 2 fuel oil by the soft-shell clam, *Mya arenaria*. Most of the uptake and distribution was obtained visually, because oil-dye emulsions were used. It was observed that the oil-dye solution passed through the gills to the stomach and diverticulum. Varying degrees of an oil-dye-mucus complex on palpi, gills, and mantle were observed in all the test animals. Exposures to OWD were carried out at 4°C and 22°C and it appears that accumulation of the oil-dye complex was much slower at 4°C than at 22°C. Although the water column contained 4.66 ppm of oil, mucus-water samples contained as much as 20 ppm of oil. When clams were exposed to No. 2 fuel oil, large quantities of mucus were produced and a complex of mucus with oil was formed. The oil-mucus complex was ingested and transported along ciliary pathways to palpi, into stomach, and along the digestive tract.

Anderson [10] has used OWD exposure conditions for clams (Table 3, Fig. 3), oysters (Table 4), and grass shrimp (Fig. 4). Analyses showed that the oyster, *Crassostrea virginica,* and the clam, *Rangia cuneata,* accumulated significant amounts of petroleum-derived hydrocarbons (Tables 3 and 4). For example, when exposed to OWD of No. 2 fuel oil (1,000 ppm) for 25 hr, *R. cuneata* accumulated 3.0 ppm of *n*-paraffins and 158 ppm of total aromatic hydrocarbons. Major components of the aromatic hydrocarbons were naphthalene, methylnaphthalenes, and dimethylnaphthalenes (Table 3). When oysters *(C. virginica)* were exposed to 1% OWD for 4 days [10], large concentrations of petroleum-derived hydrocarbons were found in the tissues (Table 4). No comparison of hydrocarbon concentrations in *R. cuneata* and *C. virginica* can be made because different concentrations and times of exposure were employed. Compositions of hydrocarbons in oysters exposed to four different oils are given in Table 4. The findings indicated that oysters exposed to No. 2 fuel oil accumulated the highest concentrations of naphthalenes (84.1 ppm) and those exposed to Kuwait crude oil accumulated the highest amounts of saturated hydrocarbons (46.0 ppm) in tissues. In the four exposure experiments, concentrations of paraffinic and aromatic hydrocarbons reached less than 0.1 ppm after the test animals were held in clean water for 24 to 52 days. Because the period of depuration for each exposure was different, no conclusion can be drawn about the effect of individual oils on depuration rates. Initial analyses by Anderson [10] were performed using gas-liquid chromatography and mass spectrometry (GLC-MS) to identify individual hydrocarbons. From these results, it was apparent that regardless of species, exposure time, and the levels of oil, naphthalene and mono- and dimethyl-derivatives were

TABLE 3

Oil-derived hydrocarbons in the tissue of the clam, Rangia
cuneata, *following exposure to oil-in-water dispersions of
No. 2 fuel oil*

Hydrocarbon	Hydrocarbons in tissues of clams[a] (ppm)
n-Paraffins	
C_{13}	0.1
C_{14}	0.3
C_{15}	0.1
C_{16}	0.2
C_{17}	0.3
C_{18}	0.2
C_{19}	0.1
Total	3.0
Aromatics	
Tetralin	9.2
Naphthalene	22.4
2-Methylnaphthalene	37.2
1-Methylnaphthalene	20.8
Dimethylnaphthalene	44.0
Trimethylnaphthalene	5.2
Misc. di- and triaromatics	6.1
Total	158.0

Adapted from Anderson [10] *in API publication 4249.*

[a] The clams were exposed for 24 hours to a 1,000 ppm (μg/ml)
oil-in-water dispersion; concentrations are based on μg/g,
wet weight.

preferentially and rapidly accumulated by marine organisms in
each experiment. Thus in subsequent challenge experiments,
the authors used ultraviolet spectrophotometry [11] to monitor concentrations of naphthalenes as an index of accumulation of petroleum hydrocarbons. For example, *R. cuneata* accumulated 10 ppm of naphthalene when exposed to dilute OWD in
which 384 ppm of oil was added and the resulting concentration of naphthalene in the water column was less than 1 ppm
(Fig. 3). The concentrations of naphthalenes in the OWD decreased continuously up to 20 hr due to evaporation; however,
this decrease was accompanied by an increase in the concentration of naphthalenes in the animal. This evidence was
presented [10,11] to show that a significant bioaccumulation
of naphthalenes took place in clams exposed to OWD. (The
bioaccumulation factor is defined as concentration of hydro-

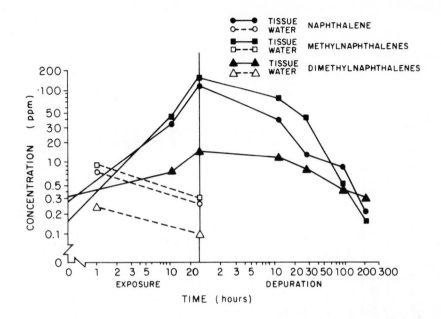

Fig. 3. Concentration of oil-derived naphthalenes in the tissues of the clam, Rangia cuneata, *during exposure to dilute oil-in-water dispersions of No. 2 fuel oil (384 ppm oil added) and following return to oil-free seawater. Each data point represents the average concentration of the hydrocarbon in the tissues (μg/g, wet weight) of five clams. Adapted from Anderson [10] in API publication 4249.*

carbons in tissue divided by the concentration of hydrocarbons in water.) Figure 3 illustrates that when the challenged clams were placed in clean water, levels of naphthalenes slowly decreased in the tissues over a period of 250 hr. By this time, the test animals contained low concentrations of naphthalenes comparable to controls.

Anderson [10] studied the accumulation of naphthalenes by grass shrimp, *Palaemonetes* sp., exposed for 10 hr to OWD of No. 2 fuel oil containing 0.07 ppm of total naphthalenes. The concentration of naphthalene in shrimp tissue (Fig. 4) began to decline after about 7 hr, whereas concentrations of methylnaphthalenes and dimethylnaphthalenes did not decrease until after about 9 hr of exposure.

It is interesting to compare the results with shrimp (Fig. 4) to those obtained with clams (Fig. 3) in which the concentrations of naphthalenes continuously increased over a 20-hr period. Compared to clams, considerable bioaccumulation of aromatic hydrocarbons occurred in the grass shrimp. For

TABLE 4

Oil-derived hydrocarbons in tissues of oysters, Crassostrea virginica, following exposure to oil-in-water dispersions

Hydrocarbon	Hydrocarbons in tissues of oysters[a] (ppm)			
	No. 2 fuel oil	S. Louisiana crude oil	Bunker C fuel oil	Kuwait crude oil
C_{16} *n*-paraffin	0.7	2.2	0.3	5.3
C_{17} *n*-paraffin	0.6	1.7	0.4	4.5
Total C_{12}-C_{25} *n*-paraffins	3.1	13.8	1.1	46.0
Naphthalene	6.3	1.8	1.3	4.3
2-Methylnaphthalene	15.4	5.5	8.5	5.7
1-Methylnaphthalene	9.4	4.2	7.0	4.8
Dimethylnaphthalene	35.6	19.8	18.8	23.2
Trimethylnaphthalene	17.4	12.7	5.7	17.1
Total	84.1	44.0	41.3	55.1
Biphenyl	0.2	0.5	0.1	0.3
Methylbiphenyl	1.0	0.6	0.2	0.3
Fluorene	1.2	0.5	0.4	0.4
Dimethylbiphenyl	0.7	0.5	0.1	0.1
Methylfluorene	1.7	1.7	0.7	1.1
Dibenzothiophene	0.6	0.1	0.1	0.6
Phenanthrene	1.7	0.9	1.3	0.4
Dimethylfluorene	0.5	1.0	0.4	0.8
Methylphenanthrene	1.7	1.7	1.7	1.5
Dimethylphenanthrene	0.2	0.5	0.5	0.5
Total	9.5	8.0	5.0	6.0
Total oil-derived hydrocarbons	96.7	65.8	47.4	107.1

Adapted from Anderson [10].

[a] The oysters were exposed for four days to 1% oil-in-water dispersions, concentrations are based on μg/g, wet weight.

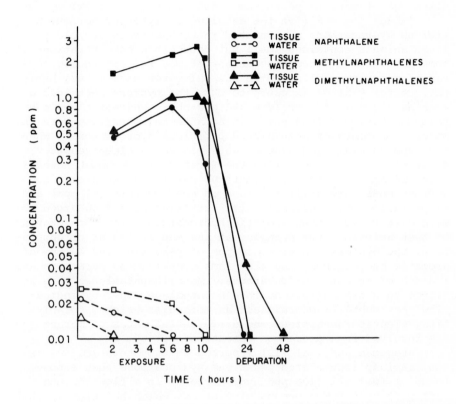

Fig. 4. The concentration of naphthalenes in the tissues of specimens of Palaemonetes *during a 12-hr exposure to OWD (0.07 ppm total naphthalenes) of No. 2 fuel oil and during 48 hr in clean water (depuration). Tissue content values (μg/g, wet weight) are derived from the analysis of four to five animals at each time interval. Adapted from Anderson [10].*

example, the concentration of methylnaphthalenes after 6 hr was 0.025 ppm in water compared to 2.5 ppm in the shrimp (Fig. 4), a bioaccumulation factor of two orders of magnitude. In a comparable time period, the bioaccumulation factor for *R. cuneata* was about 30 (Fig. 3). When the exposed shrimp were placed in clean water, the concentrations of naphthalenes rapidly declined within 48 hr to levels below 0.01 ppm.

A group of oysters *(C. virginica)* and clams *(R. cuneata)* were exposed to OWD (≅400 ppm petroleum hydrocarbons) in a flow-through system [12]. No. 2 fuel oil was continuously mixed in the inflow stream and subsequently passed through a metering pump to insure efficient mixing of the oil and water. Both animals were exposed under identical conditions for 8 hr; therefore, it was possible to compare the extent of uptake and discharge of various petroleum hydrocarbons in the two species.

Tables 5 and 6 give the detailed analyses of various petroleum hydrocarbons accumulated in both oysters and clams. These animals contained small but detectable concentrations of some petroleum hydrocarbons at zero time, reflecting low levels of petroleum pollution in the Galveston Bay, Texas, habitat. After 8 hr of exposure to OWD, the oysters contained as much as 312 ppm of petroleum hydrocarbons, whereas clams contained a maximum of 89 ppm. In both tests, paraffins were the major components of accumulated petroleum hydrocarbons. When the exposed clams and oysters were placed in clean seawater, depuration of tissues during the first 3 hr was rapid; however, after 24 hr, substantial amounts of paraffins and aromatic hydrocarbons were still retained in both oysters (67 ppm) and clams (8.1 ppm). Interestingly, paraffins were discharged much more rapidly than aromatic hydrocarbons from both groups of test animals. For example, at the end of 120 hr of depuration, the oysters contained 10 ppm of paraffins and 44 ppm of aromatic hydrocarbons and the clams contained no paraffins and 1.4 ppm of aromatic hydrocarbons. Methylnaphthalenes were retained to a greater extent than naphthalene, thereby indicating that subtle factors, such as molecular weight, polarities, electron densities, and differential rates of metabolism are involved in hydrocarbon retention.

Stegeman and Teal [13] reported that oysters (*C. virginica*) rapidly accumulated petroleum hydrocarbons when exposed to No. 2 fuel oil (106 ppm hydrocarbons) in a flow-through system at 20°C. Two groups of oysters, which had high (1.62%) and low (0.95%) lipid contents, were used. The extent of uptake of petroleum hydrocarbons declined with time for both groups and the slope of the uptake curve (i.e., rate) changed significantly after 10-14 days for both groups (Fig. 5). The oysters with high lipid content accumulated higher concentrations of petroleum hydrocarbons (334 µg hydrocarbons/g, wet weight) than those with lower lipid content (161 µg hydrocarbons/g, wet weight). These findings imply that petroleum hydrocarbons are accumulated and stored in lipid deposits and that a direct correlation exists between the amount of lipid and the concentrations of petroleum hydrocarbons accumulated in the oyster. The authors [13] noted that when test oysters were held in clean water there was a rapid decline in the hydrocarbon concentration resulting in the loss of about 90% of the accumulated hydrocarbons over a period of 2 weeks. Thereafter the rate of discharge slowed considerably. Such a biphasic mode of release was explained in terms of a "compartmentation phenomenon." The authors [13] proposed that some

TABLE 5

Accumulation of petroleum hydrocarbons by the oyster, Crassostrea virginica, during exposure to dispersed No. 2 fuel oil in a flow-through system and subsequent release of hydrocarbons when the oysters were returned to oil-free seawater

Time (hr)	Petroleum hydrocarbon concentration (ppm; μg/g, wet weight)														
	n-p	N	1-MN	2-MN	DMN	TMN	B	MB	F	MF	DBT	P	MP	DMP	Total
Exposure															
0	–	0.2	0.1	0.3	1.0	0.8	–	–	–	–	–	–	–	–	2.4
8	235	14.7	8.7	15.0	21.8	9.1	0.3	0.5	1.0	1.2	0.3	1.9	1.9	0.3	312
Depuration															
3	156	12.0	8.4	12.0	22.7	10.8	0.3	0.4	0.7	0.7	0.3	1.3	1.3	0.2	228
6	68	7.3	5.1	7.3	13.2	5.7	0.1	0.2	0.4	0.2	0.1	0.6	0.6	0.1	109
24	18	6.5	5.7	7.6	14.8	9.5	0.2	0.2	0.5	0.7	0.2	1.2	1.3	0.3	67
120	10	8.2	4.7	6.8	13.4	4.9	0.1	0.1	0.2	0.1	0.1	0.4	0.4	0.2	54
672	–	–	–	0.1	0.5	0.9	–	–	–	–	–	–	–	–	1.5

Reproduced from Neff et al. [12] with permission.

Abbreviations used: n-p, n-paraffins; N, naphthalene; 1-MN, 1-methylnaphthalene; 2-MN, 2-methylnaphthalene; DMN, dimethylnaphthalene; TMN, trimethylnaphthalene; B, biphenyl; MB, methylbiphenyl; F, fluorene; MF, methylfluorene; DBT, dibenzothiophene; P, phenanthrene; MP, methylphenanthrene; DMP, dimethylphenanthrene.

TABLE 6

Accumulation of petroleum hydrocarbons by the clam, Rangia cuneata, during exposure to dispersed No. 2 fuel oil in a flow-through system and subsequent release of hydrocarbons when the clams were returned to oil-free seawater

Time (hr)	Petroleum hydrocarbon concentration (ppm; µg/g, wet weight)														
	n-p	N	1-MN	2-MN	DMN	TMN	B	MB	F	MF	DBT	P	MP	DMP	Total
Exposure															
0	-	-	-	-	-	-	-	-	-	-	-	-	0.2	-	0.2
8	66	3.8	2.6	3.9	7.4	3.6	0.1	0.1	0.3	0.3	0.1	0.5	0.8	0.1	89
Depuration															
3	23	2.2	1.7	2.6	4.2	1.8	-	-	0.1	-	-	0.2	0.2	-	36
6	1.1	2.0	1.9	2.9	4.9	1.9	-	0.1	0.1	0.2	0.1	0.3	0.5	-	16
24	1.0	0.6	0.7	1.1	2.5	1.3	-	-	0.1	0.2	-	0.3	0.3	-	8.1
120	-	-	0.1	0.1	0.6	0.6	-	-	-	-	-	-	-	-	1.4
672	-	-	-	-	-	-	-	-	-	-	-	-	-	-	0

Reproduced from Neff et al. [12] with permission.

Abbreviations used: n-p, n-paraffin; N, naphthalene; 1-MN, 1-methylnaphthalene; 2-MN, 2-methylnaphthalene; DMN, dimethylnaphthalene; TMN, trimethylnaphthalene; B, biphenyl; MB, methylbiphenyl; F, fluorene; MF, methylfluorene; DBT, dibenzothiophene; P, phenanthrene; MP, methylphenanthrene; DMP, dimethylphenanthrene.

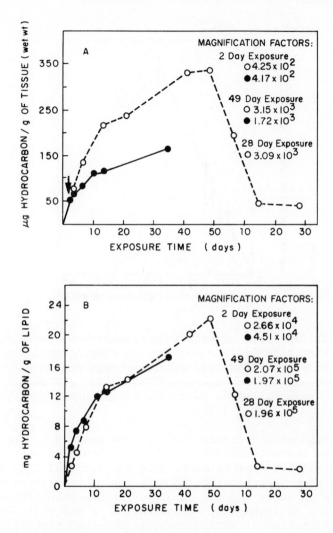

Fig. 5.   Uptake and release of petroleum hydrocarbons by high
fat-content (---o---) and low fat-content (---●---) oysters,
C. virginica.   Concentration of hydrocarbons expressed on (A)
wet weight basis, (B) lipid weight basis.   The concentration
of hydrocarbons in the water was 106 μg/l.   At Day 50, high
fat-content oysters were transferred to the system with 11 μg
of hydrocarbon per liter of water.   Each point represents determination of hydrocarbons in oysters, with determinations
in duplicate samples of three at Days 2 and 14.   Magnification factors refer to concentration of hydrocarbon in organism or lipid over the concentration in water.   Concentration
in low-fat oysters at Day 49 was determined by extrapolation.
Adapted from Stegeman and Teal [13].

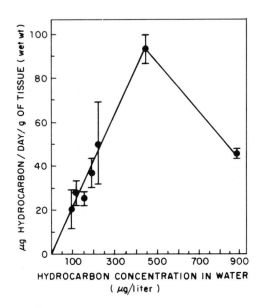

*Fig. 6.   Initial rate of petroleum hydrocarbon uptake by oys-
ters* (C. virginica) *versus hydrocarbon concentration in the
water.   Oysters were assayed after two days exposure at indicated hydrocarbon concentration.   Each point represents average of two determinations using high fat-content oysters.
From Stegeman and Teal* [13].

of the accumulated hydrocarbons may have entered a "stable"
compartment characterized by low hydrocarbon turnover.
        In a different experiment, Stegeman and Teal [13] demon-
strated a direct correlation between the concentration of hydrocarbons in water and the extent of uptake into oysters up
to a maximum environmental concentration of 450 µg/l (Fig. 6).
At a concentration of 900 µg, oysters remained tightly closed,
thereby suggesting that after certain maximum concentrations
of petroleum hydrocarbons are reached in water, the oysters
avoid contact with the contaminated environment.
        The uptake by bivalves of paraffinic hydrocarbons from
outboard motor fuel was studied by Clark and Finley [14].   An
outboard motor was operated in a barrel of clean seawater until 100 ml of the outboard lubricating oil, plus 4,800 ml of
gasoline were utilized in the operation of the motor.   The
seawater which now contained both dissolved and emulsified
petroleum products was diluted with clean seawater to make a
10% solution and was used in a flow-through system.   Both oysters *(Ostrea lurida)* and mussels *(M. edulis)* were exposed to
this solution for 10 days at 10°-12°C.   In 1 day, mussels

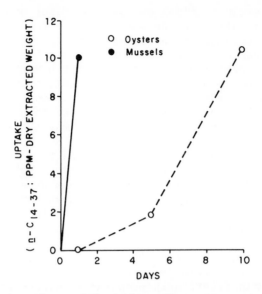

Fig. 7. Uptake of paraffin hydrocarbons by oysters and mussels from 10% outboard motor effluent. From Clark and Finley [15] with permission from Environmental Science and Technology. Copyright by the American Chemical Society.

rapidly accumulated 10 ppm of paraffinic hydrocarbons (Fig. 7), whereas oysters accumulated similar levels in the course of 9-10 days. The authors [14] suggested that the rapid uptake of hydrocarbons in mussels, together with the high mortality, implies that the mussels were susceptible to adverse affects from petroleum because of their inability to prevent hydrocarbons from entering through their byssal openings. By comparison, oysters may close their shells tightly for long periods, thus preventing the uptake of waterborne contaminants. Further, the more highly refined petroleum products are apparently accumulated more rapidly and retained over a long period of time by the mussels, whereas more viscous oils are not taken up as rapidly [14]. This difference is presumably due to the fact that viscous material does not pass as easily through the byssal opening, as does lighter, more fluid material.

In another experiment, Clark and Finley [15] used a model aquarium designed to simulate conditions on a beach surface exposed to tidal flow of seawater containing either No. 2 or No. 5 fuel oil. The experimental regime consisted of an aquarium set at 25°C into which artificial seawater was pumped twice a day to simulate flood tide; the ebb tide was simulated by siphoning out the seawater. Two groups of organisms were used; one was placed in the intertidal zone held by horizontally placed glass rods, and the other was placed below the

extreme low levels of tidal sweep. The first group was exposed to oil floating on the water surface during tidal sweep,
whereas the second group was totally immersed in seawater at
all times. The latter animals were exposed to dissolved (WSF)
and dispersed (OWD) fractions of oil, but never came directly
in contact with the oil slick. The mussels on the shallow
simulated beach surface accumulated much higher concentrations
(about 100 ppm) of paraffinic hydrocarbons than the animals
(29 ppm) that were totally submersed in water. The authors
[15] pointed out that animals exposed to No. 5 fuel oil accumulated much less paraffinic hydrocarbons than those exposed
to No. 2 fuel oil. Both groups of animals discharged 75% of
the accumulated hydrocarbons within a week when held in oil-
free seawater. Nevertheless, after 35 days, small amounts of
petroleum hydrocarbons were still detected in the group exposed to No. 2 fuel oil.

Water-Soluble Fraction (WSF) Studies
     A number of experiments were carried out using a WSF of
petroleum. This fraction is prepared by mixing known amounts
of petroleum with seawater for periods up to 20 hr. The water
and oil are allowed to separate over a period of a few hours
and the aqueous phase is removed. The aqueous phase may be
diluted with oil-free seawater to appropriate concentrations
for use in flow-through or static bioassay studies. In static
bioassay, a more frequently used method, concentrations of
aromatic hydrocarbons and volatile paraffins decreased with
time, especially when the solutions were aerated (see Chapter
1). The concentration and composition of hydrocarbons in the
aqueous phase would be obviously different from the parent oil
as more soluble components, such as aromatics and short-chain
paraffins, would be concentrated in the aqueous phase. Table
7 shows hydrocarbon profiles of the WSF obtained from four
different test oils (South Louisiana crude oil, Kuwait crude
oil, No. 2 fuel oil, and Bunker C residual oil) [5].
     Hardly any information is available on the bioaccumula-
tion of petroleum components in plankton exposed to a WSF.
Most of the work was conducted on crustacea with the following
few exceptions.
     Rossi and coworkers [16] studied the accumulation of hy-
drocarbons in the tissues of marine worm, *Neanthes arenaceodentata,* on exposure to a WSF (100% from South Louisiana crude
oil and No. 2 fuel oil) for 4 hr under static bioassay conditions (no aeration). The tissues were analyzed by GLC-MS for
the presence of petroleum hydrocarbons. The animals exposed
to a WSF of No. 2 fuel oil accumulated 20 ppm of aromatic hydrocarbons and 5 ppm of paraffins; those exposed to a WSF of
South Louisiana crude oil accumulated 10 ppm of aromatics and
6 ppm of paraffins (Table 8). It appeared from toxicity

TABLE 7

Hydrocarbon content of water-soluble fractions of four test oils

Compound	Hydrocarbon content of water-soluble fraction (ppm)			
	S. Louisiana crude oil	Kuwait crude oil	No. 2 fuel oil	Bunker C residual oil
Alkanes				
Ethane	0.54	0.23	$-^a$	-
Propane	3.01	3.30	-	-
Butane	2.36	3.66	-	-
Isobutane	1.69	0.90	0.39	0.05
Pentane	0.49	1.31	-	-
Isopentane	0.70	0.98	-	-
Cyclopentane + 2-methylpentane	0.38	0.59	0.02	0.005
Methylcyclopentane	0.23	0.19	0.019	0.004
Hexane	0.09	0.29	0.014	0.004
Methylcyclohexane	0.22	0.08	0.03	0.002
Heptane	0.06	0.09	0.02	0.004
C_{16} n-Paraffin	0.012	0.0006	0.008	0.0012
C_{17} n-Paraffin	0.009	0.0008	0.006	0.0019
Total C_{12}-C_{24} n-paraffins	0.089	0.004	0.047	0.012
Aromatics				
Benzene	6.75	3.36	0.55	0.04
Toluene	4.13	3.62	1.04	0.08
Ethylbenzene + m-, p-xylenes	1.56	1.58	0.95	0.09
o-Xylene	0.40	0.67	0.32	0.03
Trimethylbenzenes	0.76	0.73	0.97	0.11
Naphthalene	0.12	0.02	0.84	0.21
1-Methylnaphthalene	0.06	0.02	0.34	0.19
2-Methylnaphthalene	0.05	0.008	0.48	0.20
Dimethylnaphthalenes	0.06	0.02	0.24	0.20
Trimethylnaphthalenes	0.008	0.003	0.03	0.10
Biphenyl	0.001	0.001	0.011	0.001
Methylbiphenyls	0.001	0.001	0.014	0.001
Dimethylbiphenyls	0.001	0.001	0.003	0.001
Fluorene	0.001	0.001	0.009	0.005
Methylfluorenes	0.001	0.001	0.009	0.004
Dimethylfluorenes	0.001	0.001	0.002	0.002
Dibenzothiophene	0.001	0.001	0.004	0.001
Phenanthrene	0.001	0.001	0.010	0.009
Methylphenanthrenes	0.002	0.001	0.007	0.011
Dimethylphenanthrenes	0.001	0.001	0.003	0.003
Total saturates	9.86	11.62	0.54	0.081
Total aromatics	13.90	10.03	5.74	1.28
Total dissolved hydrocarbons measured	23.76	21.65	6.28	1.36

Adapted from Anderson et al. [5].

[a] Showed unresolved GC peaks, probably includes some olefins.

TABLE 8

Oil-derived hydrocarbons in the tissues of Neanthes arenaceodentata *exposed to water-soluble fractions of petroleum
and fuel oil*[a]

Hydrocarbon	Southern Louisiana crude oil (ppm)	No. 2 fuel oil (ppm)
C_3-benzenes	2.5	-[b]
C_4-benzenes	1.0	1.9
Naphthalene	1.1	0.9
1-Methylnaphthalene	1.4	3.0
2-Methylnaphthalene	0.7	3.7
Dimethylnaphthalenes	1.5	5.8
Trimethylnaphthalenes	-	1.5
Total aromatics	10.0	20.0
Total paraffins	6.0	5.0

Adapted from Rossi and coworkers [16].

[a] Exposure time was 4 hr; all concentrations are in µg/g, wet weight.
[b] Below the level of detection (<0.2 ppm).

studies that *N. arenaceodentata* was less sensitive to the WSF
of oils than *C. capitata* under static bioassay conditions;
however, *C. capitata* was more tolerant of environmental pollution under field conditions [17]. It was suggested that a
combination of factors, such as contents of oxygen and organic
matter in the water, are more important in influencing the
fate and effect of petroleum in marine organisms than previously assumed.

The fact that a multitude of factors may be important in
determining uptake, metabolism, and discharge of petroleum
hydrocarbons is further emphasized by the following experiment
[12]: A group of clams *(R. cuneata)* was exposed to a WSF of
No. 2 fuel oil (total hydrocarbons, 6.28 ppm) for 24 hr under
static bioassay conditions. The exposed clams were then
transferred to clean seawater for 24 hr (Table 9). At first
glance, it appeared that bioaccumulation of hydrocarbons within an organism was directly related to the molecular weight;
that is, higher molecular weight compounds were accumulated to
a greater extent than lower molecular weight compounds. Thus
the order of accumulation was naphthalene < methylnaphthalene
< dimethylnaphthalene < trimethylnaphthalene. However, fur-
ther scrutiny of the data reveals that there is a slight but
distinct difference in the bioaccumulation factors for 1-
methylnaphthalene (8.5) and 2-methylnaphthalene (8.1) which

TABLE 9

Accumulation and release of naphthalenes by the clam, Rangia cuneata, exposed to a water-soluble fraction of No. 2 fuel oil

No. 2 fuel oil hydrocarbon	Concentration in:		Bioaccumulation factor[a]	Concentration in tissue of exposed clams after 24 hr depuration (ppm)	Amount released in 24 hr (%)
	Exposure water[a] (ppm)	Tissues of clams exposed for 24 hr (ppm)			
Naphthalene	0.84	1.9	2.3	0.4	79
1-Methylnaphthalene	0.34	2.9	8.5	1.9	34
2-Methylnaphthalene	0.48	3.9	8.1	1.9	51
Dimethylnaphthalenes	0.24	4.1	17.1	2.8	32
Trimethylnaphthalenes	0.03	0.8	26.7	0.4	50

Adapted from Neff et al. [12] *with permission.*

a Bioaccumulation factor = $\dfrac{\text{(concentration of hydrocarbon in tissue)}}{\text{(concentration of hydrocarbon in water)}}$

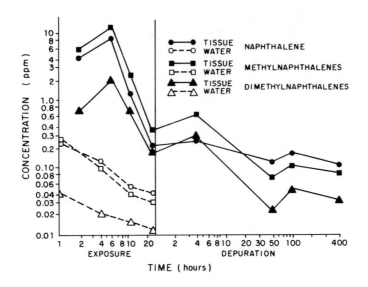

Fig. 8. The concentration of naphthalenes in the tissues of specimens of Palaemonetes *during a 24-hr exposure to a 30% WSF of No. 2 fuel oil and after various periods in clean water (depuration). Each value shown for tissue content (μg/g, wet weight) was derived from the analysis of four to five animals. Adapted from Anderson [10] in API publication 4249.*

have the same molecular weight. Moreover, the 1-isomer was retained to a greater extent than the 2-isomer during depuration. Naphthalene, which was accumulated to the smallest extent in *R. cuneata,* was released most readily (Table 9).

Anderson [10] studied the uptake and release of naphthalene by grass shrimp, *Palaemonetes,* exposed to a 30% WSF of No. 2 fuel oil for 24 hr (Fig. 8). The levels of naphthalene and methylnaphthalenes increased rapidly in tissues reaching a maximum after about 6 hr. The levels then began to drop and declined continuously to the end of the exposure period (24 hr). Similar results were obtained when grass shrimp were exposed to OWD of No. 2 fuel oil as discussed in the previous section. In both experiments, the bioaccumulation factor for naphthalene was about 20 after an exposure of 2 hr. The concentrations of naphthalenes in the test animals reached maximum values after about 6 hr of exposure in the OWD system and then began to decline during the rest of the exposure period. Metabolites of naphthalenes were not identified; however, an obvious decline in the levels of naphthalenes in the shrimp during exposure raises the possibility that naphthalenes were metabolized.

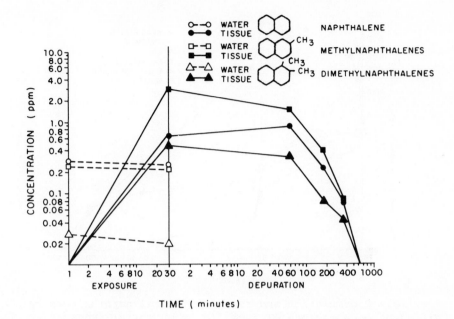

Fig. 9. Uptake and release of naphthalenes from a 30% WSF of No. 2 fuel oil by the brown shrimp, Penaeus aztecus. *The exposure water initially contained approximately 1.95 ppm total oil hydrocarbons. Tissue concentrations are based on wet weight. Adapted from Anderson et al.* [18].

When a group of brown shrimp, *Penaeus aztecus,* were exposed to a 30% WSF of No. 2 fuel oil for 30 min (Fig. 9), the animals accumulated ten times as much naphthalene as that present in the water [18]. When the test animals were placed in oil-free seawater, the naphthalenes were gradually discharged over a period of 10 hr. These results indicate that even in a few minutes naphthalenes are accumulated in the tissues of exposed animals to a substantial degree. Such a rapid uptake is followed by a gradual release of the hydrocarbons when the organisms are returned to clean seawater [19]. Because metabolic products were not determined, the question of whether these compounds accumulated in tissues remains unanswered.

A study of the distribution of naphthalene derivatives in a crustacean was carried out by Neff and coworkers [12]. It was shown that when a group of juvenile brown shrimp were exposed to a 20% WSF of No. 2 fuel oil for 20 hr the digestive gland continuously accumulated naphthalenes, whereas the gills, exoskeleton, abdomen, and head regions accumulated maximum concentrations within an hour (Fig. 10). The digestive gland, which has a function similar to that of the liver in vertebrates, accumulated as high as 70 ppm of naphthalenes in 20 hr.

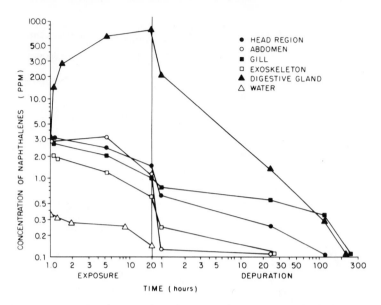

Fig. 10. Accumulation and release of total naphthalenes by different body regions of juvenile brown shrimp, Penaeus aztecus, *exposed to a 20% dilution of the water-soluble fraction of No. 2 fuel oil. Tissues from three shrimp were pooled for each data point, and background values were subtracted. Concentrations are based on µg/g, wet weight. Adapted from Neff et al. [12].*

When shrimp were placed in clean seawater, an initial rapid decline in the levels of naphthalenes occurred in all tissues; however, the initial phase was followed by a lag phase during which naphthalenes were released rather slowly. At the end of the depuration of 250 hr, concentrations of naphthalenes in all tissues were similar to those in tissues of control animals.

Feeding Studies
    An entirely different mode of exposure entails incorporation of petroleum into food or bottom sediments upon which benthic animals feed.
    Two recent studies [20,21] have demonstrated that benthic deposit-feeder organisms *(N. arenaceodentata* and *Phascolosoma agassizii)* do not accumulate significant amounts of hydrocarbons when exposed to sediments mixed with oil. Fossato and Canzonier [22] reported that when mussels, *M. edulis,* were exposed to 200-400 ppb of diesel fuel adsorbed on kaolin particles for a period of 41 days in a flow-through system, the levels of hydrocarbons in tissues were 1,000 times the level in the water. On transfer of the test animals to a relatively

clean environment, there was a rapid loss of accumulated hydrocarbons for the first 15-20 days (biological half-life = 2.7 to 3.5 days). Subsequent elimination was much slower, and after 32 days of depuration the test animals still contained considerable amounts of hydrocarbons. These results support the view [13] that under chronic exposure conditions bivalves tend to sequester a certain fraction of hydrocarbons in a "stable" form having limited accessibility for exchange when the contaminated animals are transferred to a clean environment.

Blackman [23] showed that brown shrimp, *C. crangon,* fed on sunken crude oil, especially when starved. The ingested oil apparently remained in the foregut until molting. Fresh crude oil was ingested to a lesser extent than weathered crude oil. The authors inferred from these observations that fresh crude oil was more toxic than sunken topped crude oil. The ingested material remained in the gastric mill and foregut as compacted masses of oil and sand or as globules and smears.

Marine Fish

On comparison to invertebrates, very few challenge experiments have been carried out on fish exposed to petroleum. Most studies were either conducted with a WSF under static bioassay conditions or with individual hydrocarbons.

Water-Soluble Fraction (WSF) Studies

In one study [10] killifish, *Fundulus similis,* were exposed to a "full-strength" WSF of No. 2 fuel oil, and samples were removed for analyses at various stages of exposure as the test animals exhibited abnormal symptoms (e.g., swimming in vertical position). In each group, the gallbladder accumulated the highest concentrations of naphthalenes; however, gut, liver, and brain also accumulated significant amounts of these hydrocarbons. Interestingly, gills contained relatively low levels of naphthalene. In another experiment, *F. similis* were exposed to a WSF of No. 2 fuel oil (concentration of naphthalene in water was 1.9 ppm) under static bioassay conditions [10]. The fish accumulated 43.2 ppm of total naphthalenes in 2 hr. The distribution of naphthalenes in tissues was not determined in this work; however, in a subsequent paper, Neff et al. [12] reported a detailed distribution of naphthalenes in various tissues of *F. similis* (Fig. 11). The fish were exposed to a WSF of No. 2 fuel oil containing approximately 2 ppm total naphthalenes for 2 hr. The concentration of naphthalenes in various tissues of the fish increased rapidly and reached a maximum in about 1 hr, after which the levels declined to the end of the exposure period. The gallbladder accumulated the highest concentrations of naphthalenes (2,300 ppm), and the brain accumulated substantial levels (620 ppm).

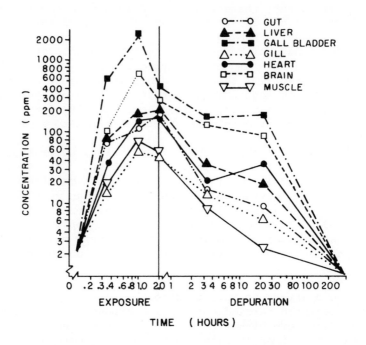

Fig. 11. *Distribution of total naphthalenes in various tissues (µg/g, wet weight) of Gulf killifish,* Fundulus similis, *during exposure to the water-soluble fraction of No. 2 fuel oil and at different times following exposure. The water-soluble fraction contained approximately 2 ppm total naphthalenes. Adapted from Neff et al. [12].*

The concentrations of naphthalenes in gut and liver were relatively small; however, as concentrations of the metabolic products were not determined these values do not necessarily provide an estimate of the actual amount of petroleum-derived products in tissues. When fish were placed in clean seawater, the brain and gallbladder released naphthalenes at a much slower rate than most other tissues (Fig. 11). After 30 hr of depuration, the brain and gallbladder contained about 100 and 200 ppm of total naphthalenes, respectively. Rapid accumulation and subsequent slow release of naphthalenes in vital organs, such as the brain of killifish, merits special attention when considering the physiological effects of petroleum. Muscle tissues released naphthalenes at a greater rate than all other tissues. Depuration period of 366 hr was required for the levels of naphthalenes to reach background values for all the tissues. The animals accumulated substantial concentrations of naphthalenes in 1 hr but required over 300 hr to discharge the hydrocarbons.

Rice and coworkers [24] studied uptake of naphthalenes and alkanes in pink salmon fry (Oncorhynchus gorbuscha) exposed to WSF of three oils: No. 2 fuel oil, Prudhoe Bay crude oil, and Cook Inlet crude oil. One percent oil in seawater was mixed gently for 20 hr and each WSF was used for the exposure studies. Fish were exposed for 96 hr in aerated aquaria at 10°-12°C. Concentrations of paraffinic and aromatic hydrocarbons in gills, viscera, and muscle were determined. These tissues accumulated straight-chain alkanes (C_{15}-C_{19}); however, in the gut, a continuous decline of the alkanes was observed. The authors [24] suggested that this decline may be due to the failure of the fish to feed during the challenge period. In gill tissues, paraffins having chain lengths of C_{12}-C_{30} were detected during the first 10 hr of exposure. The findings of Rice and coworkers [24] indicated that aromatic hydrocarbons were accumulated to the highest concentration in the gut at the 10-hr exposure time. Both gills and muscle also contained small levels of aromatic hydrocarbons, expressed in terms of naphthalene equivalents measured by ultraviolet spectrophotometry. The levels of aromatic compounds declined in all three tissues after 10 hr. The authors suggested that the high levels of naphthalenes in the gut imply that oil is being actively metabolized in the liver yielding products excreted via the gallbladder; however, possible metabolic products were not identified.

Feeding Studies

Hardy and coworkers [25] determined changes in the pattern of n-alkanes isolated from the liver of cod (Gadus morhua) exposed to Kuwait crude oil in the diet. The fish were fed an oil-rich diet for six months and gas-liquid chromatograms of alkanes from the livers of the test and control fish were examined (Fig. 12). The n-alkanes from the test fish contained mainly even-numbered hydrocarbons (C_{26}-C_{28}). The profile of the alkanes in the test fish did not resemble that of Kuwait crude oil (Fig. 12), indicating preferential retention, metabolism, and excretion of individual hydrocarbons. In a subsequent experiment the authors showed that G. morhua did not accumulate hexadecane, a major constituent of Kuwait crude oil, to a significant extent. These results suggest that some caution should be exercised in attempts to determine the origin of hydrocarbons in organisms based on comparisons of hydrocarbon profiles in oil with those in the tissues.

SELECT ALIPHATIC AND AROMATIC HYDROCARBONS

Petroleum contains a complex mixture of aliphatic, alicyclic, and aromatic hydrocarbons. We have seen that marine organisms exposed to petroleum selectively accumulate certain

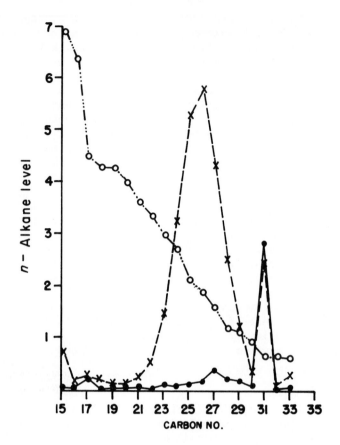

Fig. 12. Distribution of n-*alkanes. X, livers from codling fed crude oil for six months; •, control liver (both in ppm) and, 0, the crude oil used in the experiment (in µg alkanes per 100 mg crude oil). The liver results are from a mean of three fish. Concentrations are based on µg/g, wet weight. Adapted from Hardy et al. [25].*

types of hydrocarbons, particularly the aromatic compounds. This selective accumulation may relate to the physical and chemical nature of the compounds, to the conditions of exposure of the compounds, to the organisms, and to the capacity of the organisms to metabolize the particular compounds.

Most of the challenge experiments described in this section can be defined as water immersion studies involving use of a single petroleum hydrocarbon component in static bioassay or flow-through systems. A few feeding studies were reported in which the hydrocarbon was mixed with food. Experiments with individual hydrocarbons were generally free from the complexities inherent in working with mixtures; moreover, they

have the distinct advantage of allowing the use of radioactively labeled molecules to facilitate the detection of
even trace amounts of hydrocarbons and their metabolites in
tissues.

Plankton and Invertebrates

Most of the studies on plankton deal with biological effects, rather than the fate of petroleum in exposed organisms.

Water Immersion Studies

Kauss et al. [26] demonstrated the accumulation of radioactively labeled naphthalene in cells of the algae, *Chlamydomonas angulosa*. The medium contained 30 ppm of carbon-14
labeled naphthalene and the initial cell concentration was 50
x 10^4 cells/ml. The mixture was incubated at 20°C for 7 days.
Cells continued to accumulate radioactive naphthalene for the
entire 7-day period (Fig. 13). The concentration of naphthalene ranged from 0.76 to 8.0 x 10^4 disintegrations per minute
per cell, indicating that the algae are able to accumulate
significant amounts of aromatic hydrocarbons from surrounding
water.

Lee [27] challenged several planktonic crustaceans with
radioactively labeled petroleum hydrocarbons. In addition to
amphipods, crab zoea, ctenophores, and jellyfish, copepods
from California, British Columbia, Canada, and Fletcher's Ice
Island in the Arctic were used. The animals were exposed to
carbon-14 labeled benzo[a]pyrene, naphthalene, and octadecane
and tritiated benzo[a]pyrene and 20-methylcholanthrene under
static bioassay conditions. In experiments with tritiated
benzo[a]pyrene, small amounts of No. 2 fuel oil were also added to the exposure water. Lipids were extracted from the
exposed animals and concentrations of hydrocarbons in tissues
were calculated. It was determined that 10 to 15% of the
radioactive hydrocarbons were adsorbed to the sides of glass
beakers and certain losses (up to 10%) were sustained due to
evaporation. In the case of naphthalene, however, evaporative
losses were much greater. Certain losses due to oxidation
were also likely.

Results on the uptake of tritiated benzo[a]pyrene by the
copepod, *Calanus plumchrus,* are given in Fig. 14. The initial
steep increase in the concentration of accumulated benzo[a]-
pyrene in *C. plumchrus* during the first day of exposure was
followed by a gradual increase on the second and third day.
No increase in the concentration of the hydrocarbon was noted
after 3 days of exposure. Similar patterns of accumulation
were observed with the other zooplankton.

The results on uptake and discharge of various hydrocarbons by the zooplankton are given in Table 10. Findings with
C. plumchrus demonstrate that octadecane is accumulated to a

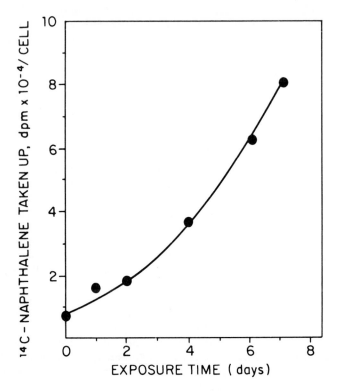

Fig. 13.   Uptake of ^{14}C-naphthalene by Chlamydomonas angulosa.
*Cells were left in closed flasks for 0, 1, 2, 4, 6, and 7 days
prior to the assessment of naphthalene concentrations.   From
Kauss et al.* [26].

smaller extent than aromatic hydrocarbons such as methylcho-
lanthrene and benzo[a]pyrene. Moreover, octadecane was discharged or degraded more rapidly than the aromatic hydrocarbons (Table 10). After 3 days of exposure, concentrations of
hydrocarbon decreased in most cases; thus the animals were
generally capable of metabolizing hydrocarbons.

The data in Figure 14 and Table 10 show that the arctic
copepod, *C. hyperboreus,* (2.2 mg, dry weight), maintained at
$3°C$, accumulated 11×10^{-4} µg of benzo[a]pyrene; *C. plumchrus,*
(1.0 mg, dry weight), maintained at $10°C$, accumulated 22×10^{-4}
µg of the hydrocarbon (Fig. 14). Thus it appears that exposure temperature influences the degree of accumulation and
metabolism of hydrocarbons in copepods. However, because two
different species were compared, such a conclusion is only
tentative.

Data from two recent reports [28,29] on the relation of
temperature to uptake and retention of naphthalene in clams,

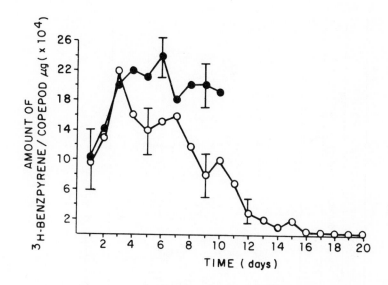

Fig. 14. Uptake and discharge of ^{3}H-benzpyrene by the copepod Calanus plumchrus. ● Copepods exposed to one μg of ^{3}H-benz-pyrene in one liter of seawater. ○ copepods exposed to one μg of ^{3}H-benzpyrene in one liter of seawater. After three days of exposure copepods were transferred to radioactive-free sea-water. From Lee [27].

R. cuneata and Prototheca staminea [28], and copepods, C. hel-golandicus [29], seem to indicate that retention of naphtha-lene in test organisms is inversely proportional to exposure temperature. Harris et al. [29] observed that retention of naphthalene in C. helgolandicus decreased by about 3.23 pg (picograms) per gram of total lipid for an increase of 10°C in exposure temperature. Accordingly, the concentration of naphthalene retained in the animals challenged at 6°C would be 44% higher than that in animals challenged at 10°C. In stud-ies with clams, Fucik and coworkers [28] found the greatest uptake of naphthalene in animals exposed at 10°C and the low-est in animals exposed at 30°C.

Lee [27] demonstrated that copepods, amphipods, crab zoea, and euphausiids were able to metabolize both aromatic and aliphatic hydrocarbons to yield hydroxy derivatives, whereas the ctenophore, Pleurobranchia pileus, was not able to metabolize benzo[a]pyrene. All zooplankton retained very small (<1%), yet detectable, levels of hydrocarbons even after 28 days of depuration.

TABLE 10

Uptake and discharge of hydrocarbons by zooplankton

| Hydrocarbon organism | Temp (°C) | Concentration of hydrocarbons per animal[a] (µg × 10⁴) | | | | | | | | | | | |
| | | Days of exposure: | | | | Days of depuration after 2 days exposure: | | | | | | | |
		1	2	3	4	1	2	3	6	8	9	14	28
³H-benzpyrene (1 µg) + No. 2 fuel oil (40 µg)													
Calanus helgolandicus	16	5.0	5.6	-	-	4.4	3.6	2.2	-	-	0.1	-	-
Calanus hyperboreus	3	7.7	8.1	11.2	7.0	7.4	5.0	3.1	-	1.0	-	-	<0.1
³H-benzpyrene (15 µg)													
Paranthemisto pacifica	14	11.0	10.0	-	-	5.0	-	2.0	-	-	-	<0.1	-
Cyphocaris challengeri	14	13.0	15.0	-	-	-	-	7.0	<0.1	-	-	-	-
³H-methylcholanthrene (0.2 µg)													
Calanus plumchrus[b]	14	5.2	-	-	-	4.4	2.8	1.6	-	0.3	-	-	-
Euchaeta japonica	10	4.8	5.6	-	-	3.8	-	1.8	-	0.2	-	-	-
¹⁴C-1-naphthalene (80 µg)													
Euchaeta japonica	10	10.0	5.0	7.0	5.0	2.0	1.0	-	-	<0.1	-	-	-
¹⁴C-1-octadecane (5 µg)													
Calanus plumchrus	14	3.1	4.6	5.2	2.2	-	-	0.1	-	-	-	-	-

Adapted from Lee [27].

a Each beaker contained six animals in 800 ml of seawater with designated amount of hydrocarbon.

b Depuration was carried out after 1-day exposure.

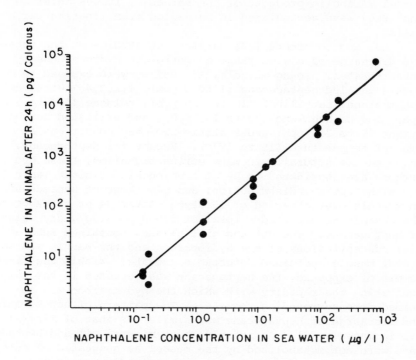

Fig. 15. Uptake of radioactivity in 24 hr by adult female Calanus in seawater solutions of naphthalene-1-^{14}C. Relationship such that y = 1.055x + 1.57; correlation coefficient = 0.990. From Corner et al. [30] with permission of Cambridge University Press.

In a recent study, Corner et al. [30] noted that the co-pepod, *C. helgolandicus,* accumulated significant concentrations (3.6 pg/animal) of naphthalene in 24 hr at 10°C when concentration of the hydrocarbon in the water was as low as 0.1 µg/l. The authors [30] also showed that there was a linear relation between the concentration of accumulated hydrocarbons in copepods and the levels in water (Fig. 15) over the range 0.1 to 1,000 µg/l. The accumulated hydrocarbon was rapidly released by animals over a period of 10 days; however, small amounts remained in test animals at the end of the depuration period.

Studies on bioaccumulation of hydrocarbons in invertebrates have focused primarily on benthic organisms. It was reported [31] that small amounts (not specified) of anthracene, phenanthrene, fluoranthrene, 1,12-benzperylene, and benzo[a]pyrene were present in the barnacle *(Tetraclita squamosa rubescens).* Because such compounds are unlikely to be

normal metabolic products of the barnacle, it was inferred
that they were accumulated in barnacles from floating tar
balls.

Lee and coworkers [32] carried out studies on the uptake
and discharge of a wide range of petroleum hydrocarbons by
invertebrates. Young mussels, *M. edulis,* were exposed to car-
bon-14 labeled heptadecane (1 to 8 ppm), 1,2,3,4,-tetrahydro-
naphthalene (tetraline) (10 to 100 ppb), toluene (100 to 500
ppb), and naphthalene (32 to 100 ppb), and tritiated benzo[a]-
pyrene (2 to 200 ppb) under static bioassay conditions at
ambient temperature (15 to 17°C). Except for heptadecane,
which occurs naturally in many marine organisms, these hydrocarbons are considered to be of nonbiogenic origin. Table 11
gives the uptake, distribution, and discharge of heptadecane
in mussels over a period of 15 days. After 24 hr of exposure,
the mussels accumulated a total of 6,000 ppm (μg/g dry weight)
of heptadecane. The gut and gill tissues contained substantial concentrations of the hydrocarbon and the mantle and adductor muscle contained detectable amounts. Within the first
20 min of exposure, the heptadecane was detected in the animal
indicating the rapidity with which the hydrocarbon was absorbed from surrounding seawater. The pattern of accumulation
and discharge of heptadecane was similar to that of mineral
oil in mussels [8]. Apparently, both mineral oil and heptadecane were not metabolized by the mussel as suggested by auto-
radiography of extracted lipids. Mussels discharged most of
the heptadecane when placed in clean seawater for 24 hr; however, the subsequent increase in levels of heptadecane was not
explained (Table 11). At the end of the depuration period
(360 hr) the gut contained the highest level of heptadecane
and the gills contained a substantial concentration.

Table 12 presents data on the uptake and discharge of
carbon-14 labeled naphthalene by mussels [32]. A substantial
amount (7 μg/g dry weight) of the hydrocarbon was taken up by
the mussels at the end of the 4-hr exposure to 32 ppb of waterborne naphthalene; the gills and gut accumulated the highest concentrations of naphthalene and the adductor muscle
accumulated a substantial amount. The mussels accumulated
significant concentrations of both toluene and benzo[a]pyrene
when exposed to relatively small amounts of these compounds in
water.

In the study by Lee and coworkers [32] with mussels,
naphthalene in the gills increased steeply from 9 μg to 22 μg
(Table 12) 2 hr after animals were transferred to clean seawater. Naphthalene in all other tissues decreased during this
time period. Excised gills exposed to radioactive naphthalene
accumulated detectable levels of these hydrocarbons rapidly,
whereas excised mantle or adductor muscle did not. It is of
interest that naphthalene continued to increase in gills when

TABLE 11

Uptake and discharge of [^{14}C]heptadecane by the mussel, Mytilus edulis

Treatment [a]	Total elapsed time (hr)	[^{14}C]heptadecane in tissues of mussels (mg/g, dry weight)				
		Whole	Gill	Mantle	Adductor muscle	Gut [b]
Exposure	2	0.14	0.57	0.08	0.01	0.16
	3	0.19	0.48	0.21	0.11	0.06
	24	6.0	13.0	7.8	1.4	20.0
Depuration	48	1.0	–	–	–	–
	120	2.8	–	–	–	–
	360	3.2	2.8	1.3	0.4	4.2

Adapted from Lee and coworkers [32]. Copyright 1972 by The American Association for the Advancement of Science.

[a] Each mussel was placed in a 2 liter beaker containing 6.2 mg of [^{14}C]heptadecane in 1 liter of seawater. After 24 hr of exposure to the hydrocarbon, the mussels were transferred to seawater free of hydrocarbon.

[b] Gut refers to all tissues other than gill, mantle, and adductor muscle.

TABLE 12

Uptake and discharge of [^{14}C] *naphthalene by the mussel,*
Mytilus edulis

Treatment	Total elapsed time (hr)	[^{14}C] naphthalene in tissues of mussels (µg/g, dry weight)				
		Whole	Gill	Mantle	Adductor muscle[a]	Gut[b]
Exposure	4	7	9	2	6	7
Depuration	6	4	22	2	4	3
	76	3	4	1	1	2

Adapted from Lee and coworkers [32]. *Copyright 1972 by the
American Association for the Advancement of Science.*

[a] Each mussel was placed in a 2 liter beaker containing 32 µg
of [^{14}C] naphthalene in 1 liter of seawater. After 4 hr of
exposure to the hydrocarbon, the mussels were transferred
to seawater free of hydrocarbon.

[b] Gut refers to all tissues other than gill, mantle, and
adductor muscle.

mussels were transferred to clean seawater. The authors [32]
proposed that gills have a micellar layer through which hydrocarbons are absorbed and subsequently transported to other
tissues. This would explain the rapid uptake of hydrocarbon
in this tissue (Tables 11,12), but does not explain the continuous increase in gills during depuration. Are gill tissues
involved in the discharge of hydrocarbons? This seems to be
an attractive explanation for the findings. Unfortunately,
little information is available on excretory mechanisms for
hydrocarbons. Further studies in this area are needed to
broaden our understanding of the fate of petroleum in marine
biota. Because concentration of hydrocarbons slowly increased
to substantial levels in the gut (Tables 11,12) of the test
mussels, it was believed that the hydrocarbons may be stored
in the hepatopancreas. No metabolic products were detected in
the study with mussels; therefore, as with heptadecane, none
of the aromatic hydrocarbons were apparently metabolized.

An interesting study on relations between temperature and
the rate of elimination of hydrocarbons was conducted by
Fossato [33]. Six depuration experiments over a 12-mo period
were carried out using mussels, *M. galloprovincialis*. Mussels
were collected from a heavily polluted area of the Lagoon of
Venice, Italy, and transferred to the relatively clean water

of Malamocco, Italy. The initial level of aliphatic hydrocarbons was determined for each group of mussels prior to a
depuration experiment. The extent of hydrocarbon discharge
was then monitored over 2 to 7 days. The data in Table 13
show that the discharge was independent of the environmental
temperature between 7.5° and 26°C. During the warmer months
the mussels released as much as 90% of the initial concentrations of hydrocarbons during each depuration experiment of
about 4 weeks. However, during November and December when the
temperature was between 4.5° and 11.5°C, mussels retained as
much as 35% of the initial concentration of hydrocarbons.
These results suggest that environmental temperature is an
important parameter in evaluating the impact of petroleum on
marine biota. Fossato [33] noted that in all samples initial
depuration was rather rapid in the first 10 to 15 days; in the
subsequent several months there was very little discharge.
Total elimination of hydrocarbons was not achieved even after
several months of depuration. The author postulated that
accumulated hydrocarbons were stored at two different sites
within the animal; the fraction that was stored in lipid deposits was not eliminated rapidly, whereas the other fraction,
which accumulated at different sites, was eliminated rapidly.
This observation supports the compartmentation theory initially put forward by Stegeman and Teal [13]. Further, it should
be noted that mussels having low lipid content were able to
eliminate accumulated hydrocarbons more completely than those
having high lipid content.

Dunn and Stich [34] studied the release of benzo[a]pyrene
from mussels, M. edulis. Mussels were taken from a heavily
polluted area and divided into three groups. The first group
was immediately analyzed for initial benzo[a]pyrene concentration, the second group was kept out of water at 15°C, and a
third group was kept in a flow-through system of clean seawater at 7°-9°C for a period up to 45 days. Mussels from the
third group were examined for benzo[a]pyrene at various intervals and the results are depicted in Figure 16. In mussels
kept in the flow-through system the original concentration of
benzo[a]pyrene (45 ppb) declined exponentially with time,
reaching background levels of 2 ppb in 6 weeks. Mussels kept
out of water remained alive for 3 days with tightly closed
shells. No apparent change in the level of benzo[a]pyrene
was observed in these mussels, whereas the mussels in the
flow-through system had lost 20% of accumulated benzo[a]pyrene
in 3 days. These findings indicating that mussels are not capable of metabolizing benzo[a]pyrene are in agreement with
previous findings [25,32].

Neff and Anderson [36] studied accumulation and tissue
distribution of benzo[a]pyrene in clam, Rangia cuneata. A
group was exposed to seawater containing 31 ppb of carbon-14

TABLE 13

Hydrocarbon depuration of Mytilus galloprovincialis

Lot number of mussels[a]	Period of depuration	Temperature range during depuration period(°C)	Hydrocarbon content of mussels[b], wet weight (mg 100 g^{-1})	
			Initial	Final
1	21 March-24 April 1973	9.0-12.8	7.3	1.2
2	1 June-19 June	20.0-22.0	3.0	1.0
3	4 July-27 August	24.0-26.0	23.8	2.8
4	6 July-30 July	24.5-25.5	4.3	0.8
5	19 Nov.-19 Dec.	4.5-11.5	8.5	3.3
6	1 Feb.-8 March 1974	7.5-10.0	25.6	2.9

Adapted from Fossato [33].

a   Mussels collected from hydrocarbon polluted areas of the Lagoon of Venice, Italy, were transferred to the relatively unpolluted port entrance of Malamocco, Italy.

b   Mean hydrocarbon level in mussels native to the port entrance of Malamocco was equivalent to 0.8±0.2 mg 100g^{-1}, based on ten samples collected during the experiment.

214

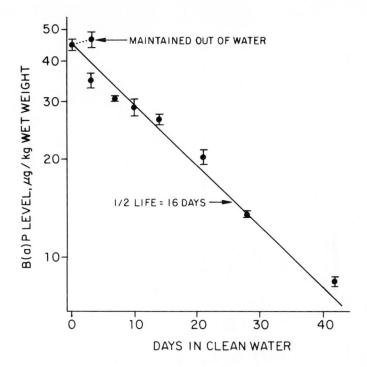

*Fig. 16.   Release of benzo[a]pyrene (B(a)P) from mussels.
Data are the mean ± S.E.M. of four to six samples.   From
Dunn and Stich [34].*

labeled benzo[a]pyrene for 24 hr at 20°C.   The animals accumulated a total of 7.2 ppm (µg/g, wet weight) of benzo[a]pyrene
(Table 14).   Nearly 75% (5.38 ppm) of the total radioactivity
was found in the viscera, which included the digestive tract,
gonads, and heart.   The mantle, gills, adductor muscle, and
foot contained 0.72, 0.49, 0.35, and 0.25 ppm of benzo[a]-
pyrene, respectively.   These findings showing viscera to be
the primary site of accumulation of benzo[a]pyrene are consistent with the results of Lee [32] showing the hepatopancreas to be a significant storage site of hydrocarbons in
mussels.   In the former study [36], when exposed clams were
placed in clean seawater, benzo[a]pyrene was released over 30
to 58 days.   The clams rapidly accumulated benzo[a]pyrene from
surrounding water, but released the hydrocarbon relatively
slowly; as much as 29% of the accumulated hydrocarbon remained
in the clams after 10 days of depuration (Table 14).   These
results [36] show that, as in other invertebrates, aromatic
hydrocarbons are rapidly accumulated and concentrated in *R.
cuneata* (bioaccumulation factor ≅236).

TABLE 14

Uptake, tissue distribution, and release of benzo[a]pyrene-C14 (BAP) in Rangia cuneata exposed to 0.03 ppm BAP-C14 for 24 hours

Sampling time	Mean total ppm BAP per animal ± S.D.	Percent of 24-hr. conc. remaining	Mean percentage total radioactivity per tissue fraction ± S.D.					
			Viscera	Mantle	Gill	Adductor	Foot
24-hour uptake (1 day)	7.2 ± 12.8(5)[a]	–	74.7±15.1	10.1±6.5	6.8±4.3	4.9±2.7	3.5±2.0
144-hour depuration (6 days)	6.5 ± 5(4)	90	81.2±14.9	7.1±6.2	2.9±2.5	5.0±3.5	3.9±3.0
240-hour depuration (10 days)	2.1 ± .97(5)	29	82.2±12.3	5.8±3.3	4.1±4.4	4.5±3.2	3.4±1.6
312-hour depuration (13 days)	1.4 ± .94(4)	19	82.7±8.8	7.4±3.2	2.8±2.8	4.4±1.8	2.8±2.6
480-hour depuration (20 days)	0.10(1)	1.4	58.8	14.3	7.1	9.4	10.5

Adapted from Neff and Anderson [36].

[a] Number of clams sampled.

Lee and coworkers [37] challenged blue crabs, *Callinectes sapidus,* with tritiated benzo[a]pyrene (2.5 ppb), and methyl-cholanthrene (1 ppb), and carbon-14 labeled fluorene (30 ppb)in seawater at ambient temperature. Within 48 hr, approximately 10% of each hydrocarbon was taken up by the crabs. The concentration of hydrocarbons did not increase after 48 hr although uptake from the water continued. Subsequent exposures were terminated after 2 days and animals were placed in clean sea-water. The distribution of benzo[a]pyrene and metabolites in various tissues of crabs is given in Table 15. Gills and hep-atopancreas accumulated high levels of the hydrocarbon: 110 x 10^{-4} µg and 160 x 10^{-4} µg in 24 hr, respectively; maximum val-ues of 290 x 10^{-4} µg and 280 x 10^{-4} µg, respectively, were reached in 2 days. Stomach and muscle accumulated relatively low levels of the hydrocarbon. At the end of the exposure pe-riod of 48 hr, benzo[a]pyrene (Table 15) as well as methylcho-lanthrene and fluorene were extensively metabolized to their po-lar derivatives. The crabs exposed to benzo[a]pyrene contained 84 x 10^{-4} µg of hydroxybenzo[a]pyrene and 210 x 10^{-4} µg of un-identified polar metabolites in the hepatopancreas (Table 15).

Lee and coworkers [37] observed that the elimination of benzo[a]pyrene from the blue crab was rapid for the first 3 days. More than 50% of accumulated benzo[a]pyrene and its me-tabolites were released within 6 days. At the end of the de-puration period of 20 days (Table 15) most tissues (e.g., gills, stomach, muscle), except for hepatopancreas, had lost virtually all accumulated hydrocarbon and metabolic products. The hepatopancreas still contained 29 x 10^{-4} µg of polar meta-bolites.

Sanborn and Malins [38] exposed spot shrimp *(Pandalus platyceros)* larvae to 8-12 ppb of carbon-14 labeled naphtha-lene or naphthalene complexed with bovine serum albumin (BSA) in a flow-through system at 10°C. This treatment resulted in a 100% mortality of Stage I and Stage V larvae in 24-36 hr. The shrimp exposed to naphthalene accumulated 820 ppb of naph-thalene, whereas those exposed to the naphthalene-BSA complex (Fig. 17) accumulated 220 ppb of naphthalene. These values represent a bioaccumulation factor of 100 and 25, respective-ly. Higher uptake of naphthalene over that of naphthalene-BSA complex may have been related to the higher lipid solubility of the former structure.

The larval tissues were examined for the presence of naphthalene metabolites; the maximum concentrations of metabo-lites expressed as naphthol were 42 ppb for naphthalene-ex-posed larvae and 49 ppb for naphthalene-BSA-exposed larvae. The ratio of naphthalene metabolites to naphthalene was sub-stantially greater at each time interval in larvae exposed to the naphthalene-BSA complex in comparison to larvae exposed to naphthalene alone. When the exposed organisms were placed in

TABLE 15

Distribution of ^3H-3,4-benzopyrene (BAP) and metabolites in tissues of blue crab (Callinectes sapidus) on exposure to water-borne BAP[a]

Product	Total time (days)	$(\mu g) \times 10^4$				
		Gill	Blood	Hepatopancreas	Stomach	Muscle
Total	1	150±70	90±17	270±90	14±2	10±3
	2	410±85	85±20	590±210	11±6	18±7
	4	100±32	80±52	300±18	10±4	8±5
	8	70±55	65±21	210±16	4±5	4±3
	12	35±12	20±13	320±74	6±2	2±2
	20	1±2	6±5	40±26	2±1	2±3
Benzopyrene	1	110	50	160	3	4
	2	290	35	280	2	2
	4	70	12	40	1	2
	8	22	8	21	T	1
	12	10	1	32	T	T
	20	T	1	2	T	T
Hydroxybenzopyrene	1	10	27	20	2	2
	2	15	12	84	2	2
	4	5	21	90	2	1
	8	11	9	40	T	T
	12	7	6	24	1	T
	20	T	2	5	T	1

continued on next page

Product	Total time (days)	$(\mu g) \times 10^4$				
		Gill	Blood	Hepatopancreas	Stomach	Muscle
Polar metabolites	1	15	10	89	8	2
	2	30	26	210	6	8
	4	12	32	140	7	4
	8	17	36	130	2	2
	12	11	10	224	2	1
	20	T	2	29	1	1

Adapted from Lee and coworkers [37].

[a] Each crab (wet weight between 25 and 30 g) was placed in an aquarium containing 5 μg of
^{3}H-3,4-benzopyrene in 2 liter of filtered seawater for 2 days. Results are expressed as
the total amount of radiolabeled material in each tissue which is composed of benzopyrene,
hydroxybenzopyrene, polar metabolites and non-extractable compounds. After 2 days of
exposure, crabs were transferred to clean seawater in order to allow depuration of
hydrocarbon from the tissues. The results for each time interval are the mean values
for three crab separately analyzed with standard deviation for the total amount of
radiolabeled compounds in each tissue. T: detectable, but less than the 0.5×10^{-4} μg.

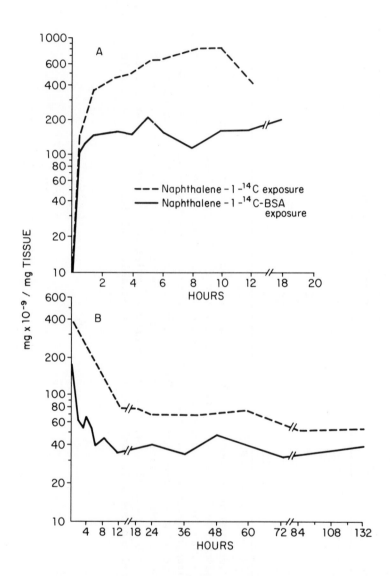

*Fig. 17. Uptake (A) and depuration (B) of waterborne naphtha-
lene-1-^{14}C-BSA complex in Stage V spot shrimp (Pandalus platyceros) after exposure to 8-12 ppb of waterborne naphthalene.
(A) Concentration of naphthalene (ng/g, wet weight) during exposure.   (B) Concentration of naphthalene during depuration.
Adapted from Sanborn and Malins [38].*

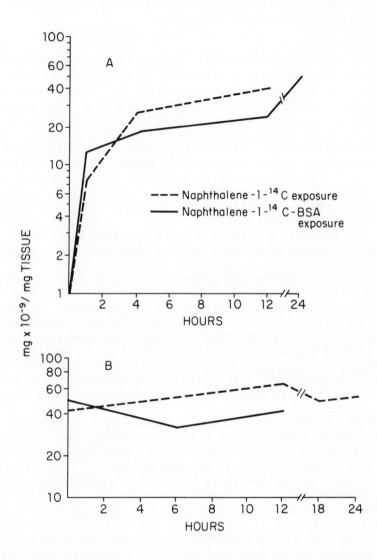

*Fig. 18.   Accumulation and depuration of metabolic products
of naphthalene (expressed as naphthol) after exposure of
Stage V spot shrimp (Pandalus platyceros) to 8-12 ppb of water-
borne naphthalene-1-14C and naphthalene-1-14C-BSA complex for
12 and 24 hours, respectively.   (A) Concentration of metabolic
products during exposure (ng/g, wet weight); (B) Concentration
of metabolic products during depuration.   Adapted from Sanborn
and Malins [38].*

clean seawater, naphthalene presented in each chemical form was released rapidly within 36 hr (Fig. 17); however, metabolic products of naphthalene were quite resistant to depuration in both test groups (Fig. 18).

Feeding Studies

Few experiments have been reported in which marine invertebrates were exposed to petroleum hydrocarbons in the diet. A challenge experiment was carried out by Corner et al. [30] using the copepod, *C. helgolandicus*. The diet was prepared by soaking *Biddulphia* cells or freshly liberated nauplii of the barnacle, *Elminius modestus*, for 3 days in naphthalene solutions (200-300 ppb). After 3 days, the radioactively labeled organisms were washed carefully to remove adsorbed hydrocarbon. These organisms were then offered to the copepods as a diet for 24 hr. The amount of food captured by the copepods was determined by estimating the number of cells before and after the experiment.

The authors [30] carried out a parallel experiment to study the uptake of naphthalene directly from water by copepods. The results are described in the previous section. The data from the feeding and water immersion studies showed that the copepods accumulated significantly higher concentrations of naphthalene from the diet than from the water. Furthermore, the naphthalene accumulated from the diet was released more slowly than that accumulated directly from seawater (Fig. 19). The loss of hydrocarbon and its metabolites in the urine and fecal pellets was monitored. Most of the radioactivity was lost in the urine; a very small amount of radioactivity was discharged through the fecal pellets. Most of the radioactivity lost during the depuration period was in the form of metabolites. These results are in agreement with those of Lee [27] showing that copepods are able to metabolize aromatic hydrocarbons. However, Corner et al. [30] found that radioactivity remaining in test animals at the end of the depuration period was primarily in the form of unchanged hydrocarbon, whereas Lee [27] found that most of the remaining hydrocarbon was in the form of metabolites. Sanborn and Malins [38] found that after depuration, naphthalene-exposed shrimp larvae retained mainly metabolites. With regard to these differences, it is important to note that in the experiment of Corner et al. [30] naphthalene was administered in the diet, whereas in the studies of Lee [27] and Sanborn and Malins [38] naphthalene was presented in seawater.

In another experiment [37], blue crabs *(C. sapidus)* were fed radioactively labeled benzo[a]pyrene, fluorene, hexadecane, naphthalene, and methylnaphthalene. The hydrocarbons were dissolved in ethanol and injected into frozen shrimp, which were subsequently fed to the crabs over two days.

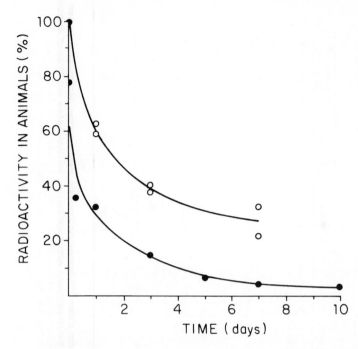

Fig. 19. Release of radioactivity by adult female Calanus
*that had accumulated naphthalene-1-^{14}C from solution (●-●) and
from a diet of* Biddulphia *cells (o-o). Losses expressed as
percentages of the original levels of radioactivity (equivalent to 170 pg naphthalene per animal for* Calanus *taking up
radioactivity from solution and 250 pb per animal for those
incorporating it from the diet). From Corner et al. [30]
with permission of Cambridge University Press.*

Initially, high concentrations of hydrocarbons were found in
the stomach of the test animals (Table 16). No radioactivity
appeared in the blood for 18 hr, whereas detectable radioactivity appeared in the hepatopancreas after 6 hr. The test
organisms accumulated approximately 7-10% of the hydrocarbons
administered in the diet (Table 16). Similar to results obtained from water immersion studies [37] with crabs, the highest concentrations of the hydrocarbons were found in the hepatopancreas. It is interesting to note that Petrocelli et al.
[39] showed that chlorinated hydrocarbons accumulated in the
hepatopancreas of shrimp and lobsters exposed to these compounds in either water or food. In the crab study [37] after
2 days, all hydrocarbons were extensively metabolized. When
the crabs were exposed to aromatic hydrocarbons in water, a
similar result occurred, indicating that crabs are able to

TABLE 16

Fate of hydrocarbons in the food of blue crabs, Callinectes sapidus

$(\mu g) \times 10^4$

Product	Stomach	Blood	Hepatopancreas	Gill	Muscle	Gonad	Excreted Material
Dotriacontane total	1,400±780	1,700±500	7,000±810	3,500±1,200	700±65	200±150	340,000±18,000
dotriacontane	930	210	630	2,200	50	110	290,000
dotriacontanol	220	1,280	2,500	610	120	11	8,000
polar metabolites	50	15	1,100	240	240	T	19,000
Methylnaphthalene total	200±45	1,200±780	18,700±7,800	900±520	60±45	600±25	75,000±7,000
methylnaphthalene	27	280	1,100	470	45	240	68,000
hydroxymethyl-naphthalene	32	480	4,800	110	12	280	2,700
polar metabolites	110	250	8,300	80	T[b]	6	2,800
Naphthalene total	300±80	6,000±1,300	14,000±6,600	1,500±870	300±280	1,500±80	55,000±2,300
naphthalene	18	2,600	1,700	830	180	500	18,000
naphthol	24	1,700	7,700	160	25	680	16,000
polar metabolites	170	460	2,800	120	T	T	4,500
Benzopyrene total	1,100±890	1,700±490	8,000±6,200	800±190	580±190	470±320	180,000±87,000
benzopyrene	720	410	4,600	610	320	110	195,000
hydroxybenzopyrene	130	720	700	29	130	80	4,000
polar metabolites	10	230	2,900	55	20	140	42,000

Adapted from Lee et al. [37].

a Crabs were fed shrimp containing either ^{14}C-labeled benzopyrene, dotriacontane, methylnaphthalene or naphthalene. There were 30 μg of radiolabeled benzopyrene, methylnaphthalene, and naphthalene and 70 μg of dotriacontane. Two days after feeding, the crabs were dissected and tissues analyzed for radioactivity. The mean values of three crabs is given for each hydrocarbon. Standard deviation is given for the total amount of radiolabeled compounds in each tissue.

b T: detectable, but less than 0.5×10^{-4} μg.

metabolize both alkanes and aromatic hydrocarbons arising from
either water or from food (Tables 15,16). After depuration of
25 days, virtually all of the activity in the hepatopancreas
was associated with metabolites.

Marine Fish

Water Immersion Studies

Studies on the accumulation and discharge of petroleum
hydrocarbons by marine fish have been largely restricted to
alkanes and aromatic hydrocarbons; virtually no information
exists on the uptake and elimination of alicyclic hydrocarbons. The literature indicates that challenge studies with
alkanes primarily involve hydrocarbons administered in the
diet. Few studies were conducted using waterborne aromatic
hydrocarbons.

Lee and coworkers [40] investigated the uptake, metabolism, and discharge of two polycyclic aromatic hydrocarbons,
carbon-14 labeled naphthalene and tritiated benzo[a]pyrene,
in mudsucker (Gillichthys mirabilis), sculpin (Oligocottus),
and sanddab (Citharichthys stigmaeus). Each species accumulated more naphthalene than benzo[a]pyrene (Table 17). These
hydrocarbons presumably entered through the gills and were
subsequently metabolized in the liver. The hydrocarbons and
metabolites were then transferred to the bile and finally
excreted. The gallbladder was a major depository of labeled
hydrocarbons and metabolic products. Each labeled hydrocarbon
was rapidly excreted in the urine and naphthalene and its
metabolites were depurated at a faster rate than benzo[a]-
pyrene and its metabolites.

Anderson et al. [18] studied the rate of uptake and discharge of naphthalene and 1-methylnaphthalene in sheepshead
minnow (Cyprinodon variegatus). The minnows were exposed to
1 ppm of either hydrocarbon for 4 hr under static bioassay
conditions. The fish accumulated 205 ppm of methylnaphthalene
and 60 ppm of naphthalene. The rate of discharge of the hydrocarbons, when the fish were placed in clean seawater, was
rapid at first and then declined slowly. After the depuration
period of 29 hr, the fish contained 10 ppm of naphthalene and
30 ppm of methylnaphthalene. The distribution of hydrocarbons
in various tissue sites was not determined.

Feeding Studies

Few feeding studies using alkanes or aromatic hydrocarbons are reported in the literature. In one experiment, Hardy
et al. [25] fed cod (G. morhua) a single dose of 2 µC of car-
bon-14 labeled hexadecane mixed in a squid diet. Only 0.4% of
the administered radioactivity was recovered from liver and
represented largely unchanged hexadecane. Studies with crude

TABLE 17

Uptake and discharge of benzo[a]pyrene and naphthalene in marine fish

Fish hydrocarbon	Duration of exposure (hr)	Duration of exposure (hr)	Hydrocarbon content of tissue (µg/g, dry weight)					
			Liver	Gut	Gill	Flesh	Gall bladder	Heart
Gillichthys mirabilis								
³H-3,4-benzopyrene	1	–	7	3	33	2	4	8
	1	24	5	3	1	3	190	2
	2	–	8	10	25	2	4	12
	2	120	1	2	1	0.5	630	–
¹⁴C-naphthalene	1	–	14.1	1.9	2.7	1.1	1.9	4.8
	1	24	0.8	0.7	0.1	0.1	5.7	2.6
	2	–	40.6	5.6	6.0	1.9	4.2	6.7
	2	1	37.4	2.2	4.0	1.1	7.9	1.1
	2	24	1.2	0.1	0.2	0.2	5.5	1.1
	2	138	0.2	0.4	0.1	0.2	6.9	0.9
Citharichthys stigmeus								
³H-3,4-benzopyrene	1	–	13	1	40	3	9	15
¹⁴C-naphthalene	1	–	14.2	2.4	17.1	8.2	3.4	3.9

Adapted from Lee et al. [40].

oil [25] showed that when cod were fed the petroleum in the diet, straight-chain alkanes having chain lengths of C_{16} were not retained in detectable amounts; however, higher molecular weight, odd-chain hydrocarbons were retained in the liver.

Whittle et al. [41] studied the uptake of carbon-14 labeled hexadecane in juvenile herring (Clupea harengus). The isotopically labeled n-alkane was mixed in ground squid and administered to herring. Much of the radioactivity was recovered in the mesenteric fat and lipid fractions of the stomach, pyloric caeca, liver, bile, intestine, muscle, brain, and gills. Substantial amounts of metabolic products of hexadecane accumulated in the same organs. The tendency for herring [41] to accumulate n-alkanes in lipid deposits is consistent with the finding of Roubal [42] who, working with salmonids, studied the dietary uptake of spin-labeled nonane and heptadecane. The n-alkanes containing nitroxide spin labels tended to be associated with the lipid portion of the biomembrane. Roubal [42] showed that neural tissues, such as brain, spinal cord, and lateral line nerve, incorporated substantial amounts of the nitroxide-labeled n-alkanes. When the animals were fed a diet free of the nitroxide-labeled n-alkanes, the concentrations of nitroxide-labeled molecules substantially decreased in neural tissues. A significant amount of the radioactivity appeared in fatty acids suggesting that n-alkanes are actively metabolized in the liver to yield fatty acids which are then utilized in lipid metabolism. Insufficient evidence is presently available on the uptake, metabolism, and excretion of n-alkanes of petroleum to adequately evaluate their fate in marine fish.

Roubal and coworkers [43] administered carbon-14 labeled benzene, naphthalene, and anthracene to young coho salmon (O. kisutch) in the food and by intraperitoneal injection. Regardless of the mode of exposure, carbon-14 (percent administered dose) accumulated in liver, brain, and muscle in following order: Anthracene > naphthalene > benzene (Fig. 20). These studies indicated that benzene, naphthalene, and anthracene accumulate in key organs in relation to the number of benzenoid rings in the molecules. Moreover, the retention was inversely proportioned to the solubility of these compounds in water. These results [43], together with those of Hardy and coworkers [25], indicate that substantial differences occur in the retention of the various petroleum hydrocarbons in marine life. Whether such differences are due primarily to discrimination at the site of absorption or during metabolism and excretion is not certain. However, the presence of one hydrocarbon apparently influences the uptake of others [44]. Thus it is likely that differences in the accumulation and retention of hydrocarbons are the result of many factors acting in concert [45,46].

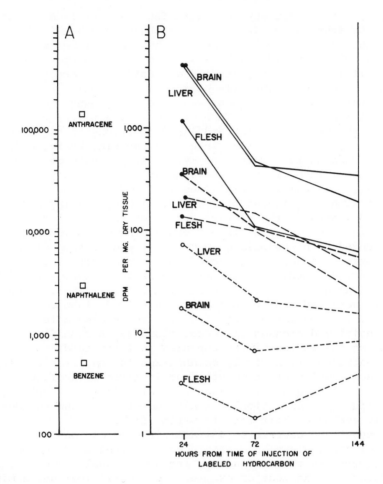

Fig. 20. *Radioactivity in tissues of coho salmon receiving* ^{14}C-*labeled hydrocarbons (2.5 μCi) by intraperitoneal injection. (A) 24 hr values for radioactivity in the gallbladder of injected fish; (B) Anthracene radioactivity (———), naphthalene radioactivity (— — —), and benzene radioactivity (-----). From Roubal et al. [43].*

Although benzene is acutely toxic to fish [47], Roubal et al. [43] found that this hydrocarbon was rapidly discharged from liver and muscle tissues of coho salmon (*O. kisutch*) in comparison to naphthalene and anthracene. It is possible that benzene may affect the respiratory processes of gills rather than exert an acutely toxic effect on internal organs. In the study of Whittle et al. [42], carbon-14 labeled benzo[a]pyrene and hexadecane were fed to juvenile herring (*C. harengus*) and, after 45 hr, the distribution of radioactivity in various

tissues was determined. The lipid of the stomach tissue of
the benzo[a]pyrene-fed fish contained 79.6% of the total car-
bon-14 present in the entire fish. The greater portion of the
remaining carbon-14 was found in the lipid of the intestine
(10.3%) and lipid-free residues of stomach, pyloric caeca, and
intestine (4.9%). More than 50% of the total radioactivity
appeared in the muscle of fish fed carbon-14 labeled hexadecane [42]; mesenteric fat, liver, and brain contained 7.2,
6.9, and 0.3% of total radioactivity in fish, respectively.
The highest proportion of the carbon-14 in the non-lipid portion was found in the bile as aqueous phase after extraction.
The work of Whittle et al. [41] demonstrated that aromatic
hydrocarbons are actively sequestered by lipid deposits in
marine fish. In another experiment with codling (G. morhua),
Whittle and coworkers [48] found that the benzo[a]pyrene-
fed fish accumulated significant radioactivity in the bile;
40% of the radioactivity was found in the stomach. In contrast to results obtained with herring, no radioactivity was
detected in codling muscle. Long-term experiments are required before conclusions can be drawn on the mode of uptake and discharge of hydrocarbons in different species of
fish.

ENZYME SYSTEMS GOVERNING THE METABOLISM
OF AROMATIC HYDROCARBONS

It is a generally accepted view that the metabolism of
aromatic hydrocarbons is mediated by the "mixed-function oxidases" (or "oxygenases") present in the endoplasmic reticulum
of animal cells. These enzymes, which are NADPH-dependent,
catalyze the introduction of oxygen into the aromatic nuclei
[49]. The oxygenases participate in electron-transport systems involving the terminal cytochrome P-448 and P-450. The
general reaction involved is as follows:

$$RH + NADPH + O_2 + H^+ \rightarrow NADP^+ + H_2O + ROH$$

The oxygenases, often referred to as aryl hydrocarbon hydroxylases (AHH) or drug-metabolizing enzymes, are believed to
account for the formation of virtually all of the primary metabolic products of aromatic hydrocarbon degradation [49]. It
is not certain that the metabolic conversion of aromatic hydrocarbons to oxygen-containing products is a prerequisite for
the production of cytotoxicity. Nevertheless, a significant
amount of evidence suggests that it is [50-54]. Substantial
evidence supporting this view was obtained by Grover and Sims
[49] who showed that aromatic hydrocarbons became covalently
bound to macromolecules (i.e., DNA) of rat liver only when
cofactor requirements for microsomal oxygenases were present.

Further evidence to support the view that aromatic hydrocarbons are activated by enzymes in animal tissues to produce oxygenated derivatives was obtained by a number of other workers [53-60]. In recent years, electrophilic intermediates (such as the epoxide group) in the formation of the hydroxy derivatives, have been viewed with considerable interest. The epoxide group has been implicated in various interactions with genetic materials [49-54] which result in deleterious alterations in life processes. Figure 21 depicts the conversion of benzo[a]anthracene to the epoxide, phenol, and glutathione conjugate [61]. Reactions involving the conjugation of epoxides and phenols with water-soluble substances give rise to mercapturic acid derivatives, glucuronides, sulfates, and glycosides in liver and kidney. The glutathione-S-transferases [49] are considered to be important because reactions catalyzed by these enzymes substantially diminish the presumed toxic properties of arene oxides through the conversion of the epoxide group to polar derivatives.

ARYL HYDROCARBON HYDROXYLASES IN MARINE ORGANISMS

An interest in the AHH of marine organisms developed recently because of the obvious importance of these enzymes in the metabolism of aromatic hydrocarbons in petroleum [62]. Until 1962 it was believed that fishes lacked the NADPH and oxygen-requiring microsomal enzymes for the metabolism of aromatic hydrocarbons [63]; however, it is well recognized now that fish possess a microsomal hemoprotein analogous to mammalian cytochrome P-450 [64-66]. Bend and coworkers [66] recently reported the resolution of hepatic microsomal cytochrome P-450, NADPH-cytochrome-C-reductase, and phospholipid components of the mixed-function oxidase system for the elasmobranch fish, *Raja erinacea*. Thus a similarity between mammalian and fish mixed-function oxidases is indicated.

Phytoplankton [1,35] and certain zooplankton [35] do not possess active AHH enzyme systems; however, a number of other marine organisms contain these degradative systems. Lee [27] and Corner et al. [30] have demonstrated by isolating metabolic products that planktonic crustaceans, such as copepods, are able to metabolize both aliphatic and aromatic hydrocarbons. Other invertebrates, such as the mussel *(M. edulis)*, scallop *(Placopecten* sp.*)*, and snail *(Littorina littorea)* do not possess detectable AHH activity [35]. However, studies on crab [37] and shrimp larvae [38] showed that marine crustaceans possess enzyme systems for hydroxylation of aromatic hydrocarbons. Lee and coworkers [40] demonstrated that both benzo[a]pyrene and naphthalene were actively metabolized in marine fish (Table 17). Evidence for AHH in marine organisms was obtained to a large degree from studies in which metabolic

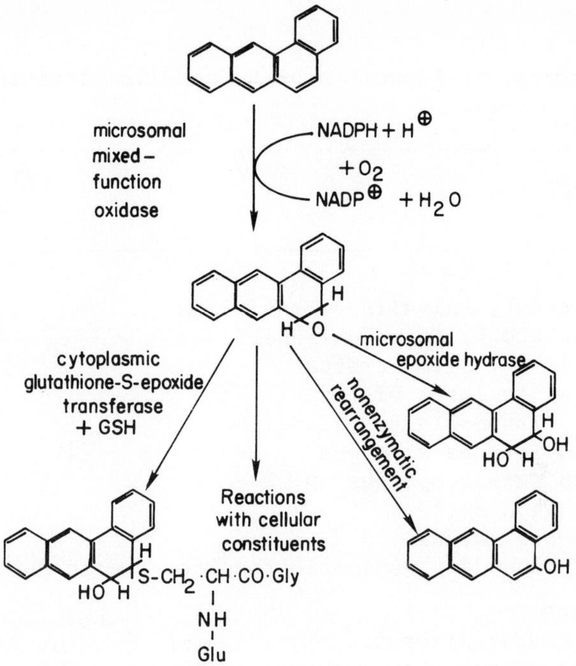

microsomal
mixed-
function
oxidase

NADPH + H$^\oplus$

+ O$_2$

NADP$^\oplus$ + H$_2$O

cytoplasmic
glutathione-S-epoxide
transferase
+ GSH

microsomal
epoxide hydrase

nonenzymatic rearrangement

Reactions
with cellular
constituents

S-CH$_2$·CH·CO·Gly
NH
Glu

*Fig. 21. Pathways involved in the metabolism of benzo[a]-
anthracene. From Swaisland and coworkers [61] with permission
from Pergamon Press.*

products were isolated from exposed animals. However, in the
last few years an increasing number of reports have been published on the direct measurement of AHH activity [35,64-69] in
marine organisms.

It is evident [35,64-79] that the livers of fish possess
active microsomal enzyme systems capable of metabolizing aromatic hydrocarbons and a variety of xenobiotics such as *p*-
nitrobenzoic acid and *p*-aminobenzoic acid (Tables 18-19).
Pedersen et al. [68] have demonstrated that rainbow trout
(Salmo gairdneri) possess the capability of hydroxylating
benzo[a]pyrene (Table 20). Diamond and Clark [69], in studies
with cell structures from bluegill *(Lepomis microchirus)* fry
and rainbow trout *(S. gairdneri)* embryonic gonad, demonstrated
the presence of enzymes capable of metabolizing benzo[a]pyrene.
Moreover, Payne [70], in attempting to compare AHH activity in
gills and liver of cunner *(Tautogolabrus adspersus)* demonstrated that benzo[a]pyrene was readily metabolized in liver
preparations (Table 21). Studies on elasmobranch [67,76,79]
indicate that some species possess very little AHH activity;
for example, the little skate *(R. erinacea)*, stingray *(Dasya-
tis sayi)*, and dogfish shark *(Squalus acanthias)* possess only

TABLE 18

Hepatopancreas or hepatic aryl hydroxylase activity in marine species

Species	Aryl hydroxylase activity
Teleosts	
Brook trout, *Salvelinus fontinalis*	+
Rainbow trout, *Salmo gairdneri*	+
Brown trout, *Salmo trutta*	+
Capelin, *Mallotus villosus*	+
Cunner, *Tautogolabrus adspersus*	+
Herring, *Clupea harengus*	+
Sculpin, *Myoxocephalus* sp.	+
Skate, *Raja* sp.	+
Cod, *Gadus morhua*	+
Winter flounder, *Pseudopleuronectes americanus*	+
Crustaceans	
Crab, *Cancer irroratus*	+
Lobster, *Homarus americanus*	+
Echinoderms	
Sea urchin, *Strongylocentrotus droebachiensis*	+
Sea star, *Asterias* sp.	+
Mollusks	
Mussel, *Mytilus edulis*	−
Scallop, *Placopecten* sp.	−
Snail, *Littorina littorea*	−
Squid, *Illex illecebrosus*	+
Algae	
Fucus sp.	−
Ascophyllum sp.	−
Mixed phytoplankton and zooplankton samples	−

Reproduced from Payne [35] *with permission.*

a slight capacity to hydroxylate benzo[a]pyrene. However, both teleosts and elasmobranchs contained hepatic cytochrome P-450 similar to that in rat hepatic microsomes [71,79]. The data given in Table 18 show the wide variety of marine organisms that possess AHH activity as well as those in which the enzyme is virtually absent [35].

The enzyme epoxide hydrase is of interest because it governs the conversion of epoxides (Fig. 21) to diols. Bend and colleagues [67,76,79,80] have examined epoxide hydrase

TABLE 19

Nitro-reductase activity in liver of various piscine species

Fish	Temp. (°C)	Nitro-reductase (µmoles *p*-aminobenzoic acid formed/g liver per hour)
Saltwater		
Lemon shark	26	0
Dogfish	37	0
Stingray	26	0
Skate	37	0.49
Barracuda	26	0.50
Yellow-tail snapper	26	0.66
Freshwater		
Pacific lamprey	25	0.02
Flathead catfish	25	0.05
Channel catfish	25	0.06
Yellow perch	25	0.07
White crappie	25	0.07
White sturgeon	25	0.08
Bluegill	25	0.09
Northern pike	25	0.14
Silver salmon	25	0.17
Smallmouth bass	25	0.18
Steelhead trout	25	0.18
Rainbow trout	25	0.21
Chinook salmon	25	0.21
Sockeye salmon	25	0.31
Carp	25	0.33
American shad	25	0.48
Coarsescale sucker	25	0.63

From Adamson [72] with permission from Federation Proceedings.

activity in the liver or the hepatopancreas of certain invertebrates, teleosts, and elasmobranchs. Spiny lobster (*Panulirus argus*), clam (*Mya arenaria*), blue crab (*Callinectes sapidus*) and the rock crab (*Cancer irroratus*), exhibited significant microsomal epoxide hydrase activity. The mussel (*M. edulis*), however, showed very low epoxide hydrase activity which is consistent with data obtained for benzo[a]pyrene hydroxylase activity [35]. Thus it appears that this organism possesses very little capacity to hydroxylate aromatic hydrocarbons. Sheepshead (*A. probatocephalus*) and eel (*A. rostrata*) exhibited significant epoxide hydrase activity with respect to styrene-7,8-oxide and benzo[a]pyrene-4,5-oxide. The eel

TABLE 20

Hydroxylation of benzo[a]pyrene to 3-OH-benzo[a]pyrene by hepatic enzymes of various strains of rainbow trout

| Strain | μmol 3-hydroxybenzo[a]pyrene formed/g protein per min[a] | | | Range statistic[b] |
	Male	Female	Combined sexes	
Chambers Creek	2.29±2.66 (12)	2.26±3.07 (13)	2.28±2.82 (25)	
Spokane	1.76±0.23 (9)	1.35±0.39 (7)	1.51±0.38 (16)	
Mt. Whitney	1.35±0.49 (9)	1.33±0.46 (9)	1.34±0.43 (18)	
Hagerman	0.44±0.11 (2)	0.70±0.38 (8)	0.65±0.35 (10)	
Donaldson	0.57±0.20 (56)	0.50±0.15 (36)	0.55±0.18 (92)	
Chester Morse	0.04±0.04 (5)	0.05±0.04 (7)	0.04±0.04 (12)	

Adapted from Pedersen et al. [68].

[a] Values indicated are mean specific activities ±1 Standard deviation. Number of determinations is indicated in parentheses.

[b] Strains bracketed do not differ statistically. Strains not bracketed do differ. Significance level chosen was $P < 0.01$.

TABLE 21

Benzo[a]pyrene hydroxylase specific activity in liver and gills of cunner

Site[a]	Number of samples	Specific activity[b] (units/mg of protein)	
		Liver	Gills
1 (Refinery)	10	53.2±25.2	0.27±0.23
2 (Harbor	8	46.6±6.7	-
3 (Control)	10	16.0±7.6	0.0
4 (Control)	9	19.9±6.6	-

Adapted from Payne [70].   Copyright 1976 by The American Association for the Advancement of Science.

[a] Sites 1 and 2 differed significantly from controls. P<0.005 for liver activity between sites 1 and 4. P<0.025 for gill activity between sites 1 and 3. There was no signigicant difference between control sites 3 and 4.

[b] Specific activity refers to arbitrary units of fluorescence of alkali-soluble reaction produce (3-hydroxybenzo[a]pyrene) per milligram of protein; values are mean ± standard deviations.

also showed significant epoxide hydrase activity with octene-1,-2-oxide.   The microsomal fractions from the livers of Atlantic stingray *(D. sabina)*, dogfish shark *(S. acanthias)*, and little skate *(R. erinacea)* generally exhibited epoxide hydrase activity with each substrate employed (Table 22).   Overall, it appears that considerable variations in the activity of the epoxide hydrase occur among different marine species [79]. Recently, Bend and coworkers [67] showed with lobster *(H. americanus)* that microsomal preparations of hepatopancreas, green gland, egg masses, and gills possess considerable epoxide hydrase activity.   Gills exhibited the lowest enzyme activity, whereas the hepatopancreas showed the highest when styrene-7,8-oxide and octene-1,2-oxide were used.

INDUCTION OF ARYL HYDROCARBON HYDROXYLASES

Petroleum hydrocarbons and a variety of other chemicals are known to alter the activity of mixed-function oxidase activity with respect to substrates, such as benzo[a]pyrene [71-74].   Payne [75] showed that benzo[a]pyrene hydroxylase was induced in the gills and liver of capelin *(Mallotus villosus)*

TABLE 22

Hepatic epoxide hydrase and glutathione S-transferase activities in crustacea and marine fish, with styrene oxide as a substrate

Species	Epoxide Hydrase Activity[a]	Glutathione S-transferase Activity[b]
Crustacea		
Blue crab	7.5±3.2(3)	0.4±0.3(3)
Rock crab	15.1±3.1(4)	0.3±0.2(4)
Spiny lobster	23.4±4.4(8)	1.1±0.3(8)
Lobster	21.9±2.4(4)	1.3±0.6(4)
Fish		
Atlantic stingray	7.6±0.7(8)[c]	5.1±1.6(8)
Bluntnose ray	2.4,4.7	4.8
Little skate	0.4±0.2(17)	2.4±0.5(17)
Large skate	1.8±0.2(5)	2.6±0.3(3)
Thorny skate	--	7.1±2.8(4)
Dogfish shark	7.6±2.4(4)	9.3
Sheepshead	6.1±2.6(16)[c]	25.5±7.7(16)
Drum	4.7±2.0(13)	16.1±5.2(13)
Mangrove snapper	2.5,1.6[d]	4.2±0.8(4)[d]
Black sea bass	0.6	2.1
Southern flounder	2.1	6.6
Winter flounder	2.0±1.4(4)	4.4±0.9(4)
King of Norway	1.8±0.4(3)	2.6±0.5(3)

Adapted from James and coworkers [79].

[a] Nmoles styrene glycol formed/min per mg microsomal protein.

[b] Nmoles S-(2-hydroxy-1-phenylethyl)glutathione formed/min per mg 176,000 xg supernatant fraction protein.

[c] Data expressed as mean ± S.D.(n). Individual values are given where less than 3 fish were assayed.

[d] Pools of liver from up to 15 fish were required to obtain sufficient microsomal protein for assay.

TABLE 23

Induction of aryl hydroxylase activity by petroleum in marine organisms

Species	Aryl hydroxylase activity
Crab	−
Lobster	−
Snail	−
Sea urchin	−
Mussel (collected near refinery outfall)	−
Cunner	+
Brown trout	+
Rainbow trout	+
Capelin	+
Algae (collected near refinery outfall)	−
Cunner	+

Reproduced from Payne [35] *with permission.*

by 1 ppm of petroleum. Several marine organisms in which aryl hydroxylase activity can be induced by petroleum are given in Table 23 [35]. A brief study of the AHH system in fish *(F. heteroclitus)* living in clean waters and in oil-polluted waters suggested that petroleum contamination induces high levels of mixed-function oxidase activity in fish [74]. Further, Payne and Penrose [78] showed that fish from petroleum-contaminated marine waters had elevated levels of benzo[a]pyrene hydroxylase activity in both liver and gills (Table 24). Payne and Penrose [78] suggested that AHH activities could be used as a monitor of marine petroleum pollution. James and coworkers [79] reported an increase in benzo[a]pyrene hydroxylase activity in sheepshead treated with 3-methylcholanthrene and 1,2,3,4-dibenzanthracene; however, pretreatment with 3-methylcholanthrene did not increase either cytochrome P-450 content or induce benzo[a]pyrene hydroxylase in stingray (Table 25). The findings of Lee et al. [81] suggest that fuel oil induces AHH in blue crab *(C. sapidus)* and polychaete *(Nereis)*. Further, Gruger et al. [82] reported that hepatic AHH activity of salmon *(O. kisutch)* was significantly induced in animals exposed to 150 ppb of the WSF of Prudhoe Bay crude oil for 6 days in a flow-through system. Stegeman and Sabo [64] found that when teleost fish *(Stenotomus versicolor)* received intraperitoneal injections of either 3-methylcholanthrene or 5,6-benzoflavone, a moderate induction in benzo[a]pyrene hydroxylase activity (Table 26) occurred. It appears, therefore, that contamination of marine organisms, especially fish, by petroleum hydro-

TABLE 24

Induction of aryl hydrocarbon hydroxylase in fish by petroleum[a]

Exposure (days)	Number of fish per group	Aryl hydrocarbon hydroxylase specific activity (units/mg protein±S.D.)[c]			
		Liver		Gill	
		Control	Oil treated	Control	Oil treated
Trout (May 1974)					
0	2	102			
16-17	6	68±14	240±88	0.07±0.51	8.7±6.1
		(t = 4.72, P < 0.001)		(t = 3.46, P < 0.01)	
Capelin (July 1974)					
0	6[b]	28.86			
7-8	4	27.2±16.7	58.1±17.3	0.043±0.083	1.07±1.26
		(t = 2.57, P < 0.05)		(t = 1.62, N.S.)	
15-16	6	27.0±10.7	130.6±34.0	0.037±0.085	3.24±1.05
		(t = 7.11, P << 0.001)		(t = 7.45, P << 0.001)	

Adapted from Payne and Penrose [78].

[a] Fish were exposed to water soluble fractions of Tia Juana medium Venezuela crude oil (average level: 1 ppm oil).

[b] Sexes evenly distributed among groups. Livers pooled before homogenizing.

[c] S.D.: Standard deviation.

TABLE 25

Effect of pretreatment with inducing agents

Species	Treatment (number)	Cytochrome P-450[a]	Benzpyrene hydroxylase[b]	7-Ethoxycoumarin[c] O-deethylase
Sheepshead	Corn oil (9)[d]	0.28±0.09	1.41±0.49	0.051±0.028
	3-Methylcholanthrene (6)[e]	0.44±0.17	15.21±8.19	0.227±0.080
Stingray	Corn oil (5)[d]	0.43±0.07	0.60±0.24	0.040±0.007
	3-Methylcholanthrene (5)[f]	0.40±0.12	0.75±0.67	0.050±0.028
Little Skate	Corn oil:acetone (6)[d]	0.24±0.02	1.22±0.17	0.360±0.058
	TCDD (5)[g]	0.25±0.03	18.40±3.00	0.563±0.096
Flounder	Corn oil:acetone (6)[d]		36.70±12.8	0.199±0.068
	TCDD (4)[h]		59.20±4.6	0.418±0.070
Little Skate	Corn oil (3)[d]	0.16±0.03	0.61±0.19	
	Dibenzanthracene (3)[i]	0.15±0.04	5.04±2.26	

Reproduced from James and coworkers [79] with permission.
a Nmol/mg microsomal protein.
b F.U./min per mg protein.
c Nmol/min per mg protein.
d Controls received the solvent vehicle by the same route and at the same time as the treated animals.
e Two doses of 3-MC (20 mg/kg, i.p.) on days 1 and 3, animals sacrificed on day 6.
f Two doses of 3-MC (20 mg/kg, i.p.) on days 1 and 4, animals sacrificed on day 6.
g Two doses of TCDD (4.5 µg/kg,i.p.) on days 1 and 3, animals sacrificed on day 7.
h Two oral doses of TCDD (4.5µg/kg) on days 1 and 3, animals sacrificed on day 8.
i Two doses of dibenzanthracene (10 mg/kg, i.p.) on days 1 and 3, animals sacrificed on day 8.

TABLE 26

Hepatic microsomal cytochrome P-450 and benzo[a]pyrene hydroxylase in treated Stenotomus versicolor

Sample	N (pooled)	Reduced CO-ligated absorption maximum (nm)	Cytochrome P-450 specific content (nmol/mg micro-somal protein)	Benzo[a]pyrene hydroxylase (units/mg micro-somal protein)[b]
Control	6	450	0.352	126
5, 6-benzoflavone[a]	5	450	0.387	217
3-methylcholanthrene[a]	3	450	0.393	219

Adapted from Stegeman and Sabo [64].

[a] Animals received a total of 150 mg/kg over 8 days, injected intraperitoneally.

[b] Activity was determined in isolated microsomes and units are expressed as 3-OH-benzo[a]pyrene equivalents produced per minute.

carbons is associated with altered levels of mixed-function oxidases.

Other factors that influence the metabolism of hydrocarbons in animal systems are of interest with respect to marine organisms. Compounds such as phenol, dimethylnitrosamine [83], polychlorobiphenyls (PCB) [84-86], trace metals [87], and epoxides [52] are known to alter AHH activity in mammals. Accordingly, attention should be given to possible synergistic or antagonistic effects of a variety of chemicals on the enzyme systems in attempting to relate AHH activities to petroleum pollution. Lidman et al. [85] showed that PCB induce the drug-metabolizing enzymes in rainbow trout *(S. gairdneri)*. Also, Gruger et al. [82] reported that 1 ppm of PCB in the diet over a 2-month period resulted in stimulation of hepatic AHH in *O. kisutch,* whereas the same treatment with Prudhoe Bay crude oil was not successful in the induction of the hepatic AHH.

Aside from chemicals, other factors influence mixed-function oxidases. Dewaide [73] showed that metabolism of several xenobiotics in rainbow trout was lower at higher temperatures (Table 27). Furthermore, Pedersen and coworkers [68] found that significant differences in the induction of AHH activity occurred among rainbow trout *(S. gairdneri)* obtained from different geographic regions (Table 28). Stegeman and Sabo [64] observed similar population differences in benzo[a]pyrene hydroxylase activity in *F. heteroclitus* sampled from different geographic areas. Large individual variations in AHH activity in challenge experiments with *O. kisutch* were reported by Gruger and Wekell [88]. Thus it appears that genetic differences, sex, size, and other undefined factors may be responsible for wide variations in AHH activities of aquatic species.

CONJUGATING ENZYMES

The conjugating enzymes are responsible for converting potentially toxic metabolic products to presumably less toxic and more water-soluble compounds, such as glycosides, glucuronides, sulfates, and mercapturic acids. The biliary excretion of xenobiotics and their conjugated metabolites is believed to constitute an important step in the discharge of xenobiotics in marine organisms [89]. In mammals, biliary excretion of xenobiotics is often associated with glutathione conjugation mediated by glutathione-*S*-transferase. The conjugating enzymes occur in the liver and kidney of the rat, but little is known about their presence or distribution in marine organisms. Recently, marine fish were shown to conjugate products of aromatic hydrocarbon metabolism [43], as indicated by the isolation and characterization of individual metabolites. In addition to such evidence, certain studies [67,79,

TABLE 27

Influence of change of environmental temperature on drug metabolism[a]

Animal	Temperature (°C)	N-demethylation of aminopyrine			
		Activity per g fresh liver	Activity per mg liver protein	Activity per mg liver DNA	Activity per 100 g body-weight
Roach (starved)	5	3.49±1.17(44)	0.0278±0.0096(42)	1.62±0.61(45)	8.16±2.06(32)
	18	2.45±0.86(39)	0.0174±0.0067(39)	0.74±0.34(38)	4.01±1.76(28)
		P<0.01	P<0.01	P<0.01	P<0.01
Trout (fed)	5	1.51±0.41(38)	0.0125±0.0038(38)	1.05±0.46(38)	2.57±0.95(26)
	18	0.90±0.30(37)	0.0083±0.0036(37)	0.39±0.23(36)	1.31±0.39(25)
		P<0.01	P<0.01	P<0.01	P<0.01
Trout (starved)	5	1.35±0.50(16)	0.0114±0.0051(16)	0.83±0.51(16)	1.73±0.59(16)
	18	0.71±0.16(9)	0.0061±0.0015(9)	0.35±0.09(9)	0.77±0.19(9)
		P<0.01	P<0.01	P<0.01	P<0.01
		p-hydroxylation of aniline			
Roach (starved)	5	1.09±0.46(40)	0.0082±0.0038(37)	0.48±0.23(40)	2.67±0.93(32)
	18	0.62±0.18(36)	0.0044±0.0015(36)	0.19±0.10(36)	1.12±0.60(28)
		P<0.01	P<0.01	P<0.01	P<0.01
Trout (fed)	5	0.39±0.08(38)	0.0032±0.0008(38)	0.27±0.09(38)	0.63±0.20(26)
	18	0.31±0.11(37)	0.0027±0.0010(37)	0.12±0.04(36)	0.37±0.15(25)
		P<0.01	P<0.01	P<0.01	P<0.01
Trout (starved)	5	0.37±0.07(16)	0.0030±0.0008(16)	0.22±0.12(16)	0.46±0.10(16)
	18	0.17±0.03(9)	0.0015±0.0002(9)	0.09±0.03(9)	0.18±0.05(9)
		P<0.01	P<0.01	P<0.01	P<0.01

Adapted from Dewaide [73].
a Activity defined as μmoles, formaldehyde or p-aminophenol produced per hour; values are means ±S.D.; the number of animals is given in parentheses.

TABLE 28

Hydroxylation of benzo[a]pyrene to 3-OH-benzo[a]pyrene by induced hepatic enzymes of various strains of rainbow trout

Strain[a]	nmol product formed/g protein per min[b]			Range statistic[c]
	Male	Female	Combined sexes	
Chambers Creek	6.50±4.71(5)	6.96±3.81(5)	6.73±4.05(10)	
Spokane	4.14±1.80(2)	5.52±1.18(4)	5.39±1.24(6)	
Mt. Whitney	3.01±0.58(3)	3.57±0.87(5)	3.36±0.78(8)	
Chester Morse	2.11 (1)	1.86±0.85(4)	1.91±0.74(5)	
Donaldson	1.40±0.74(11)	1.12±0.43(10)	1.27±0.61(21)	

Adapted from Pedersen et al. [68].

[a] Animals were injected intraperitoneally 48 hr prior to being killed with approximately 75 mg of 3-methylcholanthrene/kg body weight.

[b] Values indicated are mean specific activities ± standard deviation. Number of determinations is indicated in parentheses.

[c] Strains bracketed do not differ statistically. Strains not bracketed do differ. Significance level chosen was P < 0.01. Examination of the Hagerman strain was not performed due to unavailability of fish.

91] showed that several invertebrates, teleosts, and elasmobranchs possess the ability to convert various epoxides (e.g.,
styrene-7,8-oxide, benzo[a]pyrene-4,5-oxide, and octene-1,2-
oxide) to glutathione derivatives (Table 22). James and coworkers [79] found that the invertebrates, lobster *(H. ameri-*
canus), mussel *(M. edulis)*, clam *(M. arenaria)*, blue crab *(C.*
sapidus), and rock crab *(C. irroratus)* showed generally lower
glutathione-*S*-transferase activity than fish [winter flounder
(Pseudopleuronectes americanus), sheepshead *(A. probatocepha-*
lus), and dogfish *(S. acanthias)*]. The distribution of this
enzyme in liver and various extrahepatic tissues of the little
skate *(R. erinacea)* was determined using styrene-7,8-oxide and
benzo[a]pyrene-4,5-oxide. Of the tissues examined (e.g., liver, kidney, gills, spiral valve, mucosa, spleen, testes,
heart, and pancreas), liver and kidney possessed the highest
glutothione-*S*-transferase activity. Bend et al. [67] investigated induction of glutathione-*S*-transferase by hydrocarbons
in marine fish; 3-methylcholanthrene did not stimulate the
enzyme in *R. erinacea* when styrene-7,8-oxide and benzo[a]py-
rene-4,5-oxide were used as substrates. The few studies carried out on the conjugating enzyme systems suggest that wide
variations exist among individual animals as well as among
different species. Much more work is needed to obtain a better understanding of the role played by these enzyme systems
in the conversion of epoxides to other metabolic products. In
addition, the role of the conjugated metabolites in the biliary and renal excretion of xenobiotics in marine organisms is
of obvious interest.

FORMATION AND STRUCTURE OF METABOLIC PRODUCTS

Findings showing that microsomal enzyme systems exist in
aquatic invertebrates and vertebrates that mediate the metabolism of aromatic hydrocarbons lead to an interest in the specific structures formed [90]. Sims and Grover [49] described
the types of products formed in animal systems from the metabolism of aromatic hydrocarbons. In the first stages of metabolism, compounds such as mono- and di-hydroxy derivatives are
formed; however, as discussed previously in this review, these
metabolites undergo further conversion by conjugation with
glucuronic acid or sulfuric acid. The more water-soluble metabolites, such as glucuronides and sulfates, are prominent
constituents of the urine. Nevertheless, such excretion products often appear in body tissues and comprise a significant
portion of the total metabolites found. Figure 21 depicts the
products formed in the metabolism of benzanthracene in animal
systems [61].

To ascertain whether marine crustaceans are able to metabolize petroleum hydrocarbons, Corner and coworkers [92] fed

naphthalene to *Maia squinado*. The urine of the challenged animals contained detectable levels of unchanged naphthalene as
well as several metabolites, such as 1,2-dihydroxynaphthalene,
the glycoside derivative of this product, 1-naphthyl sulfate,
1-naphthyl glucoside, and 1-naphthyl mercapturic acid. The
finding of unchanged naphthalene in the urine was unexpected.
The authors suggested that naphthalene may be bound to macromolecules (e.g., protein) and the complex may have been degraded during laboratory extraction procedures. Animals dosed
with 1-naphthol excreted 1-naphthol, 1-naphthyl glucoside, and
1-naphthyl sulfate in their urine. In previous work [93] it
was shown that *Maia* contained considerable amounts of β-glucuronidase, thus suggesting that the glucuronides may have
been hydrolyzed in the digestive tract before excretion. Corner and coworkers [93] found that the hepatopancreas of *Maia*
contained substantial levels of aryl sulfatase despite the
fact that naphthyl sulfate was found in substantial quantities
in the urine of animals dosed with either naphthalene or 1-
naphthol. No detailed quantitative information on the distribution of metabolic products of naphthalene in *Maia* was included [92].

Lee [27] studied the metabolic fate of petroleum hydrocarbons in marine zooplankton, including copepods, euphausiids, amphipods, crab zoea, and ctenophores. These animals
were exposed to radioactively-labeled benzo[a]pyrene, methyl-
cholanthrene, and naphthalene in water. Each of these hydrocarbons was metabolized to form a number of hydroxylated metabolites by the crustaceans but not by the ctenophores. Of
the zooplankton species studied, the amphipod, *Parathemisto
pacifica*, showed the most rapid degradation of accumulated
hydrocarbons. In 24 hr, over half of the ingested naphthalene
benzo[a]pyrene, and methylcholanthrene was metabolized by this
amphipod. Lee [27] identified a number of metabolites in the
crustacea examined, including naphthol, hydroxybenzpyrene, and
hydroxy-methylcholanthrene (Table 29). The metabolites were
separated by thin-layer chromatography (TLC) and identified
against marker compounds. In a study with the copepod *(C.
plumchrus)*, Lee [27] compared the metabolism of carbon-14 labeled octadecane with that of the aromatic hydrocarbons.
Octadecane was rapidly metabolized and excreted in comparison
to slower metabolic losses encountered with the aromatic hydrocarbons. Analyses by TLC suggested that hydroxyoctadecane
was a product of octadecane metabolism in *C. plumchrus*.

In a recent study with blue crab *(C. sapidus)*, Lee and
coworkers [37] investigated the fate of petroleum hydrocarbons
acquired from both food and water. Radioactively-labeled paraffins and aromatic hydrocarbons, including benzo[a]pyrene,
fluorene, naphthalene, methylnaphthalene, hexadecane, heptadecane, and dotriacontane, were employed in the study as des-

TABLE 29

Uptake and discharge of ^3H-benzo[a]pyrene (^3H-BP) by the copepod, Calanus plumchrus[a]

Time with ^3H-BP (days)	Depuration time (days)	Amount of ^3H-BP per copepod[b] ($\mu g \times 10^4$)	Amount of ^3H-hydroxyBP per copepod[c] ($\mu g \times 10^4$)	Amount of ^3H-polar metabolites of BP per copepod[c] ($\mu g \times 10^4$)
1	—	10	0	1
2	—	14	1	2
3	—	22	1	3
3	1	16	2	6
3	2	14	1	3
3	3	15	0	1
3	4	16	0	1
3	5	12	1	1
3	6	8	1	5
3	7	10	1	1
3	8	7	1	4
3	9	3	1	4
3	10	2	0	3
3	17	<0.1	<0.1	<0.1

Adapted from Lee [27].

a Each one-liter beaker contained 6 copepods, 800 ml of filtered seawater at 14°C, 50 ppb of a water extract of No. 2 fuel oil, and 1 μg of ^3H(G)-benzo[a]pyrene (50 x 10^6 cpm).

b For the depuration experiments, copepods were transferred to one liter of filtered seawater.

c The radioactivity listed for each time interval is the mean for 6 copepods extracted and counted separately.

cribed in the previous section. Regardless of the mode of exposure a main route for the elimination of hydrocarbons and
metabolites was through fecal material. All of the hydrocarbons were metabolized by the crab to a considerable degree
within 48 hr (Tables 15,16). The fact that 50% of the radioactivity (unchanged hydrocarbons and their metabolites) accumulated by the crabs occurred in the hepatopancreas was interpreted to mean that this organ was a major site of hydrocarbon
metabolism. Twenty-five days after exposure to radioactively-
labeled hydrocarbons, a significant level of radioactivity was
still found in the hepatopancreas and was due entirely to
highly polar hydrocarbon metabolites which included dihydroxy
compounds and their conjugated derivatives. Monohydroxy and
dihydroxy aromatic compounds were found in the blood of test
animals and, in contrast to studies with a number of other marine organisms, no evidence was found for the storage of hydrocarbons in any of the crab tissues. Identification of hydroxylated derivatives was based on the use of authentic standards in TLC using two-solvent systems. In addition, certain
structural determinations were made using spectrophotometric
techniques [37].

Although some data are available on the accumulation of
aromatic hydrocarbons in larval forms, it was only recently
that information became available on the capability of marine
larval forms to metabolize aromatic compounds. Sanborn and
Malins [38] exposed Stage V spot shrimp (P. platyceros) to
seawater solutions of 8-12 ppb of carbon-14 labeled naphthalene and naphthalene as the BSA complex. Total metabolic
products of naphthalene in the larval tissues exposed to the
naphthalene and naphthalene-BSA reached a maximum of 9 and
21%, respectively, of total radioactive compounds, based on
the molecular weight of naphthol (Figs. 17,18). Of particular interest was the fact that naphthalene was almost entirely discharged from the tissues in 24-36 hr, whereas metabolic
products remained at virtually constant levels for up to 24 hr
after animals were transferred to clean seawater. Individual
metabolites were not identified because a relatively small
amount of carbon-14 was incorporated into the larvae. It remains to be seen whether other marine organisms show a comparable preference for the retention of aromatic metabolites.
The work of Sanborn and Malins [38] raises the question of
whether the toxic effects of very low levels of naphthalene on
spot shrimp larvae are related to the inability of such forms
to discharge toxic metabolic products at a rate comparable to
other marine forms.

Lee and coworkers [40] in studies with mudsucker (G.
mirabilis), sculpin (O. maculosus), and sanddab (C. stigmaeus)
showed that the major product of benzo[a]pyrene metabolism
was 7,8-dihydro-7,8-dihydroxybenzo[a]pyrene. The principal

product of naphthalene metabolism was 1,2-dihydro-1,2-dihydroxynaphthalene (Table 17). The authors observed that gallbladder accumulated the highest percentages of metabolites and that the urine was a major medium for the excretion of water-soluble products. In studying the depuration of tissues it was shown that fish could discharge naphthalene and its metabolites at a greater rate than benzo[a]pyrene and its metabolites. Roubal and coworkers [43] observed with young coho salmon (O. kisutch) that benzene was more rapidly metabolized than naphthalene and anthracene (Figs. 20,22). For example, 6 hr after the intraperitoneal injection of carbon-14 labeled benzene, the liver and gallbladder contained 32 and 63%, respectively, of total radioactivity as metabolic products. The radioactivity in the brain, muscle, and carcass, however, was almost entirely associated with unchanged aromatic hydrocarbons (Fig. 20). An examination of animals receiving naphthalene showed that after 24 hr, 13 and 72% of the radioactivity in the liver and gallbladder, respectively, was associated with metabolic products; however, in the same time period, less than 5% of the radioactivity in brain, heart, muscle, and carcass was present as metabolites. After 72 hr, substantial amounts of metabolic products appeared to arise in the latter tissues. At this time, 24% of the radioactivity in the brain was attributed to metabolic products. Similarly, fish receiving intraperitoneal injections of carbon-14 labeled anthracene accumulated high percentages (64 to 90%) of metabolic products in liver and gallbladder in 24 hr, and Roubal and coworkers [43] identified via TLC a number of individual metabolites formed in key organs of coho salmon receiving intraperitoneal injections of carbon-14 labeled naphthalene (Fig. 22). After 24 hr, the proportions of different metabolic products were evaluated in brain, liver, gallbladder, heart, and muscle. The principal metabolites in the brain were 1-naphthol and 1-naphthyl glucuronic acid. The liver comprised primarily 1-naphthol, mercapturic acid, 1-naphthyl glucuronic acid, and 1,2-dihydro-1,2-dihydroxynaphthalene (Fig. 22). The main product of naphthalene metabolism in the gallbladder was 1-naphthyl glucuronic acid (75%). Interestingly, 1-naphthol comprised 61% of the metabolites of naphthalene in heart. The 1,2-dihydro-1,2-dihydroxynaphthalene and 1-naphthyl glucuronic acid comprised 26 and 13%, respectively, of the total metabolites in this organ. Neither mercapturic acid nor glycoside and/or sulfate fractions were detected. The muscle was rich in 1-naphthol (47%), glycoside and/or sulfate fraction (26%), and 1-naphthyl glucuronic acid (14%). The findings discussed imply that a variety of metabolic products accumulate in marine organisms exposed to aromatic hydrocarbons. Moreover, substantial differences exist in the proportions of metabolic products formed depending upon the organ or tissue site. No

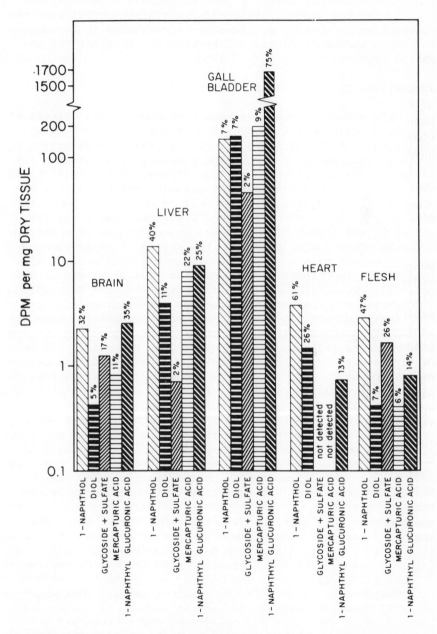

Fig. 22. Metabolic products of naphthalene in the tissues of coho salmon (Oncorhynchus kisutch)*. Adapted from Roubal and coworkers* [43].

information is available on the isolation and characterization
of epoxides in marine organisms exposed to aromatic hydrocarbons. Because most marine organisms contain relatively low
epoxide hydrase and glutathione-S-transferase activities, the
question as to whether epoxides are accumulated in key organs
following hydrocarbon exposure remains an important yet un-
solved problem.

ALTERATIONS IN BIOCHEMICAL SYSTEMS

    Only a few studies have been conducted on the effects of
petroleum hydrocarbons on the biochemical systems of marine
organisms. The results suggest that certain components of petroleum are capable of perturbing biochemical systems in organisms from phytoplankton through fishes. Nuzzi [94] showed
that No. 2 fuel oil produces certain alterations in phytoplankton cultured **axenically** as well as on natural populations
of phytoplankton. The WSF of No. 2 fuel oil had a significant
effect on the growth of the algae, *Phaeodactylum tricornutum*.
Although there was no effect on the growth of *Chlamydomonas*
sp. the growth of *Skeletonema costatum* was completely inhibited in one experiment by the addition of 1 ml of WSF of No. 2
fuel oil. Thus, although specific effects of the fuel oil on
biochemical systems were not studied, the findings of Nuzzi
[94] indicate that biochemical processes are altered when certain phytoplankton are exposed to a WSF of petroleum. Pulich
and coworkers [95] studied the effects of No. 2 fuel oil and
two crude oils on the growth and photosynthesis of microalgae.
The WSF of No. 2 fuel oil alters growth in several microalgae
including two blue-green algae, two green algae, a diatom, and
a dinoflagellate. In the case of the sensitive organism,
Thalassiosira pseudonana, strain 3H, 5 ml of seawater equilibrated with No. 2 fuel oil was found to be lethal in the range
of 40-400 ppb. In laboratory experiments [95], exposure of
organisms, such as green algae and blue-green algae, resulted
in a substantial depression in photosynthesis (Fig. 23).
Pulich and coworkers [95] suggested that observed toxic effects of petroleum can be attributed primarily to the medium-
and high-boiling fractions of petroleum. Furthermore, the
authors found that considerable variations occurred in toxicities of fuel oil to microalgae depending upon the species involved. Whether these differential effects lead to enrichment
of "oil-hardy" species in the natural environment is unknown
but remains a question of considerable interest. Hellebust et
al. [96] conducted experiments on the effects of crude petroleum on small subarctic phytoplankton, periphyton, and attached aquatic vegetation. Of main interest were alterations
in population composition, seasonal succession, and biomass;
however, it was also noted that crude oil caused an immediate

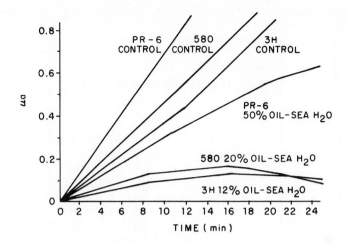

Fig. 23. Effect of a water-soluble fraction of No. 2 fuel oil on photosynthesis of three microalgae: Thalassiosira pseudonana *(3H),* Agmenellum quadruplicatum *(PR-6), and* Chlorella autotrophica *(580). Conditions: No. 2 fuel oil equilibrated for 24 hours stirring with filtered seawater; seawater separated and filtered through 0.45 nm Millipore filter and added to algal suspension 8 minutes before light turned on. Concentration of this water-soluble fraction is given in percent, v/v (e.g., 12.5% = 1.4 ml of algal suspension plus 0.2 ml of seawater = oil solubles). Controls: seawater plus medium ASP-2. The algal concentrations for PR-6, 3H and for 580 are approximately 1 x 10^7 cells/ml in medium ASP-2. Electrode current at air saturation, medium ASP-2 = 3.4 μa. Light intensity, limited by Baird-Atomic Hot Mirror (34-01-2) to 350 to 80 nm, was μW/cm^2 at level of electrode chamber, measurement temperature, 30°C. From Pulich et al. [95] with permission.*

reduction in chlorophyll content of macrophytes upon contact and that significant decreases in biomass occurred in follow-up studies of experimental oil spills in macrophyte communities. The fact that aqueous fractions of crude oil substantially altered photosynthetic rates in the blue-green algae, *Oscillatoria limnetica,* isolated from Hanna Lake, Canada, is evident from the data presented in Figure 24. Davavin and co-workers [97] showed that petroleum hydrocarbons inhibit the biosynthesis of deoxyribonucleic acid (DNA) and ribonucleic acid (RNA) in certain Black Sea algae *(Ulva lactuca, Grateloupia dichotoma,* and *Polysiphonia opaca).* An experiment was carried out in which red algae were exposed for three days to a ml/l concentration of petroleum in water. In the case of *Polysiphonia,* there was a 25% reduction in the content of both

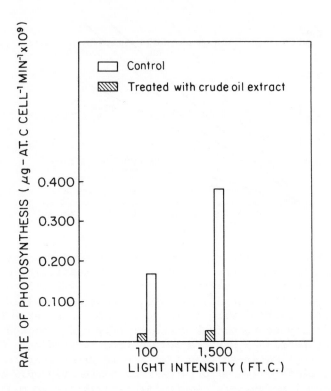

Fig. 24. Photosynthetic rates for the blue-green alga Oscillatoria limnetica *(Clone X_A), isolated from Hanna Lake, incubated for 15 min with* $NaH^{14}CO_3$, *at 20°C and 100 or 1,500 ft.c. Filaments of exponentially growing cultures were suspended in control media (open bars) and media containing aqueous crude oil extracts (striped bars) and incubated for 1 hr at 20°C and 100 ft.c. prior to the photosynthesis experiments. From* Hellebust et al. *[96].*

DNA and RNA in the test algae compared to the control. In the case of *Grateloupia,* the reduction in DNA content (35%) was greater than the reduction of RNA (6%) (Table 30). The influence of petroleum on the algae was related to the polymerization of the deoxyribonucleic acids. Kauss et al [26] showed that naphthalene (30 ppm) exposure had a significant effect on the photosynthetic capacity and motility of *C. angulosa* cells (Table 31; Fig. 25). Further, the authors [26] studied the toxicity of crude oil and its components to freshwater algae. They found that the toxic effects produced (e.g., growth inhibition) with *Chlorella* and *Chlamydomonas* resulted primarily from components of the aqueous fraction which were readily lost by volatilization. Such findings raise the possibility

TABLE 30

Nucleic acid content of Polysiphonia opaca *and* Grateloupia
dichotoma

Organism Sample	Nucleic acid content (mCi/g per 100 mg, dry weight)			DNA/RNA
	DNA	RNA	Total	
Polysiphonia opaca				
Control	1,136	5,390	6,526	0.21
Experiment	861	4,051	4,912	0.21
Grateloupia dichotoma				
Control	1,077	6,018	7,095	0.17
Experiment	692	5,664	6,358	0.12

Adapted from Davavin and coworkers [97].

that the toxic effects on the algal cells are of short duration after an oil spill; however, studies conducted with the
green algae *Chlamydomonas* in a medium containing carbon-14
labeled naphthalene showed that this hydrocarbon was rapidly
taken up from the medium by the algal cells, even under "open"
conditions (Fig. 13). The naphthalene was slowly released
from viable cells and the rate of release appeared to be dependent upon cell division. Thus it was concluded that the
more volatile aromatic hydrocarbons such as naphthalene may
be persistent in the freshwater algae although they may not
necessarily be lethal. The question remains whether accumulations of naphthalenes in algae result in hydrocarbon accumulation in the food chain.

Petroleum and certain hydrocarbon fractions induce alterations in key physiological and biochemical processes in marine invertebrates and vertebrates. Eisler [98] studied sublethal and lethal effects of petroleum on Red Sea macrofauna.
Rabbit fish *(Siganus rivulatus)* that survived exposure for
168 hr to relatively high concentrations of crude oil exhibited substantial reductions in blood hematocrit values and increases in somatoliver indices [(liver weight/body weight) x
100]. Fish exposed to 0.010 ml/l of a chemical dispersant
exhibited a significant reduction on blood hematocrit values
and a slight increase in somatoliver index (Table 32).

When mussels were exposed to 3 ml/l of Iranian crude oil
for 168 hr, 40% failed to adhere to aquarium walls or to other
mussels utilizing byssal threads. In attempting to explain

TABLE 31

Effect of naphthalene on the bicarbonate uptake and motility of Chlamydomonas angulosa *in open systems, with and without aeration*

Treatment[a]	Evaporation time (hr)	$H^{14}CO_3^-$ uptake (as % of control)[b]	Cell motility
No aeration	0	7.4	non-motile
	1	12.0	non-motile
	2	11.0	non-motile
	20	59.0	motile
Aeration for 5 hours	0	7.4	motile
	1	31.0	motile
	2	30.0	motile
	20	68.0	motile

Adapted from Kauss et al. [26].

[a] The cells were exposed to 30 ppm ($\mu g/l$) naphthalene.

[b] [(Uptake of $H^{14}CO_3$ in test cells)/(uptake of $H^{14}CO_3$ in control cells)] x 100.

toxic effects produced in the animals, the author [98] noted that: (1) water-soluble phenolic compounds together with volatile aromatic hydrocarbons are very toxic, (2) the olefins and higher-boiling saturated aromatic compounds are most likely to induce behavioral changes, and (3) non-hydrocarbon components of crude oil are comparable to the aromatic hydrocarbons in toxicity and in inducing behavioral changes. Generally, the introduction of crude oils and chemical oil-dispersants markedly alters established behavioral, metabolic, and survival patterns of Red Sea macrofauna.

Gilfillan [99] studied the effects of a WSF of crude oil on carbon budgets in two species of mussels. Exposure of *M. edulis* and *Modiolus demissus* to crude oil tended to decrease the net carbon balance for each species. As little as 1 ppm induced a reduction in net carbon balance which did not vary directly with oil concentration. Thus, small amounts of petroleum hydrocarbons can decrease the amount of available energy for maintenance, growth, and reproduction.

Heitz et al. [100] studied the acute effects of Empire Mix crude oil on enzymes in oysters, shrimp, and mullet.

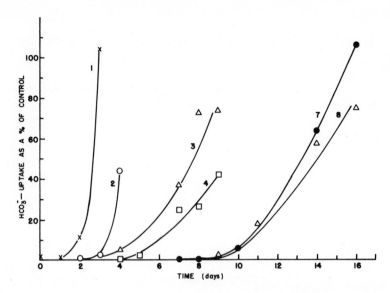

Fig. 25. Effect of exposure time on the rate of recovery of photosynthetic capacity of Chlamydomonas angulosa. *Cells were exposed to 30 ppm naphthalene in closed flasks for 1 (X), 2 (o), 3 (Δ), 4 (□), 7 (●), or 8 (Δ) days prior to opening of flasks. Adapted from Kauss et al. [26].*

Shrimp *(Penaeus* sp.) were exposed to 8 ppm of emulsified Empire Mix (OWD) for 12 hr under static bioassay conditions. Stomach-hepatopancreas homogenates from several specimens were pooled and enzyme levels were assayed in the mitochondrial and supernatant fractions. No detectable effects were observed in any of the enzymes under investigation. Oysters *(C. virginica)* were exposed to 75 ppm of emulsified Empire Mix crude oil for up to seven days (Table 33). No significant effects related to crude oil exposure were found in acetylcholinesterase, acid phosphatase, alkaline phosphatase, cytochrome oxidase, glutamic-oxaloacetic transaminase (mitochondrial), glutamic-oxaloacetic transaminase (supernatant), leucine aminopeptidase, and malate dehydrogenase. The enzymes in the test group which showed statistically different activities with respect to control groups are presented in Table 33. It is of interest that exposure of the organisms to crude oil did not significantly affect the activities of a wide spectrum of enzyme systems. Heitz et al. [100] suggested that the lack of effect may be related to the fact that the exposures were of short duration.

Recent studies of Stegeman and Sabo [64] and Sabo and Stegeman [65] demonstrate that certain aspects of lipid metabolism were altered in fish exposed to low levels of petro-

TABLE 32

Effect of two crude oils and a dispersant on blood hematocrit and somatoliver index (SLI) of juvenile rabbitfish, Siganus rivulatus

Treatment[a] (ml/l)	Hematocrit	SLI[b]
Iranian crude oil		
0.30	-7	+55[d]
1.00	-26	+105[d]
Sinai crude oil		
10.0	-16	+158[d]
Dispersant		
0.001	-10	+2
0.003	+2	+5
0.010	-18[c]	+21

Adapted from Eisler [98].

[a] Fish surviving exposure for 168 hours under static conditions were used. Values are percent deviation from controls. Control values were 47.18 for hematocrit and 1.155 for SLI.

[b] SLI = (liver weight/body weight) x 100.

[c] Values significantly different from controls at 0.05 level.

[d] Values significantly different from controls at 0.01 level.

leum: *S. versicolor* and *F. heteroclitus* were exposed to 125-200 ppb of No. 2 fuel oil in a flow-through system for a period of up to 30 days. There was as much as 90% reduction in the rate at which ^{14}C-acetate was incorporated into hepatic lipid of some exposed fish (Table 34). Moreover, the lipid content of liver was signficantly lower in exposed fish. Further, histological examination revealed a much smaller number of intracellular lipid droplets in the exposed fish (Table 34). The decreased rate of lipogenesis in the exposed fish was reflected in a decrease of ^{14}C-acetate incorporation into triglycerides, a major component of the hepatic lipid droplets. There was a decrease in the rate of synthesis of phospholipids and an increase in the synthesis of cholesterol as revealed by TLC (Table 35). Low levels of petroleum appeared to cause reduction in the storage of triglycerides and also bring about alterations in the synthesis of two major lipid components of the cellular membrane (i,e., phospholipid and cholesterol)[65].

TABLE 33

Enzyme levels in oysters (Crassostrea virginica) treated with Empire Mix crude oil [a]

Enzyme[b]	Fraction[c]	Specific activity[d]			
		Control	2 day	4 day	7 day
→B-GLU	SS	958.05±82.99(23)[d]	1275.21±114.25(11)	1370.97±112.35(15)	848.18±148.10(17)[e]
GPT	M	34.31±3.09(27)	39.00±3.68(19)	26.45±7.74(13)	58.94±7.26(21)[e]
GPT	S	39.58±2.51(26)	51.20±2.36(19)	37.74±3.17(15)	40.91±2.58(20)[f]
LAP	S	421.92±74.14(21)	160.37±69.95(14)	501.79±76.52(15)	312.84±71.39(17)[g]
MDH	M	440.00±36.54(22)	326.05±30.38(15)	341.11±38.13(15)	468.21±34.03(17)[h]

Reproduced from Heitz et al. [100] with permission.

[a] Oysters were exposed to oil-water dispersions containing 75 ppm of oil. The resulting concentration of oil in the water column was about 4 ppm.

[b] →B-GLU = β-glucuronidase (β-D-glucuronide glucuronohydrolase; 3.2.1.31)
  → LAP = Leucine aminopeptidase (3.4.1.1)
  → MDH = Malate dehydrogenase (L-malate:NAD oxidoreductase; 1.1.1.37)
  → GPT = Glutamic-pyruvic transaminase (L-alanine:2-oxoglutarate aminotransferase; 2.6.1.2)

[c] M fraction is defined as that portion of an 800 g/10-min supernatant sedimented at 8000 g for 15 min.
  S fraction is defined as the supernatant from an 8000 g/15-min centrifugation.
  SS fraction is defined as the supernatant of a 110,000 g/30-min centrifugation of a homgenate which had been sonified at 35 w for 0.5 min.

[d] (Millimicromoles of product formed/min per mg protein, mean ± SE.) Number in parentheses is number of replications.

[e] 4-day treatment mean significantly different from 7-day treatment mean ($p < 0.05$).

[f] 2-day treatment mean significantly different from 4- and 7-day treatment means ($p < 0.05$).

[g] 2-day treatment mean significantly different from 4-day treatment mean ($p < 0.05$).

[h] Control and 7-day treatment means significantly different from 2- and 4-day treatment means ($p < 0.05$).

257

TABLE 34

Incorporation of acetate-1-14 into hepatic lipid and hepatic lipid content in Stenotomus versicolor and Fundulus heteroclitus

Sample	Days treatment[a]	Control				Experimental			
		N[b]	cpm/100 mg tissue[c]	% liver lipid	Lipid vacuoles per cell[d]	N[b]	cpm/100 mg tissue[c]	% liver lipid	Lipid vacuoles per cell[d]
S. versicolor	30	3	2895(±434)	1.8(±1.1)	–	3	179(±23)[f]	1.1(±0.12)[g]	–
F. heteroclitus (Sippewissett)	5	5	1885(±305)	3.1(±0.3)	13.2	6	250(±150)[f]	2.4(±0.2)[e]	1.5[g]
F. heteroclitus (Wild Harbor)	5	11	440(±311)	2.4(±0.4)	12.8	11	300(±145)	1.8(±0.3)	0.6[g]

Reproduced from Stegeman and Sabo [64] with permission.

[a] Continuous exposure in a flow-through system with 180–200 µg #2 fuel oil (API)/liter.

[b] Samples were of mixed sexes, pooled, and the numbers in parentheses indicate S.E.M. of 2 to 9 replicates.

[c] cpm of lipid extracted following 2 hr incubation with acetate-1-^{14}C at 21(±1) °C.

[d] Values given are averages of visible lipid vacuoles counted in 25 randomly selected hepatocytes in histological preparations from each group.

[e] Significantly different from control at P $\leq$ 0.10 (e); P $\leq$ 0.01 (f); P $\leq$ 0.001 (g). Values determined using 2 x 2 contingency tables and Fisher's exact test, Student's t-test or a one-way anova and F test.

TABLE 35

Percent Contribution to Total Lipid by Lipid Class in
Fundulus heteroclitus *after exposure to 180 ppb No. 2*
fuel oil for 8 days

Lipid Class	Acetate-1-^{14}C	
	Control	Oil
Phospholipid	27.8	19.5
Cholesterol	12.7	50.6
Fatty Acid	12.7	11.8
Triglyceride	17.2	10.2
Cholesterol Ester	9.5	2.3

Reproduced from Sabo and Stegeman [65] *with permission.*

Hydrocarbons tend to associate with the lipid portion of the
biomembrane [42] and may alter the fluidity of the membrane.
Thus, changes in the proportions of the membrane lipids in
the contaminated fish (Table 35) [65] may be an effort to preserve membrane architecture. In considering the numbers and
types of studies reported on the interactions of petroleum
hydrocarbons with various biochemical systems of marine organisms, it becomes apparent that additional work needs to be
conducted. While it is obvious that a number of biochemical
systems can be perturbed in animals exposed to petroleum,
virtually no data are available to relate these events to durations and levels of exposure, environmental temperature, and
other significant experimental parameters. Accordingly, obvious difficulties arise in attempting to evaluate realistically the significance of the various changes induced in the
biochemical and physiological processes of marine organisms
on exposure to petroleum hydrocarbons.

FOOD WEB MAGNIFICATION

It is clear from previous discussion that the uptake of
petroleum hydrocarbons from seawater is a major pathway in
bioaccumulation. Another important pathway for the uptake of
petroleum hydrocarbons is via the diet. Parker and coworkers
[6] and Conover [1] have shown that copepods and barnacle
larvae exposed to petroleum contain considerable amounts of
oil in the gut which is excreted via fecal pellets. Thus,
when plankton graze on hydrocarbons from an oil slick, petroleum in their fecal material would be released into the environment. The fecal pellets, being heavier than the water,
would tend to drop to the bottom and associated petroleum

would become available to bottom feeders. Thus, oil from the slick would be transported into marine biota. Parker and co-workers [6] calculated that a copepod *(C. finmarchicus)* could graze up to 1.5×10^{-4} g of oil per day; therefore, a shoal of *C. finmarchicus* at a population of 2,000 individuals per m^3 covering an area of 1 km^2 to a depth of 10 m could encapsulate as much as 3 tons of oil per day when the level of oil is 1.5 ppm or higher. Such biological transport of oil constitutes an important factor in the food web. Soft-shelled clams *(M. arenaria)* [9] accumulated oil in an oil-mucus complex, thus transporting the oil to a denser particle, which, when re-leased, would accumulate in the sediment. In relation to this process, it is interesting that Blackman [23] found that the shrimp, *C. crangon,* is apt to eat sunken oil from sediment and the oil remains in the gut over a long period. This oil is available to predators of shrimp until they are molted. In another experiment Blackman and Mackie [101] observed that the plaice (*Pleuronectes platessa)* was capable of ingesting both clean and petroleum-contaminated shrimp offered as food. The live shrimp were dropped into the tank containing plaice and the feeding pattern of the fish was observed. The authors [101] concluded that the contaminated shrimp were eaten more frequently than the clean shrimp, presumably because the for-mer shrimp were easier to catch. Unfortunately, levels of pe-troleum hydrocarbons either in shrimp or plaice were not de-termined to learn if any biomagnification of petroleum oc-curred in plaice with respect to shrimp.

The findings discussed so far in this section merely im-ply the presence of mechanisms for biomagnification of petro-leum in the food web. Whether these mechanisms for biomagni-fication are a significant factor in the biological transport of petroleum remains to be determined. Nevertheless, several factors suggest that biomagnification of petroleum through the food web may not be a major route to the accumulation of pe-troleum in higher forms. Most marine organisms are able to accumulate substantial amounts of hydrocarbons directly from seawater; bioaccumulation of 200-300 times over the levels in the water occur in crustacea and fish. Yet, when these ani-mals are placed in clean water, most of the accumulated hydro-carbons are eventually discharged, often in hours or one or two days. On the basis of several studies it can be concluded that the concentrations of petroleum in tissues probably do not significantly increase at higher tropic levels, although in most of the species examined the rate of uptake was much greater than the rate of elimination.

Recent study [38] demonstrated that metabolic products of naphthalene were retained with little change in spot shrimp larval forms while parent hydrocarbon was almost entirely dis-charged. These findings raise questions about the transfer of *metabolic products* through the food web; however, virtually no data are available on this subject.

PROSPECTUS

The findings discussed were carried out primarily at 10°-20°C and most of the organisms considered are indigenous to arctic and subarctic regions. Because of a lack of direct information on the metabolic fate and biological effects of petroleum on marine biota in arctic regions the literature reviewed provides the only evaluation possible of the impact of petroleum on organisms inhabiting this area. A need exists to conduct more challenge experiments at low temperatures and under other conditions prevailing in the arctic. Challenge experiments investigating effects of temperature and salinity on bioaccumulation and metabolism of petroleum in marine biota would greatly enlarge our knowledge of the biological consequences of petroleum pollution. Another important area of research that has been largely overlooked is food chain transfer of petroleum and its metabolic products. Detailed studies involving bioaccumulation of petroleum products in organisms from different stages of the food chain would be desirable to obtain a better perspective of whether biomagnification of petroleum in the food web is an important process in the accumulation of hydrocarbons in higher organisms. Very few studies have been reported on bioaccumulations and biological effects of petroleum hydrocarbons in developmental stages of marine organisms. Investigations on how petroleum affects various life stages (e.g., eggs, larvae) of the same organisms would provide a better understanding of the overall impact of petroleum on marine environments. Most of the investigations on bioaccumulation and discharge of petroleum hydrocarbons have dealt with parent hydrocarbons; however, recent studies [37, 38] have shown that metabolic products of the hydrocarbons may be retained to a significant extent when parent hydrocarbons are minimal during depuration. Thus, studies with invertebrates and fish which actively metabolize petroleum hydrocarbons should be directed toward characterization of metabolic products, as well as toward their rate of formation and excretion. Moreover, enzymes (mixed function oxidases, epoxide hydrases, and conjugating enzyme systems) involved in the metabolism of aromatic hydrocarbons merit an important place in future work.

REFERENCES

1. Conover, R.J. (1971). Some relations between zooplankton and Bunker C oil in Chedabucto Bay following the wreck of the tanker *Arrow*. J. Fish. Res. Board Can. 28:1327-30.
2. Morris, R.J. (1973). Uptake and discharge of petroleum hydrocarbons by barnacles. Mar. Pollut. Bull. 4:107-9.
3. Clark, R.C., Jr., J.S. Finley, B.G. Patten, D.F. Stefani, and E.E. DeNike (1973). Interagency investigations of a persistent oil spill on the Washington Coast. Animal population studies, hydrocarbon uptake by marine organisms, and algae response following the grounding of the troopship *General M.C. Meigs*. In: Proceedings of 1973 Joint Conference on Prevention and Control of Oil Spills, p. 793-808. American Petroleum Institute, Washington, D.C.
4. Blumer, M., G. Souza, and J. Sass (1970). Hydrocarbon pollution of edible shellfish by an oil spill. Mar. Biol. (Berl.) 5:195-202.
5. Anderson, J.W., J.M. Neff, B.A. Cox, H.E. Tatem, and G.M. Hightower (1974). Characteristics of dispersions and water-soluble extracts of crude and refined oils and their toxicity to estuarine crustaceans and fish. Mar. Biol. (Berl.) 27:75-88.
6. Parker, C.A., M. Freegarde, and C.G. Hatchard (1971). The effect of some chemical and biological factors on the degradation of crude oil at sea. In: Water Pollution by Oil (P. Hepple, ed.), p. 237-44. Institute of Petroleum, London.
7. Cohen, Y. (1973). Effects of crude oil on the Red Sea alcyonanian *Heteroxenia fuscescens*. M.S. Thesis, Hebrew University, Jerusalem, Israel.
8. Lee, R.F., J. Hirota, J.C. Nevenzel, R. Sauerheber, A.A. Benson, and A. Lewis (1972). Lipids in the marine environment. Calif. Mar. Res. Commu. *CalCOFI* Rep. 16:95-102.
9. Stainken, D.M. (1975). Preliminary observations on the mode of accumulation of No. 2 fuel oil by the soft shell clam *Mya arenaria*. In: Proceedings of 1975 Joint Conference on Prevention and Control of Oil Pollution, p. 463-8. American Petroleum Institute, Washington, D.C.
10. Anderson, J.W. (1975). Laboratory studies on the effects of oil on marine organisms: An overview. Am. Petrol. Inst. Publ. 4249, p. 1-70.
11. Neff, J.M. and J.W. Anderson (1975). An ultraviolet spectrophotometric method for the determination of naphthalene and alkylnaphthalenes in the tissues of oil-contaminated marine animals. Bull. Environ. Contam. Toxicol. 14:122-8.

12. Neff, J.M., D. Dixit, B.A. Cox, and J.W. Anderson (1976). Accumulation and release of petroleum derived aromatic hydrocarbons by marine animals. Mar. Biol (Berl.), In press.

13. Stegeman, J.J. and J.M. Teal (1973). Accumulation, release, and retention of petroleum hydrocarbons by the oyster, *Crassostrea virginica*. Mar. Biol. (Berl.) 22: 37-44.

14. Clark, R.C., Jr., J.S. Finley, and G.G. Gibson (1974). Acute effects of outboard motor effluent on two marine shellfish. Environ. Sci. Technol. 8:1009-14.

15. Clark, R.C., Jr. and J.S. Finley (1975). Uptake and loss of petroleum hydrocarbons by the mussel, *Mytilus edulis*, in laboratory experiments. Fish. Bull. 73:508-15.

16. Rossi, S.S., J.W. Anderson, and G.S. Ward (1976). Toxicity of water-soluble fractions of four test oils for the polychaetous annelids, *Neanthes arenaceodentata* and *Capitella capitata*. Environ. Pollut. 10:9-17.

17. Reish, D.J. (1957). The relationship of polychaetous annelid *Capitella capitata* (Fabricus) to waste discharge of biological origins. In: Biological Problems in Water Pollution (C.M. Tarzell, ed.), p. 195-200. Public Health Service, Washington, D.C.

18. Anderson, J.W., J.M. Neff, B.A. Cox, H.E. Tatem, and G.M. Hightower (1974). The effects of oil on estuarine animals: toxicity, uptake and depuration, respiration. In: Pollution and Physiology of Marine Organisms (F.J. Vernberg and W.B. Vernberg, eds.), p. 285-310. Academic Press, New York.

19. Anderson, J.W., R.C. Clark, Jr., and J. Stegeman (1974). In: Petroleum hydrocarbons. Marine Bioassays Workshop Proceedings, p. 36-75. American Petroleum Institute, Washington, D.C.

20. Rossi, S.S. (1976). Interactions between petroleum hydrocarbons and the polychaetous annelid, *Neanthes arenaceodentata:* Effects on growth and reproduction; fate of diaromatic hydrocarbons accumulated from solutions or sediments. Ph.D. Thesis, Texas A & M University, College Station, Tex.

21. Anderson, J.W., L.J. Moore, J.W. Blaylock, D.L. Woodruff, and S.L. Kiesser (1977). Bioavailability of sediment-sorbed naphthalenes to the sipunculid worm, *Phascolosoma agassizii*. In: Proceedings of Symposium on Fate and Effects of Petroleum Hydrocarbons in Marine Ecosystems and Organisms (D. Wolfe, ed.). In press. Pergamon Press, New York.

22. Fossato, V.U. and W.J. Canzonier (1976). Hydrocarbon uptake and loss by the mussel *Mytilus edulis*. Mar. Biol. 36:243-50.

23. Blackman, R.A.A. (1972). Effects of sunken crude oil on the feeding and survival of the brown shrimp, *Crangon crangon*. Int. Counc. Explor. Sea C.M. 1972/K:13. p. 1-6.

24. Rice, S.D., R.E. Thomas, and J.W. Short (1976). Effect of petroleum hydrocarbons on breathing and coughing rates and hydrocarbon uptake-depuration in pink salmon fry. In: Symposium on Pollution and Physiology of Marine Organisms. In press. Academic Press, New York.

25. Hardy, R., P.R. Mackie, K.J. Whittle, and A.D. McIntyre (1974). Discrimination in the assimilation of *n*-alkanes in fish. Nature 252:577-8.

26. Kauss, P., T.C. Hutchinson, C. Soto, J. Hellebust, and M. Griffiths (1973). The toxicity of crude oil and its components to freshwater algae. In: Proceedings of 1973 Conference on Prevention and Control of Oil Spills, p. 703-14. American Petroleum Institute, Washington, D.C.

27. Lee, R.F. (1975). Fate of petroleum hydrocarbons in marine zooplankton. In: Proceedings of 1975 Conference on Prevention and Control of Oil Pollution, p. 549-53. American Petroleum Institute, Washington, D.C.

28. Fucik, K.W., J.M. Neff, and M.L. Byington (1977). Effects of temperature and salinity on naphthalenes uptake in the temperate clam, *Rangia cuneata* and the boreal clam *Prototheca staminea*. In: Proceedings of Symposium on Fate and Effects of Petroleum Hydrocarbons in Marine Ecosystems and Organisms (D. Wolfe, ed.). In press. Pergamon Press, New York.

29. Harris, R.P., V. Berdugo, E.D.S. Corner, C.C. Kilvington, and S.C.M. O'Hara (1977). Factors affecting the retention of a petroleum hydrocarbon by marine planktonic copepods. In: Proceedings of Symposium on Fate and Effects of Petroleum Hydrocarbons in Marine Ecosystems and Organisms (D. Wolfe, ed.) In press. Pergamon Press, New York.

30. Corner, E.D.S., R.P. Harris, C.C. Kilvington, and S.C.M. O'Hara (1976). Petroleum compounds in the marine food web: Short-term experiments on the fate of naphthalene in *Calanus*. J. Mar. Biol. Assoc. U.K. 56:121-33.

31. Zechmeister, L. and B.K. Koe (1952). The isolation of carcinogenic and other polycyclic aromatic hydrocarbons from barnacles. Arch. Biochem. Biophys. 35:1-11.

32. Lee, R.F., R. Sauerheber, and A.A. Benson (1972). Petroleum hydrocarbons: Uptake and discharge by the marine mussel *Mytilus edulis*. Science 177:344-6.

33. Fossato, V.U. (1975). Elimination of hydrocarbon by mussels. Mar. Pollut. Bull. 6:7-10.

34. Dunn, B.P. and H.F. Stich (1976). Release of carcinogen benzo[a]pyrene from environmentally contaminated mussels. Bull. Environ. Contam. Toxicol. 15:398-401.

35. Payne, J.F. (1976). Personal communication. Newfoundland Biological Station, St. John's Newfoundland.

36. Neff, J.M. and J.W. Anderson (1975). Accumulation, release, and distribution of benzo[a]pyrene-C^{14} in the clam *Rangia cuneata*. In: Proceedings of 1975 Conference on Prevention and Control of Oil Pollution, p. 469-71. American Petroleum Institute, Washington, D.C.

37. Lee, R.F., C. Ryan, and M.L. Neuhauser (1976). Fate of petroleum hydrocarbons taken up from food and water by the blue crab, *Callinectes sapidus*. Mar. Biol. (Berl.), In press.

38. Sanborn, H.R. and D.C. Malins (1977). Toxicity and metabolism of naphthalene: A study with marine larval invertebrates. Proc. So. Exp. Biol. Med. 154:151-5.

39. Petrocelli, S.R., J.W. Anderson, and A.R. Hanks (1975). Biomagnification of dieldrin residues by food chain transfer from clams to blue crabs under controlled conditions. Bull. Environ. Contam. Toxicol. 13:108-16.

40. Lee, R.F., R. Sauerheber, and G.H. Dobbs (1972). Uptake, metabolism and discharge of polycyclic aromatic hydrocarbons by marine fish. Mar. Biol. (Berl.) 17:201-8.

41. Whittle, K.J., J. Murray, P.R. Mackie, R. Hardy, and J. Farmer (1976). Fate of hydrocarbons in fish. Int. Counc. Explor. Sea, In press.

42. Roubal, W.T. (1974). *In vivo* and *in vitro* spin-labeling studies of pollutant host interaction. In: Mass Spectrometry and NMR Spectroscopy in Pesticide Chemistry (R. Hague and F.J. Biros, eds.), p. 303-23. Plenum Press, New York.

43. Roubal, W.T., T.K. Collier, and D.C. Malins (1977). Accumulation and metabolism of carbon-14 labeled benzene, naphthalene, and anthracene by young coho salmon *(Oncorhynchus kisutch)*. Arch. Environ. Contam. Toxicol., In press.

44. Boehm, P.D. and J.G. Quinn (1976). The effect of dissolved organic matter in sea water on the uptake of mixed individual hydrocarbons and No. 2 fuel oil by a marine filter-feeding bivalve *(Mercenaria mercenaria)*. Estuarine Coastal Mar. Sci. 4:93-105.

45. Farrington, J.W. and P.A. Meyers (1975). Hydrocarbons in the marine environment. In: Environmental Chemistry (G. Eglinton, ed.), Vol. I, p. 109-36. The Chemical Society, London.

46. Stegeman, J.J. (1976). Biological and ecological effects of petroleum in the marine environment. In: Proceedings of second UNESCO Intergovernmental Oceanographic Commission-World Meteorological Association Workshop on Marine Pollution (Petroleum) Monitoring. Monte Carlo, Monaco.

47. Meyerhoff, R.D. (1975). Acute toxicity of benzene, a component of crude oil, to juvenile striped bass *(Morone saxatilis)*. J. Fish. Res. Board Can. 32:1864-6.

48. Whittle, K., P.R. Mackie, and R. Hardy (1974). Hydrocarbons in the marine ecosystems. S. Afr. J. Sci. 70: 141-4.

49. Sims, P. and P.L. Grover (1974). Polycyclic aromatic hydrocarbons. In: Advances in Cancer Research (G. Klein, S. Weinhouse, and A. Haddow, eds.), Vol. 20, p. 165-274. Academic Press, New York.

50. Magee, P.N. (1974). Activation and inactivation of chemical carcinogens and mutagens in the mammal. In: Essays in Biochemistry (P.N. Campbell and F. Dickens, eds.), Vol. 10, p. 105-36. Academic Press, New York.

51. Wood, A., W. Levin, A.Y.H Lu, H. Yagi, O. Hernandez, D.M. Jerina, and A.H. Conney (1976). Metabolism of benzo[a]pyrene and benzo[a]pyrene derivatives to mutagenic products by highly purified hepatic microsomal enzymes. J. Biol. Chem. 251:4882-90.

52. Yang, C.S. and F.S. Strickhart (1975). Effects of some epoxides on aryl hydrocarbon hydroxylase activity. Biochem. Pharmacol. 24:646-648.

53. Weinstein, I.B., A.M. Jeffrey, K.W. Jennette, S.H. Blobstein, R.G. Harvey, C. Harris, H. Autrup, H. Kazai, and K. Nakanishi (1976). Benzo[a]pyrene diol epoxides as intermediates in nucleic acid binding *in vitro* and *in vivo*. Science 193:592-4.

54. Malaveille, C., H. Bartsch, P.L. Grover, and P. Sims (1975). Mutagenicity of non-K-region diols and diol-epoxides of benz[a]anthracene and benz[a]pyrene. Biochem. Biophys. Res. Commun. 66:693-700.

55. Grover, P.L. and P. Sims (1968). Enzyme-catalyzed reactions of polycyclic hydrocarbons with deoxyribonucleic acid and protein *in vitro*. Biochem. J. 110:159-60.

56. Gelboin, H.V. (1969). Microsome-dependent binding of benzo[a]pyrene to DNA. Cancer Res. 29:1272-6.

57. Wang, I.Y., H.S. Marver, R.E. Rasmussen, and T.T. Crocker (1971). Enzymic conversion of benzo[a]pyrene hydroxylation versus DNA-binding. Arch. Intern. Med. 128:125-30.

58. Hey-Ferguson, A. and E. Bresnick (1971). Binding of 3-methylcholanthrene to macromolecular components of rat liver preparations. Mol. Pharmacol. 7:183-90.

59. Bogdan, D.P. and Z.F. Chmielewicz (1973). Studies on interactions between polynucleotides and benzo[a]pyrene in the presence of aryl hydrocarbon hydroxylase. Proc. Am. Assoc. Cancer Res. 14:49.

60. Meunier, M. and J. Chauveau (1973). Binding of benzo[a] pyrene metabolites to main and satellite calf thymus DNA *in vitro*. FEBS (Fed. Eur. Biochem. Soc.) Lett. 31: 327-31.

61. Swaisland, A.J., P.L. Grover, and P. Sims (1973). Epoxides in polycyclic aromatic hydrocarbon metabolism and carcinogenesis. Biochem. Pharmacol. 22:1547-56.

62. Malins, D.C. (1977). Biotransformation of petroleum hydrocarbons in marine organisms indigenous to the arctic and subarctic. In: Proceedings of Symposium on Fate and Effects of Petroleum Hydrocarbons in Marine Ecosystems and Organisms (D. Wolfe, ed.). In press. Pergamon Press, New York.

63. Brodie, B.B. and R.P. Maickel (1962). Comparative biochemistry of drug metabolism. In: Proceedings of the First International Pharmacology Meeting (B.B. Brodie and E.G. Erdos, eds.), Vol. 6, p. 299. MacMillan, New York.

64. Stegeman, J.J. and D.J. Sabo (1976). Aspects of the effects of petroleum hydrocarbons on intermediary metabolism and xenobiotic metabolism in marine fish. In: Sources, Effects, and Sinks of Hydrocarbons in the Aquatic Environment. In press. American Institute of Biological Sciences, Washington, D.C.

65. Sabo, D.J. and J.J. Stegeman (1976). Some metabolic effects of petroleum hydrocarbons in a marine fish. In: Pollution and Physiology of Marine Organisms II (A. Calabrese and J.F. Vernberg, eds.). In press. Academic Press, New York.

66. Bend, J.R., R.J. Pohl, E. Arinc, and R.M. Philpot (1976). Hepatic microsomal and solubilized mixed-function oxidase systems for the little skate *(Raja erinacea)*, a marine elasmobranch. Proceedings of Third International Symposium on Microsomes and Drug Oxidation, Berlin, Germany, July, 1976.

67. Bend, J.R., M.O. James and P.M. Dansette (1977). *In vitro* metabolism of xenobiotics in some marine animals. Ann. N.Y. Acad. Sci., In press.

68. Pedersen, M.G., W.K. Hershberger, P.K. Zachariah, and M.R. Juchau (1976). Hepatic biotransformation of environmental xenobiotics in six strains of rainbow trout *(Salmo gairdneri)*. J. Fish. Res. Board Can. 33:666-75.

69. Diamond, L. and H.F. Clark (1970). Comparative studies of the interaction of benzo[a]pyrene with cells derived from poikilothermic and homeothermic vertebrates. I. Metabolism of benzo[a]pyrene. J. Natl. Cancer Inst. 45:1005-11.

70. Payne, J.F. (1976). Field evaluation of benzopyrene hydroxylase induction as a monitor for marine petroleum pollution. Science 191:945-6.

71. Buhler, D.R. and M.E. Rasmussen (1968). The oxidation of
     drugs by fishes. Comp. Biochem. Physiol. 25:223-39.
72. Adamson, R.H. (1967). Drug metabolism in marine inverte-
     brates. Fed. Proc. 26:1047-55.
73. Dewaide, J.H. (1970). Species differences in hepatic
     drug oxidation in mammals and fishes in relation to ther-
     mal acclimation. Comp. Gen. Pharmacol. 1:375-84.
74. Burns, K.A. and D. Sabo (1975). Environmental contamina-
     tion and the induction of microsomal mixed-function oxi-
     dases in an estuarine fish, *Fundulus heteroclitus*. Fed.
     Proc. Abst. 34(3):810.
75. Payne, J.F. (1976). Benzo[a]pyrene hydroxylase as a bio-
     chemical barometer for petroleum in the marine environ-
     ment. Proc. Can. Fed. Biol. Soc. 19, Abst. No. 404.
76. Philpot, R.M., M.O. James, and J.R. Bend (1976). Metabo-
     lism of benzo[a]pyrene and other xenobiotics by micro-
     somal mixed function oxidases in marine species. In:
     Sources, Effects, and Sinks of Petroleum in the Marine
     Environment. In press. American Institute of Biological
     Sciences, Washington, D.C.
77. Pohl, R.J., J.R. Bend, A.M. Guarino, and J.R. Fouts
     (1974). Hepatic microsomal mixed-function oxidase ac-
     tivity of several marine species from coastal Maine.
     Drug Metab. Disposition 2:545-55.
78. Payne, J.F. and W.R. Penrose (1975). Induction of aryl
     hydrocarbon (benzo[a]pyrene) hydroxylase in fish by pe-
     troleum. Bull. Environ. Contam. Toxicol. 14:112-6.
79. James, M.O., J.R. Fouts, and J.R. Bend (1976). Xenobio-
     tic metabolizing enzymes in marine fish. In: Pesticides
     in the Aquatic Environment. In press. International
     Congress of the Entomology Society, Washington, D.C.
80. James, M.O., J.R. Fouts, and J.R. Bend (1974). *In vitro*
     epoxide metabolism in some marine species. Bull. Mt.
     Desert Island Biol. Lab. 14:41-6.
81. Lee, R.F., E. Furlong, and S. Singer (1977). Metabolism
     of hydrocarbons in marine invertebrates. Aryl hydrocar-
     bon hydroxylase from the tissues of the blue crab, *Cal-
     linectes sapidus*, and the polychaete worm, *Nereis* sp.
     In: Pollutant Effects on Marine Organisms. Delibera-
     tions and Recommendations of the Biological Effects
     Program Workshop. In press. D.C. Heath and Co.,
     Lexington, Mass.
82. Gruger, E.H., Jr., M.M. Wekell, P.T. Numoto, and D.R.
     Craddock (1976). Induction of hepatic aryl hydrocarbon
     hydroxylase in salmon exposed to petroleum dissolved in
     seawater and to petroleum and polychlorinated biphenyls,
     separate and together, in food. Bull. Environ. Contam.
     Toxicol., In press.

83. Arcos, J.C. and M.F. Fouts (1974). Chemical induction of Cancer. Structural Bases and Biological Mechanisms. Academic Press, New York, 360 p.

84. Litterst, C.L. and E.J. Van Loon (1974). Time-course of induction of microsomal enzymes following treatment with polychlorinated biphenyl. Bull. Environ. Contam. Toxicol. 11:206-12.

85. Lidman, U., L. Forlin, O. Molander, and G. Axelson (1976). Induction of the drug metabolizing system in rainbow trout *(Salmo gairdneri)* liver by polychlorinated biphenyls (PCBs). Acta Pharmol. Toxicol. 39:262-72.

86. Pohl, R.J., J.R. Fouts, and J.R. Bend (1977). Response of hepatic microsomal mixed-function oxidases in the little skate, *Raja erinacea,* and the winter flounder, *Pseudopleuronectes americanus,* to pretreatment with TCDD (2,3, 7,8-tetrachlorodibenzo-*p*-dioxin) or DBA (1,2,3,4-dibenzanthracene). Bull. Mt. Desert Island Biol. Lab., In press.

87. Yoshida, T., Y. Ito, and Y. Suzuki (1976). Inhibition of hepatic drug metabolizing enzyme by cadmium in mice. Bull. Environ. Contam. Toxicol. 15:402-5.

88. Gruger, E.H., Jr. and M.M. Wekell (1977). Effects of chlorinated biphenyls on the induction of aryl hydrocarbon hydroxylase by petroleum hydrocarbons. In: Proceedings of Symposium on Fate and Effects of Petroleum Hydrocarbons in Marine Ecosystems and Organisms (D. Wolfe, ed.). In press. Pergamon Press, New York.

89. Gaurino, A.M., P.M. Briley, J.B. Anderson, M.A. Kinter, S. Schneiderman, L.D. Klipp, and R.H. Adamson (1972). Renal and hepatic excretion of foreign compounds by *Squalus acanthias.* Bull. Mt. Desert Island Biol Lab. 12:41.

90. Malins, D.C. (1977). Metabolism of aromatic hydrocarbons in marine organisms. Ann. N.Y. Acad. Sci., In press.

91. Bend, J.R. and J.R. Fouts (1973). Glutathione *S*-aryltransferase: distribution in several marine species and partial characterization in hepatic soluble fractions from little skate *Raja erinacea* liver. Bull. Mt. Desert Island Biol. Lab. 13:4-8.

92. Corner, E.D.S., C.C. Kilvington, and S.C.M. O'Hara (1973). Qualitative studies on the metabolism of naphthalene in *Maia squinada* (Herbst). J. Mar. Biol. Assoc. U.K. 53: 819-32.

93. Corner, E.D.S., Y.A. Leon, and R.D. Bulbrook (1960). Steroid sulphatase, aryl sulphatase, and β-glucuronidase in marine invertebrates. J. Mar. Biol. Assoc. U.K. 39: 51-61.

94. Nuzzi, R. (1975). Effects of water-soluble extracts of oil on phytoplankton. In: Proceedings of 1975 Joint Conference on Prevention and Control of Oil Pollution, p. 809-13. American Petroleum Institute, Washington, D.C.

95. Pulich, W.M., Jr., K. Winters, and C. Van Baalen (1974). The effects of a No. 2 fuel oil and two crude oils on the growth and photosynthesis of microalgae. Mar. Biol. (Berl.) 28:87-94.

96. Hellebust, J.A., B. Hanna, R.G. Sheath, M. Gergis, and T.C. Hutchinson (1975). Experimental crude oil spills on a small subarctic lake in the MacKenzie Valley, N.W.T.: Effects on phytoplankton, periphyton, and attached aquatic vegetation. In: Proceedings of 1975 Joint Conference on Prevention and Control of Oil Pollution, p. 509-15. American Petroleum Institute, Washington, D.C.

97. Davavin, I.A., O.G. Mironov, and I.M. Tsimbal (1975). Influence of oil on nucleic acids of algae. Mar. Pollut. Bull. 6:13-5.

98. Eisler, R. (1975). Toxic, sublethal, and latent effects of petroleum on Red Sea macrofauna. In: Proceedings of 1975 Joint Conference on Prevention and Control of Oil Pollution, p. 535-40. American Petroleum Institute, Washington, D.C.

99. Gilfillan, E.S. (1975). Effects of sea water extracts of crude oil on carbon budgets in two species of mussels. In: Proceedings on 1975 Joint Conference on Prevention and Control of Oil Pollution, p. 691-5. American Petroleum Institute, Washington, D.C.

100. Heitz, J.R., L. Lewis, J. Chambers, and J.D. Yarbrough (1974). The acute effects of Empire Mix crude oil on enzymes in oysters, shrimp, and mullet. In: Pollution and Physiology of Marine Organisms (F.J. Vernberg and W.B. Vernberg, eds.), p. 311-28. Academic Press, New York.

101. Blackman, R.A.A. and P. Mackie (1974). Effects of sunken oil on the feeding of plaice on brown shrimps and other benthos. Int. Counc. Explor. Sea C.M. 1974/E:24, p. 1-7.

Chapter 4

SUBLETHAL BIOLOGICAL EFFECTS OF PETROLEUM HYDROCARBON EXPOSURES: BACTERIA, ALGAE, AND INVERTEBRATES

FREDERICK G. JOHNSON
Environmental Conservation Division

Northwest and Alaska Fisheries Center
National Marine Fisheries Service
National Oceanic and Atmospheric Administration
U.S. Department of Commerce
Seattle, Washington 98112

INTRODUCTION

The future value of a marine ecosystem in terms of food
resources, waste disposal, and recreation, will depend upon
its resilience to perturbations. To determine the ability of
a marine ecosystem to withstand petroleum-induced perturbations and still retain its usefulness, information is needed
regarding the lowest levels of petroleum which cause biological effects, and what impact these subtle biological changes
eventually have on the marine organisms themselves and on the
marine environment as a whole. Knowing the level of pollutant
that an organism can withstand in a certain period of time
(LC_{50}) is not very helpful in terms of ecological forecasting
if critical processes other than survival of the organism are
affected at lower pollutant dosages.

This review addresses the sublethal effects of petroleum
hydrocarbon exposures on physiology, behavior, growth, development, and reproduction of marine bacteria, algae, and invertebrate animals. It is worth noting that a sublethal response
induced in a marine organism under laboratory conditions may,
in effect, be a lethal response in the marine environment if
an animal's ability to avoid predators or cope with physiological stress is impaired.

The hydrocarbon concentrations cited in this review are
presented in the units used by the original authors, and, for
convenience, are followed by the equivalent (or nearly equivalent) values in parts per million (ppm). These values often
reflect added doses rather than measured concentrations and
may generally be taken as the upper limit of the hydrocarbon
levels to which the test organisms were exposed.

In the following sections, literature is summarized and
assessed with respect to the sublethal consequences of oil
pollution on marine organisms. Invertebrate chemoreception
and behavior will be the particular focus of this review, as
these processes appear to be especially sensitive to small
amounts of oil.

BACTERIA

Bacteria are important to all marine ecosystems exposed to petroleum-related contaminants, since they are essential in the biochemical processing of both the contaminants and biogenic substances. The consequences of petroleum hydrocarbon exposures on bacterial physiology and reproduction have been discussed in detail in Volume I, Chapter 3, and will not be treated in this section. The effects of petroleum hydrocarbons on bacterial behavior (chemotaxis), however, are included below.

BEHAVIOR

Many marine bacteria are motile and some "prey" upon various microorganisms including other bacteria, phytoplankton, fungi, and viruses, besides utilizing dead organic material [1]. These bacteria also play an important role in mediating the biodegradation of organic matter in the marine environment and in the recycling of nutrients. Chet, Fogel, and Mitchell [2] showed that members of the large, motile group of marine bacteria display positive chemotactic behavior by moving toward living prey. Adler [3] described some of the underlying biochemical mechanisms enabling such behavior.

Mitchell, Fogel, and Chet [1] found that chemosensory attraction was completely inhibited by phenol, toluene, and crude oil. Bacteria were isolated from seawater samples near Woods Hole, Massachusetts, and cultured on seawater nutrient agar. Chemotaxis was determined by placing a suspension of test bacteria isolate in seawater on a microscope slide into which a capillary tube containing various chemical attractants (in seawater) was immersed. After responsive bacteria entered the capillary tube, the contents of the tube were plated on seawater nutrient agar to yield quantitative data. Bacterial movement to the attractant, glucose, was eliminated by 0.6% phenol, 0.6% toluene, or Kuwait crude oil in the test suspension. This inhibition was sublethal and reversible; motility rates remained normal but were randomly directed. When the bacteria were washed free of the hydrocarbons, they regained the ability to detect and move toward the substrate. Thus, assessment of the viability of indigenous marine microflora exposed to low-level hydrocarbon contamination by means of bacterial plate counts would not reflect such behavioral disruption. Furthermore, the loss of the ability to detect food could limit the capacity of bacteria in self-purification processes of the sea. The threshold concentrations for inhibition of bacterial chemotaxis by a number of water pollutants were determined by Walsh and Mitchell [4]. They reported the concentrations of several petroleum products sufficient to

reduce by 50% the chemotaxis of marine bacteria, mainly
Pseudomonas sp., without affecting their ability to move.
Some representative values (in ppm) were: Kuwait crude oil,
10; kerosine, 12; benzene, 0.1; and phenol, 120. The authors
suggested that such chemotactic inhibition was due to reversible blocking of the chemoreceptors since positive chemotaxis
was regained in clean seawater.

ALGAE

Numerous efforts have been made to determine the effects
of petroleum products on gaseous exchange, photosynthesis, and
growth of marine algae.

PHYSIOLOGY

Photosynthesis results in the gaseous exchange of CO_2 and
O_2. The flux of these gases is typically employed to assess
photosynthetic rates. Schramm [5] found that thin films of
three crude oils (Iranian, Libyan, and Venezuelan), 0.1 to
0.0001 mm thick, coating emersed macroalgae *(Fucus vesiculo-*
sus, Laminaria digitata, Porphyra umbilicalis, and *Enteromor-*
pha sp.) generally reduced the CO_2 uptake of the algae. The
oil films also reduced water loss (desiccation), which allowed
photosynthesis of oiled plants to continue for longer periods
than the photosynthesis of emersed untreated plants. Photosynthesis was depressed, however, when the oil-treated plants
were returned to clean seawater. The author concluded that
the crude oil films reduced the CO_2 exchange of the macroalgae
both by lowering the gaseous diffusion rates and by exerting a
toxic effect on photosynthesis. Giant kelp *(Macrocystis* sp.)
exposed to petroleum contamination in the marine environment
reportedly secrete a mucus which prevents contact between the
petroleum and plant tissues, thereby preventing extensive damage to the plant [6].

In manometric experiments, Clendenning and North [7] exposed fronds of the giant kelp, *M. pyrifera,* to petroleum hydrocarbons in seawater. Cresols and phenol at levels of 5-10
ppm and dispersed diesel oil at 10-100 ppm reduced photosynthesis of the fronds by about 50% after a 4-day exposure period. The reaction of the fronds to the diesel oil dispersion
was delayed for about two days, suggesting delayed penetration
of the oil constituents into the plant tissues. In other experiments with *M. pyrifera* [8], exposure of the fronds to 10
ppm of benzene, toluene, or *n*-hexane, produced no effects during the first 48 hr. After 96 hr, there was still no effect
on photosynthesis of the fronds exposed to *n*-hexane, a slight
depression in fronds exposed to benzene, and a 75% reduction
in fronds exposed to toluene. The toluene-treated fronds

displayed "visible injuries."

Net photosynthesis (as measured by oxygen production) of the intertidal seaweeds *Polysiphonia lanosa, Porphyra umbilicalis, Spongomorpha arcta, Porphyra miniata, Gigartina stellata,* and *Fucus vesiculosus* was relatively unaffected by seawater extracts of various crude oils (Kuwait, California, Venezuela, Persian Gulf) following 24-hr exposures [9]. However, *Palmaria palmata* photosynthesis was reduced in some cases after 24-hr exposures to 100% Persian Gulf crude oil extract, as was *P. umbilicalis* photosynthesis under longer exposures (24 to 96 hr) to 50% Kuwait crude extract.

Using the carbon-14 method, Shiels, Goering, and Hood [10] assessed the effects of Prudhoe Bay crude oil extracts on the phytosynthesis of several marine macroalgal species from Port Valdez, Alaska, during 2- to 4-hr exposures. Variable results were noted: at 7 ppm, crude oil inhibition of photosynthesis occurred in the green algae *Cladophora stimpsonii* and *Ulva fenestrata* and the brown alga *Laminaria saccharina,* while other species (including *Fucus distichus, Palmaria palmata, Halosaccion glandiforme, Costaria costata,* and *Alaria tenuifolia)* were relatively unaffected at that concentration. At lower crude oil extract concentrations, photosynthetic rates increased; at 0.7 ppm for *Ulva* and *Alaria,* and at 0.007 ppm for *Costaria.* The production of oxygen by the green alga *Enteromorpha intestinalis* was reduced by 80% after the plant was exposed to a 10-12 ppm concentration of the Prudhoe Bay crude oil extract for 4 hr [10].

The rate of photosynthesis by marine phytoplankton and macroalgae may be stimulated or repressed depending upon the level of hydrocarbons present and method of exposure. Using radioactive carbon techniques, Gordon and Prouse [11] examined the effect of seawater extracts of three oils (No. 2 fuel oil, Venezuelan crude oil, and No. 6 fuel oil) on the photosynthetic rates of endemic phytoplankton from the Bedford Basin area of the western Atlantic Ocean. The phytoplankton assemblages were exposed to the petroleum extracts for 18 hr prior to a 5- to 7-hr incubation with carbon-14. A 0.15 ppm concentration of No. 2 fuel oil reduced photosynthesis by about 50%. The No. 2 fuel oil had the highest saturated hydrocarbon content of the three oils tested. Venezuelan crude oil and No. 6 fuel oil were less inhibitory than No. 2 fuel oil to photosynthesis. The authors concluded that the hydrocarbon levels in the Bedford Basin area were high enough to depress photosynthetic activity of the phytoplankton a few percent, but the hydrocarbon levels present in the open ocean were not sufficient to depress such activity. Pulich, Winters, and van Baalen [12] found that soluble fractions of No. 2 fuel oil at concentrations on the order of 0.04 to 0.40 ppm reduced photosynthesis of the diatom *Thalassiosira pseudonana* and affected photosynthesis of certain green and blue-green algae as well.

The effects of selected aliphatic and aromatic hydrocarbons on photosynthesis of the diatom *Skeletonema costatum* have been determined [13]. Photosynthesis was assessed using carbon-14 techniques. The median effective concentrations and approximate threshold concentrations of hydrocarbons (reflecting added dosages), are tabulated below (from Parker [13]):

Treatment of diatom		Concentration (ppm) causing 50% reduction in photosynthesis	Highest concentration (ppm) causing no effect
Hydrocarbon	Exposure time (hr)		
Benzene	7	200	10
Benzene	8	300	10
Benzene	12	80	11
Toluene	8	20	2
Hexane	8	0.3	0.07
Octane	9	0.1	0.001
Decane	9	0.005	0.001

Surprisingly, the aliphatic hydrocarbons, generally considered to be less toxic than aromatics, produced a greater inhibition of photosynthesis of *S. costatum*.

In considering the mode of action of phytotoxic oils on (terrestrial) plants, van Overbeek and Blondeau [14] suggested that the primary toxic effect of such oils is their disruption of the bimolecular lipid structure of the cell membrane. The protein-lipid membrane structure is fundamental to all higher organisms. Baker's [15] publication provides an in-depth discussion on the physiological aspects of oil toxicity to plants including respiratory and photosynthetic disruption.

In a more recent review, Vandermeulen and Ahern [16] considered the physiological effects of petroleum and its constituents in unicellular algae. Their discussion included a detailed examination of the inhibitory effects of naphthalene on the photosynthesis and ATP production of *Monochrysis lutheri*. Their findings suggest that unicellular algae are physiologically sensitive to small changes in the concentration of aromatic hydrocarbons and that for short-term exposures (less than 12 hr) the inhibitory effects are reversible.

BEHAVIOR

Gametes of the fucoid macroalgae *Fucus serratus* and *F. vesiculosus* display chemotactic behavior. Chemical substances from the *Fucus* egg attract the motile spermatozoa. A variety of low-molecular weight hydrocarbons produced a similar attraction of *Fucus* sperm [17]. Cook and Elvidge determined the relative effects of specific hydrocarbons and petroleum fractions on the chemotactic behavior by preparing seawater-soluble hydrocarbon extracts and testing their ability to attract the sperm into capillary tubes at various dilutions (in seawater). The hydrocarbon extracts which demonstrated attractive activity at the greatest dilutions were as follows: *n*-hexane, 1:120; *n*-heptane, 1:70; *n*-pentane, 1:60; 1-hexene, 1:100; and various light petroleum fractions, 1:25 to 1:110. Later, Mueller [18] established the identity of the gamone that attracts sperm to the eggs of *F. serratus* as the volatile hydrocarbon 1,3,5-octatriene.

GROWTH AND REPRODUCTION

Recent work by Steele [19] demonstrated the effects of No. 2 fuel oil, Willamar crude oil, and two jet fuels on growth of *Fucus edentatus* zygotes. Growth of the fucoid zygotes was completely inhibited following addition of 20 ppm No. 2 fuel oil to the seawater test medium. Additions of 200 ppm crude oil reduced growth (in length) of the zygotes by about half. A more surprising result was obtained, however, when the macroalgal receptacles were exposed to the oils during gamete release and fertilization. Even at the lowest amounts of oil added, 0.2 ppb of No. 2 fuel oil or Willamar crude oil, there was no growth or germination of the zygotes. Apparently, fertilization did not occur in the presence of the petroleum products. If the gamete-bearing receptacles were exposed to the petroleum products prior to fertilization, which was allowed to take place in clean seawater, fertilization was successful. Growth of the zygotes in this latter experiment was similar to the growth of petroleum-treated zygotes in the first experiment. From these results, Steele concluded that spermatozoa during release and fertilization were extremely sensitive to the presence of petroleum.

Research concerned with the effects of petroleum hydrocarbons on growth and reproduction have been carried out with a wide variety of microalgae. Mommaerts-Billiet [20] unsuccessfully attempted to elucidate fine-structural changes in cell morphology due to Libyan crude oil acting on the marine nanoplankter *Platymonas tetrathele,* although diminished growth rates were observed. Mommaerts-Billiet went on to discuss the possibility that petroleum pollution could be responsible for far-reaching ecological effects if phytoplanktonic growth were jeopardized, since zooplankton grazing can only be counterbalanced by sufficiently high phytoplankton growth rates. (For the purpose of this review the terms growth, as it pertains to phytoplankton cultures, and reproduction, meaning microalgal cell division, are synonymous.)

Like photosynthesis, the growth rates of marine plants may either be stimulated by low levels of petroleum hydrocar-

bons or inhibited by higher levels. Galtsoff et al. [21] prepared water-soluble extracts of Lake Pelto crude oil by stirring one part oil in two parts seawater for 2-12 hr, and letting the mixture stand 2-10 days. The aqueous fraction was
then drawn off and sterilized by boiling. A 12% extract concentration (by volume) stimulated growth of cultures of the
diatom *Nitzschia closterium* in most cases; a 25% extract concentration retarded growth of most of the cultures, and a 50%
extract concentration retarded growth of all of the cultures.

Prouse, Gordon, and Keizer [22] studied the effects of
oil extracts on unialgal phytoplankton cultures under static
bioassay conditions during 9- to 16-day exposure periods.
Growth of cultures of *Fragilaria* sp. was significantly stimulated by a 50 µg/l (0.05 ppm) concentration of No. 2 fuel oil
present at the onset of the exposure period. Growth of *Dunaliella tertiolecta* was stimulated at initial concentrations of
55-320 µg/l (0.06-0.32 ppm) of Kuwait crude oil in seawater,
of which 12-38 µg/l (0.01-0.04 ppm) remained at the end of the
exposure period. The authors suggested that growth of phytoplankton can be stimulated by petroleum at levels less than
100 µg/l (0.1 ppm) and can be inhibited by petroleum at levels
greater than 100 µg/l (0.1 ppm).

Soluble seawater extracts (WSF) of No. 2 fuel oil strongly inhibited growth of *Phaeodactylum tricornutum (Nitzschia
closterium* var. *minutissma)* cultures [23]. One percent fuel
oil mixtures were shaken and the aqueous phase was filtered
(millipore 0.22 µ) to yield a water-soluble extract. A 30%
solution of this extract in seawater completely inhibited
growth of the diatoms. Similar extracts prepared from No. 6
fuel oil and outboard motor oil were ineffective in retarding
growth of *Phaeodactylum*. Other phytoplankton species whose
growth was inhibited by the No. 2 fuel oil extracts were *Skeletonema costatum* (complete inhibition in 10% extract) and
Chlorella sp. (complete inhibition in 60% extract). *Chlamydomonas* sp. was relatively unaffected at any of these levels
[23].

Mironov [24] determined the concentrations of oil necessary to delay or eliminate cell division of 11 algae from the
Black Sea over 5-day exposures. These values, expressed in
milliliters of oil per liter of seawater and ppm (oil to seawater) are: *Glenodinium foliaceum,* 0.1-0.01 (100-10 ppm);
Chaetoceros curvisetus, 0.01 (10 ppm); *Gymnodinium wulffii,*
0.01-0.0001 (10-0.1 ppm); *Gymnodinium kovalevskii,* 0.001-
0.0001 (1-0.1 ppm); *Prorocentrum trochoideum,* 0.1-0.00001
(100-0.01 ppm); *Licmophora ehrenbergii,* 0.1-0.001 (100-1 ppm);
Platymonas viridis, 0.1-0.001 (100-1 ppm); *Coscinodiscus
granii,* 1.0-0.1 (1,000-100 ppm); *Peridinium trochoideum,* 1.0
(1,000 ppm); and *Melosira moniliformis,* 1.0-0.1 (1,000-100
ppm).

Growth of cultures of the marine diatom *Cylindrotheca fusiformis* were shown to be inhibited by a water-soluble extract of crude oil, the degree of inhibition being roughly proportional to the extract concentration and the exposure time. In addition, the chloroplasts were distorted following exposure to the extracts [25].

Anderson, Neff, and Petrocelli [26] determined the concentrations of water-soluble fractions (WSF) of two refined and two crude oils necessary to inhibit the growth and reduce the chlorophyll-*a* content of cultures of three marine phytoplankters--*Isochrysis galbana*, *Cyclotella nana*, and *Glenodinium halli*. The concentrations of WSF of four test oils accounting for 50% reductions in cell number during 72-hr exposures (expressed in ppm total hydrocarbons) are tabulated below (adapted from Anderson [26]):

Species	Concentrations (ppm) of the WSF of:			
	Bunker C fuel oil	No. 2 fuel oil	Kuwait crude oil	South Louisiana crude oil
Isochrysis galbana	0.4	0.6	4.0	5.5
Cyclotella nana	0.7	0.5	6.6	4.4
Glenodinium halli	0.6	0.6	6.4	3.2
Ratio: (Aromatics: Paraffins)	(77.9:1)	(42.6:1)	(18.8:1)	(3.4:1)

The concentrations of WSF which reduced the chlorophyll-*a* content of the cultures by 50% were nearly the same as those for inhibition of growth. Hence, WSF of refined oils with proportionately more aromatics were found to be most toxic, producing effects at concentrations of less than 1 ppm.

Clearly, different petroleum products present different toxicities to a given plant and different plants respond variously to a given petroleum product. Often the inhibitory effects on plant activities are diminished for crude oils that have weathered [27,28]. Dunstan, Atkinson, and Natoli [29] attempted to assess the relative efficacies of benzene, toluene, xylene, and the low-molecular weight fractions of No. 2 fuel oil in stimulating and inhibiting growth of four phylogenetically distinct phytoplankton cultures. Closed culture vessels with seawater media were used, and growth was analyzed on the second or third day of logarithmic growth. Mixtures of No. 2 fuel oil at concentrations of 10^3 µg/l (1 ppm) or less in seawater media stimulated growth of the green flagellate *Dunaliella tertiolecta* by nearly 200%. *Dunaliella* growth was stimulated by low concentrations (1 µg/l; 0.001 ppm) of benzene, toluene, xylene, or No. 2 fuel oil. If the No. 2 fuel

oil mixtures were aerated (promoting escape of volatile hydrocarbons), they did not stimulate growth of the alga. At a
concentration of 10^4 µg/l (10 ppm) of No. 2 fuel oil, both the
aerated and the non-aerated fractions retarded growth of
Dunaliella; the non-aerated fraction, which retained the more
volatile components, showed the greater inhibition. At a concentration of 10^5 µg/l (100 ppm), toluene proved most inhibitory of the three hydrocarbons, reducing growth of *Dunaliella*
by 25%. Growth of the diatom, *Skeletonema costatum,* on the
other hand, was not enhanced by any of the hydrocarbons tested; growth was inhibited by mixtures of No. 2 fuel oil $>10^2$
µg/l (>0.1 ppm) and seawater, by aerated No. 2 fuel oil mixtures $>10^3$ µg/l (>1 ppm), and by seawater mixtures of benzene,
toluene, or xylene $>10^4$ µg/l (>10 ppm). Growth of the cocco-
lithophorid *Criscosphaera carterae* was inhibited by $>10^4$ µg/l
(>10 ppm) toluene or benzene, and somewhat stimulated by $<10^4$
µg/l (<10 ppm) concentrations of toluene or xylene. Of the
four phytoplankton tested, the dinoflagellate *Amphidinium
carterae* was the most sensitive, in terms of growth inhibition, to the petroleum hydrocarbons. Growth of *Amphidinium*
was inhibited by concentrations of toluene or benzene at 10^2
µg/l (0.1 ppm) or more and by concentrations of xylene greater
than 10^4 µg/l (10 ppm) in seawater. These results serve to
illustrate the species-specificity of various effects of petroleum on marine phytoplankton, and hence the caution that
must be taken in making generalizations about such effects.
Nevertheless, the authors concluded that since petroleum products affect various phytoplankton species differently at a
given level of contamination, these effects could lead to alterations of natural phytoplankton community structure [29].

    Pulich, Winters, and van Baalen [12] also used closed
growth systems to determine the highest concentrations of two
crude oils that permitted growth of various species of marine
microalgae. The crude oils were added directly to the algal-
culture medium. Under the conditions of the test, the cultures would be exposed to the water-soluble fractions of the
crude oil in the media and would also be in direct contact
with particles of undissolved crude oil and its fractions.
The two most sensitive species, the diatom *Thalassiosira
pseudonana* and the green alga *Chlorella autotrophica* were unable to grow in culture media containing Kuwait crude oil in
concentrations greater than 10 µg/25 ml of medium (400 ppm)
or South Louisiana crude oil in concentrations greater than
5 µl/25 ml (200 ppm). The filamentous blue-green alga *Microcoleus chthonoplastes* was unable to grow in culture media containing greater than 25 µl/25 ml (1,000 ppm) of either of the
two crude oils, and the green alga *Dunaliella tertiolecta* and
the blue-green alga *Agmenellum quadruplicatum* were unable to
grow in media containing either of the crude oils in concen-

trations ranging from 40-200 μl/25 ml (1,600-8,000 ppm).
Following further growth experiments with pure hydrocarbons
and various petroleum distillate fractions, the authors concluded that the toxicity of the crude oils was mainly associated with the medium- and high-boiling fractions [12]. In a
subsequent study, Winters et al. [30] investigated the toxicity of four fuel oils to growth of several marine microalgae.
The authors identified a particularly toxic fuel-oil component,
p-toluidine, which inhibited growth of *Agmenellum quadruplicatum* at 100 μg/l (100 ppb) in liquid culture.

   Davavin, Mironov, and Tsimbal [31] found that the biosynthesis of nucleic acids by macroalgae *(Grateloupia dichotoma*
and *Polysiphonia opaca)* was inhibited by 3 days' exposure to
1.0 ml/l (1,000 ppm) Romashkinskaya oil emulsified in seawater. Boney [32] showed that some aromatic hydrocarbons
(including known carcinogens such as 3,4-benzpyrene) cause
"cancerous" growths in seaweeds *(Antithamnion plumula)* at concentrations of 0.3 to 3 mg/l (0.3 to 3 ppm). Boney and Corner
[33] noted that while low concentrations of various carcinogenic aromatic hydrocarbons stimulate cell growth of algal
sporelings, high concentrations of the same aromatics and low
concentrations of structurally similar but not carcinogenic
aromatics inhibit growth.

COELENTERATES

   Investigations dealing with the effects of petroleum
products on coelenterates have yielded some information on
various states of sublethal (or prelethal) distress in hy-
droids, corals, and medusae, largely through behavioral observations.

BEHAVIOR

   Chipman and Galtsoff [34] found that the hydrozoan *Tubu-
laria crocea,* which grows on pilings, responds adversely to
dilute seawater extracts of crude oil (one part crude oil to
2,000 parts seawater) by shedding its hydranths during the 24-
hr exposures. This was taken as the death point in the study,
and was preceded by loss of the transluscent pink color, and
reduced tentacular responses to mechanical stimulation.

   Elgershuizen and DeKruijf [35] determined the ability of
stony coral *(Madracis mirabilis)* polyps to retract upon mechanical stimulation following 24-hr exposure to three crude
oils (Nigeria, Forcados, and Tia Juana Pesado). The crude
oils caused a loss of the response in half of the test corals
when mixed with the seawater medium at 602, 696, and 540 ppm,
respectively.

   Eisler [36] exposed the octocoral *Heteroxenia fuscesens*
from the Red Sea to 10 ml/l (10,000 ppm) of Iranian crude oil

under continuous-flow test conditions. The crude oil was added to the surface of the seawater in the test containers
where it formed a slick. The octocorals 0.2 m from the surface exhibited no tentacular contractions (100% reduction from
the activity of control animals); those 1.0 m from the surface
showed a 60% reduction in their tentacular contraction activity; and those 1.8 m from the surface showed a 40% reduction.

Lewis [37] conducted laboratory tests on the effect of
crude oil on four Caribbean corals, *Porites porites, Agaricia
agaricites, Favia fragum,* and *Madracis asperula.* The corals
were held under static bioassay conditions in closed test containers. Crude oil was introduced into the test containers
absorbed onto paper strips which were placed out of contact
with the coral colonies. Octocorals exposed in this manner
to 10-1,000 ppm of crude oil in the seawater medium for 24 hr
developed ruptures in the oral disc, displayed tentacular
withdrawal, and exhibited reduced feeding activity. When
allowed to recover in clean seawater, feeding activity was not
restored, although partial recovery of tentacular activity was
shown by two of the corals.

Reimer [38] studied sublethal effects of diesel oil on
four Panamanian corals, *Pocillopora* cf. *damicornis, Pavona
gigantea, Psammocora (Stephanaria) stellata,* and *Porites fur-
cata.* One milliliter of diesel oil was added to the 250 ml
test containers to form a surface slick over the coral colonies, and the slick was left for 30 or more minutes and then
washed away with clean seawater. Exposures to the diesel oil
produced feeding behavior in the corals, which was prolonged
for abnormally long periods of up to 17 days.

Feeding behavior of the zoanthid *Palythoa variabilis* is
markedly affected by diesel oil and Bunker C fuel oil [39].
Reimer presented strips of filter paper which had absorbed the
oils to the polyps. These elicited feeding responses from the
corals and led to ingestion of the oiled strips. Two feeding
stimulants, the heterocyclic amino acid proline and brine
shrimp juice introduced on paper strips also elicited the
feeding behavior. Oil-induced feeding behavior was abnormal,
however, taking longer to initiate and complete and resulting
in premature egestion of the test strips. In other tests, the
zoanthid polyps were exposed to a 2% mixture of diesel fuel
oil in seawater for 30 min, and then tested with either pro-
line-treated or untreated filter paper strips. For 3-5 days
following exposure to the diesel oil, the polyps were not able
to discriminate between the treated and untreated test strips.

Many corals are intimately associated with internal sym-
biotic zooxanthellae and surface-dwelling microflora [40].
Exposure of coral colonies to marine diesel and Bunker C fuel
oils has led to extrusion of the zooxanthellae or "bleaching"
of coral colonies [38,41]. Mitchell and Chet [40] have eluci-

dated an indirect toxic mechanism of crude oil acting on Red
Sea corals *(Platygera* sp.). Coral colonies exposed to 100 ppm
crude oil for 24 hr dramatically increased their mucus production. This in turn stimulated bacterial activity on the coral
surface which led to death of the colonies within 4 to 8 days.
Corals exposed to as much as 1,000 ppm crude oil in the presence of antibiotics also increased their mucus production, but
survived in the absence of the bacteria.

Anemones, *Anthopleura* sp., are reportedly quite resistant
to petroleum products in field conditions [42,43]. *Anthopleura*
elegantissima exhibits chemoreceptive alarm behavior which is
elicited by a pheromone from wounded conspecific anemones [44].
Behavioral studies with *A. elegantissima* suggested that this
chemoreceptive alarm behavior was not disrupted when the animals were held in seawater containing approximately 0.1-0.2
ppm soluble fraction of Prudhoe Bay crude oil under continuous-
flow conditions (Leigh Hanson, NOAA, NMFS, Northwest and
Alaska Fisheries Center, Seattle, Washington, unpublished results). During the two-week test period, however, oil-exposed
anemones attempted to withdraw from the test chambers, while
control animals held in clean seawater did not.

Percy and Mullin [45] found that crude oil disrupted the
locomotory behavior of the Arctic medusa *Halitholus cirratus*.
Medusae were exposed to light (9 ppm), medium (13 ppm), and
heavy (130 ppm) dispersions of Norman Wells crude oil in seawater for 24 hr prior to behavioral observations; activity
scores were assigned to the animals. The locomotory activity
of medusae held in the light dispersion was reduced by 45%;
the activity of those in the medium dispersion was reduced by
55%; and the activity of those in the heavy dispersion was reduced by 100%. The animals exposed to the light and medium
oil-in-water dispersions resumed swimming activity after 24 hr
of depuration in clean seawater, but those exposed to heavy
dispersions were incapable of swimming, although 60% of them
demonstrated weak contractions (30% recovery of activity).
Subsequent tests revealed that Pembina crude oil was more
toxic, and Venezuela and Atkinson Point crude oils were less
toxic, than the Norman Wells crude oil to locomotory activity
of the medusae.

GROWTH AND REPRODUCTION

Growth of colonies of the Panamanian coral *Porites fur-*
cata was inhibited following 1-hr and 2-1/2-hr exposures to
Bunker C fuel oil [41]. The corals were exposed to 100 ml
Bunker C fuel oil in seawater (the oil formed a 2.4 mm thick
surface slick in the test containers) and were then transferred to the marine sites from which they were collected.
Growth of the corals was observed over a 61-day period, and

throughout this period both oil-treated and control colonies appeared healthy.

ANNELIDS

Observations of polluted marine environments suggest that some adult polychaetes are resistant to petroleum in the sediments [46,47]. It is curious that a relatively sensitive organism, *Capitella capitata,* in terms of acute toxicity data (see Chapter 1), should also be abundant in petroleum-affected sediments [47]. Laboratory studies concerning the effects of No. 2 fuel oil and South Louisiana crude oil on another polychaete, *Neanthes arenaceodentata,* revealed that young stages in the life cycle are even more resistant to the oils than the adult worms [49].

PHYSIOLOGY

Yentsch, Gilfillan, and Sears [9] found no significant alterations in the oxygen consumption rate of *Neanthes (Nereis) virens* exposed to crude oil extracts. (In fact, no respiratory changes were detected in worms exposed to near-lethal levels of copper [49].)

BEHAVIOR

Chia [50] found that the larvae of three polychaetes succumbed to diesel oil exposures, showing loss of movement and sinking. While exposed to 0.5% mixtures of No. 2 diesel oil in seawater (5,000 ppm), trochophore larvae of *Nereis brandti* and *Serpula vermicularis* were immobilized after 48 hr and 3 hr, respectively, and metatroch larvae of *N. vexillosa* were immobilized after 48 hr. Carr and Reish [51] noted that narcosis frequently preceded death in five species of annelids chronically exposed to No. 2 fuel oil and South Louisiana crude oil.

Kasymov and Aliev [52] showed that the oligochaete *Nais elinguis* was more sensitive to seawater extracts of Artem crude oil than was the polychaete *Nereis diversicolor.* Oligochaetes exposed to "high" oil concentrations tended to swim in a vertical position near the surface of the test medium, while the control animals held in untreated seawater remained at the bottom of the test containers. Oligochaetes exposed to low oil levels, 0.3-1.4 mg/l (0.3-1.4 ppm), showed a gain in weight; those exposed to moderate oil levels, 1.4-3.0 mg/l (1.4-3.0 ppm), showed a loss in weight. At higher levels, the animals were killed quickly. The polychaetes exposed to 7-20 mg/l (7-20 ppm) crude oil developed convulsive movements and eversion of the proboscis, followed by a condition of immobility and flaccidity.

GROWTH AND REPRODUCTION

Field studies with *Cirriformia tentaculata* and *Cirratulus cirratus* indicated that spawning, growth, and mortality of the polychaetes were unaffected in sediments contaminated by fuel oil [46]. Similarly, chronic oil contamination did not significantly disrupt settlement and growth of *Pomatoleios kraussii* on artificial substrates in the Arabian Gulf at Kuwait [53].

The effects of phenol on the eunicid polychaete *Ophryotrocha labronica* has been studied by Åkesson [54], who noted reductions in growth and reproduction of the worms. Phenol in the seawater test medium at 100 ppm markedly inhibited growth of *O. labronica* larvae. At 25 ppm phenol, reductions occurred in the number of egg masses produced per adult female, and the number of eggs per egg mass. This resulted in a 56% reproductive potential (as compared with untreated controls) at 25 ppm phenol, and at 50 ppm the reproductive potential was only 15% of that for control worms.

The effects of No. 2 fuel oil and South Louisiana crude oil on reproduction of *Ctenodrilus serratus* and *Ophryotrocha* sp. were determined during 28-day bioassays [51]. Significant reductions in production of offspring by *C. serratus* occurred at 2.2 ppm No. 2 fuel oil and 9.9 ppm South Louisiana crude oil in seawater. Reproduction of *Ophryotrocha* sp. was impaired at 1.3 ppm No. 2 fuel oil and 9.9 ppm South Louisiana crude oil.

ARTHROPODS

Considerable data has been published regarding sublethal effects of oil pollution on marine crustaceans. Different permeabilities of arthropod exoskeletons between species and in a given species at different ontogenetic and molt stages may account for much of the wide range of sensitivity to contaminants in this diverse group.

PHYSIOLOGY

The respiration rates of various crustaceans are sensitive to the presence of petroleum, but the direction or magnitude of respiratory change that may be produced by a given dose of petroleum is unpredictable. Anderson and coworkers [26,55] showed that the oxygen consumption rate of the mysid *Mysidopsis almyra* increases with exposure to water-soluble fractions of No. 2 fuel oil (0.10-0.58 ppm total naphthalenes) and to the oil-water dispersion of No. 2 fuel oil (1-10 ppm total hydrocarbons). The maximum respiratory rate enhancement for *M. almyra* occurred at 0.4 ppm total naphthalenes for both water-soluble fraction and oil-water dispersion exposures.

Grass shrimp *(Palaemonetes pugio)* exposed to 3.0 to 3.6 ppm of the oil-water dispersion of No. 2 fuel oil (containing 0.10 ppm total naphthalenes) for 5 hr showed a decrease in respiration rate, concomitant with a body tissue naphthalene content of 2.0 ppm [55,56]. After the oil-exposed grass shrimp were allowed to depurate in clean seawater for seven days, the tissue naphthalene content had decreased to background levels and the respiration rate had returned to normal. The respiration rate of postlarval brown shrimp, *Penaeus aztecus,* also tended to decrease during exposure to low concentrations of the WSF of No. 2 fuel oil or South Louisiana crude oil. At higher concentrations, the brown shrimp developed an increased respiration rate accompanied by increased locomotor activity and abnormal swimming behavior. These effects were more pronounced with larger animals. The responses exhibited by the brown shrimp were also greater when the animals were exposed to the WSF of No. 2 fuel oil than when exposed to the WSF of South Louisiana crude oil. The authors noted that levels of hydrocarbons in the tissues and the size (or stage of development) of the shrimp may be factors influencing their respiratory response to petroleum hydrocarbons. Steed and Copeland [57] found that petrochemical waste, at levels below that required to produce 50% mortality in 48 hr, depressed the respiration rate of *P. aztecus,* but increased the respiration of *P. duorarum* (pink shrimp).

Rice et al. [58] studied the effects of the WSF of Cook Inlet crude oil on the respiration of Alaska king crab *(Paralithodes camtschatica).* They found that a 5-hr exposure of the juvenile crabs to sublethal levels (<6 ppm) of the WSF had little effect on respiration, but exposure to levels which would kill the animals within 96 hr (>6 ppm) caused a prompt depression in oxygen consumption. The shore crab *Carcinus maenas* developed a variable pattern of respiratory responses when exposed to a seawater extract of Mid-Continent (United States) sweet crude oil [9]. A mixture containing 1% of the extract in seawater (about 0.125 ppm total hydrocarbons) caused a slight reduction (about 20%) in oxygen consumption of the crabs; however, a mixture containing 10% extract (1.25 ppm total hydrocarbons) caused an increase in the respiration rate by about 50%.

Percy and Mullin [45] reported that the Arctic marine amphipod *Onisimus affinis* also exhibited variable respiratory responses when placed in dispersions of crude oil in seawater. Four crude oils were tested: Atkinson Point, Venezuela, Pembina, and Norman Wells. Oxygen consumption of the amphipods was invariably depressed (by 7 to 22%) at the lower concentrations of all oils tested. This effect was reversed at higher concentrations of crude oil. "Heavy" dispersions of

all the crude oils with the exception of Atkinson Point crude
oil stimulated respiratory rates of the amphipods by as much
as 40% over control rates. The oils which produced the greatest respiratory depression at low concentrations generally
produced the least stimulation at high concentrations. Respiration of cell-free homogenates, however, was enhanced 10-
45% by exposure to seawater dispersions of Norman Wells crude
oil at all concentrations tested.

Anderson and coworkers [26] provided evidence suggesting
that osmoregulation may also be disrupted by WSF. Groups of
adult brown shrimp held at 20 ^{O}/oo salinity were transferred
to 10 ^{O}/oo salinity or 30 ^{O}/oo salinity after 10-hr exposures
to 20% soluble fractions (1.7 ppm total petroleum hydrocarbons) of No. 2 fuel oil. Oil-exposed shrimp experienced wider
fluctuations in body fluid chloride content than control
shrimp which were transferred to different salinities but not
exposed to oil. Both depression of the respiratory rate of
grass shrimp and disruption of osmotic regulation in brown
shrimp may be related to body burdens of hydrocarbons, since
both processes became more "normal" as depuration proceeded.

The process of ecdysis, or molting, in arthropods is a
necessary prerequisite of growth and is likely to enhance vulnerability of the organisms to stresses imposed by pollution.
Wells [59] and Wells and Sprague [60] found that the greatest
mortality of first-stage lobster larvae exposed to crude oil
occurred when the larvae were molting, and that sublethal concentrations of oil delayed molting in early larval stages.
Likewise, Rice et al. [58] reported that toxicity of WSF of
Cook Inlet crude oil to pandalid shrimp larvae *(Pandalus
hypsinotus)* was greatest at the time of molting. Katz [61]
also noted that a seawater extract of Venezuelan crude oil
seemed to retard molting in larvae of the estuarine decapod
Neopanope texana.

Karinen and Rice [62] investigated the molting success of
juvenile Tanner crabs *(Chionoecetes bairdi)* exposed to Prudhoe
Bay crude oil in static bioassays and found that oil-exposed
crabs autotomized their limbs shortly after or during ecdysis.
Of Tanner crabs exposed to 0.56 ml oil/l seawater (560 ppm),
64% were alive after 24 hr of exposure and had lost an average
of 3.3 legs per crab. The crabs became progressively less
vulnerable to oil-induced autotomy with time after molting.
Exposure of premolt Tanner crabs to 1 ml/l (1,000 ppm) crude
oil for 48 hr, 1 to 4 weeks prior to molting, appeared to reduce the proportion of successful molts. Karinen and Rice
[62] suggested that oil pollution may affect molting of all
crustaceans. Diverse arthropodan taxa possess remarkable similarities in molting physiology [63]. However, Cox and
Anderson [64] found no changes in molting frequency or in the

growth of small brown shrimp *(P. aztecus)* held for 6 weeks
under weekly exposures to 0.97 ppm of the WSF of No. 2 fuel
oil, or following a single exposure to 4.54 ppm of the WSF.
It has been suggested that delay of molting of crab larvae
may be a general response to environmental stress [65].

BEHAVIOR

A general effect of hydrocarbons is narcosis. This effect has been thoroughly investigated by Crisp and coworkers
[66] dealing with locomotor behavior of barnacle *(Elminius
modestus)* nauplii. The authors distinguished reversible
narcosis or "physical toxicity" from irreversible "chemical
toxicity." The molecular and thermodynamic properties of a
wide range of compounds (including saturated cyclic and
aromatic hydrocarbons) were taken into account relative to the
narcotic potency of the compounds. The substitution of polar
groups into paraffin structure or increased molecular symmetry
caused greater narcotic potency, while increased molecular
volume reduced narcotic potency. In terms of narcotic potency: phenol > benzene > cyclohexane > heptane. Their results
are in agreement with the space-occupying theory of narcotic
action, which states that narcotic potency is proportional to
the volume fraction of space that narcotic molecules occupy in
the biophase [66].

Sanborn and Malins [67] observed narcotization of larval
spot shrimp *(Pandalus platyceros)* and Dungeness crab *(Cancer
magister)* zoeae exposed to 8-12 ppb naphthalene-1-^{14}C in seawater under continuous-flow conditions. Naphthalene-exposed
larvae were narcotized in 18-24 hr, and died in 24-36 hr. In
further testing, labeled naphthalene was complexed with protein (BSA) prior to its introduction, and similar results
were obtained.

Corner and coworkers [68] also determined changes in locomotor behavior of *E. modestus* exposed to petroleum hydrocarbons. They found 50% inactivation of Stage II nauplii exposed
for 8 min to 10 ppm kerosine extract. Stage II nauplii were
unaffected when exposed to the same mixture pre-aerated for
2 hr.

Investigations regarding cirral beating activity (associated with feeding) of *E. modestus* spat exposed to a 100 ppm
suspension of Kuwait crude oil showed that 4-hr exposures reduced beating by 50%; 48-hr exposures reduced cirral activity
by 90%. Retarded shell growth was also noted for the juvenile
barnacles. Similar exposure (24 hr at 100 ppm) produced a
significant reduction in the mean rate of cirral beating among
adult *Elminius* [68].

Chipman and Galtsoff [34] followed the behavioral progress of barnacles *(Balanus balanoides)* exposed to sand which had been treated with crude oil to make a final oil concentration of 2% in the static test containers. Throughout the duration of the experiments the control barnacles maintained a pattern of rapid and full sweeping of their cirri and prompt reactivity to touch (by cirral retraction and valve closure). After 6 hr, the oil-exposed animals demonstrated a reduced cirral-sweep rate, and after 23 hr, the extent of the sweeps was reduced as well. By 30 hr of exposure, cirral activity had ceased, with the valves open and cirri partly extended, and by 70 hr the animals had died (lost their ability to respond to mechanical stimulation). It is interesting to note that the control containers readily became fouled due to a copious discharge of fecal material, but the oiled containers remained clear, presumably because defecation was inhibited by the oil.

Swedmark, Granmo, and Kollberg [69] documented the effects of Oman crude oil dispersions on the locomotor behavior of various crustaceans. They found that the locomotion of prawns *(Leander adspersus)* was inactivated at all concentrations tested (<350 ppm) during 96 hr of exposure. Impaired activity was also noted for spider crabs *(Hyas araneus)*, hermit crabs *(Eupagurus bernhardus)* and prawns exposed to diesel oil emulsions. Partial recovery of locomotor behavior was achieved following depuration in clean seawater.

In static bioassay tests, Bean, Vanderhorst, and Wilkinson [70] observed behavioral modification in pandalid shrimp *(Pandalus danae)* exposed to low concentrations of crude oil extracts (Prudhoe Bay and South Louisiana crude oils). Shrimp exposed to extracts containing 1 to 2 mg/l of hydrocarbons (1 to 2 ppm) displayed "agitated" and possibly "searching" behavior, moving rapidly about the test chambers, usually in an upright position. Control animals invariably assumed "resting" positions. At higher oil-extract concentrations, the shrimp began to form tightly aggregated groups, which became more pronounced with higher concentrations, and "clawing" behavior was noted within such assemblages. Shrimp that were in the aggregated state for an extended period were able to recover during exposure in at least one instance. Post-aggregation stage shrimp which turned on their sides or backs and displayed only random movements died.

Exposure to seawater emulsions of two crude oils (Venezuelan and Norman Wells) has been shown to markedly reduce the locomotor activity of the amphipod *Onisimus affinis* [45]. The locomotor activity of the isopod *Mesidotea entomon* was not significantly altered by similar treatments with emulsions of Norman Wells crude oil. Tatem [56] reported that larvae of

the grass shrimp *Palaemonetes pugio* exposed continuously to
No. 2 fuel oil WSF (0.52–0.85 ppm total hydrocarbons, 0.27–
0.34 ppm total naphthalenes) were not nearly as active as
control larvae. The activity of adult grass shrimp exposed
to higher No. 2 fuel oil WSF concentrations (2.6 ppm total
hydrocarbons, 0.55 ppm total naphthalenes) for 24 hr increased, and the shrimp swam in spiral patterns near the surface.

Rice et al. [58] reported the doses of water-soluble
crude oil fractions sufficient to render the larvae of various crustaceans from Alaska incapable of normal locomotion
("moribund") following 96-hr exposures. The concentrations of
Prudhoe Bay crude oil causing 50% immobilization were 0.75 ppm
for shrimp larvae *(Pandalus hypsinotus* and *Eualus fabricii)*
and 1.20 ppm for Tanner crab larvae *(Chionoecetes bairdi)*. In
48-hr tests, Dungeness crab *(Cancer magister)* larvae were immobilized at 1.7 ppm Prudhoe Bay crude oil. These crude oil
levels were substantially lower than those necessary to kill
the animals. Chia [50] found that nauplius larvae of the
barnacle *Balanus cariosus* were able to maintain locomotor activity for 12 hr while exposed to a mixture of 0.5% No. 2
diesel oil in seawater.

Mironov [24] documented preliminary symptoms of crude oil
toxicity (0.01 ml/l; 10 ppm) to hermit crabs *(Diogenes pugila-
tor)*, including sluggish activity and a tendency to evacuate
the shells. Sandberg et al. [71] observed similar prelethal
behavior in amphipods and crabs. Hermit crabs *(Pagurus longicarpus)* consistently vacated their shells before they died and
in addition appeared incapable of coordinated movements.
Amphipods *(Neohaustorius biarticulatus)* held in seawater with
oiled sand at similar oil concentrations displayed a loss of
burrowing activity after 12 hr and died in 24 hr.

The presence of Venezuelan crude oil in sediments was
shown to affect the burrowing behavior of post-larval American
lobster larvae *(Homarus americanus)* [60]. The lobsters did not
discriminate between clean and oiled substrates with respect
to burrowing sites, but they dug more burrows when exposed to
increasing oil concentrations. Unexposed post-larvae and
those exposed to 17 to 18 mg/l (17 to 18 ppm) crude oil dug a
single burrow, while those exposed to 174 and 1,740 mg/l (174
and 1,740 ppm) dug up to three burrows each.

Feeding and reproduction of marine crustaceans are in
part dependent upon exogenous chemical signals. Reception of
these signals may be disrupted or modified by low levels of
petroleum. Atema and Stein [72] found that 10 ppm of La Rosa
crude oil added to seawater caused a doubling of the time period between noticing and pursuing food by lobsters *(Homarus
americanus)*. The hydrocarbon concentration of the seawater in

the lobster tanks was 17.2 µg/l (17.2 ppb) as determined by
gas chromatography. In other experiments [73], kerosine was
separated into three fractions (straight-chain, branched-chain
and cyclic, and aromatic water-soluble hydrocarbons), and each
fraction was tested against the behavior of the lobsters.
Whole kerosine and branched-cyclic fractions adsorbed on paper
strips and placed in seawater induced searching and feeding
behavior in the lobsters that led to ingestion of the test
strips. Whole kerosine was slightly less attractive than the
branched-cyclic fraction, possibly because of the aromatic
fraction present in the kerosine. The aromatic fraction alone
produced searching behavior in the lobsters at a distance, but
was repulsive at close range. The straight-chain fraction had
no effect on feeding behavior. The authors surmised that the
lobsters responded to hydrocarbon levels less than 60 ppb.

     The above results may be compared with those put forth by
Steinhardt and coworkers [74] who dealt with inactivation of
various insect chemoreceptors by some soluble straight-chain
hydrocarbons (lower alcohols and long-chain amines). Salt,
water, and sugar receptors of labellar sensillae of the blow-
fly *(Phormia regina)* were acted upon by the hydrocarbons in
two stages; first, a reversible inhibition of receptivity developed (as measured electrophysiologically) and then injury
of the receptors occurred. The primary effects on these receptors were studied quantitatively and applied to kinetic
models. The effects of the chemical substances on the salt
and water receptors resembled simple hydrocarbon-induced narcosis of nerve cells (directly proportional to hydrocarbon
concentrations). From the standpoint of the kinetic analysis,
the primary effect on the sugar receptors superficially resembled competitive inhibition. However, the authors suggested
that a non-specific inhibitory effect on sugar receptor sites
is a more likely explanation. Previously reported data which
indicated that insects "reject" such hydrocarbons may actually
reflect the possibility that hydrocarbons merely inhibit reception of the sugar stimulus.

     In studies of two arctic marine amphipods, *(Onisimus
affinis* and *Gammarus oceanicus)*, and an isopod, *(Mesidotea
entomon)*, Percy [75] found that none of the organisms were
attracted to crude oil. Both amphipods were repelled by masses of Atkinson Point crude oil, Norman Wells crude oil, and
a Venezuela crude oil (listed in order of decreasing avoidance response). The isopod was essentially unaffected by all
of the crude oil masses but may have demonstrated a slight
avoidance response to Norman Wells crude oil. Weathering of
the crude oils (except Norman Wells crude oil) and pre-exposure of the animals to the oils (24 hr at 0.5 ml/l seawater;
500 ppm) also moderated the repellent effect. When offered a

choice between clean and oiled sediments, *O. affinis* rejected sediments contaminated by all but the highest concentrations of Pembina and Norman Wells crude oils [45]. With higher concentrations in the sediments, reduced discrimination was perhaps caused by impairment of physiological processes which mediate selectivity. Avoidance of oil-tainted sediments was reduced after weathering the treated sediments for one week prior to experimental use, and reduced selectivity at higher crude oil levels was also less evident after weathering. The isopods *M. entomon* and *M. sibirica* and the amphipod *Corophium clarencense* were not significantly attracted or repelled by crude oil in the sediments.

Further investigations established that feeding preference was also species-specific [75]. The amphipod *O. affinis* preferred fish pieces untainted by crude oil, while the isopod *M. entomon* showed no such preference. *O. affinis* was scarcely attracted to oil-tainted food when it was offered the food alone.

Exposure to emulsions of Anastasiyevka crude oil reduced the feeding rates (as measured by fecal excretion) of an amphipod, *Gammarus olivii*, from the Black Sea, and an isopod, *Idotea baltica basteri* [76]. Oil concentrations of 0.1 ml/l (100 ppm) appreciably reduced feeding rate, and concentrations of 1.0 ml/l (1,000 ppm) eliminated feeding by *G. olivii*. One ml/l (1,000 ppm) reduced feeding by *I. baltica basteri* by two-thirds. Feeding rates of the common shore crab *Carcinus maenas* were unaffected over 12 weeks of exposure to 200 ppm Kuwait crude oil in experimental aquaria [77]. Wells and Sprague [60] showed that exposure of American lobster (*Homarus americanus*) larvae to Venezuelan crude oil reduced the food consumption of the larvae. The initial oil concentration responsible for this effect was 0.19 mg/l (0.19 ppm) and the average oil concentration over the 30-day test period was about 0.11 mg/l (0.11 ppm).

Rice et al. [58] noted that planktonic larvae of the Dungeness crab *Cancer magister* were not repelled by a crude oil slick and were prone to repeatedly contact the slick. Actual ingestion of oil by crustaceans has been documented under both field [78] and laboratory [79] conditions. According to Conover [78] planktonic copepods, mainly *Temora longicarpus* in Chedabucto Bay, Nova Scotia, ingested and defecated significant quantities of Bunker C fuel oil, following wreckage of the tanker *Arrow*.

Blackman [79] found that the shrimp *Crangon crangon* was likely to ingest sunken Kuwait crude oil, especially when starved. There was evidence that contact with oil reduced the feeding rates of the shrimp, and that fresh crude oil was less readily ingested than 20% topped crude oil. Ingested oil

adhered to the foregut where some remained until the next
molt. Such oil is therefore available to predators and apparently increases the rate of fish (plaice) predation upon the
shrimp by reducing the specific gravity and perhaps disrupting
the behavior of the shrimp [80].

The shore crab *Pachygrapsus crassipes* responds positively
to various amino acids in seawater; a feeding response was
elicited by 20 µl aliquots of 3 mM taurine dispensed near the
crabs [81]. Following a 24-hr exposure of crabs to low levels
(possibly less than 10 ppb) of soluble crude oil fractions,
the feeding response to taurine was eliminated. Moreover, the
inhibition was persistent; from three to six days were required for the crabs to regain sensitivity in clean seawater.
Further experimentation established that fuel oil dialysates
and monoaromatic and polynuclear aromatic hydrocarbons inhibited the feeding response of the crabs. Inhibition by monoaromatic hydrocarbons was brief; the crabs recovered sensitivity in about 30-60 min. In contrast, polynuclear aromatic
hydrocarbons caused a prolonged inhibition of the feeding response. One µg/l (1 ppb) naphthalene delayed recovery of the
feeding response for 3 or more days, and anthracene exposure
delayed recovery for 13 days.

Reproductive behavior was also eliminated by exposure of
low (possibly below 10 ppb) amounts of soluble crude oil fractions [81]. Crustecdysone, a steroid molting hormone for
many, if not all, arthropods [62] has been shown to possess
sex pheromone properties for three crabs, *Pachygrapsus crassipes, Cancer antennarius,* and *C. anthonyi* [82]. Male shore
crabs (*P. crassipes)* respond to 10^{-8} M crustecdysone (also
called β-ecdysone or ecdysterone) by rearing up on their dac-
tyls in a "mating stance." This mating stance is not exhibited in the presence of the soluble crude oil fractions (10
ppb) [81]. The male crabs respond with searching behavior to
even lower levels of crustecdysone (10^{-13} M), presumably to
find the female that is releasing the pheromone. Crustacean
distance chemoreceptors, sensory structures which are thought
to facilitate such chemosensory acuity, are thin projections
of the cuticle called aesthetascs and are located on the an-
tennules. The aesthetascs are water-permeable and contain
many neuronal dendritic tips. Kittredge, Takahashi, and
Sarinana [83] believed that the exposures to oil destroyed the
dendritic tips in the aesthetascs.

Although Blumer et al. [73] did not detect (by light and
electron microscopy) any morphological changes in the odor receptors of oil-exposed American lobsters, they noted that the
chemoreception-mediated behavior of the organisms was disrupted. They established that a large portion of the lipids
present in the test aquaria prior to the addition of an oil

slick was absent after contact with the oil. If lipid fractions are selectively taken up into the oil phase, the possibility that steroids and other chemical messages are also
taken up by oil masses in the marine environment cannot be
discounted.

Observations of the behavior of marsh fiddler crabs *(Uca
pugnax)* following the West Falmouth No. 2 fuel oil spill indicated that the reproductive behavior of the crabs was abnormal
in heavily and moderately oiled marshes [84]. Male and female
crabs reportedly displayed breeding colors and males demonstrated threat postures past the normal breeding season.

GROWTH, DEVELOPMENT, AND REPRODUCTION

No generalizations can be made with regard to the effects
of petroleum pollution on the growth (or body weight) of marine arthropods. Growth of juvenile brown shrimp, *P. aztecus,*
was unaffected by limited exposures to the WSF of No. 2 fuel
oil [64]. However, No. 2 fuel oil significantly reduced the
growth rate of larval grass shrimp *(Palaemonetes pugio)*. Tatem
[56] exposed the grass shrimp larvae to 0.52-0.85 ppm total
hydrocarbons (0.27-0.34 ppm total naphthalenes) for 12 days.
Growth of Black Sea isopods (*I. baltica basteri)* was reduced
at oil concentrations of 0.01 ml/l seawater (10 ppm), and unaffected at 0.001 ml/l (1 ppm) [76]. Benthic chironomids
(Chironomus albidus) of the Caspian Sea have been shown to
increase in weight in the presence of 0.3-0.7 mg/l (0.3-0.7
ppm) Artem crude oil and decrease in weight at higher oil concentrations [52].

The hatching rate of grass shrimp *(P. pugio)* larvae was
reduced following exposure of gravid female shrimp to hydrocarbons from No. 2 fuel oil for 72 hr [56]. No hatches occurred during the oil exposure period. Female grass shrimp
exposed to 1.44 ppm total hydrocarbons (0.62 ppm total naphthalenes) and held afterward in clean seawater bore an average
of 9 larvae each. Control females which were not exposed to
the No. 2 fuel oil fraction bore an average of over 45 larvae
per female. In addition, WSF of No. 2 fuel oil at 0.3 ppm or
greater reportedly disrupt the development of barnacles
(Balanus amphitrite niveus) [13].

Wells and Sprague [60] found that Venezuelan crude oil
retarded development of lobster *(Homarus americanus) larvae.*
Development of larvae which survived to the fourth stage in
30-day tests was retarded at crude oil concentrations of 0.24
mg/l (0.24 ppm) or greater.

Some data are available on the effects of oil pollution
on the reproductive success and recruitment of marine arthropods, stemming in large part from studies following accidental
discharges of crude oil in the Santa Barbara Channel in south-

ern California. Straughan [85] offered evidence to indicate
that oil pollution did not affect breeding of two high—intertidal sessile barnacles *B. glandula* and *Chthamalus fissus*. In
contrast, breeding of the gooseneck barnacle, *Pollicipes polymerus,* which inhabits lower intertidal areas, was reduced in
oil-impinged localities. Furthermore, settlement of the larvae of all three species of barnacles was apparently retarded
on oiled substrates. This was especially true for *P. polymerus;* the larvae set preferentially on conspecific adult
stalks (peduncle), but would not set where the stalks were
visibly contaminated with oil. *B. glandula,* which secretes a
basal plate, recolonized oiled substrates more rapidly than
did *C. fissus,* which does not form basal plates [85]. Although the impact on reproduction is unknown, heavy fuel oil
has been shown to contribute to gonadal abnormalities (lesions)
in male crabs, *Carcinus maenas* [86].

MOLLUSCS

   The two classes of marine molluscs which have been
studied with respect to petroleum pollution, *Gastropoda* and
Bivalvia, consist of animals with sharply contrasting adult
habits. The gastropods are mostly free-living epibenthic animals. The following section deals with the effects of petroleum hydrocarbons on gastropod behavior. Most adult bivalves
are either sessile or sedentary burrowing forms. Many bivalve
life functions are carried on in an all-or-none fashion con-
tingent upon whether or not the animal is pumping seawater
through its mantle cavity (ventilating). The behavior, physiology, growth, and reproduction of bivalves are so interdependent with respect to ventilation that no attempt has been
made to treat them separately in this review.

BEHAVIOR (GASTROPODS)

   Several sublethal effects of oil have been noted in gastropods, ranging from simple narcotization to loss of chemo-
sensitivity. Dicks [87] demonstrated that the limpet *Patella
vulgata* was unable to maintain pedal attachment to its rocky
substrate after contact with Kuwait crude oil, but detachment
did not occur upon contact with an inert paraffin oil. Crude
oil-affected animals were able to regain pedal sensitivity and
reattach if washed in clean seawater for a period of one to
three hours. Inability to maintain pedal attachment appears
to be the result of an anesthetic effect of the crude oil on
the foot of the limpet, and may be partly dependent on the
natural activity cycle of the animal (since locomotor activity
maximized the chances for a limpet to contact the oil). Dicks
verified his laboratory results in the field and stated that
reattachment of the limpets to substrates in the marine envi-

ronment following oil-induced detachment was unlikely to occur.

Ehrsam et al. [88] also found that petroleum fractions had a narcotic effect on two gastropods native to Puget Sound (the limpet *Notoacmaea scutum* and the snail *Thais lamellosa*). Fifty percent of the limpets exposed to 41.0 ppm No. 2 diesel oil in test aquaria for 24 hr became detached from the aquarium walls. In 48-hr exposures, 23.5 ppm No. 2 diesel oil also caused detachment of half of the limpets. The limpets generally avoided the surface slick. In response to the diesel oil, the snails became less responsive to tactile stimulation, extruded their foot and mantle before withdrawal into the shell, and secreted copious amounts of mucus. They were less sensitive to a given concentration of diesel oil than were the limpets, however.

Griffith [89] found that Arabian light crude oil had a narcotic effect on the intertidal periwinkle *Littorina littorea*. The snails were exposed to the weathered crude oil (which had lost 11-12.5% of its volume through evaporation) under simulated tidal conditions in the laboratory. The narcotic effect was reversible; most narcotized animals placed in clean seawater recovered within 24 hr. Narcotization ensued more rapidly (2-4 hr) at 11°C than at 4.6°C (10-12 hr), but recovery time (14-18 hr) was largely unaffected by temperature.

Hargrave and Newcombe [90] determined the effects of a seawater extract of Bunker C fuel oil on crawling and respiration rates of *L. littorea*. Clear-cut results were not obtained at 4°C, but at 18°C, 30-min exposures to 750-800 µg/l (750-800 ppb) oil in seawater increased oxygen uptake by 34% and crawling rate by 28%, the two responses being interdependent to a large degree. Crawling rates were determined while the snails were in the oil-treated seawater, but respiration rates were measured after the snails had been transferred to untreated seawater. It is noteworthy that the direction of crawling movement was upwards. Snails returned to clean flowing seawater were able to regain normal activity.

Exposure of periwinkles, *L. saxatilis,* to oil refinery effluents containing 12 ppm petroleum hydrocarbons for 30 min resulted in reduced activity of the gastropods after they had been transferred to untreated seawater under laboratory conditions [91]. The animals eventually regained normal activity in the untreated seawater. In a field test, oil refinery effluent introduced into unpolluted rock pools caused 50% of the indigenous *L. saxatilus* to crawl up the rocks and out of the pools. The author (Baker [91]) also presented evidence suggesting that limpet *(P. vulgata)* densities and size distributions are affected in areas receiving chronic oil refinery effluent discharges. Activity of pelagic gastropods is also susceptible to petroleum. No. 2 fuel oil was shown to inhibit swimming of the pelagic pteropod *Creseis acicula* [13]. At 0.2

ppm, the pteropods retracted their epipodia and ceased to swim.

Perhaps the most striking example of behavioral modification by low concentrations of WSF concerns chemotaxis in the mud snail *Nassarius obsoletus*. *N. obsoletus* responds positively to dilute concentrations of food (oyster and scallop) extracts on the order of 0.3 to 3 ppm in seawater by crawling upstream toward the source. Jacobson and Boylan [92] demonstrated that a calculated concentration of one part per billion of soluble kerosine fraction in seawater reduced the snail's attraction to oyster extract to levels not significantly different from control levels (without food stimulus). This kerosine fraction consisted mostly of benzenes and naphthalenes, and similar fractions are present in seawater extracts of crude oils [93].

Food finding is of fundamental importance to all marine animals, and is mediated by chemosensitive orientation in gastropods as well as in other invertebrates [94]. Blake [95] showed that oyster drills *(Urosalpinx cinerea)* are attracted to chemicals released by their bivalve prey. Eisler [36] found that the predation rate of a Red Sea drill, *Drupa granulata,* on its mussel prey was three times higher in drills kept in clean seawater than in drills exposed to sublethal mixtures of seawater and Iranian crude oil (10 ml/l; 10,000 ppm) for 168 hr prior to the predation experiments in clean seawater. The fecundity (oviposition) of the drills was also reduced, perhaps due to their poor nutritional status. Other than those mussels consumed by drills, no mortalities occurred in either species. In field and laboratory studies, Brown, Baissac, and Leon [96] determined the sublethal effects of crude oil on the sand-beach gastropod *Bullia digitalis* including failure to be attracted to its normal food.

PHYSIOLOGY, BEHAVIOR, GROWTH, DEVELOPMENT, AND REPRODUCTION (BIVALVES)

The ability of oil-exposed American oysters *(Crassostrea virginica)* to compensate osmotically and ionically for changes in test medium salinity has been investigated. Anderson and Anderson [97] found that exposure of the oysters to 1% oil-water dispersions of South Louisiana crude and No. 2 fuel oil exerted no long-term effects on the pericardial fluid of the bivalves following their transfer from the acclimation salinity (20 ^{o}/oo) to test salinities (10 ^{o}/oo and 30 ^{o}/oo). Oysters exposed to the No. 2 fuel oil dispersions, however, adjusted to the test salinities more slowly than did control of crude oil-treated oysters.

The ability of bivalves to regulate their ventilation rate, and thereby somewhat control their exposure to pollutants, is well documented. Furthermore, ventilation in bivalves serves several purposes, including respiration, feeding, and waste and gamete discharge. Thus a pollutant which affects ventilation may be expected to exert multiple effects on these organisms. Swedmark, Granmo, and Kollberg [69] investigated the shell closure ability of bivalves exposed to dispersions of Oman crude oil, finding that mussels (Mytilus edulis) were unaffected, cockles (Cardium edule) closed their shells during the entire exposure period (96 hr), and scallops (Pecten opercularis) rapidly lost their ability to maintain shell closure at the highest concentration (1,000 ppm) of the crude oil in seawater. The authors noted that byssal activity of mussels was more sensitive than shell closure activity; impairment of byssal thread production occurred within 96 hr at less than 350 ppm of oil. Recovery of byssal activity was noted when exposed mussels were placed in clean seawater, but recovery did not occur among any of the bivalves that had lost the ability to close their shells [69].

Comparing the responses of mussels (M. edulis) and oysters (Ostrea lurida) following 24-hr exposure to a 10% concentration of soluble components derived from the use of a two-cycle outboard motor, Clark and Finley [98] found that the oysters merely closed their shells. Most of the mussels were gaping and may have suffered gill tissue degeneration. Oysters (O. lurida) exposed five and ten days to this concentration of components also showed gill tissue degeneration. With exposure to increasing concentrations of No. 2 fuel oil, oysters (Crassostrea virginica) showed less readiness to ventilate (and feed) and at 900 µg/l (0.9 ppm) remained closed entirely [99]. Syazuki [100] determined the threshold concentrations of phenol in seawater sufficient to produce shell closure (following 1 hr exposure) and increased oxygen consumption rates (following 24 and 48-hr exposures) of short-necked clams, Venerupis phillipinarum. The threshold phenol concentration affecting shell closure was 2 ppm, and that causing increased respiration rate was 20 ppm.

Alterations in metabolism may arise from the regulatory closure (and concomitant interruption of feeding) of oil-impinged bivalves, as the results of Gilfillan [101] seem to indicate. Concentrations as low as 1 ppm of Mid-Continent (United States) sweet crude oil reduced the net carbon-flux of mussels (M. edulis and Modiolus demissus). Respiration rate, however, was increased in the presence of small amounts of crude oil (in 31 °/oo salinity seawater). In some cases the amount of carbon available would fall below maintenance requirements, and any reduction in energy reserves may affect subsequent spawning success. Mussels (M. edulis) which survived the West Falmouth oil spill failed to spawn the following year. Straughan's data [85] which indicated reduced breeding in M. californianus from oil-contaminated intertidal areas,

also lend credence to the notion. Generally, *M. edulis* appears
to be more resistant to oil than *M. demissus* [101]. Besides
oil extract concentration and oil type, the nutritional state,
salinity, and acclimation state were shown to affect the mussels' respiratory response [9] and these factors combined to
produce a complex and variable spectrum of responses.

A later study by Gilfillan and coworkers [102] showed
that a population of soft-shell clams *(Mya arenaria)* from sediments exposed to a spill of No. 6 fuel oil gained carbon at
half the rate at which clams from an unoiled site did. These
results are consistent with the hypothesis that physiological
disruptions caused by petroleum exposure in the marine environment can lead to a reduction in carbon available for reproduction and growth. In comparison, Harger and Straughan [103]
found that the body weights of mussels *(M. edulis and M. californianus)* did not appreciably differ between oil-impinged and
unimpinged areas for three years following the 1969 Santa
Barbara oil spill. The spill occurred, however, during a period of minimal growth for the mussels.

Unlike Gilfillan's findings with mussels, other workers
have noted oil-induced inhibition of respiratory rate among
bivalves. Sublethal exposures to Arabian light crude oil in
concentrations of 10 and 25 ml/l in seawater (10,000 and
25,000 ppm) were found to depress the respiratory rates (oxygen consumption) of the mussel *Brachidontes variabilis* and the
clam *Donax trunculus* by over 50% in some cases [104]. With
higher concentrations (up to 100 ml/l; 100,000 ppm) respiratory inhibition was less pronounced. Dunning and Major [105]
found that WSF of Esso Extra oil (a premium lubricating oil)
and No. 2 fuel oil reduced the oxygen consumption rates of
M. edulis at 12% of total WSF in seawater. At 24% WSF, respiration virtually ceased. Further investigation revealed
that oil-induced closure of the bivalve (avoidance response)
was partly responsible for the reduced respiration rate. Animals that were exposed to the oil extracts after their adductor muscles had been severed (rendering shell closure impossible), had greater respiratory rates than did exposed mussels
with intact adductors, but still lower rates than unexposed
mussels with cut adductors. Twenty-four percent Esso Extra
oil WSF was also shown to significantly reduce the respiration
rate of isolated gill tissue. The authors suggested that inhibition of gill ciliary activity might account for the remaining oil-induced respiratory inhibition. In this context, the
filtration rate of mussels exposed to 12% Esso Extra oil WSF
was found to be much slower than that of unexposed animals.
In addition, the glycogen stores of the posterior adductor
muscles of the *M. edulis* exposed to the extracts were reduced.
These results further suggest that hydrocarbon contamination

may lead to reduction in energy reserves. Mussels exposed to the oil extracts failed to secrete byssus threads, unlike the unexposed animals. The more volatile hydrocarbon constituents of these extracts appear to be associated with the toxic effects, because the abnormal responses did not occur unless the test aquaria were covered and fresh extracts of the oil were used [105].

Anderson [55] presented data indicating that 96-hr exposure to 1% oil-seawater dispersions of various crude and fuel oils exert little effect on oyster *(C. virginica)* growth over 105 days. Mackin and Hopkins [106] reported studies by various workers which revealed that growth of oysters *(C. virginica)* kept under a crude oil slick for more than one year under field conditions and setting of new spat were unaffected. In laboratory studies, the heartbeat and shell movements of oysters exposed to a 0.1% concentration of WSF were also unchanged. In other studies, concentrations of a seawater-soluble crude oil fraction greater than 50% in seawater reduced oyster pumping rates, and 10% concentrations of oil field bleedwater in seawater produced similar effects. In field studies near an oil field bleedwater discharge, the shell growth and glycogen accumulation of oysters were reduced at distances of approximately 150 feet or less from the discharge point.

Lund [107] investigated the effects of petroleum fracions on the pumping and clearance (filtration) rates of oysters *(C. virginica)* and found that filtration rate was the more sensitive physiological index. Threshold concentrations of bleedwater of 3-6% affected the rate of filtration of a turbid suspension by the oysters, while 10% bleedwater concentrations were necessary to affect pumping rate. A 6% concentration of WSF of crude oil obtained by countercurrent exchange with seawater was ineffective in altering the filtration rates of oysters.

Chipman and Galtsoff [34] reported experiments establishing the inhibition of ventilation and the inducement of valve closure activities of oysters *(C. virginica)* by crude and diesel oils. Their findings indicate that both muscular and ciliary activity were depressed. Anderson [108], however, found that filtration rates of the soft-shelled clam *Mya arenaria* increased when the clams were held in emulsions of 0.9% Bunker C fuel oil in seawater, but the rates were not affected by 0.9% WSF in seawater. Kittredge et al. [83] found that 1 ppm naphthalene affected two types of ciliated gill tissue of *C. virginica* differently; the activity of cilia involved in food-gathering was accelerated, while the activity of cilia which pump water through the gills was decreased. Exposure of arctic bivalves, *Yoldiella intermedia,* to crude oil WSF re-

sulted in an initial cessation of feeding followed by a resumption of feeding. The duration of the non-feeding stage
varied directly with the oil concentration [45].

Field studies on production (weight) of soft-shelled
clams, *M. arenaria,* in intertidal sediments contaminated by an
oil spill (unknown type) showed that growth and production of
the clams were reduced [109]. Two years after the spill, production of the clams had decreased by 20% in contaminated sediments but had increased by 250% in adjacent uncontaminated
mudflats. These results support findings of Gilfillan and coworkers [101,102] with respect to long-term ramifications of
petroleum-induced physiological disruptions in bivalves. Dow
cited evidence indicating soft-shelled clams may surface from
their burrows in response to petroleum contamination.

Two additional studies have yielded information regarding
the disruption of burrowing activities among bivalves exposed
to petroleum constituents. Taylor, Karinen, and Feder [110]
found that a WSF of Prudhoe Bay crude oil caused many buried
clams *(Macoma balthica)* to come to the sediment surface. In
static bioassays, these effects on clams were noted within 3
days exposure to 0.331 ppm of the WSF (expressed in naphthalene equivalents) and within 9 days at 0.036 ppm. In flow-
through bioassays, such WSF also caused buried clams to surface and inhibited burrowing of some unburied clams. At a
concentration of 0.361 ppm (in naphthalene equivalents) of
oil, 50% of the buried clams surfaced within 3 days. At 0.233
ppm, 50% of the unburied clams were inhibited from burrowing
within 60 min. Burrowing of the bivalve *Tellina tenuis* is inhibited by phenol under both static and continuous-flow conditions [111]. Phenol concentrations ranging from 10-500 mg/l
(10-500 ppm) in seawater inhibited burrowing. Some of the
clams exposed to crude oil fractions or phenol were able to
recover normal activity when returned to clean seawater.

Most bivalves are sessile as adults, and must select and
attach to favorable substrates in order to survive. Previous
work has shown that among some bivalves substrate selection is
mediated in part by chemoreception [66,112,113]. Cardwell
[114] demonstrated that low levels of No. 2 diesel oil (0.005
to 0.040 ml/l; 5 to 40 ppm) were sufficient to inhibit the
byssal attachment of young mussels *Mytilus edulis).* The 24-hr
EC_{50} for this effect was 0.017 ml/l (17 ppm), and the 48-hr
EC_{50} was nearly the same (0.016 ml/l; 16 ppm). Complete recovery (reattachment) occurred within 24 hr after the mussels
were placed in clean running seawater. Swedmark and coworkers
[69] observed impairment of byssal activity in *M. edulis* following 96-hr exposures to 350 ppm Oman crude oil. Reduced
substrate attachment was also noted for Red Sea mussels, *M.
variabilis,* exposed for 168 hr to 3-30 mg/l (3-30 ppm) of
Sinai and Arabian crude oils under static conditions [36].

Larvae of marine animals are often more sensitive to toxic agents than adults, and many workers have turned to assessment of larval development as a method for sensitive pollutant bioassays. Legore [115] showed that petroleum and its components affect the early development of larvae of the Pacific oyster *Crassostrea gigas*. He found that less than 1 ml/l (1,000 ppm) of Alaskan crude oil produced abnormal development in 50% of the oyster larvae within 48 hr. Threshold doses for inducement of abnormalities in oyster larvae by benzene, toluene, and xylenes were 3.1-3.6 mg/l (3.1-3.6 ppm). Of many pure fractions tested, *n*-propyl benzene, naphthalene, and cyclooctane were found to be most toxic, and paraffins were least toxic. Renzoni [116] extended such a study to *Crassostrea angulata* and *Mytilus galloprovincialis,* and showed that fertilization was probably more sensitive to oil than early larval development. Later work by Renzoni [117] established that the sperm were more sensitive to crude oil WSF than eggs of the estuarine bivalve *Mulinia lateralis*. Fertilization and normal development of both *M. lateralis* and *C. virginica* and growth of *M. lateralis* larvae were adversely affected in proportion to WSF concentrations from 0.001 to 1 ml/l (1-1,000 ppm) of Prudhoe Bay, Nigerian, and Kuwait crude oils.

The effects of *n*-hexane-soluble components of crude oil and phenol on the clam *Meretrix lusoria* have been assessed by Lee and coworkers [118]. The crude oil components at 3 ppm caused abnormalities in cleavage and development of larvae, and caused a reduction in the oxygen consumption rate of isolated gill tissue of adult *M. lusoria*. Ten parts per million of phenol produced similar effects.

Jeffries [119] described a stress syndrome in quahaugs *(Mercenaria mercenaria)* whereby hydrocarbon pollution brought about a measurable change in the tissue taurine-to-glycine ratio, and possibly led to enhanced infection by the annelid *Polydora*.

ECHINODERMS

Owing to their possession of a water-vascular system, echinoderms may be expected to be in intimate physiological contact with water-borne contaminants. Despite this, very little work has been done concerning the effects of petroleum hydrocarbons on these forms.

PHYSIOLOGY

The oxygen consumption rate of the sea urchin *Strongylocentrotus droebachiensis* may be slightly stimulated by exposures to crude oil extracts [9].

BEHAVIOR

Sea urchins may be particularly susceptible to oil pollution since exposure to oil emulsions weakens adherence to the
substrate, allowing the animals to be swept inshore or otherwise debilitated. North and coworkers [42] found that exposure for 20 min or less of urchins *(S. purpuratus)* to 0.1%
diesel oil emulsions produced retraction of the tube feet.
Normal behavior was regained after the animals were placed in
fresh seawater, but less rapidly with longer exposures to the
oil emulsions.

Starfish *(Asterias vulgaris)* have been shown to detect
their oyster prey at a distance of at least 120 cm upstream
through chemoreception. Whittle and Blumer [120] were successful in making partial purifications of the active fractions of oyster extract and establishing the threshold concentrations necessary to produce a positive response in the
starfish. Additions of 1, 4, and 40 mg non-detergent motor
oil per liter (1, 4, 40 ppm) to the test chambers produced an
observable decrease in the response (more than 40 mg/l would
have been required to eliminate the response) of the starfish
to 50 ppb of the partially purified extract [121]. Crapp [77]
also gave evidence that oil pollution can affect predation
rates of starfish. In his experiments the rates of predation
by *A. rubens* on the mussel *M. edulis* were reduced in the presence of 2 ml Kuwait crude oil per 10 liters of seawater.

Chia [50] noted large differences in the sensitivities of
four echinoderm larvae to a 0.5% mixture of No. 2 diesel oil
in seawater. Immobility of brachiolaria larvae of the asteroid *Crossaster papposus* did not ensue until 200 hr of exposure, while gastrulae of the asteroid *Pisaster ochraceus,*
bipinnariae of *Luidia foliata,* and pluteus larvae of the echi-
noid *Dendraster excentricus* were immobilized after only 12,
15, and 21 hr, respectively.

GROWTH, DEVELOPMENT, AND REPRODUCTION

Fertilization of eggs of the sea urchin *S. purpuratus* was
shown to be relatively insensitive to extracts of various
crude and fuel oils (25 ml oil/500 ml seawater [122]); however,
cleavage and development of the early embryos was markedly
affected. Extract concentrations of 6.25% and greater in seawater significantly disrupted development of the embryos in
most cases following 2-and 4-hr exposures to the 16 different
petroleum extracts. Of the extracts tested, crude and heavy
bunker oil extracts were most inimical to development of the
embryos.

Lönning and Hagström [123] investigated the effects of crude oil on fertilization and development of sea urchin *(Psammechinus miliaris* and *Paracentrotus lividus)* embryos. Fertilization rate was retarded, although 100% fertilization was achieved in the presence of 1,000-20,000 ppm Kuwait or Ekofisk crude oil. A moderate retarding effect on fertilization was also produced following a 2 min pre-exposure of sperm to the oil. Crude oil treatment produced substantial developmental abnormalities, however. Regardless of the onset of the exposure period (pre-hatching or at 2-cell stage) the various crude oil treatments caused a reduction of skeletal formation in the pluteus larvae. The authors concluded that this effect would prevent normal development and metamorphosis.

CONCLUSIONS AND PROSPECTUS

These concluding comments focus on the lowest concentrations of petroleum hydrocarbons that have been shown to affect biological processes of marine bacteria, algae, and invertebrates. Most of this information is derived from research conducted on plants and animals from temperate marine environments in the northern hemisphere.

PHYSIOLOGY

A wide range of physiological changes are brought about by exposure of marine organisms to petroleum contamination. Petroleum hydrocarbon concentrations on the order of 1 ppm induce alterations in the carbon flux of mussels [101], ciliary activity of oysters [44], ionic regulation of shrimp [26], and the respiration rates of various marine invertebrates [9,26,90]. At levels between 0.4 and 0.04 ppm of crude oil or No. 2 fuel oil, inhibition of the respiration rate of a crab and the photosynthetic rates of microalgae occur [9,12]. Aliphatic hydrocarbon concentrations as low as 5 ppb significantly reduce the photosynthetic rate of a diatom [13].

Despite the variety of oil-induced physiological disruptions that have been reported, relating the importance of these disruptions to the viability of affected organisms is difficult. This is especially true for alterations in respiratory rates when respiration is the only parameter assessed. Respiration rates are covariant with other biological functions such as activity and nutrition. Monitoring the effects of petroleum on respiratory rates while simultaneously considering other associated biological processes is most revealing, however. Unfortunately, only in a very few studies, such as the work of Gilfillan and coworkers [101,102], has this been done. From their work, which relates oil-affected respiratory

and nutritive functions to their combined effect in marine organisms, we can just begin to appreciate the significance of
such physiological disruptions.

BEHAVIOR

Behavioral disruptions attributable to petroleum hydrocarbon exposures have been reported among diverse marine organisms from bacteria and gametes of fucoid algae through invertebrates. These behavioral disruptions themselves are as
varied as the organisms that experience them, and include
alterations in patterns of locomotor, reproductive, habitat-
selection, and feeding activities. Despite this array of
diverse behavioral effects, those effects produced by the
lowest concentrations of petroleum hydrocarbons are similar
in one respect; they are disruptions of behavioral events
which are initiated by the organism's recognition of exogenous
chemical cues.

Low concentrations of petroleum hydrocarbons, principally
aromatics, are capable of disrupting feeding and reproductive
behaviors mediated by chemoreception. One part hydrocarbon
(kerosine fractions or naphthalene) per billion parts seawater
eliminated the responses of snails and crabs to chemical substances that normally initiate feeding behavior [81,92].
Roughly ten times that level of hydrocarbons (10 ppb) derived
from crude oil eliminated chemoreceptive feeding and reproductive displays of crab [81]. At 100 ppb, benzene inhibited
chemotaxis of marine bacteria [4]. These observations suggest
that concentrations of aromatic hydrocarbons on the order of a
few parts per billion are sufficient to impair chemosensory
behavior. Moreover, these effects are produced by short-term
(24 hr or less) exposures to hydrocarbons, and are reversible
in some cases.

It is not known which events in the sequence beginning
with reception of the chemical stimulus and ending with the
behavioral response of an organism are disrupted by petroleum
hydrocarbons. The fact that aromatic hydrocarbons inhibit
chemoreception-dependent bacterial behaviors may be significant. Bacteria do not possess a nervous system. Therefore,
the inhibition of chemotactic behavior of bacteria cannot be
due to hydrocarbon-induced impairment of the nervous system
as it could in higher organisms. This emphasizes the importance of peripheral cell membrane function as a target for
research relevant to a mode of action of toxic hydrocarbons.

At this time there is no compelling reason to believe
that the primary effects of petroleum hydrocarbons on chemoreceptive cells are any different than the primary effects of
such agents (including anesthetics) on other excitable or non-

excitable cells [124]. Many narcotic effects of petroleum
hydrocarbons on marine invertebrates have been noted in this
review [34,35,36,45,50,66,67,68,69,87,88,89]. The variety of
petroleum-induced effects on the behavior of marine organisms
may simply reflect the variety of functions with which the
petroleum-affected cells are endowed.

GROWTH, DEVELOPMENT, AND REPRODUCTION

Unfortunately there is little information relevant to the
effects of petroleum hydrocarbons on growth, development, and
reproduction of marine organisms.

Petroleum hydrocarbon concentrations as low as 1 ppm adversely affect fertilization or development of various bivalve
larvae [115,117]. Phytoplankton are affected at even lower
levels. The growth rate of phytoplankton cultures, a measure
of the rate of division or reproduction of individual algal
cells, is either stimulated or inhibited by petroleum hydrocarbons. Algal cell division was inhibited by petroleum hydrocarbon concentrations as low as 10 ppm [24]. At even lower
levels (1 ppb), stimulation of phytoplankton reproduction can
take place [29].

The most dramatic case of reproductive failure caused by
low levels of petroleum concerns complete inhibition of fertilization of *Fucus edentatus* eggs. This occurs when the mature macroalgae are exposed to 0.2 ppb or more of No. 2 fuel
or crude oil [19].

RISK AND THE PAUCITY OF INFORMATION PROBLEM

Clearly, petroleum and its components in seawater can induce changes in the life processes of marine bacteria, algae,
and invertebrates at concentrations far lower than those necessary to kill the organisms outright. Many factors must be
considered before extrapolating the sublethal biological
changes induced by petroleum contamination under one set of
conditions, such as those in a laboratory, to those that would
be induced by the same contaminants under other conditions,
such as those in a marine environment. Examples of these factors, along with those mentioned in other chapters of this
review, include:

1. Environmental factors. Does addition of a contaminant to a medium under one set of conditions lead to an exposure of the organisms within the medium that is equivalent to
the exposure produced by addition of the same contaminant to
a different medium, under other conditions? These conditions
may be chemical, physical, or biological in nature.

2. Cyclic chronobiological factors. The physiology of

most organisms undergoes cyclic flux as a function of seasonal, lunar, or daily cycles. Assuming equivalent biological
exposure, it is possible that such exposures would exert different sublethal effects on organisms with respect to the
phase of the chronobiological processes taking place at the
time of exposure. For example, would exposure of marine organisms to petroleum at a time when feeding or reproductive
activities were at a peak have more effect than when such
biological activities were minimal?

3. Serial chronobiological factors. Organisms also undergo progressive fluxes; their physiological and morphological states change as a function of their age and ontogenetic
status. Would a given dose of oil affect adults of a marine
species differently than larvae?

4. Other biological factors. Does the nutritional state,
size, stage of moult, prior experience, or a myriad of other
biological states of an organism moderate the sublethal effects of a contaminant on that organism?

5. Interactive factors. Do the parameters mentioned
above, in all their combinations and permutations, interact in
an additive, synergistic, or antagonistic fashion with respect
to the cumulative effects that a contaminant may have on an
organism? Moreover, how will the effects of such exposures
ramify through the impinged ecosystem or through unimpinged
ecosystems connected to the first through numerous biotic and
abiotic interactions? Will reduced growth or reproductive
success of invertebrates deleteriously affect fish populations
dependent upon those invertebrates for food, or affect other
resources not so directly linked?

Solutions to problems such as those outlined above will
greatly enhance our ability to predict biological consequences
of petroleum pollution. Nevertheless, it is necessary to draw
upon present knowledge, whatever its shortcomings, to provide
the most accurate ecological forecasts possible. These forecasts should provide quantitative guidelines, or "critical
concentrations" that should represent thresholds below which
deleterious effects would not be anticipated, and should be
accompanied by some idea of effective exposure times.

Before arriving at a critical concentration it is helpful
to consider several points. First, what are the benefits,
aside from petroleum-related endeavors, which man expects to
glean from the given marine environment? In other words, what
is this concentration critical to? Would significant changes
in species composition necessarily be undesirable? Second, it
is best to bear in mind the fact that critical contaminant
levels decrease as research efforts intended to determine the
effects of those contaminants increase. The work of Mearns
and coworkers [125] illustrates this point. These workers
studied the effects of chromium on the marine polychaete,

Neanthes arenaceodentata, and found that hexavalent chromium
at concentrations of about 3 ppm in seawater killed 50% of the
worms in 4 days. The authors reared the worms over three generations (440 days), and in doing so discovered that hexavalent chromium concentrations as low as 0.0125 ppm or greater
reduced the brood size (reproductive success) of the worms.
Hence, while a short-term study yielded a concentration sufficient to reduce a worm population, a longer-term effort
yielded a concentration over 200 times lower that also reduced
the density of the worms. Comparisons of water quality criteria over a successive number of years would also indicate
that critical concentrations are adjusted only to lower levels. Thirdly, it is quite possible that the level of hydrocarbons in tissues, and the dynamic processes that determine
them, relate more directly to their toxic effects than the
concentrations of those hydrocarbons in seawater. Tissue hydrocarbon concentration factors of 100-fold and greater over
test medium hydrocarbon concentrations have been noted (see
Volume II, Chapter 3). Finally, it cannot be overemphasized
that we actually know very little about the primary sublethal
effects of petroleum hydrocarbons on marine organisms, much
less their ramifications through the ecosystem. Taking the
above considerations into account, the critical concentrations
represent those concentrations which, if achieved in a marine
environment, carry with them the *risk* of disrupting important
biological processes.

REFERENCES

1. Mitchell, R., S. Fogel, and I. Chet (1972). Bacterial
    chemoreception: An important ecological phenomenon inhib-
    ited by hydrocarbons. Water Res. 6:1137-40.
2. Chet, I., S. Fogel, and R. Mitchell (1971). Chemical de-
    tection of microbial prey by bacterial predators. J.
    Bacteriol. 106:863-7.
3. Adler, J. (1976). The sensing of chemicals by bacteria.
    Sci. Am. 234:40-7.
4. Walsh, F. and R. Mitchell (1973). Inhibition of bacterial
    chemoreception by hydrocarbons. In: The Microbial Degra-
    dation of Oil Pollutants (D.G. Ahearn and S.P. Meyers,
    eds.), p. 275-8. Publ. No. LSU-SG-73-01. Center Wetland
    Resources, Louisiana State University, Baton Rouge, La.
5. Schramm, W. (1972). Untersuchungen uber den Einfluss von
    Olverschumtsungen auf Meeresalgen. I. Die Wirkung von
    Rohofilmen auf den CO_2- Gaswechsel ausserhalb des Wassers.
    [Investigations on the influence of oil pollution on ma-
    rine algae. 1. The effect of crude-oil films on the CO_2
    gas exchange outside the water.] Mar. Biol. (Berl.)
    14:189-98.

6. Mitchell, C.T., E.K. Anderson, L.G. Jones, and W.J. North (1970). What oil does to ecology. J. Water Pollut. Control Fed. 42(5, part 1):812-8.

7. Clendenning, K.A. and W.J. North (1959). Effects of wastes on the giant kelp, *Macrocystis pyrifera*. In: Proceedings of the First International Conference on Waste Disposal in the Marine Environment (E.A. Pearson, ed.), p. 82-91. Pergamon Press, New York.

8. California State Water Quality Control Board (1964). An investigation of the effects of discharged wastes on kelp. Publ. 26, p. 50-120.

9. Yentsch, C.S., E.S. Gilfillan, and J.R. Sears (1973). The fate and behavior of crude oil on marine life. AD-678584. National Technical Information Service, U.S. Dep. of Commerce, Springfield, Va., 62 p.

10. Shiels, W.E., J.J. Goering, and D.W. Hood (1973). Crude oil phytotoxicity studies. In: Environmental Studies of Port Valdez (D.W. Hood, W.E. Shiels, and E.J. Kelley, eds.), p. 413-46. University of Alaska, Inst. Mar. Sci. Occas. Publ. 3.

11. Gordon, D.C., Jr. and N.J. Prouse (1973). The effects of three oils on marine phytoplankton photosynthesis. Mar. Biol. (Berl.) 22:329-33.

12. Pulich, W.M., Jr., K. Winters, and C. van Baalen (1974). The effects of a No. 2 fuel oil and two crude oils on the growth and photosynthesis of microalgae. Mar. Biol. (Berl.) 28:87-94.

13. Parker, P.L. (ed.) (1974). Effects of Pollutants on Marine Organisms. Deliberations and Recommendations of the NSF/IDOE Effects of Pollutants on Marine Organisms Workshop. Sidney, British Columbia, Canada, 11-14 August 1974, 46 p.

14. van Overbeek, J. and R. Blondeau (1954). Mode of action of phytotoxic oils. Weeds 3:55-65.

15. Baker, J.M. (1970). The effects of oils on plants. Environ. Pollut. 1:27-44.

16. Vandermeulen, J.H. and T.P. Ahern (1976). Effect of petroleum hydrocarbons on algal physiology: review and progress report. In: Effects of Pollutants on Aquatic Organisms (A.P.M. Lockwood, ed.), p. 107-25. Cambridge University Press, Cambridge.

17. Cook, A.H. and J.A. Elvidge (1951). Fertilization in the Fucaceae: investigations on the nature of the chemotactic substance produced by eggs of *Fucus serratus* and *F. vesiculosus*. Proc. R. Soc. Lond. B. Biol. Sci. 138:97-114.

18. Mueller, D.G. (1972). Sex attractants in brown algae. Ber. Dtsch. Bot. Ges. 85:363-9.

19. Steele, R.L. (1977). Effects of certain petroleum products on reproduction and growth of zygotes and juvenile stages of the alga *Fucus edentatus* De la Pyl (Phaeophyceae: Fucales). In: Proceedings of Symposium on Fate and Effects of Petroleum Hydrocarbons in Marine Ecosystems and Organisms (D. Wolfe, ed.). In press. Pergamon Press, New York.

20. Mommaerts-Billiet, F. (1973). Growth and toxicity tests on the marine nanoplanktonic alga *Platymonas tetrathele* G.S. West in the presence of crude oil and emulsifiers. Environ. Pollut. 4:261-82.

21. Galtsoff, P.S., H.F. Prytherch, R.O. Smith, and V. Koehring (1935). Effects of crude oil pollution on oysters in Louisiana waters. Bull. Bur. Fish. 48:158-210.

22. Prouse, N.J., D.C. Gordon, Jr., and P.O. Keizer (1976). Effects of low concentrations of oil accommodated in sea water on the growth of unialgal marine phytoplankton cultures. J. Fish. Res. Board Can. 33:810-8.

23. Nuzzi, R. (1973). Effects of water soluble extracts of oil on phytoplankton. In: Proceedings of 1973 Joint Conference on Prevention and Control of Oil Spills, p. 809-13. American Petroleum Institute, Washington, D.C.

24. Mironov, O.G. (1970). The effect of oil pollution on flora and fauna of the Black Sea. In: Proceedings FAO Technical Conference on Marine Pollution and its Effects on Living Resources and Fishing, MP/70/E92. Food and Agriculture Organization of the United Nations, Rome, 4 p.

25. Mitchell, F.M. and H.J. Bennett (1972). The susceptibility of bluegill sunfish *Lepomis macrochirus* and channel catfish *Ictalurus punctatus* to emulsifiers and crude oil. Proc. La. Acad. Sci. 35:20-6.

26. Anderson, J.W., J.M. Neff, and S.R. Petrocelli (1974). Sublethal effects of oil, heavy metals, and PCBs on marine organisms. In: Survival in Toxic Environments (M.A. Kahn and J.P. Bederka, Jr., eds.), p. 83-121. Academic Press, New York.

27. Hellebust, J.A., B. Hanna, R.G. Sheath, M. Gergis, and R.C. Hutchinson (1975). Experimental crude oil spills on a small subarctic lake in the Mackenzie Valley, NWT: effects on phytoplankton, periphyton, and attached aquatic vegetation. In: Proceedings of 1975 Conference on Prevention and Control of Oil Pollution, p. 509-15. American Petroleum Institute, Washington, D.C.

28. Kauss, P.B. and T.C. Hutchinson (1975). The effects of water-soluble petroleum components on the growth of *Chlorella vulgaris* Beijerinck. Environ. Pollut. 9:157-74.

29. Dunstan, W.M., L.P. Atkinson, and J. Natoli (1975). Stimulation and inhibition of phytoplankton growth by low molecular weight hydrocarbons. Mar. Biol. (Berl.) 31:305-10.

30. Winters, K., R. O'Donnell, J.C. Batterton, and C. van Baalen (1976). Water-soluble components of four fuel oils: Chemical characterization and effects on growth of microalgae. Mar. Biol. (Berl.) 36:269-76.

31. Davavin, I.A., O.G. Mironov, and I.M. Tsimbal (1975). Influence of oil on nucleic acids of algae. Mar. Pollut. Bull. 6:13-4.

32. Boney, A.D. (1974). Aromatic hydrocarbons and the growth of marine algae. Mar. Pollut. Bull. 5:185-6.

33. Boney, A.D. and E.D.S. Corner (1962). On the effects of some carcinogenic hydrocarbons on the growth of sporelings of marine red algae. J. Mar. Biol. Assoc. U.K. 42:579-85.

34. Chipman, W.A. and P.S. Galtsoff (1949). Effects of oil mixed with carbonized sand on aquatic animals. U.S. Fish. Wildl. Serv., Spec. Sci. Rep. 1, 52 p.

35. Elgershuizen, J.H.B.W. and H.A.M. DeKruijf (1976). Toxicity of crude oils and a dispersant to the stony coral *Madracis mirabilis*. Mar. Pollut. Bull. 7:22-5.

36. Eisler, R. (1975). Toxic, sublethal, and latent effects of petroleum on Red Sea macrofauna. In: Proceedings of 1975 Conference on Prevention and Control of Oil Pollution, p. 535-40. American Petroleum Institute, Washington, D.C.

37. Lewis, J.B. (1971). Effects of crude oil and oil-spill dispersant on reef corals. Mar. Pollut. Bull. 2:59-62.

38. Reimer, A.A. (1975). Effects of crude oil on corals. Mar. Pollut. Bull. 6:39-43.

39. Reimer, A.A. (1975). Effects of crude oil on the feeding behavior of the zoanthid *Palythoa variabilis*. Environ. Physiol. Biochem. 5:258-66.

40. Mitchell, R. and I. Chet (1975). Bacterial attack of corals in polluted seawater. Microb. Ecol. 2:227-33.

41. Birkeland, C., A.A. Reimer, and J.R. Young (1976). Survey of Marine Communities in Panama and Experiments with Oil. EPA-60013-76-028. U.S. Environmental Protection Agency, Narragansett, R.I., 177 p.

42. North, W.J., M. Neushul, and K.A. Clendenning (1965). Successive biological changes observed in a marine cove exposed to a large spillage of mineral oil. In: Symposium Commission internationale exploration scientifique Mer Mediterranée, Monaco, 1964, p. 335-54.

43. Foster, M., M. Neushul, and R. Zingmark (1971). The Santa Barbara oil spill. Part 2. Initial effects on intertidal and kelp bed organisms. Environ. Pollut. 2:115-34.

44. Howe, N.R. and Y.M. Sheikh (1975). Anthopleurine: A sea anemone alarm pheromone. Science 189:368-88.

45. Percy, J.A. and T.C. Mullin (1975). Effects of crude oils on Arctic marine invertebrates. Beaufort Sea Tech. Rep. 11, Environment Canada, Victoria, B.C., 79 p.

46. George, J.D. (1971). The effects of pollution by oil and oil-dispersants on the common intertidal polychaetes, *Cirriformia tentaculata* and *Cirratulus cirratus*. J. Appl. Ecol. 8:411-20.

47. Rossi, S.S., J.W. Anderson, and G.S. Ward (1976). Toxicity of water-soluble fractions of four test oils for the polychaetous annelids, *Neanthes arenaceodentata* and *Capitella capitata*. Environ. Pollut. 10:9-18.

48. Rossi, S.S. and J.W. Anderson (1976). Toxicity of water-soluble fractions of No. 2 fuel oil and South Louisiana crude oil to selected stages in the life history of the polychaete, *Neanthes arenaceodentata*. Bull. Environ. Contam. Toxicol. 16:18-24.

49. Raymont, J.E.G. and J. Shields (1963). Toxicity of copper and chromium in the marine environment. Int. J. Air Water Pollut. 7:435-43.

50. Chia, F. (1973). Killing of marine larvae by diesel oil. Mar. Pollut. Bull. 4:29-30.

51. Carr, R.S. and D.J. Reish (1977). The effect of petrochemicals on the survival and life history of polychaetous annelids. In: Proceedings of Symposium on Fate and Effects of Petroleum Hydrocarbons in Marine Ecosystems and Organisms (D. Wolfe, ed.). In press. Pergamon Press, New York.

52. Kasymov, A.G. and A.D. Aliev (1973). Experimental study of the effect of oil on some representatives of benthos in the Caspian Sea. Water Air Soil Pollut. 2:235-45.

53. Mohammad, M.B.M. (1974). Effect of chronic oil pollution on a polychaete. Mar. Pollut. Bull. 5:21-4.

54. Åkesson, B. (1975). Bioassay studies with polychaetes of the genus *Ophryotrocha* as test animals. In: Sublethal Effects of Toxic Chemicals on Aquatic Animals (J.H. Koeman and J.J.T.W.A. Strik, eds.), p. 121-35. Elsevier, New York.

55. Anderson, J.W. (1975). Laboratory studies on the effects of oil on marine organisms: An overview. Am. Petrol. Inst. Publ. 4249, 70 p.

56. Tatem, H.E. (1976). Accumulation of naphthalenes by grass shrimp: Effects on respiration, hatching, and larval growth. In: Proceedings of Symposium on Fate and Effects of Petroleum Hydrocarbons in Marine Ecosystems and Organisms (D. Wolfe, ed.). In press. Pergamon Press, New York.

57. Steed, D.L. and B.J. Copeland (1967). Metabolic responses of some estuarine organisms to an industrial effluent. Publ. Inst. Mar. Sci. Univ. Tex. 12, p. 143-59.

58. Rice, S.D., J.W. Short, C.C. Brodersen, T.A. Mecklenburg, D.A. Moles, C.J. Misch, D.L. Cheatham, and J.F. Karinen (1976). Acute toxicity and uptake depuration studies with Cook Inlet crude oil, Prudhoe Bay crude oil, No. 2 fuel oil, and several subarctic marine organisms. Northwest and Alaska Fisheries Center, NMFS, NOAA, U.S. Dep. of Commerce, Auke Bay Fisheries Laboratory, P.O. Box 155, Auke Bay, Alaska. Processed report, 114 p.

59. Wells, P.G. (1972). Influence of Venezuelan crude oil on lobster larvae. Mar. Pollut. Bull. 3:105-6.

60. Wells, P.G. and J.B. Sprague (1976). Effects of crude oil on American lobster *(Homarus americanus)* larvae in the laboratory. J. Fish. Res. Board Can. 33:1604-14.

61. Katz, L.M. (1973). The effects of water soluble fraction of crude oil on larvae of the decapod crustacean *Neopanope texana* (Sayi). Environ. Pollut. 5:199-204.

62. Karinen, J.F. and S.D. Rice (1974). Effects of Prudhoe Bay crude oil on molting Tanner crabs, *Chionoecetes bairdi*. U.S. Natl. Mar. Fish. Serv. Mar. Fish. Rev. 36:31-7.

63. Krishnakumaran, A. and H.A. Schneiderman (1970). Control of molting in mandibulate and chelicerate arthropods by ecdysones. Biol. Bull. (Woods Hole) 139:520-38.

64. Cox, B.A. and J.W. Anderson (1973). Some effects of No. 2 fuel oil on the brown shrimp *Penaeus aztecus*. Am. Zool. 13:1308 (abstract).

65. Epifanio, C.E. (1971). Effects of dieldrin in seawater on the development of two species of crab larvae, *Leptodius floridanus* and *Panopeus herbstii*. Mar. Biol. (Berl.) 11:356-62.

66. Crisp, D.J., A.O. Christie, and A.F.A. Ghobashy (1967). Narcotic and toxic action of organic compounds on barnacle larvae. Comp. Biochem. Physiol. 22:629-49.

67. Sanborn, H.R. and D.C. Malins (1977). Toxicity and metabolism of naphthalene: A study with marine larval invertebrates. Proc. Soc. Exp. Biol. Med. 154:151-55.

68. Corner, E.D.S., A.J. Southward, and E.C. Southward (1968). Toxicity of oil-spill removers ('detergents') to marine life: an assessment using the intertidal barnacle *Eliminius modestus*. J. Mar. Biol. Assoc. U.K. 48:29-47.

69. Swedmark, M., A. Granmo, and S. Kollberg (1973). Effects
     of oil dispersants and oil emulsions on marine animals.
     Water Res. 7:1649-72.

70. Bean, R.M., J.R. Vanderhorst, and P. Wilkinson (1974).
     Interdisciplinary study of the toxicity of petroleum to
     marine organisms. Battelle Pacific Northwest Laborato-
     ries, Richland, WA 99352, 48 p.

71. Sandberg, D.M., A.D. Michael, B. Brown, and R. Beebe-
     Center (1972). Toxic effects of fuel oil on haustoriid
     amphipods and pagurid crabs. Biol. Bull. (Woods Hole)
     143:475-76.

72. Atema, J. and L. Stein (1974). Effects of crude oil on
     the feeding behavior of the lobster, *Homarus americanus*.
     Environ. Pollut. 6:77-86.

73. Blumer, M., J.M. Hunt, J. Atema, and L. Stein (1973).
     Interaction between marine organisms and oil pollution.
     U.S. Environmental Protection Agency, Office of Research
     and Monitoring, Washington, D.C. Ecol. Res. Serv. No.
     EPA-R3-73-042, 97 p.

74. Steinhardt, R.A., H. Morita, and E.S. Hodgson (1966).
     Mode of action of straight chain hydrocarbons on primary
     chemoreceptors of the blowfly, *Phormia regina*. J. Cell.
     Physiol. 67:53-62.

75. Percy, J.A. (1976). Responses of arctic marine crusta-
     ceans to crude oil and oil-tainted food. Environ. Pol-
     lut. 10:155-62.

76. Milovidova, N.Y. (1974). The effect of oil pollution on
     some coastal crustaceans of the Black Sea. Hydrobiol. J.
     4:76-9.

77. Crapp, G.B. (1971). Chronic oil pollution. In: Pro-
     ceedings of the Ecological Effects of Oil Pollution on
     Littoral Communities (E.B. Cowell, ed.), p. 187-206.
     Institute of Petroleum, London.

78. Conover, R.J. (1971). Some relations between zooplankton
     and Bunker C oil in Chedabucto Bay following the wreck of
     the tanker *Arrow*. J. Fish. Res. Board Can. 28:1327-30.

79. Blackman, R.A.A. (1972). Effects of sunken crude oil on
     the feeding and survival of the brown shrimp *Crangon
     crangon*. Int. Counc. Explor. Sea CM 1972/K:13, 8 p.

80. Blackman, R.A.A. (1974). Effects of sunken oil on the
     feeding of plaice on brown shrimps and other benthos.
     Fisheries Improvement Committee Int. Counc. Explor. Sea
     CM 1974/E:24, 7 p.

81. Takahashi, F.T. and J.S. Kittredge (1973). Sublethal ef
    fects of the water soluble component of oil: Chemical
    communication in the marine environment. In: The Micro-
    bial Degradation of Oil Pollutants (D.G. Ahearn and S.P.
    Meyers, eds.), p. 259-64. Publ. No. LSU-SG-73-01. Cen-
    ter Wetland Resources, Louisiana State University, Baton
    Rouge, La.

82. Kittredge, J.S., M. Terry, and F.T. Takahashi (1971).
    Sex pheromone activity of the molting hormone, crustecdy-
    sone, on male crabs (*Pachygrapsus crassipes, Cancer an-
    tennarius* and *C. anthonyi*). Fish. Bull. 69:337-43.

83. Kittredge, J.S., F.T. Takahashi, and S.O. Sarinana
    (1974). Bioassays indicative of some sublethal effects
    of oil pollution. In: Proceedings Marine Technological
    Society, p. 891-7. Washington, D.C.

84. National Academy of Sciences (1975). Petroleum in the
    marine environment. Washington, D.C., 107 p.

85. Straughan, D. (1971). Breeding and larval settlement of
    certain intertidal invertebrates in the Santa Barbara
    Channel following pollution by oil. In: Biological and
    Oceanographical Survey of the Santa Barbara Channel oil
    spill 1969-1970, Vol. 1, p. 223-44. Allan Hancock Foun-
    dation, University of Southern California, Los Angeles.

86. Albeaux-Fernet, M. and C.M. Laur (1970). Influènce de la
    pollution par le mazout sur les testicules de crabes
    (étude histologique). [Influence of pollution by fuel oil
    on crab testicles (histologic study)]. Natl. Acad. Sci.,
    Paris 270:170-3.

87. Dicks, B. (1973). Some effects of Kuwait crude oil on
    the limpet *Patella vulgata*. Environ. Pollut. 5:219-29.

88. Ehrsam, L.C., Jr., T.S. English, J. Matches, D. Weitkamp,
    R. Cardwell, R.S. Legore, R.W. Steele, and R. Orhiem.
    (1972). Biological assessment of diesel spill in the vi-
    cinity of Anacortes, Wash., Sept. 1971, Final Report.
    Texas Instruments, Inc., Dallas, Tex., 82 p.

89. Griffith, D. de G. (1970). Toxicity of crude oil and de-
    tergents to two species of edible molluscs under artifi-
    cial tidal conditions. In: FAO Technical Conference on
    Marine Pollution and its Effects on Living Resources and
    Fishing, MP/70/E16. Food and Agriculture Organization of
    the United Nations, Rome, 12 p.

90. Hargrave, B.T. and C.P. Newcombe (1973). Crawling and
    respiration as indices of sublethal effects of oil and a
    dispersant on an intertidal snail *Littorina littorea*.
    J. Fish. Res. Board Can. 30:1789-92.

91. Baker, J.M. (1973). Biological effects of refinery ef-
    fluents. In: Proceedings of 1973 Joint Conference on
    Prevention and Control of Oil Spills, p. 715-24.
    American Petroleum Institute, Washington, D.C.

92. Jacobson, S.M. and D.B. Boylan (1973). Effect of sea-water soluble fraction of kerosene on chemotaxis in a marine snail, *Nassarius obsoletus*. Nature 241:213-5.

93. Boylan, D.B. and B.W. Tripp (1971). Determination of hydrocarbons in seawater extracts of crude oil and crude oil fractions. Nature 230:44-7.

94. Kohn, A.J. (1961). Chemoreception in gastropods. Am. Zool. 1:291-308.

95. Blake, J.W. (1960). Oxygen consumption of bivalve prey and their attractiveness to the gastropod *Urosalpinx cinerea*. Limnol. Oceanogr. 5:273-80.

96. Brown, A.C., P. Baissac, and B. Leon (1974). Observations on the effects of crude oil pollution on the sandy-beach snail, *Bullia* (Gastropoda:Prosobranchiata). Trans. R. Soc. S. Afr. 41(Part 1):19-24.

97. Anderson, R.D. and J.W. Anderson (1975). Effects of salinity and selected petroleum hydrocarbons on the osmotic and chloride regulation of the American oyster, *Crassostrea virginica*. Physiol. Zool. 48:420-30.

98. Clark, R.C., Jr. and J.S. Finley (1974). Acute effects of outboard motor effluent on two marine shellfish. Environ. Sci. Technol. 8:1009-14.

99. Stegeman, J.J. and J.M. Teal (1973). Accumulation, release, and retention of petroleum hydrocarbons by the oyster *Crassostrea virginica*. Mar. Biol. (Berl.) 22:37-44.

100. Syazuki, K. (1964). Studies on the toxic effects of industrial wastes on fish and shellfish. J. Shimonoseki Coll. Fish. 13:157-211.

101. Gilfillan, E.S. (1975). Decrease of net carbon flux in two species of mussels caused by extracts of crude oil. Mar. Biol. (Berl.) 29:53-7.

102. Gilfillan, E.S., D. Mayo, S. Hanson, D. Donovan, and L.C. Jiang (1976). Reduction in carbon flux in *Mya arenaria* caused by a spill of No. 6 fuel oil. Mar. Biol. (Berl.) 37:115-23.

103. Harger, J.R. and D. Straughan (1972). Biology of Sea mussels before and after the Santa Barbara oil spill (1969). Water Air Soil Pollut. 1:381-8.

104. Avolizi, R.J. and Nuwayhid, M. (A.) (1974). Effects of crude oil and dispersants on bivalves. Mar. Pollut. Bull. 5:149-53.

105. Dunning, A. and C.W. Major (1974). The effect of cold seawater extracts of oil fractions upon the blue mussel, *Mytilus edulis*. In: Pollution and Physiology of Marine Organisms (F.J. Vernberg and W.B. Vernberg, eds.), p. 349-66. Academic Press, London.

106. Mackin, J.G. and S.H. Hopkins (1961). Studies on oysters in relation to the oil industry. Publ. Inst. Mar. Sci. Univ. Tex. 7:1-315.

107. Lund, E.J. (1957). Effect of bleedwater, "soluble fraction" and crude oil on the oyster. Publ. Inst. Mar. Sci. Univ. Tex. 4:328-41.

108. Anderson, G.E. (1972). The effects of oil on the gill filtration rate of *Mya arenaria*. Va. J. Sci. 23:45-7.

109. Dow, R.L. (1975). Reduced growth and survival of clams transplanted to an oil spill site. Mar. Pollut. Bull. 6:124-5.

110. Taylor, T.L., J.F. Karinen, and H.M. Feder (1976). Response of the clam *Macoma balthica* (Linnaeus), exposed to Prudhoe Bay crude oil as unmixed oil, water-soluble fraction, and sediment adsorbed fraction in the laboratory. Northwest and Alaska Fisheries Center, NMFS, NOAA, U.S. Dep. of Commerce, Auke Bay Fisheries Laboratory, P.O. Box 155, Auke Bay, Alaska. Processed Report, 27 p.

111. Stirling, E.A. (1975). Some effects of pollutants on the behavior of the bivalve *Tellina tenuis*. Mar. Pollut. Bull. 6:122-4.

112. Hidu, H. (1969). Gregarious setting in the American oyster *Crassostrea virginica* (Gmelin). Chesapeake Sci. 10:85-92.

113. Hidu, H., F.P. Veitch, Jr., and P.E. O'Brien (1970). Gregarious setting in the American oyster. Proc. Natl. Shellfish Assoc. 60:4.

114. Cardwell, R.D. (1973). Acute toxicity of No. 2 diesel oil to selected species of marine invertebrates, marine sculpins and juvenile salmon. Ph.D. Thesis, University of Washington, Seattle, 124 p.

115. Legore, R.S. (1974). The effect of Alaskan crude oil and selected hydrocarbon compounds on embryonic development of the Pacific oyster, *Crassostrea gigas*. Ph.D. Thesis, University of Washington, Seattle, 189 p.

116. Renzoni, A. (1973). Influence of crude oil, derivatives and dispersants on larvae. Mar. Pollut. Bull. 4:9-13.

117. Renzoni, A. (1975). Toxicity of three oils to bivalve gametes and larvae. Mar. Pollut. Bull. 6:125-8.

118. Lee, B.D., T.Y. Lee, and P. Chin (1975). Effects of crude oil ingredients on the development and oxygen uptake of hard clam *Meretrix lusoria* (Roding). Publ. Inst. Mar. Sci. Nat. Fish. Univ. Busan 8:31-8.

119. Jeffries, H.P. (1972). A stress syndrome in the hard clam, *Mercenaria mercenaria*. J. Invertebr. Pathol. 20:242-51.

120. Whittle, K.J. and M. Blumer (1970). Interactions between organisms and dissolved organic substances in the sea. Chemical attraction of the starfish *Asterias vulgaris* to oysters. In: Symposium on Organic Matter in Natural Waters (D.W. Hood, ed.), p. 495-508. University of Alaska, Inst. Mar. Sci. Occas. Publ. 1.

121. Zafiriou, O., K.J. Whittle, and M. Blumer (1972). Response of *Asterias vulgaris* to bivalves and bivalve tissue extracts. Mar. Biol. (Berl.) 13:137-45.

122. Allen, H. (1971). Effects of petroleum fractions on the early development of a sea urchin. Mar. Pollut. Bull. 2:138-40.

123. Lönning, S. and B.E. Hagström (1975). The effects of crude oils and the dispersant Corexit 8666 on sea urchin gametes and embryos. Norw. J. Zool. 23:121-29.

124. Seeman, P. (1972). The membrane actions of anesthetics and tranquilizers. Pharmacol. Rev. 24:583-655.

125. Mearns, A.J., P.S. Oshida, M.J. Sherwood, D.R. Young, and D.J. Reish (1976). Chromium effects on coastal organisms. J. Water Pollut. Control. Fed. 48:1929-39.

Chapter 5

SUBLETHAL BIOLOGICAL EFFECTS OF PETROLEUM HYDROCARBON EXPOSURES: FISH

BENJAMIN G. PATTEN
Environmental Conservation Division

Northwest and Alaska Fisheries Center
National Marine Fisheries Service
National Oceanic and Atmospheric Administration
U.S. Department of Commerce
Seattle, Washington 98112

INTRODUCTION

The objective of this review is to present information on the behavioral and physiological responses of marine fishes to petroleum hydrocarbons at sublethal concentrations. Of major concern are marine species indigenous to arctic and subarctic waters; since this information is meager, data on organisms from other geographic environments will be included to demonstrate effects that may generally relate to a variety of species.

In challenge experiments, the concentration of hydrocarbons in the test media was often cited in terms of gravimetric or volumetric admixtures. This may not represent the exact hydrocarbon concentration in a solution. Recently, more precise analytical techniques have been used and these will be denoted as GC (gas chromatography), IR (infrared spectrometry) or UV (ultraviolet spectrometry). In most experiments, the initial test mixture was not renewed through exposure periods and some compounds may have vaporized. For other tests, the mixture was renewed or a flow-through system was used; this will be noted in the discussions of long-term exposures.

BEHAVIOR

Fish exposed to sublethal concentrations of petroleum in the environment show various behavioral responses. Responses which have been studied are conditioned responses, avoidance reactions, and changes in locomotor activity patterns.

AVOIDANCE REACTION

Hasler and Wisby [1] determined, in conditioned response tests, that the freshwater bluntnose minnow *Pimephales notatus* can detect a 0.0005 mg/l (0.5 ppb) concentration of phenol. In contrast, Jones [2] found that the freshwater dace *Phoxinus phoxinus* was apparently unable to detect phenol at any of 12 concentrations ranging from 3 to 400 ppm in a flow-through apparatus. Rainbow trout *(Salmo gairdneri)* [3] failed to show avoidance reaction to phenol at sublethal concentrations of 0.001 to 10.0 mg/l (1 ppb to 10 ppm) under similar exposure conditions. Also, the freshwater green sunfish *Lepomis cyanellus* did not react to phenol at concentrations of 0.5 ml/l (500 ppm) or 20 mg/l (20 ppm), nor was it distinctly repelled by benzene at 400 mg/l (400 ppm) in a flow-through [4] and a static system [5]. The freshwater orangespotted sunfish *L. humilis* and rock bass *Ambloplites rupestris* displayed different reactions to 5 ppm naphthalene; the bass demonstrated avoidance behavior while the sunfish did not. In addition, the sunfish showed no reaction to benzene at 0.04 ml/l (40 ppm), but both the sunfish and bass avoided more dilute solutions (benzene concentration not given) [4].

In seawater, goby *(Chaenogobius heptacanthus)*, crescent perch *(Therapon jarbua)*, and striped mullet *(Mugil cephalus)* showed avoidance reactions to phenol and phenolic coal-gas waste at a concentration of 23 to 25 ppm in a flow-through system [6]. The avoidance threshold concentrations for these same species to a variety of oils dispersed on seawater were: lamp oil at 1.4 ppm; heavy oil (probably Bunker C fuel oil) at 3.5 ppm; "Mobile" oil at 48 ppm; and crude petroleum at 0.7 ppm.

In tests with Atlantic cod *(Gadus morhua)*, Atlantic herring *(Clupea harengus harengus)*, and plaice *(Pleuronectes platessa)* larvae exposed to three types of crude oils (Venezuela, Libya, or Iran), Kuhnhold [7] stated "larvae do not seem to be able to avoid oil-contaminated water, especially dispersions, as the chemoreceptors are probably blocked or destroyed rather quickly at the first contact with oil compounds." Pink salmon *(Oncorhynchus gorbuscha)* fry avoided the water-soluble fraction (WSF) of Prudhoe Bay crude oil in both fresh water and seawater in a laboratory flow-through apparatus but with considerable differences in avoidance thresholds [8]. In early summer, pink salmon fry displayed an avoidance reaction to a lethal concentration of the WSF extracted from 497 mg oil/l (497 ppm) in fresh water, but not to a sublethal solution of a WSF extracted from 89 mg/l of oil (Table 1). At the same time other pink salmon fry of identical age, but adapted to seawater, avoided a WSF made from 16.0 mg oil/l (16.0 ppm) but not a WSF from 8.8 mg/l (8.8 ppm). Fry tested again 2-1/2 months later in seawater showed avoidance to a WSF extracted from 1.6 mg/l (1.6 ppm).

TABLE 1

Avoidance thresholds of Prudhoe Bay crude oil by pink salmon fry

Response	Fry in fresh water on June 5 (temp. 5°C)	Fry in seawater on June 5 (temp. 7.5°C)	Fry in seawater on August 27 (temp. 11.5°C)
Avoidance level[a]	497 mg/l	16.0 mg/l	1.6 mg/l
Nonavoidance level	89 mg/l	8.8 mg/l	0.75 mg/l

From Rice [8]
[a] At the 95% confidence level.

COUGH RESPONSE

Cough responses or convulsive respiratory reactions of fish probably denote irritation levels of toxicant. Rice, Thomas, and Short [9] studied the cough response of pink salmon fry exposed to the WSF of Prudhoe Bay crude oil, Cook Inlet crude oil, and No. 2 fuel oil. The fry were exposed to sublethal concentrations of the oils ranging from 0.35 to 2.22 ppm total hydrocarbons (IR) for 22 hr. The cough response developed shortly after the fish were exposed to the petroleum, reached a maximum rate in 3 hr, and diminished gradually thereafter. The cough rate of fry exposed to petroleum at

0.63 to 1.03 ppm also peaked at 3 hr, but by the end of the test period the response rates of exposed and untreated fry were similar. The authors suggested that the cough response was induced by aromatic compounds in the petroleum, and that the progressive reduction in coughing rate was due to a loss of the aromatics from the water through volatilization. Rainbow trout did not develop a cough response when exposed for 10 min to 10 to 30 mg/l (10 to 30 ppm) of phenol in fresh water [3].

PHYSIOLOGY

The limited data available concerning physiological effects of petroleum hydrocarbons on fish primarily involve alterations in metabolism and activity patterns. Although a number of physiological changes have been found after petroleum exposure in laboratory tests, their significance is not clear. Whether or not the changes detected in respiratory rates, for example, in several studies are deleterious mostly remains to be demonstrated.

METABOLISM

Respiration of fishes has been estimated by measurement of oxygen used, or by the rate of opercular movement. The correlation of opercular movement and oxygen consumption of a fish in clean water (uncontaminated by hydrocarbons) is supported, but there are no data relating the rate of opercular movement with oxygen consumption of fish in waters contaminated by hydrocarbons.

Syazuki [6] studied the rate of oxygen consumption of the goby *C. heptacanthus* exposed to phenol, lamp oil, or heavy lubricating oil in seawater at concentrations of from 3 to 12 ppm for tests of durations of 1 and 24 hr. With increasing concentrations of phenol or suspended heavy oil, there was a decrease in oxygen consumption; with increasing concentrations of lamp oil, oxygen consumption increased. Brocksen and Bailey [10] determined the oxygen consumption of juvenile chinook salmon *(O. tshawytscha)* and striped bass *(Morone saxatilis)* after test groups had been exposed to benzene in fresh water for 24, 48, 72, or 96 hr. Oxygen consumption of chinook salmon after they had been exposed to 5 or 10 ppm (GC) of benzene increased and was maximal after a 48-hr exposure but then decreased for longer exposures up to 96 hr. The oxygen consumption of the striped bass after exposure to 5 ppm or 10 ppm varied. For those that had been exposed to 5 ppm benzene, oxygen consumption was greater than that of the controls after a 24-hr exposure but dropped to control levels for

longer exposures up to 96 hr. At 10 ppm benzene, oxygen consumption remained at the same level as, or slightly less than,
that for the control fish. In an additional experiment, salmon and bass were first exposed to 10 ppm (GC) of benzene for
24 hr, then they were placed in clean water and their oxygen
consumption was measured for 10 days. Initially, oxygen consumption increased for chinook salmon and decreased for the
striped bass. In both species, oxygen consumption gradually
approached the rate for the control fish during the 10 days of
observation. Struhsaker, Eldridge, and Echeverria [11] exposed Pacific herring *(C. harengus pallasi)* larvae to either
13.0 or 19.1 ppm of benzene (GC) in seawater for 24 hr; the
oxygen consumption rate of the larvae increased by 25% and
45%, respectively (Table 2).

The oxygen consumption of the warm-water, estuarine,
sheepshead minnow *Cyprinodon variegatus* was measured in a respiratory chamber following a 24-hr exposure of the organism
to four test oils [12]. The test mixtures were WSF consisting
of 19.8 ppm South Louisiana crude oil, 10.4 ppm Kuwait crude
oil, 8.7 ppm No. 2 fuel oil, or 6.3 ppm Bunker C fuel oil;
concentrations were in total hydrocarbons (IR). At dilutions
of the stock WSF ranging from 30 to 50% for No. 2 fuel oil and
at 60 to 100% for Kuwait crude oil, oxygen consumption increased. However, the South Louisiana crude oil first induced
respiratory depression at 60% dilution of the WSF followed by
an increase in oxygen consumption at the 80 and 100% dilutions. The effect of Bunker C fuel oil on oxygen consumption
of the minnow was different from that of the other oils tested. Oxygen consumption increased at 50% dilution of the stock
WSF, it was normal at 60% dilution, and it then became depressed at 70% dilution.

Unpublished data of Foster cited by Anderson et al. [13]
indicated that embryos of warm-water, estuarine mummichog
(Fundulus heteroclitus) exposed to 10 and 50% WSF of South
Louisiana crude oil (the 100% WSF contained 20 ppm total hydrocarbons [IR], including 0.3 ppm total naphthalenes [UV])
for 24 hr had respiration rates 50 to 80% greater than those
of controls.

Oxygen consumption of pink salmon fry was estimated from
their operculum movements during exposure to the WSF of
Prudhoe Bay crude oil in flow-through chambers [14]. Operculum movements increased when the fish were exposed to 3 to 4
ppm total hydrocarbons (IR) of the oil for 9 to 12 hr, but
were normal thereafter to 23 hr. The operculum rates for
salmon exposed to 0.015 to 1.55 ppm were normal throughout the
23-hr test. When embryos of the warm-water fishes sheepshead
minnow, mummichog, and longnose killifish *F. similis,* developed an observable heartbeat, they were exposed to two oils
in water of 20 °/oo salinity to determine sublethal effects

[13]. The 100% WSF of the No. 2 fuel oil contained 10 ppm total hydrocarbons (IR) including 2 ppm total naphthalenes, and the 100% WSF of South Louisiana crude oil contained 20 ppm total hydrocarbons (IR) including 0.3 ppm total naphthalenes (UV). Heartbeat rates of the mummichog and sheepshead minnow were determined daily for 5 to 9 days. For those exposed to 25% of the WSF of No. 2 fuel oil, the rate of beat was similar to controls; for those exposed to 50% WSF or higher, the rates were depressed. For longnose killifish, there was no apparent relation between heartbeat rates and concentrations ranging from 0 to 50% of the WSF of South Louisiana crude oil over a 17-day period to the time of hatching. At concentrations from 70 to 100% of the WSF, the rate was depressed. In this study, heartbeat rates of embryos did not provide a useful measure of sublethal levels of hydrocarbon contaminants because concentrations of hydrocarbons reducing the heartbeat rate were of a lethal level.

LOCOMOTOR AND ACTIVITY PATTERNS

Larvae of the winter flounder *Pseudopleuronectes americanus* became narcotized after being held in seawater containing 0.1% (1,000 ppm) Bunker C fuel oil for 42 hr [15]. They remained inactive at the bottom of the test containers and reacted only when stimulated by prodding. Following exposure, the larvae were returned to clean water where they rapidly regained normal activity (time for recovery was not stated).

Prelarvae of the Black Sea flatfish-kalkan *Rhombus maeoticus* perished within 2 days in seawater containing 0.001 to 0.1 ml/l (1 to 100 ppm) of either Bunker C fuel oil, solar oil, or Malgobek oil [16]. At concentrations of 0.00001 and 0.0001 ml/l (10 and 100 ppb) of these oils, the survival rates of the exposed and control prelarvae were similar but the activity patterns of the contaminated prelarvae were abnormal. Prelarvae placed in the test mixtures immediately sank to the bottom of the container where they remained inactive and responded weakly to prodding. After 2 to 3 hr in the test mixture, the prelarvae exhibited normal activity. Kuhnhold [7] studied the effect of Venezuela, Iran, and Libya crude oils on the activity of larvae of Atlantic cod, Atlantic herring, and plaice. When the larvae were placed in seawater containing about 10 ppm (method of analysis not stated) of the WSF of crude oil, swimming activity initially increased and then diminished (times of events were not given). Larvae that reached the "critical point" (no response to prodding) never recovered even when placed into clean water. Struhsaker and coworkers [11] exposed larvae of the Pacific herring to concentrations of 6.7 and 12.1 ppm (GC) of benzene (daily additions were made to maintain initial concentration) for 48 hr and then placed the larvae in clean water. The exposed larvae showed initial reduced levels of feeding (Table 2) and swimming in the clean water, but returned to normal levels (same as the controls) in about 5 days.

Petroleum hydrocarbons have similar effects on the locomotor activity of juvenile and adult fish. Waluga [17] subjected 4- to 5-year-old bream (Abramis brama) to an average concentration of 2.6 ppm (range 0.4 to 10 ppm; test solution was replaced every 12 hr) of phenol in fresh water for 7 days. During the first day of exposure the fishes' equilibrium was upset and respiration became irregular with some violent movements. During the third and fourth day, the bream became progressively weaker and showed signs of unrest. By the sixth or seventh day, the fish developed permanent loss of equilibrium and rarely attempted to swim; moreover, respiratory movements of the mouth and opercules were weak.

The tropical marine fish Kuhlia sandvicensis exposed to 2 ppm of phenol displayed rapid swimming movements, gulping at the water surface, and erratic motion [18]. At 20 ppm of phenol, the fish swam very rapidly and convulsively, then became paralyzed and died within 2 to 3 min of exposure (in both cases duration of test was not given). Kristoffersson and coworkers [19] investigated the effect of phenol on northern pike (Esox lucius) inhabiting brackish water (5 to 6 °/oo salinity) in a flow-through system. The highest phenol concentration causing no mortality over a 7-day exposure period was 5 ppm. During the first day of exposure (4.4 ppm phenol concentration) the pike showed strong convulsive movements. They were sensitive to bright light and vibration during the first 2 to 3 days, but by the end of the 7-day exposure period the fish appeared normal and unstressed. Morrow [20] recorded the reactions of juvenile coho and sockeye salmon (O. kisutch and O. nerka) exposed in seawater to Prudhoe Bay crude oil poured on the surface at concentrations of 500 to 3,500 ppm. At all concentrations of crude oil, the fish swam at the surface of the water after 45 min of exposure. After 24 hr, the fish showed loss of equilibrium and reduced swimming activity. Some of the fish swam in a vertical (head-up) position and did not recover. The survivors which recovered after 96 hr of exposure lived in the contaminant (that had presumably lost some volatile fractions) for 30 days.

Cardwell [21] exposed juvenile chinook, chum (O. keta), and pink salmon to No. 2 diesel oil layered on seawater and fresh water at concentrations of 0.15 to 3.00 ml/l (150 to 3,000 ppm). In general, after exposure for 24 hr, the fish showed signs of narcosis, were unresponsive to fright stimuli, and swam at the surface of the water. As exposure time continued, the fish had increasing difficulty in maintaining equilibrium, began to swim in a vertical position near the

TABLE 2

Summary of effects of benzene on eggs and larvae of Pacific herring. Percents are approximate estimates of the significant differences from control levels (P < 0.05). NS = Not significant, LD = Larval day

Stage exposed	Approximate concentration range (ppm)	Exposure time (hr)	Survival hatching LD 0	Survival larvae LD 3	Abnormal larvae hatching	Mean % feeding LD 1-7	Respiration rate	Stand. length LD 1-7	Developmental rate
Egg day 0	3- 5	24	NS	NS	NS	--	--	--	NS
	15-20		NS	NS	NS	--	--	--	NS
	35-45		-15%	-10%	+20%	--	--	--	Delayed
Egg day 0.1	3- 5	48	NS	NS	NS	--	--	--	NS
	15-20		NS	NS	NS	--	--	--	NS
	35-45		-15%	-10%	+20%	--	--	--	Delayed
Egg day 0,1,2,3	3- 5	96	NS	NS (LD 7)	NS	--	--	--	NS
	15-20		NS	-10%	NS	--	--	--	Delayed
	35-45		-15%	-10%	+25%	--	--	--	Delayed
Larval day 2	5-10	24	Not exp. until LD 2	NS		--	--	NS	NS
	10-15			-10%		-25%	+25%	NS	Delayed
	30-35			-25%		-30%	+45%	NS	Delayed
Larval day 2,3	5-10	48		NS		-25%	--	Smaller	Accelerated
	10-15			NS		-25%	--	Smaller	Delayed
	30-35			-70%		-50%	--	Smaller	Delayed

From Struhsaker, Eldridge, and Echeverria [11]

surface of the water, and finally lost their equilibrium completely. Through these stages, the salmon showed excessive opercular ventilation. Eventually the fish became completely immobile, except for an occasional respiratory effort. Cardwell noted an increasingly greater degree of stress in chinook salmon at the higher concentrations of No. 2 diesel oil. At the end of a 96-hr test in fresh water, 13, 83, and 100% of the salmon surviving exposure to respective concentrations of 0.100, 0.398, and 0.794 ml/l (100, 400, and 800 ppm) of oil showed signs of distress (rapid opercular movements, lack of response to stimuli, or having difficulty maintaining equilibrium). Following exposure, the salmon were placed in clean water for 48 hr. At the end of the 48-hr post-exposure period, 15% of the salmon from all exposures remained distressed (100% were distressed at start), and 5% showed equilibrium loss (53% showed equilibrium loss at start). There was no relation between the activity of the fish in clean water and prior exposure concentration 48 hr after exposure.

The reaction of the longnose killifish subjected to the WSF of No. 2 fuel oil at a concentration of 7 ppm total hydrocarbons (IR), including 2 ppm naphthalenes (UV), in seawater was studied by Anderson [22] and Dixit and Anderson [23]. As a result of individual degrees of tolerance to the WSF, some fish were swimming normally after one hour of exposure, but soon after became hyperactive followed by floating in a vertical head-up position. Other fish were floating at the surface or swimming in an inverted position after a 15- to 20-min exposure; subsequently these fish sank to the bottom of the tank in an inverted position and showed only slow opercular activity. After the longnose killifish had lain on the bottom of the tank, they were placed in clean seawater where they recovered within 3.5 hr.

Exposure of fish to petroleum hydrocarbons may also affect schooling behavior. Gardner [24] exposed adult Atlantic silverside *(Menidia menidia)* to 0.167 ml/l (167 ppm) of the WSF of Texas-Louisiana crude oil in seawater for a period of 7 days. During the pre-test period in clean seawater, the fish displayed a distinct schooling behavior; however, at onset of exposure and during the entire test period the fish were disoriented and showed no tendency to congregate in schools. Gardner attributed this abnormal behavior to damage of the olfactory organs and the lateral line of the fish.

Abnormal behavior of fish after exposure to hydrocarbon contamination may be in part related to anoxia. For example, Meyerhoff [25] suspected that possible mechanisms leading to anoxia of exposed fish could be central nervous system depression, loss of oxygen-carrying capacity of erythrocytes, and cardiac disruption and failure.

DELAYED EFFECTS

There is little detailed information concerning delayed or long-term effects of oil contamination on survival, growth rate, and fecundity of fish; however, several reports on these subjects have been published.

SURVIVAL

Kuhnhold [7] exposed eggs of Atlantic cod to the WSF of crude oil from Libya, Iran, or Venezuela at concentrations of 10 ppm and less for 100 hr and then placed them in clean water. The mortality rate of the eggs to time of hatching (10 days) was greater with increasing concentration of oil. Most of the larvae that survived were deformed; the deformity was apparent in the gastrula stage in some embryos. Some eggs did not hatch even though the embryos appeared normal. Kuhnhold also noted that embryos were more resistant than the larvae and the larvae became less resistant with resorption of the yolk sac. In other experiments, Kuhnhold found that the larvae of plaice were more resistant than the larvae of cod to petroleum hydrocarbons; the larvae of Atlantic herring were the least resistant. Also, Libya crude oil was more toxic to fish eggs and larvae than Iran or Venezuela crude oil. Hakkila and Niemi [26] exposed eggs of the northern pike at the pre-gastrula stage to floating Russian crude oil (concentrations not indicated) in brackish water for 30 min in a static system. Post-exposure survival of the oil-treated eggs ranged from zero in two groups to 15.3% in the third group while the controls had a 57.7% survival over the 16-day observation period. Oil-treated ova had small oil droplets attached to the egg surface (this contrasts with the findings of James [15] where cod, *Gadus* sp., eggs mixed with oil were not coated by Bunker C fuel oil). Hakkila and Niemi also noted that 40.9% of the larvae from the treated eggs were deformed, but only 10% of the larvae from the control eggs were abnormal. In a flow-through apparatus, these authors subjected northern pike ova in the pre-gastrula stage to the WSF extracted from 1, 3, and 10 ppb of Russian crude oil in brackish water for 48 hr. These eggs were placed in clean water after treatment. The eggs from all exposure concentrations showed normal survival, but the numbers of deformed larvae were proportionally greater than for the controls.

Struhsaker, Eldridge, and Echeverria [11] exposed eggs and larvae of Pacific herring and northern anchovy *(Engraulis mordax)* to various levels (from 3 to 55 ppm, GC) of benzene for 24, 48, or 96 hr (daily additions of benzene were made for tests of 48 hr or more to maintain the initial concentration).

Following transfer to clean seawater, the eggs and larvae
treated with 3 to 15 ppm of benzene generally showed a normal
rate of development, while those exposed to the 30 to 45 ppm
of benzene showed a delay in rate of development (Table 2).
The larvae were more sensitive than the eggs to benzene, and
some abnormalities were noted in the embryos. Delayed deaths
also occurred in pink salmon eggs pretreated for 96 hr with
the WSF of Prudhoe Bay crude oil at a concentration of 25 ppm
(IR) in fresh water [27]. Sixty-six percent of the salmon
eggs failed to hatch over a period of "several weeks."

Eggs of warm-water fishes, the sheepshead minnow, mummichog, and longnose killifish, were exposed to two oils in
20 $^\text{O}$/oo salinity water [13]. The 100% WSF of the No. 2 fuel
oil used contained 10 ppm total hydrocarbons (IR) including
2 ppm total naphthalenes (UV); the 100% WSF of South Louisiana
crude oil used only for tests on the longnose killifish contained 20 ppm total hydrocarbons (IR) including 0.3 ppm total
naphthalenes (UV). After an approximate 8-day exposure to a
100% WSF of the test oils, all of the test fish of both species died; at an initial 50% concentration of the WSF of No. 2
fuel oil, sheepshead minnows and mummichog had 40 to 62% survival to hatching. The longnose killifish had a 72% survival
to hatching at a 50% WSF of South Louisiana crude oil (replaced daily). These authors also removed the chorion of eggs
of sheepshead minnows and exposed them to an initial 50% WSF
of No. 2 fuel oil for about 11 days. Survival to hatching was
similar between eggs with and without the chorionic membrane,
indicating that the membrane was not a barrier to hydrocarbons.
In other tests on sheepshead minnows, the test media of No. 2
fuel oil were replaced daily; mortality was complete in concentrations of 30% of the WSF and survival to hatching was 82%
in 10% of the WSF. Exposing longnose killifish eggs to 10 to
50% of the WSF of South Louisiana crude oil (replaced daily)
resulted in abnormal periods of hatching where some eggs
hatched 7 days in advance of or 3 days after the controls. At
70% of the WSF, only 4% of the eggs hatched. In the controls,
hatching was within 4 days. Differences in the concentrations
of the two oils causing an approximate 50% mortality of the
embryos may have been related to their naphthalene content.
This level of mortality occurred with 25% of the WSF of No. 2
fuel oil (2.5 ppm total hydrocarbons including 0.5 ppm total
naphthalenes) for sheepshead minnows or with 60% of the WSF of
South Louisiana crude oil (12 ppm total hydrocarbons including
0.2 ppm total naphthalenes) for longnose killifish where species differences were assumed not significant. Fry hatching
from exposed eggs from the experiments with South Louisiana
crude oil were maintained under test conditions [13].   After
2 weeks, all of the fry in the 10 and 30% WSF survived, as did
89% of the fry in the 50% WSF.

The long-term survival of juvenile fish after an initial exposure to oil contamination has been studied for several species. Mironov [28] found that *Mugil saliens* developed in a normal manner for several months in clean seawater after exposure to 0.25 ml/l (250 ppm) of crude oil in seawater for many days (exact duration not given). Cardwell [21] exposed pink salmon fry, tidepool sculpin *(Oligocottus maculosus)*, and tadpole sculpin *(Psychrolutes paradoxus)* to No. 2 fuel oil at concentrations ranging from 0.100 to 0.398 ml/l (100 to 398 ppm) in seawater. The sculpins were transferred to clean water after 66 hr; the salmon were transferred upon reaching complete immobility. The 10 pink salmon exposed to 398 ppm of No. 2 fuel oil became immobile after 18 to 42 hr; after they were transferred to clean seawater, 4 died within 24 hr and the remaining 6 appeared healthy after 5 days. Delayed mortalities did not occur for sculpins exposed to concentrations of 100 and 158 ppm. Some of the sculpins exposed to 398 ppm of oil showed loss of equilibrium; none of these recovered when transferred to clean water. Of the sculpins that appeared healthy after a 66-hr exposure, there was a 57% delayed mortality for those that had been subjected to 0.251 ml/l (251 ppm) of oil and a 29% delayed mortality for those subjected to 0.398 ml/l (398 ppm) of oil.

Atlantic silversides exposed to waste motor oil in aerated seawater at an initial concentration of 250 ppm died within 7 days; at 100 ppm, there were no deaths in 36 days; and at 20 ppm, there were no deaths in 60 days [29].

GROWTH AND FEEDING

Pink salmon alevins were exposed to a WSF of Prudhoe Bay crude oil for 10 days at concentrations ranging from 0.73 to 5.73 ppm total hydrocarbons (IR) in fresh water [27]. Approximately 50 days after exposure, length and weight measurements were taken. Alevin growth was inversely related to the WSF concentration, with this effect more pronounced at later stages of development. Growth was delayed for 6 days in Pacific herring larvae exposed to 6.7 or 12.1 ppm (GC) benzene (daily additions were made to maintain initial concentration) for 48 hr (Table 2) [11]. The herring were lethargic for 2 days after exposure to the contaminant. Within 6 days most individuals regained the ability to move about and feed. An average of 75% of the herring larvae subjected to 6.7 ppm benzene and 74% subjected to 12.1 ppm benzene had food in their gastrointestinal tracts, compared to 100% for the controls.

Food uptake of the marine goby *C. heptacanthus* over a 4-day period was affected by exposure (presumably in static baths) to varying concentrations of five types of hydrocarbons [6]. Their appetite declined during exposure to progressively greater concentrations of contaminant beyond a threshold limit. The threshold concentration was about 3 ppm for phenol, 0.3 ppm for suspended lamp oil, 2 ppm for suspended heavy oil, 4 ppm for suspended "Mobile" oil, and 0.2 ppm for crude oil.

The feeding response, weight, percent fat, and caloric content were determined for juvenile striped bass held in benzene at a high concentration of 6 µl/l (6 ppm average, range 3.6 to 8.1 ppm), or a low concentration of 3.5 µl/l (3.5 ppm average, range 1.5 to 5.4 ppm) (GC) in seawater over a 4-week period [30]. Feeding ability was reduced for both groups initially. At the end of the test, feeding success was normal for the low concentration group and reduced for the high concentration group. The high concentration group was initially unable to locate and consume food but at the end of 4 weeks they consumed 50% of their rations while the controls had consistently consumed all of their rations. The mean dry weight of the control fish was 0.8721 g whereas it was 0.8137 g for fish of the low concentration group and 0.7242 g for fish of the high concentration group at the end of the test. The dry weight of fish of the high concentration group was significantly less than the other two groups. Fat content of striped bass used as controls was 39.2%, while it was 34.1% for the low concentration group and 32.2% for the high concentration group. Caloric contents of the test and control fish were similar.

REPRODUCTION

In a recent experiment [31], Prudhoe Bay crude oil was incorporated into the diets of 3-year-old rainbow trout for 6 to 7 mo prior to their reaching maturity. The purpose was to assess the effect of this treatment on the reproductive success of the fish. The test food was prepared by mixing 2 g of Prudhoe Bay crude oil with 2 kg of Oregon moist pellets and it was fed at the rate of 2% of their body weight per day for 5 days per week. Eggs were artificially fertilized where one or both parents had been subjected to hydrocarbon contamination to determine ova viability. Spectrophotofluorometric curves from egg extracts derived from oil-fed parents indicated they were contaminated with hydrocarbons. The mean hatching success of ova from oil-fed parents was 86.4% (range 32.4 to 99.5%) and that of non-oil-fed fish was 90.3% (range 79.2 to 96.8%); this was not a statistically significant difference. The average survival of alevins of non-oil-fed parents was higher (91.0%) than that from oil-fed parents (76.1%), but again not significantly so. Under the experimental procedures used, these data do not indicate a significant deleterious effect on the reproductive potential of rainbow trout as a result of including Prudhoe Bay crude oil in their diet.

PROSPECTUS

The impact of petroleum on the behavior and physiology of fish is at present poorly understood, largely because of variability within and among species and variability of oils, and because of environmental factors that affect both the fish and the oil. Material presented in this review simply emphasizes the lack of a sufficient data base to accurately predict, in most instances, the reactions of marine fish encountering an oil spill or possible physiological effects from either acute or chronic exposures to petroleum.

REFERENCES

1. Hasler, A.D. and W.J. Wisby (1950). Use of fish for the olfactory assay of pollutants (phenols) in water. Trans. Am. Fish. Soc. 79:64-70.
2. Jones, E.J. (1951). The reactions of the minnow, *Phoxinus phoxinus (L)*, to solutions of phenol, ortho-cresol and para-cresol. J. Exp. Biol. 28:261-70.
3. Sprague, J.B. and D.E. Drury (1969). Avoidance reactions of salmonid fish to representative pollutants. In: Advances in Water Pollution Research (S.H. Jenkins, ed.), Vol. I, p. 169-79. Pergamon Press, New York.
4. Shelford, V.E. (1917). An experimental study of the effects of gas wastes upon fishes, with especial reference to stream pollution. Bull. Ill. Lab. Nat. Hist. 11: 381-412.
5. Summerfelt, R.C. and W.M. Lewis (1967). Repulsion of green sunfish by certain chemicals. J. Water Pollut. Control Fed. 39:2030-8.
6. Syazuki, K. (1964). Studies on the toxic effects of industrial waste on fish and shellfish. J. Shimonoseki Coll. Fish. 13:157-211.
7. Kuhnhold, W.W. (1970). The influence of crude oils on fish fry. In: FAO Technical Conference on Marine Pollution and its Effects on Living Resources and Fishing. MP/70/E-64. Food and Agriculture Organization of the United Nations, Rome, 10 p.
8. Rice, S.D. (1973). Toxicity and avoidance tests with Prudhoe Bay oil and pink salmon fry. In: Proceedings of 1973 Joint Conference on Prevention and Control of Oil Spills, p. 667-70. American Petroleum Institute, Washington, D.C.

9.   Rice, S.D., R.E. Thomas, and J.W. Short (1977). Effect of petroleum hydrocarbons on breathing and coughing rates, and hydrocarbon uptake-depuration in pink salmon fry. In: Symposium on Pollution and Physiology of Marine Organisms (F.J. Vernberg, A. Calabrese, F.P. Thurberg, and W.B. Vernberg, eds.), p. 259-77. Academic Press, New York.

10. Brocksen, R.W. and H.T. Bailey (1973). Respiratory response of juvenile chinook salmon and striped bass exposed to benzene, a water-soluble component of crude oil. In: Proceedings of 1973 Joint Conference on Prevention and Control of Oil Spills, p. 783-92. American Petroleum Institute, Washington, D.C.

11. Struhsaker, J.W., M.B. Eldridge, and T. Echeverria (1974). Effects of benzene (a water-soluble component of crude oil) on eggs and larvae of Pacific herring and northern anchovy. In: Pollution and Physiology of Marine Organisms (F.J. Vernberg and W.B. Vernberg, eds.), p. 253-84. Academic Press, New York.

12. Anderson, J.W., J.M. Neff, B.A. Cox, H.E. Tatem, and G.M. Hightower (1974). The effects of oil on estuarine animals: Toxicity, uptake and depuration, respiration. In: Pollution and Physiology of Marine Organisms (F.J. Vernberg and W.B. Vernberg, eds.), p. 285-310. Academic Press, New York.

13. Anderson, J.W., D.B. Dixit, G.S. Ward, and R.S. Foster (1976). Effects of petroleum hydrocarbons on the rate of heart beat and hatching success of estuarine fish embryos. In: Pollution and Physiology of Marine Organisms (F.J. Vernberg, A. Calabrese, F.P. Thurberg, and W.B. Vernberg, eds.), p. 241-58. Academic Press, New York.

14. Thomas, R.E. and S.D. Rice (1975). Increased opercular rates of pink salmon (*Oncorhynchus gorbuscha*) fry after exposure to the water-soluble fraction of Prudhoe Bay crude oil. J. Fish. Res. Board Can. 32:2221-4.

15. James, M.C. (1926). Report of the United States Bureau of Fisheries: Preliminary investigation on effect of oil pollution on marine pelagic eggs, April 1925. In: Preliminary Conference on Oil Pollution of Navigable Waters, Washington, D.C. Append. 6, p. 85-92. U.S. Government Printing Office, Washington, D.C.

16. Mironov, O.G. (1967). Effect of low concentrations of oil and oil products upon the developing eggs of the Black Sea flatfish - Kalkan (*Rhombus maeoticus* Pallasi). Vopr. Ikhtiol. 7:577-80.

17. Waluga, D. (1966). Phenol effects on the anatomico-histopathological changes in bream (*Abramis brama* L.). Acta Hydrobiol. 8:55-78.

18. Hiatt, R.W., W. Naughton, and D.C. Matthews (1953). Effects of chemicals on a schooling fish, *Kuhlia sandvicensis*. Biol. Bull. (Woods Hole) 104:28-44.

19. Kristoffersson, R., S. Broberg, and A. Oikari (1973). Physiological effects of a sublethal concentration of phenol in the pik (*Esox lucius* L.) in pure brackish water. Ann. Zool. Fenn. 10(2):392-7.

20. Morrow, J.E. (1973). Oil-induced mortalities in juvenile coho and sockeye salmon. J. Mar. Res. 31:135-43.

21. Cardwell, R.D. (1973). Acute toxicity of No. 2 diesel oil to selected species of marine invertebrates, marine sculpins, and juvenile salmon. Ph.D. Thesis, University of Washington, Seattle, 114 p.

22. Anderson, J.W. (1975). Laboratory studies on the effects of oil on marine organisms: An overview. Am. Petrol. Inst. Publ. 4249, 70 p.

23. Dixit, D. and J.W. Anderson (1977). Distribution of naphthalenes within exposed *Fundulus similus* and correlations with stress behavior. In: Proceedings of 1977 Oil Spill Conference (Prevention, Behavior, Control, Cleanup), p. 633-6. American Petroleum Institute, Washington, D.C.

24. Gardner, G.R. (1974). Chemically induced lesions in estuarine or marine teleosts. In: The Pathology of Fishes (W. Ribelin and G. Migaki, eds.), p. 657-93. University of Wisconsin Press, Madison.

25. Meyeroff, R.D. (1975). Acute toxicity of benzene, a component of crude oil, to juvenile striped bass (*Morone saxatilus*). J. Fish. Res. Board Can. 32:1864-6.

26. Hakkila, K. and A. Niemi (1973). Effects of oil and emulsifiers on eggs and larvae of northern pike (*Esox lucius*) in brackish water. Aqua Fenn., p. 44-59. Cited in: Selected Water Resources Abstracts 8(1):54.

27. Rice, S.D., D.A. Moles, and J.W. Short (1975). The effect of Prudhoe Bay crude oil on survival and growth of eggs, alevins, and fry of pink salmon (*Oncorhynchus gorbuscha*). In: Proceedings of 1975 Conference on Prevention and Control of Oil Pollution, p. 503-7. American Petroleum Institute, Washington, D.C.

28. Mironov, O.G. (1970). The effect of oil pollution on flora and fauna of the Black Sea. In: FAO Technical Conference on Marine Pollution and its Effects on Living Resources and Fishing. MP/70/E-92. Food and Agriculture Organization of the United Nations, Rome, 4 p.

29. Gardner, G.R., P.P. Yevich, and P.F. Rogerson (1975). Morphological anomalies in adult oyster, scallop, and Atlantic silversides exposed to waste motor oil. In: Proceedings of 1975 Conference on Prevention and Control of Oil Pollution, p. 473-7. American Petroleum Institute, Washington, D.C.

30. Korn, S., J.W. Struhsaker, and P. Benville, Jr. (1976). Effects of benzene on growth, fat content, and caloric content of striped bass, *Morone saxatilis*. U.S. Fish. Wildl. Serv. Fish. Bull. 74, p. 694-8.

31. Hodgins, H.O., W.D. Gronlund, J.L. Mighell, J.W. Hawkes, and P.A. Robisch (1977). Effect of crude oil on trout reproduction. In: Proceedings of Symposium on Fate and Effects of Petroleum Hydrocarbons in Marine Ecosystems and Organisms (D. Wolfe, ed.). In press. Pergamon Press, New York.

Chapter 6

EFFECTS OF PETROLEUM ON ECOSYSTEMS

HERBERT R. SANBORN
Environmental Conservation Division

Northwest and Alaska Fisheries Center
National Marine Fisheries Service
National Oceanic and Atmospheric Administration
U.S. Department of Commerce
Seattle, Washington 98112

BACKGROUND

Previous chapters have dealt with the effects of petroleum on individual species. The use of acute and sublethal tests for ecological prediction is limited to instances where there is previous field experience with similar compounds or where the ecological significance of the observed parameters has been established [1]. In this chapter the literature dealing with the consequences of petroleum on arctic and sub-arctic habitats, populations, and communities will be reviewed. Petroleum is a mixture of hundreds of substances with widely different properties and toxicities that may directly and indirectly affect all the elements (habitats, populations, communities) of the marine ecosystems [2]. The assessments of the biological consequences of petroleum contamination are further complicated by the interaction of the organisms and their environment. Studies made at spill sites have given some insights into habitat changes, changes in diversity and community structure, and general ecological consequences; but any statement of impact on biological systems is not simple and inevitably will be a mixture of fact and supposition [3]. Prediction of the behavior of a specific oil spill in most areas is currently impossible and little is known of long-term effects of petroleum on the marine environment [2].

Studies of spills have shown ecological consequences which were described as ranging from negligible to catastrophic [4]. This variability in biological impact is a result of the interaction and relative contribution of each of the following parameters identified by Straughan [5].

Factors which relate to the spill itself include:

1. Type of petroleum spilled. Diesel oil contains more aromatic compounds, is more soluble in water, and is dispersed more rapidly than crude oil. The toxicity of different crude oils will vary depending in part on the relative amounts of aromatic hydrocarbons they contain [6]. In the arctic, the low temperatures reduce the rate of evaporation of the aromatic hydrocarbons allowing them to remain in the marine system for a longer time than they would in the subarctic. Ottway [6] found that the black, thick crude oils (which are also the most obvious) are less toxic than the translucent, thin brown oils (which are often virtually invisible).

2. Oil dosage. The volume of oil spilled is obviously important. Spills in confined areas have greater biological impact than spills of the same volume that occur in the open ocean or that are able to spread over a larger area where toxic concentrations are reached only in a few isolated places. In the arctic, however, open ocean areas and confined areas are not necessarily mutually exclusive during conditions where sea ice is present.

3. Method of oil spill cleanup. Mechanical methods are the least damaging for cleanup at present [7]. The use of dispersants, sinking agents, and absorbants has limitations; however, large scale adverse effects may occur from misuse of these products.

Factors which relate to physical movement and the bioavailability of the hydrocarbons include:

4. Oceanographic conditions. The currents, wave action, temperature, and coastal formations are important in the mixing, dissolution, dilution, and distribution of the spilled oil.

5. Meteorological conditions. Wind associated with storms may have a definite effect on the movement and mixing of the petroleum in the water. The winds can direct the movement of the oil on or off shore. Wind also can mix the oil in the water column reducing its toxic effect by dilution. This dispersion of the petroleum, however, increases the availability of the oil to the biota in the water column. Wind may also increase the mixing of oil and sediment in the intertidal zone. High sediment loads in runoff areas can act as adsorptive agents which sink oil, preventing it from reaching the shore, perhaps to the detriment of the subtidal benthos (see Chapter 2 of Volume I).

Factors which relate to biological distribution are:

6. Biota of the area. Species in the community respond differently to the same oil spill depending on factors such as morphology, reproductive strategy, feeding type, and age.

7. Season. There are certain months when the very sensitive gametes and larvae are present in the water or when newly metamorphosed animals are present on the substrate. There is also a seasonal component of community structure with different species and numbers of individuals being present at certain times of the year. Straughan [5], for example, indicated that there may be seasonal differences in tolerance to oil by the mussel, *Mytilus californianus*. Seasonal variation might also include changes in salinity or temperature which affect an animal's tolerance to oil.

Factors which relate to biological adaptation of the community are:

8. Previous exposure of the area to oil. Organisms exposed to oil at chronic low levels from seeps, industrial areas, oil installations, or harbors may develop a tolerance which reduces mortality from a spill. Although some natural seeps occur in the Arctic, the general lack of human habitation and industrialization leaves these organisms without a detailed history of oil exposure.

9. Exposure to other pollutants. Oil may act synergistically with other pollutants to increase the toxicity or may concentrate other pollutants. There is some information which shows a correlation between chlorinated hydrocarbons and oil in the sediment [8]. This is attributed to the increased solubility of the chlorinated hydrocarbons in oil and suggests a concentration of these compounds prior to their entry into the marine food web.

In considering the complexity of the interrelationship of these nine factors, it is easy to understand the difficulty in predicting possible ecosystem effects from a spill or for that matter in evaluating the consequences of one spill in relation to another.

The biological consequences of a spill include the impacts at all levels of biological organization from subcellular components through the ecosystem. The impact at each level is dependent on the impact at the previous level plus variables unique to each level. The impact at higher levels of organization is dependent on the specific community structure of the area [9].

When considering only one level of biological organization, specific effects can be delineated. Moore and Dryer [10] identified five specific effects of oil on individual organisms: (1) Direct lethal toxicity, (2) sublethal disruption of physiological and behavioral activities, (3) direct coating, (4) incorporation of the hydrocarbons into the organism, and (5) habitat alterations, especially alterations of substrate characteristics. Adaptive change was mentioned as a possible additional effect, which may be short-term such as acclimation (an increase in the resistance to oil due to repeated exposure to contaminants) or it may be long-term, such as genetic change producing a population of more tolerant individuals. Discussions of the toxic effects, sublethal disruptions, and incorporation of hydrocarbons into organisms are contained in other chapters of this volume. Coating effects and habitat alterations will be covered in this chapter.

HABITATS

Habitat disruption is one of the most important factors that determine the biological consequences of a spill. We will use a rather broad definition of habitat disruption: The physical or chemical alterations of the environment that result in a change in species composition or in geographic distribution [10]. Two general habitats will be considered; the intertidal zone and the subtidal zone. These habitats are not meant to be a comprehensive list but will serve to present the available literature on habitat effects.

INTERTIDAL ZONE

The intertidal zone includes the areas of the marine environment that are most visible. Oil and the consequences of an oil spill are directly visible in areas of public use. The animals that inhabit the intertidal zone, however, must be extremely hardy or adaptable for their environment is one of extremes and constant change. These animals are subjected to radiant heating, freezing, long exposure out of water, wave action, intermittent high sediment loads, and other stresses. Ecological adaptations, such as streamlined, tightly-fitting shells, of the intertidal animals to environmental stresses helps them to survive many of the direct effects of an oil spill, such as fouling, smothering, and direct poisoning. However, community change may take place due to a change in habitat that allows an opportunistic species to proliferate. The intertidal zone can be classified by type of substrate: rocky intertidal, sandy intertidal, and mud flat. Each of these zones have physical and biological factors which differ considerably, warranting discussion of each zone separately.

Rocky Type

In the rocky intertidal area certain physical factors are important in determining the effects of a spill: (1) The type and thickness of oil; (2) the latitude, climate, and time of year; and (3) the exposure of the habitat to wave and sand abrasion [11]. Oil can deposit on the substrate and cover any attached fauna or flora, resulting in direct toxic effects or in smothering [7]. As the tide recedes, oil is trapped in intertidal pools leaving small amounts of water and a relatively large amount of oil [7]. The surf can cause emulsified oil droplets to adsorb to sedimentary particles forming a sludge which is then deposited on the rocks [4]. Oil stranded on rocks may warm in the sunlight and spread or may weather to an asphaltic pavement which persists for years. Some animals can set or will graze on this material [11,12] but their survival may be low due to increased heat stress and desiccation [13].

Sandy Type

Nelson-Smith [14] stated that petroleum tends not to penetrate sandy beaches unless emulsified by chemical means or by wave action but rather tends to be washed to the strandline. This is only true for oil washed ashore during the incoming tide. Oil stranded on falling tide on a sandy beach tends to percolate into the sediment where it may come in direct contact with the infauna [7]. The amount of crude oil in the sediment is a function of (1) sediment-particle size, (2) strength of vertical mixing, (3) water depth, and (4) time after spill or extent of weathering [9]. Deposits of oil can be transported by sedimentary processes to other areas [7] or can be buried by clean sand [11]. Once the oil is buried beneath the aerobic layer, degradation is slow due to the lack of oxygen necessary for microbial attack [7,9,15]. Oil trapped in the beach can persist for years [8,14] to be uncovered at a later time by erosion.

Mud Flats

Little has been studied on the effect of petroleum on mud flats. These areas are often high in organic material, have sediments high in clay particles, and are often rich with fauna. The areas are characteristically protected from wave action and currents. Oil stranded in these areas would not be

subjected to the forces of scouring. Since oil adsorption is
the function of particle surface areas, there may be more oil
in a clay sediment than in a sandy sediment [9]. After the
wreck of the tanker *Arrow*, there was very little decrease in
the Bunker C fuel oil in the soft sediments after 26 mo [16].

SUBTIDAL ZONE

The subtidal zone has received much less attention than
the more visible intertidal zone, yet habitat disruption is
possible through a number of different mechanisms. Oil usually floats but can sink by adsorbing to sedimentary particles
[17]; this can occur in the surf [17], from stranding [18],
and from sedimentary runoff [19]. Once incorporated into the
sediment, the oil can be transported to deep waters, extending
pollution of the area [18]. It is also possible that, because
of the high biological oxygen demand of oil, areas of low oxygen content might become anoxic.

POPULATIONS AND COMMUNITIES

PLANKTON

Because plankton are present in the upper layers of the
ocean and are unable to avoid contaminated areas, they are especially vulnerable to an oil spill. The unicellular algae
that make up the phytoplankton are the principal primary producers in the ocean. The zooplankters are the principal herbivores and secondary consumers that form a critical link in
the marine food web. ⸝Thus, an oil spill affecting the plankton may have the consequences of reducing the productivity and
the diversity of the community which in turn may directly impact the food web.⸝ The ingestion of oil by these animals and
the incorporation of petroleum components into tissues can be
the point of entry of petroleum hydrocarbons in the marine
food web producing possible biomagnification and tainting at
higher trophic levels.

Laboratory studies have shown that the degree of influence of petroleum hydrocarbons on phytoplankton varies with a
number of parameters. The concentration necessary to cause
change differs with season, temperature, light level (higher
toxicity at higher light levels), the amount and type of petroleum, and the species composition [20]. Floating oil can
also influence the spectral quality as well as the quantity of
penetrating solar radiation [21,22]. Aromatic hydrocarbons
vary in effect from inhibition, to no effect, to stimulation
of growth [23]. Venezuela crude oil, No. 2 fuel oil, and a
No. 6 fuel oil were shown to have similar effects on a natural
phytoplankton population in the North Atlantic [24]. Two

species of algae tested with the water-soluble fraction from
No. 2 fuel oil and a crude oil reacted quite differently: One
species was indifferent and the other very sensitive [25].
Thus, petroleum can act to disrupt the natural selective processes resulting in an alteration of the natural phytoplankton
community structure [23,26].   Community change and the possibility of incorporation of hydrocarbons in algal cells directly impacts the herbivores.   The selectivity and dependence of
some herbivores on specific sizes or specific species of algae
is discussed by Fisher and Wurster [25] and mentioned by
Spooner [11].   Since many of the herbivores are larval stages
of invertebrates and vertebrates, changes in phytoplankton
communities directly impact all trophic levels.

Lee [27-29], using a controlled ecosystem to study the
effects of petroleum hydrocarbons on plankton, provided some
proof of the plankton community changes hypothesized from laboratory studies.   In a controlled experiment with naturally
occurring plankton enclosed in large containers, a major
change in the community was noted after treatment with a water
extract of No. 2 fuel oil with a non-volatile hydrocarbon concentration of 50 ppb (IR method).   A drastic decline in the
number of diatoms took place followed by a bloom of microfla-
gellates which became the dominant phytoplankton.   This was in
turn followed by an increase in tintinnids and rotifers.   In a
control enclosure, a single diatom species was dominant during
the course of the experiment.   Thus, he noted "As a result of
the addition of fuel oil there was a major change in the ecosystem enclosure in terms of the type of primary and secondary
producers." [28].

Aqueous extracts of crude oil prepared from a 20:1 preparation and naphthalene at approximately 3 ppm caused immediate
and almost complete loss of photosynthesis in the green flagellate *Chlamydomonas angulosa*.   The naphthalene was accumulated for seven days and was immediately released when the algae were placed in fresh water.   However, when the algae were
retained in the original media after the naphthalene was allowed to escape, the decrease in naphthalene content of the
cells was dependent upon resumption of cell division and occurred in a stepwise manner indicating cell retention rather
than loss to the media [30,31].

Field observations of the effects of actual spills on
plankton are limited.   Some kills among phytoplankton were observed following the *Torrey Canyon* spill [31].   The Santa Barbara blowout, however, produced no detectable harmful effect
on phytoplankton productivity [33].   A study of the Caspian
Sea has shown that, after receiving intense and continuous oil
pollution, phytoplankton productivity decreased markedly from
1962 to 1969.   This general decline in primary productivity

was also reflected in zooplankton production and in production at higher trophic levels [3].

The zooplankton comprise not only the larvae and adults of animals that spend their entire life history as planktonic forms, but also include, seasonally, the eggs and larvae of benthic invertebrates. The majority of bottom invertebrates on the continental shelf (except in high latitudes) pass through a pelagic larval phase during development [34]. The adults of many of these invertebrates are of commercial importance, and the survival and maintenance of these animals are determined by the survival of the pelagic larvae.

Petroleum and petroleum components have varying effects on the different types of zooplankton. Several species of copepods will ingest oil from suspension with no apparent effect [11]. Following the wreck of the tanker *Arrow* in Chedabucto Bay, Nova Scotia, it was found that zooplankton ingested small particles of oil dispersed through the water column. As much as 10% of the oil in the water column was associated with feces of the zooplankton. The feces contained 7% by weight Bunker C fuel oil and it was estimated that, in addition to normal sedimenting processes, 20% of the particulate oil was deposited as zooplankton feces [35]. This uptake of oil at the surface and deposition of feces at depth during normal diel migration could cause dispersion of the oil through the water column [11]. Uptake of oil by zooplankton also represents a possible route for oil to enter the food chain [11].

Some plankton and planktonic larvae of benthic invertebrates are highly sensitive to oil pollution [36]. The mortalities of the larvae are the result of either direct poisoning or of changes in faunal structure and the surrounding environment [34]. Perhaps the two most critical periods in the larval history are at the extrusion of the gametes and at the time of metamorphosis and settling on the benthic substrate. Studies on the effects of crude oil and water-soluble fractions of crude oils have shown that the sperm which is exuded into the water is much more sensitive than the following larval stages [37,38]. During the settling period the animals drift over the substrate, delaying metamorphosis until suitable substrate is encountered. Mileikovsky [34] listed four causes which could induce mortalities in settling larvae in areas of pollution: (1) Eutrophication and the resultant formation of toxic metabolites, (2) changes in sediment structure so that no suitable substrate is available for settlement, (3) accumulation of pollutants in sediments or concentration of pollutants by filter feeders, causing the larvae to be poisoned when in contact with the sediment, and (4) the disappearance from communities of species whose larvae are gregarious during settlement and the subsequent failure of resettlement by drifting larvae from other communities.

Observations of the Santa Barbara spill and the wrecks of the *Torrey Canyon* and *Arrow* indicate no harmful effects of the oil on the zooplankton [32,35]. Effects on the larvae of benthic invertebrates would be difficult to document since the effects may only become apparent years after the spill and in localities removed from the original site of the pollution. The effects on the benthic larvae, however, may be of much greater import to the ecosystem. The permanent zooplankton display large seasonal changes and generation times in weeks or months; however, benthic animals require years to attain maturity and thus any adverse effect on larval success may endure longer [11].

NEUSTON

The ecology of the assemblage of organisms living at or just below the surface of the ocean is poorly known; consequently, virtually no studies have been made on the effects of petroleum on these communities. These animals and plants are especially vulnerable since they occur in the top few centimeters of the water column where they are in direct contact with any spilled oil. It is not surprising that petroleum components occur in the plants and animals associated with the *Sargassum* community of the North Atlantic due to the direct contact of these organisms with floating oil [41]. The effect of petroleum on the ecology of the organisms, however, can only be surmised [13]. Though no community studies have been carried out, a small amount of information is available on the important constituent of the neuston, the pelagic eggs and larvae of fish. Petroleum and petroleum products at concentrations down to 10^{-5} ml/l are highly toxic to the developing eggs of the Black Sea flatfish, *Rhombus maesticus*. The hatched prelarvae appeared to be more resistant, but development to larvae was not studied [39]. Following the *Torrey Canyon* crude oil spill, eggs of pilchard sampled from the water column showed high mortality [11]. General information on the toxicity of petroleum products to some fish eggs and larvae is available [40], but no specific information is available on the effects of an altered phyto-zooplankton community on the ichthyoplankton or on the effect of petroleum on larval development and metamorphosis.

NEKTON

The continental shelves are the most productive areas of the ocean. These areas support the only fisheries of economic importance with the exception of the tuna fisheries [3]. They also are the sites of offshore oil fields, the routes of the greatest ship traffic, and are, therefore, subject to chronic

oil pollution [3].   The effect of petroleum on the ecology of
fishes is largely unknown [3].   Changes in adaptive behavior,
such as schooling, resulting from pollution is poorly understood and virtually no information is available on changes in
fecundity, natality, recruitment, and other factors [36,42].
There is even less information on the lethal effects of
spilled oil on fish [13].   There are, however, five possible
ways that oil can damage a local population of fish: (1) Eggs
and larvae can die in spawning or nursery areas due to coating
or direct toxic effects; (2) adults can die or fail to reach
spawning grounds in critical, narrow, or shallow contaminated
waterways; (3) local breeding populations may be lost due to
contamination of spawning grounds or nursery areas; (4) fecundity or spawning behavior may be changed; and (5) local food
species of the adults, juveniles, fry, or larvae may be adversely affected or eliminated [43].

Fish can become contaminated with petroleum by feeding on
contaminated organisms or by feeding in contaminated areas.
Large amounts of tar were found in the stomachs of three saury
(*Scomberesox saurus*) from the Mediterranean [44].   A laboratory study showed that plaice, *Pleuronectes platessa*, would
catch and eat oiled shrimp and would search and eat burrowing
benthic animals in oiled substrates.   It also appeared that
the plaice intentionally ingested oil as a potential food
source rather than ingesting oil incidentally while in the act
of feeding.   The oiled shrimp were preferentially chosen because they were easier to catch [45].

Studies of the North and Baltic Seas, areas subjected to
petroleum contamination for decades, provide no convincing evidence to indicate that oil pollution has had any direct effect on fish populations [3].   These are large bodies of water,
well flushed, where oil is quickly diluted and transported
from the region.   However, the east coast of the United States
with its estuary-like bays, is much more vulnerable.   The Caspian Sea is relatively enclosed and has shown marked drops in
primary productivity as a result of intense petroleum pollution [3]; zooplankton production has declined and there has
been a subsequent reduction in the commercial fishery.   Since
1930, sturgeon catches dropped by two-thirds and salmon, bream,
carp, pike, and sild catches have also dropped to almost one-
tenth of the 1930 catch [3].

BENTHOS

Almost all of the studies at actual spill sites have
dealt with the effects of petroleum on the intertidal communities.   This has occurred because: (1) There is a belief that
oil always floats; (2) the heavy deposits of oil are often
visible from shore; (3) historically, the intertidal zone has

been a prime study area; and (4) the intertidal environment is more accessible than the subtidal areas [13]. This situation has led to a neglect of the subtidal zone where oil pollution may have a major effect on the benthic communities.

From past studies at actual spill sites, there is a reasonably clear impression of the consequences of an oil spill on the intertidal communities. The stranded oil smothers animals, may be directly toxic to organisms, or may mechanically impede the littoral animals [3,46]. The attached algae may be covered with oil, may be directly affected by the toxic components, or may be torn loose by wave action because of the added weight of the oil. A considerable portion of most marine plants can be damaged without necessarily destroying their capacity to recover. Large brown algae have a mucilaginous covering that is not easily wetted by fresh oil [47]. However, an oil spill can change the entire ecological character of rocky intertidal areas where there is a delicate balance between the settlement and growth of seaweed and the grazing of the herbivores [3]. The algae occupy the space available to settling organisms such as barnacles and mussels and the moving fronds sweep other rock surfaces rendering them unusable by settling organisms [47]. The algal growth is kept in check by herbivores such as gastropods which graze on the young plants. By removing the algae and the gastropods, the rocky areas become populated with barnacles and mussels [3]. The selective loss of herbivores causes a proliferation of algae that creates competition with other settling organisms for space.

The barnacles that inhabit the rocky intertidal area are generally resistant to oil contamination unless completely smothered [47]. This resistance is due, in part, to the ability of the animals to close tightly and to their streamline shape [48]. It has been shown that barnacles will recolonize oil-treated fouling plates preferentially under conditions in which algae will not settle; the barnacles may be attracted to the black color of the plates [49]. In some spills, however, large mortalities of barnacles have taken place [37,50]. This may be due to the type and freshness of the oil that arrives at the beach. The effect of the petroleum on the organism may also be a function of the location of the organism in the intertidal zone. The upper and mid-intertidal zone animals are covered with oil at high tide and are not washed until the following high tide. This leaves them exposed to high concentrations of oil for long periods of time. The lower intertidal zone and the animals in this zone are exposed for relatively short periods of time to the concentrated oil [51].

The oil that is stranded in rocky areas may be removed by the browsers, such as chitons and limpets, which clean the rocky surfaces for food and inadvertently remove oil with no apparent effect to the animals [11,51].

Little information is available on the consequences of a petroleum spill on the animals associated with sandy intertidal areas of the subtidal zone. The animals in these areas are often buried or are very motile and thus are not as available to study as the organisms of the rocky intertidal. Usually they are only noted if a large number of dead organisms wash up on the shore.

A few reports, however, do document the magnitude of the possible effect and the animals that are affected. Large kills of Pismo clams (*Tivela stultorum*) occurred after the diesel oil spill by the *Tampico* [17] and a large kill of razor clams (*Siliqua patula*) occurred on the coast of Washington following a spill of gasoline and diesel fuel [52]. A spill of No. 2 fuel oil mixed with JP5 jet fuel in Searsport, Maine, caused immediate and continued mortality in a *Mya* population. In the three years following the spill an estimated 50 million clams were killed representing 85% of the harvestable population. There was no evidence that other factors such as heavy metals, a toxic plankton bloom, or predation contributed to this mortality [53]. Dow [54] indicated that in the two years following oil pollution in a Maine tide flat, production of *Mya* was reduced by 20% while adjacent mudflats increased production by 250% [54]. A spill in the lower York River, Virginia, of cracking residue thinned with No. 2 fuel oil caused mortalities in the polychaete and crustacean populations. After one year, the species richness and faunal similarity of the population had returned to pre-spill conditions but the number of individuals remained low [55]. Effects other than mortalities have been noted from only a few spills. After the Searsport, Maine, spill, it was noted that there was a high incidence of gonadal tumors in the contaminated clams which in some cases, replaced the normal gonadal tissue [43,53]. This is of obvious import to maintenance of the population.

Eisler [56] studied the effect of exposure of mussels (*Mytilus variabilis*) and the gastropod drill (*Drupa granulata*) to crude oil under laboratory conditions. Exposure of the animals to crude oil caused a reduction in predation of the oysters by the drills. The fecundity of the drills was directly related to the number of mussels destroyed with reduced predation causing reduced fecundity. Thus oil alters established behavior and survival patterns of these animals and constitutes a potential threat to population stability [56].

Oil that sinks following a spill provides another source of contamination for the benthic forms. Animals that only have a passive reliance on the substrate (animals that are attached to the substrate) are less affected than those forms which are buried in the substrate or feed directly on the sediment. Chemical analysis of clams showed evidence of contamination nine years after a spill of crude oil in Casco Bay, Maine [43]. Blackman [57] demonstrated that starved or well-fed shrimp (*Crangon crangon*) will ingest oil which, once ingested, remains in the gastric mill and foregut until it is sloughed when molting takes place. The oil may compose as much as 1% of the weight of the shrimp. The oil or metabolic products may then be transferred to predator species.

SALT MARSH

The salt marsh is one of the most productive and important features of an estuarine ecosystem. The marsh is important for shoreline stabilization, as a waterfowl nesting and feeding area, and perhaps most importantly, as a source of organic material. The salt marsh is a eutrophic high net-yield system that provides energy to the trophic structure of the tidal estuary by the biodegradation of cellulose and chitin [58]. Any disruption or alteration of this complex biological system affects a basic stage in the food web. A shift in productivity directly affects the biomass kinetics of the locality [58]. It is thus somewhat alarming that salt marshes also act as natural sites for trapping and holding oil while the biodegradation and breakdown of the petroleum occurs [59]. In general, however, the marshes can recover unless they are exposed to multiple spills, chronic pollution, emulsifiers, or very heavy contamination [14,58,59].

Oil can affect the marsh grasses directly by penetrating the soil where it affects the root system, by inhibiting germination, and by destroying foliage, and indirectly by inhibiting oxygen diffusion into the substrate [59,60,61]. Repeated monthly sprayings of a salt marsh with fresh crude oil killed the vegetative parts of *Spartina* and *Puccinella* by increasing the reducing condition in the substrate [62]. The plants recovered by producing new shoots; however, oiling that occurred in spring and summer reduced the flowering and seed production. Any degradation of a salt marsh system can reduce the energy flow within the associated biological systems.

ECOSYSTEMS

Prediction of the effects of oil spills on ecosystems is largely a matter of conjecture. The limited information on the effects of petroleum on marine habitats, populations, and communities allows only the most tentative speculation about possible ecosystem ramifications produced by a spill of petroleum. The estuarine ecosystem is perhaps one of the most vulnerable systems to petroleum contamination. Many established species are living near the limit of their tolerance range,

and additional stress could exclude them from the estuary
[63].   Changes in the trophic structure of the estuary could
directly affect the many commercial species of fish and shellfish that utilize the estuary as a nursery area./ Periods of
flushing from heavy rainfall may allow contaminated organisms
to release some of the accumulated contaminants [64].   However, the system which enables the estuary to concentrate and
recycle nutrients may also allow the estuary to become a pollution sink [63].   The consequences of an estuarine spill
could almost certainly cause major alterations in the ecosystem.

Predictions of the effects of petroleum on the biota of
the continental shelf are, perhaps, even more conjectural than
those on the estuaries due to the magnitude of the area and
the paucity of information about oil effects on the indigenous
populations; however, due to a lack of confinement of the oil,
the overall effect would probably not be as serious.   Local
kills would be expected following a spill, but drifting larvae
would repopulate and some animals subjected to the oil would
drift or swim free of the contamination.   Small amounts of oil
might be ingested by the filter-feeding plankton which then
could be passed up the food chain to taint commercial species.
Local reproductive success may decline, but adjacent populations would help to repopulate depleted areas.   Green [22]
stated that petroleum pollution of the continental shelf may
cause serious reduction in exploitable food resources through
declining production, reduced abundance, and the tainting of
commercial species [22].

PROSPECTUS

Any discussion of the possible effects of petroleum on
the arctic ecosystems must be phrased in the same speculative
terms as the discussion of subarctic ecosystems plus the added
disadvantage of a lack of knowledge of many of the interrelationships of arctic populations and communities.   There are
certain abiotic and biotic factors, however, which will influence the effects of an oil spill.

The severity of the climate creates a greater risk in the
exploration and transport of oil in the arctic than elsewhere.
Sea routes for the transport of oil are exposed, difficult to
navigate, and follow enormous lengths of remote and inaccessi-
ble coastline.   This inaccessibility and remoteness may cause
problems in effective salvage and cleanup [3].   There are also
other reasons that might increase the seriousness and duration
of arctic oil spills: (1) Cold temperatures do not permit a
rapid evaporation of the highly-toxic aromatic fraction, (2)
bacterial degradation is slower, (3) limited daylight reduces
photochemical oxidation, (4) the marine biota is generally

long-lived, has low reproductive potentials, and does not have
wide ranging dispersal stages, and (5) arctic food chains are
relatively short, increasing their vulnerability to disruption
at any given level [13,55,65]. It would seem then that any
spill will have longer and perhaps a more marked effect on
arctic biota than similar spills in other regions.

There are three distinct habitats in the arctic marine
waters - the sub-ice, the neritic, and the benthic [66]. Each
has particular physical and biological characteristics that
are unique to the arctic. General information about the basic
ecology and physiology of the majority of the inhabiting species is lacking. The basic knowledge of ecological concern
centers on the species of economic importance, particularly
the marine mammals and waterfowl [66]. This leaves a great
paucity of information on the forms that comprise the food web
on which the higher forms depend.

The physical phenomena associated with these habitats are
also unique. Sea-ice eliminates the intertidal communities by
its scouring action; however, there is a tendency for oil to
accumulate at the sea-ice and benthic habitat interface. The
oil that accumulates in pockets at the sea and ice interface
is potentially of particular significance since it weathers
slowly, can be transported considerable distances, will decrease little in toxicity, and then can be reintroduced into
the water column at spring breakup, a time of intense biological activity [66].

The ice acts as a substrate for an under-ice diatom flora
which is the primary link in the relatively simple food chain.
The food chain may be as simple as diatom-copepod-fish-mammal,
leaving few options for the species at each level. Some food
chains may be more complex but the trophic sequences are usually short with few links and options [65]. It is therefore
obvious that the sea-ice interface represents both an area of
critical importance to the food web and an interface where oil
accumulates. The fact that crude oil can inhibit primary production has been shown in laboratory studies using a natural-
ly-occurring algal population from an arctic marsh [67]. The
algae were incubated in 275 ml water to which 0.5 ml crude oil
that had weathered for two months in the arctic was added
without shaking. A tenfold reduction in primary productivity
occurred in a population that had a naturally low productivity.
The assessment of the impact of a spill in this habitat is
thus of importance.

The basic biological composition of the south Beaufort
Sea is dependent on the balance between the surface outflow of
low salinity Mackenzie River water overlaying the intruding
relatively higher salinity Arctic Ocean waters. This estuarine system requires an unaltered input of water of fairly
constant quantity and quality. The estuary supports a low

rate of primary and secondary biological production, probably subject to considerable variation, but supporting fish and mammal populations [65]. Oil introduced into this estuarine system would be expected to spread to all areas of the river plume and contaminate all levels of the biological system.

In assessing the areas of further study it should be noted that the general lack of knowledge about the physical and biological aspects of the ecosystem render any pertinent information of value. Of interest are the physical factors that dictate nutrient availability, water movements, ice formation, and plankton distribution. Probably of most importance biologically is a better knowledge of the ecology and physiology of the non-commercial arctic biota, and the effect that oil has on these organisms. Trophic relationships also need to be described with details of available options, alternate pathways, and the impact and cycling of petroleum through the system.

REFERENCES

1. Wilson, K.W. (1975). The laboratory estimation of the biological effects of organic pollution. Proc. R. Soc. Lond. B. Biol. Sci. 189:459-77.
2. Holcomb, R.W. (1969). Oil in the ecosystem. Science 166:204-6.
3. Clark, R.B. (1971). The biological consequences of oil pollution of the sea. In: David Davies Memorial Institute of International Studies. Report of a conference on water pollution as a world problem, Aberystwyth, 11-12, July 1970, p. 53-77. Europa Publications, London.
4. Mitchell, C.T., E.K. Anderson, L.G. Jones, and W.J. North (1970). What oil does to ecology. J. Water Pollut. Control Fed. 42:812-8.
5. Straughan, D. (1972). Factors causing environmental changes after an oil spill. J. Pet. Technol. (March 1972):250-4.
6. Ottway, S.M. (1971). The comparative toxicity of crude oils. In: The Ecological Effects of Oil Pollution on Littoral Communities (E.B. Cowell, ed.), p. 172-80. Institute of Petroleum, London.
7. National Academy of Sciences (1975). Petroleum in the Marine Environment. Washington, D.C., 107 p.
8. Murphy, T.A. (1971). Environmental effects of oil pollution. J. Sanit. Eng. Div. Proc. Am. Soc. Civ. Eng. 8221: 361-71.
9. Moore, S.F., R.L. Dwyer, and A.M. Katz (1973). A preliminary assessment of the environmental vulnerability of Machias Bay, Maine to oil supertankers. Mass. Inst. Technol. Rep. MITSG 73-6, 162 p.

10. Moore, S.F. and R.L. Dwyer (1974). Effects of Oil on Marine Organisms - A Critical Assessment of Published Data, Vol. 8, p. 819-22. Pergamon Press, Oxford.

11. Spooner, M. (1969). Some ecological effects of marine oil pollution. Pollut. Abstr. 1:70-4.

12. Nelson-Smith, A. (1968). The effects of oil pollution and emulsifier cleansing on shore life in Southwest Britain. J. Appl. Ecol. 5:97-107.

13. Boesch, D.F., C.H. Hershner, and J.H. Milgram (1974). Oil Spills and the Marine Environment. Ballinger Publishing Co., Cambridge, Mass., 114 p.

14. Nelson-Smith, A. (1972). Effects of the oil industry on shore life in estuaries. Proc. R. Soc. Lond. B. Biol. Sci. 180:487-96.

15. Reish, D.J. (1973). Marine and estuarine pollution. J. Water Pollut. Control Fed. 45:1310-9.

16. Scaratt, D.J. and V. Zitko (1972). Bunker C oil in sediments and benthic animals from shallow depths in Chedabucto Bay, N.S. J. Fish. Res. Board Can. 29:1347-50.

17. North, W.J., M. Neushul, Jr., and K.A. Clendenning (1964). Successive Biological Changes Observed in a Marine Cove Exposed to a Large Spillage of Oil. In: Symposium Commission Internationale Exploration Scientifique Mer Mediterranee, Monaco, 1954, p. 335-54.

18. Blumer, M., H.L. Sanders, J.F. Grassle, and G.R. Hampson (1971). A small oil spill. Environment 13:1-12.

19. Kolpack, R.L., J.S. Mattson, H.G. Mark, Jr., and T.-C. Yu (1971). Hydrocarbon content of Santa Barbara Channel sediments. In: Biological and Oceanographical Survey of the Santa Barbara Channel Oil Spill, 1969-1970 (R.L. Kolpack, ed.), Vol. 2, p. 276-95. Allan Hancock Foundation, University of Southern California, Los Angeles.

20. Shiels, W.E., J.J. Goering, and D.W. Hood (1973). Crude oil phytotoxicity studies. In: Environment Studies of Port Valdez (D.W. Hood, W.E. Shiels, and E.J. Kelley, eds.), p. 413-46. Univ. Alaska Inst. Mar. Sci. Occas. Publ. 3.

21. Green, K.A. (1974). The effects of petroleum hydrocarbons on organisms of the continental shelf. Biologist 56:165-79.

22. Holmes, R.W. (1969). The Santa Barbara oil spill. In: Oil on the Sea (D.P. Hould, ed.), p. 15-27. Plenum Press, New York.

23. Dunstan, W.M., L.P. Atkinson, and J. Natoli (1975). Stimulation and inhibition of phytoplankton growth by low molecular weight hydrocarbons. Mar. Biol. (Berl.) 31:305-10.

24. Gordon, D.C., Jr. and N.J. Prouse (1973). The effects of three oils on marine phytoplankton photosynthesis. Mar. Biol. (Berl.) 22:329-33.

25. Pulich, W.M., Jr., K. Winters, and C. Van Baalen (1974). Effects of a No. 2 fuel oil and two crude oils on the growth and synthesis of microalgae. Mar. Biol. (Berl.) 28:87-94.

26. Fisher, N.S. and C.F. Wurster (1974). Impact of pollutants on plankton communities. Environ. Conserv. 1:189-90.

27. Lee, R.F., M. Takahashi, J.R. Beers, W.H. Thomas, D.L. Seibert, P. Koeller, and D.R. Green (1976). Controlled Ecosystems: Their Use in the Study of the Effects of Petroleum Hydrocarbons on Plankton (J. Vernberg and A. Calabrese, eds.). In press. Academic Press, New York.

28. Lee, R.F. and M. Takahashi (1976). The fate and effect of petroleum in controlled ecosystem enclosures. In: Petroleum Hydrocarbons in the Marine Environment. Rapp P-V Reun. Cons. Int. Explor. Mer. No. G5, In press.

29. Lee, R.F. and J.W. Anderson (1976). Fate and effect of naphthalenes in controlled ecosystem enclosures. Bull. Mar. Sci., In press.

30. Soto, C., J.A. Hellebust, T.C. Hutchinson, and T. Sawa (1975). Effect of naphthalene and aqueous crude oil extracts on the green flagellate *Chlamydomonas angulosa*. I. Growth. Can. J. Bot. 53:109-17.

31. Soto, C., J.A. Hellebust, and T.C. Hutchinson (1975). Effect of naphthalene and aqueous crude oil extracts on the green flagellate *Chlamydomonas angulosa*. II. Photosynthesis and the uptake and release of naphthalene. Can. J. Bot. 53:118-26.

32. Smith, J.E. (1968). *Torrey Canyon* Pollution and Marine Life: A Report by the Plymouth Laboratory, Vol. xiv. Cambridge University Press, Cambridge, 196 p.

33. Straughan, D. (1971). Oil pollution and fisheries in the Santa Barbara Channel. In: Biological and Oceanographical Survey of the Santa Barbara Channel Oil Spill, 1969-1970 (D. Straughan, ed.), Vol. 1, p. 245-54. Allan Hancock Foundation, University of Southern California, Los Angeles.

34. Mileikovsky, S.A. (1970). The influence of pollution on pelagic larvae of bottom invertebrates in marine nearshore and estuarine waters. Mar. Biol. (Berl.) 6:350-6.

35. Conover, R.J. (1971). Some relations between zooplankton and Bunker C oil in Chedabucto Bay following the wreck of the tanker *Arrow*. J. Fish. Res. Board Can. 28:1327-30.

36. Mironov, O.G. (1970). The effect of oil pollution on flora and fauna of the Black Sea. In: FAO Technical Conference on Marine Pollution and its Effects on Living Resources and Fishing. MP/70/E-92. Food and Agriculture Organization of the United Nations, Rome, 4 p.

37. O'Sullivan, A.J. and A.J. Richardson (1967). The *Torrey Canyon* disaster and intertidal marine life. Nature 214: 448, 541-2.

38. Ramamurthy, V.D. (1974). Oil tanker disaster in Northwest coast of India. Curr. Sci. (Bangalore) 43:293-4.

39. Mironov, O.G. (1967). Effect of low concentrations of oil and oil products upon the developing eggs of the Black Sea flatfish - Kalkan (*Rhombus maeoticus* (Pallas)). Vopr. Ikhtiol. 7:577-80.

40. Environmental Protection Agency (1974). Semi-annual Report, January to July, 1975. Environmental Research Laboratory, Narragansett, R.I., 137 p.

41. Burns, K.A. and J.M. Teal (1973). Hydrocarbons in the pelagic *Sargassum* community. Deep-Sea Res. 20:207-11.

42. Goldberg, E.D. (convener) (1972). Baseline studies of pollutants in the marine environment and research recommendations. In: Deliberations of IDOE Baseline Conference, May 24-26, 1972, 51 p.

43. Council on Environmental Quality (1974). OCS Oil and Gas - An Environmental Assessment. Report to the President by the Council on Environmental Quality 1, p. 103-14.

44. Horn, M.H., J.M. Teal, and R.H. Backus (1970). Petroleum lumps on the surface of the sea. Science 168:245-6.

45. Blackman, R.A.A. (1974). Effects of sunken oil on the feeding of plaice on brown shrimps and other benthos. Int. Counc. Explor. Sea. CM 1974/E:24, 7 p.

46. Crapp, G.B. (1971). The ecological effects of stranded oil. In: The Ecological Effects of Oil Pollution on Littoral Communities (E.B. Cowell, ed.), p. 181-6. Institute of Petroleum, London.

47. Nelson-Smith, A. (1970). The problem of oil pollution of the sea. Adv. Mar. Biol. 8:215-306.

48. Nelson-Smith, A. (1968). Biological consequences of oil pollution on shore cleansing. In: The Biological Effects on Oil Pollution on Littoral Communities (J.D. Carthy and D.R. Arthur, eds.), Suppl. to Field Studies, Vol. 2, p. 73-80. Obtainable from E.W. Classey, Ltd., Hampton, Middx., England.

49. Straughan, D. (1971). The influence of oil and detergents on recolonization in the upper intertidal zone. In: Proceedings of 1971 Conference on Prevention and Control of Oil Spills, p. 437-40. American Petroleum Institute, Washington, D.C.

50. Chan, G.L. (1975). A study of the effects of the San Francisco oil spill on marine life. Part II: Recruitment. In: Proceedings of 1975 Conference on Prevention and Control of Oil Pollution, p. 457-61. American Petroleum Institute, Washington, D.C.

51. George, M. (1961). Oil pollution of marine organisms. Nature 192:1209.

52. Tegelberg, H. (1964). Washington's razor-clam fishery in 1964. Wash. Dep. Fish. Annu. Rep. 74:53-6.

53. Dow, R.L., J.W. Hurst, Jr., D.W. Mayo, C.G. Cogger, D.J. Donovan, M. Barry, and P.P. Yevich (1975). The ecological, chemical and histopathological evaluation of an oil spill site. Mar. Pollut. Bull. 6:164-73.
    Dow, R.L. and J.W. Hurst, Jr. Part I: Ecological Studies.
    Mayo, D.W., C.G. Cogger, and D.J. Donovan. Part II: Chemical Studies.
    Barry, M. and P.P. Yevich. Part III: Histopathological Studies.

54. Dow, R.L. (1975). Reduced growth and survival of clams transplanted to an oil spill site. Mar. Pollut. Bull. 6:124-5.

55. Bender, M.E., J.L. Hyland, and T.K. Duncan (1974). Effect of an oil spill on benthic animals in the Lower York River, Virginia. In: Marine Pollution Monitoring (Petroleum). Natl. Bur. Stand. Spec. Publ. 409, p. 257-9.

56. Eisler, R. (1975). Toxic, sublethal, and latent effects of petroleum on Red Sea macrofauna. In: Proceedings of 1975 Conference on Prevention and Control of Oil Pollution, p. 535-40. American Petroleum Institute, Washington, D.C.

57. Blackman, R.A.A. (1972). Effects of sunken crude oil on the feeding and survival of the brown shrimp - *Crangon crangon*. Int. Counc. Explor. Sea CM 1972/K:13, 8 p.

58. Meyers, S.P., D.G. Ahearn, S. Crow, and N. Berner (1973). The impact of oil on marshland microbial ecosystems. In: The Microbial Degradation of Oil Pollutants (D.G. Ahearn and S.P. Meyers, eds.), p. 221-8. Publ. No. LSU-SG-73-01. Center for Wetland Resources, Lousiana State University, Baton Rouge, La.

59. Stebbings, R.E. (1970). Recovery of salt marsh in Brittany sixteen months after heavy pollution by oil. Environ. Pollut. 1:163-7.

60. Cowell, E.B. and J.M. Baker (1969). Recovery of a salt marsh in Pembrokeshire, Southwest Wales, from pollution by crude oil. Biol. Conserv. 1:291-6.

61. Baker, J.M. (1971). Oil and salt marsh soil. In: The Ecological Effects of Oil Pollution on Littoral Communities (E.B. Cowell, ed.), p. 62-71. Institute of Petroleum, London.
62. Baker, J.M. (1971). Successive spillages. In: Proceedings of the Symposium on the Ecological Effects of Oil Pollution on Littoral Communities (E.B. Cowell, ed.), p. 21-32. Institute of Petroleum, London.
63. Odum, W.E. (1970). Insidious alteration of the estuarine environment. Trans. Am. Fish. Soc. 99:836-47.
64. Anderson, J.W., J.M. Neff, and S.R. Petrocelli (1974). Sublethal Effects of Oil, Heavy Metals, and PCBs on Marine Organisms (M.A.Q. Fahn and J.P. Bederke, Jr., eds.). Academic Press, New York, 553 p.
65. Grainger, E.H. (1975). Biological productivity of the southern Beaufort Sea: The physical-chemical environment and the plankton. Beaufort Sea Tech. Rep. 12a, Environment Canada, Victoria, B.C., 82 p.
66. Percy, J.A. and T.C. Mullin (1975). Effects of crude oils on arctic marine invertebrates. Beaufort Sea Tech. Rep. 11, Environment Canada, Victoria, B.C., 167 p.
67. Dickman, M. (1971). Preliminary notes on changes in algal primary productivity following exposure to crude oil in the Canadian Arctic. Can. Field-Nat. 85:249-51.

Chapter 7

BIOLOGICAL EFFECTS OF
PETROLEUM ON MARINE BIRDS

W. N. HOLMES and J. CRONSHAW

Department of Biological Sciences
University of California
Santa Barbara, California   93106

INTRODUCTION

Seepage of petroleum through parts of the ocean floor is an ancient geological phenomenon and for many centuries man has made use of this oil. For example, the coastal Indians of Southern California used weathered crude oil to waterproof their rude coracles and Christopher Columbus and Sir Francis Drake in the 15th and 16th centuries used tar from oil seeps in the Caribbean Sea and the Santa Barbara Channel to caulk the decks and planks of their ocean ships.

In regions of natural seepage, crude oil has been present in the local seawater for many thousands of years and organisms living in these areas have evolved with petroleum as an

integral part of their environment. The prolonged presence of
petroleum in these regions has been construed to suggest that
petroleum has little adverse effect on the flora and fauna in
these areas. Since we know nothing about the abundances of
organisms in these environments prior to the onset of natural
seepage, this argument is misleading. Nevertheless, this rea-
soning has been extended by some to suggest that periodic accidental spillages of petroleum into coastal waters have
little permanent effect on the local flora and fauna. The
amounts and concentrations of petroleum pollutants that are
now present in some of our estuarine and coastal waters, however, far exceed those in areas of natural seepage and the
comparison is not justified. Indeed, the amount of petroleum
entering the marine environment by natural seepage through the
ocean floor may account for less than 10% of the total worldwide petroleum pollution.

EFFECTS OF SPILLAGE ON MORTALITY

The effects of heavy petroleum pollution on marine bird
populations are probably more rapid and more conspicuous than
they are on other forms of wildlife. Accidental spillage of
crude oil often leads to high mortality of birds in the vicinity of the spill and one of the earliest accounts of such an
accident was published by Jenny Mothersole [1]. She reported
that in 1907 the seven-masted schooner, Thomas W. Ralston, released 2 million gallons of crude oil into the waters around
the Isles of Scilly. One of these isles, Annet, had a seabird
colony that was reputed to include more than 100,000 puffins
and "vast numbers" of these birds were reported to have died
as a result of this spillage. Since then several more incidents have occurred in the area and today only about 100 puffins are left on Annet. Other colonies of puffins in the
Western Approaches have also been reduced proportionately during the past 50 yr [2,3] and there is little doubt among ornithologists that persistent spills of petroleum have been a
major factor contributing to their decline [4].
Numerous other reports on the effects of oil spills were
published during the period between World War I and World War
II but estimates of the number of birds affected in these incidents were poorly documented. Since 1945, however, the
worldwide consumption and transportation of petroleum has increased dramatically and concomitantly the accidental spillage
at sea has become more frequent and more extensive. Occasional catastrophic spillages caused by leakage from shipwrecked
tankers and blowout accidents on offshore drilling rigs have
focussed public attention on the seriousness of the problem.
Although ornithologists had long realized that large numbers
of seabirds perish as a result of these spills, it was not

until oil pollution reached a serious level that a general public awareness of the problem developed and there was publication of more complete records of mortalities among bird populations. These reports fall roughly into four categories. The most abundant records deal with the effects of spillage in terms of total seabird mortality. A few reports examine the mortalities of individual species within the resident population. Other reports deal mainly with the implied effects of mortality sustained during periods of acute and chronic spillage on the size and growth of surviving colonies and finally there are one or two reports dealing with the differential mortality rates observed among different species exposed to similar degrees of contamination.

TOTAL MORTALITY

Although the very high levels of contamination which occur immediately after a catastrophic spillage may be short-lived, the effects of the petroleum on birds may persist long after the environment has returned to a relatively pristine state. For instance, the estimates of mortality recorded during the first few days after a spill will be derived mainly by counting beached carcasses. No estimate can be made of the number of carcasses that sank or were devoured. During subsequent weeks birds that have been collected into cleansing centers will die and this number must be added to the initial estimates. Since some of the cleansed birds may survive several weeks, data from all sources may not be collected and included in the final estimate. Thus, quite apart from the fact that not all casualties are found, serious inaccuracies may occur during the collection of mortality data from these sources.

In contrast to the acute contamination resulting from major accidents, the petroleum pollution occurring in the industrialized areas of the world is often continuous and more persistent; this type of chronic pollution results from minor spillage from tankers and offshore rigs, leakage from transmission lines, jettisoning of bilge washings, etc. The total effect of this chronic petroleum pollution on bird populations, which may be monitored more reliably and certainly less hurriedly than the effects resulting from catastrophic spillage, may exceed the effects of major spillages. However, casualties counted by observers following both acute contamination and during chronic low-level leakage may represent only a small fraction of the actual mortality.

In 1967, the tanker *Torrey Canyon* became grounded off the Cornish Coast of England and more than 100,000 tons of Kuwait crude oil were released. The total number of birds killed during the 3-week period following the accident may have exceeded the estimated 20,000-30,000 (Table 1). Less than 2 yr later, on 28 January 1969, a blowout occurred on an off-shore drilling operation in the Santa Barbara Channel, California and during the next 10 days approximately 18,000 tons of crude oil were released into the surrounding water; seabird carcasses collected on the beaches and deaths reported by cleansing centers during the next 6 weeks indicated that approximately 3,600 birds died.

TABLE 1

The estimated mortalities sustained by seabird populations following some of the major oil spills that have occurred since 1937

Incident	Spillage	Mortality	Species	Reference
March 1937 San Francisco Bay USA	Crude oil 9,000 tons	10,000 (1.1 birds/ton)	Murre, grebe, scoter	5
Jan. 1953 Howacht Bay Baltic Sea	Oil residues 500 tons	10,000 (20 birds/ton)	Eider, merganser, scoter	6
Jan. 1955 Gerd Maersk Elbe River, Germany	Crude oil 8,000 tons	275,000 (34.4 birds/ton)	Scoter	6
Sept. 1956 Seagate, Washington, USA	Bunker C fuel oil	6,000	Scoter, guillemot	7
1962 Gotland, Sweden	No record	30,000	Long-tail duck	8
March 1967 Torrey Canyon, SW England	Crude oil 117,000 tons	30,000 (0.26 birds/ton)	Guillemot, razorbill	9
Feb. 1969 N. Zeeland, Denmark	No record	10,000	Eider, common scoter	10
Feb. 1969 Terschelling, Holland	Crude oil	30-35,000	Eider, common scoter	11
March 1969 Santa Barbara, Calif., USA	Crude oil 11,000 tons	3,600 (0.3 birds/ton)	Western grebe, loon, scoter, cormorant	12,13
April 1969 Hamilton Trader, Irish Sea	Heavy fuel oil 600-700 tons	6,000 (9.2 birds/ton)	Guillemot, razorbill	14
May 1969 Palva, Kökar, Finland	Crude oil 150 tons	3,000-3,500 (21.7 birds/ton)	Eider, long-tail duck	15
Jan. 1970 NE Britain	Fuel oil 1,000 tons	50,000 (50 birds/ton)	Sea duck, auk	16
Feb. 1970 East Jutland, Denmark	No record	12,000	Eider, common scoter, velvet scoter	10
Feb. 1970 Delian Apollon Tampa, Florida, USA	Bunker C fuel oil 80-100 tons	9,000 (90 birds/ton)	No record	17
Feb.-April 1970 Arrow & Irving Whale Newfoundland & Nova Scotia	Bunker C fuel oil 10,000 tons	12,800 (0.8 birds/ton)	Sea duck, auk, alcid, eider, ducks	18
Feb.-March 1970 Kodiak Oil Spill Alaska	Tanker ballast	10,000	Alcid, sea duck, gull, kittiwakes	19
Dec. 1970-Jan. 1971 South Kattegat	No record	15,000	Eider, scoter	10
Jan. 1971 San Francisco Bay, Calif. USA	Bunker C fuel oil 300-350 tons	7,000 (21.5 birds/ton)	Grebe, guillemot, scoter	20
March 1972 Jutland	No record	30,000	Eider, scoter	21
Dec. 1972 Danish Waddenzee	No record	30,000	Eider, common scoter	21

The *Torrey Canyon* and Santa Barbara Channel accidents were typical of the two major types of catastrophic spills that may occur somewhere in the world several times in every decade. Other major spills have had equally devastating effects on local seabird populations and between 1955 and 1972 more than 1 million deaths have been recorded following these incidents. However, data on the quantities of oil spilled, the number of birds killed, and the species involved in these accidents are almost always incomplete and they are frequently recorded in obscure publications and reports. In Table 1 we have attempted to assemble a representative listing of total bird mortalities recorded after some of the major accidents which have occurred since 1937; we emphasize, however, that this list is incomplete and the data are only estimates of the true values.

It is of interest to note that accidents involving partially purified petroleum products, such as fuel oil and Bunker C, seem to have caused more deaths per unit mass of oil spilled than comparable accidents involving unrefined crude oil (Table 1). Several other factors, however, may also have contributed to the high mortalities recorded following spills of refined product. For example, irrespective of the material spilled, contamination of the water in a confined bay that sustains a high seabird population may be expected to cause more deaths than a similar accident occurring in an open coastal channel at a time when the density of marine birds on a migratory flyway is low. These two factors alone may have accounted for the difference in mortality rates observed following the 1971 spillage of Bunker C fuel oil in the San Francisco Bay and the 1969 leakage of crude oil into the Santa Barbara Channel (Table 1). In contrast, however, the *Torrey Canyon* spill occurred when the seasonal migration of birds was in full swing and yet in spite of a high seabird population, the records indicate that less than one bird was killed per ton of crude oil released. The possibility exists, therefore, that under similar circumstances, refined products may be more hazardous to birds than crude oil and this topic is worthy of detailed examination.

In addition to these major accidents, either the continuous or the frequent intermittent leakage of lesser amounts of petroleum products into the marine environment may account for many more seabird deaths than those recorded following the major incidents recorded in Table 1. Spilling incidents of this type are quite frequent, as indicated by the records of the Liverpool Underwriters Association who reported 91 tanker groundings (17 spillages) and 238 tanker collisions (22 spillages) between June 1964 and April 1967; although this number of accidents is extremely small compared to the total number of sailings, the number of spills is clearly much larger than the number of major oil spills reported during the same period (Table 1).

In Great Britain, the Royal Society for the Protection of Birds, and in Europe, the International Beached Bird Surveys have attempted to monitor annually the effects of these minor spillages along beaches. In an attempt to standardize these surveys, measured lengths of beach have been monitored regularly and mortalities have been expressed as recorded deaths per unit length of coastline (Tables 2 and 3). The serious effects of persistent minor spillage are further emphasized by the personal records of Mr. W. E. Williams (reported in 4) who, from 1952 to 1963, counted the total number of contaminated birds that were washed ashore and estimated the amount of spilled oil appearing along 160 yd of beach in St. Agnes in Cornwall, England (Table 4). It is interesting to note that these records do not show any correlation between the estimated annual bird mortality and the quantities of oil washed ashore. However, on the basis of these data, Mr. Williams estimated that the annual mortality rates were equivalent to a total mortality between 1952 and 1963 of 100,000 birds along the shoreline of Cornwall. Indeed, it has been suggested that the effects of this low-level pollution around the world may greatly exceed the effects of the less frequent but larger accidental spillages [27].

VULNERABILITY OF SPECIES

There are several published reports regarding the comparative vulnerability of different species to petroleum contamination [4,22-26,28-33]. Most of these surveys have estimated this vulnerability in terms of the incidence of beached carcasses in areas where active regular surveys have been conducted. Some results of this type of study are summarized in Tables 2 and 3.

The effect of chronic persistent spillage may vary from year to year and the total number of recorded deaths will be roughly correlated to the amount of oil spilled. Records of the South African National Foundation for the Conservation of Coastal Birds (SANCCOB) show quite clearly that the mortality and incidence of oil contamination among colonies of jackass penguins is closely correlated with the incidence of oil spillage. Before 1967 there were only two recorded instances, one in 1948 and another in 1952, when petroleum spillage had affected colonies of these species. But, following closure of the Suez Canal in 1967, large numbers of fully-laden westbound tankers became susceptible to accident while rounding the Cape and the threat of persistent oil pollution became apparent for the first time. These shipping accidents that occurred between

TABLE 2

Annual total of oil-contaminated birds found on British beaches

	1951-52	1952-53	1966-67	1968-69	1969-70	1970-71	1971-72	1972-73	1973-74
Divers/Grebes	253	161	71	89	78	60	66	78	25
Gannet	-	-	60	9	46	29	40	53	47
Cormorant/Shag	-	-	59	21	72	24	58	72	133
Wildfowl (primarily ducks)	-	-	229	80	772	105	99	104	271
Waders	-	-	73	16	194	18	18	14	249
Gulls/Terns	4,700	331	1,141	353	290	303	462	311	529
Auk	1,065	402	1,417	1,878	2,646	620	1,315	837	1,559
Other	101	105	30	43	60	29	42	62	144
Total	6,722	1,408	3,080	2,511	4,158	1,188	2,100	1,489	2,957
Beach surveyed (km)	ca 220	ca 175	ca 600	2,839	4,009	4,605	9,826	11,942	12,517
Oiled birds/km	ca 30.6	ca 8.1	ca 5.1	0.89	1.04	0.26	0.21	0.13	0.24

From Bourne [4] and Bourne and Devlin [22,23].

TABLE 3

Annual total of oil-contaminated birds found on British (UK) and European (EU) beaches

	UK 1969	UK 1970	UK 1971	UK 1972	EU 1972	UK 1973	EU 1973
Divers/Grebes	16	33	27	13	123	19	102
Gannet	9	11	6	5	16	6	43
Cormorant/Shag	2	50	14	11	3	18	1
Wildfowl (primarily ducks)	30	283	55	47	329	15	923
Waders	3	43	9	5	77	3	20
Gulls/Terns	160	162	96	122	351	69	352
Auk	345	1,398	169	402	205	167	264
Other	9	55	12	9	5	2	26
Total	574	2,035	388	614	1,109	299	1,731
Beach surveyed (km)	753	1,529	1,489	1,964	1,181	2,336	1,769
Oiled birds/km	0.76	1.33	0.26	0.31	0.94	0.13	0.98

From Bourne and Devlin [22,23] and Bibby and Bourne [24,25,26].

TABLE 4

An estimate of the amount of oil and the number of birds washed ashore each year along 160 yards of beach at St. Agnes, Cornwall, England

Year	Estimated oil waste (kg)	Number of dead birds collected	Number of deaths per 100 kg of oil waste
1952	4,325	ca 80	1.8
1953	3,655	ca 80	2.2
1954	535	318	59
1955	235	74	32
1956	190	36	19
1957	185	56	30
1958	145	66	46
1959	1,240	33	2.7
1960	?	?	?
1961	50	27	54
1962	150	37	21
1963	150	37	25

From private records of W. E. Williams cited in 4.

1967 and 1974 and affected the colonies of jackass penguins along the South African Coast are recorded in Table 5.

The mortality sustained by individuals of a particular species, however, may be also correlated with their behavior. The relative abundance of some species in an area varies according to their seasonal migrations. In areas where their appearance and disappearance is abrupt, the changing effect of chronic petroleum spillage will be most pronounced. But, for a variety of reasons, the recorded mortality rates of some migratory species may not always show clear seasonal cyclicity. Species characteristics such as short migrations, prolonged periods during which individuals arrive and depart from an area, and the existence of sub-species and races with ill-defined and perhaps different patterns of migration are only a few of the factors that may tend to obscure true differences in seasonal mortality rates. Also, annual variations in climatic conditions may influence the frequency of marine accidents and the distribution of spilled petroleum; these physical factors may tend to further obscure seasonal differences in mortality.

Data purporting to show seasonal changes in the mortality of common guillemot exposed to chronic petroleum contamination are illustrated in Figure 1. These data were derived from weekly surveys of selected beaches in Great Britain by members of the Royal Society for the Protection of Birds [28]. During 1970-71 when 942 km of beach were surveyed and 260 oil-contaminated carcasses were found, the monthly mortality rate showed an apparent seasonal cyclicity; the mortality being highest during the autumn and winter months when the birds spend long periods on the water and lowest during the summer breeding period. However, when a similar census was conducted in 1973-74, a clear seasonal difference in mortality was not apparent, in spite of the fact that more beach was surveyed (12,465 km) and four times the previous number of dead birds were collected. At best, therefore, these data may be interpreted to indicate nothing more than the combined effect of seasonal differences in the location of the birds, climatic conditions, and incidence of oil spillage (Fig. 1).

The feeding behavior and defense postures assumed by some marine birds may also tend to increase their vulnerability to contamination by oil slicks. Breeding penguins are particularly vulnerable to contamination when oil slicks surround the coastal islands they inhabit [34]. The birds, being flightless, must swim through the oil when leaving and returning to the islands at feeding time.

Field observations suggest that although thin films of oil on seawater evoke little or no response, thicker patches of oil cause some species to dive below the surface [4]. The pattern of diving seems to be random and the birds do not

TABLE 5

Oil pollution incidents along the cape coast, South Africa, affecting jackass penguins, and the numbers of oiled penguins recovered, cleaned and released by SANCCOB 1968-1974

Origin (*name of ship*) or location of spill	Date	Spillage (tons)	Number of contaminated birds (minimum)	Number treated	% released
Esso Essen	April 1968	15,000	1,700	1,300	73
Cape Point slick	August 1969	–	52	52	94
Simonstown slick	August 1970	–	51	51	71
Kazimah	November 1970	200	599	414	64
Wafra	February 1971	25,000	1,216	1,139	64
Dassen Island slick	March 1972	–	>2,100	1,706	60
Oswego Guardian	September 1972	?	400	400	63
Oriental Pioneer	July 1974	?	488	488	65
TOTAL	1968-1974	–	6,606	5,550	65

From Frost, Siegfried, and Cooper [34], Westphal and Rowan [35], and Percy, Westphal, and Westphal [36].

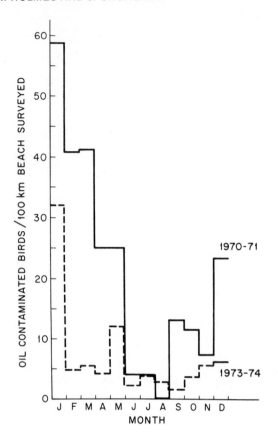

Fig. 1. *The numbers of oil-contaminated common guillemot found along measured beaches in Great Britain during 1970-71 and 1973-74. These data are derived from the results of surveys conducted by the Royal Society for the Protection of Birds (Redrawn from IMCO [28]).*

appear to select oil-free areas in which to surface. Thus, in regions of extensive spillage the probability of birds surfacing through the slick will increase and this is believed to be a serious cause for the selective contamination of diving seabirds [4]. Diving is also a primary means of foraging among many seabirds and of course this activity will be equally hazardous in areas of oil spillage. However, there seems to be no substantial evidence that birds actively seek oil slicks and suggestions that their vulnerability is increased because oil slicks either render the surface of the water smooth (and therefore attractive) or resemble shoaling fish and rip tides, etc., seem to be based on conjecture.

EFFECT ON FUTURE POPULATIONS

The volume, the chemical composition, and the geographical location of a spill, together with the prevailing climatic
conditions, are some of the physical factors that will determine the vulnerability of seabirds to a spillage of petroleum.
The interactions between these factors and the biological
characteristics of an affected species will influence the future recovery of a diminished population. For example, the
frequency of breeding and the duration of postnatal care will
either separately or in combination influence the rate of increase in population size. The alcids (guillemots, razorbills, other auks, and puffins), which have suffered steady
severe losses in recent years, do not reach sexual maturity
for 3 or more years and then during each breeding season they
may lay only one egg. Furthermore, mature adults may not
breed every year, and when they do, the period of postnatal
care is often long and the chicks are vulnerable to attack by
predators. It has been shown that within colonies of
Brunich's and the common guillemot, the average annual population recruitment to the fledgling stage of development is
only 0.2 individuals per breeding pair [37,38] and that even
without any mortality due to oil pollution it might take about
50 yr for a guillemot colony to double in size [39]. Clearly,
a serious mortality within colonies of these species will have
a more serious effect on the rate of growth of the surviving
population than a similar reduction in the population of
mallard ducks; a species that lays 8 to 14 eggs in each
clutch, does not engage in prolonged postnatal care of the
rapidly maturing chicks, and where the size of a colony may
double within a single breeding season.

However, annual estimates of seabird numbers do provide
some convincing circumstantial evidence that crude oil and
petroleum products have been implicated in the decline of
many seabird colonies. The populations of puffins in the
Scilly Isles [2,3,40], common guillemots on Ailsa Craig [41],
razorbills on the Newfoundland Coast [42], and the long-tail
ducks migrating across Finland [43] have all declined drasti-
cally in recent years. More specifically, population studies
on seabird colonies on Sept Ile, Brittany, suggest that mortalities resulting from the *Torrey Canyon* accident may have
reduced the breeding pairs of common guillemots by 81%, razorbills by 89% and puffins by 84% [44].

Frost and his coworkers, however, have suggested that
the magnitude of the effect of petroleum contamination on the
jackass penguin populations along the South African coast may
be much less than is popularly believed [34]. The average
annual rate of contamination of these birds is estimated to
be about 0.7 to 0.9% of the total population. This figure is

well below the probable annual mortality rate (8.5%) of adult
birds. They have concluded, therefore, that petroleum contamination alone may be relatively unimportant, though in combination with others factors it may adversely affect future
populations of penguins.

DIFFERENTIAL MORTALITIES OF SPECIES

The comparative mortalities of seabird species exposed
to similar types of external contamination have been examined
objectively in only one study [12]. In this instance the sur-
vivals of several species were compared following routine
cleansing of contaminated individuals. We must emphasize,
however, that these studies do not necessarily reflect differ-
ing systemic sensitivities of the various species to petroleum
contamination. A more accurate assessment of their significance would be that they demonstrate different responses of
the individuals from several species to the sequence of events
and treatments following external contamination with petroleum.

During the 33-day period following the Santa Barbara oil
spill, 652 contaminated birds representing 26 species were
cleansed at a small local zoo in Santa Barbara, California.
The proportion of survivors and the survival time of the individuals from each species were carefully recorded for groups
consisting of 10 or more individuals of each species [12].
Although the degree of contamination in this sample ranged
from light patches of oil that did not interfere with the
bird's movements to a heavy coating that completely covered
the bird, no correlation between survival and the amount of
oil was apparent. However, even though 88% of the birds died
during the 33-day period, the mortality rate and survival time
of some species were much lower than others. In Figure 2 the
survival records are illustrated for the groups of each species. It is clear that the gulls, mergansers, and scoters
survived the effects of oil and cleansing much better than did
other species such as the grebes, ruddy ducks, and loons.
Furthermore, under these conditions of cleansing and maintenance, the mean survival time or mean time to death of a species was positively and significantly correlated ($r = 0.9$,
$P < 0.01$) with the survival rate observed for that species.
Thus, there was no evidence to suggest that acute toxicity occurred among those individuals that succumbed.

Survival records maintained by Mr. David C. Smith at the
International Bird Rescue Research Center in Berkeley, California, show that a total of 502 contaminated seabirds consisting of 11 or more individuals of 11 species were cleansed
at the Center during 1973. The overall survival rate of
these cleansed birds was 41.6% which is considerably higher

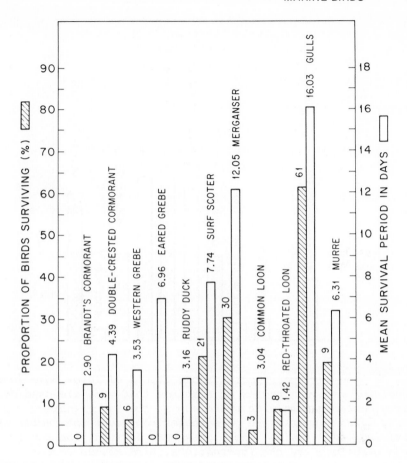

Fig. 2. The survival records among groups of 10 or more individuals of various species cleansed following contamination with crude oil during March 1969 in Santa Barbara, California (Redrawn from Drinkwater, Leonard, and Black [12]).

than the survival achieved following the Santa Barbara oil spill [cf. 12]. However, although this survival rate reflects improvements in the cleansing techniques that have occurred since 1969, these records nevertheless confirm that different species of seabirds show differential survival rates following contamination and cleansing (Fig. 3).

Members of the South African National Foundation for the Conservation of Coastal Birds have been particularly successful in cleaning and rehabilitating contaminated jackass penguins (Table 5). From 1968 to 1974 they released over 3,500 of the 5,550 birds cleaned and this represented each year a success rate of approximately 60%. Between 1971 and 1974, however, 1,440 of the released birds were marked with flipper

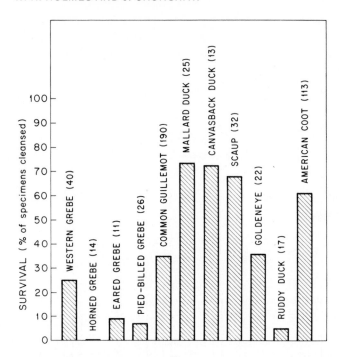

Fig. 3. *The survival records among groups of 10 or more indi-*
viduals of various species of seabirds that were cleansed fol-
lowing contamination with petroleum in the San Francisco Bay
during 1973. Numerals in parentheses represent the number of
surviving individuals. These data were derived from the re-
cords maintained by the International Bird Rescue Research
Center, Berkeley, California and they were made available to
us by the Director, Mr. David C. Smith.

bands and to date 1.8% of these birds have been recovered dead
[34]. At the same time a banded control group consisting of
5,250 uncontaminated penguins were released but during the
same period less than 1% of these banded controls have been
found dead. These data suggest that the mortality among the
rehabilitated birds may have been somewhat higher than it was
among uncontaminated birds and the true successes of the rehabilitation procedures were probably lower than they appeared
to be at the time the birds were released.

PHYSICAL AND SYSTEMIC EFFECTS OF PETROLEUM

The death of seabirds following petroleum contamination
is in most instances not sudden and, especially among a
cleansed population, mortality may continue for several weeks.

The precise reasons for these deaths may be numerous and they are not always clear. In general, however, they fall into two categories; some effects may be external and physical whereas others may be systemic and result directly or indirectly from the ingestion of petroleum. The external and physical effects are the most frequent consequences of acute contamination whereas systemic effects may result from either acute or chronic exposure of birds to petroleum contamination. For the purposes of this discussion, we have defined the physical ef-- fects of oil on birds to include only those effects that are directly and indirectly associated with contamination of the integument. The systemic effects, therefore, will include all those instances where ingested petroleum has been shown to either affect specific physiological processes or cause struc- tural and pathological changes in tissues.

PHYSICAL EFFECTS

When seabirds become heavily contaminated with petroleum, the entrapped air between the feathers is eliminated and the resulting loss of buoyancy may lead to death through drowning. In instances where birds have sustained less severe contamina- tion, such as when only the breast feathers become soaked with petroleum, the effective body weight may be increased substan- tially. For example, we have noted that even light to moder- ate smearing of the breast feathers with Bunker C oil in- creases the effective body weight of a 1.2 kg mallard duck by 7-18% and moderate smearing of a 2.5 kg Pekin duck increases its effective body weight by 25%. Such added burdens must surely contribute to the physical exhaustion of contaminated birds. Contamination of the flight feathers, even with small amounts of petroleum, may prevent them from sliding easily over one another as the wings change shape during flight. Thus, the aerodynamic properties of the wings will become less efficient and in some cases this may even prevent active flight. The added body weight and possible impaired flight of contaminated birds, therefore, may adversely affect their abilities to forage and these factors may account for the lean or emaciated condition of so many beached birds that are only lightly contaminated with petroleum.

In less extreme instances, and particularly after at- tempts have been made to cleanse the feathers of contaminated birds, the elimination of entrapped air from between the feathers leads to a loss of thermal insulation. The experi- mental application of quite small amounts of oil to the breast feathers of mallard and black ducks can eliminate sufficient air from between the feathers to cause their thermal conduc- tivity to increase significantly. Therefore, the basal metab- olism of the bird must increase to compensate for the

resulting high rate of heat loss [45]. Similar metabolic responses occur when any one of a variety of petroleum products
are applied to the feathers and in each case the increase in
metabolism appears to be dose-dependent. The response in each
case is believed to be due entirely to changes in the physical
properties of the feathers and not due to systemic toxicity or
irritation of the skin. Figure 4 illustrates the type of

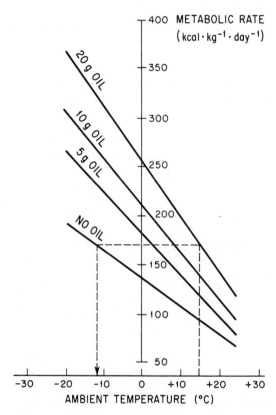

Fig. 4. The metabolic rates of black ducks following contamination of the breast feathers with different quantities of a
lubricating oil (Redrawn from Hartung [45]).

changes observed in the basal metabolic rates of black ducks
following contamination of the feathers with different doses
of lubricating oil. These data show quite clearly that at an
environmental temperature of 15°C, contamination of a 900 g
black duck with only 20 g of oil will cause almost a twofold
increase in metabolic rate and that this rate of energy consumption would be equivalent to that necessary to maintain the
normal body temperature of an uncontaminated bird living at

less than -10°C (Fig. 4).   Thus, even a moderately contaminated bird would have to double its food intake to achieve the
level of metabolism necessary to offset the loss of thermal
insulation.

Field studies have frequently shown that oil-contaminated
birds become isolated from their food supply and their food
intake may be reduced to zero [46-48]. Under these conditions,
the increased utilization of body fat will lead to accelerated
starvation and death when the stores of fat are depleted; also
survival studies of experimentally-contaminated birds maintained at low environmental temperatures have suggested that
adverse weather may accelerate the death of birds contaminated
at sea [45].

Although the topic has not been examined experimentally,
the increased metabolism and the attendant increase in respiration rate of the oil-contaminated birds will also lead inevitably to higher rates of respiratory water loss; in some
birds, particularly juveniles, this additional water loss will
exacerbate the osmoregulatory imbalance that occurs following
ingestion of petroleum (see section on "Effects on Juveniles").

SYSTEMIC EFFECTS

The domestic Pekin duck, and its ancestor the common mallard duck, can live equally well in either freshwater or
marine environments. For this reason, these birds make good
experimental models and have been used frequently for studies
on the adaptive responses of birds exposed to simulated conditions of the marine environment and the possible effects of
ingested petroleum on these adaptive mechanisms.

Laboratory studies have shown that both juvenile and
adult ducks will eat food that has been contaminated with petroleum and petroleum products and, although concentrations of
up to 3 ml crude oil per 100 g dry mash do not seem to diminish the palatability of the food, similar concentrations of
petroleum products such as No. 2 fuel oil are not consumed
with such characteristic voracity. In the wild, contaminated
food may be ingested in the form of organisms that have themselves consumed petroleum or plant material to which petroleum
may have adhered. Drinking water, particularly at the shoreline or other places where wave action occurs, may also contain droplets of petroleum in suspension. Ingestion of petroleum in the form of contaminated food and drinking water, however, is not the only way in which seabirds may ingest petroleum. Observers in the field have reported that birds attempt
to clean their feathers immediately after they become contaminated by an oil slick on the surface of the ocean [e.g., 4] and
it has been shown that ducks will preen up to 5% of the

contaminating oil from their feathers during the first 8 days after exposure [49]. Studies using radioactively labelled crude oil have indicated that contaminated ducks may ingest up to 7 ml of oil per kg body weight per day in the course of preening their plumage [50].

The results of recent studies in these and other laboratories suggest that, at least in ducks, the apparent systemic effects of petroleum may be different at several stages of development. For reasons of clarity, therefore, we have summarized all experimental studies according to the effects that petroleum may have on birds during prenatal, juvenile, and adult phases of their life cycles.

Effects on Developing Embryos

The fact that further embryonic development is arrested in eggs that have been sprayed with oil has been known for many years [51]. This effect has been attributed mainly to the impaired passage of respiratory gasses through the shells of contaminated eggs. In the 1930's, A.O. Gross of Bowdoin College, Maine, suggested that spraying eggs with oil might be used as a method to control the herring gull populations in some parts of New England. His recommendations were adopted by the U.S. Fish and Wildlife Service and records suggest that some decline in population size occurred between 1940 and 1952 when the program was discontinued; some details of this program have been reviewed by Kadlec and Drury [52]. In 1956, Rittinghaus [53] also noted that eggs that had become contaminated with petroleum from the feathers of brooding Cabot's tern did not hatch, and a similar effect of petroleum was observed by Birkhead et al. in 1973 [54] for great black-backed gulls.

This effect was tested experimentally by Hartung [55] who smeared small volumes of mineral oil over the shells of fertile duck eggs that were being incubated artificially. He also applied the same material to the breast feathers of brooding mallard ducks. Coating the eggs with mineral oil reduced their hatchability to 20% compared to a value of 80% normally found among uncontaminated eggs. When fertilized eggs were incubated naturally by oil-contaminated females, none of the embryos survived. Also, in a study designed to evaluate the effects of herbicide and pesticide solvents, Kopischke found that when fertile pheasant eggs were sprayed with diesel oil, their hatchability was reduced to zero [56].

In Hartung's [55] and Kopischke's [56] experiments, most of the shell surfaces were coated with oil and there is little doubt that the embryonic mortality they observed was due to impaired gaseous exchange through the egg shell. However, recent studies by investigators at the Patuxent Wildlife Research Center at Laurel, Maryland, have focussed attention on

the possibility that some petroleum hydrocarbons may penetrate
the shell and affect embryonic development through a systemic
action [57,58]. These workers, using fertile mallard and
eider duck eggs, have applied very small volumes of a No. 2
fuel oil to only a portion of the total egg shell surface.
Significant increases in mortality have been observed when
less than 2% of the surface of mallard duck eggs are contaminated with 1 μl of this oil; when larger volumes of oil are
applied, the mortality among the developing embryos is increased further (Table 6). They have also observed that, compared to the effect of a similar volume of fuel oil, the application of a mixture of saturated paraffins causes the death
of fewer embryos at a much later stage of their development,
even though samples of the paraffin mixture and the fuel oil
covered similar areas of the egg shells (Table 6). These data
provide convincing evidence that some constituents in fuel oil
may penetrate the shell and arrest the development of embryos.
Partial confirmation of these observations has been obtained
from a similar series of experiments on eider duck eggs [58].
Eggs from this species, however, were collected in the field
and the oil samples were applied to the shells at a later
stage of embryonic development. Nevertheless, a significant
increase in mortality occurred when the eggs were contaminated
with very small volumes of No. 2 fuel oil and again it is improbable that the effect was due to impaired gaseous exchange.

Effects on Juveniles

Response to Dose
    In earlier experiments we had observed that, although
ducklings would eat contaminated food, the mortality rates
were high. We therefore designed a series of experiments to
examine more precisely the effect of different quantities of
ingested crude oil on the mortality of seawater-adapted ducklings. Each group consisted of 30 birds that had been adapted
to seawater for 3 days and during this time their daily food
intake was monitored. On the fourth day, the uncontaminated
food was replaced with weighed amounts of food containing
known volumes of South Louisiana crude oil. Even at the highest concentrations of crude oil used in these experiments, the
birds consumed normal quantities of food (10 g dry weight per
100 g body weight) during the first two days. Thus, although
the intake of food containing the high concentrations of oil
diminished markedly on the third day, we are confident that
proportionate volumes of oil were consumed by each experimental group of birds during the first and second days.
    Very few deaths occurred when birds were fed food con-
taining only 5% crude oil and 87% of the experimental group
was still alive at the end of the 6-day experiment (Fig. 5).

TABLE 6

The survival of developing mallard duck embryos following contamination of the egg shell with various quantities of petroleum and petroleum hydrocarbons. After the fertility of the eggs had been confirmed on the eighth day of incubation, the shells were contaminated in the region of the air sac with the indicated volumes of either petroleum or the petroleum hydrocarbon mixture

Treatment	Area of shell contaminated with oil (% total shell area)	Mortality (% of total number of eggs incubated)	Mean age of embryos at death (days)	Mean body weight of survivors (g)	
				24 hr after hatching	29 days after hatching
Untreated controls	0	2-12	23.7	43.3	738
Paraffin mixture[a] (50 μl)	34.0	28	21.6	41.1	756
No. 2 fuel oil[b]					
1 μl	1.3	37	10.8	42.3	743
5 μl	5.0	55	11.1	43.0	756
10 μl	11.5	88	10.1	41.5	670
20 μl	20.2	98	9.4	–	–
50 μl	32.1	100	8.5	–	–

From Albers [57].

a The following paraffin compounds were mixed in equal proportions: pentadecane, hexadecane, heptadecane, octadecane, nonadecane, 2,2,4,6,6-pentamethylheptane, 2,2,4,6,8,8-heptamethyl-nonane, 2,6,10,14-tetramethylpentadecane, decahydronaphthalene.

b American Petroleum Institute Reference Oil No. III containing 38.2% aromatic hydrocarbons.

380

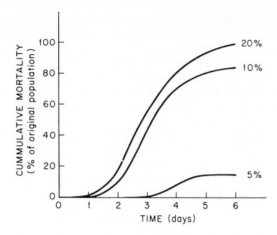

Fig. 5. The cumulative mortality among groups of 30 Pekin
ducklings given food contaminated with 5, 10, and 20% (v/w),
South Louisiana crude oil (Holmes, Cronshaw, and Crocker, unpublished).

This low mortality rate was in marked contrast to that observed in the group of birds given food containing 10% crude
oil. In this group, 73% of the colony died during the first
4 days and although the mortality rate declined thereafter,
only 4 birds survived to the end of the 6th day (Fig. 5).
When the concentration of crude oil in food was doubled once
more, 80% of the colony died during the first 4 days and none
survived after 6 days (Fig. 5).
      To our surprise, many of the surviving birds seemed to be
able to withstand contaminated food indefinitely, although
their growth rates were somewhat lower than those of control
birds. This was particularly apparent among the survivors of
the group fed 5% crude oil in their food. These birds were
fed the oil-contaminated food for a further 2 weeks after the
experiment and no further deaths were recorded.

Changes in Intestinal Transfer
      During the course of these experiments, we noted that
those seawater-adapted ducklings that died following the ingestion of crude oil often showed signs of impaired electrolyte balance. Furthermore, their symptoms resembled those
seen in birds that failed to adapt to a seawater diet. This
failure is associated with an acute dysfunction of one or more
of the interdependent osmoregulatory mechanisms that have
evolved in marine birds. These mechanisms enable the birds to
absorb ingested seawater from the gut and excrete the large
amounts of salt, particularly Na^+, without incurring an excessive loss of water. To this end the nasal glands have

developed as extrarenal excretory organs and by augmenting the limited excretory capacity of the kidney, successful adaptation to a marine habitat is assured. Both neural and hormonal regulators are involved in the initiation and continuation of the renal, extrarenal, and intestinal homeostatic mechanisms [59-61]. Included among these regulators are the adrenal steroid hormones. We have shown that when ducklings are fed seawater, the rates of Na^+ and water transfer across the intestinal mucosa are increased and the development of this increase seems to be stimulated through the action of the adrenocortical hormones [62]. Furthermore, the ingestion of a specific corticosteroid inhibitor, such as spironolactone, prevents the development of this increase and the survival of seawater-fed ducklings is threatened [62,63]. As a working hypothesis, therefore, we proposed that the necessary development and continuation of increased mucosal transfer in seawater-adapted ducklings might also be sensitive to the presence of petroleum hydrocarbons in the small intestine.

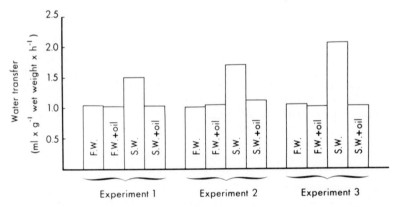

Fig. 6. The effect of a single oral dose (0.2 ml) of Santa Barbara crude oil on the rates of mucosal transfer in the small intestine of ducklings maintained on either fresh water or seawater. In Experiments 1 and 2 the transfer rates were measured 24 hr and 4 days respectively after the oil was given, and in Experiment 3 the birds were allowed to adapt to seawater for 3 days, the oil was given at the beginning of the fourth day of adaptation and the mucosal transfer rates were determined 24 hr later (From Crocker, Cronshaw, and Holmes [64]).

In these experiments we fed small volumes of ingested crude oil to ducklings and its acute effect on the intestinal mucosa was measured *in vitro* [64]. Although the administration of crude oil had no effect on the basal rate of mucosal transfer found in ducklings maintained on fresh water, the adaptive response in birds given seawater was inhibited (Fig. 6). This effect was apparent 24 hr after the oil was administered, and the effect of a single dose persisted for at least 4 days (Fig. 6). Furthermore, the increment in mucosal transfer that had developed during a previous 3-day exposure to seawater was abolished 24 hr after a single dose of crude oil had been given (Fig. 6). The degree to which the adaptive response of the intestinal mucosa was inhibited by different crude oils varied according to their geographic origins

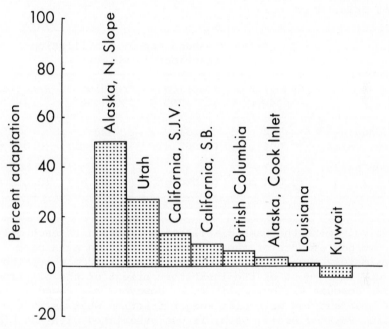

Fig. 7. *A comparison of the effects of crude oils from different locations on the adaptive responses occurring in the small intestinal mucosa of ducklings maintained on seawater. Each bird received 0.2 ml of a crude oil at the time of transfer to seawater and the increase in mucosal water transfer observed 4 days later was expressed as a percentage of the increase which occurred in untreated birds similarly adapted to seawater.*

$$\% \ Adaptation = \frac{\left(T_{SW+oil} - T_{FW} \right)}{\left(T_{SW} - T_{FW} \right)} \cdot 100$$

where T_{FW}, T_{SW} and T_{SW+oil} represent respectively the mucosal water transfer rates (ml/g wet tissue per hr) in untreated birds maintained on fresh water and seawater or seawater-maintained birds given a single dose of crude oil (From Crocker, Cronshaw, and Holmes [65]).

(Fig. 7). Furthermore, when the effects of distillation fractions prepared from two crude oils of disparate composition were compared (Table 7), the inhibition was not associated

TABLE 7

Relative abundances of the distillation fractions derived from two chemically different crude oils. The values in parentheses indicate the volumes of each distillation fraction present in 0.2 ml of the San Joaquin Valley, California, and Paradox Basin, Utah, crude oils

Source	Relative abundance of distillation fractions (% weight)			
	Fraction 1 <240°C	Fraction 2 245°-399°C	Fraction 3 399°-482°C	Fraction 4 >482°C
San Joaquin Valley, Calif.	2 (0.004 ml)	31 (0.062 ml)	20 (0.04 ml)	47 (0.094 ml)
Paradox Basin, Utah	27 (0.054 ml)	32 (0.064 ml)	13 (0.026 ml)	28 (0.056 ml)

exclusively with the same distillation fraction of each oil. The combined effects of these fractions were in each case approximately equal to that of the whole oil from which they were derived. Most of the inhibitory effect of the oil from the San Joaquin Valley, California, however, was found in the least abundant low molecular weight fraction whereas in the oil from Paradox Basin, Utah, it was associated with the highest molecular weight fraction (Fig. 8).

We have recently observed that the adrenal steroid hormone, corticosterone, will induce high rates of mucosal transfer in the small intestine of freshwater-maintained ducklings [63]. In this context, therefore, it is interesting to note that if seawater-maintained ducklings are treated with this hormone prior to receiving small doses of crude oil the mucosal transfer rates are not suppressed (Fig. 9). In addition, to providing a circumstantial insight into the nature of the inhibitory action of ingested crude oil, these findings suggest that a simple therapy based on the administration of corticosterone may be effective in increasing the survival rate of some oil-contaminated birds.

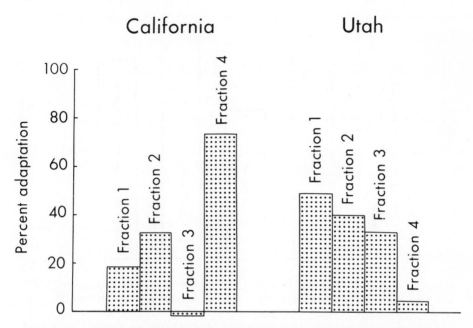

Fig. 8.   A comparison of the effects of distillation fractions derived from a California (San Joaquin Valley) and a Utah (Paradox Basin) crude oil on the adaptive responses occurring in the intestinal mucosa of ducklings maintained on seawater. At the time of transfer to seawater each bird received a single oral dose equivalent to the volume distilled from 0.2 ml of crude oil (see Table 7). The mucosal water transfer was measured 4 days later and the adaptive response was calculated as in Figure 7 (From Crocker, Cronshaw, and Holmes [65]).

Effects on Mature Birds

Responses to Environmental Stress

In an earlier section, we have mentioned that the ducklings which survived an initial period of exposure to oil-contaminated food seemed to be able to tolerate this diet almost indefinitely. These birds, however, were maintained in a relatively protected environment where two or three birds were housed together in cages. But when some of them were transferred to open runs, where the population was comparatively dense, many died within a few days and at autopsy, we found that the adrenal glands were enlarged and the lymphoepithelial tissues were atrophic. These observations suggested that the prolonged consumption of oil-contaminated food may have

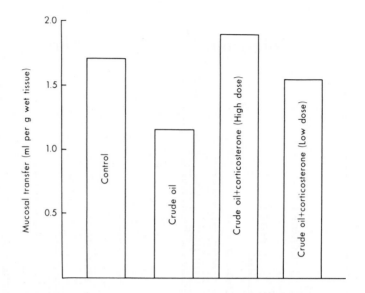

Fig. 9. *The effect of 0.2 ml of ingested crude oil (Kuwait) on the mucosal water transfer rates of ducklings given sea-water to drink. The suppression of water transfer, that char-acterizes the effect of crude oil ingestion in ducklings, did not occur when the birds were pretreated with the adrenal steroid hormone, corticosterone (From Crocker and Holmes [63]).*

constituted a physiological stress to these birds and that when they were exposed to an additional stress, such as that imposed through competition with other birds, they succumbed.

To test this hypothesis, a series of experiments was planned to examine the effects of ingested petroleum on groups of seawater-adapted ducks maintained under stressful and non-stressful environmental conditions. Known volumes of Kuwait and South Louisiana crude oil were mixed each day with weighed amounts of dry poultry food and the experimental groups were given their respective mixtures of contaminated food at 0800 hours each day. At 1600 hours the food remaining in the trays was weighed and the daily intakes of food and petroleum were estimated. The birds were maintained on this feeding regimen for 100 days and during this period their mean daily food intake was similar to that of the birds fed uncontaminated food (70 g dry food/kg body weight per day). For the first 50 days the birds were maintained in a room at 27°C. During this period no deaths occurred among either the control birds or those given food mixed with Kuwait crude oil and only one died in the group fed South Louisiana crude oil (Fig. 10). After

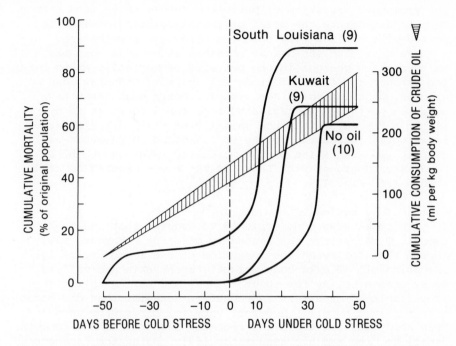

Fig. 10. A comparison of the cumulative mortalities observed among groups of mature Pekin ducks fed uncontaminated food and constant daily amounts of either South Louisiana or Kuwait crude oil. After each group of birds had been maintained at 27°C for 50 days the temperature of the room was lowered to 5°C. Throughout the 100-day experimental period the mean daily consumptions of petroleum by the birds given food containing South Louisiana and Kuwait crude oils were 3.0 and 2.4 ml per kg body weight. Numerals in parentheses indicate the number of birds in each group (From Holmes, Cronshaw, and Gorsline [66].

each group of birds had been maintained at 27°C for 50 days, the temperature of the room was lowered to 5°C. Three days later the birds fed South Louisiana crude oil started to die and the mortality continued until only one bird was alive after 23 days of exposure to cold (Fig. 10). The birds fed Kuwait crude oil started to die after 10 days of exposure to cold and after 25 days of exposure to cold two-thirds of the group had died (Fig. 10). However, the birds fed uncontaminated food were also unable to tolerate prolonged exposure to cold, although compared with the birds fed oil-contaminated food, the onset of mortality occurred later and fewer birds died during the experimental period (Fig. 10). In summary, therefore, the effects of cold-stress on birds subjected to the prolonged ingestion of petroleum-contaminated food seemed only to accelerate the onset of mortality and diminish the period of sustained cold that the birds could withstand.

We have also shown that stresses other than cold may cause similar changes in the patterns of mortality among birds fed chronic low doses of crude oil (Holmes, Cronshaw, and Crocker, unpublished). For example, Pekin ducks that have consumed petroleum-contaminated food for 2 mo start to die within a few days after the salinity of their drinking water is abruptly increased from 60 to 75% standard seawater and graphic representation of the mortality rates among these birds are congruent with those of the birds exposed to cold stress (cf. Fig. 10).

Ovarian Dysfunction

There is also some evidence to suggest that ingested petroleum may affect the fecundity of birds. Hartung [55] showed that following the ingestion of small amounts of lubricating oil (2 g/kg body weight), both Pekin and mallard ducks ceased to lay for about 2 weeks and during this time they displayed much less reproductive behavior than did birds that received no oil. However, very few birds were used in this study and the topic has recently been reexamined in more detail by Grau and his associates [67]. Using the Japanese quail as their experimental model, these workers have shown that a single large dose of Bunker C fuel oil will completely inhibit laying for 6 to 8 days and that smaller doses not only reduce the rate of laying but the hatchability of the eggs laid during the days immediately following the administration of oil is also reduced. Indeed, when the dose of Bunker C fuel oil was insufficient to reduce the rate of laying, the hatchability of the eggs was still slightly lower than normal for several days whereas comparable doses of mineral oil and refined safflower seed oil affected neither the rate of laying nor the hatchability of the eggs. Differential effects on oviposition and hatchability were also identified following the ingestion of a crude oil. Thus, when a relatively high dose of Kuwait crude oil was given, the rate of laying remained almost normal but the hatchability of the eggs laid during the next 3 days was reduced below 50% of that found among eggs laid by the control birds. The results of these studies are summarized in Table 8.

When quail are maintained on a simulated daylight schedule (14 hr light, 10 hr dark), they normally deposit a ring of dark-staining yolk during the daylight hours and a ring of light-staining yolk during the hours of darkness [68]. However, the eggs laid during the few days following ingestion of

TABLE 8

The egg production and hatchability of eggs laid by Japanese quail following the administration of single oral doses of petroleum or vegetable oil on day zero. Production is expressed as eggs laid per day per 100 birds and hatchability is expressed as the percentage hatched from eggs containing live embryos after 7 days incubation.

Oil administered	Egg production	Hatchability
Mineral oil or safflower oil	>90%	>80%
500 mg Bunker C	Zero for 6-8 days	Zero
200 mg Bunker C	Reduced to 40% on day 2, 30% on day 3; and returned to normal by day 6	<70% on day 1 <50% on day 2 <30% on day 3 <70% on day 4 Normal on day 5
100 mg Bunker C	Normal (>90%)	Slightly reduced for 3 days (>80%)
800 mg Kuwait crude	Slightly reduced for 3 days	<50%
800 mg Prudhoe Bay crude	Reduced to 52% on day 1, 44% on day 2, 72% on day 3; returned to normal by day 4	Unaffected
800 mg Cook Inlet crude	Reduced to 58% on day 1, 50% on day 2, 71% on day 3; returned to normal by day 5	Unaffected

From Grau, Roudybush, Dobbs, and Wathen [67] and unpublished data of these authors.

a single dose of petroleum show irregularities in these patterns of yolk deposition [67]. Less than normal amounts of yolk, consisting of abnormally small yolk spheres (10-30 microns in diameter), are deposited during the first night after dosing and during the next day a narrow band of dense staining yolk is deposited. Also, during formalin fixation, prior to

staining with potassium dichromate, cracks often develop between the spheres of yolk deposited in the days immediately
following ingestion of petroleum. After high doses of petroleum, when laying and hatchability of eggs are diminished,
this pattern of yolk deposition may persist for at least 2
days [67].

Although the mechanism of petroleum action on ovarian
function is not known, the effects are clearly systemic. It
is possible that some components of petroleum are absorbed
from the intestinal tract and following transportation to the
liver and the ovary they may be deposited in the yolk. In
seabirds, however, it is also possible that ingested petroleum
may act indirectly to modify ovarian function; partial inhibition of the Na^+ and water uptake mechanisms in the intestinal
mucosa may cause changes in the ion composition of yolk and
thus influence embryo survival [64,65,67].

PATHOLOGICAL EFFECTS

There have been several pathological examinations of tissues collected from oil-contaminated seabirds. Some workers
have described conditions that may have been caused by the
ingestion of crude oil or petroleum derivatives but others
have been unable to show any pathological symptoms attributable to petroleum.

Hartung and Hunt [50] claimed to identify several pathological conditions both in dead birds that had been contaminated with crude oil in the wild and in birds that had been
fed commercial crude oil derivatives in the laboratory. Several oils caused irritation of the gastrointestinal mucosa and
these birds showed a slight anemia that was attributed to
hemorrhage. A high incidence of lipid pneumonia was observed
in birds that had ingested oil and other conditions reported
included fatty degeneration of the liver, acinar atrophy of
the pancreas, adrenocortical hyperplasia, and toxic nephrosis.
Laboratory studies also showed that the plasma glutamic-oxa-
lacetic transaminase levels were increased significantly and
the bromsulphalein liver function tests showed significantly
increased retention of the dye after the ingestion of high
doses of diesel oil.

Clark and Kennedy [8] reported that Beer examined over a
hundred oil-contaminated birds that had died in captivity following the *Torrey Canyon* disaster and the most common diseases
he found were enteritis, aspergillosis, and infective arthri-
tis.

Necropsies were also performed on 119 birds that died in
captivity after exposure to the Bunker C fuel oil that was
spilled in the San Francisco Bay in 1971 [69]. These birds,
which had been captured by volunteer workers and had been

subjected to initial cleansing, were further cleansed with mineral oil, Basic H, and poly complex A-11. Severe tissue damage was found in the intestinal tract, liver, and kidneys. However, these workers also found that Bunker C fuel oil was not lethal when fed to juvenile chickens and mallard ducks.

In another experimental study over a hundred mallard ducks were contaminated with Santa Barbara crude oil [70]. Some of these birds were later cleansed and at autopsies performed during a subsequent one-month period no pathological changes were observed. We also have been unable to detect any histological differences between intestinal tissue from control and oil-treated ducklings even though Na$^+$ and water transfer by the intestinal mucosa of these birds had been severely attentuated through oil ingestion [64,65].

In another experimental series we gave 90 successive daily doses of petroleum to a group of mature Pekin ducks that had been previously adapted to seawater. The petroleum was given by stomach tube each day immediately before feeding. Two birds received 5 ml of Santa Barbara crude oil and similar doses of Kuwait crude oil and No. 2 fuel oil were given to two other pairs of birds. One of the birds received 10 ml of Santa Barbara crude oil. With the exception of one of the birds given Kuwait crude oil, all birds ate normal quantities of food and they either maintained or increased their body weights during the period of treatment. Occasional regurgitation of oil caused some contamination of the feathers and in the birds given crude oil a characteristic dark colored material that resembled petroleum was seen in the feces, and feathers around the cloaca became stained by a black contamination.

At autopsy, none of the birds showed any gross abnormal clinical conditions and, except for the liver and adrenal weights in some birds, all organ weights were within ranges found normally in seawater-adapted birds. The liver and adrenal weights of birds given No. 2 fuel oil were low and resembled those found in birds maintained on fresh water. The adrenal weights of the birds given Santa Barbara and Kuwait crude oils were high and there was a corresponding reduction in the lymphoepithelial tissues suggesting possible high levels of adrenocortical activity.

In all birds, the lungs, liver, and intestine appeared normal, healthy, and indistinguishable from these tissues in untreated birds. Although occasional regurgitation of administered oil occurred, none of the birds showed symptoms of lipid pneumonia and none died during the experimental period. In the case of birds treated with the Santa Barbara and Kuwait crude oils, an accumulation of black bituminous material was found in the caecal pouches; these oils contained approximately 5.0% by weight of asphaltenes. In contrast,

there was no black deposit in the caecal pouches of birds
given No. 2 fuel oil and this product contained no asphaltenes.

The intestines of birds treated with the crude oils
showed changes in the organization of the villi. Mucosal tissue from uncontaminated control birds normally show elongated
villi with rounded or pointed tips but many of the birds given
petroleum showed villi with flattened tips and the mucosal
epithelial cells were frayed-out at the tips. There was no
evidence of granuloma or necrosis and there was no evidence of
inflammation as judged by the normal population of plasmo-
cytes, eosinophils, or polymorphonuclear leucocytes in the mucosal region of the gut. There was a distinct increase in the
number of lymphocytes in the *lamina propria* and also the number of muscle fibers in this region appeared greater than in
the control birds. The crypts of Lieberkühn appeared normal
in all specimens and contained many mitotic figures.

The adrenal glands of birds given either a crude oil or
No. 2 fuel oil showed a distinct zonation which was not apparent in the control birds. This zonation was due to an increase in the size and number of lipid droplets in the interrenal cells of the subcapsular zone of the glands. In the
inner parts of the glands the interrenal cells were smaller
and polygonal.

These pathological studies seem to indicate that mature
ducks maintained under laboratory conditions tolerate well the
chronic administration of at least two crude oils and one petroleum distillation product. The increase in body weight of
some of the birds and the absence of mortality in any of the
groups studied was remarkable and quite unexpected. This is
especially so since one of the birds consumed almost a liter
of Santa Barbara crude oil and the remainder of the birds consumed 450 ml of either Kuwait crude oil or No. 2 fuel oil during the 90-day experimental period. The histological patterns
of the adrenal glands in birds treated with oil, however, suggest a higher than normal level of adrenocortical function
occurs under conditions of chronic petroleum ingestion. The
development of this hyperadrenocortical condition may account
for the high mortality seen when the birds fed petroleum-contaminated diets were exposed to cold-stress (cf. Fig. 10).

SCIENTIFIC NAMES OF BIRDS CITED

Coot, American, *Fulica americana*
Cormorant, Brandt's, *Phalocrocorax penicillatus*
Cormorant, double-crested, *Phalocrocorax auritus*
Guillemot, Brunich's, *Uria lonvia*
Guillemot, common, *Uria aalge*
Duck, black, *Anas rubripes*

Duck, canvasback, *Aythya valisineria*
Duck, eider, *Somateria mollissima*
Duck, golden eye, *Bucephala clangula*
Duck, long-tail, *Clangula hyemalis*
Duck, mallard, *Anas platyrhynchos*
Duck, Pekin, *Anas platyrhynchos*
Duck, ruddy, *Oxyura jamaicensis*
Grebe, eared, *Podiceps caspicus*
Grebe, horned, *Podiceps auritus*
Grebe, pied-billed, *Podilymbus podiceps*
Grebe, western, *Aechmorphorus occidentalis*
Gull, *Larus sp.*
Gull, great black-backed, *Larus ridibundus*
Gull, herring, *Larus argentatus*
Kittiwake, *Rissa tridactyla*
Loon, common, *Gavia immer*
Loon, red-throated, *Gavia stellata*
Merganser, *Mergus merganser*
Murre, common, *Uria aalge*
Penguin, jackass, *Spheniscus demersus*
Puffin, *Fratercula arctica*
Quail, Japanese, *Coturnix coturnix*
Razorbill, *Alca torda*
Scaup, *Aythya marila*
Scoter, surf, *Melanitta perspicillata*
Scoter, velvet, *Melanitta fusca*
Tern, Cabot's, *Thalasseus sandvicensis*

REFERENCES

1. Mothersole, J. (1910). The Isles of Scilly, Their Story, Their Folk and Their Flowers. Religious Tract Society, London.
2. Parslow, J.L.F. (1967). A census of auks. Br. Trust Ornithol. News 23:8-9.
3. Parslow, J.L.F. (1967). Changes in status among breeding birds in Britain and Ireland. Br. Birds 60:2-47, 97-122, 177-202.
4. Bourne, W.R.P. (1968). Oil pollution and bird populations. In: The Biological Effects of Oil Pollution on Littoral Communities (J.D. Carthy and D.R. Arthur, eds.), Suppl. to Field Studies, Vol. 2, p. 99-121. Obtainable from E.W. Classey, Ltd., Hampton, Middx., England.
5. Aldrich, J.W. (1938). A recent oil pollution and its effect on the water birds in the San Francisco Bay area. Bird Lore 40:110-4.
6. Goethe, F. (1968). The effects of oil pollution on populations of marine and coastal birds. Helgol. Wiss. Meeresunters 17:370-4.

7.   Richardson, F. (1956). Sea birds affected by oil from
      the freighter *Seagate*. Murrelet 37:20-2.
8.   Clark, R.B. and J.R. Kennedy (1968). Rehabilitation of
      oiled seabirds. Report to the Advisory Committee on Oil
      Pollution of the Sea (U.K.), p. 1-57. Department of
      Zoology, The University of Newcastle upon Tyne, England.
9.   Bourne, W.R.P., J.D. Parrack, and G.R. Potts (1967).
      Birds killed in the *Torrey Canyon* disaster. Nature 215:
      1123-5.
10.   Joensen, A. (1971). Olieforureninger 1970. Dansk Vildt-
      forskning 1970-71:53-5.
11.   Swennen, C. and A.L. Spaans (1970). De Sterfte van
      Zeevogels door Olie in Februari 1969 in het Waddengebied.
      Het Vogeljaar 18:233-45.
12.   Drinkwater, B., M. Leonard, and S. Black (1971). Oil
      pollution and sea birds. In: Biological and Oceano-
      graphical Survey of the Santa Barbara Oil Spill (D.
      Straughan, ed.), p. 313-24. Allan Hancock Foundation,
      University of Southern California, Los Angeles.
13.   Straughan, D. (1971). Oil pollution and seabirds. In:
      Biological and Oceanographic Survey of the Santa Barbara
      Oil Spill 1969-1970 (D. Straughan, ed.), Vol. I, p. 307-
      12. Allan Hancock Foundation, University of Southern
      California, Los Angeles.
14.   Hope-Jones, P., G. Howells, E.I.S. Rees, and J. Wilson
      (1970). Effect of *Hamilton Trader* oil on birds in the
      Irish Sea in May 1969. Br. Birds 63:97-110.
15.   Woikkeli, M. and J. Virtanen (1972). The *Palva* oil
      tanker disaster in the Finnish south-western archipelago.
      II. Effects of oil pollution on the eider population in
      the archipelagos of Kökar and Föglö, south-western Fin-
      land. Aqua. Fenn., p. 122-8.
16.   Greenwood, J.J.D., R.J. Donally, C.J. Feare, N.J. Gordon,
      and G. Waterston (1971). A massive wreck of oiled birds:
      northeast Britain, Winter 1970. Scott. Birds 6:235-50.
17.   Clark, R.B. (1973). Impact of acute and chronic oil
      pollution on seabirds. In: Background Papers for a
      Workshop on Inputs, Fates, and Effects of Petroleum in
      the Marine Environment II, p. 619-34. Ocean Affairs
      Board, National Academy of Sciences, Washington, D.C.
18.   Brown, R.G.B. (1970). Bird mortality caused by the *Arrow*
      and *Irving Whale* oil spills. Can. Wildl. Serv., unpub-
      lished administration report, 23 p.
19.   U.S. Department of the Interior (1970). Kodiak oil pol-
      lution incident, February-March 1970: Summary Report,
      Federal Water Quality Administration, Washington, D.C.,
      23 p.
20.   Orr, R.T. (1971). Oil, wildlife and people. Pac. Dis-
      covery 24:24-9.

21. Joensen, A.H. (1973). Danish seabird disasters in 1972. Mar. Pollut. Bull. 4:117-8.

22. Bourne, W.R.P. and T.R.E. Devlin (1969). Birds and oil. Birds 2:176-8.

23. Bourne, W.R.P. and T.R.E. Devlin (1971). The pollution plot thickens. Birds 3:190-2, 207.

24. Bibby, C.J. and W.R.P. Bourne (1971). More problems for threatened birds. Birds 3:307-9.

25. Bibby, C.J. and W.R.P. Bourne (1972). Trouble on oiled waters. Birds 4:160-2.

26. Bibby, C.J. and W.R.P. Bourne (1974). Pollution still kills. Birds 5:30-1.

27. Croxall, J.P. (1975). The effect of oil on nature conservation, especially birds. In: Petroleum and the Continental Shelf on North West Europe, Environmental Protection, Vol. 2, p. 93-101. Applied Science Publishers, Ltd., Barking, England

28. IMCO (1973). The environmental and financial consequences of oil pollution from ships. Report of Study No. 6, submitted by the U.K. Appendix 3, The biological effects of oil pollution of the oceans, U.K., Atomic Energy Authority, Programmes Analysis Unit, Chilton, Didcot, Berks.

29. Joensen, A.H. (1972). Oil pollution and seabirds in Denmark 1935-1968. Dan. Rev. Game Biol. 6(8):1-24.

30. Joensen, A.H. (1972). Studies on oil pollution and sea birds in Denmark, 1968-1971. Dan. Rev. Game Biol. 6(9): 1-32.

31. Joiris, G. (1972). The behavior of oil covered birds at sea. Aves 9:136-7.

32. Vermeer, K. and G.G. Anweiler (1975). Oil threat to aquatic birds along the Yukon Coast, Canada. Wilson Bull. 87:467-80.

33. Vermeer, K. and R. Vermeer (1975). Oil threat to birds on the Canadian West Coast. Can. Field-Nat. 89:278-98.

34. Frost, P.G.H., W.R. Siegfried, and J. Cooper (1976). Conservation of the jackass penguin (*Speniscus demersus* (L)). Biol. Conserv. 9:79-99.

35. Westphal, A. and M.K. Rowan (1971). Some observations on the effects of oil pollution on the jackass penguin. Ostrich Suppl. 8:521-26.

36. Percy, J.F., A. Westphal, and E.O.J. Westphal (1972). The rescue and cleaning of oil polluted seabirds in South Africa, Aug. 1969-July 1972. Report to SANCCOB, South African National Foundation for the Conservation of Coastal Birds, Cape Town, 23 p. (Mimeograph).

37. Upenskii, S.M. (1956). Bird bazaars of Novaya Zemlya Academy of Sciences, Moscow, USSR. Eng. Translation: Can. Wildl. Serv., Transl. Russ. Game Report No. 4.

38. Southern, H.N., R. Carrick, and W.G. Potter (1965). The natural history of a population of guillemots (*Uria aalge* Pont.). J. Anim. Ecol. 34:649-65.

39. Tuck, L.M. (1961). The murres: Their distribution, populations and biology, a study of the genus *Uria*. Can. Wildl. Ser. 1, Monogr. Nat. Parks Branch, Ottawa.

40. Cramp, S., W.R.P. Bourne, and D. Saunders (1974). The Seabirds of Britain and Ireland. Collins, London, 287 p.

41. Fisher, J. and R.M. Lockley (1954). Seabirds. Collins, London.

42. Giles, L.A. and J. Livingston (1960). Oil pollution on the seas. Trans. N. Am. Wildl. Nat. Resour. Conf. 25: 297-302.

43. Lemmetyinen, R. (1966). Damage to waterfowl in the Baltic caused by waste oil. Suom. Riista 19:63-71.

44. Monnat, J.Y. (1969) Statut actuel des oiseaus marins incheurs en Bretagne 6 ème partie, Haut Trégor et Grelo (de Trebeurdon à Paimpol). Ar. Vran. 2:1-24.

45. Hartung, R. (1967). Energy metabolism in oil-covered ducks. J. Wildl. Manage. 31:789-804.

46. Hawkes, A.L. (1961). A review of the nature and extent of damage caused by oil pollution at sea. Trans. N. Am. Wildl. Nat. Resour. Conf. 26:343-55.

47. Hunt, G.S. (1961). Waterfowl losses on the lower Detroit River due to oil pollution. In: Proceedings of the Fourth Conference, Univ. Mich., Great Lakes Res. Dir., Inst. Sci. Technol. Publ. 7, p. 10-26.

48. Erickson, R.C. (1963). Oil pollution and migratory birds. Atl. Nat. 18:5-14.

49. Hartung, R. (1963). (Wildlife) Ingestion of oil by waterfowl. Pap. Mich. Acad. Sci. Arts Lett. 48:49-55.

50. Hartung, R. and G.S. Hunt (1966). Toxicity of some oils to waterfowl. J. Wildl. Manage. 30:564-70.

51. Bourne, W.R.P. (1969). Chronological list of ornithological oil-pollution incidents. Seabird Bull. 7:3-8.

52. Kadlec, J.A. and W.H. Drury (1968). Structure of the New England Herring gull population. Ecology 49:644-76.

53. Rittinghaus, H. (1956). Etwas über die "indirekte" verbreitung der Ölpest in einem Seevogelsschutzgebeit. Ornithol. Mitt. 8:43-6.

54. Birkhead, T.R., C. Lloyd, and P. Corkhill (1973). Oiled seabirds successfully cleaning their plumage. Br. Birds 66:353.

55. Hartung, R. (1965). Some effects of oiling on reproduction of ducks. J. Wildl. Manage. 29:872-4.

56. Kopischke, E.D. (1972). The effect of 2,4-D and diesel fuel on egg hatchability. J. Wildl. Manage. 36:1353-56.

57. Albers, P.H. (1976). Effects of external applications of oil on hatchability of mallard eggs. In: Proceedings of Symposium on Fate and Effects of Petroleum Hydrocarbons in Marine Ecosystems and Organisms (D. Wolfe, ed.). In press. Pergamon Press, New York.

58. Szaro, R.C. and P.H. Albers (1976). Effects of external applications of oil on common eider eggs. In: Proceedings of Symposium on Fate and Effects of Petroleum Hydrocarbons in Marine Ecosystems and Organisms (D. Wolfe, ed.). In press. Pergamon Press, New York.

59. Holmes, W.N., J.G. Phillips, and I. Chester Jones (1963). Adrenocortical factors associated with adaption of vertebrates to marine environments. Recent Prog. Horm. Res. 19:619-72.

60. Holmes, W.N. (1972). Regulation of electrolyte balance in marine birds with special reference to the role of the pituitary-adrenal axis in the duck (*Anas platyrhynchos*). Fed. Proc. 31:1587-98.

61. Holmes, W.N. and J.G. Phillips (1976). The adrenal cortex of birds. In: General, Comparative and Clinical Endocrinology of the Adrenal Cortex (I. Chester Jones and I.W. Henderson, eds.), p. 293-420. Academic Press, London.

62. Crocker, A.D. and W.N. Holmes (1971). Intestinal absorption in ducklings (*Anas platyrhynchos*) maintained on fresh water and hypertonic saline. Comp. Biochem. Physiol. 40A:203-11.

63. Crocker, A.D. and W.N. Holmes (1976). Factors affecting intestinal absorption in ducklings (*Anas platyrhynchos*). Proc. Soc. Endocrinol. (May, 1976) 71:88P-89P.

64. Crocker, A.D., J. Cronshaw, and W.N. Holmes (1974). The effect of a crude oil on intestinal absorption in ducklings (*Anas platyrhynchos*). Environ. Pollut. 7:165-78.

65. Crocker, A.D., J. Cronshaw, and W.N. Holmes (1975). The effect of several crude oils and some petroleum distillation fractions on intestinal absorption in ducklings (*Anas platyrhynchos*). Environ. Physiol. Biochem. 5:92-106.

66. Holmes, W.N., J. Cronshaw, and J. Gorsline. The effects of cold stress on seawater-maintained ducks given food contaminated with petroleum. Manuscript in preparation.

67. Grau, C.R., T. Roudybush, J. Dobbs, and J. Wathen (1977). Altered yolk structure and reduced hatchability of eggs from birds fed single doses of petroleum oils. Science 195:779-81.

68. Grau, C.R. (1976). Ring structure of avian egg yolk. Poult. Sci. 55:1418-22.

69. Snyder, S.B., J.G. Fox, and O.A. Soave (1973). Mortali-
     ties in waterfowl following Bunker C fuel exposure. An
     examination of the pathological, microbiological, and oil
     hydrocarbon residue findings in birds that died after the
     San Francisco Bay oil spill Jan. 18, 1971. Mimeo report
     on work supported by a grant from the Standard Oil Corp.
     and by the National Institute of Health, Bethesda, Md.,
     Research and Resources Grant No. RR00282-06, p. 1-48.

71. Griner, L.A. and R. Herdman (1970). Effects of oil pol-
     lution on waterfowl. A study of salvage methods. Re-
     search Grant No. 14-12-574, Water Quality Office, Envi-
     ronmental Pollution Agency. U.S. Govt. Printing Office,
     Washington, D.C., 35 p.

Chapter 8

CONSEQUENCES OF OIL
FOULING ON MARINE MAMMALS

JOSEPH R. GERACI

Wildlife Disease Section
Department of Pathology
Ontario Veterinary College
University of Guelph
Guelph, Ontario, Canada

and

THOMAS G. SMITH

Arctic Biological Station
Fisheries and Marine Service
Department of Fisheries and the Environment
P.O. Box 400
Ste. Anne de Bellevue, Quebec, Canada

BACKGROUND

There is increasing concern over the possible impact of oil fouling on marine mammals. This is prompted by the advent of offshore drilling sites and the high risks involved with marine oil transport. Over the past 10 yr, reports by the media and some scientific review articles have alluded to definitely implicated oil as the cause of death of seals, sea lions, sea otters, dolphins, and both small and large whales. The incident which has received the most attention is that of the January 1969 blowout of Union Oil's offshore well in the Santa Barbara Channel. Several conflicting news and popular article accounts of the incident speculated that grey whales, *Eschrichtius gibbosus*, had died as a result of the spill. Newsweek (10 Feb. 1969) reported on the presence of a stranded dolphin with an oil-clogged blowhole and lung hemorrhage. Similar accounts involved northern elephant seals, *Mirounga angustirostris*, California sea lions, *Zalophus californianus*, and the northern fur seal, *Callorhinus ursinus*.

Critical assessments of the Santa Barbara spill on marine mammals later pointed out that in no case could death be unequivocally linked with the presence of oil. It was shown, in fact, that the rates of natural mortalities documented during the spill were no higher than seen in previous years [1-4].

Reports on seals contaminated in other oil spill situations follow a similar pattern. There have been two accounts in Alaskan coastal waters involving a total of 900 marine mammals, mostly seals (species not specified) [5]. Though the animals were contaminated with oil, there were no deaths noted with the exception of one sea otter, *Enhydra lutris*, carcass which was found coated with oil.

Following the *Arrow* spill of 1969 at Chedabucto Bay, Nova Scotia, it was inferred that a small number of seals had died due to suffocation caused by plugging of vital orifices with Bunker C fuel oil [6]. Details of these observations are not available and therefore the account cannot be assessed critically. In another report of a Bunker C fuel oil spill in the Gulf of St. Lawrence, 500-2,000 harp seals, *Phoca groenlandica*, were observed to be coated with oil. Some dead seals were found and it could not be determined whether the oil was directly involved. Davis and Anderson [7] studied the differences between oiled and uncontaminated grey seals (*Halichoerus grypus*) off the west coast of Wales following an oil spill of undetermined origin. They observed two dead pups which were encased in oil. The remainder of the exposed seals showed no differences in behavior or survival which could be linked with oil.

A CONTROLLED STUDY ON SEALS

In view of such equivocal and controversial reports, it became necessary to do a controlled study on the behavioral, physiological, and pathological consequences of crude oil contact on at least one group of marine mammals. As part of an overall environmental impact study stemming from oil exploration in the Beaufort Sea, we carried out such an investigation on ringed seals, *Phoca hispida* [8,9].

Two oil immersion studies were carried out, one in natural seawater pens in the arctic, the other in a southern laboratory. In the arctic experiment prior to immersion in oil, each of six seals was immobilized with ketamine [10], blood samples were taken, and a sonic temperature telemetry pill was administered. Seals were then placed in a pen 2.4 x 2.4 x 1.2 m high that had a plywood floor and sides which allowed water to circulate through a 3 cm opening 35 cm below the oil-water interface (Fig. 1). Seals were in the pen for 12 hr

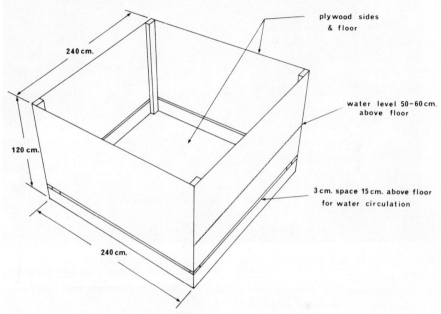

Fig. 1. Plywood holding pen used in the field oil immersion study. The pen was constructed to allow a free exchange of seawater below the level of the floating crude oil.

before oil was introduced. Body temperatures were monitored every 3 hr and blood samples were drawn to establish control values. Crude oil, sufficient to create a 1 cm thick surface layer (60 liters), was poured into the pen. Sea ice was then added to cool the water to about 8°C. Seals were left for 24 hr, then removed, sampled, examined, photographed, and placed in a clean-water pen. They were monitored continually, and a subsample was killed by gunshot at 2-day intervals and necropsied.

Next, a small group of ringed seals was taken to holding facilities at the University of Guelph, Ontario, where the second immersion study was conducted. The oil immersion study at Guelph was carried out in pools 3 x 3.6 x 1.2 m deep, containing water of 24°/oo salinity, at about 13°C (Fig. 2). The three seals used were apparently in good health and eating Atlantic herring, *Clupea harengus harengus*, and rainbow smelts, *Osmerus mordax*. After 2 mo of acclimation in captivity, they

Fig. 2. Ringed seals in the holding pen containing a 1 cm thick surface layer of crude oil. In the field study, all six seals survived a 24-hour exposure. In the laboratory study, all three seals died within 71 minutes.

were exposed to oil in the same manner as in the field experiment.

Nine, 3-4 week-old whitecoat harp seals, *P. groenlandica*, were used to assess the effects of oil coating on temperature regulation in pups. This was done because ringed seal pups were not available for study. The harp seal study was carried out in March 1975 on the Magdalen Islands. Core body temperatures were monitored with the aid of a YSI telethermometer (Yellow Springs Instrument Co., Inc., Yellow Springs, Ohio) fitted with an internal rectal probe. Temperatures were recorded every 4 hr for 48 hr prior to oiling and continued for up to 4 days after. Six seals were designated as experimentals and three as controls. The experimental seals were well coated by brushing Norman Wells crude oil onto the hair over the entire body. The next day, as a measure of assurance they were recoated in the same manner using crude oil from Mildale, Saskatchewan. Four experimental seals and two controls were killed 3 days after oiling and the remaining ones a day later. All the animals were weighed before and at the end of the experiment. Postmortem examinations were carried out on the dead seals.

In the arctic study, the six immersed seals showed immediate signs of distress; they thrashed, shook their heads, and were obviously agitated. All showed signs of eye disturbance, i.e., lacrimation, squinting, conjunctivitis, swollen nictitating membranes, and in one case, corneal erosions (Figs. 3, 4).

Fig. 3. A ringed seal in oiled water showing the typical surface attitude which results in the inevitable constant exposure of eyes and mucous membranes.

Twenty-four hours later, the seals were removed to clean water pens. By the third and fourth days, there was almost no evidence that they had been in oil. The eye problems disappeared and the behavior was normal. At no time during the 7-day follow-up period was there any consistent evidence of hematologic, biochemical or physiological disturbances. At necropsy small amounts of oil were found in the mouth, but chemical analysis of tissues showed the presence of petroleum oil in all organs except lung. The highest concentrations were found in the urine and bile, suggesting these organs as possible

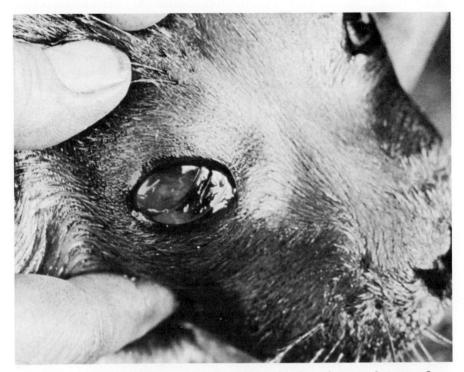

Fig. 4. Conjunctivitis and swollen nictitating membrane of a ringed seal after 24 hours exposure to oil. This condition was one of the most obvious oil-induced effects.

routes of excretion [11]. This was further supported by some evidence of kidney lesions in at least one seal.

The findings from the laboratory immersion study were in marked contrast with those from the field study. Immediately upon exposure to the contaminated water, all three animals began to shake vigorously and all died within 71 min. Blood studies before and after death revealed significant differences in six hematologic and plasma parameters pointing to stress as the underlying factor in the cause of death. Oil simply acted as a trigger.

The oil coating experiment on 2-3 week-old harp seal whitecoat pups was designed to assess the effects of crude oil on thermoregulation. Here, there were no significant differences between the oiled and control seals; there were no behavioral or pathological changes resulting from oil coating (Fig. 5).

Two separate oil ingestion studies were conducted to determine the effects and fate of oil consumption by seals. A high level, single-dose ingestion study was carried out on 2-3

Fig. 5. Harp seal whitecoat pups, one of which is coated with crude oil. No behavioral or thermoregulatory changes were observed over the four-day study.

week-old fasting harp seal pups.   Seals were divided into two groups, each containing six experimental and one control animal.   One group was fed 75 ml of Norman Wells crude oil, the other 25 ml, as a single dose.   One seal from each group was killed 1, 2, 4, 6, 8, and 10 days after ingestion of the oil. Controls were also killed on the 10th day.   Blood samples were drawn from all seals 6-8 hr before ingestion of the oil, and again just prior to death.   Crude oil was excreted and began fouling the fur within 1½ hr after dosing.   Yet there were no obvious behavioral or chemical alterations noted.   Blood enzyme studies showed mild changes in muscle enzymes, most probably resulting from handling stress.   When oil labelled ^{3}H-benzene was given to healthy ringed seals, highest tissue activity was seen after the second day of dosing with a sharp decline thereafter.   Tissue biopsy samples showed pronounced activity after the second day of ingestion, greater in liver and blubber than in muscle.   Activity in all tissues and fluids declined to low levels by 28 days.

IMPLICATIONS

Our study showed that up to 75 ml of ingested crude oil is not irreversibly harmful to seals. The liver is generally regarded as a prime target organ for hydrocarbon damage in mammals. The effects of such damage have been well documented [12]. If sufficient quantities of these hepatotoxic substances are administered, liver enzymes are released into plasma and are detectable. The degree and duration of enzyme release is generally a function of the quantity and toxicity of the substance(s). Geraci [13] induced measurable liver damage in grey seals, using 5 and 10 ml quantities of carbon tetrachloride, a rather potent fraction. In our study there was only transient liver enzyme release. If there was liver damage, it was negligible.

Reports which suggest that oil might affect seals by acute intoxication through ingestion should be viewed cautiously [14]. Our experience has shown that immersed seals ingest very small quantities. Seals are not known to be carrion feeders, and any oil which they might consume from live contaminated prey would be negligible. Seals exposed to oil at sea may well swallow small amounts. As for carcasses found with oil in the alimentary tract, they could have been fouled after death, much in the same way that sand and debris are found in the stomachs of stranded seals and whales (Geraci, personal observations). Though the immersed seals did accumulate petroleum hydrocarbons in their tissues, the exact route of entry is not known, nor is the level at which these would begin to be toxic. The crude oil used in our study was highly volatile, and likely to be highly toxic.

Surface contact with oil had a far greater impact on the seals than did absorption. Eye damage was a significant finding in the field oil study. At least some of the damage appears to have been done by volatile components of the oil. Nearly all of the investigators experienced eye irritation when exposed to the pungent fumes in the seal pen. The eye inflammations in the seals subsided soon after they were placed in clean water. It is reasonable to assume that continued exposure to oil would have resulted in severe and possibly permanent eye disorders. Nelson-Smith [15], quoting an unidentified source, stated that oil damage in seals frequently includes severe eye irritation, and made reference to a female seal, now blind, which was rescued during an oil spill. Eye damage and blindness has been observed in wild and captive seals [16,17], and the occurrence in nature need not be linked with oil or other noxious substances. Nevertheless oil is irritating and damaging to eyes and the severity of damage is likely to be related to exposure time and to the concentration of volatile components.

Oil fouling with Norman Wells crude oil did not cause any mechanical damage such as sticking of the flippers to the body or the plugging of body openings. It should be pointed out that Norman Wells crude oil, which is similar to Beaufort Sea oil, is relatively light, and of low viscosity. It is unlikely that such an oil can be compared to the more viscous crudes and to fractionated products such as Bunker C fuel oil, in its physical fouling characteristics. Literature does exist indicating that seal deaths have been associated with heavy oils [6], in one case by plugging vital body orifices [6] and in another by pups being encased and then unable to swim [7].

No thermoregulatory problems were observed in our study, nor were they expected. Hair in postweaned hair seals contributes little to their overall insulation [18]. Seals between the time of birth and the laying down of the blubber are more dependent on hair for insulation and, presumably, would be vulnerable to the thermal effects of oil coating. Even the young seals in our study had developed a blubber layer, which apparently was enough to prevent surface heat loss.

This brings up an interesting question of the differences, if any, on the effects of oil between phocid seals we have studied and the otariid seals which depend more on the insulative property of hair. They, as well as sea otters and polar bears, also dependent on fur for insulation, would likely be more adversely affected by contact with oil [19,20].

The markedly different responses of seals immersed in oil indicate an important factor to be considered in assessing the impact of oil spills on marine mammal populations. The laboratory immersed seals died of stress.

Generally, stress had been regarded as a condition of captivity. The exact mechanism is unknown, but it is probably related to adrenal insufficiency [21]. Affected animals become uncoordinated, display muscle quivering, and have electrolyte disturbances. When further stressed in any way, they often die with little or no warning [13,21]. Our study adds oil to the growing list of factors which can trigger the death of stressed seals.

Recently, we have shown that stress also occurs and can be assessed hematologically in wild ringed seals [22]. The electrolyte disturbances which characterize the condition have been found in emaciated and late molting animals (Geraci and Smith, unpublished observations). Assuming that animals so stressed respond as do captive stressed seals, then any severe disturbances, including contact with oil, would conceivably have a selective effect on the populations, eliminating those animals in poor general condition. Typically, this would include isolated seals that are diseased and heavily parasitized, older seals, or seals during a particularly vulnerable time in their life cycle. Adverse environmental conditions which result in low food production may further complicate the effects of oil by selectively affecting the stressed seals in poor nutritional condition.

The cetacean story with respect to our knowledge of oil fouling is indeed brief. Following the Santa Barbara oil leak, various popular articles described a gruesome picture of grey whales which had died as a result of oiling. Brownell [1] laid the stories to rest. Following an investigation of each incident, he concluded that "no positive evidence was obtained to show that any grey whales died on their northward migration from the effects of crude oil pollution." In fact, of the five whales reported, one had stranded almost one year previous to the spill.

Brownell's final account is in no way intended to minimize the impact of oil fouling on cetaceans. The fact is that there is simply no evidence to show how such fouling might affect the animals.

Most cetaceans are not shore dwelling, and would likely not be exposed to the shoreline-accumulated oil as are the pinnipeds. Should they move through a spill, it is equally unlikely that they could accumulate oil on their body surface to the same degree as seals can.

Yet surface accumulation is not necessarily the key issue with regard to fouling. The eye problems in seals, as well as the ultimate influence of oil on stress, may be as functional in cetaceans, especially those species which appear to be most sensitive to changes in the environment, such as the common harbor porpoise, Phocoena phocoena. Polar dwelling species which become confined to small breathing spaces during the winter months would of course have maximum exposure both because of their dependence on the area and because oil might tend to accumulate in open leads.

Many factors would be involved in determining the eventual consequences of oil spills or oil well blowouts on marine mammals. The importance of the area for the marine mammals occupying it as an overwintering site, feeding area and migration corridor, and the availability of alternate areas, would have a direct bearing on the length and type of exposure to oil. Climatic conditions affecting productivity, feeding success, and the health status of the population prior to and during exposure to oil would have a strong influence on the outcome. Many years of data are needed to document the response of a wild population to natural environmental stresses. In the case of the Beaufort Sea ringed seal study, our results were interpretable largely because of a considerable number of years of prior research in the area. In many cases for other marine mammals, this kind of information is lacking. The difficulties involved in conducting controlled experiments on the larger animals such as whales will probably preclude such studies. At the same time, it is dangerous to generalize about the effects on different species, as they will obviously differ in their reaction to oil.

REFERENCES

1. Brownell, R.L. (1971). Whales, dolphins and oil pollution. In: Biological and Oceanographical Survey of the Santa Barbara Channel Oil Spill 1969-1970. Biology and Bacteriology (D. Straughan, ed.), Vol. 1, p. 255-76. Allan Hancock Foundation, University of Southern California, Los Angeles.
2. Brownell, R.L. and B.J. LeBoeuf (1971). California sea lion mortality: Natural or artifact? In: Biological and Oceanographical Survey of the Santa Barbara Channel Oil Spill 1969-1970. Biology and Bacteriology (D. Straughan, ed.), Vol. 1, p. 287-306. Allan Hancock Foundation, University of Southern California, Los Angeles.
3. LeBoeuf, B.J. (1971). Oil contamination and elephant seal mortality: A "negative" finding. In: Biological and Oceanographical Survey of the Santa Barbara Channel Oil Spill 1969-1970. Biology and Bacteriology (D. Straughan, ed.), Vol. 1, p. 277-85. Allan Hancock Foundation, University of Southern California, Los Angeles.
4. Simpson, J.G. and W.G. Gilmartin (1970). An investigation of elephant seal and sea lion mortality on San Miguel Island. Bioscience 20:289.
5. Morris, R. (1970). Alaska Peninsula oil spill. Event No. 36-70. Smithson. Inst. Annu. Rep., p. 154-7.
6. Anon. (1970). Report of the task force-operation oil (clean-up of the *Arrow* oil spill in Chedabucto Bay) to the Minister of Transport. Information Canada, Ottawa, 2, p. 46-7.
7. Davis, J.E. and S.S. Anderson (1976). Effects of oil pollution on breeding grey seals. Mar. Pollut. Bull. 7:115-8.
8. Smith, T.G. and J.R. Geraci (1975). The effect of contact and ingestion of crude oil on ringed seals of the Beaufort Sea. Beaufort Sea Tech. Rep. 5, Environment Canada, Victoria, B.C., 67 p.
9. Geraci, J.R. and T.G. Smith (1976). Direct and indirect effects of oil on ringed seals (*Phoca hispida*) of the Beaufort Sea. J. Fish. Res. Board Can. 33:1976-84.

10. Geraci, J.R. (1973). An appraisal of ketamine as an im-
    mobilizing agent in wild and captive pinnipeds. J. Am.
    Vet. Med. Assoc. 163:574-7.
11. Engelhardt, F.R., J.R. Geraci, and T.G. Smith (1977).
    Uptake and clearance of petroleum hydrocarbons in the
    ringed seal, *Phoca hispida*. J. Fish. Res. Board Can., In
    press.
12. Cornelius, C.E. and J.J. Kaneko (1963). Clinical bio-
    chemistry of domestic animals. Academic Press, New York,
    678 p.
13. Geraci, J.R. (1972). Experimental thiamine deficiency in
    captive harp seals, *Phoca groenlandica*, induced by eating
    herring, *Clupea harengus*, and smelts, *Osmerus mordax*.
    Ph.D. Thesis, McGill University, Montreal, Quebec, 144 p.
14. Duguy, R. and P. Babin (1975). Acute intoxication by
    hydrocarbons observed in a harbour seal (*Phoca vitulina*).
    Rapp. P.-V. Reun. Cons. Int. Explor. Mer, Marine Mammal
    Committee, C.M. 1975/N:5.
15. Nelson-Smith, A. (1970). The problem of oil pollution of
    the sea. Adv. Mar. Biol. 8:215-306.
16. King, J.E. (1964). Seals of the World. Trustees of the
    British Museum (Natural History), London, p. 124-5.
17. Ridgway, S.H. (1972). Homeostasis in the aquatic envi-
    ronment. In: Mammals of the Sea - Biology and Medicine,
    p. 590-747. Charles C. Thomas, Publisher, Springfield,
    Ill.
18. Irving, L. and J.S. Hart (1957). The metabolism and in-
    sulation of seals as bare-skinned mammals in cold water.
    Can. J. Zool. 35:498-511.
19. Hartung, R. (1967). Energy metabolism in oil-covered
    ducks. J. Wildl. Manage. 30:564-70.
20. McEwan, E.H., N. Aitchison, and P.E. Whitehead (1974).
    Energy metabolism of oiled muskrats. Can. J. Zool. 52:
    1057-62.
21. Geraci, J.R. (1972). Hyponatremia and the need for di-
    etary salt supplementation in captive pinnipeds. J. Am.
    Vet. Med. Assoc. 161:618-23.
22. Geraci, J.R. and T.G. Smith (1975). Functional hematol-
    ogy of ringed seals (*Phoca hispida*) in the Canadian arc-
    tic. J. Fish. Res. Board Can. 32:2559-64.

Chapter 9

EFFECTS OF OIL SPILLS IN
ARCTIC AND SUBARCTIC ENVIRONMENTS

ROBERT C. CLARK, JR. AND JOHN S. FINLEY
Environmental Conservation Division

Northwest and Alaska Fisheries Center
National Marine Fisheries Service
National Oceanic and Atmospheric Administration
U.S. Department of Commerce
Seattle, Washington 98112

INTRODUCTION

The potential for a major oil pollution incident in arctic and subarctic waters has increased dramatically over the
past several years and will probably continue to increase as
petroleum exploration is pushed farther into the arctic regions. Dunbar [1] suggested that pollution from petroleum development and production is now the most serious and immediate
threat facing the arctic ecosystem. Our inability to predict

the impact of such activities is due to a lack of understanding of both the short- and long-term fate and effects of petroleum on marine ecosystems. Little reliable information is available on the basic ecology and physiology of almost all of the arctic marine species. Lack of reliable data makes it extremely difficult to predict the interaction of oil with arctic and subarctic marine ecosystems; most existing knowledge was gained from field and laboratory studies of temperate and tropical marine environments [2].

In this chapter we have outlined those results which we felt give the best evidence for understanding the damage to arctic and subarctic ecosystems from petroleum. Because little or no information on cold water environments was available, we have had to rely on data relating to temperate waters and species yet realizing the limitations involved in attempting to apply observations from temperate ecosystems to those of the arctic and subarctic.

DEFINITION OF ARCTIC AND SUBARCTIC MARINE ENVIRONMENTS

First it seems pertinent to define arctic and subarctic waters. We know so little about the climate, life, and geography of the northern portion of our planet that considerable variations occur in the interpretation of the terms used to denote or delineate the various portions of the arctic and subarctic. We are indebted to Sater [3] for his attempt to define the terms and to set forth some boundaries of the arctic region. The word "arctic" is derived from the Greek "arktos" (a bear), denoting the region beneath the Big Dipper or "Great Bear." The term "arctic" has been used to denote the entire area within the Arctic Circle [3]. "Arctic waters" have been defined as those marine areas containing certain biological indicator organisms, such as a certain species of plankton [1,4,5]. Johnson [6] defined the marine arctic as the area of northern seas and oceans normally covered by perennial sea ice. Oceanographers, according to Sater [3], consider the arctic as that region in which only pure arctic water, having a temperature at or near 0°C and a salinity of about 30 °/oo (parts per thousand), is found at the surface. In our discussion, we have taken a liberal view and have defined arctic waters as those waters covered by extensive sea ice at least part of the year. We have not included in this definition the small shallow bays or inlets occasionally covered by winter ice. In the Pacific Ocean, arctic waters would encompass the southern limit of sea ice in the Bering Sea extending westward from southern Bristol Bay along roughly 56°N latitude to the Komandorski Islands, and thence to the Kamchatka Peninsula and southward along the Okhotsk Sea [7]. In the open ocean areas, this boundary would be a wide band, encompassing the southern limit of the sea ice (the limit may vary from year to year) (Fig. 1).

In the north Atlantic Ocean, arctic waters would be those north of a looping line from northern Labrador around southern Greenland, north of Iceland, northeastward to Spitzbergen, east to Novaya Zemyla, and southwestward to the Kola Peninsula in European Russia (based on winter seasonal surface ice coverage of greater than 10%) [3]. Arctic lands are defined climatically as those areas where the temperature does not exceed 10°C (50°F) and the lowest temperature is not above 0°C (32°F) [8].

Marine "Subarctic waters" are more difficult to define. Johnson [6] designated subarctic marine waters as those having a seasonal sea ice cover. Dunbar [1] referred to the region as having mixed arctic and non-arctic water in the upper 200 to 300 m. Sverdrup, Johnson, and Fleming [9] defined Pacific subarctic waters as those in the Gulf of Alaska region of the North Pacific that contain no arctic water. We have chosen to use the concept of Dodimead, Favorite, and Hirano [7]. They defined subarctic waters as those waters lying between the southern boundary of sea ice (previously defined as "arctic waters" boundary; see Fig. 1) and a band of water along 40°N latitude from Japan to California. The southern boundary of subarctic waters is approximately the southern limit of the 3°C water isotherm at 100 m depth. This boundary becomes indefinite near the continental margins.

The subarctic waters of the North Atlantic region are arbitrarily defined as those waters lying between the southern boundary of the arctic (previously defined) and the northern influence of the Gulf Stream, which traverses a generally northerly route to Iceland, and thence to northern Norway (Fig. 1). The waters around the British Isles and the North Sea would not be included in this definition, nor would some of the major North American estuaries which are influenced by local oceanographic and climatic conditions.

Subarctic land masses have been defined as those land areas where the temperature is over 10°C (50°F) for not more than four months during the year, and the lowest temperature is less than 0°C (32°F) [8].

PROBLEMS IN PREDICTING BIOLOGICAL IMPACTS OF OIL SPILLS

The biological effects of an oil spill in any marine or estuarine environment are difficult to predict because each spill is unique. The variables associated with a spill are specific only to the one time and one place. A complex variety of organic compounds (more than tens of thousands in a typical crude oil), showing a wide range of physical and chemical properties singly or in combination, can be introduced

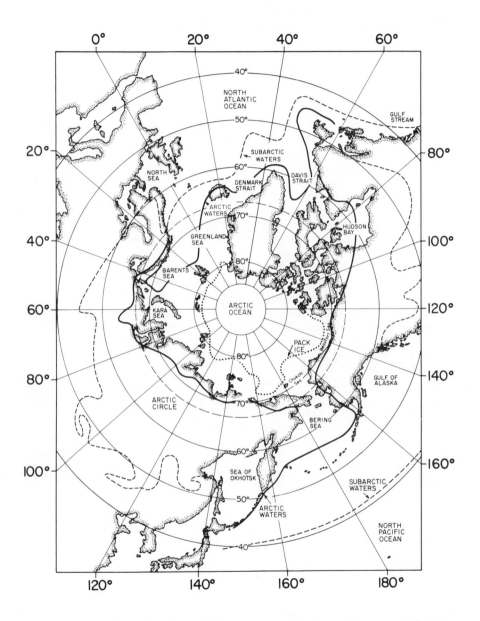

FIG. 1. Arctic and subarctic regions showing the approximate
southern boundaries of marine and terrestrial ranges for arctic and subarctic species, based on references 1,3,7,8,10,11.

into an infinite combination of environmental conditions (see
Chapter 2 of Volume I). Experiments in the laboratory on the
toxicity of petroleum to aquatic organisms provide data which
can be used to suggest but not to completely predict the effects of an oil spill in the environment. In addition, techniques for petroleum hydrocarbon analyses and damage assessment in the field have become sophisticated enough only in the
last five years to provide sufficiently accurate and reliable
data for the possible development of predictive theories or
models.

Many factors determine the degree and duration of damage
from a petroleum spill. These include (1) the chemical composition and physical properties of the petroleum, (2) the quantity of the petroleum and duration of the spill, (3) seasonal,
oceanographic, and meteorological conditions, (4) nature of
the exposed biota, (5) habitat type and substrate, (6) geographic location, and (7) type of spill cleanup employed.

The physical properties and chemical composition of crude
petroleums of different origins vary widely (see Chapter 1 of
Volume I). The toxicity of the various fractions has been attributed primarily to the low molecular weight aromatic hydrocarbons such as benzene, alkylated benzenes, and xylenes, some
of the medium and high molecular weight aromatics, and certain
phenolic components such as the naphthenic acids [12]. Under
laboratory conditions, fresh crude oil is more toxic to marine
organisms than the aged residue. Also, the various crude oils
show different degrees of toxicity to certain organisms; for
example, Ottway [13] found that the snail, *Littorina littorea*,
displayed a wide degree of sensitivity when exposed to each of
20 different crude oils (see Chapter 1).

Immediate effects on marine organisms occur from a single
large infusion of petroleum into the marine environment, usually from a spill incident. High mortality of marine organisms may occur almost simultaneously with, or at any time
after, a spill incident. Many spills occur within confined
marine areas, such as bays or estuaries, where the concentrations of oil may remain high for extended periods. These circumstances may result in relatively severe impacts on the
biota. Accidental spills are generally large in volume compared with chronic inputs and, unfortunately, commonly occur
in coastal areas where humans make maximum use of the marine
resources.

Sublethal effects may be associated with the chronic exposure of marine organisms to petroleum hydrocarbons released
into the marine environment on either a continuous or intermittent basis. Other pollutants, such as heavy metals, pesticides, or waste heat, may act synergistically with components
of the oil increasing damage to the biota [14]. Physical alteration of the marine environment can also increase the

susceptability of marine organisms to petroleum; for example, the dredging and filling of marshes can modify habitats and may increase the vulnerability of individual organisms to petroleum contaminants.

A summary of the biological impacts of several major oil spill incidents has already been presented in the report "Petroleum in the Marine Environment" prepared by the National Academy of Sciences [15].   Although accidental petroleum spills are occasionally spectacular events which attract considerable public attention, they account for less than 10% of the total estimated input of petroleum into the marine environment (see Table 1 in Chapter 2 of Volume I).

ARCTIC AND SUBARCTIC OIL SPILLS

TERRESTRIAL

We have included a discussion of petroleum spills in the nearshore terrestrial environment and inland rivers of the arctic and subarctic because these environments have a direct influence on and can be influenced by the marine environment. These aquatic habitats support anadromous fish stocks and provide a supply of nutrients and food for nearshore marine and estuarine organisms.

Hunt and coworkers [16] believed that the high sensitivity of the terrestrial biota in the arctic to an oil spill or to any ecological disturbance is related to the low level of biological activity in these areas of low air and soil temperatures.

In the arctic, an annual negative heat balance (heat flows from the warmer earth to the colder air) commonly occurs at the ground-atmosphere interface because of the low air temperature; the soil remains perennially frozen, a condition referred to as permafrost [16].   The depth of the summer thaw is influenced by the type and degree of vegetative cover (trees, bushes, grass, moss).   When this thermal regime is altered (e.g., high localized temperatures following removal of the protective vegetation), damage may include flooded drainage channels, excessive headward erosion of the soil, and shifting and cracking of buildings and other structures [16,17].   In fact, extensive sections of the Trans-Alaska Pipeline from Prudhoe Bay to Valdez were built above ground to minimize permafrost disturbances from hot crude oil (49°-63°C, 120°-150°F) flowing through the pipeline [18,19].

A serious consequence that might arise from petroleum spills in the arctic and subarctic, particularly if mechanical cleanup methods are used, is a drastic alteration of the permafrost.   Soil types especially susceptible to permafrost degradation are ice-rich frozen silty materials which show very low cohesiveness when thawed. The use of vehicles or heavy machinery in such areas in the summer could sufficiently disrupt the soil to upset the delicate balance between the permafrost and the summer melting cycle [16]. Only the passage of years will heal the scars of some of these past damages to permafrost environments.

Between 1942 and the mid-1970's the U.S. Army operated a pipeline in Alaska and Canada for the transportation of military fuels. Spills occurred along the 1,007-km Haines to Fairbanks section; however, no data are available on the number of spills or on the amount of oil discharged. Nevertheless, extensive kills of vegetation occurred in areas exposed to spilled oil. There was little indication of serious soil erosion or slope instability, presumably because the dead moss layer provided an effective insulating zone. Where this moss layer was uplifted by the roots of fallen trees killed by the fuel oil, erosion became significant if the permafrost was directly exposed [16].

A jet fuel spill sprayed over a luxuriant, moist, coastal forest community near Haines, Alaska, resulted in the complete kill of all vegetation in contact with the fuel. Fuel oil was still present in the soil three to four years later to a depth of at least 50 cm, and an oil film was present in a small stream passing through the impacted area. Apparently, after rainfall had leached the fuel oil from the upper soil layers, herbs and shrubs reappeared [16].

A No. 2 fuel oil spill at an inland Yukon Territory, Canada, site eliminated all vegetation in a willow and alder environment. After three to four years the revegetation occurred only with the fireweed and reedgrass typically found on disturbed terrains. The oil spread to an intermediate-age stand of white spruce and associated understory, killing all plant coverage within the path of the fuel oil. No new vegetation appeared in the kill areas within three to four years after the spill [16].

A jet fuel oil spill in Yukon Territory, Canada, in permafrost terrain typical of interior Alaska killed almost all of the vegetative cover. After five to six years, recovery had approached about 65% of the prespill condition. Most of the vegetative regrowth occurred in areas where mineral soil was exposed in the root scars of fallen trees or where the organic mat over mineral soil was shallow. An obvious increase in permafrost thaw occurred where the fuel oil killed the vegetation [16].

Light refined petroleum products can have an immediately devastating effect on plants. Soil contamination at a level of 6,000 ppm of a No. 2 fuel oil, for instance, resulted in the death of corn seedlings. In this phytotoxic process the oil interfered with the water uptake mechanism in the plant

root, and only those plants whose roots extend well below the
depth of contaminated soil survived. In warm climates,
spilled fuel oils have a relatively short life in the soil due
to evaporation, chemical degradation, and degradation and assimilation by soil microflora [20].

McCowen and coworkers [21] demonstrated contact herbicid-
al effect of crude oil on arctic vegetation, especially the
low-growing mosses and liverworts. The depth of oil penetration into the active soil layer, a function of the water content of the soil, appeared to be a critical factor. Standing
water prevented the downward penetration of the oil, so that
damage was confined largely to above-ground portions of the
vegetation.

It is assumed that revegetation following oil spills in
arctic terrestrial regimes would be facilitated by microbial
breakdown of the petroleum components. Westlake and Cook [22]
found that a high proportion of the microorganisms in arctic
oil samples were capable of degrading crude oil at room temperature but showed extremely reduced activity at low temperatures. ZoBell and Agosti [23] isolated low-temperature hydro-
carbon-decomposing bacteria from oil seepage areas on the
Alaskan North Slope. Apparently oil may be decomposed at low
temperatures by natural soil microbial populations [2], although the rates may be slow (see Chapter 3 of Volume I).

Hutchinson and Freedman [24] carried out experimental
field spills of Norman Wells (Canada) crude petroleum on taiga
and tundra sites in the Canadian Arctic. The petroleum was
applied in two ways: in the first method the ground and vegetation were coated evenly with a relatively small amount of
crude oil (9 $1/m^2$); the second method involved a point discharge of a large volume (50 bbl, 7,950 l) of crude oil. Both
spills had a devastating effect on most plant species. The
vegetation showed very little evidence of recovery even after
the third summer following the spills. Lichens and mosses,
lacking a protective cuticle and being especially susceptible
to oiling because of their low ground-hugging habit, were destroyed. The oil seemed to act as a contact herbicide. Damage
(defined as a reduction in the number of species and the percent vegetational cover of the surviving plants) increased
during the second year after the spill as a result of winter
killing factors. Large black spruce trees took three seasons
to die in the spill areas, emphasizing the necessity for long-
term assessment of terrestrial oil spill damage. Tundra vegetation was affected somewhat less severely than the boreal-
taiga due to the presence of some very resistant species.
Even in the third summer following the spill, the number of
plants producing flowers were few and plant reproduction was
severely reduced.

Winter spills had a less severe effect than summer spills due to the absence of actively growing foliage. There was a decrease in albedo in the oiled sites, as well as a decrease in evapotranspiration and an increase in infrared reradiation of energy from the oiled ground surface. Permafrost was little affected, despite changes in the energy budgets (e.g., slight increases in soil heat flux from oiled areas) [24].

In test spills on two Canadian freshwater lakes, the surface oil film not only was toxic to, but also served to entrap, certain surface aquatic organisms such as the gerrids, the corixids, and adult *Haliplus* beetles. The surface film induced changes in the chemistry of the water and in the production and distribution of phytoplankton and periplankton. Increases in seston, particulate nitrogen, and particulate carbon (but not particulate phosphorus) occurred within three weeks and appeared to be the result of increased microbial activity and phytoplankton blooms. There was a striking development of blue-green algae suggesting an eutrophic effect from the surface oil film [25].

In another experimental spill of Norman Wells (Canada) crude oil on a subarctic Canadian lake, no significant effect occurred on the phytoplankton composition or abundance throughout the summer growth season. A marked inhibitory effect on most members of the periphyton developed, perhaps because the periphyton were trapped on a solid substratum that also trapped oil components. Growth of the blue-green algae increased. Shoots of sedge and horsetail, and moss populations contaminated with oil, showed considerable losses of chlorophyll; a large percentage of the shoots were killed. Parts of plants below the water level appeared to survive well, allowing considerable recovery by the next growing season. Laboratory studies on three algae isolated from the lake indicated that the effects on phytoplankton may be most serious if the spill occurs early or late in the growth season when temperature and light conditions are suboptimum [26].

Petroleum spilled into arctic or subarctic water may be harmful to fresh water aquatic life in the following ways [27]:

(1) Free oil and emulsions may act on the epithelial surfaces of fish by adhering to gills and interfering with respiration.

(2) Free oil and oil-water emulsions may coat and destroy algae and other plankton, which may serve as sources of food for higher forms.

(3) Oily materials may coat the bottom and destroy benthic organisms and damage spawning areas.

(4) Heavy coatings of free oil on the surface of the water may interfere with aeration and photosynthesis.

(5) Water-soluble fractions may exert a direct acute or chronic toxic action on fish or lower members of the food web.

The effects of an oil spill on arctic or subarctic freshwater biota depend on a number of factors including the location of the spill, the amount and type of petroleum, temperature, season of the year, water level and flow, sediment load, and the effectiveness of containment and cleanup. The shallow summer melt water zone between the arctic shore and the pack ice, an estuarine system unique to the arctic, is especially susceptible to petroleum pollution. Vast quantities of plankton are produced in this zone during the short arctic summer. About 20 species of marine, anadromous, and freshwater fish inhabit the shallow nearshore zone of the Beaufort Sea. The arctic char, one of the most important anadromous species, frequents areas near the mouths of arctic rivers and thus would be particularly susceptible to oil contamination [27].

The impact of arctic or subarctic terrestrial oil spills on larger organisms (birds and mammals) is not well documented except for such obvious effects as entrapment in pools of standing oil, saturation of pelage or plumage leading to loss of insulative qualities, and the destruction of available food supplies (see Chapters 7 and 8). By means of the beach vegetation and carrion links in the food web, it is possible that petroleum pollution of intertidal zones could affect terrestrial mammals and birds that either constantly or intermittently use the beaches. For example, deep winter snows force the deer on the islands and mainland around Prince William Sound, Alaska, onto beaches where tidal action has cleared the snow. During these periods the deer rely heavily on sedges and washed-up kelp to supplement their meager diet. Oil may destroy these food sources or make them unpalatable to the deer; or, the animals might ingest contaminated vegetation [28].

MARINE

Reference Oil Spills

In providing information on the wide range of conditions associated with petroleum pollution of the marine environment, we have included a discussion of two significant oil spill incidents that occurred in the temperate zone: the crude oil spill from the *Torrey Canyon* into the English Channel and the medium-grade fuel oil spill from the *Tampico* off the coast of Baja California. Although specific results of these two examples may not be directly applicable to the arctic and subarctic, some aspects of the fates and effects of the oil may be common to all three environments.

Torrey Canyon

The first great loss of crude petroleum at sea occurred on 18 March 1967 when the supertanker *Torrey Canyon* grounded and broke up on Pollard Rock of the Seven Stones located 24 km (15 mi) west of Land's End and 11 km (7 mi) northeast of the Isles of Scilly off the southwest coast of Great Britain (Fig. 2). The 296-m (970-ft) *Torrey Canyon* was bound for Milford Haven from the Persian Gulf and carried some 860,000 bbl (117,000 tons, 137 million l) of Kuwait crude oil within her eighteen cargo tanks. Six of the tanks tore open with the impact of the vessel striking the reef at 32 km/hr (17 kn). The vessel remained on the reef in progressive stages of disintegration for six weeks, after which time she was a submerged and broken wreck containing no more oil [29].

The prevailing southwesterly winds swept the crude oil from the hulk toward great stretches of coastline in the English and Bristol Channels. Approximately 15% of the petroleum came ashore along 225 km (140 mi) of the British shoreline at Land's End and on the north and south coasts of Cornwall. A slightly smaller amount came ashore along another 120 km (75 mi) of the north coast of Brittany in France and in the Channel Islands [29]. The actual surface area of contaminated shore will never be accurately known. However, Ranwell [31] calculated that the whole of the petroleum released to the sea (ca. 100,000 tons) would fit into a theoretical cube not much more than 33 m (100 ft) on a side; if 1/100 of this amount (1,000 tons) washed onto a beach 9 m (30 ft) wide, it could form a layer 12 mm (0.5 in) thick for 32 km (20 mi).

Extensive efforts were made to limit the amount of oil headed for shore by (1) igniting the oil remaining in the stricken tanker, (2) dispersing the oil by the use of detergents (dispersants, emulsifiers), and (3) sinking the oil at sea by applying powdered chalk. Burning of the oil in the tanker was not a particularly successful operation. The powdered chalk appeared to sink large portions of the drifting surface oil before it could reach the French coast. The solvents used in the detergents for dispersal and shoreline cleaning tended to have a high degree of toxicity. These detergents were chemically different from household detergents [32]. The use of the toxic detergents for cleaning the intertidal rocky shores and sandy beaches is now believed to have caused as much, if not more, biological damage as the untreated oil itself.

At least 11 million l (3 million gal) of detergent-solvent mixtures were used in shoreline decontamination activities in southwest England. The mixtures were generally effective in rapidly clearing the surface of all but the worst affected beaches and shorelines. Their use, however, extended the oil contamination deeper into sand and throughout the

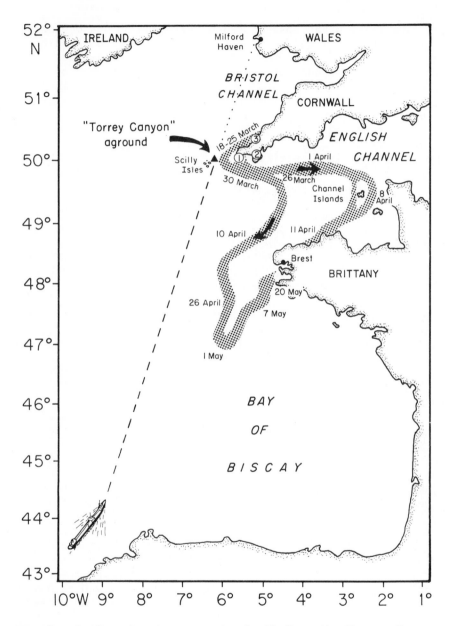

FIG. 2. *Surface-borne movement of oil from the* Torrey Canyon
*in 1967. Numbers refer to locations discussed in text: 1 -
Land's End and Sennen Cove; 2 - Porthleven; and 3 - Godrevy.
Adapted from Smith [29] and Nelson-Smith [30].*

water column, enabling the oil to spread more easily to uncontaminated parts of the English coast. Highly toxic elements in the detergents destroyed some of the shore organisms, such as the limpets, which might have survived the ciling alone. Furthermore, it was believed that the detergent solvent materials generally increased the mortality of the marine organisms on the shore and in the sublittoral zone down to depths of at least 15 m at Cornwall [31].

The greatest damage to coastal habitats occurred on the predominantly rocky shorelines where most of the crude oil was stranded. Among the plants, the intertidal algae and some lichen suffered extensive mortality from direct smothering with thick deposits of oil [31]. One of the most obvious consequences of oiling the rocky shore was the almost complete disappearance of gastropods. Sennen Cove, which received probably the heaviest oiling of the Cornwall coast, was treated extensively with detergents, and the rocks were thoroughly cleaned. Ten days after the oil first washed ashore (April), the topshells and dog whelks, *Nucella* sp., had disappeared, except for a few empty shells that had become wedged in crevices. No large periwinkles were present although conditions locally were obviously suitable for them; however, specimens of the snail, *Littorina neritoides*, which occupy small crevices and empty barnacle shells, seemed surprisingly unaffected.

The common limpet, *Patella vulgata*, was completely destroyed at Sennen Cove; empty shells collected in gullies, and some dead, shell-free bodies were still attached to the crystalline granite. At Porthleven, several kilometers to the east on the south Cornwall coast where rocks were a smooth sandstone, only the house scars of the limpets ground into the rock or showing as bare patches in the coralline encrustation of tidal pools remained. A number of *Patella aspera* survived on the lower shore, where the sea anemone, *Actinia* sp., also appeared healthy. Elsewhere, the sea anemones were discolored, flaccid, and easy to detach; some of them showed protruding gut structures. About half of the large population of barnacles, *Chthamalus stellatus*, were unhealthy or moribund, particularly those at the higher intertidal levels. The few *Balanus balanoides* barnacles in the lower intertidal levels at Porthleven seemed unaffected [33].

Intertidal algae were also affected by the oil. *Ulva* (sea lettuce), *Porphyra* (laverweed), and other red algae were flaccid and either lacked color or had developed abnormal tints. *Himanthalia*, a large brown thong-weed which exists at Sennen Cove at the lowest intertidal level, developed a greenish color (more typical of fucoid algae when preserved in formalin). The *Corallina* and *Lithothamnia* lining the tide pools

had completely lost their pinkish-purple color and were a
stark white [33].

Six months after the spill, Nelson-Smith [33] visited
Sennen Cove and found only a few *Littorina neritoides*, one or
two sea anemones, *Actinia*, and a few of the largely sublittoral tube-worms, *Pomatoceros*. Mortality of the *Chthamalus* barnacles was greater than estimated six months earlier (April),
although in the meantime a moderate spatfall had occurred.
Mortality of the intertidal algae was also greater than that
estimated in April; most of the seaweeds of the upper intertidal zone had disappeared and the few large plants of *Ascophyllum* sp. and *Fucus vesiculosus* that remained were dry,
blackened, brittle, and obviously dead. The shore areas of
the middle and lower intertidal zone were clothed with a
bright green mat of *Enteromorpha intestinalis*, an alga that is
typically found in sheltered bays and brackish estuaries.
Living specimens of those algae which normally ranged over a
considerable vertical intertidal distance were present only in
the lower intertidal zone. There were, however, clear signs
of recovery at Porthleven where the shore is exposed to wave
action.

At Porthleven, Nelson-Smith [33] found that the periwinkle, *Littorina neritoides*, was surprisingly numerous and
occupied a more extensive range than during the April survey.
Many *Chthamalus* barnacles had survived, and there was a relatively heavy settlement of barnacle spat. A few topshells and
dogwhelks, two or three stringwinkles (*Ocenebra*), and the
young of the true winkle (*Littorina obtusata*), were present in
the middle intertidal zone. *Patella aspera* were no longer in
the lower intertidal zone, although two or three common limpets were found on the beach [33].

The seaweeds of the upper intertidal zone and the higher
level seaweeds of the lower intertidal zone were gone; however, all species, especially the *Himanthalia* in the lower
level of the lower intertidal zone, appeared healthy. The
Enteromorpha extended over the entire intertidal region, min-
gling in the middle and upper intertidal zones with the blad-
derless form of *Fucus vesiculosus* (typical of exposed coast-
lines) and joined lower down by the dark-green floats of the
oyster-thief, *Colpomenia*, which was apparently another new-
comer to this contaminated shore [33].

At Godrevy in Cornwall, the shoreline had been only
lightly polluted with the crude oil and had not been treated
with detergents. Six months after the spill, Nelson-Smith
[33] found that 50 to 80% of the barnacles associated with
hardening patches of oil were dead. Barnacles in nearby oil-
free areas were normal and only a few empty shells were noted.
There were many healthy limpets and winkles everywhere, even
on the oily streaks. The apparent ability of limpets, and

perhaps winkles, to graze away a thin layer of oil without
toxic effects might be due to the immiscibility of oil and
water. Detergents enable the oil to wet the surfaces of the
intertidal organisms and to penetrate their systems [33].
They also enable the oil to spread into areas not originally
polluted or to disperse throughout the water column of rocky
tide pools where it otherwise might have only floated on the
surface. Thus, most of the sessile animals are unable to escape emulsified oil; however, some have adaptive capabilities
which increase their chances of survival. The small winkles,
Littorina neritoides, for example, are sheltered deep in small
crevices in the upper intertidal zone, and mussels can close
their shells tightly and are streamlined so that the oil will
drain rapidly from the shells. Certain winkles attempt to escape pollutants by releasing their grip on the rocky substrate, but such action merely increases their exposure to
danger because they roll into gullies and pools containing the
oil [33].

Certain factors influence the rate of recovery of various
members of the intertidal community after a major oil spill.
Limpets, hardy, moderately mobile organisms, produce planktonic larvae that can rapidly recolonize a short section of contaminated shoreline provided the planktonic forms are ready to
settle, or are from adjacent uncontaminated intertidal areas.
Other gastropods deposit their eggs on the shore; *Littorina
obtusata* (winkle) leave jelly-like egg masses on brown algae
and *Nucella* snails deposit little urn-like cases beneath
stones. These brood structures were found on both the north
and south shores of Cornwall, but the young were found only at
Porthleven [33]. Where neither the adults nor young of a vi-
viparous species survive, as apparently happened at Sennen
Cove, a long time may be required for the species to become
reestablished. The season of the year is undoubtably very important to community recovery. Barnacle larvae swim for a
long time in the planktonic stage. It appeared that larvae of
Balanus balanoides were at the point of settling on the Cornwall coast as the oily emulsion was being washed off the rocky
substrate. Barnacle spat in the area six months after the
spill (September) appeared to be of the later-settling species, *Chthamalus stellatus*.

The first stages of a disturbance of the seaweed-to-graz-
er balance occurred at Cornwall six months after the spill,
but many marine community balances were also disturbed with
less obvious results. It took several years to redress some
of these imbalances. However, the ultimate effects of a single polluting incident, even as severe as that of the *Torrey
Canyon*, may be less than those from repeated pollution in the
vicinity of some oil ports and commercial harbors [33].

Only a few extensive areas of salt marsh were exposed to oil from the *Torrey Canyon*; areas in Brittany, France, were more severely contaminated than those in Cornwall, England. Salt marsh and other coastal plants are most susceptible to oil damage when they are actively growing, and fresh oil is more toxic (short-term toxicity, on a weight basis) than weathered oil. Nevertheless, *Puccinellia maritima*, one of the chief component grasses of European salt marshes, was killed by oil which had weathered at sea for at least seven days [31]. Baker has studied the long-term effects of repeated oilings of salt marsh plants [34,35].

Damage to sand dunes and cliff top communities along the Cornwall coast was caused largely by the decontamination teams as they trampled the areas and spread the detergent. About 10% of the wind-borne sand from treated beaches was contaminated with oil-detergent mixture and part of this sand had been distributed above the shoreline to contaminate backbeach areas. At least 100 species of algae, lichen, flowering plants, and ferns were killed at Cornwall by the oil or the detergent; some of them were rare or locally-distributed species. Recovery of plants and animals to pre-spill densities took several years, but the organizational structure of the new community remained altered.

The mortality of subtidal shellfish was limited following the *Torrey Canyon* incident; however, some shellfish acquired sufficient petroleum taint to render them unmarketable. Tainting of the shellfish food products can originate from three sources: (1) surface oil coatings; (2) oil ingested into the gut of the organisms; and (3) petroleum components assimilated into tissues. Surface contamination of shellfish may not seriously affect the animal; however, when the contaminated animal is cooked, even a small amount of oil can cause serious taint. Several months or more may be required for a tar-like residue on intertidal shellfish to disappear [36]. Filter-feeders, such as mollusks, may ingest oil droplets produced by wave action or by the use of detergents, often without harm; nevertheless, considerable periods of time may be required for depuration if the ingested oil is assimilated into the tissue (see Chapter 3). Even though the shellfish are normal (i.e., continue to exhibit normal growth and reproduction), the presence of extremely low levels of certain petroleum components may render them unsuitable for human consumption [37]. Stegeman and Teal [38], Anderson et al. [39], and Clark and Finley [40] showed that petroleum hydrocarbons are retained in shellfish tissue at levels below taste or odor thresholds for extended periods.

Crabs and lobsters may become tainted but they are more mobile and are capable of moving out of a heavily-polluted area. However, these organisms are detritus feeders and can consume other organisms which are contaminated with oil. Tainted lobsters were found in areas where detergents had been employed following the *Torrey Canyon* grounding. When a researcher bit into the eggs of a "berried" or egg-carrying female lobster, a paraffin taste was detected. This paraffin taste was not evident until the eggs were actually penetrated in this manner, indicating that the contaminant had become incorporated within the eggs and was not just adhering to the surface [36]. Unfortunately, no long-term studies were conducted on the offspring of these lobsters to evaluate effects on the viability of their eggs. The question of whether the hydrocarbons are incorporated into the undeveloped young deserves further investigation.

The impact of the *Torrey Canyon* oil spill on sea birds was serious, affecting an estimated 10,000 birds. When the oil reached the most important seabird colony in France at Sept Îles, it wiped out five-sixths of the entire French puffin (*Fratercula arctica*) population as well as 80 percent of the resident guillemot (*Uria aalge*) and 90 percent of the razorbill (*Alca torda*) populations [41]. In Cornwall and Brittany, there appeared to be a noticeable reduction in the population of adult auks, a considerable loss of immature auks from more northernly colonies, a limited setback to shags and gannets (unlike the other species, the shags and gannets can recover quite quickly), and transient damage to coastal habitats [42].

TAMPICO

One of the first well-documented accounts of the damage caused by a refined petroleum product on an intertidal community involved the grounding of the diesel oil-laden tanker *Tampico* (or *Tampico Maru*) off Baja California, Mexico, about 145 km (90 mi) south of the United States border in the spring of 1957. This study is unique for several reasons: (1) the area, though remote and previously unchanged by humans, had been surveyed briefly a few months prior to the spill, so something of the prevailing conditions prior to the disaster were known; (2) the biota and habitat of a natural area were suddenly and almost totally destroyed, and (3) no attempts were made to control the disaster or mitigate the effects; subsequent adaptions to the trauma were singularly the result of natural forces.

The oil tanker *Tampico* was headed for the port of Ensenada. After groping for two days in a thick fog off the coast of Mexico, on 29 March 1957 the vessel ran against a pinnacle of lava on the nearshore bottom and tore a long gash in the hull near the bow. The forward section of the hull sank after filling with seawater, and the surf swung the stern around so that the tanker lay broadside across the entrance to a small cove allowing the crew to escape safely.

The cargo of about 60,000 bbl (8,000 tons, 9,540,000 l) of dark diesel oil rapidly leaked from the tanker and spread along the shore. The oil was carried by wind and waves and soon covered the cove, which was scarcely ten times the size of the stricken vessel. The diesel oil was rapidly emulsified by the surf. When the turbid emulsion contacted sand and shell particles, greasy surface films and a suffocating sludge formed and settled to the bottom of the cove. In addition, the oil and seawater emulsion covered many of the tide pools. The hull of the *Tampico* formed a breakwater across the mouth of the cove, thereby reducing wave action and, in turn, lowering the oxygenation of the cove water. The luxurious submarine kelp gardens of the cove perished, and seaweed and dead and dying animals littered the beach. The oil coated beaches for several kilometers beyond the small cove, killing pismo clams and other sessile marine organisms.

One month after the disaster, oil still fouled the sea; visibility was limited to only a few centimeters into the extremely cloudy water. Although considerable numbers of dead animals had washed ashore, many more were floating in the water or decomposing on the sea floor. Only a few animal species were left alive in the lagoon. One survivor was the tiny periwinkle, *Littorina planaxis*, whose habitat is normally in the spray zone above high water and was, fortunately, above the limits of the oil spill. A large green anemone, *Anthopleura xanthogrammica*, also survived, but this species has been found in salt water pipelines of oil refineries that use seawater as a coolant; thus it is believed to be tolerant to petroleum. Among the dead species were lobsters, abalone, sea urchins, starfish, mussels, barnacles, crabs, clams, a few fish and hosts of other smaller marine forms [43]. In the subtidal zone, destruction of benthic animal species reached to depths of 4.6 meters [44]. During the first few months, however, small patches of apparently undisturbed mixed marine populations as close as 30 meters from the wreck were found. As additional oil leaked out during the first year, these patches of marine organisms disappeared [45].

The oil caused an immediate, obvious, and widespread destruction of the fauna; however, clearcut effects on the flora were initially restricted to the shallow waters in the immediate vicinity of the wreck. The amount of cast-up algae on the beach was not determined, because algae normally drifted ashore in this locality. Only a few moribund coralline algae tufts occurred in the tide pools near the wreck. In subsequent years the same pools always contained luxurious covers of seaweeds; thus North [45] believed there must have been substantial plant losses following the *Tampico* spill.

Some intertidal animals up to 8 km from the hulk displayed abnormal behavior patterns. A number of *Tegula fune-
bralis* snails, that prefer to remain submerged or beneath damp
seaweed, had moved to dry rock at low tide. Many mussels perished, and large numbers still living did not respond to physical stimulation (e.g., tapping the shell) [44].

The polluted condition lasted about three months and by
summer (3-4 months after the spill) the oil had disappeared;
the cove was again fresh and clean with a profuse bloom of
subtidal algae. With the hulk of the *Tampico* forming a breakwater from the relentless pounding by the surf, the cove became a protected environment for returning mobile animals,
such as large fishes, sea lions, and lobsters. Tiny organisms
whose life-spans were but a few weeks or months began to recolonize the barren rock. Since the shore was no longer exposed to wave action from the open sea and seaweed-grazing
animals had been eliminated, the seaweeds (particularly *Macrocystis pyrifera* or giant kelp) grew at a fantastic rate and
formed a massive and almost impenetrable jungle of tangled
stems, blades, and bladders.

The following winter several severe storms broke up the
hulk and destroyed the protective barrier to the cove. The
Tampico broke in half in early December. Subsequent winter
storms completed the demolition, strewing wreckage over the
bottom of the cove. With the breakwater action of the hulk
removed, the seaweeds were soon ripped up by the waves and the
cove again became barren. Small protected niches were recolonized by new plants and animals; the cove gradually returned
to a new balance with nature.

This cove has been studied each year for more than a decade, and the plant and animal distributions at a dozen locations were recorded. Gradually, the different forms of marine
life returned. Ten years after the accident there were 69
species of animals, compared with only two surviving species
immediately following the disaster. Moreover, there were 57
species of plants ten years later compared with only four remaining species that initially survived. It appeared that at
least one species, the giant kelp (*Macrocystis*), is now more
abundant than before the spill. The variety of marine animal
species had changed; only a few specimens of some prespill
species were present after ten years, whereas numerous dead
specimens of the same species were found immediately following
the spill. At least two species, the green abalone (*Haliotis
fulgens*) and the coastal mussel (*Mytilus californianus*), were
less abundant ten years after the spill than they were originally. Photographs taken immediately after the spill showed
populations of dead but attached mussels in areas inhabited by
other species more than ten years after the spill [45]. Although many of the marine plants and animals have reestablish-

ed themselves in the cove since the spill, there seems to have been a realignment of marine plant and animal species dominance indicating a change in the biotic community of the cove [43].

North [43] stated that the *Tampico* incident prompts a sobering thought: when humans disturb nature on a grand scale, many years may be required for a new natural balance to become established. The time required for the reestablishment of a species in a disturbed environment often substantially exceeds the time required for that species to develop to maturity. One cannot predict the rate of return of marine life to a damaged marine area just on the basis of the growth rates of the organisms under laboratory conditions [43]. The time between the occurrence of a spill and the reappearance of several shellfish species and other invertebrates nearly always exceeds the larval lifespans of these organisms [45].

Arctic

Fortunately, few major petroleum spills have occurred in the Arctic; in fact, as of 1972 Deslauriers [46] could find reports of only a total of 24 oil spills in ice-infested waters, some of which were in fresh water environments under winter conditions. Because the spills were small and occurred in remote areas, they were inadequately studied; however, reports of some subjective observations are available. The following discussion will consider the fuel oil spills in Deception Bay, Quebec, and Resolute Bay, Northwest Territories, Canada (Fig. 3).

Deception Bay Fuel Oil Spill

About 10,500 bbl (441,000 gal, 1,670,000 l) of Arctic diesel fuel oil and 1,700 bbl (71,000 gal, 269,000 l) of gasoline spilled following a slush slide through a tank farm at Deception Bay, Quebec, in western Hudson Strait in early June of 1970. The spill from the six tanks in the farm occurred during a period of small tidal ranges at a location where the tidal range varied from about 3.6 to 5.8 m (12-19 ft). Moreover, the sea was completely covered with a 1.2-m (4-ft) thick layer of ice. Most of the oil was contained within the large blocks of ice in the intertidal zone immediately in front of the slide and on the surface of the water in nearby pools along the tidal hinge. As the tidal range increased later in the month, oil moved out of the area of containment in the intertidal zone. Considerable quantities of the oil were burned either within the intertidal zone or after having been pumped out onto the sea ice, allowing cleanup at the expense of some air pollution and biological damage [47,48].

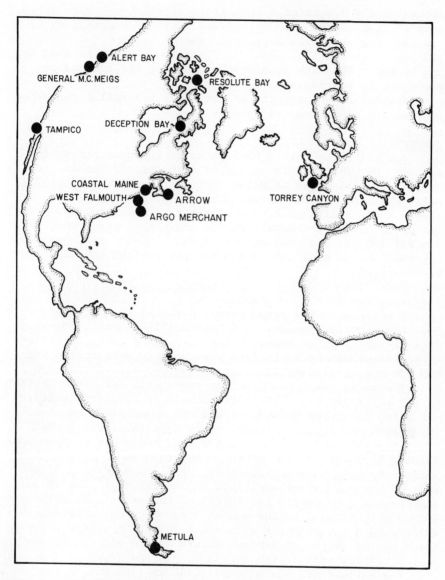

FIG. 3. Locations of major oil spills discussed in this chapter.

Resolute Bay Fuel Oil Spill

A 86 bbl (3,600 gal, 14,000 l) spill of a mixture of diesel fuel oil and a heavier fuel oil, perhaps as heavy as Bunker C fuel oil, occurred at Resolute Bay in Canada's Northwest Territories in late August 1970. The heavy oil was probably the tank or hose cleanings from an oil products tanker.

Approximately 1.8 km of a nonuniform gravel beach were oiled, some of it heavily, with an average depth of penetration of 7.6 cm. For about six days after the spill, the ice cover (80-90% of the surface area) confined the oil to the head of the harbor. When the wind changed much of the ice and oil moved out to sea [48,49].

Neither of the reports of the above oil spills contained information on biological damage.

Subarctic

Several major spills have occurred in subarctic marine waters. We will discuss spills of fuel oil off Chedabucto Bay, in coastal areas of Maine, off West Falmouth, a spill in Alert Bay off western Canada, a spill off the Washington coast, a crude oil spill in the Strait of Magellan, and a fuel oil spill on Georges Bank. Spills near the coastal margins of central [50,51] and southern California [52-54] are considered intermediate to subarctic and subtropic regions and will not be discussed.

The Arrow Incident at Chedabucto Bay

The steam tanker Arrow struck Cerberus Rock in Chedabucto Bay, Nova Scotia, Canada, on 4 February 1970 causing a major loss of its cargo of Bunker C fuel oil. The Liberian-registered vessel was en route from Venezuela to Nova Scotia with 108,000 bbl (17,700 metric tons, 4,540,000 gal, 17,200,000 l) of oil when it ran aground amidst heavy rain and winds gusting to 110 km/hr (60 kn). The forward half of the Arrow suffered extensive damage on grounding, and oil immediately began to spill from the ruptured tanks. Four days later the Arrow broke in half, and four days after that the stern section containing at least a third of the cargo sank in 27 m (90 ft) of water. By this time approximately half, or more than 50,000 bbl, of the oil had escaped into Chedabucto Bay. The total loss amounted to nearly two-thirds of the cargo. An estimated 40,000 bbl, trapped in the sunken stern section, were successfully pumped out by means of a steam injection system necessitated by the extremely viscous nature of the oil at the low winter temperatures of the bay [54].

The spilled oil coated nearly 240 km (150 mi) of shoreline [55], became imbedded in ice [48], and was dispersed in the water as particles of oil up to 1 mm in diameter to at least 80 m in depth extending 180 km in a band 10-25 km wide [56]. There were several features of the Arrow oil spill that make the results of special significance. This was the first time that an extensive research program was quickly organized to study the spill and to determine the effects of Bunker C fuel oil on a cold water environment and its marine biota. Secondly, the water temperature at the time of grounding and

for several months following was at or close to freezing; in
addition, ice was present. Thirdly, detergents were not used
extensively so that the biological impact was due primarily to
the oil rather than to oil and detergent [57].

The Bunker C fuel oil that came ashore behaved differently on the varied types of beach materials. In the intertidal zone, the oil uniformly coated the bedrock, boulders,
and boulder beaches and flowed into crevices and hollows. The
oil was not removed during tidal submergence. The oil that
came ashore on sand and gravel beaches remained on the surface
and formed discrete particles, which tended to float free and
become concentrated along the high water strandline. The
rather viscous Bunker C fuel oil did not penetrate sandy
beaches but acquired a surface coating of sand particles. On
gravel beaches oil permeated as deep as about 50 cm [55].

Following the grounding and subsequent sinking of the
Arrow in the winter of 1970, large slicks contaminated over
half of the shoreline in Chedabucto Bay, and leaks from the
hulk continually released small amounts of oil throughout the
following spring and summer. The slicks produced by these
leaks were a great deal smaller and thinner than the one immediately following the accident but were large enough, nevertheless, to recontaminate many of the beaches. In addition,
shoreline recontamination occurred as wave action reworked the
contaminated sediments and as high spring tides and storm
waves flushed oil-contaminated tide pools.

Conover [58] found that several species of copepods fed
on Bunker C fuel oil droplets without apparent harm and suc-
ceeded in compacting some of the oil into fecal pellets which
sank because they were considerably denser than seawater. On
the basis of this fact, Conover suggested that zooplankton
grazing on dispersed oil droplets constituted an important
natural cleanup system. The only detrimental effect on some
of the *Calanus* copepods was the collection of a few rather
large "oil" particles in the foregut which could lead to a
fatal blockage.

Scarratt and Zitko [59] found residues of Bunker C fuel
oil (see Tables 8 and 10 in Chapter 2 of Volume I) in many organisms and sediments 26 months after the *Arrow* had stranded.
Generally, samples from shallow stations (3.5 m in depth) contained more oil than samples from deeper stations (12 m).
After this period of time there was no visible evidence of oil
in the water column, and carnivorous species had a generally
lower Bunker C fuel oil content (based on fluorescence emis-
sion spectroscopy) than the browsing species.

On Chedabucto Bay shores, the Venezuelan Bunker C fuel
oil was deposited in heavy layers, which adhered tenaciously
to rock, algae, and ice. Thick coatings of oil remained for
extended periods of time, and in some places where populations

had been smothered, no communities were apparently reestablished. The surface of the stranded oil weathered to a firm
consistency; however, the surface skin was thin and during
subsequent warmer weather, oil from beneath the weathered skin
softened and flowed.

The plants in the spill area were heavily coated with oil
and these stranded plants served as reservoirs for oil, no
doubt contributing to the reoiling of the area. According to
Thomas [57], the reoilings, which continued for two years after the spill, produced low-level chronic contamination. Degradation of the oil was slow because the layers were thick
and the surface had developed a firm, weathered coating. The
oil disappeared fairly rapidly from the rock and other exposed
areas [57].

Rafts of mixed seaweeds and oil that stranded on the
beaches soon after the grounding were made up predominantly of
Fucus serratus, which ordinarily occurs in the lower intertidal zone. Midtide seaweeds, such as the dominant *Ascophyllum nodosum* or *Fucus vesiculosus*, were not prominent in
the rafts although they had been exposed to the most severe
oiling. Thomas [57] assumed that these two species were protected by a mucous layer which prevented adhesion of oil.

Fixed littoral epifauna, such as barnacles, were not
abundant in the area prior to the spill, probably due to harsh
winter conditions and to ice scour. These species would have
given better evidence of the immediate effects of the oil than
the dominant intertidal periwinkle species; any dead or inactive periwinkles would have been washed away. Nevertheless,
the complete absence of all fauna from the very heavily oiled
shores suggested rapid inactivation or death [57]. The immediate and apparent effects of the Bunker C fuel oil on Chedabucto Bay intertidal biota were severe only where oiling was
exceptionally heavy; elsewhere the effects were less obvious.

Information on the long-term effects on the biota was
better documented, but even so the trends were not entirely
clear. Most rocky shore fauna showed no evidence of adverse
effects after several years. Sets of barnacle spat appeared,
and the abundance and distribution of the dominant periwinkle
did not change except where seaweed mortalities occurred. The
eradication of the upper intertidal alga, *Fucus spiralis*, was
the sole example of extensive mortality on the rocky shores.
These plants died off slowly from prolonged exposure to the
oil. This alga was particularly vulnerable to the oil pollutant because of its location high in the intertidal zone where
natural attrition of the oil is slowest [57]. In Chedabucto
Bay the most abundant lagoonal biota had been soft-shell clams
and salt marsh cord grass; both were adversely affected by the
Bunker C fuel oil.

Effects on the intertidal biota were most noticeable in
the sheltered lagoons that suffered an initial heavy oiling
and repeated summer reoilings. But even there Thomas [57] observed extensive mortalities in only two species, the soft-
shell clam, *Mya arenaria*, and the salt marsh cord grass, *Spartina alterniflora*. The presence of ice may well have prevented accurate assessment of the mortalities of clams, since dead
clams were found after the ice had receded several months later in May of 1970. Apparently some clams were killed while in
the substratum and others were killed after leaving their burrows. Thomas [57] suggested that some of the clams apparently
tried to avoid the oil pooled in the bottom of their burrows.
It was also possible that oil sealed the mouth of the burrow,
thereby reducing gaseous exchange between air and sediment.
Many clams continued to die in their burrows; the mortalities
were directly proportional to the percentage of oil cover on
adjacent sediments. The exact cause of the mortalities was
not established, but the clams retained oil for a long period
after the spill.

Mollusks make up a large percentage of the benthic fauna
in the low-energy intertidal zones of Nova Scotia; marine bivalves contribute significantly to the total turnover of sedimented materials by epibenthic and benthic fauna. *Mya arenaria* (soft-shell clam), *Mytilus edulis* (blue mussel), and *Ostrea
edulis* (European oyster) lack the enzyme systems (aryl hydrocarbon hydroxylases) to degrade polycyclic aromatic hydrocarbons. According to Vandermeulen and Penrose [60], the apparent inability of these mollusks to degrade polycyclic aromatic
hydrocarbons and the tendency of such pollutant compounds to
accumulate in mollusk tissues present an opportunity for unaltered aromatic hydrocarbons to enter the marine food web. A
detailed discussion of the enzyme systems governing the biotransformation of aromatic hydrocarbons in marine organisms
had been presented by Malins [61] and is summarized in Chapter
3 of this volume.

Inshore, shallow water fish, such as *Ulvaria subbifurca-
ta, Myoxocephalus scorpius*, and *Liparis atlanticus*, may have
been adversely affected by the oil although suspicion has been
also cast on the chemicals introduced as solvents or ignition
agents [57]. The crustacean, *Gammarus oceanicus*, died or
moved away from severely oiled locations. The periwinkles
(*Littorina* sp.) appeared to migrate from oiled to clean areas,
remaining active in spite of their oiled shells; however, the
L. littorea exhibited abnormal behavior in rock pools [54].

A visual assessment was made of the abundance and distribution of oil and of any damage to the sublittoral zone in
Chedabucto Bay. Because of the relatively high density of
this Bunker C fuel oil (0.950 specific gravity; see Table 5 in
Chapter 2 of Volume I), any small increase in density or in

turbulence could have facilitated the distribution of the oil
from the surface down into the water column. Actually, particles and globules of oil were more abundant in the water column than at the bottom, but there was no clear pattern of distribution. With the exception of the heavily oiled sublittoral alga, *Chondrus crispus* (Irish moss), no conclusive visual
evidence was found of any significant short-term damage to the
sublittoral fauna or flora of Chedabucto Bay [54]. Scarratt
and Zitko [59] conducted chemical analyses on a variety of
sublittoral animals (see Table 8 in Chapter 2 of Volume I) and
found petroleum hydrocarbons in the digestive tract, certain
other organs, and muscle tissues.

The fish of Chedabucto Bay (groundfish, lobster, mackerel, herring, smelt, salmon) and their associated industry
(four fish processing plants) represent a primary source of
income to local residents. The oil threatened the lobster
beds in particular, but apparently did not reduce the catch or
affect the flavor of the meat. Contamination of fishing gear,
ships, and docks caused serious inconvenience and some economic loss [54].

An estimated 2,000 dead birds washed ashore shortly after
the oil spill in Chedabucto Bay. In addition, an estimated
5,000 birds had washed ashore on Sable Island. Some of the
casualties may have been due to natural causes; however, the
total dead at sea was estimated to be from 6 to 25 times the
number washed ashore [54]. An assessment of the long-term effects on the bird population of the Bay was hampered by the
lack of reliable background information on natural mortality
rates.

The oil pollution and the actions of an unusually heavy
influx of inquisitive humans probably caused the harbor seals
to move out of Chedabucto Bay. On Sable Island, more than 160
km (100 mi) to the south, the seals were invariably oil-covered. The oil from the *Arrow* mainly affected the vital orifices, causing considerable suffering and occasionally death
by suffocation rather than by toxicity [54] (see Chapter 8).

Large quantities of Bunker C fuel oil lost from the *Arrow*
remained stranded along the shoreline of Chedabucto Bay five
years after the spill. This oil was not static but was slowly
released into the intertidal and sublittoral environments; apparently the principal route was through the sediment and interstitial water. High levels of compounds derived from the
original components of the oil were still present in the burrowing soft-shell clam and in the rooted eel-grass, *Zostera*,
but not in the macroalga, *Fucus*. Zooplankton and phytoplankton probably experienced little or no detectable direct effects from the low concentrations (about 1 ppb) of hydrocarbons still present in the water column above oil-contaminated
beaches. However, nearshore epibenthic biota and meiobiota

must have encountered amounts of petroleum hydrocarbons (about 200 µg/l at the sediment-water interface and at least as high as 1,000 µg/l in the interstitial waters) considered delete-rious to growth, respiration, and chemoreception [62]. The beach sediments in Chedabucto Bay appeared to act as a natural sink for the petroleum hydrocarbons, sequestering interstitial oil at levels up to 5 mg/g of sediment (see Table 10 in Chap-ter 2 of Volume I). Analysis of beach sediments (5, 10, and 15 cm depths) from a low-energy beach 5 yr after the *Arrow* spill indicated a considerable degradation of sediment-bound oil, with an almost total loss of the *n*-paraffins (relative to the unresolved envelope in the gas chromatogram pattern). This degradation, believed to be caused by microbial activity, was rapid with almost total degradation of the *n*-paraffins from the Bunker C oil residues occurring in the top few centi-meters of the beach surface. A considerable aromatic and cy-cloparaffinic fraction remained for potential reentry into the water column [63]. Based on laboratory experiments using con-taminated Chedabucto Bay sediment, Vandermeulen and Gordon [62] estimated that sediment-bound oil may remain as a con-tinuing source of contamination for extremely long periods of time, perhaps in excess of 150 years!

Coastal Maine

Approximately 36,500 bbl (5,000 tons, 1,500,000 gal, 5,800,000 l) of Iranian (Aghi Jari) crude oil was lost when the Liberian tanker *Northern Gulf* ran aground on West Ledge, Casco Bay, Maine, in November of 1963. Stranded oil occurred along 64 km of coastline between the mean high tide and ex-treme low tide levels. All commercial shellfish, principally the soft-shell clam, *Mya arenaria*, in the growing sites within the affected area were contaminated by oil. One area could not be harvested for two years. The total two-year market loss of clams from the spill was estimated at between a mini-mum of 60 and a maximum of 209 metric tons of edible meats.

Five tidal lobster (*Homarus americanus*) storage impound-ments were also located within the spill area. Immediate to-tal loss of 28,800 lobsters, weighing an estimated 15.2 metric tons, was reported by three of the impoundment operators. The persistence of the hydrocarbons from the Aghi Jari crude oil was evidenced by the presence of petroleum isoprenoid hydro-carbons in the sediment from the lobster impoundment areas, even after eleven years. Clams transplanted into contaminated sediments ten years after the oiling showed a 99% mortality (compared to 40% for clams transported to uncontaminated con-trol sites) after 29 days; the surviving clams showed a rapid absorption of petroleum hydrocarbon residues [64].

A continuous spill of No. 2 fuel oil mixed with JP-5 jet fuel from a shoreline tank farm occurred at Searsport, Maine.

The spill started on 16 March and lasted until at least 30
June 1971. The spill had an immediate and long-lasting effect
on the local soft-shell clam industry. Over the following
three and a half years, systematic interdisciplinary studies
were carried out on one cove directly contaminated by the
spill. During the first two years after the spill the following mortalities of clams had occurred [65]: after 6 days - 3%
dead; 13 days - 13% dead; 30 days - 25% dead; 1 year - 55%
dead; and 2 years - 86% dead.

Chemical analysis indicated that contamination of the
area with fresh petroleum material from the leaching of oil-
saturated sediments at higher beach elevations continued up to
eighteen months following the initial detection of the spill.
After two to four weeks of exposure, the flesh of the soft-
shell clams showed a petroleum hydrocarbon pattern similar to
that of the sediment [66].

Histopathological examination of surviving contaminated
clams revealed a high incidence of gonadal tumors. The area
of highest oil impact had the highest percent of tumorous
clams; none of the unexposed control clams (from nearby uncontaminated areas) showed any indication of tumors. The tumors
were malignant neoplasms, although the causative factors were
not specifically investigated [67] (see Chapter 2).

The West Falmouth Oil Spill
During a strong southwest gale on 16 September 1969, the
barge *Florida* transporting 14,000 bbl (1,867 tons, 2,200,000
l) of No. 2 fuel oil (aromatic content 41%) came ashore in
Buzzards Bay off West Falmouth on southwest Cape Cod, Massachusetts (Fig. 4). From 650 to 700 tons of the oil was released. Compared to other incidents, the West Falmouth spill
was a relatively small one; the amount of oil lost from the
Torrey Canyon was 150 times larger. The strong gale-force
winds carried the oil toward West Falmouth and Wild Harbor
which was closed by a floating boom. The waters of Wild Harbor and the Wild Harbor River were converted into a coffee-
colored emulsion, and the shoreline became littered with continuous windrows of dead and dying fish and marine invertebrates [68]. After two or three days, the wind shifted to the
northeast, and the remaining oil slick moved out of Buzzards
Bay. Detergents were applied in limited areas for a short
time [69]. The oil continued to spread and severely contaminated the coastal waters, salt marshes, offshore sediments,
and shellfish resources of Falmouth and Bourne, Massachusetts.
Oil incorporated into the sediments extended to at least 10 m
of water depth, probably because of the intense mixing of oil
and water by the gale-force winds [70].

Three distinct, though partially overlapping, phases followed the spill. In the first phase, covering the first sev-

eral days after the incident, there was a very heavy mortality
of those organisms coming in contact with the oil. A drastic
kill of fish, worms, crustaceans, and mollusks occurred almost
immediately, before detergents had been applied. The kill extended to the inshore areas upstream from the floating booms.

The second phase covered the period from several days to
nearly a year after the spill. The oil continued to spread to
areas that had not been immediately affected, inflicting additional mortalities to both marine plants and animals. The local commercial and recreational shellfish resources were ren-
dered unacceptable for human consumption [71]. Eight months
after the accident, the actual area directly affected by the
spill (including sea bottom, marshes, and tidal rivers) was
far more extensive than was first estimated from the visual
assessment of the limits of the surface-borne oil slicks.
Also, the dispersal of the high aromatic content No. 2 fuel
oil was far greater than expected, based on observations from
previous spills [72]. The area offshore, polluted to depths
of 13 m, covered 20 km^2 (5,000 acres), an area ten times
greater than the area directly impacted with oil immediately
after the spill. In addition, 2 km^2 (500 acres) of tidal
rivers and salt marshes were affected [72].

Depending on the location, the third phase started several months to a year after the spill, and lasted for three to

FIG. 4. The barge Florida aground at West Falmouth, Massachusetts. Photo courtesy of The Falmouth Enterprise.

five years. Residues of oil in the sediment prevented resettlement of the original fauna. The persistence of petroleum
hydrocarbons in sediment and marine organisms was unexpected
in view of the high levels of low-boiling (volatile) aromatic
compounds in the No. 2 fuel oil [73]. After the passing of
several seasons, biochemical and physical processes led to a
gradual reduction of the oil content in the contaminated sediments. Concurrent with the degradation, there was a gradual
reduction in the toxicity of the oil in the sediments. These
changes permitted resettlement of the polluted region, first
in the outlying less affected areas by the most resistent opportunistic species, followed later by a more varied and more
normal distribution of fauna.

A major investigation of the West Falmouth oil spill and
its effect on the marine environment was carried out by a multidisciplinary team of scientists from the Woods Hole Oceanographic Institution and the Marine Biological Laboratory over
a period of more than five years. To assess the biological
effects of the oil on the macroorganisms, the scientists carried out detailed and periodic biological observations and
chemical analyses of the small (retained by a 0.297 mm mesh
screen), highly-sensitive components of the intertidal and
benthic soft-bottom fauna.

The severity of the kill of benthic organisms correlated
well with the concentration of the oil in the sediment samples
collected along with the animals. Even in marginal areas,
where the sediment contained only low levels of oil, some
faunal components were adversely affected, especially the various species of sensitive ampeliscid amphipods. At the heavily oiled intertidal and inshore subtidal areas of Wild Harbor,
the classic marine opportunist worm, *Capitella capitata*, was
one of the few survivors; however, in areas of the greatest
oil pollution even this worm was eliminated. *C. capitata* is
highly resistant to oil pollution and can withstand the severe
stress characteristic of areas heavily contaminated by a variety of pollutants; moreover, it requires only three to four
weeks to become sexually mature. Within three months of the
spill, the *C. capitata* population had explosively increased.

Ten months after the spill by the summer of 1970, some
biodegradation of the oil in the surface sediments had occurred, and other less opportunistic species appeared. The *C.
capitata* population dropped precipitously in response to competition, predation, and the overuse of food resources. Other
species gradually reestablished themselves in intertidal areas
around the spill site, although certain species were still
missing from local intertidal areas for as long as four years
after the incident [74].

Chemical analyses showed that oysters, soft-shell clams,
quahaugs, and scallops had taken up fuel oil [69]. The con-

taminated region had to be closed to the harvesting of shellfish. Continuing analyses revealed that the level of contamination in the 1970 shellfish crop was as severe as that in
the 1969 crop, but in addition, more distant areas in 1970
contained shellfish contaminated by fuel oil; thus these
newly-polluted shellfish grounds had to be closed as well.
Blue mussels, *Mytilus edulis*, that were juvenile at the time
of the accident generally were sexually sterile in the next
season; they survived but had developed almost no eggs or
sperm [72].

At the less-affected localities, faunal densities remained much reduced for nearly a year after the spill. During
the second year most of the species reestablished themselves
but, as expected, the populations consisted of inordinately
high percentages of young individuals. At the marginally affected localities, only a few species showed stress, and recovery was relatively rapid; however, recovery was stopped
following a fresh infusion of less degraded oil from the initial spill site. These fresh infusions of oil probably origi-
nated from reservoirs in the marsh or from deposits on the
beach. The redistributed oil produced secondary mortality at
certain localities [74].

Four to five years later the numbers of benthic species
at the offshore stations and in the marsh were slightly, but
significantly, lower than those at control stations not affected by the spill. At the offshore stations for both exposed and control sites, the population densities in the control and contaminated areas were similar. However, in the
marsh environment the exposed areas had less than 20,000 individuals per square meter compared with nearly 110,000 for the
control area. Michael and coworkers [75] warned of misinter-
pretation inherent in the use of subjective visual observa-
tional methods in assessing oil pollution damage. Up to the
time of the West Falmouth spill most subtidal damage assessments had been (1) non-quantitative and limited to the dominant species only, (2) conducted for only a restricted time
period, or (3) both. It is now well-established that certain
species, such as oysters, barnacles, and mussels, are much
more tolerant to oil than other marine organisms. Growth ring
studies showed that the mussel, *Modiolus demissus*, from Wild
Harbor survived the spill quite well; a significant number of
individuals had five or more annual growth rings in 1974 indicating that their life span interval started before the time
of the oil spill. After several years, the intertidal region
of the initially heavily-oiled Wild Harbor boat basin supported an abundance of *Littorina* snails, whereas the subtidal area
a few meters removed was still heavily affected by the oil.
If the assessment of the effects of the spill had been limited
to such dominant species, one might have concluded erroneously,

according to Michael and coworkers [75], that the area had fully recovered. Except for river and marsh portions, the intertidal regions, the area where the greatest study effort is normally made, represents only a tiny fraction of the total geographic area ordinarily affected by a spill. Fuel oil residues were detected in the benthic habitats more than a kilometer off the entrance to Wild Harbor, as was evidence of biological effects [75].

The petroleum hydrocarbons seemed to persist in the sediments; even after eight months, essentially unaltered No. 2 fuel oil was recovered from the sediments of the most heavily polluted areas. By the end of the first year, changes in the gas chromatographic fingerprint pattern of the oil provided evidence that bacterial degradation had taken place [71,73]. Nevertheless, only partial loss of petroleum components from the sediments had occurred. Bacteria in the surface sediments appeared to attack the paraffinic hydrocarbons first, and analyses showed that some of the medium and higher molecular weight aromatic hydrocarbons remained in the sediments [72].

Geochemical conditions in the subsurface region of the sediment appeared to be relatively stable. The degree of degradation of the No. 2 fuel oil between 2.5 and 7.5 cm depth lagged by 14 months the degree of degradation of the oil in the surface two centimeters. Rapid degradation of the oil in subsurface sediments will probably occur only when the sediment is reworked by mechanical or biological means. The presence of relatively unchanged and potentially toxic petroleum in the subsurface sediment presents a hazard to burrowing marine organisms [71].

Environmental degradation of the No. 2 fuel oil spilled at West Falmouth proceeded relatively slowly. Although slow degradation of the *n*-paraffins in moderately contaminated sediment might start soon after a spill, several months may elapse in heavily polluted sediment before rapid degradation commences. Furthermore, *n*-paraffins seem to persist above background levels in the sediment environment and in marine macroorganisms even though some microorganisms present in the sediment show a preference for degrading *n*-paraffins [71].

Blumer and Sass [71] found that degradation rates of petroleum products determined under laboratory conditions could not be applied to the assessment of petroleum degradation in the estuarine environment affected by the spill off West Falmouth. The branched and cyclic hydrocarbons were degraded more slowly than the *n*-paraffins. Even after two years, isoprenoid and cyclic saturated and aromatic hydrocarbons were still present in the sediments and in organisms of Buzzards Bay and adjacent marshes. The loss of aromatic hydrocarbons appeared to Blumer and Sass [71] to proceed mostly through dissolution rather than through microbial utilization. The

more soluble lower molecular weight and less-highly substitut-
ed aromatic hydrocarbons of the fuel oil disappeared gradually, while the alkyl-substituted and higher boiling aromatic
hydrocarbons persisted. The preferential microbial degradation of some saturates and the simultaneous dissolution of
certain aromatics preserved the overall saturate-to-aromatic
ratio in the fuel oil remaining in the sediment but the distribution of specific hydrocarbons was altered.

It is still not possible to construct a model of the marine environment which can predict actual physical and chemical changes that may take place in the course of an oil spill.
Petroleum contaminants may be distributed among all the many
compartments of the marine ecosystem and may be altered in
many ways depending upon the availability of water, oxygen,
and macro- and microorganisms. The persistence after two
years of a fraction of "readily degradable" n-paraffins in the
sediment off West Falmouth raises some doubt about the possible effectiveness of intentional bacterial seeding as a means
of reducing environmental petroleum residues [71].

Evaporation played a minor role in the weathering of the
oil at West Falmouth. The boiling point distribution of the
components of the residue in the sediments two years after the
spill was still close to that of the original No. 2 fuel oil;
hydrocarbons as low as C_{12} remained in sediments and organisms. Oil taken up by organisms and sediments cannot evaporate; and, the West Falmouth experience demonstrated the retention, for extended periods, of compounds representing almost the entire boiling range of even low boiling oil components, such as a No. 2 fuel oil. Environmental weathering of
the oil does not severely alter the ratios between adjacent
members of homologous series, such as the ratio of pristane to
phytane. Each crude oil may exhibit characteristically different hydrocarbon distribution ratios; the persistence of
these characteristic ratios during the aging (weathering) of
the oil provides a basis for "fingerprinting" or "tagging" a
particular oil introduced into the environment from a spill or
other sources [71] (see Chapter 1 of Volume I).

Alert Bay Heavy Fuel Oil Spill
The freighter *Irish Stardust* ruptured two heavy fuel oil
tanks on striking Haddington Reef in 1973 and spilled roughly
1,340 bbl (200 tons, 61,000 gal, 232,000 l) into Broughton
Strait near Alert Bay between Vancouver Island and the British
Columbia mainland in western Canada. Several miles of upper
intertidal beaches were contaminated and, except for one semi-
exposed bay that was left undisturbed for scientific study,
were subjected to cleanup operations.

The oil quickly spread along a 1.5-m band downward from
the high tide line and completely covered beaches, rock faces,

logs, and seaweeds with a 1- to 5-cm thick coat. Beach sand was oiled but not completely coated, and below mid-tide in several areas the beach and rock faces appeared totally oil-free. Six weeks after the spill biological damage appeared to be limited to those flora (*Fucus* sp., rockweed) and fauna (limpets and periwinkles, primarily) smothered by the heavy oil. The wave and tidal action had not visibly altered the initial pattern of contamination in the bay.

Eight months after the accident, oil was still present along the rock faces and on the rock and gravel portions of the affected beach. A surface slick was produced during each advancing tide from oil leached from the beach. Significant recolonization of limpets or periwinkles on the oiled rock faces had not occurred. A superficial examination of the bay one year after the spill might have led to the conclusion that the oil had disappeared, but closer examination revealed that coagulated oil had immobilized the gravel on the most heavily contaminated portion of the beach. Oiled marsh grass stands previously noted to be 15 to 25 cm high (non-contaminated stands were 15-30 cm high) were now about 3-5 cm high, indicating physical damage. Limpets had not begun to recolonize the previously oiled rock faces, but periwinkles were found under rocks in areas previously devoid of the organisms.

Gas chromatograms of the oil collected on the beach during the first six weeks following the spill showed very similar hydrocarbon patterns to those based on a Japanese 1,000 second oil (less viscous than a Bunker C fuel oil) from the fuel tanks of the freighter. After four and a half months, the beached oil showed a definite loss of the *n*-paraffin hydrocarbons of carbon number less than C_{25}. After summertime weathering, nearly all of the normal paraffin compounds had been degraded, although the isoprenoid compounds, pristane and phytane, remained. After a year the level of isoprenoid compounds had also diminished. Green and coworkers [76] considered that this loss of isoprenoid hydrocarbons indicated that bacterial degradation was the main mechanism for altering the chemical character of the heavy fuel oil. If so, the process took one year to complete the degradation of the *n*-paraffin hydrocarbons, leaving an asphalt-like residue (estimated at 5-10% of the original volume) on the beach.

General M.C. Meigs Incident off Washington

The grounding and breakup of the *General M.C. Meigs* provided an opportunity for study of the effects on the marine environment of a long-term, low-level release of a well-aged Navy Special fuel oil (similar to Bunker C fuel oil) into a rich, subarctic open coastal intertidal environment. On 9 January 1972, the *General M.C. Meigs*, a 190-m (620-ft) unmanned troopship, was being towed from Puget Sound, Washington, to San Francisco Bay, California, when 17 km (10 mi) south of Cape Flattery on the northwest Washington coast a winter storm broke the vessel's tow line, swept the ship ashore, and broke it into two segments (Fig. 5). It was esti- mated that the vessel was carrying 2,750 bbl (410 tons, 437,000 l) of oil, or about 16% of the vessel's fuel capacity, in 19 tanks. Until this accident, it was standard practice to leave some oil, usually stripped of its diesel oil-like cutter stock by forced ventilation, in military vessels placed in re- serve status to inhibit corrosion and provide ballast.

An estimated 50 bbl of the aged fuel oil spilled as the main amidships center tank was ripped open on grounding. The oil was largely contained along the immediate shoreline as the vessel acted as a barrier to the seaward flow of oil and by the onshore winds (83 to 93 km/hr, 45 to 50 kn). Considerable quantities of oil globules varying from 5 to 30 cm in diameter and a large amount of heavily oiled debris, shoring, and crib- bing from the deck cargo washed up on the beach. A decision was made not to try to salvage the vessel because of its con- dition and remote location. The oil that came ashore was re- moved by hand using rakes and was placed in heavy plastic bags; the bags were air-lifted by helicopter to a land-fill disposal site. The oil-soaked debris was burned. No deter- gents were used, nor were attempts made to remove the oil re- maining in the hulk because of its gelatinous condition and the hazardous location of the wreck in the surf zone. Up to 180 kg (500 lb) of oil and oil-soaked debris were collected daily for several weeks on beaches within one kilometer of the grounded hulk. Progressively decreasing amounts were removed during the next several months. Small quantities of newly- released oil globules were being continuously washed up at the high tide drift line during periods of extreme low tide for the next three years [77,78].

The small cove immediately inshore from the wreck that received the greatest concentration of fuel oil was studied to determine if plant and animal life was adversely affected by the spill. Using modern analytical chemical techniques, in- vestigators were able to detect n-paraffin hydrocarbon resi- dues in the plants and animals of the cove. The "residual" hydrocarbon patterns of exposed organisms after correction for biogenic hydrocarbons resembled the patterns of the petroleum pollutant [79].

Analyses [80] showed that n-paraffin residues remained in certain marine organisms for at least nine months after the initial grounding and oil spill; n-paraffins remained in cer- tain species of algae for more than a year. Accurate assess- ment of uptake and discharge of petroleum components by marine organisms was difficult because the oil was released contin- ually at a slow rate over the 31-month study period. In addi-

FIG. 5. The General M.C. Meigs aground on the Washington coast. Size is indicated by the two persons in a raft at lower center.

tion, the amount of oil released varied with environmental conditions over the seasons in a manner which could not be estimated [78]. It is not clear whether the persistence of the petroleum components in the marine organism tissues was due to normal retention by the organisms or by recontamination of the organisms by tar globules; current methods did not permit a differentiation between the two possibilities. Nevertheless, the pattern and level of n-paraffin hydrocarbons in the tissues reflected the degree of exposure of the organism to the pollutant [78].

Certain marine plants and animalshad suffered some damage during the first ten months after the spill. Several species of seaweeds in the lower intertidal zone had lost portions of their fronds and several species in the upper intertidal zone showed bleached thalli. In small localized areas, many of the purple sea urchins, *Strongylocentrotus purpuratus*, were dead or had lost sufficient spines to make their survival improbable. After 32 months, no damaged urchins could be found in the area that could be attributed to the spill.

The abundance of marine plants and animals two months after the incident was not significantly different from that 31 months after the spill, except for differences attributable to normal seasonal variations. Few changes in abundance of marine animals occurred during the first ten months after the accident, but a slight decline took place subsequently. It is possible that the breakwater effect of the hulk favored the growth of algae over the competing intertidal animals on the same substrate [78].

Although the *General M.C. Meigs* incident involved a relatively minor oil spill, based on volume and type of petroleum material involved, evidence of organism damage and pollutant uptake by the intertidal species was found. This emphasized the sensitivity and vulnerability to pollution of those organisms that are generally considered hardy by virtue of the environmental stresses they normally encounter [77].

Metula Crude Oil Spill in the Strait of Magellan

On 9 August 1974, the *Metula* (a VLCC - very large crude carrier), loaded with more than 1.45 million bbl (197,000 metric tons, 230 million l) of Light Arabian crude oil, ran aground on Banco Satelite (Satellite Patch) in the eastern portion of the Strait of Magellan (Fig. 6). The 325-m (1,067-ft) long supertanker was steaming at nearly full speed (27 km/hr, 14.5 kn) when it struck bottom (loaded draft of 19 m) ripping open five forward compartments. Some 6,100 tons of oil were spilled. Two days later the ship shifted under the force of a strong flood tide current at high water, and the engine and steering engine rooms filled with seawater; as a result the ship lost all power [81].

FIG. 6. VLCC Metula *grounded in the Strait of Magellan. Photo courtesy of the MESA Program Office, U.S. Department of Commerce, Boulder, Colorado.*

Oil leaked from the hulk as it was buffeted by tides and currents. Major oil losses occurred during the next two weeks as additional cargo tanks were breached. By 22 August, 20% of the cargo was lost; another 25% was transferred to smaller tankers by 25 September when the *Metula* was refloated and towed to a safe anchorage. The estimated discharge into the Strait of Magellan was slightly more than 50,000 tons of crude oil and about 2,000 tons of Bunker C fuel oil. Winds (to 130 km/hr, 70 kn) and currents (to 4.8 m/s, 9.3 kn) transported the oil throughout the eastern third of the Strait. At times oil slicks covered about 2,600 km^2 (1,000 mi^2); however, no efforts were made to contain, disperse, or cleanup the oil on the water nor to contain or remove the oil on the Tierro del Fuego beaches [82].

The intertidal zone in the spill area consisted primarily of shingle, gravel, and sand; in addition, the area contained some mud flats, salt marshes, and shorelines having boulders and large stones [83]. Two distinct types of oil deposits appeared as two distinct bands on the gravel beaches; a "dark mousse" (consisting of oil, about 5% water, sand, seaweed, marine worms, and other detritus) was located at the high-tide strandline and a "light mousse" (containing about 30% water) occurred in the intertidal zone [82]. Hann [84] estimated that 60,000 m^3 (2.1 million ft^3) of mousse appeared along the most heavily oiled beach section (about 77 km) of the south side of the Strait.   This represented about 40,000 tons of oil.   Beach deposits of oil were generally 2 to 50 m wide and 0.5 to 15 cm deep.   When the tide went out, prevailing winds tended to keep the mousse on or near the shore.   Oil was also carried several kilometers into two tidal estuaries on the Tierro del Fuego side [82].   The mousse was mixed into the beach material; some oil refloated as small lumps, and sheens occurred [83].

Five months after the spill, Hann [85] estimated that at least half of the mousse that developed immediately after the spill was still on the beaches.   On the heavily-oiled beaches, oil extended as much as 50 cm below the beach surface but depth of penetration and horizonal distribution along the beach were quite variable.   Oil had flowed, apparently aided by diurnal and seasonal heating, from the upper part of the beach to the lower part.   The oil flow, aided by wave erosion of oily sand and gravel layers, and the resuspension of oil and mousse by high tides continued to discolor the surf along several beaches [82].

Within three months of the spill, the mousse in all areas where sand or coarse gravel beaches existed had been buried. There was still a band of weathered, dried-out mousse at the high tide strandline.   Two to three months later at the heavily oiled locations, sand covered a thick layer of mousse that was still fresh and only partially mixed with sand in many places.   There was a generally eastward drift of mousse toward protected areas of little wave action where the oil tended to collect.

One of the most visible adverse ecological impacts in-volved the water birds.   A two-day survey one month after the spill showed that 408 cormorants (*Phalacrocorax* spp.), 66 Magellan penguins (*Speniscus magellanicus*), 23 ducks (*Lopho-netta specularioides*), and 84 kelp gulls (*Larus dominicanus*), were killed because of heavy oiling.   Other estimates put the number of dead birds as high as 2,000 [82].   Five months after the spill, observers reported sickness and mortality among the cormorants, penguins, and other birds related to oiling and the ingestion of oil-contaminated food.   Baker and coworkers [83] estimated that 3,000 to 4,000 birds may have been killed during the first six months.

Biological damage occurred in the littoral zone, espe-cially near the spring low water tide line, where rich popu-lations of mussels (*Mytilus chilensis*) and some limpets (*Nacella* sp.), anemones (*Corynactis* sp.), and starfish were coated with oil [82].   In the lower intertidal areas, where generally much less mousse was deposited, the algae associated with mussel beds (e.g., laverweed [*Porphyra*], sea lettuce [*Ulva*], and other species) had been damaged [83].

Due to the active nature of many of the gravel beaches, the affected shores had low densities of intertidal flora and fauna; however, toward the sublittoral zone there was a much richer flora and fauna (i.e., greater densities and more species) [83]. Intertidal surveys after five months indicated continuing mortality among invertebrates. The number of species in heavily oiled areas was consistently lower than in unpolluted areas. Straughan [86] found large numbers of empty shells in good condition and noted that mussel communities were previously more extensive. While these observations do not conclusively imply a cause and effect relation, Straughan concluded that the oil spill caused these detrimental effects because: (1) mortalities were recent; (2) oil was present in large amounts for five months; and (3) changes in numbers of species could not be related to natural physical changes in the sediment.

In some areas, deaths of the marine organisms that occurred during and a few months after the spill may have been related to the toxicity of the low-boiling petroleum components, suffocation, and habitat destruction by the mousse, rather than from continued leaching of soluble components. Surviving mussels, containing 1,000 to 5,000 µg/g of petroleum-derived hydrocarbons, were smaller for their shell size than uncontaminated mussels, containing 10 to 15 µg/g hydrocarbons from control areas [86,87].

Chemical analyses of contaminated materials (sediment and tissue) showed large amounts of petroleum components similar, as determined by gas chromatography and mass spectrometry, to those in the oil taken directly from the *Metula*. The patterns differed only in the levels of the lower boiling hydrocarbons; practically all of the hydrocarbons boiling below n-C_{13} were lost as well as significant amounts of those in the n-C_{13-17} range. Warner [87] suggested, on the basis of the gas chromatographic results, that most of the benzenes and naphthalenes had been lost but the phenanthrenes, dibenzothiophenes, and other higher boiling components remained. He found no evidence of any significant amount of selective microbiological modification of n-paraffins in the 41 sediment and 7 tissue samples analyzed.

Many of the oiled salt marsh plants (perennials) showed new shoots five months after the spill. Since the spill occurred toward the end of winter, the contamination involved only the old shoots from the previous summer [83]. However, studies after the *Arrow* spill in Chedabucto Bay showed that, for as long as two years after the incident, oil in estuaries continued to harden (weather) to an asphalt-like consistency; as a result plants that had already grown through the oil layer may be eventually killed [86].

Several months after the spill, crusty, partially-dried, weathered mousse and oil were found along the extreme high tide strandline, in the splash zone, and among the oil-covered, blackened marsh plants; it tended to harden into the black asphaltic material [82].   The long-term consequence of petroleum-induced physical alteration of some beach and estuarine habitats (e.g., change in drainage patterns, rocks being cemented together by the oil, reduction of oxygen levels) have yet to be assessed.   The contaminated beaches in the Strait of Magellan have been subjected to a long and high dosage of a crude oil capable of forming extensive amounts of mousse.   Since the oil in the lower intertidal zone was in the form of mousse six months after the spill, Straughan [86] found that the oil had not dried sufficiently to become a substrate suitable for the settlement of sessile organisms but remained in a sticky state. Aside from any direct chemical toxicity of this mousse, the physical modifications of the intertidal habitat by its presence could have a significant long-term effect on the capability of the biota to recover from one of the largest oil spills to date.

Two tidal estuaries on the south side of the Strait of Magellan were seriously affected by the oil.   One estuary in the eastern part of the heavily oiled section on Tierro del Fuego contained large amounts of wind-driven oil months after the incident.   During high tides and gale winds the oil was pushed as far as 5 km into smaller tidal channels and over flat grasslands, leaving pools of oil up to 30 cm deep and killing vegetation.   The rise and fall of oil by tidal action caused recoating of channel walls and vegetation [82].

Kelp (*Macrocystis pyrifera*) beds commonly occur in this part of Chile.   A brief survey of oiled kelp beds one month after the spill revealed the presence of a large number and variety of healthy animals.   Except for one complaint of tainted fish, no reports were received of damage to commercial fisheries, most of which are well to the south of the affected area [83].

Hann [85a] revisited the *Metula* spill site in January, 1976, 1-1/2 years after the grounding.   By this time, an estimated 200 to 240 km (125 to 150 mi) of beach were contaminated with oil from the spill.   In some heavily contaminated areas the mousse had combined with sand, gravel, shells, and debris, and the mass had weathered to an asphalt-like hard pavement, termed "moussecrete."   The oil residues on some beaches showed substantial weathering but residues on many other beaches had formed 5- to 30-cm thick layers of moussecrete which existed in bands as large as 5 to 25 m wide and 2 to 4 km long.

The east tidal estuary on the south side of the Strait remained a desolate wasteland.   Banks and flat areas were still clogged or covered with oil deposits.   The deposits in the flat areas were soft and soupy and had a black surface film but showed little evidence of crusting or hardening.   In the west estuary, the oil deposits had blackened and hardened somewhat from exposure and had penetrated further into the sediment.   In the intertidal zone, dispersion of the oil occurred only on the high-energy beaches, in channels having high-velocity flow of water, and on exposed beach top areas [85a].

The seaward 100-m stretch of the intertidal zone exposed only at the spring low tides was not coated with significant amounts of oil.   This zone was rich in algae and some mussels; algae had become attached to the surface of the hardened pavement in some areas.   Hann [85a] found substantially more dense populations of mussels, limpets, crustaceans, worms, and other organisms on the relatively uncontaminated north shore of the Strait of Magellan than on the impacted south shore.   Although many adult mussels survived at the low tidal level of the impacted beaches, there was a scarcity of juvenile mussels, juvenile and adult limpets and an absence of crustaceans in the affected intertidal areas.

The remoteness of the area and lack of facilities and equipment made it impossible to conduct a timely study of the effects of dissolved or finely-dispersed oil on behavior, growth, reproduction, and survival of plankton and the young of commercial and other species.   Microbiological studies could not be carried out immediately.   No ecological studies of communities of the affected area existed prior to the spill so the immediate, and even some of the long-term, effects of this spill cannot be adequately assessed.   Straughan [88] found that it was impossible to compare control and contaminated sites because areas outside those contaminated by the oil have, in general, a different physical structure from those in the areas impacted by the oil spill.   Because of its remoteness, economic impacts of the spill on the local environment (e.g., fishing, tourism, recreation) were not significant [82,83].

The *Metula* spill, like the *Tampico* spill, afforded an opportunity for the assessment of the long-term effects of petroleum on the biota and the progress of natural weathering of a massive quantity of oil in a remote area where the forces of nature alone determine the course of the readjustment of a marine community.   Human efforts to minimize the spill were directed toward removing as much oil as possible from the hulk rather than toward containment or dispersal of the free oil. This circumstance was due in part to: (1) the severe weather conditions; (2) the problems of remoteness and unavailability of manpower and equipment; (3) the initial uncertainties in estimating the amount of spilled oil; (4) lack of baseline data on the impacted marine environment; (5) the possibility of additional damage to the environment from such operations; and (6) questions about legal and financial responsibilities [82].

Argo Merchant Fuel Oil Spill

In the morning of 15 December 1976, the *Argo Merchant*, a 23-year old, 195-m (640-ft), 28,691-dwt (deadweight tons) tanker, ran aground on Fishing Rip, an area of treacherous Nantucket Shoals 43 km (27 mi) off Nantucket Island (southeast of Massachusetts). The visibility at the time was 6 to 10 km (4 to 6 mi) and the tanker was 47 km (29 mi) off course [89]. The tanker was carrying 182,600 bbl (about 27,300 tons, 7.67 million gal, 29.0 million l) of No. 6 fuel oil (similar to a Bunker C fuel oil) from two different Venezuelan sources. The vessel was travelling at a speed of 15 km/hr (8.5 kn) when it ran aground in sand from midships to stern. The screw was reversed for 13 min before a pipe broke resulting in the slow flooding of the engine room. By that afternoon, oil slicks had appeared and plans were made for offloading the oil. It was predicted that offloading would take from two to four weeks, weather permitting. Because the pour point temperature (see p. 6, Chapter 1 of Volume I) of this industrial oil was near that of the seawater (4.6°C), the oil could not be pumped from the tanks without first being heated [90].

During the first night after the grounding, the *Argo Merchant* was buffeted by 1 to 2.5-m (3 to 8-ft) waves and 19 to 37 km/hr (10 to 20 kn) winds. However, weather conditions deteriorated and flooding of the cargo tanks and engine room with seawater increased. By the next day, the spill control team was forced to abandon the stricken vessel. The *Argo Merchant* had lost more than 20% of her cargo at this point. Increasing winds carried the viscous fuel oil more than 105 km eastward off the southern edge of Georges Bank, one of the richest fishing grounds in the world. Concern was expressed that these valuable fishery resources might be affected by the oil spill, especially the bottom-dwelling crustaceans and mollusks such as lobsters, ocean quahaugs, surf clams, and scallops, as well as major finfish stocks, such as cod, haddock, sole, and flounder. Oiled herring gulls (*Larus argentatus*) were washed ashore on Nantucket Island several days after the spill. By 20 December, approximately 500 oiled seabirds were sighted on the northern tip of Nantucket Island [90].

After six days of being battered by high seas, the tanker broke into two pieces and 40 to 60% of the original cargo was spilled, bringing the total loss to about 80% of the cargo (146,000 bbl); thus, the *Argo Merchant* spill was the largest to occur near American shores. Because of continuing bad weather (winds to 92 km/hr, 47 kn) and heavy seas (to 6 m, 20 ft), no oil had been offloaded. The next day (7 days after the grounding) the forward section split releasing the remaining 36,000 bbl of No. 6 fuel oil from the hulk. The only portion of the vessel above the surface was the tip of the bow and the antennae of the superstructure.

The trapezoid-shaped oil slick had affected an estimated area of 7,870 km^2 (3,040 mi^2) and extended 220 km east of the wreck. Fifty-six kilometers east of the grounding site, currents and rip tides broke the congealed oil into patches. Because of offshore winds, only about 6% of the spilled oil had reached Georges Bank during the first week and none had reached the New England shores or beaches [90].

However, during the second week, it was estimated that the oil slick covered as much as 20% of the water overlying Georges Bank. Concern was expressed that the heavy fuel oil might sink because its density was near that of the seawater (see p. 29-31, Chapter 1 of Volume I for a discussion of the physical properties of heavy fuel oils). Once oil sinks to the sea floor, it can move horizonally with bottom currents (for further discussion see p. 121, Chapter 2 of Volume I). Based on oceanographic conditions of the area, it was predicted by the use of a computer that the movement of near-bottom oil would be toward the southern New England coast [91]. Plans to burn the surface slicks were abandoned when it became impossible to find patches of oil large enough to burn.

Preliminary surveys made in the weeks following the grounding revealed that the dense oil did not sink and cover large portions of the productive Georges Bank, although oil apparently was present in bottom sediments in the immediate vicinity of the sunken wreck. A number of scientific cruises were made to the Georges Bank area east and north of the *Argo Merchant* to investigate physical, chemical, and biological impacts; however, severe weather frequently hampered these efforts. Within two weeks of the grounding, more than 115 water, 48 sediment, 10 plankton, 10 neuston, and 50 intertidal samples were taken and the bottom area was trawled several times during 8 cruises. Analysis of the samples are in progress as of the printing of this volume.

It is too early at this time (March 1977) to offer any definite conclusions about damage to the biota. Preliminary observations of marine mammal populations suggest that whales and dolphins were distributed randomly throughout the spill area and showed no apparent response to the presence of floating oil. In the first two weeks after the spill, no marine mammals were seen to be in direct contact with oil patches. When oiled seabirds were seen offshore, usually half of the seabirds (e.g., murres, gulls, loons, auks) were fouled with oil on the breast, abdomen, or wings, although none appeared to be crippled or entrapped in the oil. A total of 160 oiled birds were collected on Nantucket and Cape Cod within the first month of the spill [92].

Evidence from preliminary surveys suggested that ichthyoplankton were significantly and adversely affected in the area of the spill. Pollock eggs found at stations within the slick area showed high mortalities (70% of the eggs appeared moribund, based on microscopic examination of the net tow samples) and nearly all of the eggs had adhering oil globules. A greater percentage of the cod eggs found adjacent to the spill were viable but 64% of the cod eggs showed evidence of oil contamination. Cytogenetic studies on these eggs indicated a high incidence of abnormal development and high percentages of dead or morbid eggs. Zooplankton biomass was significantly reduced in the area of the spill. Because of normally patchy distribution of zooplankton, it was impossible to draw any conclusions until further information was obtained. Large percentages of copepods and amphipods had oil particles clinging to their feeding appendages or stored in their digestive tracts [92].

Weathering of the spilled oil was studied to provide data for the development of a better spill trajectory model. It was calculated that the oil patches (about 25 mm thick) moved at only 1.1 to 1.2% of the wind speed, for wind speeds of 18 to 32 km/hr (10 to 17 kn) (see p. 104, Chapter 2 of Volume I). Once free of the wreck, the oil formed pancakes which built up in thickness as they moved seaward. After one to two weeks on the sea surface, the oil increased in thickness from 25 to 50 mm to about 300 mm [92].

LONG-TERM BIOLOGICAL EFFECTS OF OIL SPILLS

Investigations following an oil spill have always revealed some biological damage. The case studies cited in the previous section have shown that various effects can occur due to differences in amount and duration of the spill, type of oil, weather conditions, type of environmental habitat, and methods used to reduce the impact of the pollution. In some cases there have been immediate and obvious deaths of marine plants and animals from the oil (*Tampico* and *Arrow* spills); in other cases the effects have been more subtle, such as the slow loss of certain intertidal algae species or a shift in the dominant species over a period of several seasons (*Tampico* and *General M.C. Meigs* spills). The effects of remedial actions, such as the improper use of detergents, appear to be as great, if not greater, than the impact of the oil alone (*Torrey Canyon* spill). The *Tampico*, West Falmouth, *General M.C. Meigs* and *Argo Merchant* spills provided opportunities for studying the impact of refined products in the absence of remedial actions, while the *Metula* spill provided an opportunity for a study of crude oil effects.

These studies show that, in some instances, oil pollution increases in area (West Falmouth) over a period of time and that the extent of the increase is related directly to the type of petroleum spilled and to the degree of agitation of the oil in the marine system. Once in the environment, especially in the sediments, petroleum tends to degrade quite slowly (Chedabucto Bay [*Arrow*], coastal Maine, West Falmouth, Alert Bay, and Strait of Magellan [*Metula*]), although the modification of various hydrocarbon components (e.g., loss of *n*-paraffins) may be dependent on how the oil is incorporated into the sediments (*Arrow* vs. West Falmouth spills).

Depending on the type of oil spilled and on climatic conditions, weathering can be rather slow. For instance, in low-energy shore areas (Chedabucto Bay [*Arrow*], Alert Bay, and parts of the Strait of Magellan [*Metula*]), oil remained buried in intertidal beaches for years, often retaining its high-boiling aromatic hydrocarbons. Oil splashed on rock faces above the normal high tide level can last for years (*General M.C. Meigs* spill; [78]).

Over a long period of time, alteration of the intertidal population structure, such as increased algal densities when grazing animals are depleted (*Torrey Canyon* and *Tampico* spills), frequently occurs. Some effects take months to years; for instance, intertidal algae took several months to die and become bleached (Cornwall [*Torrey Canyon*] and Washington [*General M.C. Meigs*]), while a lack of maturation in contaminated mussels took a year to become apparent (West Falmouth). The immediate effects of oil on biota, however, are usually limited to the local areas of greatest concentration of the oil [15].

The shift in balance of an ecosystem from a severely altered one immediately following a major oil spill to a stable ecosystem can require many years; for example, the cove inshore from the *Tampico* oil spill site had reached ecological stability after ten years but the actual populations before the spill and now are different. Stability, in the context of this discussion, is defined as the ability of a biological system to return to its initial state or to maintain a new state after an external perturbation [93].

Certain organisms can be killed by water-soluble fractions (WSF) of oil in the 0.1 to 100 ppm range (see Chapter 1) and may exhibit sublethal responses at much lower concentrations (1 to 10 ppb) (see Chapters 3, 4, and 5). According to Hyland and Schneider [93], the ecological significance of these responses can only be considered at the population level or above (e.g., community, ecosystem, or biome level) of biological organization. An individual organism may be very sensitive to oil when exposed under laboratory bioassay conditions but in the environment, under conditions of effective reproductive and dispersal capabilities, high birth rates, normal maturation rates, and possibilities of migration, an entire population may recuperate rapidly from the severe perturbation of a major oil spill. The expected rapid recovery of a community proven resistant in the laboratory may, nevertheless, be seriously delayed under natural conditions as a result of community interactions, such as competition for food and space, dependence on a specific food source, or ability to compete with other recovery species [93]. North [43] found the recolonization by marine animals at the *Tampico* site was very slow; the population balance among the various barnacles was upset after the *Torrey Canyon* incident because the spill coincided with the annual spawning period of one important barnacle species [33].

These observations should reinforce the concept that it is not possible to make accurate general assessments of the future impact of major oil pollution beyond the point that certain demonstrable short- and long-term damage can be expected. The impacts of petroleum on specific organisms and ecosystems have been discussed in greater detail in the preceding eight chapters of this volume. In general, the effects of oil on marine organisms can be categorized [94] as (1) direct lethal toxicity (Chapter 1); (2) sublethal disruption of biochemical, physiological, and behavioral activities (Chapters 2, 4, and 5); (3) effects of direct coating by the oil (Chapters 6, 7, and 8); (4) assimilation of hydrocarbons (Chapter 3); and (5) alteration of habitat, especially substrate character (Chapter 6 and this chapter).

PACIFIC SUBARCTIC AND ARCTIC OCEAN AS POTENTIAL OIL SPILL AREAS

PACIFIC SUBARCTIC

Crude oil and refined products are shipped in large amounts over the waters of the Pacific Subarctic. The variety and quantity of products are steadily increasing in response to expanding industrial needs. In the last two decades, the markets for petroleum have increased while the production of crude oil on the continental margins of the Pacific Subarctic and nearby contiguous areas has started to decrease. Consequently, it has become expedient to build new refineries nearer the developing markets and supply these plants by tanker, because the nearest domestic and foreign oil fields may be many thousands of miles away. Completion of the Trans-Alaska pipeline from Alaska's North Slope oil fields to the ice-free port of Valdez and the transshipment of crude oil aboard supertankers to the West Coast of North America will add to the increased level of the marine transportation of petroleum and its refined products (Fig. 7). Clark [95] has described the historical changes in the marine transportation of petroleum and pollution input sources in the northeast Pacific Ocean.

The projected capacity of the Trans-Alaska pipeline will eventually reach two million barrels per day. The crude oil will be loaded into a planned fleet of at least 35 large,

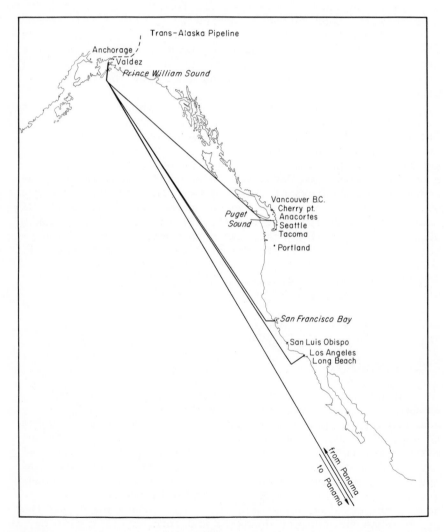

FIG. 7. *Crude oil transportation routes from the southern terminal of the Trans-Alaska Pipeline System at Valdez to west coast ports. From Clark [95].*

modern tankers (45,000 to 150,000 tons, deadweight capacity)
for delivery to refineries in Puget Sound, San Francisco Bay,
and southern California. On the return run to Valdez, the
tankers will not be able to use the load-on-top techniques for
cleaning ballast water from cargo tanks [30], because the West
Coast runs are too short to allow proper separation of the
oily residue from the ballast water. At Valdez, the oily ballast water will be treated ashore and will be discharged as an
effluent containing not more than 10 ppm of oil.

A major loss of petroleum to the marine environment
arises from accidental discharges from vessels (see Table 1,
Chapter 2 of Volume I), involving collisions, groundings,
structural failures, rammings by vessels of fixed structures,
fires, explosions, breakdowns, and various human errors. One
study [96] indicated that 75% of the major oil spills were
from vessels, 90% of which were tankers; half of the spills
were due to tanker groundings. Eighty-five percent of the
major spills occurred within 80 km (50 mi) of a port.

The potential for accidents in the coastal waters of the
Pacific Subarctic is high due to a combination of factors.
The marine transportation of crude petroleum from Valdez involves the navigating of 120 km (75 mi) of deep and narrow
passages between the tanker terminal and the open waters of
the Gulf of Alaska; occasionally these passages contain gla-
cially-produced icebergs. Frequently, severe storms lash the
Gulf of Alaska area through which these supertankers will have
to pass. Even with all the modern weather prediction capabilities, navigation equipment, and construction requirements for
seagoing vessels, ships are still lost to the elements in the
Subarctic Pacific Ocean.

Reception facilities will probably be located in protected waters already carrying a large volume of ship traffic,
such as Cherry Point, Washington, in Puget Sound (220 km or
140 mi, from the 100-meter depth curve offshore), Upper San
Francisco Bay, California (105 km, 65 mi), or Long Beach Harbor, California (16 km, 10 mi). Also with the advent of exploratory drilling for petroleum in the outer continental
shelf of the Gulf of Alaska, the risk of associated accidents
is high considering the inhospitable climate of this region.
The intentional discharge of ballast water into the Gulf of
Alaska beyond a specified distance from shore, as permitted by
state, federal, and international regulations, will add to the
petroleum pollutant burden of the Gulf of Alaska.

The available information [15,28,96-98] indicates that
accidents and intentional discharges of oil will continue to
occur in spite of technological advances and the most strin-
gent regulations. Thus a gradual accumulation of pollutant
hydrocarbons might be expected in the Pacific Subarctic, especially in the nearshore areas [95]. The Pacific Subarctic is

relatively unpolluted compared with much of the world's ocean areas [99]. The background hydrocarbon level is relatively low in Port Valdez, Prince William Sound, and in Puget Sound. Although it is not clear what the acute and long-term effects of oil upon the marine environment will be, the biological effects will, undoubtably, be most apparent in these nearshore environments [28]. Although potential pollution of the Gulf of Alaska area from accidental and unregulated discharges appear to offer a definite threat to the marine ecosystem, the precise adverse effects cannot be predicted as yet because too many variables are involved. Compounding the problem, is the fact that the currents in the Gulf of Alaska could transport spilled oil to areas far distant from the original discharge site [28].

A similar discussion could be put forth for the Atlantic Subarctic region as well, but it would undoubtably result in basically the same conclusions, taking into account the same unknown parameters, differences in existing marine petroleum transportation and consumption patterns, and proposed outer continental shelf petroleum development.

THE ARCTIC OCEAN

Oceanographic Description
    Butler and Berkes [54] in 1972 reviewed the state of knowledge on the impact of oil pollutants in the Canadian Arctic. The following discussion is drawn heavily for their review.
    The main exchange of the Arctic Ocean water is with the Atlantic Ocean through the gap between Greenland and Spitsbergen (Fig. 1) that has a sill depth of 1,500 m. The Bering Sea connection to the Pacific Ocean is shallower (only 50 m) and narrower, but the flow volume is still significant. Other interchanges with the Arctic Ocean are through the Canadian Archipelago via several channels leading to Baffin Bay and Davis Strait. The estimated annual water budget in cubic kilometers of seawater per year is as follows: influx through the Bering Strait (32,500), from the Atlantic (112,500), and freshwater runoff (3,800). This inflow is balanced by outflows through the Denmark Strait (112,500 km^3) and the Davis Strait (36,300 km^3). Pickard [100] estimated that the surface water of the Arctic Ocean is replaced in 3 to 10 years, and the deep water in 10 to 50 years.
    Estimates of the circulation of the upper layers of the Arctic Ocean have been made from observations of ice movements and from geostrophic calculations based on density differences of water masses. It appears that the net movement of the surface layers is clockwise in the Canadian Basin leading out to the East Greeland Current. In the Eurasian Basin, the move-

ment is by the most direct path toward Greenland and out into the East Greenland Current. The current velocities average 300-1,200 km/yr (1-4 cm/s). The tracks of drifting oceanographic ice islands north of Alaska and west of the Canadian Archipelago suggest a fairly closed clockwise circulation of surface waters. This Beaufort Sea gyre tends to retain water inside the Canadian Basin; for instance, during the 23-year period from 1946 to 1969 the American ice island T-3 had made three circuits [3]. The shorelines of the Arctic Ocean are very long and indented and, in addition, the shelf depths are shallow. These features may compound the problems of oil pollution in the Arctic Ocean [54].

The temperatures of the surface waters in the Arctic Ocean remain close to the freezing point of seawater, varying from -1.5°C at a salinity of 28 °/oo to -1.8°C at 33.5 °/oo. The salinity varies ± 1 °/oo and the temperature ±0.1°C over the seasons, with wider extremes occurring in the nearshore and river estuaries where a freshwater melt layer overspreads the colder, more saline Arctic Ocean basin water.

The Arctic sea ice (as distinct from land-formed glacier ice) can be designated by three classifications: (1) the polar-cap ice, which is present in all seasons, covers about 70% of the ocean, and is generally non-navigable by surface vessels; (2) the pack ice, which lies outside the polar cap, covers an additional 25% of the Arctic Ocean, is lighter than the polar cap ice, and is penetrable by ice breakers; and (3) the fast ice, which is anchored to the shore in winter and extends to the pack ice, but melts completely in the summer [100].

Biological Production

Dunbar [1] believed that the Arctic Ocean is impoverished in terms of biological production because of the strong layering of water masses. Since nutrients are formed by the microbial breakdown of organic matter which sinks to the bottom, the nutrient supply to the euphotic, surface layer depends on the upward transport of regenerated nutrients from the deeper waters. There is minimum replenishment of nutrients in the Arctic Ocean due to the hydrographically stable two-layer water system; consequently, biological production is low. Low plankton productivity is reflected in the absence of major fishery resources [101].

Furthermore, due to the short Arctic summer, most biological activity is compressed into a few weeks. According to McLaren [102], it is this greatly reduced period of plant production that is the true "harshness" of the Arctic waters and is ultimately responsible for the slow growth throughout the web of marine life. For example, the arrowworm, *Sagitta elegans*, takes two years to reach maturity in the Canadian eastern arctic but takes only two to three months off the south coast of the British Isles [1]. The Arctic char near Frobisher Bay on Baffin Island requires 12 years to reach sexual maturity, and even then each female spawns only every second or third year [54].

The slow growth and low reproduction rates of arctic animals means slow recovery in the event of environmental damage and has serious implications with respect to petroleum exploration, development, and production. Should a major oil pollution accident involve an arctic animal community not only the adults but also the stock of larvae could be destroyed. Replacement of the population from adjacent areas may be slow, and the reestablishment of a balanced community may require many more years in the arctic environment than in a comparable temperate community [103].

Low diversity of animal and plant species is another characteristic of Arctic ecosystems and may be associated with large fluctuations in the numbers of food organisms. Dunbar [1] attributed the fluctuation in population of food organisms to ecosystem instability. However, it has not been established that low species diversity makes the marine ecosystem of the arctic more susceptible to petroleum pollution than other parts of the biosphere [54].

Much of our estimate of the biological consequences of oil pollution on the arctic marine ecosystem has been derived from the assessment of results of related laboratory experiments and of data collected on oil pollution in subarctic regions. Butler and Berkes [54] believed that it would be unwise to be strictly limited to this approach, because most arctic organisms show certain metabolic adjustments for life at low temperatures. Furthermore, Dunbar [1] suggested that arctic animals exhibit metabolic activity levels similar to those of temperate and tropical forms. One question that also remains is how abundant are hydrocarbon-oxidizing types among the bacteria that function effectively under arctic temperatures and conditions [54].

Dunbar [104] suggested that the impact of an oil spill would be greater in arctic waters than in more southern seas. He reached this conclusion by considering the effect of low temperatures on the degradation and dissipation rates of petroleum hydrocarbons, the potential for accumulation and spread of oil between seawater and ice, and the biological characteristics of the high latitude ecosystems. He pointed out, further, that oil could have a direct effect on two groups of marine animals, sea mammals and sea birds. A secondary effect might be reflected in the native Eskimo populations who use these animals as a source of food. In any large-scale oil spill, the seals, polar bears, walrus, ducks, murres, terns, and other species would be bound to suffer to

some extent. These animals are the most valuable food resources of the arctic seas, and the Eskimos have depended on
them for centuries.

Possible Impact of Oil Spills
Intertidal Habitat

In a report on the effects of petroleum on arctic marine
invertebrates, Percy and Mullin [2] also evaluated the impact
of petroleum on a number of different arctic habitats. The
most dramatic and readily visible biological impact associated
with oil pollution incidents in temperate and tropical waters
occurs when drifting slicks are driven ashore and smother the
biota in the large areas of the biologically-rich intertidal
zone. The intertidal zone of the western Arctic Ocean, however (Beaufort and Chukchi Seas), is barren of marine life as
a result of intense sea ice scouring. The investigators further suggested that petroleum damage to the invertebrate fauna
in the western arctic intertidal zone would consequently be
minimal, although oil residues in the zone would still be
available for reintroduction into other areas of the marine
environment.

Sub-Ice Habitat

Most information to date on the biology of arctic species
was gathered during the summer months, but very little is
known about the organisms during the remaining ten months of
the year [105]. Among phytoplankton communities, rich algal
blooms form on and within the lower surface of ice in spring
and constitute an important fraction of the total primary production in the Arctic Ocean [5]. In addition, a variety of
marine invertebrates congregate in the general vicinity of
this ice-water interface, perhaps due to the presence of the
associated algal blooms. Virtually nothing is known about the
general ecology and trophic interrelationships of the animal
and phytoplankton components of this community or to their
sensitivity to oil pollution.

Oil released under the ice or transported there by currents will tend to accumulate in the pockets on the underside
of floating ice (see Chapter 2 of Volume I). Percy and Mullin
[2] suggested that the impact of oil on organisms in the sub-
ice habitat may be similar to the impact of oil on intertidal
fauna in other areas. In both situations animals are subjected to smothering and fouling by viscous oil masses.

Oil that accumulates under the sea ice does not undergo
significant weathering over the course of many months. Crude
oil in a spill in temperate or tropical waters can weather
rapidly and lose most of its acutely toxic fractions while
drifting on the sea surface. Clearly, rapid weathering of oil
does not occur following under-ice spills in the arctic.

Percy and Mullin [2] found that the toxicity of a crude oil
recovered from ice six months after a spill was not significantly lower than that of the fresh oil.

The oil from a late summer oil well blowout could accumulate under the ice over a long period of time and be transported long distances with little or no loss of toxic components [2]. The toxic components of the accumulated oil could
be preserved unchanged until spring breakup, when much of the
trapped oil could be reintroduced into the water column. In
the Arctic, spring breakup of ice is the period of intense
biological activity in the water column and may be the worst
possible time for the reintroduction of unweathered oil into
the seawater [2].

Water-Column Habitat

Oil can occur in the water column in both dispersed and
dissolved states; as such, it is likely to spread most widely
through the ecosystem and interact with the greatest number of
species. Experimentally, it has been difficult to differentiate between the biological effects resulting from dissolved
and finely dispersed components of oil. Under usual weather
conditions, much of the oil from a spill is quickly dispersed
in the water column where increasing quantities of the soluble
components start to dissolve. Finely dispersed oil appears to
be more toxic to marine life than the soluble fractions; however, this may be due largely to the fact that much higher
concentrations of oil can be accommodated in seawater in a
dispersed state than in the truly soluble state.

On the basis of short-term toxicity studies, Percy and
Mullin [2] found that most of the arctic neritic, or open
water, invertebrate species tested appeared to be relatively
tolerant of high concentrations of dispersed crude oil. Even
with the so-called "sensitive" species, dispersed oil concentrations of 100 ppm or greater were required to cause significant mortality during 96-hr exposure bioassays. These authors
believed that massive initial mortality among adult organisms
inhabiting the water column, as a consequence of contact with
particulate or sub-particulate crude oil, will be limited to
relatively small areas in close proximity to a spill or to
areas where large accumulations of under-ice oil are released
into the seawater at breakup. Furthermore, only the particularly sensitive species within these areas are likely to be
severely affected over the short-term. Information directly
relating to the susceptibility of larval stages to such oil
pollution is not available; however, a number of invertebrate
larval forms are killed in hours by less than one ppm of a
water-soluble fraction of petroleum [106] (see also Chapter
3).

Benthic Habitat

The high sediment load carried by some arctic rivers, involving massive and visually impressive plumes, poses special problems in the event of a major oil spill. This would be particularly true for the Mackenzie River, which empties into the Beaufort Sea, and the Yukon River, which flows into the Bering Sea. Kolpack [53] found that the slick from the crude oil blowout off Santa Barbara, California, penetrated the heavy sediment plume for only a short distance in the inshore areas before being absorbed on the suspended particles and thus carried to the bottom. At first glance, this sedimentation of the oil might appear to be a rather effective self-purification process, but in fact it actually compounds the pollution problem [2]. Sedimentation does not remove the oil pollutants from the ecosystem but rather concentrates them in one ecologically important part of the marine environment. We know that (1) microbial degradation occurs in sediment, (2) hydrocarbon-utilizing organisms are found in most seawater samples, and (3) sediments function as filters for some alkanes and perhaps for some aromatics [62,105]. The problem is that our knowledge of degradation conditions in arctic sediments is still too inadequate to allow us to predict degradation rates from more temperate environments (see Chapter 3 of Volume I).

Little is known about the effects of oil-contaminated sediments upon arctic benthic fauna and infauna. Percy and Mullin [2] found that certain benthic species were killed by short-term exposure to oiled sediments, but only at very high oil concentrations. Of considerable ecological concern is the fact that certain species are capable of detecting low concentrations of oil in the sediment, and may migrate from areas of contamination to adjacent clean areas. Certain benthic species which tend to avoid burrowing in oil-contaminated sediment may be subjected to increased predation during such migration.

Once incorporated into the surface of bottom sediments, the oil is likely to have a long-term effect on the benthic community. Studies by Blumer and Sass [73,107] in coastal subarctic areas (West Falmouth) suggested that oil trapped in sediments may be degraded very slowly. In the sub-zero temperatures of arctic marine sediments, the rate of degradation may be even slower. The results of Percy and Mullin [2] further indicate that the rate of decline in toxicity of sediment-bound oil varies markedly with different oil types.

Oil-contaminated bottom sediments may not be static. Sediments in the Beaufort Sea are intermittently eroded and redeposited by bottom current so that the potential exists for contamination of a much wider area of the sea floor than originally affected [2]. In both the Santa Barbara crude oil

spill [53] and the West Falmouth spill [72], the oil incorporated into shallow water sediments was later transported and
redeposited in deeper areas.

Summary of Potential Impacts of Oil
Pollution in the Arctic Ocean

According to Percy and Mullin [2], the problem of assessment of the impact of petroleum pollution of the arctic is
compounded by the fact that the variety of marine species exhibit differences in response to crude oil. These responses
relate to degree of tolerance to various levels of petroleum,
the nature and magnitude of sublethal behavioral dysfunction
resulting from exposure to petroleum, and the sublethal behavioral effects from exposure to the various states (dissolved,
or dispersed, or in the form of emulsions, films, or particles) of the various petroleum materials. Because of the differential sensitivity of the species, it is quite likely that
the diversity of organisms would be reduced in the immediate
vicinity of an oil spill. The selective elimination of certain sensitive species over wide areas could result in significant disruptions of the ecosystem [2].

In all three marine habitats (sub-ice, water column, and
benthic) in the arctic, the sublethal physiological and behavioral effects of marine organisms are likely to be of greater
ecological significance in the long run than the immediate
lethal effects because low concentrations of oil, over a long
period, may occur over fairly extensive areas of the arctic
environment. Percy and Mullin [2] found that some marine species suffered severe impairment of locomotor activity and respiratory metabolism following exposure to oil. Such disruption of physiological activity of the organisms may result in
serious ecological consequences over the long run by adversely
altering feeding responses and by enhancing vulnerability to
predation (see Chapters 4 and 5).

The effects of petroleum on respiratory metabolism are
rather complex. At low oil levels, such as are likely to occur in the water column in the wake of a major arctic oil
spill, the metabolic rate of some species may be depressed
significantly and accompanied by reduction in locomotor activity. With increasing oil concentrations a reversal of the inhibition occurs and at very high oil levels the metabolic rate
may even be enhanced [2].

Although the immediate biological effect on marine organisms in a limited area may be severe following an oil spill in
the arctic, the overall biological effect may not be so severe
when considered on a broad geographic scale.

The cumulative effects of chronic introduction of oil into the environment during exploration, production, and transportation of oil in the arctic and subarctic land margins may

be far more important [2]. The critical point of balance in
the broad ecological sense is the point at which the processes
following an accidental input of oil into the environment can
be effectively neutralized by natural processes. Indications
are that in the arctic seas the rate of input necessary to exceed the effective rate of natural removal may be considerably
lower than that in temperate and tropical seas.

PROSPECTUS

The conclusion we can draw from data on observations of
oil spills is that it is very difficult to make generalizations about the biological effects of petroleum in the marine
environment. Each case study adds to our appreciation of the
complexity of the fate and effects of petroleum but frequently
raises new and perplexing questions. These questions tend to
make us less confident in our understanding of vital processes
and in our ability to predict what might happen in the next
major pollution incident. Since the majority of the well-
studied major oil spills have not occurred in arctic or subarctic environments, we feel even more uncomfortable about our
lack of knowledge, predictive ability, and capability for
dealing with a major pollution incident should it occur in
this sensitive environment. We need, as soon as possible, detailed studies involving a wider group of scientific disci-
plines using a coordinated systems approach to investigate
major oil spill impacts. Such an approach would involve an
analysis of the specific problem areas, followed by an orderly
development of the research program needs, and a systematic
study of the entire ecosystem. This is a difficult task because major oil pollution incidents seldom occur at a time and
place convenient to the scientist. But small-scale field and
laboratory exposure studies frequently do not give sufficient
information to allow for the extrapolation of data to a much
larger-scale incident in the complex systems of the environment. Therefore, any specific suggestions for necessary research on the fate and effects of petroleum in the arctic and
subarctic marine environments would only echo those recommendations already presented in other chapters of these volumes.

REFERENCES

1.   Dunbar, M.J. (1968). Ecological Development in Polar Re-
      gions. Prentice-Hall, Inc., Englewood Cliffs, N.J.,
      119 p.
2.   Percy, J.A. and T.C. Mullin (1975). Effects of crude
      oils on arctic marine invertebrates. Beaufort Sea Tech.
      Rep. 11, Environment Canada, Victoria, B.C., 167 p.

3. Sater, J.E. (coordinator) (1969). The Arctic Basin. Arctic Institute of North America, Washington, D.C., 319 p.

4. Dunbar, M.J. (1954). The amphipod crustacea of Ungava Bay, Canadian Eastern Arctic. J. Fish. Res. Board Can. 11:709-98.

5. Dunbar, M.J. (1975). Biological oceanography in Canadian arctic and subarctic waters. J. Fish. Res. Board Can. 32:2276-83.

6. Johnson, G.L. (1976). Marine research. Arct. Bull. 2(8):42-6.

7. Dodimead, A.J., F. Favorite, and T. Hirano (1963). Salmon of the North Pacific Ocean. Part II. Review of oceanography of the Subarctic Pacific region. Int. North Pac. Fish. Comm. Bull. 13:1-195.

8. Encyclopedia of Science and Technology (1971). Arctic and subarctic islands, Vol. 1, p. 571-4. McGraw-Hill, New York.

9. Sverdrup, H.U., M.W. Johnson, and R.H. Fleming (1942). The Oceans. Prentice-Hall, Inc., New York, 1087 p.

10. Weltatlas (1949)(printing 3-10-949-a-L). Karl Wenschow GMBH, Munich, Germany, 34 p.

11. Kimble, G.H.T. and D. Good (1955). Geography of the Northlands. American Geographical Society and John Wiley and Sons, New York, 534 p.

12. Mackay, D. and W.Y. Shui (1976). Aqueous solubilities of weathered northern crude oils. Bull. Environ. Contam. Toxicol. 15:101-9.

13. Ottway, S.W. (1971). The comparative toxicities of crude oils. In: The Ecological Effects of Oil Pollution on Littoral Communities (E.B. Cowell, ed.), p. 172-80. Institute of Petroleum, London.

14. National Academy of Sciences (1975). Petroleum in the Marine Environment. Washington, D.C., 107 p.

15. Malins, D.C. (1977). Metabolism of aromatic hydrocarbons in marine organisms. Ann. N.Y. Acad. Sci., In press.

16. Hunt, P.G., W.E. Rickard, F.J. Neneke, F.R. Koutz, and R.P. Murrman (1973). Terrestrial oil spills in Alaska: Environmental effects and recovery. In: Proceedings of 1973 Joint Conference on Prevention and Control of Oil Spills, p. 733-40. American Petroleum Institute, Washington, D.C.

17. Brooks, J.W., J.C. Bartonek, D.R. Klein, D.L. Spencer, and A.S. Thayer (1971). Environmental influences of oil and gas development in the Arctic Slope and Beaufort Sea. U.S. Bur. Sport Fish. Wildl. Resour. Publ. 96, 24 p.

18. Lachenbruch, A.H. (1970). Some estimates of the thermal effects of a heated pipeline in permafrost. U.S. Geol. Surv. Circ. 632, 23 p.

19. Anon. (1976). Pipeline insulation travels 1,800 miles-- by rail. Alaska Constr. Oil 17(5):50-3.

20. Swader, F.N. (1975). Persistence and effects of light fuel oil in soil. In: Proceedings of 1975 Conference on Prevention and Control of Oil Pollution, p. 589-93. American Petroleum Institute, Washington, D.C.

21. McCown, B.H., J. Brown, and R.P. Murmann (1971). Effect of oil-seepages and spills on the ecology and bio-chemistry in cold-dominated environment. Ann. Rep. 1, Earth Sciences Branch, U.S. Army Cold Regions Research and Engineering Laboratory, Hanover, N.H. (Cited in: Hutchinson, T.C. and W. Freedman (1975). Effects of experimental crude oil spills on taiga and tundra vegetation of the Canadian arctic. In: Proceedings of 1975 Conference on Prevention and Control of Oil Pollution, p. 517. American Petroleum Institute, Washington, D.C.)

22. Westlake, D.W.S. and F.D. Cook (1973). Microbial modification of crude oils. In: Oil and the Canadian Environment. Proceedings of the Conference of the Institute for Environmental Studies, p. 95. University of Toronto, Canada. (Cited in: Hutchinson, T.C. and W. Freedman (1975). Effects of experimental crude oil spills on taiga and tundra vegetation of the Canadian arctic. In: Proceedings of 1975 Conference on Prevention and Control of Oil Pollution, p. 518. American Petroleum Institute, Washington, D.C.)

23. ZoBell, C.E. (1973). Bacterial degradation of mineral oils at low temperatures. In: The Microbial Degradation of Oil Pollutants (D.G. Ahearn and S.P. Meyers, eds.), p. 153-61. Publ. No. LSU-SG-73-01. Center for Wetland Resources, Lousiana State University, Baton Rouge, La.

24. Hutchinson, T.C. and W. Freedman (1975). Effects of experimental crude oil spills on taiga and tundra vegetation of the Canadian arctic. In: Proceedings of 1975 Conference on Prevention and Control of Oil Pollution, p. 517-25. American Petroleum Institute, Washington, D.C.

25. Snow, N.B. and B.F. Scott (1975). The effect and fate of crude oil spilt on two arctic lakes. In: Proceedings of 1975 Conference on Prevention and Control of Oil Pollution, p. 527-34. American Petroleum Institute, Washington, D.C.

26. Hellebust, J.A., B. Hanna, R.G. Sheath, M. Gergis, and T.C. Hutchinson (1975). Experimental crude oil spills on a small subarctic lake in the Mackenzie Valley, N.W.T.: Effects on phytoplankton, periphyton, and attached aquatic vegetation. In: Proceedings of 1975 Conference on Prevention and Control of Oil Pollution, p. 509-15. American Petroleum Institute, Washington, D.C.

27. McKee, J.E. and H.W. Wolf (1963). Water quality crite-
    ria. Calif. State Water Resour. Control Board Publ. 3-A,
    548 p.

28. U.S. Department of the Interior (1972). Final Environ-
    mental Impact Statement: Proposed Trans-Alaska Pipeline.
    Evaluation of Environmental Impact, Vol. 4. PB-206-921-
    4. National Technical Information Service, U.S. Dep. of
    Commerce, Springfield, Va., 637 p.

29. Smith, J.E. (1968). *'Torrey Canyon'* Pollution and Marine
    Life. Cambridge University Press, Cambridge, 196 p.

30. Nelson-Smith, A. (1973). Oil Pollution and Marine
    Ecology. Plenum Press, New York, 260 p.

31. Ranwell, D.S. (1968). Extent of damage to coastal habi-
    tats due to the *Torrey Canyon* incident. In: The Biolog-
    ical Effects of Oil Pollution on Littoral Communities
    (J.D. Carthy and D.R. Arthur, eds.), Field Studies,
    Suppl. to Vol. 2, p. 39-47. Obtainable from E.W. Classey,
    Ltd., Hampton, Middx., England.

32. Canevari, G.P. (1973). Development of "next generation"
    chemical dispersants. In: Proceedings of 1973 Joint
    Conference on Prevention and Control of Oil Spills,
    p. 231-40. American Petroleum Institute, Washington, D.C.

33. Nelson-Smith, A. (1968). Biological consequences of oil
    pollution and shore cleansing. In: The Biological Ef-
    fects of Oil Pollution on Littoral Communities (J.D.
    Carthy and D.R. Arthur, eds.), Field Studies, Suppl. to
    Vol. 2, p. 73-80. Obtainable from E.W. Classey, Ltd.,
    Hampton, Middx., England.

34. Baker, J.M. (1971). Successive spillages. In: The Eco-
    logical Effects of Oil Pollution on Littoral Communities
    (E.B. Cowell, ed.), p. 21-32. Institute of Petroleum,
    London.

35. Baker, J.M. (1973). Biological effects of refinery ef-
    fluents. In: Proceedings of 1973 Joint Conference on
    Prevention and Control of Oil Spills, p. 715-23. Ameri-
    can Petroleum Institute, Washington, D.C.

36. Simpson, A.C. (1968). The *Torrey Canyon* disaster and
    fisheries. Ministry of Agriculture, Fisheries and Food,
    Fisheries Laboratory, Burnham-on-Crouch, U.K. Laboratory
    Leaflet (New Series) 18, 43 p.

37. Blumer, M. (1971). Scientific aspects of the oil spill
    problem. Environ. Affairs 1:54-73.

38. Stegeman, J.J. and J.M. Teal (1973). Accumulation, re-
    lease and retention of petroleum hydrocarbons by the
    oyster, *Crassostrea virginica*. Mar. Biol. (Berl.) 22:
    37-44.

39. Anderson, J.W., J.M. Neff, B.A. Cox, H.E. Tatem, and G.H. Hightower (1974). Characteristics of dispersions and water-soluble extracts of crude and refined oils and their toxicity to estuarine crustaceans and fish. Mar. Biol. (Berl.) 27:75-88.

40. Clark, R.C., Jr. and J.S. Finley (1975). Uptake and loss of petroleum hydrocarbons by the mussel, *Mytilus edulis*, in laboratory experiments. Fish. Bull. 73:508-15.

41. Bourne, W.R.P. (1970). Special review -- After the *'Torrey Canyon'* disaster. Ibis 112:120-5.

42. Bourne, W.R.P. (1968). Oil pollution and bird populations. In: The Biological Effects of Oil Pollution on Littoral Communities (J.D. Carthy and D.R. Arthur, eds.), Field Studies, Suppl. to Vol. 2, p. 99-121. Obtainable from E.W. Classey, Ltd., Hampton, Middx., England.

43. North, W.J. (1967). *Tampico*. A study of destruction and restoration. Sea Front. 13:212-7.

44. Mitchell, C.T., E.K. Anderson, L.G. Jones, and W.J. North (1970). What oil does to ecology. J. Water Pollut. Control Fed. 43:812-8.

45. North, W.J. (1973). Position paper on effects of acute oil spills. In: Background Papers, Workshop on Inputs, Fates, and Effects of Petroleum in the Marine Environment, Airlie, Va, 21-25 May, p. 758-77. National Academy of Sciences, Washington, D.C.

46. Deslauriers, P.C. (1975). Oil pollution in ice infested waters. A survey of recent development. Unpublished manuscript (9104 Red Branch Road, Columbia, MD 21045), 29 p.

47. Barber, F.G. (1970). Oil spills in ice: Some cleanup options. Arctic 23:285-6.

48. Barber, F.G. (1971). Oil spilled with ice: Some qualitative aspects. In: Proceedings of 1971 Joint Conference on Prevention and Control of Oil Spills, p. 133-7. American Petroleum Institute, Washington, D.C.

49. Barber, F.G. (1971). An oiled Arctic shore. Arctic 24: 229.

50. Chan, G.L. (1973). A study of the effects of the San Francisco oil spill on marine organisms. In: Proceedings of 1973 Joint Conference on Prevention and Control of Oil Spills, p. 741-81. American Petroleum Institute, Washington, D.C.

51. Chan, G.L. (1975). A study of the effects of the San Francisco oil spill on marine life. Part II: Recruitment. In: Proceedings of 1975 Conference on Prevention and Control of Oil Pollution, p. 457-61. American Petroleum Institute, Washington, D.C.

52. Straughan, D. (ed.) (1971). Biological and Oceanographi-
     cal Survey of the Santa Barbara Channel Oil Spill, 1969-
     1970. Vol. I. Allan Hancock Foundation, University of
     Southern California, Los Angeles, 426 p.
53. Kolpack, R.L. (ed.) (1971). Biological and Oceanographi-
     cal Survey of the Santa Barbara Channel Oil Spill, 1969-
     1970. Vol. II. Allan Hancock Foundation, University of
     Southern California, Los Angeles, 477 p.
54. Butler, M.J.A. and F. Berkes (1972). Biological Aspects
     of Oil Pollution in the Marine Environment: A Review.
     McGill University, Montreal, Canada, Mar. Sci. Cent.
     Manuscr. Rep. 22, 118 p.
55. Owens, E.H. (1971). The restoration of beaches contamin-
     ated by oil in Chedabucto Bay, Nova Scotia. Dep. of
     Energy, Mines and Resources, Ottawa, Canada, Mar. Sci.
     Branch Manuscr. Rep. Ser. 19, 75 p.
56. Forrester, W.D. (1971). Distribution of suspended oil
     particles following the grounding of the tanker *Arrow*.
     J. Mar. Res. 29:151-70.
57. Thomas, M.L.H. (1973). Effects of Bunker C oil on inter-
     tidal and lagoonal biota in Chedabucto Bay, Nova Scotia.
     J. Fish. Res. Board Can. 30:83-90.
58. Conover, R.J. (1971). Some relations between zooplankton
     and Bunker C oil in Chedabucto Bay following the wreck of
     the tanker *Arrow*. J. Fish. Res. Board Can. 28:1327-30.
59. Scarratt, D.J. and V. Zitko (1972). Bunker C oil in sed-
     iments and benthic animals from shallow depths in Cheda-
     bucto Bay, N.S. J. Fish. Res. Board Can. 29:1347-50.
60. Vandermeulen, J.H. and W.R. Penrose (1976). Absence of
     aryl hydrocarbon hydroxylase (AHH) activity in chronical-
     ly oiled (1970-1976) marine bivalves: Possible conse-
     quences. Unpublished manuscript. Marine Ecology Labora-
     tory, Bedford Institute of Oceanography, Dartmouth, Nova
     Scotia, Canada, 20 p.
61. Malins, D.C. (1977). Biotransformation of petroleum hy-
     drocarbons in marine organisms indigenous to the Arctic
     and Subarctic. In: Proceedings of the Symposium on Fate
     and Effects of Petroleum Hydrocarbons in Marine Ecosys-
     tems and Organisms (D. Wolfe, ed.). In press. Pergamon
     Press, New York.
62. Vandermeulen, J.H. and D.C. Gordon, Jr. (1976). Reentry
     of 5-year-old stranded Bunker C fuel oil from a low-ener-
     gy beach into the water, sediments, and biota of Cheda-
     bucto Bay, Nova Scotia. J. Fish. Res. Board Can. 33:
     2002-10.

63. Vandermeulen, J.H., P.D. Keizer, and T.P. Ahern (1976). Compositional changes in beach sediment-bound *Arrow* Bunker C: 1970-1976. Unpublished manuscript. Fisheries Improvement Committee, Int. Counc. Explor. Sea CM 1976/E:51, 6 p.

64. Mayo, D.W., D.J. Donovan, L. Jiang, R.L. Dow, and J.W. Hurst, Jr. (1974). Long term weathering characteristics of Iranian crude oil: The wreck of the "Northern Gulf." In: Marine Pollution Monitoring (Petroleum). Natl. Bur. Stand. Spec. Publ. 409, p. 201-8.

65. Dow, R.L. and J.W. Hurst, Jr. (1975). The ecological, chemical and histopathological evaluation of an oil spill site. Part I. Ecological studies. Mar. Pollut. Bull. 6:164-6.

66. Mayo, D.W., C.G. Cogger, D.J. Donovan, R.A. Gambardella, L.C. Jiang, and J. Quan (1975). The ecological, chemical and histopathological evaluation of an oil spill site. Part II. Chemical studies. Mar. Pollut. Bull. 6:166-71.

67. Barry, M. and P.P. Yevich (1975). The ecological, chemical and histopathological evaluation of an oil spill site. Part III. Histopathological studies. Mar. Pollut. Bull. 6:171-3.

68. Sanders, H.L. (1973). Some biological effects related to the West Falmouth oil spill. In: Background Papers, Workshop on Inputs, Fates, and Effects of Petroleum in the Marine Environment, Airlie, Va., 21-25 May, p. 778-800. National Academy of Sciences, Washington, D.C.

69. Blumer, M., G. Souza, and J. Sass (1970). Hydrocarbon pollution of edible shellfish by an oil spill. Mar. Biol. (Berl.) 5:195-202.

70. Blumer, M., J. Sass, G. Souza, H. Sanders, F. Grassle, and G. Hampson (1970). The West Falmouth oil spill. Unpublished manuscript. Woods Hole Oceanogr. Inst. Tech. Rep. 70-44, 32 p.

71. Blumer, M. and J. Sass (1972). The West Falmouth oil spill. II. Chemistry. Unpublished manuscript. Woods Hole Oceanogr. Inst. Tech. Rep. 72-19, 125 p.

72. Blumer, M., H.L. Sanders, J.F. Grassle, and G.R. Hampson (1971). A small oil spill. Environment 13(2):1-12.

73. Blumer, M. and J. Sass (1972). Oil pollution: Persistence and degradation of spilled fuel oil. Science 176:1120-2.

74. Sanders, H.L. (1974). The West Falmouth saga. How an oil expert twisted the facts about a landmark oil spill study. New Engineer (May):1-8.

75. Michael, A.D., C.R. Van Raalte, and L.S. Brown (1975). Long-term effects of an oil spill at West Falmouth, Massachusetts. In: Proceedings of 1975 Conference on Prevention and Control of Oil Pollution, p. 573-82. American Petroleum Institute, Washington, D.C.

76. Green, D.R., C. Bawden, W.J. Cretney, and C.S. Wong (1974). The Alert Bay oil spill: A one-year study of the recovery of a contaminated bay. Pac. Mar. Sci. Rep. 74-9, Environment Canada, Victoria, B.C., 42 p.

77. Clark, R.C., Jr., J.S. Finley, B.G. Patten, D.F. Stefani, and E.E. DeNike (1973). Interagency investigations of a persistent oil spill on the Washington coast. Animal population studies, hydrocarbon uptake by marine organisms, and algae response following the grounding of the troopship General M.C. Meigs. In: Proceedings of 1973 Joint Conference on Prevention and Control of Oil Spills, p. 793-808. American Petroleum Institute, Washington, D.C.

78. Clark, R.C., Jr., J.S. Finley, B.G. Patten, and E.E. DeNike (1975). Long-term chemical and biological effects of a persistent oil spill following the grounding of the General M.C. Meigs. In: Proceedings of 1975 Conference on Prevention and Control of Oil Pollution, p. 479-87. American Petroleum Institute, Washington, D.C.

79. Clark, R.C., Jr. and J.S. Finley (1973). Paraffin hydrocarbon patterns in petroleum-polluted mussels. Mar. Pollut. Bull. 4:172-6.

80. Clark, R.C., Jr. and J.S. Finley (1973). Techniques for analysis of paraffin hydrocarbons and for interpretation of data to assess oil spill effects in aquatic organisms. In: Proceedings of 1973 Joint Conference on Prevention and Control of Oil Spills, p. 161-72. American Petroleum Institute, Washington, D.C.

81. Price, R.I. (1974). Report of the VLCC Metula Grounding, Pollution and Refloating in the Strait of Magellan in 1974. Unpublished report. U.S. Coast Guard Office of Marine Environment and Systems, Washington, D.C., 40 p.

82. Gunnerson, C.G. and G. Peter (1976). The Metula oil Spill. NOAA Special Report. National Oceanic and Atmospheric Administration, U.S. Dep. of Commerce, Boulder, Colo., 37 p.

83. Baker, J.M., I. Campodonico, L. Guzman, J.J. Texera, B. Texera, C. Venegas, and A. Sanheuza (1976). An oil spill in the Straits of Magellan. In: Marine Ecology and Oil Pollution (J.M. Baker, eds.), p. 441-71. John Wiley and Sons, New York.

84. Hann, R.W., Jr. (1974). Oil Pollution from the Tanker *Metula*. Report to the U.S. Coast Guard Research and Development Program. Texas A & M University, College Station, Tex., 67 p.

85. Hann, R.W., Jr. (1975). Follow-up Field Survey of the Oil Pollution from the Tanker *Metula*. Report to the U.S. Coast Guard Research and Development Program. Texas A & M University, College Station, Tex., 60 p.

85a. Hann, R.W., Jr. (1977). Fate of oil from the supertanker *Metula*. In: Proceedings of 1977 Oil Spill Conference (Prevention, Control, Cleanup), p. 465-8. American Petroleum Institute, Washington, D.C.

86. Straughan, D. (1975). Biological Survey of Intertidal Areas of the Straits of Magellan in January 1975, Five Months after the *Metula* Oil Spill. NOAA Tech. Memo. ERL MESA-10. National Oceanic and Atmospheric Administration, U.S. Dep. of Commerce, Boulder, Colo., 57 p.

87. Warner, J.S. (1975). Determination of Petroleum Components in Samples from the *Metula* Oil Spill. NOAA Data Rep. ERL MESA-4. National Oceanic and Atmospheric Administration, U.S. Dep. of Commerce, Boulder, Colo., 72 p.

88. Straughan, D. (1976). Comments on an oil spill in the Straits of Magellan. In: Marine Ecology and Oil Pollution (J.M. Baker, ed.), p. 523. John Wiley and Sons, New York.

89. Anon. (1976). Tanker disaster. Direction finder blamed. Seattle Times 99(No. 363, 28 December):A-2.

90. Anon. (1976). *Argo Merchant* Grounding and Oil Spill. IPAN 70-76, cards 2556, 2560, 2561, and 2562. The Center for Short-Lived Phenomena, Cambridge, Mass.

91. Anon. (1976). Oil slick blown toward fishery. Seattle Post-Intelligencer 113(No. 359, 24 December):A-2.

92. Grose, P.L. (compiler) (1977). The *Argo Merchant* Oil Spill. NOAA Special Report. National Oceanic and Atmospheric Administration, U.S. Dep. of Commerce, Boulder, Colo., In press.

93. Hyland, J.L. and E.D. Schneider (1976). Petroleum hydrocarbons and their effects on marine organisms, populations, communities, and ecosystems. In: Sources, Effects and Sinks of Hydrocarbons in the Aquatic Environment, p. 463-506. American Institute of Biological Sciences, Arlington, Va.

94. Moore, S.F. and R.L. Dwyer (1974). Effects of oil on marine organisms: A critical assessment of published data. Water Res. 8:819-27.

95. Clark, R.C., Jr. (1976). Impact of the transportation of petroleum on the waters of the northeastern Pacific. U.S. Natl. Mar. Fish. Serv. Mar. Fish Rev. 38(11):20-6.

96. Gilmore, G.A., D.D. Smith, A.H. Rice, E.H. Shenton, and W.H. Moser (1970). Systems Study of Oil Spill Cleanup Procedures. Vol. I: Analysis of Oil Spills and Control Materials. Am. Petrol. Inst. Publ. 4024, 188 p.

97. Alyeska Pipeline Service Company (1971). Description of Marine Transportation Systems--Valdez to West Coast Ports. Report submitted to U.S. Dep. of the Interior, July 22, 1971, 65 p.

98. U.S. Coast Guard (1972). Marine Transportation Systems of the Trans-Alaska Pipeline Systems. Report submitted to U.S. Dep. of the Interior, Feb. 1971.

99. Butler, J.N., B.F. Morris, and J. Sass (1973). Pelagic tar from Bermuda and the Sargasso Sea. Bermuda Biol. Stn. Res. Spec. Publ. 10, 346 p.

100. Pickard, G.L. (1964). Descriptive Physical Oceanography. Pergamon Press, London, 199 p.

101. Dunbar, M.J. (1970). On the fishery potential of the sea waters of the Canadian North. Arctic 23:150-74.

102. McLaren, I.A. (1968). Marine life in arctic waters. In: The Unbelievable Land (I.N. Smith, ed.), Queen's Printer, Ottawa. (Cited in: Butler, M.J.A. and F. Berkes (1972). Biological Aspects of Oil Pollution in the Marine Environment: A review. McGill University, Montreal, Canada, Mar. Sci. Cent. Manuscr. Rep. 22, p. 75.)

103. Chia, F.S. (1970). Reproduction of arctic marine invertebrates. Mar. Pollut. Bull. 1 (NS):78-9.

104. Dunbar, M.J. (1971). Environment and Good Sense. McGill-Queens University Press, Montreal, 92 p.

105. Vandermeulen, J.H. (1976). Personal communication. Marine Ecology Laboratory, Bedford Institute of Oceanography, Dartmouth, Nova Scotia, Canada.

106. Sanborn, H.R. and D.C. Malins (1977). Toxicity and metabolism of naphthalene: A study with marine larval invertebrates. Proc. Soc. Exp. Biol. Med. 154:151-5.

107. Blumer, M. and J. Sass (1972). Indigenous and petroleum-derived hydrocarbons in a polluted sediment. Mar. Pollut. Bull. 3:92-3.

List of Abbreviations

AHH	aryl hydrocarbon hydroxylase
API	American Petroleum Institute
BAP (BP)	benzo [a]pyrene (benzpyrene)
BSA	bovine serum albumin
^{14}C	radioactive carbon-14 labeled compound
DNA	deoxyribonucleic acid
DO	dissolved oxygen
dpm (DPM)	disintegrations per minute
dwt	deadweight ton (2,240 lb)
EC	effective concentration
$ED_{50}(ED_m)$	median effective dose
EMD_{50}	50% ecological mortality dose
F	the F test
GC (GLC)	gas chromatography (gas-liquid chromatography)
GC/MS	gas chromatography and mass spectrometry
^{3}H	radioactive tritium-labeled compound
H & E	hemotoxylin and eosin
IgA	immunoglobulin A
IR	infrared spectroscopy
LC	lethal concentration
LD_{50}	median lethal dose
LT	lethal time
MS	mass spectrometry
NADP	nicotinamide adenine dinucleotide phosphate
NADPH	reduced nicotinamide adenine dinucleotide phosphate
NSFO	Navy special fuel oil
OWD	oil-in-water dispersion
PCB	polychlorinated biphenyl
r	sample correlation coefficient
RNA	ribonucleic acid
RSS	Royal Survey Ship
sal	salinity
S.E.M.	standard error of the mean
SW	seawater
S.D.	standard deviation

t	*Student's t test*
TD	*time to death*
TLC	*thin-layer chromatography*
TLm	*(TL_{50}) median tolerance limit*
(ton)	*(metric ton; 2,205 lb)*
μg-AT C cell $^{-1}$ min $^{-1}$ x 10^9	
	microgram-atoms of carbon per cell x 10^9
UV	*ultraviolet spectroscopy*
wW/cm^2	*microwatts per square centimemeter*
VLCC	*very large crude carrier (tanker)*
WSF	*water-soluble fraction*

Geographical Name Index

A

Ailsa Craig, Newfoundland, 371
Alaska, 113, 417, 461
Alaska, North Slope, 457
Alaskan coastal waters, 400
Alaskan waters, 104
Alert Bay, Canada, *431*, *432*, 443, 444, 456
American Ice Island T-3, 461
Anacortes, Washington, *458*
Annet, 360
Arabian Gulf, Kuwait, 285
Arctic 20, 21, 339, 430
Arctic, Canadian, 418, 460
Arctic Circle, 412, *414*
Arctic Ocean, 139, 351, *414*, 460-467
Arctic Ocean, western, 463
Arctic waters, 412, *414*
Atlantic, 460
Atlantic coast, 111
Atlantic, North, 345, 413
Atlantic, northeastern, 116
Atlantic Ocean, 114, 119, 413
Atlantic Ocean, eastern, 110
Atlantic Ocean, North, *414*
Atlantic Ocean, western, 110, 275
Atlantic, western, 106, 120

B

Baja California, Mexico, 420, 427-430
Baltic Sea, 103, 114, 346
Banco Satelite (Satellite Patch), Strait of Magellan, 447
Barents Sea, *414*
Bay of Biscay, *422*
Beaufort Sea, 351, 400, 420, 461, 463, 465
Bedford Basin, 275
Bering Sea, 97, 120, 127, 412, *414*, 465
Bering Strait, 460
Berkeley, California, 372, *374*
Berkeley Strait, 460
Black Sea, 292
Bourne, Massachusetts, 438

Brest, France, *422*
Bristol Bay, Alaska, 412
Bristol Channel, Great Britain, 421, *422*
Britain, NE, *362*
British beaches, U.K., *365*, *366*
British Columbia, Canada, 116, 123, 124, 205, 443
British estuary, 119
British Isles, 120, 413
Brittany, France, *422*, 426, 427
Buzzards Bay, Massachusetts, 438, 442

C

California, 110, 205, 413, 432, 459
Canada, 128, 417
Canada, eastern arctic, 461, 462
Canadian Archipelago, 461
Canadian Basin, 460, 461
Canadian freshwater lakes, 419
Canadian Pacific waters, 121
Cape Cod, Massachusetts, 455
Cape Flattery, Washington, 445
Cape Point, South Africa, *369*
Caribbean Sea, 359
Casco Bay, Maine, 114
Caspian Sea, 343
Cerberus Rock, Nova Scotia, 432
Channel Island, Great Britain, *422*
Chedabucto Bay, Nova Scotia, 292, 344, 400, 432-437, 450, 456
Cherry Point, Anacortes, Washington, *458*, 459
Chesapeake Bay, 113
Chile, South America, 451
Chukchi Sea, Alaska, 123, *414*
Cornish Coast, England, 361
Cornwall, England, 364, 422, 423, 425-427, 456

D

Dassen Island, South Africa, 369
Davis Strait, *414*, 460
Deception Bay, Quebec, Canada, 430, *431*

479

Scientific Name Index

Numbers in italics refer to figures or tables containing information

A

Abalone *Haliotis fulgens, 429*
Alder (species not indicated), 417
Algae
  Agmenellum quadruplicatum, 251,
    280, 281
  Alaria tenuifolia, 275
  Ascophyllum sp., *232*
  Chaetoceros curvisetus, 278
  Chlamydomonas, 252, 253
  Chlamydomonas angulosa, 205, 206,
    252, 254, 255
  Chlamydomonas sp., *278*
  Chlorella, 252
  Chlorella autotrophica, 251, 280
  Chondrus crispus, 435
  Cladophora stimpsonii, 275
  Corallina, 423
  Coscinodiscus granii, 278
  Costaria costata, 275
  Dunaliella tertiolecta, 278, 280
  Enteromorpha intestinalis, 424
  Enteromorpha sp., *274*
  Fragilaria sp., *278*
  Fucus, 436
  Fucus distichus, 275
  Fucus edentatus, 277, 306
  Fucus gardneri, 178
  Fucus serratus, 276, 277
  Fucus sp., *232*
  Fucus spiralis, 434
  Fucus vesiculosus, 274, 276
  Glenodinium foliaceum, 278
  Grateloupia dichotoma, 251, 253, 280
  Gymnodinium kovalevskii, 278
  Gymnodinium wulffii, 278
  Halosaccion glandiforme, 275
  Laminaria digitata, 274
  Laminaria saccharina, 275
  Licmophora ehrenbergii, 278
  Lithothamnia, 423
  Melosira moniliformis, 278
  Microcoleus chthonoplastes, 280
  Monochrysis lutheri, 276
  Oscillatoria limnetica, 251, 252
  Palmaria palmata, 275
  Peridinium trochoideum, 278
  Phaeodactylum tricornutum, 250
  Platymonas viridis, 278
  Polysiphonia opaca, 251, 253
  Porphyra, 423, 449
  Porphyra miniata, 275
  Porphyra umbilicalis, 274
  Prorocentrum trochoideum, 278
  Ulva, 423, 449
  Ulva fenestrata, 275
  Ulva lactuca, 251
  Thalassiosira pseudonana, 250, 251
Amphipods
  Anisogrammarus locustaides, 52
  Anisogrammarus sp., *52*
  Atylus carinatus, 52
  Calliopius laeviusculus, 52
  Corophium clarencense, 292
  Gammarus macronatus, 52
  Gammarus marino-gammarus olivii,
    52
  Gammarus oceanicus, 291
  Gammarus olivii, 292
  M. sibirica, 292
  Neohaustorius biarticulatus, 52, 290
  Onisimus affinis, 52, 285, 289, 291,
    292
  Orchestia traskiana, 52
  Orchomene pinguis, 52
  Parathemisto pacifica, 245
Anchovy, northern *Engraulis mordax,*
  72, 328
Anemones
  Actinia, 424
  Actinia sp., *423*
  Anthopleura elegantissima, 283
  Anthopleura sp., *283*
  Anthopleura xanthogrammica, 428
  Corynactis sp., *449*

Subject Index

103.524

COLLEGE LIBRARY
SUFFOLK UNIVERSITY
BOSTON, MASS.